FUNDAMENTALS
OF
URBAN ECONOMICS

John F. McDonald

Department of Economics
University of Illinois at Chicago

Prentice Hall, Upper Saddle River, NJ 07458

Executive Editor: Leah Jewell
Associate Editor: Teresa Cohan
Editorial Assistant: Kristen Kaiser
Editor-in-Chief: James Boyd
Production Editor: Maureen Wilson
Managing Editor: Carol Burgett
Manufacturing Buyer: Ken Clinton
Marketing Manager: Susan McLaughlin
Cover Art: Richard Berenholtz/The Stock Market

Copyright © 1997 by Prentice-Hall, Inc.
A Simon & Schuster Company
Upper Saddle River, New Jersey 07458

Library of Congress Cataloging-in-Publication Data

McDonald, John F.
    Fundamentals of urban economics / John F. McDonald.
       p.   cm.
    Includes index.
    ISBN 0-02-378852-6
    1. Urban economics.   I. Title.
HT321.M34   1997
330.9173′2—dc20   96-16026
                                 CIP

Prentice-Hall International (UK) Limited, *London*
Prentice-Hall of Australia Pty. Limited, *Sydney*
Prentice-Hall Canada, Inc., *Toronto*
Prentice-Hall Hispanoamericana, S.A., *Mexico*
Prentice-Hall of India Private Limited, *New Delhi*
Prentice-Hall of Japan, Inc., *Tokyo*
Simon & Schuster Asia Pte. Ltd., *Singapore*
Editora Prentice-Hall do Brasil, Ltda., *Rio de Janeiro*

Printed in the United States of America

10 9 8 7 6 5 4 3 2 1

For
Glena
and
Elizabeth

Contents

■ v ■

Preface

This textbook has been written primarily for undergraduate students who wish to learn about the field in which economic analysis is applied to urban areas. The title of the book has been chosen with care. The emphasis is on the fundamental methods used by economists to study cities. Those methods make use of economic models and economic data. Those who study this book should be able to conduct economic studies of an urban area. I do not mean that the student can do original academic research, but that she or he can conduct a study that is informed and well organized. One implication of this purpose for the book is that although many urban policy issues are examined, a complete catalog of urban social problems is not included. Potential users of the book should note that all of the examples and data pertain to urban areas in the United States.

The book is written presuming that the student has a background that, at a minimum, includes a strong course in the principles of microeconomics and the ability to handle algebra. The student needs to feel comfortable with the use of basic mathematics because economic analysis cannot be done without it. The book does include a few mathematical derivations that are more than two or three lines in length. Students who have had a course in intermediate microeconomic theory will find that most of the mathematical and economic concepts in the book are quite familiar. The book does not require that the student has studied calculus. All of the mathematical concepts used are covered in the appendix at the end of the book. However, the student who has had a course in basic differential calculus (e.g., math for business and economics) will find that the math is easy.

The book can be used in (at least) two ways. It can serve as a text for students who are majoring in economics. These students wish to learn about the subject matter of urban economics, but they also need to gain more practice in the use of economic theory and the underlying mathematical techniques. Several more advanced sections and appendices have been included for these students, and they should review the entire appendix to the book while they are reading the first five chapters. The book can also serve as a text for students who do not intend to become experts in economic analysis, but who wish to apply their knowledge of basic microeconomics to the urban economy. These students can use the book in slightly abbreviated form by omitting certain sections, exercises, and appendices, denoted by an asterisk (*). These students can also omit Chapter 6 without loss of continuity. They should study the appendix to the book, except for Section G (the last section). If I were teaching students in this category, I would allocate some of the time in each of the first few weeks of the course to covering the material in the appendix to the book.

The book begins with four chapters that introduce urban economics as a field and discuss the origins and economic functions of cities in the United States. The rest of the book is organized around two basic methods that are used to study urban economies. The first method studies spatial patterns within an urban area. In Chapters 5 through 10 we examine the spatial patterns of land use, population, employment, housing, and the local public sector. An analysis of urban transportation is included in this section as well. The second method for studying urban areas concentrates on the economic growth of the urban economy as a unit. The topic has recently caught the attention of a number of researchers, and there is now a substantial body of knowledge upon which to draw. This is the first modern text in urban economics that emphasizes urban economic growth. Chapters 11 through 14 present theories of urban growth, empirical evidence, and a discussion of policy. The book concludes with two chapters on the changing nature of urban economies in the United States and the attendant economic and social problems, especially poverty, homelessness, and crime.

I have been teaching urban economics to undergraduate and graduate students at the University of Illinois at Chicago since 1971, and this book draws upon that experience. My experience also tells me that undergraduate students need to do more than just read the textbook and attend lectures. They need to learn about the main data sources in the field, they need to write, and they need to read other books.

I assign a paper topic to undergraduates that requires use of some of the basic data sources, such as:

- The Census of Population and Housing
- County Business Patterns
- County data of the Regional Economic Information System, Bureau of Economic Analysis, U.S. Department of Commerce
- Census of Governments
- Census of Manufactures, Retail Trade, Wholesale Trade, and Selected Services
- Labor market data in the Monthly Labor Review
- Labor market and employment data provided by the state department of labor or employment security

The students select an urban area and a particular topic, such as housing, employment growth, or public transportation, and write a paper that is based on government data and secondary sources. The students (and I) receive assistance from the staff of the UIC library government documents section. I have found that students need practice in writing a paper that includes tables that present data on some topic. Many essentially have no idea about how to construct a table that presents data clearly, and how to write prose that describes the table and points out the most important facts contained therein. Writing in the discipline of economics is different from writing for the required English course, and the skills must be taught. This book is full of tables that have been constructed for a variety of purposes, and students can learn from them. However, they will not really learn unless they practice.

I also require that the undergraduate students write a book review, and I supply them with a list of books from which they can choose. Recommendations for books to read are made along the way in text. I make only a few recommendations of books that are readable and insightful, and they are:

- William Cronon, *Nature's Metropolis*
- Anthony Downs, *Stuck in Traffic*
- Joel Garreau, *Edge City*
- Edgar Hoover and Raymond Vernon, *Anatomy of a Metropolis*
- Jane Jacobs, *The Economy of Cities*
- Edwin Mills and John McDonald (eds.), *Sources of Metropolitan Growth*
- Thomas Stanback, *The New Suburbanization*

In fact, since I am located in Chicago, I use Cronon's fine book as one of the required texts for the course. This book is easily the most popular book with students that I have ever assigned. It gives the students a sense that they are really in touch with the economic past of the place that they inhabit.

By now you know that I set lofty goals for students in urban economics. They are to:

- Learn the models and techniques that are used in urban economic analysis
- Learn how those methods arc applied to particular topics and issues
- Learn about data sources
- Practice writing as an economist
- Gain some sense of the history of the urban area in which they live

The book does not include a descriptive discussion of every urban social policy issue because if the student succeeds in attaining these goals, he or she is capable of learning more about urban areas. In essence, the goal of the course in urban economics is for students to develop both the capacity for and the desire to learn more.

ACKNOWLEDGMENTS

I owe a great debt of gratitude to six scholars who read the entire manuscript and provided detailed comments and suggestions: Donald A. Coffin, Indiana University, Northwest; Nancy Hammerle, Stonehill College; Irving Hoch, University of Texas at Dallas; Daniel McMillen, Tulane University; James R. Prescott, Iowa State University; and Terri A. Sexton, California State University, Sacramento. I have used nearly all of their suggestions, as I hope they will see when they read the final version.

I owe much to my senior editor at Prentice Hall, Leah Jewell, who handled the manuscript with dispatch and provided wise suggestions for revisions. Editorial assistant Kristen Kaiser has also been quite helpful. Production editor Maureen Wilson and the production staff did an excellent job on a tight schedule.

I wish to thank the former professors and colleagues who have helped to teach me the lessons that are contained in this book. My partners in urban economic research include Daniel McMillen, Edmond d'Ouville, H. Woods Bowman, and Steven Balkin. My former teachers include Peter Mieszkowski, Robert Goldfarb, Guy Orcutt, Robert Haveman, Douglas Dacy, F. Ray Marshall, William Brainard, David Grether, and Marc Nerlove.

I think that many of the scholars in the field of urban economics are indebted to Edwin Mills, the founding editor of the *Journal of Urban Economics*. His work as a patient, encouraging, and wise journal editor fostered the careers of many urban economists, including mine.

Finally, I owe my career in urban economics to the Department of Economics at Yale University and to the fellowship support that the department provided during my four years there. I could not have attended Yale without that financial support. We should not forget that graduate students need financial support in these times as well.

ABOUT THE AUTHOR

John F. McDonald has been teaching urban economics at the University of Illinois at Chicago since 1971, when he received his Ph.D. in economics from Yale University. He earned the B.A. from Grinnell College, and also did graduate work at the University of Texas at Austin. He is a member of the editorial board of the *Journal of Urban Economics*, and served as President of the Illinois Economic Association during 1993–1994. He is the author of two other books, *Economic Analysis of an Urban Housing Market* and *Employment Location and Industrial Land Use in Metropolitan Chicago*, and the co-editor (with Edwin Mills) of *Sources of Metropolitan Growth*. His wife, Glena, daughter, Elizabeth, and he live in River Forest, Illinois.

C H A P T E R

1

Introduction to Urban Economics

A. THE NATURE OF URBAN AREAS AND URBAN ECONOMICS

Urban economics is the study of economies that are organized as urban areas. An *urban area* can be defined as a place with (1) a very high population density, compared to the surrounding area, and (2) a total population greater than some minimum number (to distinguish urban areas from small towns). Most urban areas have an identifiable central point where population density is at a peak and declines with distance from that point. (A few urban areas, such as Minneapolis−St. Paul, have more than one central point.) Urban economies are based on frequent contact among people and economic activities, and high population density facilitates that contact. You will be studying economies such as the New York metropolitan area, "Chicagoland," and the Dallas−Fort Worth "metroplex."

The field of urban economics is closely related to its sister field, regional economics. *Regional economics* is the study of regions that are much larger than a single urban area but are smaller than an entire nation. Regional economists are interested in the economy of the midwest, the southwest, and so on. But both urban and regional economists are interested in the variety of economic experience that can occur within a single nation. Both study economic units that are defined geographically, as opposed to industry units, demographic groups, occupational groups, or other possible disaggregations of the entire economy. Indeed, because both fields study geographic subunits of the national economy, urban and regional economics make use of some of the same economic models and methods.

Two different, complementary methods for examining the economy of an urban area are used in this book. The first is the study of location patterns within an urban area. The location decisions of households and firms within the area are the chief topics. For example, the study of the spatial pattern of population density in an urban area is a favorite topic in urban economics. Location decisions are influenced by many factors, including public policies regarding the provision of transportation facilities and other public goods and services, local taxation, and zoning and other forms of land-use control. The second method is the examination of the urban economy in the aggregate. Spatial patterns within the urban area are largely ignored; instead, the focus is on the growth or decline of economy of the urban area. An urban economy is quite "open" in the sense that imports and exports are large fractions of its total economic activity. Most urban areas specialize in the production of a certain group of goods and services for export outside the urban area. Most urban areas thus have an identifiable economic function within the larger economy. Changes in the larger economy can have a sizable impact on an urban economy and may sometimes require that the urban area undergo a significant change in its basic economic function.

These two methods for looking at an urban economy are not independent. Clearly, a major change in the economic functions performed by an urban area can have implications for the location patterns within the area. Chicago is no longer the "hog butcher of the world" but is in fact now the center of the nation's air transportation system. Location patterns within the Chicago metropolitan area have adjusted accordingly. At the same time, it is possible that the location patterns within an urban area can influence its ability to grow. Is the supply of industrial sites sufficient for further industrial growth? Do those industrial sites possess good access to transportation facilities, suppliers, and needed workers? Is the urban area an attractive place that will draw to it workers who possess skills?

B. DEVELOPMENT OF THE FIELD OF URBAN ECONOMICS

Urban economics as something of a separate field of study within economics began in the late 1930s when economists started using the tools of macroeconomics to examine urban economies and their real estate markets. Basic concepts such as gross national product, exports and imports, the multiplier, and the unemployment rate were adapted to the study of urban economies. Perhaps a date for the founding of the field is 1956, the year in which the New York Metropolitan Region Study was initiated. The book that summarizes this huge study was written by two economists, Edgar M. Hoover and Raymond Vernon, and is entitled *Anatomy of a Metropolis*. This book, which was published in 1959, carries the subtitle "The changing distribution of people and jobs within the New York metropolitan region." This study of New York succeeded in gathering an enormous volume of data that were presented in a well-organized fashion. The trends observable in the data were then discussed using a variety of forces that were hypothesized to influence the location choices of firms and households within a metropolitan area. *Anatomy of a Metropolis* is a classic study, and I recommend that you read it.

Some urban economists would place the founding of the field in 1964, the date of the publication of William Alonso's book *Location and Land Use*. Alonso laid out a basic theoretical model that can be used to study the economics of location patterns within urban areas that is still used today. Alonso's method makes use of the idea that households and firms are willing to make bids for land at various locations. Location decisions and patterns of land use can be explained by comparing the bids made by different types of households and firms. The law firm outbids others for downtown locations, the electronics plant makes the highest bid for a site near the interstate highway, the family with children bids more than others for a lot in the suburbs, and so on. These ideas are explored in detail in this book.

Since the 1960s a great deal of progress has been made in urban economics as a field of research. It is also true that urban economics is still a relatively new field of study. But what does it mean to say that progress has been made in a field of research? Research in economics can be classified as one of two fundamental types: normative and positive. *Normative economics* is the exploration of such questions as: How should the economy be organized to be efficient and/or equitable? Some ethical objective is specified and what "ought" to be done is deduced—given the facts of life. This type of research usually makes use of formal economic theory to derive such propositions as "The economy should have perfectly competitive markets" or "A tax should be placed on polluters." The task of *positive economics* is to determine the facts of economic life.

The development of positive economic knowledge in fields such as urban economics typically proceeds through five stages, which can be characterized as follows:

1. Accumulation of data pertinent to the field of study.
2. Systematic examination of these data to determine the important facts that require formal "explanation" through the development of economic models.
3. Formulation of economic models that are capable of accounting for the important facts.
4. Empirical estimation and testing of such economic models.
5. Use of the models for forecasting, policy analysis, and normative analysis.

While research may be under way simultaneously in all five stages, at a single moment, researchers often focus on only one or two stages. Also, some researchers may be engaged in work that refines or makes use of the generally accepted model (stages 4 and 5), while other researchers are in the process of questioning the generally accepted model (stages 1, 2, and 3). Sometimes those who are questioning the generally accepted model will demonstrate that the older model needs to be abandoned in favor of their newer, better approach. In other cases the older and newer models will coexist, and the matter of which model is better will be unresolved.

Given these five stages in the accumulation of positive economic knowledge, can we determine a date for the founding of the field of urban economics? Perhaps the field begins with the accumulation of facts—the first stage listed above. If that is the case, no date can be given because we do not (and perhaps can never) know when someone who resembled an economist began to collect data about cities. On the other hand, perhaps a field of study is founded when someone begins to sort through the facts and to find patterns and trends that seem to call for an economic model. Indeed, perhaps it is the *finding* of such patterns and trends that initiates a field in economic science.

Others will claim that economic science does not exist until the first economic model pertaining to those patterns and trends is actually formulated. This is why 1964, the year of the publication of Alonso's *Location and Land Use*, is often proposed as the date for the founding of the field. There is no definitive answer to this question, but a stimulating class discussion might be held to sort out the issues. How would you compare urban economics to other fields within economics, to other social sciences, and to other fields of science?

Urban economics provides several examples of competing models. For example, consider the analysis of urban economic growth. One model places emphasis on the demand for the exports of the urban area and uses macroeconomic methods (including Keynesian multipliers) to explain trends in the urban economy. Another model puts its emphasis on the supply side. The growth of an urban economy is seen as being determined largely by its supplies of labor, capital, and infrastructure. Yet another model emphasizes the life-cycle patterns of the industries that are located in the urban area. Are the industries in the urban area "mature," or are they new and vigorous? Which of these models is best at explaining the facts that need to be explained? Can these models be combined into a more comprehensive model that provides better explanations? These matters are discussed in detail in Part III of this book. For now you have learned that a field of research can contain alternative models and that the question of which model is "best" can be an unresolved issue.

My purpose in writing this book is to teach you, to the best of my ability, the nature of the progress that has been made in the field of urban economics. Both normative and positive economics are covered, but it is fair to say that this book emphasizes the positive side. This reflects caution on my part; I am not sure that we have sufficient knowledge to make detailed normative statements about some urban issues. We do have some answers, but we also have many unresolved questions.

C. TALES OF THREE CITIES: NEW YORK, LOS ANGELES, AND CHICAGO

Urban areas are the subject matter of urban economics, and the New York, Los Angeles, and Chicago metropolitan areas are, by far, the three largest in the United States. In my opinion, all students of urban economics should have some familiarity with the basic economic facts of these three dominant urban areas. Indeed, given that the North American Free Trade Agreement (NAFTA) strengthens the economic ties among the United States, Canada, and Mexico, North American students should also be familiar with the basic economic facts of Mexico City, with 20 million people the largest urban area on the North American continent. The purpose of this section is to provide a systematic presentation of some of the basic facts of metropolitan population growth and spatial patterns for the three largest urban areas in the United States since 1950, the year of the first census of population after World War II. Economic models to explain these facts are covered in later chapters. Mexico City is excluded on the grounds that it is located in a developing country and therefore may not be comparable to New York, Los Angeles, and Chicago.

The definition of the metropolitan area is the first question that must be answered in an empirical study. We wish to focus on a particular urban area viewed as an economic unit, distinct from rural areas and other urban areas. Clearly, studying only the "central city" (i.e., New York City, the city of Los Angeles, the city of Chicago) will not do. The residential suburbs must be included because they are part of the economic unit. A more difficult question concerns the inclusion of nearby cities that are satellite cities but not really residential suburbs of the main city. For example, New York has Newark, New Jersey just across the Hudson River. Chicago has a ring of old satellite cities: Waukegan, Elgin, Aurora, and Joliet in Illinois and

Gary, Indiana. Except for Gary, these cities were founded in the nineteenth century after a railroad line was built around Chicago, intersecting the major trunk rail lines that converge on Chicago. Los Angeles has a series of cities that line the coast of the Pacific Ocean and a line of cities that stretches to the east. The difficulty of this question is compounded by the fact that since 1950, some satellite cities that were really economic units separate from the major city at that time have been engulfed by the spread of the major urban area.

The U.S. Bureau of the Census has the task of defining the metropolitan areas. As a practical matter the Census Bureau defines metropolitan areas as groups of *counties* that contain a central city with a population of at least 50,000. A county is included in a metropolitan area if there is a significant amount of commuting to jobs in the county that contains the central city. Counties are used as the building blocks of metropolitan areas because their boundaries do not change and because a great many data are gathered at the county level. This procedure means that the Census Bureau changes the definition of a metropolitan area as residential and commuting patterns change. This procedure also means that there can be more than one metropolitan area, as defined by the Census Bureau, within a major urban area. For example, Newark is its own metropolitan area because it is a central city of over 50,000 population, and workers in surrounding counties commute to Newark. Consequently, the Census Bureau also defines what it calls a Consolidated Metropolitan Statistical Area (CMSA). A CMSA has a population of at least 1 million and at least two metropolitan areas that are economically integrated.

New York, Los Angeles, and Chicago all fall into the CMSA category. For purposes of this section, these three major urban areas are defined as all of the counties contained in the CMSA as of 1990. This definition means that some counties are included for 1950 that cannot be considered to be part of the main urban area at that time. However, there is a benefit from studying the *same* geographic area over time. We make a small error by including some farms and an occasional satellite city in 1950, but we make sure that we encompass the entire larger urban area for the entire 1950–1990 period. We recognize what we are doing, and keep that small error in mind. The method that is followed is to define a "core" area (e.g., the central city), an inner ring of suburban counties, and an outer ring of counties.

New York

The New York Metropolitan Area consists of 24 counties in New York, New Jersey, and Connecticut. New York City consists of its five boroughs [Manhattan (New York County), Brooklyn, Queens, the Bronx, and Staten Island (Richmond)]; each is a separate county.

Population data for 1950, 1970, and 1990 are shown in Table 1.1. The definitions of the core area, the inner ring, and the outer ring follow Hoover and Vernon (1959) and are noted in the footnotes of Table 1.1. The population of the metropolitan area was 13.9 million in 1950, and it grew by 29.6%, to 18.1 million, in 1970. The next 20 years saw population growth come to a complete halt—the 1990 population was 18.0 million. Table 1.1 also shows that the core of the metropolitan area [defined as New York City excluding Staten Island and adding Hudson County (Newark), NJ] had a small population loss of 1.8% from 1950 to 1970. Manhattan lost population

TABLE 1.1	New York Metropolitan Area		
	Population^a (thousands)		
	1950	*1970*	*1990*
Core area	8357	8208	7498
Manhattan	1960	1539	1488
New York City	7892	7895	7324
Inner ring	3671	5452	5091
Outer ring	1928	4411	5365
	13,946	18,071	17,954

^aThe core area is defined as Manhattan, Brooklyn, Queens, the Bronx, and Hudson County, NJ. New York City includes Staten Island and excludes Hudson County. Inner ring counties include three counties in New York and five counties in New Jersey. Outer ring counties include four counties in New York, seven in New Jersey, and one in Connecticut.

Source: U.S. Bureau of the Census.

while the rest of the core area gained population. The next 20 years tell a different story for the core area; population loss was a sizable 8.7%, and most of that loss occurred in the core area outside Manhattan. The population loss of 710,000 in the core area exceeds the population of the state of Wyoming and suggests the image of large expanses of abandoned territory in the Bronx.

Next consider the inner ring of eight counties that are adjacent to the core area. Population grew in this area by 48.5% (or 1.8 million) from 1950 to 1970 and then *declined* by 6.6% in the 1970–1990 period. The rapid growth of population in the metropolitan area of the earlier period translated into very rapid growth in the inner ring, but the failure of population to grow at the metropolitan level meant decline for the inner ring in the later period. The outer ring experienced more than a doubling of its population during the period 1950–1970, and growth was a more sedate 21.6% from 1970 to 1990.

These two time periods give us a remarkably clear example of what happens to the spatial distribution of population in modern urban areas under conditions of rapid and zero growth. With rapid growth, the population of the core area holds fairly steady, the inner ring grows, and the outer ring booms. However, when there is no population growth in the metropolitan area, the core area declines rather sharply, the inner ring also declines, and the outer ring experiences growth equal to the declines in the other two areas. One might hypothesize that the data for 1970 and 1990 provide us with a pretty clear picture of the underlying trend toward the "suburbanization" of the population. Even if there is no population growth, the outer suburbs still grow for a variety of reasons, such as the demand for new houses, desire to escape central city problems, local taxes, and the shift of jobs to the suburbs. The core area must cope with population decline, while the outer ring must handle rather sizable growth.

Los Angeles

The Los Angeles metropolitan area consists of five counties in California. Los Angeles County, the central county, contains the city of Los Angeles. The story of the Los Angeles metropolitan area is quite different from that of New York (Table 1.2). In 1950 it was a metropolitan area of 4.9 million people, only one-third the size of the New York metropolitan area and smaller than metropolitan Chicago. The post–World War II boom in California more than doubled the population of the entire metropolitan area from 1950 to 1970 (growth of 102%) and then added another 4.6 million people from 1970 to 1990. The Los Angeles metropolitan area added almost 5 million people in each 20-year period. Given the downturn in the California economy of the early 1990s, it is safe to say that this kind of growth is unlikely to be continuing. Nevertheless, it is remarkable for a place that large to have grown so rapidly. A glance at Tables 1.1 and 1.2 suggests that Los Angeles will soon overtake New York as the largest metropolitan area in the United States. When will Los Angeles overtake New York in metropolitan population? What is your estimate? How did you make that estimate? (Is making local population forecasts fun or what?) An exercise at the end of the chapter provides several suggestions for how to make local population forecasts.

Table 1.2 shows that the growth in total population translated into growth in all areas of the metropolitan area. The city of Los Angeles increased its population by 76.9% from 1950 to 1990, and the rest of Los Angeles County grew by 146.5% during the same 40 years. But the other counties saw explosive population growth. The inner ring counties of Orange and Ventura went from 331,000 people in 1950 to 3.1 million in 1990, and the outer ring counties of San Bernadino and Riverside added over 2.1 million people. Orange County started with 216,000 people in 1950 and had a population of 2.4 million in 1990. In short, a modern metropolitan area of very rapid population growth not only experiences increased population density in its settled areas but also spreads out in rather startling fashion. Los Angeles is a textbook case. (This is a textbook, after all.)

TABLE 1.2 Los Angeles Metropolitan Area			
	Population*a* *(thousands)*		
	1950	*1970*	*1990*
City of Los Angeles	1970	2812	3485
Rest of Los Angeles County	2182	4230	5378
Inner ring	331	1799	3080
Outer ring	451	1139	2588
	4934	9980	14,531

*a*Inner ring counties are Orange and Ventura. Outer ring counties are San Bernadino and Riverside.

Source: U.S. Bureau of the Census.

Chicago

Our third-largest metropolitan area is Chicago. It consists of eight counties in Illinois, two counties in Indiana, and one county in Wisconsin. The city of Chicago is located in Cook County, Illinois, and the city of Gary is located in Lake County, Indiana. As with the other two cities, Metropolitan Chicago experienced substantial population growth in the baby-boom years of 1950 to 1970. Table 1.3 shows that the growth was from 5.6 million to 7.8 million, or 36.7%, during those 20 years. Recall that population growth in the New York metropolitan area was 29.6% during the same period. Chicago also resembles New York in that population growth in the urban area essentially came to a halt after 1970; the growth was only 3.7% over the 1970–1990 period. Chicago began the post–World War II period as the "second city" and the "second metropolitan area," but by 1970 it was no longer second in metropolitan population, and by 1990 it had lost its title of "second city" as well. The Los Angeles metropolitan population of 10.0 million in 1970 far exceeded metropolitan Chicago's 7.8 million. By 1990 the population in the city of Chicago had dropped to 2.8 million, compared to 3.5 million in the city of Los Angeles.

The spatial patterns of population change in metropolitan Chicago follow what is now a familiar pattern. In the earlier period, when metropolitan population was growing fairly rapidly, the population of the core area [defined as the city of Chicago plus Lake County (Gary), Indiana] held steady. Table 1.3 shows that the population of the core area dropped 1.9% from 1950 to 1970. However, the city of Chicago experienced a larger decline of 7.0%. This population loss for the central city is perhaps larger than one might have expected and can probably be attributed to the opening of the system of radial expressways in the early 1960s. The 1970–1990 period is one of little overall population growth, and the core area shows a decline of 16.7%. The other areas in metropolitan Chicago display rapid population growth from 1950 to 1970. The remainder of Cook County (excluding the city of Chicago) and the inner ring counties more than doubled in population, and the outer ring counties grew by 80.7%.

TABLE 1.3   Chicago Metropolitan Area

	Population[a] (thousands)		
	1950	1970	1990
Core	3989	3915	3260
City of Chicago	3621	3369	2784
Lake County, IN	368	546	476
Remainder of Cook County	888	2125	2321
Inner ring	334	871	1298
Outer ring	481	869	1185
	5692	7780	8064

[a]Inner ring counties include DuPage and Lake in Illinois. Outer ring counties include Kane, McHenry, Will, Kendall, and Grundy in Illinois, Porter in Indiana, and Kenosha in Wisconsin.

Source: U.S. Bureau of the Census.

Population growth during the 1970–1990 period slowed down appreciably in all three areas. Growth in the rest of Cook County was only 9.2% over this period, while the inner and outer rings grew by 49.0% and 36.4%, respectively. As we shall see in later chapters, during this period the inner ring counties were the sites of substantial employment growth, partly in the form of employment subcenters. Thus metropolitan Chicago and New York both present us with the seemingly strange combination of a core area coping with sizable decline while some suburban areas are grappling with substantial growth.

D. EMPLOYMENT IN METROPOLITAN LOS ANGELES

The other half of the story is employment. This section is a brief look at employment location patterns and growth *by place of work* in the Los Angeles metropolitan area. Employment data can also be studied *by place of residence* of the workers. The data compiled by place of work reflect the location decisions made by businesses rather than households. Metropolitan Los Angeles was chosen (rather than New York or Chicago) because it experienced the greatest population growth of the three. What sort of employment growth went along with the rapid population growth? Also, it was easier to compile the necessary data, which are available by county. Metropolitan Los Angeles contains only five counties, all of which are in the same state. The New York and Chicago metropolitan areas contain more counties, and both include at least one county from each of three states.

Any discussion of employment change must acknowledge the changes that have taken place in the composition of the national economy. Employment outside agriculture can be classified broadly into industries that produce goods, industries that produce services, and government. Goods-producing industries include manufacturing, mining, and construction. Service-producing industries include wholesale and retail trade, the financial sector (including banking, insurance, and real estate), services (business services, health care, etc.), and transportation, communication, and utilities. In 1970 the goods-producing sector of the U.S. economy employed 23.6 million people and the service-producing sector, 47.3 million. Government at all levels provided 12.5 million jobs. Twenty years later the picture had changed dramatically. The goods-producing sector employed only slightly more workers, 25.0 million. By contrast, service industries had grown to an employment level of 84.8 million, and government employment had increased to 18.3 million. Total nonagricultural employment in the United States had increased by about 55% over those 20 years, but that growth was largely in service industries. This overwhelming fact about the nature of employment growth is an important piece of background information that you must bear in mind as you read this book.

The basic data for Los Angeles are shown in Table 1.4. Total employment in the metropolitan area increased from 4.40 million in 1970 to 8.04 million in 1990, an average annual rate of increase of 3.02%. Population growth over this same period was from 9.98 million to 14.53 million, an annual increase of 1.88%. Employment grew more rapidly than population because the baby-boom generation entered the workforce and because a larger proportion of women decided to work. Employment grew annually by 1.14% per year more rapidly than did population. Table 1.4 also shows

TABLE 1.4 Employment in the Los Angeles Metropolitan Area by Place of Work[a]

Geographic Area	Employment (thousands)		Annual Growth Rate (%)
	1970	1990	
LA metropolitan area			
Total	4398	8042	3.02
Manufacturing	1016	1285	1.17
Retail trade	710	1253	2.84
Services[b]	954	2508	4.83
Other[c]	1718	2996	2.78
LA County			
Total	3326	5200	2.23
Manufacturing	824	894	0.41
Retail trade	520	764	1.92
Services	746	1707	4.14
Other	1236	1835	1.98
Suburban counties			
Total	1072	2842	4.87
Manufacturing	192	391	3.56
Retail trade	190	489	4.73
Services	208	801	6.74
Other	482	1161	4.40

[a]Employment includes all full-time and part-time wage and salary employees and proprietors.

[b]Services include hotels, personal services, business services (advertising, data processing, etc.), repair services, health services, private educational and social services, legal services, membership organizations, and professional services (engineering, accounting, management consulting, etc.).

[c]Other employment includes construction, TCU (transportation, communication, and utilities), wholesale trade, FIRE (finance, insurance, and real estate), government (federal, state, and local), and all other.

Source: Regional Economic Information System, Bureau of Economic Analysis, U.S. Department of Commerce.

that employment growth varied by industry; manufacturing jobs increased by only 1.17% per year, whereas jobs in the service sector grew by 4.83% per year. The primary components of the service sector are health care, business services, private educational services, and various professional services (law, accounting, etc.) (see the Table 1.4 footnotes for more details). Other sectors as a whole, including retail trade, grew at rates that are near the overall growth rate of 3.02% per year. As we know from the national data, this comparison of industry employment growth rates is typical—manufacturing jobs grew comparatively slowly and service-sector jobs grew comparatively rapidly.

Table 1.4 also shows employment for Los Angeles County (the central county) and for the other four suburban counties. Employment in the Los Angeles metropolitan area grew very rapidly, and a good deal of that growth took place in the central county. Employment in Los Angeles County increased from 3.33 million to 5.20 million, an average annual growth rate of 2.23%. This compares to an annual rate of population growth in the county of 1.15% (Table 1.2). But the employment growth rate in the four suburban counties was more than double the rate in the central county. Employment in the suburban counties of 1.07 million in 1970 turned into 2.84 million in 1990, a rate of growth of 4.87% per year. Population growth in these suburban counties was 3.29% over the same period (Table 1.2), so employment growth in these counties exceeded population growth by 1.58% per year. Recall that employment growth exceeded population growth in the metropolitan area by 1.14% per year, so jobs were "suburbanizing" more rapidly than were residents during this period. Employment growth rates by industry show the same pattern in both locations—manufacturing jobs grew relatively slowly and service-sector employment grew relatively rapidly.

Employment growth in Los Angeles was certainly spectacular. No wonder so many people decided to locate in Los Angeles. At the same time, one could say that population growth in Los Angeles was spectacular. No wonder they created so many jobs. Which is it? It is both, of course. People follow jobs, and jobs follow people. One important goal of this book is to explain both mechanisms.

E. URBAN GROWTH CONTROLS

In the preceding two sections we have documented the spectacular growth of the suburbs in population for the three largest urban areas and employment for Los Angeles. Many observers of urban areas are concerned that suburban "sprawl" is harmful for several reasons and have suggested that actions should be taken to stop or substantially reduce the spreading out of urban areas. Urban sprawl can be characterized by:

1. Low-density development that is widely dispersed and uses large amounts of land
2. Geographic separation of essential places, such as work, residences, shopping, and schools
3. Almost complete dependence on private autos for travel.

Suburban sprawl creates costs for state and local governments to provide highways and streets, schools, and water and sewer systems. It is alleged that the residents of sprawling suburban areas do not pay the full costs of these public facilities. It is also thought that the sprawl generates more traffic and more traffic congestion.

One certainly hears a lot about the problem of urban sprawl, but has anyone in the United States done anything about it? The answer is "yes." Several urban areas in states such as California and Florida are grappling with the problem, but the best example is Portland, Oregon. Portland is the first urban area in the United States to have an Urban Growth Boundary. In 1977 the state of Oregon created the Metropolitan Service District, which is now known simply as Metro. One of Metro's primary duties is the administration of the Urban Growth Boundary, which it created in 1977. The Urban Growth Boundary separates land that can be developed for urban use from land that must remain rural until the boundary is changed, and includes the urbanized portions of three counties (the city of Portland and 23 other municipalities). The boundary includes an area of 350 square miles.

TABLE 1.5	Population in the Portland Metropolitan Area (Population in Thousands)			
	1960	*1970*	*1980*	*1990*
Central County (Multnomah[a])	523	557	563	584
Inner suburban counties				
Clackamas[a]	113	166	242	279
Washington[a]	92	158	246	312
Outer suburban counties				
Columbia	22	29	36	38
Yamhill	32	40	55	66
Clark County, Washington	94	128	192	238
	876	1038	1334	1517

[a]*Urbanized portion of county included inside Urban Growth Boundary.*
Source: U.S. Bureau of the Census.

Table 1.5 has been prepared using Census of Population data to examine the effects of the Urban Growth Boundary. The definition of the Portland Metropolitan Area in 1990 includes five counties in Oregon and one county in the state of Washington (Clark County). The county in Washington is not included in the urban growth control policy because the policy is created by an Oregon state law. The central county is Multnomah, and the city of Portland is located in this county. About half of Multnomah County is inside the Urban Growth Boundary, and the urbanized portions of Clackamas and Washington counties (in Oregon) are also included.

Table 1.5 shows that the population of the metropolitan area increased by 18.5% from 1960 to 1970. Most of that population growth took place in the two inner suburban counties in Oregon (Clackamas and Washington) and in Clark County, Washington. The populations of these counties increased by 53,000, 66,000, and 34,000, respectively. However, the population of the central county (Multnomah) increased by 34,000 (6.5%). Population growth accelerated in the decade of the 1970s to 28.5% for the metropolitan area, and the two inner suburban counties in Oregon experienced sharp increases in population. Clackamas County added 76,000 people and Washington County grew by 88,000. The population of both counties had more than doubled between 1960 and 1980, but the source of concern over urban sprawl probably emanates from the experience in the 1970s. Look at what happened in the central county. While the metropolitan area was growing by 28.5% and the two inner suburban counties in Oregon were growing by 60.5%, the central county added only 6000 people (1.1% increase). The growth of population in Multnomah County was substantially less in the 1970s than it had been in the 1960s, even though total population growth in the metropolitan area had been much greater in the 1970s.

The effect of the Urban Growth Boundary policy can be seen in the population data for 1980 to 1990. Population growth in the decade of the 1980s for the metropolitan area slowed down to 13.7%, but the central county recorded growth of 21,000 people (3.7%). Population growth took place in the urbanized portions of the two inner suburban counties in Oregon inside the Urban Growth Boundary, but the growth rates were reduced substantially from the previous two decades. Indeed, the population growth in Clackamas County was only 15.3%, just barely greater than the growth rate for the entire metropolitan area. Furthermore, it appears that population growth was not pushed into Clark County, Washington in any appreciable amount. Clark County grew by 24.0%, but Washington County, Oregon grew by 26.8%. Finally, the Urban Growth Boundary seems to have prevented population growth in one of the outer suburban counties (Columbia). The other outer suburban county (Yamhill) added 11,000 people (20% increase).

It is clear how data from the Census of Population can be used to examine the effects of a policy of urban growth control that imposes an Urban Growth Boundary. It would be possible to use the more detailed geographic data provided by the census to pinpoint the exact locations where population growth was permitted. This would be a good research topic for an independent study project or even a senior thesis.

F. PREVIEW OF COMING ATTRACTIONS

This book is organized into four parts:

    I. Economics and urban areas

   II. Location patterns in urban areas

  III. Economic growth of urban areas

  IV. The changing urban economy

The remaining three chapters of Part I continue the introduction to the field of urban economics. Chapter 2 is a discussion of schools of thought within the field of urban economics. Urban economists come in (roughly speaking) three varieties: mainstream, conservative, and Marxist. An economist's identification with a particular school of thought can influence the research questions he or she asks, the methods used to investigate those questions, and the nature of the conclusions that are drawn from research. These matters are examined in some depth in Chapter 2. Chapters 3 and 4 turn from methodological matters to the economic origins and functions of cities. The focus of Chapter 3 is the location decisions of firms and how those decisions create cities, and Chapter 4 is an examination of the economic functions of cities.

Part II contains six chapters on the location patterns of economic activity within urban areas. Basic concepts and facts are introduced in Chapter 5. Chapter 6 presents more formal economic models of location patterns in an urban area that is organized around a single central point. This chapter is, by far, the most theoretical chapter in the book. Its purposes are to demonstrate how urban location models are connected to more conventional microeconomic theory and to show how location patterns in the urban area depicted in the model respond to various changes, such as population growth and reductions in transportation costs.

The remaining four chapters of Part II turn to more practical matters. In this group of chapters we examine location decisions made by the three main actors in the urban economy: businesses, households, and local governments. One chapter is devoted to the urban transportation system through which these actors are linked. Chapter 7 is a discussion of centers of employment in urban areas. The central business district is one center of employment, of course, but most urban areas have other employment concentrations that perform various functions within the larger economy. The locations of employment centers influence the location patterns of households, although that influence operates through the urban transportation system. Chapter 8 presents the methods that are used to model the transportation system of an urban area. This chapter includes a detailed discussion of the increasing traffic congestion that plagues large urban areas, and various transportation policy alternatives are discussed. The urban housing market is examined in Chapter 9. The operation of the market for housing is described first at a more practical level, and then a useful economic model of urban housing is presented. This model considers urban housing of different quality levels (e.g., high, medium, and low quality) to be connected as a set of interrelated markets. Urban housing policy is also discussed. Part II concludes with a chapter on the public sector in urban areas. Economic functions of local government are examined, and it is concluded that their main function is to allocate resources to various local public goods and services. Two alternative models of local government resource allocation decisions are presented next. The chapter concludes with discussions of the two main sources of revenue for local governments: the tax on real estate and intergovernmental grants.

The economic growth of urban areas is treated in Part III of the book. The focus of this part is on urban area as an economic unit. As stated earlier, in Section A, spatial patterns within the urban area are largely ignored. A wide variety of theories of urban economic growth are covered in Chapter 11. These theories generally are of two types; one type emphasizes the demand side as a determinant of growth, and the other type concentrates on the supply side. Chapter 12 is devoted to the relationship of urban growth to forces of agglomeration in urban areas and to technical change. Chapter 13 is a detailed discussion of the growth of labor and capital in urban areas. The labor force in an urban area grows primarily through migration, and the quality of the labor force is enhanced by education and training. The capital stock of an urban area includes both private and public capital—both types are considered in Chapter 13.

Given the detailed presentation of the sources of urban economic growth in Chapters 11, 12, and 13, Chapter 14 is devoted to urban economic growth policy: the process of setting general economic goals, devising strategies and supporting policies, and conducting evaluations of the results of policy.

Part IV, the final two chapters of the book, is a study of the changing nature of urban areas in the United States. Chapter 15 examines how urban areas have changed in the period since the end of World War II. The emphasis in this chapter is on the interaction between the growth of the urban area and the changes in location patterns within the urban area. Research methods for carrying out this kind of task are just emerging, so much of this chapter is devoted to three specific studies by leading scholars. The strengths and weaknesses of these studies are discussed. The chapter concludes with the proposition that the economic growth of many urban areas, and the fortunes of their central cities, are being driven by the degree of economic success of their suburbs.

The final chapter of the book is devoted to selected economic and social problems that are at least partly related to urban economic trends. Chapter 16 includes discussions of crime, the problems of the urban "underclass," fiscal problems of central city governments, the apparent mismatch between job and housing location patterns, and the housing problems faced by low-income households.

G. SUMMARY

This first chapter has served to introduce you to the subject matter of urban economics and to the contents of this book. Urban economics is largely an applied field of economic inquiry in which data are collected, patterns in the data are observed, economic models are formulated and tested, and then the knowledge that is gained is used for forecasting or policymaking purposes.

Urban economics is about the economics of urban areas. Urban areas are linked to the larger economy, and one critical task is to understand those linkages. The other major part of the agenda of urban economics is to understand the spatial patterns of economic activity within an urban area and how those patterns have changed. The examples of New York, Los Angeles, and Chicago were used to illustrate some of the basic facts of modern urban areas in the United States. We learned that the absence of population growth at the metropolitan level translates into population decline in the core of the urban area because there is an underlying trend toward suburbanization even in urban areas that are not growing. We also learned that very rapid population growth in the metropolitan area leads to an increase in population densities and to a remarkable spreading out of the urban area. That tendency to spread out can, to some degree, be controlled by the use of an Urban Growth Boundary such as the one used in Portland, Oregon.

One final introductory note needs to be mentioned. Probably many students sign up for urban economics because they are interested in and concerned about a variety of economic and social problems that exist in urban areas in the United States and around the world. Students are correctly concerned about poverty, homelessness, problems with schools in central cities, racial discrimination, the welfare system, high taxes, and many other troubling aspects of urban life. Such students have come to the right place. It probably is true that quite a few professional economists who specialize in urban economics began their studies with similar concerns, and this book reflects the topics that urban economists have decided to study.

However, economists (and other social scientists, of course) know that concern about economic and social problems is not enough. Study and professional training are needed to turn concern into deeper understanding and useful contributions to debates over urban economic and social policy. That is why the emphasis in this book is on the fundamental methods that are used by urban economists. As you will see, there are many places where the more formal study of urban economics comes very close to being the study of an urban economic or social problem. However, there will also be many times when your study of this book seems to be pretty remote from more immediate urban problems. Be patient. Urban economists are probably more concerned about urban problems than are most people, but they also know that understanding urban problems is difficult work. A course in urban economics is, in my view, an essential part (but only a part) of the education that one needs to understand and address urban economic and social problems.

EXERCISES

1. Reproduce the analysis of population growth (as in Table 1.1) for the urban area of your choice. The data source for this kind of analysis is the decennial Census of Population and Housing, a critical source of information for anyone who is interested in urban areas. By the way, do not take your selection of an urban area lightly. The exercises at the end of some of the other chapters will ask you to conduct further empirical studies of this urban area.

2. In the text you were asked to make an estimate of the time when the population of the Los Angeles metropolitan area will overtake the population of the New York metropolitan area. Here are some suggestions for projecting the population of an urban area:

   (a) Assume that the population continues to grow by the same absolute amount per year as it did over the prior 20 years. For example, the population of the Los Angeles metropolitan area increased by 4.551 million from 1970 to 1990, or by 227,550 per year.

   (b) Assume that the population continues to grow at the same percentage rate as it did over the prior 20 years. In the case of Los Angeles, the increase from 1970 to 1990 was 45.6%. You can solve for the annual percentage increase by solving for r in

   $$(1 + r)^{20} = 1.456.$$

   The steps in this solution are

   $$1 + r = (1.456)^{1/20}$$
   $$\log(1 + r) = 0.05 \log 1.456 = 0.00816$$
   $$1 + r = 10^{0.00816} = 1.01897$$
   $$r = 0.019 \text{ (approximately)}.$$

   (c) Assume that the metropolitan area grows so as to be the same percentage of the nation's population as it was in 1990. The U.S. Bureau of the Census makes projections of the population of the nation that are updated frequently. They publish low-growth, moderate-growth, and high-growth projections. You can then link any particular metropolitan area to the national projections.

   (d) However, the fraction of the population of the nation that is located in the Los Angeles metropolitan area has been *rising*. You could assume that this fraction will continue to rise as it did over the 1970–1990 period. The U.S. population was 205.052 million in 1970 and 249.924 million in 1990, so the fraction of the population that was located in metropolitan Los Angeles was 4.867% in 1970 and 5.814% in 1990. This is an increase of 0.947% in 20 years. We might therefore assume that the population of metropolitan Los Angeles will be 6.761% of the U.S. population in the year 2010.

   Here is your task. Use all four methods to forecast the populations of the New York and Los Angeles metropolitan areas for the year 2010. Which forecasts make the most sense to you?

REFERENCES

Alonso, William, 1964. *Location and Land Use*. Cambridge, MA: Harvard University Press.

Hoover, Edgar and Raymond Vernon, 1959. *Anatomy of a Metropolis*. Cambridge, MA: Harvard University Press.

Schools of Thought in Urban Economics

A. INTRODUCTION

Urban economics was portrayed in Chapter 1 as a field of research in which economists are busy gathering data, building and testing models, making forecasts, conducting policy analysis, and deducing new normative propositions. All of that is true, but it leaves something out. Present within the field of urban economics (and economics in general) are three rather distinct schools of thought. Students in courses in macroeconomics are introduced to different schools of thought, such as the "Keynesians" and the "monetarists." Some textbooks in macroeconomics try to give a "balanced" treatment to the different schools of thought, while other texts present primarily the views of only one school. As you will see, adherence to a particular school of thought can influence research at every phase. On the normative side, schools of thought differ in the ethical objectives that are taken as given. On the positive side, the school of thought influences the nature of the data that are gathered, the nature of the facts that are deemed important to explain, the choice of economic model to explain those facts, and the use of the models that are formed. The existence of alternative schools of thought leads to competing economic models that can coexist. Sometimes it is not simply a matter of determining which economic model is "best" but which school of thought is "best." Often, there is no answer to this question. Often, it will be the case that a person's views on a particular question cannot be understood until that person's school of thought is identified.

What are the three schools of thought in urban economics? I shall refer to them as mainstream economics, conservative economics, and Marxian economics. These schools of thought in economics overlap with political views (liberal, conservative, socialist/Marxist), so each school of thought is discussed here both as a guide to economic research and as a political philosophy.

B. MAINSTREAM ECONOMICS

Most urban economists belong to the school of thought that is called *mainstream economics*. This school of thought is presented in most intermediate textbooks in microeconomic theory, so most students are already familiar with it. The ethical objective in mainstream economics is the maximization of the utility of the members of a society, where utility depends on the goods a person consumes and how a person spends his or her time. The society is constrained by the availability of resources, including land, capital, and (above all) the time of its members. Framing the economic question in this way as maximization subject to constraints leads to the familiar normative proposition that the marginal benefit of a particular good or activity (and hence price) should equal the marginal cost. This is so because the failure to satisfy this condition makes someone needlessly worse off. For example, suppose that a monopolist controls all the taxicabs in a particular city and charges a fare that is higher than marginal cost. This means that there are some consumers out there who are willing to pay more than marginal cost for a taxi ride, but they are unable to satisfy their demands. The benefit of the unsupplied taxi ride exceeds the benefit of the next-best use of resources (at the margin), so the consumer is made needlessly worse off. A different allocation of existing resources (more taxi rides, less of something else) could make consumers better off.

Mainstream economists believe that the allocation of resources to their various uses is, for the most part, best handled by the market. However, there are some very important exceptions to this rule that call for intervention into the economy by government. Mainstream economists argue that monopoly (and oligopoly), externalities (pollution and congestion), and public goods all call for public action to improve the allocation of resources. They also acknowledge that the market economy produces a distribution of income that is quite unequal, and they generally favor public policies to reduce income inequality. They recognize that there may be some loss of efficiency caused by income redistribution policy, but they suggest that society might be willing to tolerate some inefficiency to achieve a more equitable income distribution. They believe that government intervention in these situations will improve matters. Indeed, mainstream economists also generally advocate activist macroeconomic policies as well. They believe that the government is capable of using monetary and fiscal policy to stabilize the economy in the short run and to promote growth in the long run. Government policies can be mistaken or badly timed, but on balance the policies of a democratic government can be made to improve welfare.

The research agenda of mainstream urban economists is, to a degree, influenced by membership in this school of thought. A fair amount of their research focuses on the costs and benefits of various policy actions or proposals. Consider housing for low-income households, for example. Facts are gathered concerning the operation of the urban housing market in general and the status of low-income households in the housing market in particular. Economic models of the urban housing market are formulated and estimated. Then those models are used to discover the most efficient method for improving the housing of low-income households. Mainstream urban economists think that the facts show that the construction of public housing is a very expensive method for improving the housing of low-income households. The use of housing vouchers—certificates that increase the ability of low-income households to rent decent housing in the private market—is far more efficient. The same improvement in housing quality can be achieved with a lower government expenditure on housing vouchers, and a lower expenditure of real resources as well, than on public housing.

Now the fact is that housing policy in the United States includes only a small program that resembles housing vouchers. What explanation does the mainstream urban economist have for this seeming anomaly? First, nearly all of the public housing was constructed before we knew that housing vouchers are better policy. Now we are locked into a policy that must use the existing public housing units until they are obsolete. Second, the suppliers of public housing (and housing that is supplied by private suppliers under public subsidy) have formed political interest groups that block attempts to turn the public money for housing over directly to the low-income households. A political battle must be fought, and that battle can be waged with the results of studies that show the efficiency of housing vouchers and the waste of public housing.

The appendix to this book provides a brief review of some of the major normative propositions in mainstream microeconomics and introduces the mathematical techniques that are used in this book. You should study the first two sections of this appendix before you read Chapter 3.

C. CONSERVATIVE ECONOMICS

Conservative economics is discussed at some length here because this school of thought has been quite influential in recent years and because most students may not really know how conservative economics differs from mainstream economics. Most students know that Milton Friedman, professor emeritus from the University of Chicago and a winner of the Nobel Prize in economics, is the most prominent conservative economist. But it was Friedrich A. Hayek (another Nobel Prize winner) who wrote what conservative economists consider to be the classic statement of their values. Hayek's book *The Road to Serfdom*, published in 1944, still exerts considerable influence in conservative quarters. In its Summer 1994 issue, the conservative magazine *Policy Review* included a symposium entitled "Serfdom USA—Fifty Years Down Hayek's Road." The symposium coincides with the reissue of the book on its fiftieth anniversary.

Hayek's chief concern was with the progressive replacement of competition with planning, or the central direction of the nation's resources toward some objective. At the time he wrote, he was worried about the progressive advance of socialism in Western nations, especially England. His concern was with the *method* of centralized planning, even if the goals espoused by its advocates were admirable. He saw that the ultimate effect of socialism and other forms of central planning would be a return to serfdom, the condition of most ordinary people prior to their progressive liberation that began roughly with the Renaissance. For Hayek (1944, p. 14), the hallmark of Western civilization is "the respect for the individual man *qua* man, that is, the recognition of his own views and tastes as supreme in his own sphere, however narrowly that may be circumscribed, and the belief that it is desirable that men should develop their own individual gifts and bents." Conservatives think that the emergence of this respect for the individual was closely associated with the development of the laissez-faire market economy.

For Hayek the danger was those who advocated goals for the society other than freedom and liberty. This includes mainstream economists who advocate the maximization of utility of society's members. Hayek's central point is that the pursuit of social goals (except for those that can achieve virtually unanimous agreement), even those chosen through democratic means, must inevitably sharply restrict the freedom of individuals. The democratic decision to engage in central planning of a particular sector of the economy will lead to a delegation of substantial power to planning agencies. Hayek (1944, p. 66) stated that "The objectionable feature is that delegation is so often resorted to because the matter in hand cannot be regulated by general rules but only by the exercise of discretion in the decision of particular cases. In these instances delegation means that some authority is given power to make with the force of law what to all intents and purposes are arbitrary decisions (usually described as 'judging the case on its merits')." The attempt to plan a substantial portion of an economy will eventually cry out for an economic dictator, someone who can get things done—make the trains run on time, and so on. Free societies are governed by the rule of law, not by administrative discretion. Or as Milton Friedman suggests, the Federal Reserve should increase the money supply by a fixed percentage per year (a rule) rather than attempt to engage in discretionary monetary policy.

Hayek wrote a new forward for his book in the late 1950s, and there he recognized that socialism based upon the state as chief owner of the means of production was essentially a dead issue in the United States and Western Europe. His updated forecast was for continued "hodge-podge" development of the welfare state that would produce restrictions on human freedom that would strongly resemble full state socialism. Increasing reliance on administrative discretion rather than the rule of law was, in his view, going to be in the cards. The desire to have a welfare state would slowly produce a psychological predilection to limiting freedom. He predicted that we would get there, just at a slower pace than if we had embraced outright socialism.

Whether you believe Hayek's prediction, Milton Friedman certainly did. His 1962 book *Capitalism and Freedom* sets down the conservative's economic creed clearly and concisely. Like Hayek, Friedman's basic proposition is that human freedom is the ultimate end and that competitive capitalism is a system of economic freedom that is a necessary condition for political freedom. The secondary proposition is that the scope of government must be limited to functions that Friedman outlines and that governmental power must be dispersed rather than concentrated at the federal level. His basic statement (1962, p. 2) is that "freedom is a rare and delicate plant. Our minds tell us, and history confirms, that the great threat to freedom is the concentration of power. Government is necessary to preserve our freedom, it is an instrument through which we can exercise our freedom; yet by concentrating power in political hands, it is also a threat to freedom."

Friedman asked (1962, p. 2), "How can we benefit from the promise of government while avoiding the threat to freedom?" His answer is that government should largely be limited to certain functions that support the competitive market economy—provision of pure public goods such as the common defense, maintenance of law and order, enforcement of contracts voluntarily made, definition and enforcement of property rights, and provision of a monetary system. He found little reason for government action to regulate or operate monopolies or public policy to attempt to correct for externalities (neighborhood effects).

Friedman's view of monopoly is instructive. Monopoly means a lack of alternatives and therefore an inhibition of freedom. Friedman stated (in agreement with Hayek) that monopoly most often arises from government policy of some sort or through collusive agreements, so most monopoly can be avoided by eliminating the offending public support or by enforcement of the antitrust laws. The few instances in which monopoly arises from technological factors call for one of three courses of action: private monopoly, government regulation, or government operation. Friedman suggested (1962, p. 28) that permitting the private monopoly to operate as it will ". . . may be the least of the evils."

In matters of externalities, or neighborhood effects, Friedman follows the argument that was made by Ronald Coase, his colleague at the University of Chicago and yet another Nobel Prize winner, in a classic article [Coase (1960)]. Coase argued that if property rights are fully defined and enforced, and the costs of making "transactions" (i.e., costs of arriving at private contracts) are trivial, then externalities will not cause inefficiencies. Private negotiation can be used to arrive at an efficient allocation of resources. For example, suppose that a factory owns the right to make noise. In this case the neighbors can pay the factory owner to reduce the noise (by, perhaps, installing insulation), or they can suffer, whichever is cheaper. Or suppose that the neighbors own the right to peace and quiet. The factory owner can install insulation or can bribe the neighbors into accepting some noise (whichever is cheaper). Furthermore, all parties always have the option of moving away. Provided that a private agreement can be reached with minimal difficulties, there is no role for government to play in the regulation of factory noise. Besides, the attempt by government to regulate noise may make matters worse.

Friedman recognized that one of society's needs is the alleviation of poverty. Here he is famous for his advocacy of the negative income tax for all poor people regardless of occupation, employment status, sex, location, and so on. According to Friedman, the negative income tax has three fundamental advantages: It provides purchasing power for the poor directly, it permits markets to function in unregulated fashion, and it can be set up to provide an incentive for the poor to work. Friedman advocated the negative income tax as a more effective replacement for the myriad of programs that attempt to assist the poor. Note that Friedman's proposals follow Hayek's philosophy that we should follow simple rules of law rather than rely on the bureaucratic judgments of such people as officials of the Environmental Protection Agency and social workers.

At this point you may wonder why Friedman advocates any antipoverty policy at all. In a market economy people are paid according to their own decisions to work, obtain training for jobs, undertake risks, and so on. The income distribution is the result of choices freely made, so what's the problem? First, the economy is full of constraints on free choice. Equal educational opportunity is not available to all, minimum wage laws exist, and occupational licensure limits entry to various remunerative jobs. Friedman advocates doing away with all of these limitations on freedom, but in the meantime we have people in poverty. Furthermore, Friedman believes that the alleviation of poverty is a public good. As he put it (1962, p. 191), "I am distressed by the sight of poverty; I am benefited by its alleviation; but I am benefited equally whether I or someone else pays for its alleviation; the benefits of other people's charity therefore partly accrue to me." Given this "free-rider" problem, the alleviation of poverty must become a public program. Private charity will be insufficient to improve the welfare of *those who are not in poverty*. In this case, as in the case of other public goods, a public program enhances the personal freedom of both the poor *and* those who are not poor.

There can be no question that membership in the Conservative Economics school of thought influences one's research. These economists look for unexpected places in which the private market is working well, and they take particular delight in finding those instances in which government policy turns out to have had effects that seemingly were the opposite of those intended. In fact, George Stigler, another of Friedman's colleagues at the University of Chicago, received the Nobel Prize for founding the Chicago School of Political Economy. Members of this school concentrate some of their research efforts on the economic analysis of political decisions — equilibrium in the political marketplace for policies that help or harm certain groups. Why do public policies seem to "fail" so often? Perhaps it is because we fail to perceive the real purposes of those policies. For example, it is argued that zoning to regulate the use of urban land is needed to protect the health and welfare of the public. The legal justification for zoning in fact falls under the police power of local government. No doubt some aspects of zoning ordinances do protect the health and welfare of the public, but other aspects of zoning probably do just the opposite. Consider the requirement that some suburban zoning ordinances require that residential lots be quite large. This "large-lot" zoning has the effect of excluding households of more modest means from living in that suburb and has little to do with health and welfare of the public. Has zoning therefore "failed"? No, because the exclusion of lower-income households was the intention of the local government in the first place.

Two of Friedman's favorite examples of urban policy are public housing and urban renewal. One argument made for public housing is that slums create negative neighborhood effects. Therefore, the argument goes, the government should tear down the slums and replace them with public housing so that the negative neighborhood effects are eliminated. Friedman replies that those negative neighborhood effects may well exist and that negotiation of the sort suggested by Coase (1960) cannot handle the problem. The proper policy therefore is to levy a tax on slum housing (just as we should levy a tax on polluters) and to provide the poor with more income through a negative income tax. By the way, other conservative economists doubt that there are pervasive negative neighborhood effects associated with the housing consumed by low-income households that would call for any public action at all. Friedman then suggests that the real justification for the public housing program was paternalism — policymakers thought that the poor needed better housing more than they needed other things.

Whatever the justification for the public housing program may have been, its results seem to have been disastrous. The program of the 1950s bulldozed more housing units than were constructed, and many of the units constructed under the urban renewal program were for middle-class households. The public housing units that were constructed tended to segregate the poor into public housing developments and to concentrate and perhaps to exacerbate social problems. As opposed to the high-minded goals that were the original motivation for these programs, the actual implementation of the public housing and urban renewal programs was the result of decisions made by local officials and real estate developers who had their own agendas.

D. MARXIAN ECONOMICS

Karl Marx provided the world with a sweeping interpretation of economic history that included a prophesy for capitalism. Marx taught that the ultimate outcome of capitalism is huge industrial firms owned by the capitalist class that exploit and oppress the industrial workers, the proletariat. Capitalism ultimately fails to be of benefit to the mass of workers, who rise up and defeat the capitalist class in the final battle of the war between these two dominant social classes. The overriding theme in Marx is the class struggle between the two classes that are associated with the two primary factors of production, capital and labor.

Marxian economics survives in American universities (and a few other places), so it behooves one to understand Marxian arguments and to be able to recognize a Marxist. Marxism has been revised and adapted to the American scene, but the theme of class struggle remains intact. According to Marxists, conventional economics, including both the mainstream and conservative varieties, omits class conflict as an important factor to consider. The most prominent Marxist economists of the 1950s and 1960s were Paul Baran and Paul Sweezy, who published their major joint work, *Monopoly Capital*, in 1966. At the time of his death in 1964, Baran of Stanford was the only Marxist economist who held a tenured position in a major university economics department in the United States. He and Sweezy, who held an untenured position at Harvard in the early 1940s, led a renewal of interest in Marxist economics that has carried on to this day. How did these modern Marxists perceive American capitalism?

Baran and Sweezy began their book by asserting that the American economy is dominated by giant corporations in oligopolistic industries. The giant corporations are controlled by management, which is largely a self-perpetuating group. These firms tend to pursue maximum profits for their industries. They engage in price leadership and other policies to enhance financial strength and growth through the generation of huge amounts of retained earnings. The maximization of profits for the industry is a necessary step for the pursuit of these objectives. In the effort to maximize profits, the oligopolies continually work to cut costs and expand their markets. This hypothesis led Baran and Sweezy to their central point; under monopoly capitalism there is a tendency for what they call the *economic surplus* to rise. The economic surplus was defined as the difference between the economy's total output and the labor that is truly necessary for the production of the output. This point harks back to Marx's labor theory of value. The economic surplus is the extent to which the capitalist economy is wasteful of society's resources. In direct contrast to Marx, who believed that the rate of profit under capitalism would fall, Baran and Sweezy argued that monopoly capitalism would experience rising profits and greater waste of the ability of the economy to produce useful goods and services.

The Marxist class struggle for Baran and Sweezy was between the corporate elite (the managers of the giant corporations) and the workers in the rank and file.

Owners of small businesses and middle-class professionals did not play an important role in their class struggle.

It is important to realize that Baran and Sweezy regarded the U.S. government to be a tool of the major capitalist interests. The federal government was pursuing a policy of militarism and imperialism, so all military spending could be classified as surplus. However, Baran and Sweezy went far beyond the predictable point when they argued that (1966, p. 147) "the structure of the monopoly capitalism economy is such that a continually mounting volume of surplus simply could not be absorbed through private channels; if no other outlet were available, it would not be produced at all. What government absorbs is in addition to, not subtracted from, the private surplus." Under monopoly capitalism big government is needed to keep effective demand high, and this point has not been lost on the elite of corporate managers. Civilian spending on such things as education and welfare programs are part of the total, but under monopoly capitalism these forms of civilian spending can be expanded only to a limited degree (such as the rate of growth of the economy as a whole). According to Baran and Sweezy, influential portions of the corporate oligarchy would oppose generous welfare programs and an educational system that could be seen as a threat to the existing class system. It was therefore primarily through expanded military expenditures that the economic surplus was absorbed and effective demand maintained through the 1950s and 1960s (and 1970s and 1980s, Sweezy would no doubt argue). Military spending is useful for opening up foreign supplies of raw materials (such as oil) and foreign markets, and militaristic habit of thinking reinforces the power of the corporate oligarchy at home.

What does this sort of Marxist analysis have to do with urban areas? Plenty, according to a growing group of Marxist urbanists. For them, class conflict and the role of the state in advanced capitalism play out in urban areas. In the early 1970s Marxists began to write about how, in their view, urban problems that provoke local conflicts have their roots in national, even global, economic forces. Why has industrial investment shifted to the U.S. sunbelt and to less-developed countries? Why is the American economy shifting from an industrial to a service base? How do these forces influence class conflicts in urban areas, and what are the outcomes of those conflicts?

Marxists see class conflicts in controversies over the use of land in cities and in the funding of urban public services. Industrial workers in the United States (and in other advanced capitalist countries) failed to create national revolutionary politics based on grievances at the workplace, so Marxists have turned their attention to urban political economy because that is where they think the class conflict action is. For them capitalism will inevitably lead to class conflicts that will lead to a socialist revolution, so the questions are: "Where are the conflicts happening?" and following Lenin, "What can Marxist intellectuals do to move the revolutionary process along?" In short, the ethical objective is socialist revolution, and the gathering of facts and the formulation of theories are guided by this goal. As the Marxist urban political scientist Michael Peter Smith (1988, pp. 64–65) puts it, "both structural Marxists and other critical urban theorists were forced to come to grips with the failure of the industrial working classes in advanced capitalist societies to convert concrete grievances found in the work place into a revolutionary politics. Surveying the landscape, they turned to the arena where social conflicts in the 1960s and 1970s were most evident, the arena of urban politics." For Marxists there must be a "crisis" that reflects the inherent contradictions in the capitalist economy, but traditional Marxist analysis had not been used to examine urban areas. Marxists have disagreed over how to make Marxism fit urban political economy. In this section we describe two examples of Marxist analysis applied to urban areas.

Richard Child Hill (1978) provides one anatomy of that "crisis" in the context of urban America. He argues that the huge profits and capital accumulation of large, oligopolistic firms no longer require the older, densely concentrated central cities. Capital accumulation is taking place in the suburbs. More important, perhaps, as profits have been squeezed in the past 20 years, the major corporations have become global in scope. They seek to locate production and distribution facilities at the least expensive locations, in places such as Mexico and southeast Asia. Hill does not see all of this as a "capitalist conspiracy" but rather, as inevitable outcomes of capitalism.

The consequences of these trends include the loss of economic opportunity for central city residents (especially minority populations), financial decline of various central cities, and a host of social problems associated with the urban "underclass." Central cities have an enormous fiscal burden associated with maintaining some semblance of social control over their people who no longer have an economic function in the capitalist economy. The inherent contradiction is between the use of the economic surplus for further capital accumulation or measures for social control. For most people, questions of urban social policy are the ordinary stuff of local and national politics. Marxists seek to make clear the underlying "structural" reasons for social problems in our capitalist economy.

Another example of Marxist analysis of urban areas is Matthew Edel's (1972) essay on the conflict over the use of land near the downtown areas of major cities. He argued that as new housing was built in the suburbs for upper- and middle-class households, the older housing in the central city was relinquished to the lower-income households. However, many of the jobs held by the corporate elite and their supporters continued to be located downtown. Indeed, many downtown areas experienced renewed growth in professional and white-collar jobs in the 1980s. The continued strength of downtown as the location of jobs held by the middle and upper classes therefore creates a conflict over the use of land near the downtown business area. Edel (1972) argued that the market is not capable of converting what many regard as slums into places where the middle and upper classes wish to live. Government action is needed, and the political struggle surrounding "urban renewal" policy is an outgrowth of the market (capitalist) economy that is a conflict between social classes. Edel went on to describe examples of victories for the social elite in such land-use conflicts.

All students should learn to think critically, and in my view, the Marxist viewpoint must be given particularly close scrutiny. I shall illustrate with my own critique of Baran and Sweezy's framework and Hill's urban crisis theory.

What of Baran and Sweezy's (1966) indictment of U.S. capitalism? Baran and Sweezy created a category of expenditures called economic surplus and asserted that these expenditures served no useful function for the society. This is not a hypothesis that can be tested and found to be true or false. Anyone can divide the GNP into various categories and attach labels to those categories. Such categorization is useful to the extent that testable hypotheses rest on the distinctions being made. If we can define what might be meant by "no useful function" in the statement above, we might be able to test the usefulness of the categorization. Rather, it was Marxist ideology that defined the economic surplus, which Baran and Sweezy said included (among other things) profits, rents, interest, advertising expenditures, government spending, and lawyers. Cogent arguments can be made for the usefulness of each. For conventional economists, profits, rents, and interest serve to allocate capital to productive uses and generate economic growth. Surely some advertising expenditures are of questionable value to society, but some advertising provides useful information. The assertion that government spending is waste is surely preposterous (although conservative economists agree that a lot of government is wasteful). In short, Baran and Sweezy made some cogent criticisms of U.S. society, but their economic framework disintegrates upon close examination. We cannot determine whether their economic framework is right or wrong, but we do know that some of the items they regarded as wasteful surplus surely are not. However, we must also remember that some Marxists do not care whether their arguments are right or wrong in the ordinary sense. Following Lenin, their primary concern is whether their arguments move the society closer to the socialist revolution.

Next, consider Hill's (1978) attempt to link the problems of central cities primarily to the actions of major corporations. First, the movement of middle-class people and many jobs to the suburbs does not originate with decisions made by the elite of corporate management. Many people have a taste for living in the suburbs. The development of the automobile and government decisions to build highways were not capitalist plots. Not even Baran and Sweezy regard automobiles as part of the economic surplus. Subsequently, many employers large and small have established workplaces in the suburbs. As subsequent chapters show, one does not have to be a Marxist to understand why. Second, it is true that since the early 1970s, many of the older U.S. corporations have been under a great deal of pressure to cut costs and improve productivity. We have seen big increases in the foreign penetration of American markets (along with expanding American exports). As the Japanese, German, Korean, and other economies have grown, competition in world markets has increased. Corporate "downsizing" seems to be a way of life. Changes in technology and communications have made it feasible to disperse production activity away from traditional locations in the northeastern United States. All of these changes can be explained using the methods of mainstream economics. The social and fiscal problems of the older central cities are very troublesome and have many causes.

Marxists such as Hill cannot have it both ways. If the problems of the central cities in the current era are the product of advanced capitalism, so too were the benefits of urban areas of just a few years ago. In the period of the 1940s to the 1960s, millions of people of all races migrated to the great urban areas of the northeastern United States to work in the factories, offices, and distribution centers. Members of minority groups, especially blacks, encountered racism in the cities, but they still came because life in the city was better than life in the rural areas and small towns. The machinations of the elite of corporate managers cannot be given credit for these facts, just as they cannot be given primary blame for today's urban problems. It is not clear that the notion of class conflict in "advanced capitalism" contributes to our understanding of urban economic and social problems. Also, racism is not a product of capitalism; racism exists all over the world.

E. SUMMARY

Urban economists can generally be classified as belonging to one of three schools of thought: mainstream economics, conservative economics, or Marxist economics. Mainstream urban economists take the economy as they find it. Their first task is to understand the workings of the urban economy, and then they sometimes make policy recommendations that are designed to have benefits that are greater than costs. Conservative economists normally are distrustful of the ability of government to undertake policies that enhance individual freedom. Milton and Rose Friedman, in their best-selling book *Free to Choose*, asserted that (1980, p. xix) "in the government sphere, as in the market, there seems to be an invisible hand, but it operates in precisely the opposite direction from Adam Smith's: an individual who intends only to serve the public interest by fostering government intervention is 'led by an invisible hand to promote' private interests, 'which was no part of his intention.'" The conservative urban economist's research agenda will often include finding out why the market outcome is the best outcome, or determining just how the Friedmans' invisible hand "theorem" operates in particular cases. In complete contrast, the Marxist economist seeks to find the locus of the crisis of advanced capitalism that will lead eventually to socialist revolution. Many contemporary Marxists think that the inevitable class struggle between capital and labor is taking place in America's central cities.

You should be able now to recognize each of these schools of thought when you meet them—and I am certain that you will meet them. Your task will always be to use your ability for critical thinking to evaluate the points of view that you encounter. It is fair to say that most of the rest of this book is devoted to mainstream urban economics. Criticisms of mainstream economic thinking are included along the way, and some references to the conservative and Marxist schools of thought are also incorporated.

EXERCISE

1. Select an issue of public policy that is under debate in the news media in an urban area of your choice. For example, the issue might have to do with public housing, schools, environmental protection, public transit, and so on. Decide how a mainstream economist, a conservative economist, and a Marxist economist might approach the study of that issue and what the nature of their policy recommendations might be.

REFERENCES

Baran, Paul A. and Paul M. Sweezy, 1966. *Monopoly Capital: An Essay on the American Economic and Social Order*. New York: Monthly Review Press.

Coase, Ronald H., 1960. "The Problem of Social Cost," *Journal of Law and Economics*, Vol. 3 (October), pp. 1–44.

Edel, Matthew, 1972. "Planning, Market or Warfare? Recent Land Use Conflict in American Cities," in M. Edel and J. Rothenberg, eds., *Reading in Urban Economics*. New York: Macmillan.

Friedman, Milton, 1962. *Capitalism and Freedom*. Chicago: The University of Chicago Press.

Friedman, Milton and Rose D. Friedman, 1980. *Free to Choose*. New York: Harcourt Brace Jovanovich.

Hayek, Friedrich A., 1944. *The Road to Serfdom*. Chicago: The University of Chicago Press.

Hill, Richard Child, 1978. "Fiscal Collapse and Political Struggle in Decaying Central Cities in the United States," in W. Tabb and L. Sawyers, eds., *Marxism and the Metropolis*. New York: Oxford University Press.

Smith, Michael Peter, 1988. *City, State, and Market*. Cambridge: Basil Blackwell.

CHAPTER

$$\boxed{3}$$

Location Decisions, Agglomeration Economies, and the Origins of Cities

A. INTRODUCTION

Cities are formed by the location decisions of firms, households, and governmental bodies. In this chapter we examine the theory and some more practical aspects of how location decisions are made by firms. The chapter begins with some basic theory that explores transportation costs and other determinants of a firm's location decision. In the next section we take a further step to examine the possibility that firms in a specific industry, or firms in general, may save on costs by locating together. These ideas about economies of urban agglomeration are explored theoretically in the succeeding section. In the final section of the chapter we use some of the theoretical concepts to examine the origins of cities in the United States.

B. LESSONS IN BASIC LOCATION THEORY FOR A FIRM

The general problem faced by a firm is to choose a location at which it will assemble inputs and from which it will distribute its output to customers. Both the inputs and the customers may have dispersed location patterns, and both inputs and output are subject to transportation costs. This general problem can be very complicated, so to make some progress, economists emphasize two simple versions of the problem. The first version supposes that there is only one input that is used to produce the output and that customers are all located in one place. The second version suppresses the inputs entirely and only considers a firm that must distribute output to customers in various locations.

In the first model—the one input, one market model—the firm uses an input that is available at some location and produces an output that is sold at another location. For example, suppose that the firm's business is to take raw lumber (i.e., trees that have been cut down) available at some forest, cut the lumber into firewood, and then deliver the firewood to the market in the city. One of the things that the firm must do to maximize profits is to select the location where it cuts the trees into firewood. At any level of output that is chosen the firm can make more profits if it can cut down on transportation costs. Where does the firm perform the operation of cutting the trees into firewood? The firm could transport the raw lumber to the city first and then produce the firewood. Or the firm could cut up the trees at the forest first and then transport the firewood to market. Also, some point between the forest and the city could be selected.

Suppose that the firm decides to produce 10 tons of firewood, and assume that it takes 12.5 tons of trees to make 10 tons of firewood. (There is 20% waste in the process of turning trees into firewood, so this is a *weight-losing* process.) The firm can use a standard stake-bed truck to carry the firewood, but hauling trees calls for a larger and more expensive truck. Either type of truck is available for rent, but the truck used to haul trees is more expensive. Now consider this problem carefully. Clearly, it is cheaper to cut the trees into firewood at the forest and haul firewood to the city, compared to hauling the trees to the city first. Furthermore, and here is the more subtle point, the firm will not choose a point in between the forest and the city either. Hauling 12.5 tons of trees even 1 mile is more expensive (in this model) than hauling 10 tons of firewood. The firm will choose to locate at the source of the raw material—the trees.

This argument can be made graphically. The firm uses an input that is located at point *I* in Figure 3.1, and produces output for the market located at point *M*. Straight line *II** shows the cost of transporting the input (12.5 tons of raw lumber) needed for 10 tons of output at various distances from *I*. The slope of this line is the cost of an additional mile of transporting the input. Straight line *MM** likewise shows the cost of transporting the output (10 tons of firewood) from various locations away from point *M*. The slope of the line is −1 times the cost of transporting the output one more mile. The negative slope means that this component of transportation cost declines as distance to the market *declines*. The entire transportation cost for 10 tons of output is the sum of these two costs, which is line *M**I*. Where would you locate your firewood firm? Given the transportation costs displayed in Figure 3.1, you would choose to locate at point *I* because the point minimizes transportation costs.

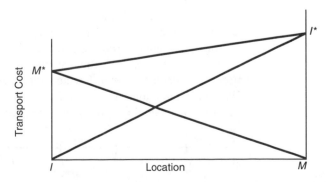

FIGURE 3.1 Transportation cost and location

FIGURE 3.2 Transportation cost and location

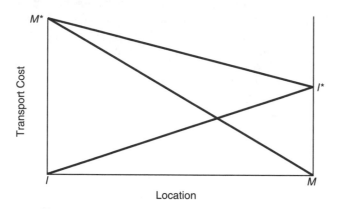

The appendix to this chapter contains a mathematical model for this location problem that connects the model to the standard theory of the firm. This appendix is recommended for those students who are familiar with microeconomic theory.

The example shown in Figure 3.1 leads to the firm's location choice at *I*, the input location. It is easy to construct cases in which the firm decides to locate at the market. Consider the case of Coca-Cola. The "secret" formula syrup is produced at point *I* and is the main input. The other input is water. The market for bottles of Coca-Cola is at point *M*. It is much cheaper to transport the input (syrup) than it is to transport the bottles of output. Figure 3.2 illustrates the matter. This is a case of a *weight-gaining* production process, and the transportation costs throw the firm to the market location.

What does this have to do with cities? Note that the firm chooses to locate either at the input location or at the market and not at intermediate points. Firms are drawn to their inputs or to their markets. Either location might become a city. Obviously, a *market-oriented firm* (as in Figure 3.2) will locate in a city, where the consumers are located. Also, an *input-oriented firm* (as in Figure 3.1) would locate in a city if the input happens to be located there. For example, the main input might be some sort of specialized labor rather than a raw material. The cumulative effect of these location decisions would create cities.

The next basic location theory model considers a firm that must distribute output to customers in various locations. It is assumed that input and production costs do not vary from place to place. The simplest version of the model presumes that customers are located along a straight line—space is only one-dimensional. Figure 3.3 shows seven customers (*A* through *G*) arrayed along a road. Each customer purchases 1 unit of the good. Ignore customer *G'* for now. The rules of the game are that the firm must select *one* location at which production takes place and then deliver the product to each customer. Furthermore, there is one delivery round trip per customer. We can assume that either the firm's delivery person or the customer makes the trip. The classic example is that of an ice cream vendor on a (linear) beach.

FIGURE 3.3 Customers on a road

Where should the firm locate to minimize transportation costs? The firm should follow the *principle of median location*, which states that transportation costs are minimized if the firm is located at the median customer. In this case the median customer is customer D. Three customers are located to the left of D and three are located to the right of D. Why does the median customer determine the minimum for transportation costs? Consider any other point—point C, for example. Assume that the distance from D to C is $\frac{1}{2}$ mile. Point C has a higher transportation cost than point D because, in moving to C, the firm is nearer to three customers (A, B, and C) and saves 3 miles in round trips but is farther away from four customers (D, E, F, and G) and adds 4 miles to total delivery cost. A similar argument holds for any other point along the line. By a similar argument, the best location cannot be off the line either. Why?

One interesting and perhaps unexpected implication of the model is that the location of the most distant customer makes no difference to the choice of location. Suppose that customer G moves to location G' in Figure 3.3. Point D is still the best location. Total delivery costs have increased, of course, but there is nothing the firm can do about that.

The principle of median location works best if there is an *odd* number of customers. If there is an *even* number of customers, the firm's location is not determined precisely. For example, suppose that customer G (and G') is eliminated. Now with six customers the firm is indifferent to all locations from C to D. As the firm hypothetically moves from C to D, it gets closer to three customers and farther away from three customers. But moving outside this range will increase transportation cost—a move away from D toward E puts the firm closer to only two customers and farther away from four.

The two basic location models for the firm in this section seem to offer contradictory advice. The one-input, one-market model leads to the conclusion that the firm should locate at the input source or at the market. However, the principle of median location tells us that the firm should locate in some sense in the "middle" of its customers. Upon closer examination the two models are not offering contradictory advice. Consider a firm with only two customers (with inputs suppressed). Such a firm is indifferent to all locations along the route from one customer to the other—provided that the cost of delivery per mile is the same for the two customers. Now suppose that the per-mile delivery cost is higher for one customer than for the other. This delivery cost difference makes the firm prefer to locate at the site of the customer with the higher delivery cost. This result is essentially the same as the result obtained in the one-input, one-market model. In short, the model that generates the principle of median location can easily be transformed into one that closely resembles the one-input, one-market model.

The principle of median location provides a reason why cities grow. Suppose that a new product is invented, and a firm decides to provide the product to the market shown in Figure 3.4. The market has five customers (A through E) located to-

FIGURE 3.4 Customers on a road   A,B,C,
D,E   F   G   H

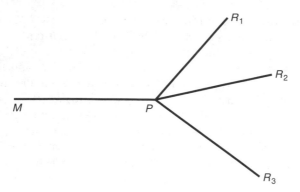

FIGURE 3.5 Production of wheat for export

gether in a city and three customers located in the "hinterlands" (*F*, *G*, and *H*). The median location is between customers *D* and *E*—in the city. The city attracts the new firm based on access to the customers.

A slightly more complex model than the two discussed so far can be used to explain the existence of port cities. A port city is a city at which goods are transferred from one mode of transportation to another. There is a cost of transferring cargo from one mode to another. For example, wheat is transported from the farms to the port by train and then exported by ship. Or foodstuffs are transported to the port by ship and then distributed by truck. In each case the cargo must undergo the costly operation of being unloaded and then loaded. These natural breaks in the transportation system, called *transshipment points*, become probable locations for cities. A transshipment point, by definition, requires a labor force for the loading and unloading operations. In addition, a transshipment point can become the location of production activity.

Consider the case of wheat production for export shown in Figure 3.5. Wheat is produced along rail lines R_1, R_2, and R_3. The market for wheat and wheat products is located at point *M*, and the port is point *P*. The distance from *P* to *M* must be traversed by ship. Now imagine that you are going to locate a flour mill somewhere in Figure 3.5. There are two locations that are likely candidates, *M* and *P*. It might be cheaper to ship raw wheat all the way to *M* and produce flour at the market. Because flour milling is a weight-losing process, it is more likely that it will be cheaper to mill flour at point *P* and ship flour to *M*. Note that you would not assemble your raw material at some other point along the routes to R_1, R_2, or R_3. Such a location would require greater shipping distances for both the wheat *and* the flour than does point *P*. The port thus becomes a center for production activity as well as transportation. Indeed, most major U.S. cities began as ports or transshipment points and grew into major centers of production. This group includes Boston, New York, Philadelphia, Baltimore, Chicago, Cleveland, Pittsburgh, New Orleans, St. Louis, Los Angeles, San Francisco, and Seattle.

The possible importance of a transshipment point can also be demonstrated in the simple one-input, one-market model. In this model it is assumed that a transshipment point exists somewhere between the location of the raw material and the location of the market. The cargo must be transferred from one transport mode to another at that point, so the costs of unloading and loading must be paid in any case. It is also assumed that there are loading and unloading costs incurred at the location of the raw material and the market, respectively. In this case clearly the firm would never wish to locate at any point other than the location of the raw material, the market, or the transshipment point because such a location would mean adding an unloading–loading operation that is unnecessary.

For simplicity assume that loading and unloading are the only transportation costs for the firm—the cost of moving the cargo is trivial compared to loading and unloading costs. The problem now boils down to a comparison of three alternatives:

1. Loading raw material at its source, unloading and loading raw material at the transshipment point, and unloading raw material at the production point (market)
2. Loading final output at the raw material source, unloading and loading final output at the transshipment point, and then unloading at the market
3. Loading raw material at its source, unloading raw material and loading final output at the transshipment point, and unloading final output at the market

Any of these three alternatives could turn out to be cheapest, depending on the various loading and unloading costs at the three locations. The point is that the transshipment point has become one of the options for the location of the production facility.

C. OTHER FACTORS IN THE LOCATION DECISION

The models discussed so far consider only transportation costs, but there are many other factors that enter into a firm's location decision. Indeed, improvements in transportation and communication have made these other factors more important than they were in the past. This is the day of interstate highways, air travel, rapid air freight, FAX machines, and the internet. A manufacturer of a product for a wide market has a large range of possible locations from the standpoint of transportation and communication costs. What can narrow that choice?

Labor Costs

One critical factor is labor. The wage rate (before taxes) that must be paid is important, but the quality of the workforce can be even more important to the firm. Firms seek locations where the workers with the needed skills are available. They also seek locations where the business climate is such that work rules can be designed to enhance the efficiency of the operation. If all the needed skills are not available at a particular location, workers must be recruited and moved. How difficult will it be to attract these workers from other urban areas? Wage rates (after taxes) matter again, of course, but another set of factors lumped into a category called *quality of life* is also quite important. Quality of life depends upon positive things such as good weather, sports and cultural amenities, good schools, recreation opportunities, universities, quality of medical care, attractive natural terrain and architecture, historical sites, and good shopping. These things are called *locational amenities*. Negative factors such as crime and pollution also play a role. Clearly, the San Francisco metropolitan area wins. What do you particularly value on this list? What would you add to the list? A good set of locational amenities will help the firm to recruit the needed workers. All of this can get quite complicated because different types of workers may prefer different groups of locational amenities.

Other Inputs: Energy, Capital, and Land

The cost and availability of other inputs may also be important. Energy costs are particularly important for the industries that require substantial amounts of this commodity. The most energy-intensive manufacturing industries are paper mills, chemicals, petroleum refining, primary metals (e.g., steel and aluminum), and stone, clay, and glass products. These industries can be expected to pay attention to energy costs. The availability of capital can be an important consideration for smaller firms. Large firms raise capital in the national capital market, but smaller firms may have to rely on local sources of loans. Do local financial institutions understand the firm's line of business? Is venture capital available? These questions can be important in particular cases. Labor, energy, and capital have been discussed. What about land and real estate? Are good sites available at reasonable prices? Do those sites have environmental problems lurking under the ground? Are needed buildings (offices, warehouses, industrial facilities) available?

Intermediate Inputs

In addition to the primary inputs, firms are also concerned with the cost and availability of goods and services that are intermediate inputs to the business in question. This can be a long list of raw materials, parts, and business services such as specialized legal, accounting, and computer services. These intermediate inputs are normally purchased from other firms, and many of them may be available in the local economy.

The Knowledge Input

Another category of inputs can be called knowledge of the industry. Is a proposed location one where the firm can more easily keep up with the latest trends in the industry? To survive and thrive, a firm may need to have rapid access to information about changes in products and/or production technologies. Television and movie producers locate in Los Angeles. Fashion designers prefer New York (and Paris and Milan). Information about these industries is "in the air" in such places.

Taxes and Public Services

The activities of the state and local governments can also be important to firms. Governments impose taxes and provide the standard public goods and services. The level of taxation imposed on the firm and the quality of the public goods and services provided to the firm must be considered. There has been disagreement about the importance of taxes and routine public services in the location decisions of firms, but a recent survey of research by Newman and Sullivan (1988) shows that when other factors are equal, taxes do matter. This result is found consistently in studies of location choice within an urban area. Taxes show up as a significant location factor less often in studies of location choice from among a group of urban areas. There are additional factors beyond the normal functions of state and local governments. Nearly all states and localities offer incentive programs for business. Businesses may be offered tax breaks, low-interest loans, job training programs targeted to their needs, construction of needed infrastructure (e.g., a highway interchange), and other inducements. Incentives for business are a part of location decisions in the modern economy. These kinds of programs are discussed at length in later chapters. Local governments also engage in a variety of regulatory activities such as building codes, zoning ordinances, and environmental regulations. Are local governments prepared to be cooperative with business?

In this section we have discussed a lengthy list of factors other than transportation costs that influence the location decisions of firms. Implicit in the discussion of many of these factors is the idea that a firm may be attracted to a location because the location possesses an agglomeration of economic activity that creates a favorable economic environment for that firm. A more systematic discussion of agglomeration factors is needed.

D. AGGLOMERATION ECONOMIES

The notion of an economy of agglomeration is one of the central concepts in urban economics, and it means that cost reductions occur *because* economic activities are *located* in one place. The original idea is attributed to Alfred Marshall (1920, Book 4, Chapter 10). Marshall never used the term *agglomeration economies*; instead, he referred to *localized industries*. He devoted an entire chapter to this concept, but the following passage [Marshall (1920, p. 225)] may give you the flavor of his discussion:

> When an industry has thus chosen a locality for itself, it is likely to stay there long: so great are the advantages which people following the same skilled trade get from near neighborhood to one another. The mysteries of the trade become no mysteries; but are as it were in the air, and children learn many of them unconsciously. Good work is rightly appreciated, inventions and improvements in machinery, in processes and the general organization of the business, have their merits promptly discussed: if one man starts a new idea, it is taken up by others and combined with suggestions of their own; and thus it becomes the sources of further new ideas. And presently subsidiary trades grow up in the neighborhood, supplying it with implements and materials, organizing its traffic, and in many ways conducing to the economy of its material.

This statement, and the rest of Marshall's chapter on the subject, includes factors that are external to the individual firm but internal to the local industry (e.g., if one person starts a new idea), as well as factors that are external to the local industry but internal to the local economy (e.g., subsidiary trades grow up). Also, Marshall mixed factors that mean lower costs in a static sense with factors that create continuing decreases in costs. A more systematic approach was needed.

In his classic volume *Interregional and International Trade*, Bertil Ohlin (1933) provided most of what is now the standard system for classifying agglomeration economies. Ohlin (1933, p. 203) suggested that it is meaningful to set up the following categories of agglomeration economies:

1. Economies of scale within the firm
2. Localization economies, which are external to the individual firm and arise from the size of the local industry

3. Urbanization economies, which are external to the local industry and arise from the size of the local economy

Hoover (1937) used the terms *localization economies* and *urbanization economies* to refer to the last two of Ohlin's categories. Ohlin's categories refer to *static* rather than dynamic agglomeration economies. Dynamic agglomeration economies are important for the growth of an urban area, and this topic is discussed in detail in Part III of this book. Ohlin added one more category to the list because an agglomeration of firms in an urban area may be the result of:

4. Interindustry linkages, which arise from transportation cost savings in purchases of intermediate inputs (i.e., inputs other than the primary inputs: labor, capital, land, and entrepreneurship)

Economies of scale within the firm refer, in this context, to economies that are created by expanding production at a single location. Average cost declines as output at that location increases. Other economies of scale may arise when the firm increases in size by adding establishments at new locations. The latter notion of economies of scale is not an agglomeration economy as here defined. The agglomeration economy called *economies of scale* can arise for a variety of reasons, including the spreading of a fixed cost over a larger output, greater specialization and division of labor, and cost reductions through bulk purchases. This form of agglomeration economy is discussed rather extensively in general courses in microeconomics, but there is a need to pursue the topic a bit more here.

In a classic article, Edwin Mills (1967) asked us to imagine an economy with *no* economies of scale. It turns out that this is difficult to do because it is an economy without cities. All goods and services can be produced in very small quantities at minimum cost, so everything is produced everywhere. What sort of economy is this? One idea is that the feudal economy of medieval times may have approximated such an economy. Each feudal manor was nearly a self-sufficient entity that produced its own food, clothing, housing, furniture, tools, weapons, livestock, medical care, religious services, and so on. Roads basically did not exist, and there was very little trade.

Now suppose that someone invents a process that creates economies of scale in some line of production. Suppose that the product involved is cloth. People on the feudal manor raise sheep, shear them, and make wool cloth for clothing. They use simple technologies for these tasks, and the making of cloth consumes a great deal of time. This particular example has been chosen because it should sound familiar. Have you ever been to a reconstructed pioneer village or a museum with articles from the United States in the first half of the nineteenth century? You undoubtedly have seen a spinning wheel. What on earth were people doing with a spinning wheel in the middle of the nineteenth century? They were making their own thread so that they could make their own cloth, of course. In fact, most of the soldiers in the Confederate army in the Civil War wore clothing that was "homespun." (By the way, clothing made out of homespun cotton cloth had a distinctive "butternut" color. Most of the Confederate soldiers did not wear the stylish gray uniforms that we see in the movies.)

This cloth can now be made by using a manufacturing production process that embodies significant economies of scale. What happens? Someone builds a factory of some size and hires workers. The cost of producing cloth in the factory is far less than the cost of making it at home. The cost of making cloth at home is the opportunity cost of spending time spinning and weaving. People on the farms can do better by growing more crops and trading the foodstuffs for cloth. The people who work in the cloth factory get paid wages, with which they buy food from the farmers. What is more, the factory is located at some particular site. To save time getting to work, the workers reside near the factory. A marketplace is set up so that people can make the exchanges that are needed. Voilà, a town has been created.

How large will this town be, and how much cloth will be produced there? The answer depends on the extent of the economies of scale, the cost of transporting the cloth to the consumers, and the population density out in the agricultural area. Suppose that the economies of scale are not very great; the cost of producing in the factory even at its most efficient size is not very much less than the cost of homespun. Further suppose that transportation costs are high (e.g., no roads exist and people walk). These assumptions mean that the output of the factory will be small, the town will be small, and the area to which the factory sells its output will be small as well. The farmers cannot save much by buying cloth from the factory, and transportation costs (in terms of time spent) are high. Beyond some rather short distance the farmers will simply decide to make their own cloth because this option is cheaper. These are the reasons why the pioneers in the first half of the nineteenth century made their own cloth even though there were sizable textile industries in New England and England at the time. On the other hand, if the economies of scale are large and transportation costs are cheap, the factory can sell its output over a wide area.

Localization economies are external to the firm and arise because of the size of the local industry. The static notion of localization economies presumes that there is a limit to the saving that arises from the size of the local industry, or otherwise there would be cumulative declines in costs for that industry. The larger the local industry gets, the lower are costs and the larger the industry gets. The first point that one might make is that firms in some (indeed, many) industries have no interest at all in locating near other firms in the same industry. Firms in the same industry are in competition. If you wish to start a grocery store, you are probably not going to locate your store next to a big supermarket. You look for a possible gap in the network of grocery stores. The same thing can be said for drugstores, video rental stores, dentists, and many others. These examples are what are called *convenience goods* in the Census of Retail Trade. But the Census of Retail Trade also has another category, called *shopping goods*. Shopping goods are goods for which the consumer invests some time comparing prices and qualities before the purchase is made. Think about purchasing an automobile. The consumer probably engages in fairly extensive comparison shopping before such a major purchase is made. Now think again about where the auto dealers are located. Many of them are located near other auto dealers! There are major streets or highways that are lined with one auto dealer after another. This spatial arrangement facilitates the comparison shopping that consumers are going to do. Many auto dealers want to be a stop on that comparison shopping trip, so they are willing to locate near their competitors. Note that auto dealers are willing to locate near dealers who sell *other* makes of autos. A Buick dealer does not wish to locate near another Buick dealer. Indeed, the Buick Division of General Motors does a careful analysis of the local market and the spatial arrangement of Buick dealers before they grant a license for another Buick dealer. In any event, this sort of shopping behavior creates an incentive for businesses in an industry to cluster together because they can save on advertising and promotion costs, the costs of attracting customers.

These shopping effects can apply to an entire industry in an urban area. If you are a wholesale buyer of clothing for a department store, you can go to New York, Paris, and Milan to see the products that are available.

Other forms of localization economies are created if there are economies of scale in the provision of inputs specific to the industry. Suppose that the industry requires workers who need a specific form of training. The workers can be trained by the firm itself, but that might be expensive. If there are enough firms in the local industry, it will be worthwhile for someone to set up an educational or training program that does the job. These programs can be set up by labor unions, private training firms, public institutions of higher education (e.g., junior colleges or universities), or local governments through the use of job training funds provided partly by the federal government. A training program that is not run as part of one of the firms is created precisely because it is the cheaper option. Or, as Marshall put it, if the local industry is large enough, the skills that are required for that industry are just "in the air." People in Los Angeles really do talk the movie business. At least some people in Chicago really do discuss the futures and options markets in their spare time. A larger local industry also creates a larger pool of labor with the requisite skills, so it may be easier for an individual firm to fill open positions. That pool of labor is created partly by people who migrate to the urban area in the hope of finding a job in that particular industry. More discussion of labor and human capital is contained in Part III of the book.

Economies of scale can also exist in the other inputs. These items were discussed in the preceding section but not in the context of economies of scale. The provision of capital for the industry may require specialized knowledge of the industry by lending officers and others who make lending decisions. If there are enough firms in the local industry, it will be worthwhile for some financial institutions to develop that specialized knowledge. The same thing goes for various types of business services, such as legal advice, accounting, advertising, management consulting, and computer services. The needs of an industry may be special, and an agglomeration economy is created when it pays someone to become the specialized lawyer, accountant, media buyer, management consultant, or computer consultant. The lawyer or accountant can work more efficiently if she works only for movie producers (or fashion designers or commodity traders) than if she has a general practice that requires jumping from one type of work to another. Other intermediate inputs can be subject to economies of scale as well. The industry may require specialized machinery and parts. The specialized machinery may require highly skilled and specialized maintenance and repair services, which in turn may require specialized training courses as well.

The last three paragraphs are written in a rather informal style, but they contain some powerful specific reasons for the existence of localization economies. Similar arguments can be made for urbanization economies, cost reductions for an industry that arise from the size of the entire local economy. We have places called *shopping centers* within an urban area. These are places that offer a wide range of goods, so shoppers hope to be able to buy everything on their lists in a single place. Similarly, shoppers such as wholesale buyers are attracted to an urban area that offers a wide range of products. Economies of scale exist in the provision of inputs that are not specific to a particular industry. An important example is the general urban infrastructure. Much of this infrastructure is provided by the public sector, and other parts are provided privately. Transportation facilities such as airports, ports, and railway service are subject to economies of scale. Air and water transportation services are provided jointly by the public and private sectors. The public sector provides the terminal facility (the airport and the port), and private firms provide the transportation services. A larger urban area provides more frequent service and a longer list of destinations that is served directly. Freight railway service is provided by private firms, but the same idea applies. The larger urban area has more convenient service.

The larger urban area also offers a deeper and more diverse set of goods and services for businesses. Does your firm need a patent attorney, an architect who can design an office building, or an economic consultant? If your firm is located in a smaller urban area, you can hire a local attorney who does not specialize in patent work, or you can bring in someone from a larger urban area who does. The quality of the work may be suspect in the former case, and the latter option may be inconvenient and expensive. The firm that is located in the larger urban area does not face these problems. The theory of the hierarchy of urban areas is discussed in Chapter 4. The basic point is that large urban areas are not just larger versions of small urban areas. The large urban areas offer goods and services that do not exist in small urban areas.

Other important features of large urban areas are cultural and recreational amenities. Large urban areas have more museums, more live theater and musical performances, and more sporting events to attend. These amenities can make it easier to attract the workers that are needed by an industry.

These are some examples of urbanization economies, but there is a "downside" to urbanization. Large urban areas also suffer from higher levels of congestion, pollution, and social problems. Competition for central locations drives up office rents and housing prices. Given that there are both benefits and costs to the size of the urban area, some researchers have tried to determine whether there is an optimal size for urban areas in general. At what point do the costs to everyone in the urban area of additional urban size outweigh the added benefits? In other words, at what level of urban size are the marginal costs equal to the marginal benefits? The research has not reached any clear conclusions. It is fair to say that we do not know the optimal size for urban areas, and it is also not likely that a general answer exists. A more meaningful way to ask the question is whether there is an optimal size for an individual urban area that performs a particular set of economic functions. Given the economic functions that each urban area performs, should New York, Los Angeles and Chicago be larger or smaller than they are? Maybe the television and movie capital of the world should be larger than the financial capital of the western hemisphere (or maybe not). This question has not been investigated.

There is a good deal of empirical evidence concerning the existence of localization and urbanization economies. The idea is to measure the effects of both the size of the local industry and the size of the local economy as a whole on the costs in that local industry. One careful study by Henderson (1986) examined labor productivity for 1972 in manufacturing industries in U. S. urban areas. Labor productivity is measured as value added (output) in the local manufacturing industry divided by the total labor input. Clearly the wage rate is the first variable that determines labor productivity. The standard result in microeconomic theory is that workers are hired by an industry up to the point at which the wage rate is equal to the value of the marginal product of the last worker. The value of the marginal product is the price of output times the marginal product. Henderson (1986) assumed that the price of output in a manufacturing industry is the same for all urban areas in the United States, so the marginal product for an urban area is higher if the wage rate is higher. Note that labor productivity is defined as *average* product, but the average product and the marginal product should change together. Henderson further hypothesized that given the wage rate, labor productivity will depend upon localization and urbanization economies. The localization effect is measured as full-time employment in the local industry, and urbanization is measured by total local population. Henderson studied 16 manufacturing industries and found statistically significant localization economies in eight of the 16. These industries are:

- Primary metals
- Electrical machinery
- Nonelectrical machinery
- Petroleum refining
- Apparel
- Wood products
- Pulp and paper products
- Food products

Henderson also found that the localization economies die out once the local industry has reached a critical size. Localization economies in these manufacturing industries do not go up without limit. The other manufacturing industries did not exhibit localization economies in U.S. urban areas, and they are:

- Textiles
- Leather products
- Printing and publishing
- Furniture
- Fabricated metals
- Rubber and plastics
- Chemicals
- Stone, clay, and glass products

One industry in the group of 16 exhibited urbanization economies: stone, clay, and glass products.

What are we to make of Henderson's (1986) results? One implication is that those industries that are subject to localization economies should be found to cluster in a relatively small number of urban areas rather than being spread out over a large number of urban areas. Henderson (1986) found evidence of a tendency for the eight industries with localization economies to cluster, and the other eight industries did not cluster. In addition, the fact that localization economies do not go up without limit means that there will be several urban areas in which an industry clusters, not just a few. The general absence of urbanization economies in manufacturing industries means that firms in these industries have no particular incentive to locate in the largest urban areas. Of course, Henderson's findings do not mean that urbanization economies do not exist in other industries, such as those that produce business services or financial services. Unfortunately, the output data required for Henderson's empirical tests are available only for manufacturing industries.

Economies that arise through interindustry linkages mean that industries with strong input–output linkages will cluster together. The tendency for interindustry clusters to emerge is explored in Chapter 4.

E. STATIC THEORY OF EXTERNAL ECONOMIES AND DISECONOMIES

In the preceding section we have examined the possibility that external economies are an important feature of urban areas. External diseconomies of urban areas were also mentioned briefly. The basic idea in each case is that the person who is making an economic decision, such as whether to produce more output, makes that decision on the basis of his own marginal costs and marginal benefits and ignores costs or benefits that affect others. The familiar case is the external diseconomy of air pollution. The individual firm makes an output decision based on its own marginal cost, which does not include a cost of air pollution. But the marginal cost to the entire urban area must also include the cost of additional air pollution that is caused by that firm. A diagram can depict the situation. Figure 3.6 shows the case of external diseconomies of urbanization. The diagram depicts a perfectly competitive market for labor in an urban area. Employment in the urban area will represent the size of the urban area for this purpose. Labor is demanded by the firms in the urban area for use in producing goods and services for export or for local use, and the demand curve for

FIGURE 3.6 External diseconomies of urbanization

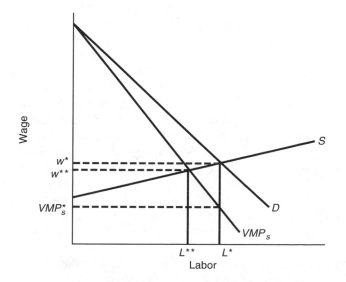

labor is denoted D. The supply curve of labor that is faced by the firms in the urban area is S, which is drawn with a positive slope. If employment in the urban area is to expand, a higher wage rate must be paid. A market equilibrium wage is established at w^*, and the employment level is L^*. Wage w^* is the wage rate that firms use to decide how many workers to hire.

External diseconomies can be introduced into the urban labor market model on the demand side. Recall that the demand curve for labor is the same thing as the value of labor's marginal product, which equals the price of output times the physical marginal product of labor. Now suppose that when a firm hires one more worker, that worker produces a marginal product for the firm *and* causes output at other firms to decline. How can this happen? The water pollution example works well. The firm decides to produce more output, so another worker is hired. That decision adds more pollution to the river. Firms that are located downstream and use the water must now use more resources to clean up the water before it can be used. A given amount of resources employed by those downstream firms will now produce a smaller quantity of output. In effect, the decision by the upstream firm to hire another worker has reduced the output of the downstream firms. Another example is traffic congestion. The decision to hire another worker means that there will be more traffic in the urban area. Truck drivers who work for the various firms will now have to spend more time in traffic, so they will produce less in a day's work. If phenomena of this type apply to all firms in the urban area, the value of the marginal product of labor to the urban area as a whole should be drawn as curve VMP_s in Figure 3.6. Curve VMP_s is below demand curve D by the amount of the external diseconomy at the margin. At employment level L^* the wage rate is equal to the value of the marginal product of labor that accrues to the firm that hired the last worker, but the actual value of the marginal product of that last worker for the urban area as a whole is only VMP_s^*.

Left to their own devices, the firms hire "too many" workers and the urban area is too large. This is a normative proposition of the kind discussed in Chapter 1. Exactly what is wrong with employment level L^*? Employment level L^* is *inefficient* because the last worker hired generated a marginal benefit to the firms in the urban area that is less than marginal cost. A firm paid wage w^* to hire the last worker, but the firms as a group only reaped a benefit of VMP_s^*. This creates a situation in which it is possible to make some firms better off and no one else worse off. For example, suppose that it is possible for the firms in the urban area, excluding the one that hired the last worker, to take up a collection and bribe that firm and the worker not to work. The firm does not need much inducement because the profits earned from hiring the last worker are small. Furthermore, the marginal worker *is* the marginal worker because the opportunity cost of his or her time is just slightly less than the wage rate. Small bribes will do for both. The firms in the urban area have amount $w^* - VMP_s^*$ available for bribery, and that is more than enough to do the trick. If this bribery scheme could be organized, everyone can be made better off.

As you may already have concluded, the efficient level of employment for the urban area is L^{**}, where the supply curve of labor crosses the value of labor's marginal product to the entire group of firms. At this point workers earn wage rate w^{**}, and the firms as a group gain output worth that same amount by hiring the last worker.

Now consider the less familiar case of an external economy. Henderson (1986)

FIGURE 3.7   Localization economies

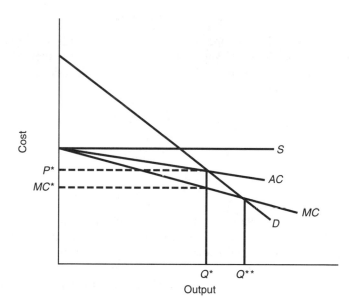

found evidence of localization economies, so the analysis will focus on an individual industry in an urban area. Supply and demand for this industry are shown in Figure 3.7. The industry faces the usual sort of demand curve, labeled *D*. The industry is made up of a large number of small, competitive firms. Each of these firms is assumed to have a long-run average cost curve that has a minimum point at some level of output. In the long run the output of the industry expands by adding more firms of this optimum size. If there is no external economy, the long-run supply curve of the industry is just horizontal line *S* in Figure 3.7. The market price is set equal to long-run average and marginal cost. This is the model that students learn in an introductory microeconomics course. Now suppose that there is an economy that is external to the firm but internal to the industry. The expansion of industry output, through the addition of another firm, will lower the average costs for the other firms. The price at which the firms in the industry will offer the good for sale now drops to the lower average cost.

The critical relationship is between the average and marginal costs of output for the industry. Define *TC* as the total cost in the industry, which equals the number of firms (*n*) times the total cost in each of those firms (*tc*), or

$$TC = n(tc).$$

Total cost in each firm is the firm's average cost (*ac*) times output (*q*), or

$$tc = q(ac).$$

Note that the average cost for the industry (*AC*) is the same as the average cost for each of the firms because

$$AC = \frac{TC}{nq} = \frac{tc(n)}{nq} = \frac{tc}{q} = ac.$$

If one firm is added to the industry, the change in total cost is

$$\delta TC = \delta n\, q(ac) + \delta ac(nq) + \delta q\, n(ac).$$

Here the δ symbol stands for "change in." Assume that the optimal output for each firm does not change, so $\delta q = 0$. The marginal cost (MC) for the industry is the change in total cost for the industry as the number of firms increases, divided by the output of the additional firm; therefore,

$$MC = \frac{\delta TC/\delta n}{q} = \frac{q(ac)}{q} + \frac{(\delta ac/\delta n)(nq)}{q}$$

$$= ac + n\left(\frac{\delta ac}{\delta n}\right)$$

$$= AC + n\left(\frac{\delta ac}{\delta n}\right)$$

The existence of an external economy means that $\delta ac/\delta n$ is less than zero; average cost declines as the industry expands. This result is very clear. It says that the marginal cost of output *for the industry* is the initial average cost minus the change in average cost in each firm times the number of firms. In other words, the marginal cost for the industry is less than the average cost by the amount $n(\delta ac/\delta n)$. Curves for AC and MC are shown in Figure 3.7.

Which of the two curves (AC or MC) is the supply curve of the industry? The supply curve is AC because firms in a competitive industry must make a price equal to average cost to make a normal profit. At price p^* the firms will offer quantity Q^*, and this is the equilibrium solution for the market. The supply curve AC is called "forward falling" because the offer price declines as industry output expands. But you probably already have realized that the equilibrium price for the output exceeds its *marginal* cost, which is the cost to the entire industry of producing 1 more unit of output. Clearly, output level Q^* is an inefficiently low output. At Q^* the benefit of producing another unit of output is p^*, but the cost to the industry of doing so is only MC^*. This industry expands by adding firms, but at price p^* no new firm will enter *unless it is bribed to do so*. At price p^* the firms in the industry are just making a normal profit. Equilibrium output will remain at Q^* even though the optimal level of output is at Q^{**}. Output level Q^{**} is the point at which the marginal benefits of the good (the price) are equal to the marginal costs. It is in the interest of the consumers of the product (i.e., the rest of society) to bribe firms to enter the industry to produce more output. At output level Q^{**} the price is below average cost, so the firms in the industry will lose money unless they are subsidized.

Figure 3.7 has produced an important theoretical result. Society will benefit by subsidizing the expansion of an industry that possesses localization economies. The matter of subsidization is discussed further in Part III of the book.

F. ECONOMIC ORIGINS OF URBAN AREAS IN THE UNITED STATES

The history of urban areas is a fascinating subject. If you enjoy reading history, you probably will also enjoy reading about the history of urban areas in general and the histories of specific urban areas. Cities around the world have their origins in a wide variety of political, military, religious, social, and economic reasons. A classic book that was published in 1961 and that still appears on many college reading lists is Lewis Mumford's *The City in History*. Mumford's book is 576 pages in length, and he did not get around to discussing the market economy until page 410. Unlike Mumford's book, the purpose of this section is not to summarize the stories of the world's major cities. Rather, the idea is to take a brief look at major urban areas in the United States. This decision narrows the focus to the more recent past, and it also means that the economic reasons for cities can be emphasized. Except for Washington, DC and some of the former and current state capitals, urban areas in the United States have origins that are almost purely economic in nature.

In 1790, the year of the first Census of Population, only 5.1% of the population of 3.9 million lived in urban places, which are defined as having a population of 2500 or more. The United States was an agricultural nation. The largest urban areas were really nothing more than towns; New York had a population of 49,000, Philadelphia had 29,000, 18,000 people resided in Boston, and Baltimore had 14,000. These and most of the other towns began life in colonial days as ports that were used to ship agricultural products out and various goods in. Ports were built where a major river empties into the ocean. A port represents a transshipment point, as discussed earlier in Section B, and ports are subject to economies of scale, as mentioned in Section C. Transshipment points are not spread out all up and down the coast but are concentrated at a few points. The New York harbor was and is, by far, the best port on the east coast. The harbor is sheltered from the ocean by Long Island, and flanked by the East River and the Hudson River, Manhattan provides a great deal of space for docking facilities. What is more, the navigable Hudson River reaches far into the agricultural hinterland. It is difficult to imagine a better setup given the transportation methods of the time.

The transportation methods of the time are critical. In 1790 cities were small partly because of limitations imposed by a transportation system that consisted of boats (without steam power), horses, and feet. The next 70 years produced what economic historians call the transportation revolution. First came improvements in transportation by water. Robert Fulton's steamboat completed its first upstream voyage from New York City to Albany in 1807, and regular service was initiated. The earliest canal projects were also completed in the first decade of the nineteenth century. The value of steamboats for use on the Ohio and Mississippi rivers was immediately apparent, and the steamboat made its first appearance on these western waters in 1811. Regular service on the western rivers was initiated in 1817, and by 1825, 80 steamboats were operating there. At the same time the era of canal building got under way. Most of the canals were financed by state governments. The Erie Canal, which was completed in 1825, was the most important canal. It connects the Hudson River with the Great Lakes (at Buffalo, on Lake Erie) and thereby provided a cheap freight connection between the upper midwest and the east coast. Many other canals were built in the first six decades of the nineteenth century. Most of the canal mileage was in the states of New York, Pennsylvania, and Ohio. The economic historian Douglas North (1973) shows that canal and upstream river freight rates declined by over 90% between 1800 and 1840.

The canal era overlaps with the era of the railroad. The first railroad was opened in England in 1825, and the Baltimore and Ohio began operation in 1830 with 23 miles of track. Total mileage of main track reached 4600 in 1845, and then the industry exploded to 30,600 miles in 1860. North (1973) shows that freight rates on the railroad dropped by over 50% from 1845 to 1860. Railroad rates were far greater than canal or river boat rates, but the railroad was much faster, could run in all seasons and in all weather conditions, and reached places that were inaccessible by water. The speed and reliability of rail service meant that timetables could be kept and meant that people, probably for the first time, had to pay close attention to the time of day. The system of standard time zones was created by the railroads in 1881.

My students know that I am fond of using anecdotes from the life of Abraham Lincoln to illustrate the economic history of this period. His first job after he left his father's household in 1830 was to transport a farmer's crop from central Illinois downriver for sale in New Orleans. He used an unpowered flatboat, and the first leg of the journey was on the Sangamon River. The Sangamon River is little more than a wide creek. He had not gone very far when the boat became stalled on a small dam next to a new pioneer village named New Salem. He cleverly freed his flatboat from its predicament, and a man who was watching told him that he had a job waiting for him in New Salem when he returned from New Orleans. Lincoln eventually made his way back to New Salem and took the job as storekeeper and postmaster. The job left him plenty of time to study law and to get elected to the Illinois General Assembly. Thirty years later President-elect Lincoln left nearby Springfield by train. He rode to Indianapolis and then to Baltimore and Washington, DC.

The transportation revolution had transformed the nation by making enormous areas of fertile agricultural land accessible and by reducing dramatically the cost of moving agricultural commodities, manufactured goods, and people. People knew very well that the eastern half of the nation was going to be settled very quickly and that an entire system of towns and cities would spring up. They knew that agricultural settlement and the growth of towns and cities would go hand-in-hand. Furthermore, they knew that the cities would be very large by the standards of the early years of the nineteenth century. Any clue as to where the large cities would be located was valuable information. For example, the *announcement* in 1829 that a canal would be built at Chicago to connect the Great Lakes to the Mississippi River system set off a tremendous land boom in what was a minor trading post.

How did people know all of this? In short, they knew that the new transportation system would lead to urban agglomeration economies. The water and rail transportation systems themselves provided services under conditions of substantial economies of scale. The emerging manufacturing industries based on steam power and standardized parts possessed some internal economies of scale. Many of the business services required by an agricultural economy, such as banking, insurance, and marketing of agricultural products, also possessed economies of scale. The economies of scale in water and rail operations tended to centralize economic activity, and the cheap freight rates permitted urban manufacturing and business services to cover a wide area. The economies of scale in manufacturing production activity became an even larger factor in urbanization after the Civil War, but the level of urbanization in 1860 is still impressive.

The percentage of the population residing in urban places increased slightly from 5.1% in 1790 to 8.8% in 1830, the year in which Lincoln struggled down the Sangamon River. When the president-elect traveled to Washington, DC, 19.8% of the

American people lived in urban places. This increase in urbanization was coupled with a huge increase in the total population of the nation. The total population in 1830 was 12.9 million, and the waves of immigrants from Germany and Ireland, coupled with a very rapid natural rate of increase, produced a population of 31.4 million in 1860. These figures mean that the population in urban places was 1.1 million in 1830 and 6.2 million in 1860, an increase of *464%*. Of these 6.2 million, 1.37 million lived in New York and Philadelphia. Recall that the total population of these two cities was 78,000 in 1790. At the end of the Civil War decade in 1870, the two cities had a total population of 2.13 million. The other major cities—Baltimore, Boston, Buffalo, Chicago, Cincinnati, New Orleans, and St. Louis—were also growing rapidly. In 1860, 42.4% of the urban population lived in the nine largest cities, each of which had populations in excess of 100,000.

Cities of such size also generated substantial diseconomies. The sanitation problems were staggering. The threats of fire and communicable diseases were ever present. The movement of both people and freight within an urban area was still rudimentary. Some of the early photographs of urban areas show traffic jams that defy description. (Note that early photographic technology required that the subjects stand still for a lengthy period. Photographs of urban traffic jams were possible nonetheless.)

Between 1790 and 1860 Americans settled almost half of the nation. Because of the transportation revolution and innovations in the production of urban goods and services, that settlement was coupled with very rapid urbanization after 1830. The first real cities in the United States were created in this period, and the economic models of this chapter provide good explanations for this first phase of urbanization.

G. SUMMARY

This chapter is an introduction to the economic theory of location choice by firms. The role of transportation costs for inputs and outputs was examined first, and then several other factors were considered. The costs of labor, land, capital, and intermediate inputs can vary over space. For some firms in some industries these costs can vary because of the level of:

1. Economies of scale internal to the firm's operation at a single location
2. Economies of scale external to the firm but internal to the local industry
3. Economies external to the local industry that arise from the size of the urban area

These are called *agglomeration economies*; the last two are called *localization economies* and *urbanization economies*, respectively. In addition, the size of the urban area may cause diseconomies such as pollution and congestion.

Empirical evidence developed by Henderson (1986) indicates that localization economies occur in several manufacturing industries but that urbanization economies in manufacturing industry are rare. These findings imply that those manufacturing industries with localization economies should be observed to cluster in a relatively small number of urban areas and that those urban areas are not necessarily very large. Henderson's findings are consistent with these hypotheses.

The existence of diseconomies of urban size and localization economies was investigated theoretically. Diseconomies of urban size generate an urban area that is inefficiently "too large," given its economic functions. Localization economies lead to an industry in an urban area that is inefficiently "too small." It would be worthwhile for the public to bribe firms to enter the local industry to create additional economies.

The chapter concluded with a brief discussion of the creation of urban areas in the United States in the first 60 years of the nineteenth century. Urbanization was particularly rapid during the 1830–1860 period as firms took advantage of the transportation revolution and agglomeration economies arising from economies of scale in manufacturing production and business services. On the eve of the Civil War, 19.8% of the population of the United States lived in urban places, and 42.4% of the urban population lived in nine large cities.

Mathematics of the One-Input, One-Market Model

In the one-input, one-market model the firm uses an input that is located at point I in Figure 3.1 The input is available at a given price at point I. The firm produces output for the market located at point M, and the firm faces a downward-sloping demand curve for output at the market. The firm must decide how much to produce and where to produce it. For example, suppose that the firm's business is to take raw lumber (i.e., trees that have been cut down) available at the forest at point I, cut the lumber into firewood, and deliver the firewood to the market at point M. Where does the firm perform the operation of cutting the trees into firewood? As discussed in the text, the firm could transport the raw lumber to point M first and then produce the firewood. Or the firm could cut up the trees first at point I and transport the firewood to market. Also, some point between I and M could be selected. The decision depends upon transportation costs.

Suppose that the firm takes 1.2 tons of raw lumber to produce 1 ton of firewood. The production process involves a little waste, so the product is known as *weight losing*. The cost of transporting 1.2 tons on raw lumber is \$$a$ per mile, and the cost of transporting 1 ton of firewood is \$$b$ per mile. Cutting the raw lumber into firewood requires L units of labor at a wage of \$$w$ per unit. The price of output at the market is \$$p$ per ton, and the price of raw lumber at point I is \$$R$ per ton. Denote the distance from point I to the firm's location as x. This is the distance that the raw lumber is transported. Let y stand for the distance from the firm's location to the market; y is the distance the output is transported. Obviously, $z = x + y$ equals the distance from I to M. Either x or y is permitted to be zero. Let us restate the definitions of the variables:

p = price of output at the market, point M

a = cost per mile of transporting 1.2 tons of raw lumber

b = cost per mile of transporting 1 ton of firewood

w = wage rate per unit of labor

L = amount of labor needed for 1 ton of firewood

R = price of raw lumber at the forest, point I

x = distance raw lumber is transported

$$y = \text{distance firewood is transported}$$

$$z = x + y = \text{distance from } I \text{ to } M$$

Given these definitions, and letting Q stand for output, the firm's profit can be written

$$\text{profit} = \text{total revenue minus total costs}$$

$$= pQ - 1.2RQ - wLQ - Q(1.2ax - by).$$

Total revenue is pQ, and the three components of total cost are

$$1.2RQ = \text{cost of raw lumber}$$

$$wLQ = \text{cost of labor}$$

$$Q(1.2ax + by) = \text{transportation cost}$$

The firm maximizes profits by selecting the output level at which the marginal change in profit is zero. In other words, Q is selected so that

$$\text{change in profit} = \text{marginal revenue minus marginal cost}$$

$$= p\,\delta Q + Q\,\delta p - 1.2R\,\delta Q - wL\,\delta Q - 1.2ax\,\delta Q - by\,\delta Q = 0.$$

Here δQ stands for a marginal change in Q, and δp is the marginal change in p. Marginal revenue for a change in output of 1 unit is $p + Q\,\delta p/\delta Q$. The condition above reduces to the usual statement that marginal revenue equals marginal cost, or

$$MR = p + \frac{Q\,\delta p}{\delta Q} = 1.2R + wL + 1.2ax + by = MC.$$

Marginal cost consists of the cost of raw lumber per ton of output ($1.2R) plus labor cost ($wL$) plus transportation costs per ton of output ($1.2ax + by).

The firm must also choose its *location* so as to maximize profits. Consider Figure A3.1. Straight line II^* shows the cost of transporting the input (raw lumber) needed for 1 ton of output at various distances from I. The slope of this line is $1.2a$. Straight line M^*M likewise shows the cost of transporting the output (firewood) from various locations away from point M. The slope of line M^*M is $-$b$, meaning that this component of costs declines by $b per mile for each ton of output. The entire transportation cost for a ton of output is the sum of these two costs, which is line M^*I^*. In algebraic form, transportation cost per ton is $1.2ax + by$. Where would you locate your firewood firm? Given the transportation costs displayed in Figure A3.1, you would choose to locate *at* point I because this point minimizes transportation costs per ton of output.

You can further convince yourself that point I is the correct choice by returning to the equation for profits. Rewrite the profit equation:

$$\text{profits} = pQ - 1.2RQ - wLQ - Q(1.2ax + by).$$

Clearly, for profits to be at a maximum at whatever output level is chosen, the firm must minimize transportation costs per unit of output, which equals $1.2ax + by$. Point I, with $x = 0$ and y equal to the total distance from I to M, is the cost-minimizing point.

FIGURE A3.1 Transportation cost and location

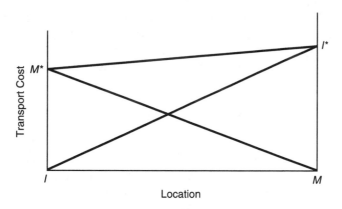

The analysis is complicated slightly by the fact that output depends upon price, which depends upon marginal cost, and marginal cost (*MC*) depends upon location. Recall that

$$MC = 1.2R + wL + 1.2ax + by.$$

The point is that in order to maximize profits, the firm must minimize marginal costs. Given that *R*, the price of raw lumber, and *w*, the price of labor, are constant, marginal costs are at a minimum if $x = 0$ (location *I* is chosen).

Consider the alternative. Suppose that some other location and output level have been chosen. The firm can increase profits (at that output level) by reducing transportation costs. Furthermore, the lowering of marginal cost by selecting the best location will also stimulate the firm to produce more output and earn even greater profits. This point is illustrated in Figure A3.2. The firm begins with the "wrong" lo-

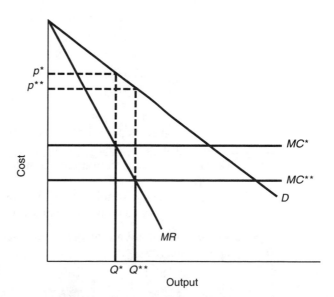

FIGURE A3.2 The Firewood Firm

cation and marginal cost level MC^*. Profit-maximizing price is p^* and output is Q^* given demand D and marginal revenue MR. Selection of the correct location lowers marginal cost to MC^{**}. If output is held at Q^*, profits increase by the amount $Q^*(MC^* - MC^{**})$. However, the firm will decide to increase output to Q^{**} because, at the lower output Q^*, marginal revenue exceeds the new marginal cost. Therefore, selection of the correct location increases profits on two counts.

EXERCISES

1. You own a firewood business that involves chopping down trees, cutting the trees up into firewood, and transporting to the market. You can cut the trees up into firewood where they are cut down, or you can transport the trees to the market and then cut them into firewood. The costs of the various operations are as follows:

Cutting down trees	$25 per ton
Cutting trees into firewood	$100 per ton
Transporting trees to market	$50 per ton
Transporting firewood to market	$35 per ton

   (a) Where should the trees be cut into firewood to minimize costs? Why? What data did you need to make this decision?
   (b) Suppose that the price of firewood at the market is $150 per ton. Where should the trees be cut into firewood now? What if the price increased to $175 per ton?

2. A business has customers located in Lubbock, Amarillo, and points in between as follows:

Lubbock	10 customers
10 miles from Lubbock	1 customer
25 miles from Lubbock	3 customers
50 miles from Lubbock	1 customer
70 miles from Lubbock	2 customers
Amarillo	6 customers

   (a) Suppose that a separate trip must be made to each customer and that transportation costs per mile are the same for all trips to any customer. Where does the business locate to minimize transportation costs?
   (b) How does the solution change if four more customers are added in Amarillo? Why?
   (c) How does the solution change if four more customers are added in Lubbock? (Assume six customers in Amarillo.) Why?

3. Imagine that there are *two* ice cream vendors on a linear beach 10 yards long. We assume that:

- Consumers are evenly distributed along the beach, located at the endpoints and spaced 3 feet apart.
- Production costs are zero.
- Both vendors sell ice cream for p cents.
- The cost to consumers of travel to the vendor is $\frac{1}{2}$ cent per yard (money equivalent of consumer's time).

(a) What are the profit-maximizing equilibrium locations for the two vendors? What do aggregate travel costs equal?

(b) What are the socially optimal locations (to minimize travel costs)? How much are aggregate travel costs reduced compared to the answer to part a?

4. Consider an industry in an urban area that is subject to localization economies. The industry faces the demand curve

$$P = 59 - 0.05Q,$$

where P is price and Q is the output of the industry. Each firm in the industy has an average cost function of

$$ac = 10 - 0.001Q.$$

The firms in the industry behave as competitive firms.

(a) What is the average cost function for the industry?

(b) What is the marginal cost function for the industry? (*Hint:* First find the total cost function.)

(c) What is the output level that this competitive industry would produce in the absence of any bribes or subsidies? What is the difference between average cost and marginal cost at this output level?

(d) What output level would be produced if there were no localization economy for the industry?

REFERENCES

Henderson, Vernon, 1986. "Efficiency of Resource Usage and City Size," *Journal of Urban Economics*, Vol. 19, pp. 47–70.

Hoover, Edgar, 1937. *Location Theory and the Shoe and Leather Industries*. Cambridge, MA: Harvard University Press.

Marshall, Alfred, 1920. *Principles of Economics*, 8th ed. London: Macmillan.

Mills, Edwin, 1967. "An Aggregative Model of Resource Allocation in a Metropolitan Area," *American Economic Review, Papers and Proceedings*, Vol. 57, pp. 197–210.

Mumford, Lewis, 1961. *The City in History*. New York: Harcourt, Brace, & World.

Newman, R. and D. Sullivan, 1988. "Econometric Analysis of Business Tax Impacts on Industrial Location: What Do We Know and How Do We Know It?" *Journal of Urban Economics*, Vol. 23, pp. 215–234.

North, Douglas, 1973. *Growth and Welfare in the American Past*. Englewood Cliffs, NJ: Prentice Hall.

Ohlin, Bertil, 1933. *Interregional and International Trade*. Cambridge, MA: Harvard University Press.

CHAPTER

Economic Functions of Cities

A. INTRODUCTION

It is obvious that urban areas are arranged in fairly regular patterns. There are many small towns, fewer large towns, even fewer cities, and a small number of major metropolitan areas. Clearly, there is a hierarchy of urban areas that is shaped roughly like a pyramid. Also, there are geographic regularities. As you know from Chapter 1, the three largest metropolitan areas in the United States are New York, Los Angeles, and Chicago (with Los Angeles gaining rapidly on New York). They are, of course, located on the east coast, the west coast, and in the middle of the nation, respectively. The urban areas that have populations in excess of 2.0 million by rank are:

Urban Area	1990 Population (millions)
New York/NE New Jersey	17.95
Los Angeles/Long Beach/Orange County	14.53
Chicago/Gary	8.06
San Francisco/Oakland/San Jose	6.23
Philadelphia/Wilmington/Trenton	5.90
Detroit/Ann Arbor	4.66
Boston/Lawrence/Salem	4.17
Washington, DC	3.92
Dallas/Fort Worth	3.89
Houston/Galveston/Brazoria	3.71
Miami/Ft. Lauderdale	3.19
Atlanta	2.83
Cleveland/Akron/Lorain	2.76
Seattle/Tacoma	2.56
San Diego	2.50
Minneapolis/St. Paul	2.46

St. Louis	2.44
Baltimore	2.38
Pittsburgh/Beaver Valley	2.24
Phoenix	2.12
Tampa/St. Petersburg/Clearwater	2.07

Notice how many of the largest urban areas are now located in the sunbelt. If Seattle is included in the sunbelt, a dubious assumption because of all the rain in Seattle, nine of the top 21 urban areas are located in the sunbelt. Large urban areas are now seemingly scattered around the nation in a pattern that surely has some regularity. Urban areas vary widely in size and in economic function; the task of this chapter is to gain an understanding of the patterns in urban size and function. The approach to this task is to examine the system of urban areas in the contemporary U.S. economy.

In the first section of the chapter we take a look at a simple geographic theory of an urban hierarchy that is based on market-oriented goods and services. This theory has severe limitations, but it points out the important relationship between economies of scale and the economic functions performed by urban areas of various sizes. The next section is an empirical investigation of the economic functions performed by urban areas. What are their basic functions, and how can they be measured? These questions are answered, and then in the next section we make use of a system for measuring fundamental economic functions to classify the 140 largest urban areas into four general categories and 11 more specific groups. The general categories are (1) diversified service centers, (2) specialized service centers, (3) production centers, and (4) consumer-oriented centers.

The field of urban economics lacks a comprehensive theory of the urban hierarchy that can explain most of the real-world pattern, but the categorization exercise is useful and may lead to a new theory. The chapter concludes with a close look at the economy of Des Moines that makes use of the classification schemes that are introduced.

B. THEORY OF THE URBAN HIERARCHY

Basic Model

There is a reasonably simple theory, based on the location decisions of market-oriented firms, that leads to a hierarchy of urban areas. The theory has several weaknesses which are discussed later, but for now it is useful to examine the theory in detail.

The first assumption of the theory is that an agricultural population lives on a plain at a population density that does not vary by location. Transportation costs are equal in all directions. Suppose that the agricultural population purchases and consumes two goods; one good can be supplied by small firms, and because of significant economies of scale, the other must be supplied by large firms. Furthermore, because of agglomeration economies such as shared roads and other public infrastructure, firms in the two industries have an incentive to locate together whenever possible. The firms in both industries are assumed to be market oriented; their inputs are assumed to be available everywhere at constant prices.

As an example, suppose that gas stations serve an area containing 1000 households, and that department stores serve an area of 7000 households. These market sizes enable the firms to make a normal profit, and firms with market sizes much in excess of these numbers will induce more firms to enter. What will happen? First, gas stations will locate at regular intervals sufficiently small to create markets of 1000 households. The markets tend to be circular in shape, and the households located in a given market will, to minimize travel, purchase gasoline at the gas station that is located in that market. Similarly, department stores will locate so as to establish market areas of 7000 households each. Recall that department stores also have a strong incentive to locate next to a gas station in order to share infrastructure. Therefore, one in seven gas stations will be accompanied by a department store. Each firm requires a workforce, of course. The workers and their families create towns. This model has created a simple hierarchy of retail "towns" with small towns that contain only a gas station and larger towns that include both a gas station and a department store. There is one larger town for every six small towns.

Suppose that the gas station in the larger town supplies the gasoline needed by the department store workers and that the department store supplies its good to the workers in the seven gas stations that fall within its market area. Also, farmers pay for their gasoline and department store goods with agricultural produce, which the workers in the towns consume. Finally, farmers produce and consume their own food, gas station workers buy gasoline at their own stations, and department store workers purchase goods at their own stores. Incomes and expenditures are in balance for these groups of workers.

More goods and services can be added to the model. For example, suppose that a hospital can provide comprehensive care to 49,000 households and all of the other people who live in 42 small towns and seven larger towns. One of those seven larger towns will then also contain a hospital (so that infrastructure can be shared) and will therefore be larger than the other six. The hierarchy is now one "city" for every six larger towns and for every 42 small towns. Further, assume that one hospital in seven contains a university that educates doctors and nurses for its own employ and for the other six hospitals in its area. One could keep on going with the exercise, but the point is now clear.

Rank-Size Rule for Urban Areas

The basic theory of the urban hierarchy as presented above is roughly consistent with what is known as the *rank-size rule* of urban areas. Suppose that the urban areas are ranked by population from the largest to the smallest (New York is number one, etc.). The rank-size rule says that for any urban area, its rank times its population size is a constant number. For New York,

$$\text{rank} \times \text{size} = 1 \times 18.0 \text{ million} = 18.$$

However, for Los Angeles

$$\text{rank} \times \text{size} = 2 \times 14.5 \text{ million} = 29,$$

and for Chicago

$$\text{rank} \times \text{size} = 3 \times 8.1 \text{ million} = 24.3.$$

Clearly, rank times size is not equal to 18 for the next two urban areas. Try out a few of the other large urban areas listed in Section A. You will note that rank times size generally is a number larger than 28 million. (For example, Baltimore is 18×2.38 million = 42.84.) The rank-size rule does not work particularly well because New York is, oddly enough, "too small."

Why is the urban hierarchy theory roughly consistent with the rank-size rule? Return to the simple model with six small towns and one larger town. The six small towns just contain one gas station, which serves 1000 rural households and the people who live in the town. The basic equation for the size of the small town is

$$p_1 = k(r + p_1),$$

where p_1 is the size of the small town, r the size of the rural population that it serves, and k the number of gas station workers needed to serve one household. The input coefficient k is most likely a small number such as 0.015; 15 gas station workers can serve 1000 households. The solution for the size of the small town is

$$p_1 = \frac{rk}{1 + k}.$$

If $r = 1000$ and $k = 0.015$, then $p_1 = 15.2$. Note that the kp_1 term is quite small (the number of gas station workers needed to serve the small town itself), and it will be ignored for simplicity. In this case we have

$$p_1 = rk.$$

Now consider the larger town. It contains a department store that serves seven rural areas, six small towns, and its own population. The larger town also contains a gas station that serves one rural area and its own population. Let us assume that a department store, as does a gas station, requires 15 workers per 1000 households served ($k = 0.015$). How large is the larger town? First, determine the number of workers in the department store. This works out to be

$$7kr + 6kp_1 + kp_2 = 7kr + \frac{6k^2r}{1-k} + kp_2,$$

where p_2 is the population of the larger town. However, the last two terms of this expression are quite small and can be ignored for the sake of simplicity. The number of workers in the gas station is

$$k(r + p_2),$$

but once again, the kp_2 term is quite small and can be ignored.

The size of the larger town is approximately

$$p_2 = 7kr + kr = 8kr,$$

or one department store plus one gas station. Given that $k = 0.015$ and $r = 1000$, $p_2 = 120$. The ratio of the population of a small town to the population of the larger town is

$$\frac{p_1}{p_2} = \frac{kr}{8kr} = \frac{1}{8}.$$

The larger town has a rank of 1 among the seven towns and a population that is sufficient to staff one department store and one gas station. The small towns have a population that is sufficient to staff one gas station and ranks of 2 through 7 (average rank of 4). Rank times size for the larger town is 120, and rank times size for the average small town is $15 \times 4 = 60$. What went wrong? Clearly, the outcome of the model depended, among other things, on the number of department store workers needed to serve 1000 households. This number was assumed to be 15, but instead, suppose it is 7. In this case the number of workers in the department store is $0.007(7r)$, and the size of the larger town is

$$0.007(7r) + 0.015r = 64.$$

This change in input coefficients makes the rank-size rule work almost exactly for the "average" rank of the small towns. Clearly, the rank-size rule is only a very rough approximation of the relationship between the size of an urban area and its rank.

Shortcomings of the Urban Hierarchy Model

The basic urban hierarchy theory does a good job of providing an explanation for a spatial hierarchy of towns and cities for retailing and consumer services. The theory can also include manufacturing and producer services provided that they are market oriented rather than input oriented. For example, suppose that a textile mill and an accompanying apparel factory use the cotton produced everywhere by farmers to produce clothing for people who live in the market area of 42 small towns, six larger towns, and one city discussed above. Where will these manufacturing firms locate? They most likely choose to locate in the one city because of urbanization economies arising from shared urban infrastructure. However, if infrastructure is not important for them, it is conceivable that they will locate in one of the towns.

Clearly, the critical feature of the model is economies of scale. As discussed in Chapter 3, if there were no economies of scale in the production of anything, each farm household would be a self-sufficient producer of all of its consumer goods and services. Households would produce their own food, clothing, shelter, tools, medical care, and so on. There would be no reason for towns and cities. In this world no one specializes in the production of anything. But as soon as we introduce the notion of specialization, we start to get reasons for towns and cities.

Consider the making of tools. Suppose initially that each farmer spends 1 hour out of a workday of 8 hours making tools. Next, consider a toolmaking "specialist" who makes tools for himself and seven other farmers. The seven farmers can now devote 8 hours per day to farming, and the eighth man is the toolmaker. However, this arrangement is better only if output increases as a result of specialization. Output will increase if the toolmaker can make more and better tools (in 8 hours) than the eight farmers can (each spending 1 hour on tool making). Furthermore, the increased output of tools (and the resulting increase in farm products) must be sufficient to compensate for the travel time expended by the farmers to get their tools from the toolmaker. But it is clear that specialization does generate economies of scale and that economies of scale are indeed very powerful forces. In the previous example of a hierarchy of urban places, imagine what would happen if each "larger town" (with a gas station and a department store) tried to have a "comprehensive" hospital staffed by one doctor who does everything. Or imagine what would happen if every hospital tried to have medical and nursing schools with a very small faculty.

The urban hierarchy theory is useful, but it leaves out some very important features of the real-world economy. Firms that are resource oriented (or input oriented in general) make location decisions, as discussed in Chapter 3, that are not based on the locations of customers. Steel once was produced exclusively where one could assemble the necessary resources: iron ore, coal, and limestone. (Now steel scrap, an input that is virtually ubiquitous, is used to produce some steel. This fact makes the steel industry tend to be more oriented to the market.) Second, the urban hierarchy theory leaves out the geographic features of real transportation systems. In particular, the theory ignores the importance of transshipment points and the port cities that are created along the lines discussed in Chapter 3. Recall that most of the major urban areas in the United States began as ports.

Third, the urban hierarchy theory leaves out localization economies. Firms in the same industry avoid each other in the urban hierarchy theory. They set up separate market areas, a result that makes sense for gas stations and (probably) for department stores. However, we know that firms that sell "shopping goods" have an incentive to locate together to facilitate the activity of shopping. All of the other arguments made in Chapter 3 regarding localization economies apply. Finally, the theory leaves out special cases such as government capitals, military centers, resort cities, and retirement communities.

Chicago is a good example of a complex case. Metropolitan Chicago began as the place where the Great Lakes water transportation system could be linked to the Mississippi River (via the Chicago River, a canal, and the Illinois River). Because of its location, by the 1850s Chicago had also become a center of the rail transport system in the midwest region. All of this meant that Chicago could become a production center for goods that are market oriented and subject to very large economies of scale. It could also become a center for the production of goods that required the assembly of inputs at a transshipment point. Chicago became a center for exporting various agricultural products from the midwest and for importing goods to the midwest from the factories of the east. Last, but not least, Chicago became a gateway for people coming to the midwest from Europe and from the other regions of the United States. Real-life urban areas that are larger than small towns usually represent complicated combinations of various location forces, of which the urban hierarchy theory presented in the section is only one. Enough information about Los Angeles has already been presented in this book to enable you to make a preliminary attempt at telling its story in the same terms I just used to discuss Chicago. This would make an excellent question for your first examination in this course, would it not?

C. INDUSTRY CLUSTERS IN URBAN AREAS

The theory of the urban hierarchy reaches the conclusion that the economic functions performed by an urban area are determined by its place in the hierarchy. In the preceding section we also noted that the basic urban hierarchy model leaves out urban areas that are centers of resource-based production, mining-based cities, transshipment points, governmental centers, military centers, centers of production for goods with localization economies, resorts, or retirement communities. The task of this section and the next is to provide a comprehensive and realistic method for classifying urban areas according to their economic functions. The first step is to enumerate the basic economic functions performed by urban areas. Methods for performing this task are discussed here. In the next section we present a functional classification of the largest 140 urban areas in the United States. Recall the discussion in Chapter 1 of the creation of economic knowledge in an applied field such as urban economics. The tasks that are being undertaken in the remainder of this chapter involve the collection of data about urban areas and the systematic examination of the data to find important patterns and trends. The next step would be to develop a more comprehensive theory of the urban hierarchy, but alas, that is a step which cannot be included in this book. It is a step that has not been taken.

Noyelle and Stanback (1983) have proposed a scheme for the enumeration and measurement of the fundamental economic functions performed in an urban area. Table 4.1 summarizes their method of classification by type of output. Noyelle and Stanback group industries (as defined by the SIC code system mentioned in Chapter 1) into eight basic functional areas. The first category of agriculture, extractive, and construction includes industries that are not necessarily urban in character, although a few urban areas specialize in one of these industries. The other seven functional areas typically are urban functions. They include the manufacturing of goods and the distribution of goods and services. Next comes the area that Noyelle and Stanback call the complex of corporate activities. This large and important urban sector includes central administrative offices; finance, insurance, and real estate (FIRE); and corporate services that include business, legal, social, and other professional services as well as membership organizations. In short, the complex of corporate activities includes the "command and control" portions of large and medium-sized companies along with the services those companies need for planning, financing, managing risk, operating within the law, expanding, and interacting with each other.

The other basic economic functions of urban areas are performed by the nonprofit services (health and education), retailing, consumer services, and government sectors. The sectors are all quite substantial in size. The health care sector alone constitutes 14% of GNP (and should probably not be called "nonprofit"). Retailing and consumer services both deal directly with consumers, but retailing involves the sale of goods (including restaurant meals and beverages). In contrast, consumer services include services such as hotel rooms, hair styling, auto repairs, and amusements. Finally, government includes the federal, state, and local levels. Everything from local public schools to the U.S. military is lumped into this category, which constitutes 20% of the economy.

TABLE 4.1 Basic Economic Functions Performed by Urban Areas	
	SIC Codes
1. Agriculture, extractive, construction	
Agriculture	01–09
Mining	10–14
Construction	15–17
2. Manufacturing	20–39
3. Distributive services	
Transportation, communication, and utilities	40–49
Wholesale trade	50–51
4. Complex of corporate activities	
4a. Central administrative offices and auxiliary establishments	A&A[a]
4b. Finance, insurance, and real estate	60–67
4c. Corporate services	
Business services	73
Legal services	81
Membership organizations	86
Misc. professional services	89
Social services	83
5. Nonprofit services	
Health	80
Education	82
6. Retailing	52–59
7. Consumer services	
Hotels, etc.	70
Personal services	72
Auto repair, garages	75
Misc. repair services	76
Motion pictures	78
Amusement and recreation services	79, 84
Private household services	88
8. Government and government enterprises	91–97

[a]*A&A stands for "administrative and auxiliary employment" for each one-digit SIC code group.*
Source: Adapted from Noyelle and Stanback (1983, pp. 9, 60–61).

    The Noyelle and Stanback system permits the analyst to break down the economy of an urban area into a relatively small number of economically meaningful sectors. However, the Noyelle–Stanback system displayed in Table 4.1 is not based on an empirical examination of urban areas. Rather, it is a system based on an *a priori* classification of output into types. It would be helpful to know if the industries included in each of the eight categories in Table 4.1 tend to cluster together in urban areas. A finding that the industries tend to cluster as shown in the table would lend credibility to the Noyelle–Stanback system.

    Research on this issue was conducted by McDonald (1992) and O'hUallachain (1992) and reported in Mills and McDonald (1992). They computed "location quotients" for the 150 largest urban areas in the United States in 1980 using employment data at the two-digit SIC code level, the same type of data used by Noyelle and Stanback to devise their classification system. A location quotient is a measure of the extent to which an urban area specializes in a particular industry. It is defined as the percentage of total employment in an urban area engaged in a particular industry divided by the corresponding percentage for the nation as a whole. In algebraic form,

$$LQ = \frac{e_i/e}{E_i/E},$$

where e_i is the employment in industry i in the subject urban area, e the total employment in the subject urban area, E_i the employment in industry i in the United States, and E the total employment in the United States. A location quotient that is appreciably greater than 1 indicates that the urban area probably is producing the good or service for export outside its own area. A location quotient smaller than 1 suggests importation of the good or service.

For example, manufacturing employment in the Des Moines metropolitan area in 1980 was 26,303 of a total of 154,178 jobs in the private sector; jobs in manufacturing were 17.1% of the private-sector total. The corresponding figure for the United States in 1980 was 28.3%, so the location quotient for manufacturing in Des Moines was 0.60. This figure indicates that Des Moines did not specialize in manufacturing. In contrast, employment in wholesale trade for Des Moines was 9.2% of total private employment. The corresponding figure for the United States was 7.0%, so the location quotient for this sector was 1.31. Such a location quotient that is substantially greater than 1.0 indicates that the Des Moines metropolitan area specializes in this industry and therefore is providing this service for a wider area.

The location-quotient data were then used to find statistical associations among the two-digit SIC code industries. The statistical method determined whether urban areas with large location quotients for one particular industry had large location quotients for other industries — whether there were industries that tended to cluster together. The results of this exercise are shown in Table 4.2. Thirteen industry clusters emerge, although only the seven that are shown are of importance to most urban areas. The first cluster is manufacturing as a whole. However, the fact is that not all 20 manufacturing industries cluster together. A separate examination of manufacturing was completed and is reported in the appendix to this chapter. The second and third clusters are financial and legal services and business and professional services. The groupings presented in Table 4.2 differ somewhat from the Noyelle–Stanback system in Table 4.1, but the basic ideas are similar. The complex of corporate activities includes two groups of supporting industries, one largely financial in nature and the other providing business and professional services.

The distribution sector in Table 4.2 is more narrowly defined than is the corresponding Noyelle–Stanback sector, but the systems are quite similar. The health, social service, and education sector in Table 4.2 corresponds to the nonprofit services sector defined by Noyelle and Stanback, with the main exception that state and local government is included in the cluster defined in Table 4.2. The retail trade and recreation services clusters in the table correspond pretty closely to the combination of the retailing and consumer services groups defined by Noyelle and Stanback. In summary, the Noyelle and Stanback system does not correspond exactly to groupings based on statistical associations, but the results in Tables 4.1 and 4.2 are quite similar. The other six industry clusters reported by McDonald (1992) are wood products, manufacturing headquarters and cultural activities, construction, the port cluster, the

TABLE 4.2 Clustering of Industries in Urban Areas[a]

	SIC Codes
1. Manufacturing	20–39
2. Financial and legal services	
FIRE	60–67
Transportation by air	45
Communication	48
Legal services	81
A&A, FIRE[b]	—
3. Business and professional services	
Business services	73
Misc. professional services	89
4. Distribution	
Trucking and warehousing	42
Wholesale trade	50–51
A&A, wholesale	—
A&A, retail	—
5. Health, social services, and education	
Health services	80
Education	82
Social services	83
Government, state and local	—
Local passenger transit	41
6. Retail trade	
Retail trade	52–59
Personal services	72
Auto repair	75
Special trade contractors	17
7. Recreation services	
Hotels, etc.	70
Amusement and recreation services	79
Museums, etc.	84

[a]*There are six more clusters that appear in selected urban areas: wood products, manufacturing headquarters and cultural activities, construction, the port cluster, the mining and oil cluster, and apparel manufacture and distribution.*

[b]*A&A stands for "administrative and auxiliary establishments."*

Source: Adapted from McDonald (1992).

mining and oil cluster, and apparel manufacturing and distribution. These clusters are important in selected urban areas, and the investigator of a local economy should check to see if one or more of them should be included in his or her study.

D. THE NOYELLE–STANBACK CLASSIFICATION SYSTEM

The book by Noyelle and Stanback entitled *The Economic Transformation of American Cities* (1983) is something of a modern classic study of the system of cities in the United States. In this book they use the system for the classification of industry sectors, as shown in Table 4.1, to classify urban areas according to their economic functions. Now let us examine their use of that industry classification system to develop a functional typology of urban areas in the United States.

The theories discussed in Chapter 3 and in this chapter lead to the conclusion that the mix of economic activity will vary from urban area to urban area. Noyelle and Stanback measured that mix as of 1976 and assigned the top 140 urban areas to different functional categories. Their basic data consisted of employment location quotients of the top 140 urban areas for the industry groups defined above in Table 4.1. They searched statistically for groupings of *urban areas*.

Noyelle and Stanback found, using the location quotient data, that the 140 urban areas tended to cluster into 11 reasonably distinct groups. These groups are given titles in Table 4.3. The first three groups fall under the heading of diversified service centers, which can pertain to the national, regional, or subregional level. These three types of urban areas all tend to have location quotients in excess of 1.10 for the corporate complex (administrative offices, FIRE, and corporate services), and the distribution sector (transportation, communication, and utilities, and wholesale trade). The next three groups of urban areas are specialized service centers. Functional-nodal centers specialize in manufacturing and corporate administration within the complex of corporate activities, but they do not specialize in FIRE, corporate services, or distribution. The government–education group in the specialized service centers consists of centers of government (e.g., state capitals) combined in most cases with employment in universities. A small number of specialized service centers (five) combine manufacturing and education.

Consumer-oriented centers include residential urban areas that are near larger urban areas (e.g., Anaheim, California) and resort–retirement communities. Both of these types of urban areas specialize in retailing and consumer services.

TABLE 4.3   Noyelle–Stanback Functional Typology of Metropolitan Areas

	Number of Metropolitan Areas	Important Industry Sectors (LQ > 1.0)
Diversified service centers		
National nodal	4	Distribution, corporate complex
Regional nodal	19	Distribution, corporate complex
Subregional nodal	16	Distribution, corporate complex
Specialized service centers		
Functional nodal	24	Manufacturing, corporate complex
Government–education	15	Government
Education–manufacturing	5	Manufacturing, nonprofit services
Consumer-oriented centers		
Residential	3	Retailing, consumer services, nonprofit services
Resort–retirement	9	Retailing, consumer services
Production centers		
Manufacturing	25	Manufacturing
Industrial–military	12	Government, retail, consumer services
Mining–industrial	7	Mining, retail, consumer services

Source: Adapted from Noyelle and Stanback (1983).

The final set of three types of urban areas consists of production centers. Manufacturing centers specialize only in manufacturing. As we know from Chapter 3, this group of urban areas is consistent with Henderson's (1986) finding of localization economies in several manufacturing industries. Industrial–military centers specialize in government, retailing, and consumer services. The last group, mining–industrial centers, have employment concentrated in mining (or oil), retailing, and consumer services.

Which urban areas fall into these groups? Table 4.4 is a partial who's what list. This table also lists the population rank of the urban area in 1976. The three largest urban areas (New York, Los Angeles, and Chicago) and San Francisco are the national nodal diversified service centers. The regional nodal group includes 19 of the 31 remaining urban areas ranked in the top 35. This group includes older urban areas such as Philadelphia, Boston, and Baltimore as well as newer urban areas such as Miami, Phoenix, and Portland, Oregon. The subregional nodal group contains smaller urban areas, ranked from 41 to 120. The largest ones in this group are Memphis, Salt Lake City, and Birmingham. The smallest members of the group are Jackson (Mississippi), Spokane, and Des Moines. Readers who are familiar with some of these urban areas will recognize this as a group of commercial centers with more limited spheres of influence.

The specialized service centers include the large functional–nodal group. This group combines manufacturing with corporate administrative employment and includes major industrial centers such as Detroit, Pittsburgh, Newark, and Milwaukee. The group also includes smaller urban areas such as Rochester (New York), Toledo, and Peoria. The government–education group includes Washington, DC, of course, and several state capitals, such as Sacramento, Albany, Austin, Baton Rouge, and Madison. The small education–manufacturing group includes New Haven, Springfield (Massachusetts), Tacoma, South Bend, and Ann Arbor.

TABLE 4.4   Examples of the Classification of Metropolitan Areas by Function (with Population Rank in 1976)

Diversified Service Centers

National nodal

New York	1	Chicago	3
Los Angeles	2	San Francisco	7

Regional nodal (examples)

Philadelphia	4	Miami	21
Boston	6	Denver	22
Dallas	10	Seattle	23
Houston	11	Phoenix	30
St. Louis	12	Portland, OR	34
Baltimore	14	Columbus	35

Subregional nodal (examples)

Memphis	41	Des Moines	110
Salt Lake City	45	Spokane	114
Birmingham	46	Jackson, MS	120
Mobile	91		

TABLE 4.4   Examples of the Classification of Metropolitan Areas by Function (with Population Rank in 1976) *(Continued)*

Specialized Service Centers

Functional nodal (examples)

Detroit	5	Toledo	50
Pittsburgh	13	Greensboro	51
Newark	16	Akron	57
Milwaukee	24	Allentown	62
Hartford	36	Peoria	103
Rochester	38	Kalamazoo	137

Government–education (examples)

Washington	8	Lansing	84
Sacramento	39	Baton Rouge	89
Albany	48	Columbia, SC	99
Raleigh–Durham	77	Trenton	112
Austin	82	Madison	113

Education–manufacturing

New Haven	54	South Bend	130
Springfield, MA	64	Ann Arbor	140
Tacoma	90		

Production Centers

Manufacturing (examples)

Buffalo	27	Canton	92
Providence	42	Chattanooga	94
Worcester	59	Davenport	98
Gary	60	Beaumont	104
Grand Rapids	71	York	107
Youngstown	72	Appleton	125
Flint	74	Rockford	134
New Bedford	80		

Industrial–military (examples)

San Diego	20	Newport News	102
San Antonio	37	Colorado Springs	128
Norfolk	49	Pensacola	132
Charleston, SC	97		

Mining–industrial (examples)

Tucson	83	Duluth	138
Corpus Cristi	118	Charlestown, WV	139

Consumer-Oriented Centers

Residential

Long Island	9	Long Beach	76
Anaheim	19		

Resort–retirement (examples)

Tampa	25	Albuquerque	95
Ft. Lauderdale	43	Las Vegas	108
Orlando	68	Santa Barbara	122

Source: Adapted from Noyelle and Stanback (1983).

Production centers primarily include smaller urban areas among the top 140. The manufacturing centers include one large urban area (Buffalo), but Gary, Flint, and Chattanooga are more typical members of this group. Recall that this group specializes in manufacturing production, and does not include much of corporate administration. Finally, the industrial–military group and the mining–industrial group are groups of urban areas dominated respectively by military bases (San Diego, Charleston, Pensacola) and mining or oil (Tucson, Corpus Cristi, Duluth).

The Noyelle–Stanback classification system of urban areas pertains to 1976, but nearly all of the urban areas probably still fall into the same groups. Here is an interesting point for discussion and perhaps for a research paper. Which urban areas may have changed in function enough since 1976 to jump from one group to another? I nominate Tucson as one possible example. The mining industry around Tucson has declined, while jobs in government–education (University of Arizona) and resort–retirement activities have grown. In other cases employment in a basic sector of the local economy has declined, but nothing has grown up to take its place. Flint is a good (bad?) example. Employment in the auto industry has declined, but no other sector has grown enough to move Flint out of the manufacturing production group.

In summary, the Noyelle–Stanback system produces a functional hierarchy for modern urban areas and classifies urban areas according to their dominant economic functions. There is no simple theory that explains fully the patterns that Noyelle and Stanback uncovered. The simple urban hierarchy model of market-oriented activities based on specialization and economies of scale tells part of the story. Localization economies appear to be important for some industries, including both manufacturing and nonmanufacturing industries. Urbanization economies appear to be important too, but may have been more critical in the early history of large urban areas than they are today. As shown in the appendix to this chapter, input–output linkages are also important and emerge as factors in the clustering of manufacturing industries. The complex of corporate activities also clearly involves input–output relationships between corporate offices and business and financial services.

Information and labor market factors surely create further urban agglomeration. But at this point we do not know the relative importance of these agglomerative forces. Finally, large urban areas are large because they grew rapidly during previous time periods. What role does each of the forces of agglomeration play in urban *growth*? A discussion of this question is deferred to Part III of the book.

E. EXAMINATION OF THE DES MOINES ECONOMY

A good theory is a useful theory. Good classification systems are also useful. In this chapter we have presented two systems for classifying industries in urban areas and one functional classification of urban areas themselves. These systems can be of use to anyone who wishes to gain some insight into the economy of a particular urban area. This section makes use of these systems to take a look at the economy of Des Moines, Iowa. The choice of Des Moines is purely arbitrary, although Des Moines has the advantage of being almost entirely contained in one county, Polk County, Iowa. What follows is an examination of this county.

From Table 4.4 we already know that Des Moines was classified by Noyelle and Stanback (1983) as a diversified service center–subregional nodal. Des Moines is grouped with urban areas such as Mobile, Little Rock, Shreveport, Spokane, and Jackson, Mississippi. Diversified service centers in this group tend to specialize in the distribution sector and the complex of corporate activities. In 1976 a population of 328,000 gave Des Moines a rank of 110 among urban areas in the United States.

Total employment in Polk County has been broken down into the industry clusters in Table 4.2 using the McDonald (1992) scheme. Employment data for 1980 and 1987 for the top six clusters are shown in Table 4.5. Des Moines is the state capital of Iowa, so government employment is a separate category in Table 4.5. Table 4.5 also displays the fraction of total private employment for each private-industry cluster and location quotients for each private-industry cluster. These figures are restricted to private industries because of the presence of the state government in Des Moines.

Table 4.5 shows that Noyelle and Stanback (1983) had it just about right. Des Moines specializes in financial and legal services and in the distribution cluster. The employment level of 23,147 in financial and legal services for 1980 translates into a share of 15.0% and a location quotient of 1.74. These are high numbers indeed. By 1987 employment in this sector had grown to 30,796, for a share of 17.9% and a location quotient of 1.83. This sector is a winner! The distribution cluster employed 21,647 in 1980. Its share was 14.0% and the location quotient was a relatively high 1.46. However, this cluster did not keep pace with financial and legal services. Employment grew to 22,727 in 1987, but its share dropped to 13.2% and the location quotient fell to 1.40. These two sectors are examined in more detail below.

TABLE 4.5 Employment in Des Moines (Polk County), Iowa

	1980			1987		
Sector	Employment	Percent Share	LQ[a]	Employment	Percent Share	LQ
Total private employment	154,178			171,945		
Manufacturing	26,303	17.1	0.60	22,850	13.3	0.60
Retail cluster	37,595	24.4	1.00	40,477	23.5	0.89
Financial and legal services[b]	23,147	15.0	1.74	30,796	17.9	1.83
Business and professional services	7,604	4.9	0.94	11,770	6.8	0.91
Distribution	21,647	14.0	1.46	22,727	13.2	1.40
Health, education, and social services	17,744	11.5	1.11	23,026	13.4	1.11
Other	20,138	13.1	0.97	20,299	11.8	0.93
Government	28,800	15.8	0.88	30,600	15.3	0.89

[a]LQ *stands for "location quotient," which equals the local share for the industry group divided by the corresponding figure for the nation. For the private sectors, percent share and* LQ *pertain to private employment only.*

[b]*Industry group includes FIRE (SIC 61–67) plus legal services (SIC 81), air transportation (SIC 45), and transportation services (SIC 47).*

Source: *County Business Patterns,* U.S. Department of Commerce; *Employment and Earnings,* U.S. Department of Labor.

The health, education, and social services cluster had a location quotient of 1.11 in both 1980 and 1987, which is only slightly in excess of 1.0. Note that to maintain its location quotient of 1.11 over these years, the sector had to grow from 17,744 to 23,026 workers and increase its share from 11.5% to 13.4%. This sector includes health care, and the sector is examined in more detail below.

Table 4.5 also shows the lack of prominence of manufacturing in the Des Moines economy. The location quotient for manufacturing was 0.60 in both 1980 and 1987, and both its level and share of employment dropped. With one exception, the other sectors listed in Table 4.5 are rather unremarkable; they show up with location quotients that are equal to or slightly less than 1.0. The exception is business and professional services. This sector has a location quotient that is less than 1.0, but it grew very rapidly in Des Moines (and in the rest of the nation as well). Table 4.5 did not take very long to construct, and it provides a nice overview of the main sectors of the Des Moines economy and how well they have been doing.

A comparison for Des Moines of employment growth by industry cluster with the United States is shown in Table 4.6. Private employment in the United States grew by 14.2% from 1980 to 1987, and Des Moines almost matched that growth, with a figure of 11.5%. However, the patterns of that growth for the Des Moines and national economies were very different. The retail cluster grew much more rapidly at the national level, and national employment growth in business and professional services and in distribution also exceeded their growth in Des Moines by a fair margin. Remember, this last cluster is one in which Des Moines specializes. Perhaps we need to take a more detailed look at these sectors so that we can pinpoint both the sources of robust employment growth and the sources of lackluster performance.

The more detailed look at the sectors is shown in Table 4.7. The data source is *County Business Patterns*, which provides employment figures by county down to the four-digit SIC code level. Most of the data shown in Table 4.7 is taken from the two-digit SIC industry level, but a few three- and four-digit SIC figures are used to examine some additional details. Four sectors will be examined in turn: financial and

TABLE 4.6	Employment Growth in Des Moines (Polk County), Iowa and in the United States, 1980–1987 (Percent)	
Sector	*Des Moines*	*U.S.*
Total private employment	11.5	14.2
Manufacturing	−13.1	−10.2
Retail cluster	7.7	23.4
Financial and legal services[a]	33.0	30.7
Business and professional services	54.8	64.2
Distribution	5.0	12.5
Health, education, and social services	29.8	32.8
Other	0.8	7.5
Government	6.2	7.2

[a]*Industry group includes FIRE (SIC 61–67), legal services (SIC 81), air transportation (SIC 45), and transportation services (SIC 47).*

TABLE 4.7	Important Industries in Des Moines (Polk County), Iowa			

| | | Employment | | Growth |
Industry		1980	1987	(%)
Financial and legal services		23,147	30,796	33.0
SIC 60	Banking	2,696	2,958	9.7
SIC 61	S&Ls	1,879	3,390	80.4
SIC 62	Security brokers	499	733	46.9
SIC 63	Insurance carriers	12,434	15,237	22.5
SIC 64	Insurance agents	1,220	2,293	88.0
SIC 65	Real estate	2,242	2,584	15.3
SIC 66–67	Other real estate and investment	432	702	62.5
A&A	Administrative	298	643	115.8
SIC 45, 47	Transportation	347	701	102.0
SIC 81	Legal services	1,100	1,555	41.4
Distribution		18,630	21,647	16.2
SIC 42	Trucking and warehousing	5,418	5,390	−0.5
SIC 50–51	Wholesale trade	12,462	14,122	13.3
A&A in retailing		750	2,135	184.7
Business and professional services		7,604	11,770	54.8
SIC 73	Business services	6,140	10,075	64.1
734	Services to buildings	1,064	1,670	57.0
736	Personnel supply	1,217	1,898	56.0
737	Computer, data processing	880	2,262	157.0
7374	Data processing	841	1,821	116.5
SIC 89	Professional services	1,464	1,695	15.8
Health, education, and social services		17,744	23,026	29.8
SIC 80	Health services	13,041	13,854	6.2
SIC 82	Education services	2,366	4,064	71.8
SIC 83	Social services	1,910	3,843	101.2
SIC 41	Local transit	427	1,265	195.6

Source: County Business Patterns, U.S. Department of Commerce.

legal services, distribution, business and professional services, and the health, education, and social services group.

Table 4.7 tells us immediately that the financial and legal services cluster is dominated by the insurance industry—the insurance carriers, as opposed to local insurance agents. Insurance carriers (SIC 63) made up 53.7% of the cluster in 1980, and that percentage fell slightly to 49.5% in 1987. It would certainly not come as news to anyone in Des Moines that insurance is big business there, but the importance of this industry is highlighted in Table 4.7. Clearly, insurance services are being exported to a wide area. What are the localization economies at work? This is a question that should be investigated by those who are vitally concerned with the Des Moines economy. However, it is also true that the other components of the financial and legal services cluster grew substantially during the 1980–1987 period. As a group their growth was far greater than the growth in the insurance industry. Employment in insurance (SIC 63) grew by 22.5% over these seven years, but employment in the rest of the financial and legal services cluster grew by 45.2%. This finding perhaps tells us that the Des Moines economy is branching out into other areas of financial and legal services, a trend that is probably a good thing. A local economy perhaps relies so heavily on a single industry at its peril.

The other major specialty for Des Moines is the distribution cluster, which consists of trucking and warehousing, wholesale trade, and administrative offices in retail trade. Table 4.7 shows that wholesale trade alone contributed 14,808 jobs to the Des Moines economy in 1987. Des Moines clearly is a center of distribution of goods to its subregion, and it also serves as a collection point for exports from Iowa. The growth in this cluster was a rather modest 5.0% during 1980–1987. Trucking and warehousing added 455 jobs, and wholesale trade added 686. Why did this sector experience this lackluster performance when the sector as a whole grew by 12.5% at the national level? What impact did the deregulation of the trucking industry in the early 1980s have on Des Moines? These questions need some answers.

The business and professional services cluster is not a specialty for Des Moines, but it experienced an impressive growth of 54.8%. This cluster has only two industries at the two-digit SIC level, business services (SIC 73) and professional services (SIC 89). Table 4.7 shows that the cluster in Des Moines is dominated by business services. Nearly all of the growth in the cluster from 1980 to 1987 was in business services. Table 4.7 shows the major components of business services (SIC 73) in Des Moines. These are services to buildings (SIC 734), personnel supply (SIC 736), and computer and data processing services (SIC 737). This last industry is dominated by data processing (SIC 7374). Services to buildings (SIC 734) means janitorial, maintenance, and repair services. This industry has been growing as building owners have decided to have their buildings serviced by professionals. This kind of service is particularly prevalent in office buildings, and clearly office employment and the office building industry have been growing in Des Moines. Personnel supply (SIC 736) consists of firms that supply temporary workers to a variety of clients. The temporary workers are usually considered to be employees of the supplying firm (e.g., Manpower, Inc.). Growth in this industry in Des Moines is part of the national trend toward hiring temporary rather than permanent workers. Firms seem to require more of the flexibility that temporary workers can provide. Finally, Des Moines experienced huge growth in data processing (SIC 7374) of 116.5% in just seven years. Almost 1000 jobs were created in this industry alone. Why did this happen? Can this growth continue? The people of Des Moines should find out.

The fourth and final cluster that is examined in Table 4.7 is health, education, and social services. Recall that this cluster grew rapidly enough to maintain its location quotient of 1.11. That growth was 5282 jobs over seven years. Table 4.7 shows that, perhaps surprisingly, the lion's share of the growth was *not* in health services. Health services made up 73.5% of the cluster in 1980, but that proportion had fallen to 60.2% in 1987. Most of the growth took place in the education services and social services industries. Once again, the people of Des Moines need to find out why this growth took place and whether more of the same could have been expected.

In this section we have, in effect, presented a report on the status of the Des Moines economy that might be of use to local officials and industry leaders. We have shown a great deal of what makes the Des Moines economy tick, but also raise some questions that need to be answered. This is certainly one valid purpose for a short report of this kind, to raise questions that are critical to a deeper understanding of the local economy.

F. SUMMARY

This chapter is a discussion of the economic functions of urban areas. An urban area fits into the system of urban areas in particular ways. The urban hierarchy model for market-oriented industries explains some of the patterns that are observed, but that model has severe limitations. Those limitations include not taking account of resource-based industries, industries that are subject to localization economies, and various types of special-purpose urban areas. The real features of the transportation system are also ignored. Unfortunately, there is no comprehensive theory that can replace the urban hierarchy theory.

In the absence of a comprehensive theory, researchers and practitioners have turned to classification systems that are based on statistical associations. Noyelle and Stanback (1983) provided an innovative classification scheme for the top 140 urban areas in the United States based on economic functions broadly defined. McDonald (1992) and O'hUallachain (1992) have introduced a classification system for industries that is based on statistical association. These classification systems can be used to gain some insights into the functions performed by a local economy, and the Des Moines economy was used as an example.

Clustering of Manufacturing Industries

It was noted in the text that not all manufacturing industries tend to cluster together. Manufacturing industries cluster in urban areas if they have strong input–output relationships or other forms of agglomeration economies, as discussed in Chapter 3. McDonald (1992) found that the two-digit SIC code manufacturing industries tended to group together statistically in 1986 as shown in Table A4.1. The procedure followed was to compute the 20 by 20 matrix of simple correlations of employment shares in total manufacturing. Of the 190 simple correlations, 18 are positive and statistically significant (at the 99% level of statistical significance). None of these simple correlations is negative and statistically significant. The 18 simple correlations led to 15 industry clusters of two industries each and one cluster of three industries. The most important clusters are listed in Table A4.1.

The clusters clearly are largely based on input–output relationships or on particular combinations of available basic resources. For example, the first cluster is food and kindred products (SIC 20) and stone, clay, and glass products (SIC 32). This cluster is consistent with the idea that food products and food containers, dishes, and so on, tend to be produced in the same urban areas. Part of the correlation probably stems from the use of glass containers as packaging for food items. In contrast, the second cluster is tobacco (SIC 21) and furniture (SIC 25). Urban areas that produce both of these products are located in the southeastern region of the nation, which has an abundance of the raw materials used in both industries. The presence of tobacco farms and forests in the same general area is simply a coincidence of nature. The third cluster of textiles and apparel is obviously based on a strong input–output relationship. The fourth cluster consists of textiles and furniture, which combine an input–output relationship (use of textile mill products in furniture) and coincidental resource availability (cotton and wood).

One can proceed through the list of cluster in Table A4.1 in this fashion and note that all of the remaining clusters are based in substantial measure on input–output relationships. For example, cluster 6 has chemicals, which need petroleum and coal products as inputs. Cluster 10 includes transportation equipment (autos, trucks) and the fabricated metals products needed for such equipment.

We have seen that manufacturing industries have clear tendencies to cluster together based largely on input–output relationships. Table A4.1 provides a summary of the major clusters.

TABLE A4.1	Major Manufacturing Clusters (Based on Correlations of Employment Shares)	
		SIC Code
1. Food and containers		
	Food and kindred products	20
	Stone, clay, and glass products	32
2. Tobacco and furniture		
	Tobacco	21
	Furniture	25
3. Textiles and apparel		
	Textile mill products	22
	Apparel	23
4. Textiles and furniture		
	Textile mill products	22
	Furniture	25
5. Furniture and fixtures		
	Furniture	25
	Fabricated metal products	34
6. Petrochemicals		
	Chemicals and allied products	28
	Petroleum and coal products	29
7. Chemical products and containers		
	Chemicals and allied products	28
	Stone, clay, and glass products	32
8. Machinery I		
	Rubber and plastic products	30
	Fabricated metal products	34
	Machinery, except electrical	35
9. Metals		
	Primary metal products	33
	Fabricated metal products	34
10. Transportation equipment		
	Fabricated metal products	34
	Transportation equipment	37
11. Machinery II		
	Machinery, except electrical	35
	Electric and electronic equipment	36

Source: Adapted from McDonald (1992), from *County Business Patterns* (U.S. Department of Commerce) data.

EXERCISES

1. In Exercise 1 of Chapter 1 you were asked to prepare population data for an urban area of your choice. Now your task is to collect data on employment for this urban area. You can use data from *County Business Patterns* to examine private employment by industry, and government employment data are provided in *Employment and Earnings*.

(a) Create a table for your urban area that shows employment by one-digit SIC code for the years 1979 and 1990. These two years are chosen because they are peaks in the national business cycle. The one-digit SIC code industries are:

- Agricultural services and mining
- Construction
- Manufacturing
- Transportation, communication, and utilities
- Wholesale trade
- Retail trade
- Finance, insurance, and real estate
- Services
- Government

Compute the location quotients for your urban area (relative to the United States). Which industries in your urban area grew rapidly? Which industries had an increase in the location quotient? Is the same list of industries the answer to both of these questions? If not, why not?

(b) Use the 1990 *County Business Patterns* data to create the industry clusters shown in Table 4.2. Compute the location quotients (relative to the United States) for these industry clusters. Also, create a table that shows the clusters of manufacturing industries as shown in Table A4.1. In what sectors does your urban area specialize? Offer some reasons for why this urban area has this particular group of specializations. In formulating these reasons, be sure to take into account the basic idea of the urban hierarchy. By the way, some of the SIC code categories were changed in 1987, so it is not possible to compare detailed SIC industries before and after this date. This is why you are asked to perform this exercise for only one year, 1990.

REFERENCES

Henderson, J. Vernon, 1986. "Efficiency of Resource Usage and City Size," *Journal of Urban Economics*, Vol. 19, pp. 47–70.

McDonald, John, 1992. "Assessing the Development Status of Metropolitan Areas," in E. Mills and J. McDonald, eds., *Sources of Metropolitan Growth*. New Brunswick, NJ: Center for Urban Policy Research, Rutgers University.

Mills, Edwin and John McDonald, eds., 1992. *Sources of Metropolitan Growth*. New Brunswick, NJ: Center for Urban Policy Research, Rutgers University.

Noyelle, Thierry and Thomas Stanback, Jr., 1983. *The Economic Transformation of American Cities*. Totowa, NJ: Rowan & Allanheld.

O'hUallachain, Breandon, 1992. "Economic Structure and Growth of Metropolitan Areas," in E. Mills and J. McDonald, eds., *Sources of Metropolitan Growth*. New Brunswick, NJ: Center for Urban Policy Research, Rutgers University.

CHAPTER

Introduction to Urban Location Patterns: Static Analysis

A. INTRODUCTION

In this chapter we introduce the static theory of the location of economic activity within urban areas. Conventional textbooks in microeconomics present theories designed to answer the following questions. *What* is produced? *How* is it produced? *For whom* is it produced? Urban economics is the branch of microeconomics that also asks: *Where* are the various economic goods produced within urban areas? The theory in this chapter and the next is what distinguishes urban economics from the rest of microeconomics. The core of the theory is developed in this chapter and in Chapter 6, and the theory is applied and extended in Chapters 7 to 10.

Economic theory is a deliberate simplification of reality. The art of theorizing (and it *is* partly an art) is to devise theories that are reasonably simple and yet powerful, able to account for significant aspects of the real world. The theory of urban location patterns presented here does indeed provide a sensible and consistent explanation for many features of real urban areas. But the theory does not explain everything. We do not expect theories to explain everything. The challenge for those who choose economics as a career is to improve the ability of economic theory to explain what is important to people. Urban economics has made great progress, but there is room for further progress.

The market for urban land is of central importance to the theory of urban location patterns. The urban land market is a highly regulated market, but it is still very useful to employ the tools of competitive market analysis to understand how land is allocated to its various potential uses. Furthermore, land is an input into the production of all goods and services. It is obvious that housing uses a great deal of land as an input. Manufacturing and commercial activities also use land. The public sector uses a great deal of land for transportation facilities (roads, highways, and airports) as well as for parks, schools, and other public buildings. The amount of land that is used to produce outputs can vary enormously—from the tall office buildings in the central business district to the vast suburban shopping malls. The land market not only determines what is produced at a particular site but influences how much is produced (per unit of land).

B. AGGLOMERATIONS OF ECONOMIC ACTIVITY IN URBAN AREAS

The theory of the urban land market begins with the observation that economic activity tends to be concentrated in certain locations within an urban area. The modern urban area contains several types of economic agglomerations: the downtown central business district, major airports and other transportation and distribution centers, industrial areas, large shopping centers, hospitals and related medical facilities, educational institutions, and government offices and facilities. An urban area contains a collection of such centers of economic activity that depends upon its economic history and its functions in the modern economy. The types and sizes of urban areas were discussed in Chapter 4.

All of the major urban areas in the United States were founded prior to the 1920s, the beginning of the age of the automobile. Indeed, except for a few that began as railroad junctions, most urban areas began as ports. For example, Chicago and its central business district are located at the mouth of the Chicago River, because this small, lifeless river was once the best of a bad set of choices for the location of a port on Lake Michigan. Other major urban areas, such as New York, Boston, Philadelphia, Miami, New Orleans, Houston, Los Angeles, San Francisco, and Seattle, began economic life as ports and continue to be major ports in the world economy. The layout of the port facility tended to dictate the nearby location of other commercial activities, such as wholesale trade, banking, and insurance companies as well as important parts of manufacturing production. The coming of the railroad in the latter half of the nineteenth century usually meant that rail lines were focused on an existing port and its related concentration of economic activity. For these reasons many urban areas in the late nineteenth and early twentieth centuries can be considered to be *monocentric*; that is, there was only one major center of economic activity around which the urban area revolved.

There are important early exceptions to monocentric cities. The largest urban areas, such as New York, Philadelphia, and Chicago, had outgrown their original downtown districts well before 1900. Important parts of the urban economy had taken up residence in other locations. The early examples of the *suburbanization* of employment usually involve one of the large-scale manufacturing facilities that date from the late nineteenth century. Chicago's Union Stockyards provide a good case in point. Chicago had a large number of small stockyards and meatpacking plants that grew rapidly in the early 1860s. These companies were located at various spots near the downtown area and very quickly ran out of space. The Union Stockyards was formed in 1865 by a consortium of meat packers and railroad companies, and a single site was chosen at the periphery of the urban area (about 5 miles to the southwest of downtown). This site was provided with both rail and water transportation, and it almost instantly developed into a huge agglomeration of industrial activity. Did the Chicagoans of the day decry the loss of jobs from the inner city? No. Rather, there was a great feeling of relief because cattle and hogs do not make very good urban neighbors. Besides, the Chicago economy was growing rapidly.

The basic message here is that the analysis of an urban land market for some point in time begins with the enumeration of the important focal points for economic activity. In some cases it is sufficient to assume a monocentric urban area, but in other cases two or more centers of employment are important enough to merit separate attention. The number and types of employment centers are matters for more detailed examination in Chapter 7.

C. SECTORS IN THE URBAN ECONOMY

One of the first things that a student in elementary economics learns is that the economy can be divided into the household and business sectors. Households supply labor to businesses, and businesses produce products and services that are sold to households. In addition, households engage in savings that are channeled ultimately into investments made by businesses. This is a simple characterization of an economy that is without a government and is closed completely to the rest of the world. A basic model of the urban economy and its land market could be based on this elementary picture. However, this model would miss some very important features of real urban areas.

It is critical to recognize that urban areas engage in a great deal of importing and exporting. This trading activity is not necessarily foreign trade—trade with foreign countries—but is simply trade with people who are located outside the urban area. Philadelphians "import" much of their food from outside their metropolitan area. There are many firms in Philadelphia that manufacture food items for Philadelphians, but these firms must purchase their basic inputs of grains, vegetables, meats, and so on, from outside the area. Also, most of Philadelphia's food-processing firms export some of their output to people who live outside the metropolitan area. Urban areas are centers of commerce. They exist to facilitate trade. Therefore, it is necessary to specify at least three business sectors: businesses that produce for export, businesses that import, and businesses that exist to produce for the local population. Some businesses may in fact engage in all three types of activities, but this complication will be ignored for now.

Another type of categorization of business sectors was introduced in Chapter 1 and used extensively in Chapter 4. The U.S. Department of Commerce classifies businesses by type of industry into the following categories:

- Agriculture, forestry, and fisheries
- Mining
- Construction
- Manufacturing
- Transportation, communication, and public utilities
- Wholesale trade
- Retail trade
- Finance, insurance, and real estate
- Services

Obviously, the first two categories are not important in most urban areas, but the other seven are. Furthermore, each of these seven major sectors has numerous components that are very different. There are 20 basic types of manufacturing industries, eight categories of retail trade establishments, and services consist of everything from hotels and personal services to health care, legal services, engineers and architects, accountants, and educational services. How many business sectors should be enumerated to gain a good understanding of urban location patterns and the urban land market? The answer is that no one is entirely sure because it depends on the nature of the questions that one is trying to investigate.

Suppose that you are mainly interested in the market for industrial land and the location patterns of manufacturing activity and employment. In this case you might divide manufacturing activity into two categories, such as heavy industry and light industry, keep a separate category for transportation, communication, and public utilities, and lump all other industries into a "commercial" category consisting largely of warehouses, stores, and offices. On the other hand, if you are interested primarily in studying whether downtown activities such as banking and finance, business and professional services, and retail trade have moved into other parts of an urban area, you would set up business sectors differently.

The household sector also consists of many components. Households differ by type (married couple with or without children, single individual, single parent with children), race, age of household head, and income level. Different schemes for the categorization of households can be used depending on the purpose at hand. One might wish to examine household location patterns and the residential land market for the various racial or income groups, for example. We examine this matter in detail in Chapter 9.

So far the role of government in an urban area has been ignored except to note at the beginning that government is a major user of land for streets, public buildings, parks, and other things. Furthermore, the use of land is regulated by the government. Any model of the urban land market that claims to be reasonably comprehensive cannot afford to ignore the various roles of government. The role of government as a major employer cannot be ignored either.

Large urban areas have professional urban planners who, among other things, collect information on the use of land. A standard set of categories for urban activities consists of the following:

- Residential
- Manufacturing
- Transportation, communication, and public utilities
- Commercial
- Public buildings
- Public open space
- Parking
- Streets
- Vacant
- Unusable (including bodies of water)

As a practical matter, analysis of the urban land market may be constrained by such data collection efforts.

D. THEORY OF RENT, LAND RENT, AND BID RENT

Basic and intermediate textbooks in microeconomics barely mention land, and if they do, the reference is usually to agricultural land. Furthermore, in the standard texts rent is defined as the price paid per year (or per month) for the services of a factor of production that is fixed in supply. *Rent* is thus a term that can be applied to the earnings of land, the price paid for the services of uniquely talented people, or the earnings of some other inelastically supplied input. Rent in this sense is sometimes called *pure economic rent*, to emphasize that it is payments per year to an input beyond the payment needed to call forth the existing supply. Babe Ruth earned $125,000 per year to play baseball (in the 1920s!), and his alternative occupation (let us suppose) was to be a bartender at a salary of $3000 per year. His pure economic rent was $122,000. Figure 5.1 illustrates the determination of rent in this kind of situation in a competitive market. The fixed supply is vertical line *SS*, and the demand is *DD*. Market equilibrium rent *R* is determined by the height of the demand curve. An increase in demand to *D'D'* gets translated directly into an increase in rent to *R'*.

The rent as illustrated in Figure 5.1 can be translated into the market value of the asset that is being rented. The market value is simply the present value of the stream of rents that the asset will earn. In a competitive market for the asset the value would be set so that buyer would not earn a higher return on his purchase than he would earn in another investment of equal risk. In equation form,

$$V = \frac{R_1}{1+r} + \frac{R_2}{(1+r)^2} + \frac{R_3}{(1+r)^3} + \cdots,$$ (1)

FIGURE 5.1 Determination of pure economic rent

where R_1 is the rent for the first year, R_2 the rent for the second year, R_3 the rent for the third year, and r the going interest rate (in decimal terms such as 0.05 for 5%). The stream of rents lasts for the life of the asset.

If the rent is expected to be the same amount R each year, then

$$V = \sum \frac{R}{(1+r)^i} \qquad (2)$$

where Σ refers to the sum over i from year 1 to year n. Furthermore, if the asset has a life of infinite length, then

$$V = \frac{R}{r}. \qquad (3)$$

The proof of this result is very easy and something you should be able to do. Return to equation (2), and multiply both sides by $(1 + r)$ to get

$$V + rV = \sum \frac{R}{(1+r)^{i-1}}, \qquad (4)$$

for i equals 1 to infinity. The first term of the summation on the right-hand side of equation (4) is R divided by $(1+r)$ taken to the zero power, or just divided by 1. The rest of the right-hand side of equation (4) is V. In other words,

$$V + rV = R + V. \qquad (5)$$

Subtraction of V from both sides and division by r yields equation (3): $V = R/r$. Alternatively, write this result as $R = rV$, which states that the annual rent on an asset of infinite life is just the value of that asset times the going interest rate written as a decimal.

Ricardo's Theory of Land Rent

The first economist to develop a theory of land rent was David Ricardo (1821, pp. 33–45), who turned his attention to agricultural land. His theory is a steppingstone on the way to the modern theory of urban land rent, so it is interesting to examine his theory as he presented it. Ricardo (1821, p. 34) defined *land rent* as "that compensation which is paid to the owner of land for the use of its original and indestructible powers." This statement refers to the fertility of agricultural land, which we now know is not indestructible. For now, assume that the fertility of a parcel of land is a given.

Ricardo's fundamental insight was to realize that agricultural land is not all of the same level of fertility. He supposed that there is a fixed supply of land of the best fertility, which he called No. 1 land. Land with a somewhat lower level of fertility was called No. 2 land, and it was fixed in supply as well. Land with even lower levels of fertility (No. 3, No. 4, etc.) was also fixed in supply. Ricardo assumed that with equal employment of capital and labor, No. 1, No. 2, and No. 3 land would yield a net produce of 100, 90, and 80 units of corn per acre.

Now consider what happens when the country under consideration is young and has a small population. A sufficient amount of No. 1 land exists to feed the entire population, with some No. 1 land left over. In this case the land rent is zero. (The most fertile land is a free good because its supply exceeds its demand, even at a price of zero.) But as Ricardo (1821, p. 35) put it, "when, in the progress of society, land of the second degree of fertility is taken into cultivation, rent immediately commences on that of the first quality, and the amount of that rent will depend on the difference in the quality of these two portions of land." No. 2 land produces 90 units of corn per acre for an equal application of capital and labor. For capital (and labor) to earn the same amount on both types of land, 10 units of corn must be paid to the owner of the No. 1 land. Therefore, land rent exists because land varies in fertility, and land of a given fertility level is fixed in quantity. Further "progress of society" will bring No. 3 land into cultivation, which will mean that No. 1 land will now receive land rent of 20 units of corn per acre and No. 2 land will begin to earn land rent of 10 units per acre. The modern economist would add that competition among farmers generates the result. A farmer who is cultivating No. 3 land would pay up to 20 units of corn to occupy No. 1 land, so the farmer who actually occupies No. 1 land must pay 20 units or lose his lease.

Ricardo (1821) introduced the crucial concepts in the theory of land rent:

1. Land varies in its natural endowment or advantage for the user.
2. Land of a given level of natural endowment or advantage is fixed in supply.
3. The land market is governed by perfect competition.
4. Land rent is determined by the differences in natural endowment or advantage of land.

The Urban Land Market

The theory of the urban land market also makes use of the concept of land rent. Henceforth in this chapter the price paid for the services of urban land is called *land rent*, to distinguish it from rent paid to factors of production in general. One important distinction between rent of the pure economic variety and land rent in an urban area concerns the assumption of fixed supply. Of course, the total land area of the earth is fixed in supply except for minor additions in Holland, land-fill areas, and erosion of coastlines. But it is also true that the market value of much of the earth's land is zero. You may have heard of the fatuous remark by Will Rogers that "land is a good investment: they ain't making any more of it." Buy land in the Sahara, Gobi, or Mojave desert and see what a good investment you have made. Unless there happens to be oil under your sand, you will lose your money. Besides, if there were oil under the ground, you would want to buy the mineral rights, not the land itself. The better (but still rather fatuous) remark is that there are three principal factors in the determination of land values: location, location, and location. What is fixed in supply is the amount of land within 5 miles of 42nd Street and Fifth Avenue in New York. There is only so much usable land within 10 miles of Chicago's O'Hare Airport.

The land that is in fixed supply is the land with particular locational attributes. This corresponds to Ricardo's assumption that there is a fixed supply of land of a given level of fertility (natural endowment or advantage). However, the supply of land for a particular *use* is *not* fixed in supply. The supply of land for urban use has expanded rapidly. Indeed, some people are of the misplaced view that urban land use is encroaching significantly on the world's supply of good farmland. Also, land within an urban area can be converted from one use to another. Sometimes land-use conversion is expensive, but it can be done. For example, in the 1950s and 1960s a great deal of urban land in a variety of uses was converted to urban freeways to facilitate the movement of auto and truck traffic. At this moment urban land developers are converting to commercial and residential uses land in older industrial cities that once housed factories.

The fundamental concept that is used in the theory of the urban land market is *bid rent*. Land rent as defined above is a market price, but bid rent is only a hypothetical price. Bid rent for a household for a particular urban site is the maximum rent per unit of land that the household can pay to reside at location x and maintain some given level of utility. Similarly, bid rent for a business is the maximum rent per unit of land that it can pay for a particular urban site and maintain a given profit level. This idea corresponds to the bid that Ricardo's farmer on No. 3 land would make for the use of No. 1 land. A *bid-rent function* for a household depicts the relationship between location and bid rent at a given utility level. There is a bid-rent function for each hypothetical utility level of the household, and there is a bid-rent function for the firm at each hypothetical profit level. The bid rent for a household changes as location changes so as to keep utility constant, and the bid rent for a firm changes as location changes so as to keep profits constant. In other words, bid rent can be thought of as a residual amount that is bid for land once the attributes of a location have been taken into account.

Bid-Rent Theory for Firms

The theory of bid rent for a firm is easier to explain than the bid rent for households. Suppose that a firm in an urban area is in business to produce a particular product that is sold for export at the port in the center of the urban area. For simplicity we shall assume that the firm occupies exactly 1 acre of land and produces Q^* units of output no matter where the firm decides to locate. The firm uses labor and capital (along with land) to produce the output, and the average cost of labor and capital for each unit of output is c dollars. The output is sold at the port at a price of p dollars per unit, but before the output can be sold, it must be transported from the plant site to the port. Assume that transportation cost is t dollars per mile for each unit of output. Finally, the firm must pay land rent R for its 1 acre of land.

Given these assumptions, the firm's profits can be written as

$$\text{profit} = pQ^* - cQ^* - txQ^* - R,$$

where x is the distance (in miles) from the plant site to the port. The basic idea of a bid rent function is to set profits at some level and then trace out how land rent varies. In this case land rent can vary with distance to the port (x). Set profits at some arbitrary level K, and solve for land rent as follows:

$$K = pQ^* - cQ^* - txQ^* - R,$$

$$R = (p - c)Q^* - K - (tQ^*)x.$$

Recall that R is the bid rent for 1 acre of land, so R is the bid rent per acre. This bid-rent function is depicted in Figure 5.2. The intercept of the function is $(p - c)Q^* - K$, and the slope of the (linear) function is $- tQ^*$. The intercept of the function indi-

FIGURE 5.2 Bid-rent functions for firms

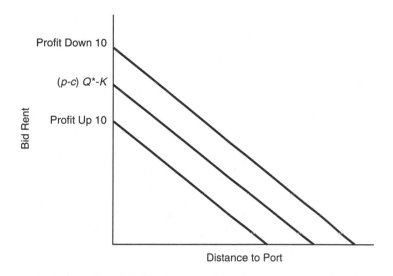

cates the bid rent at a distance to the port of zero, and the slope of the function says that bid rent declines by tQ^* dollars as distance from the port increases by 1 mile.

A family of bid-rent functions can be derived by varying the level of profits that is assumed. An increase in the level of profits from K to $K + 10$, for example, will shift the bid rent *down* by 10 dollars (as shown in Figure 5.2). Similarly, a decrease in the level of profits from K to $K - 10$ will shift the bid-rent function *up* by 10 dollars. A particularly important bid-rent function is the one that corresponds to a profit level of zero. If the firm that is depicted in the model is a member of a competitive industry, that firm will, in the long run, make zero economic profits. Each of the inputs into production (labor and capital) will earn its opportunity cost (competitive) return and no more.

Suppose that the firm does indeed earn zero economic profits. In this case the bid-rent function is just

$$R = (p - c)Q^* - (tQ^*)x.$$

This bid-rent function is shown in Figure 5.3. Why is this case so important? This is the bid-rent function that is forced upon the firm by the competition for land among all of the firms in its industry. Suppose that the firm in question bids less than the amount indicated by this bid-rent function for an acre of land at some distance x. Let this "underbid" amount be Z, or the bid is now

$$\text{bid} = (p - c)Q^* - (tQ^*)x - Z.$$

If this bid were to be accepted, the firm obviously would be making economic profits of Z. If competition for land is operating perfectly, the other firms in the industry will not permit the firm in question to earn economic profits. Some firm will come along and make a higher bid. The process of making higher bids for the acre of land will end when the last bidder ends up with zero economic profits, or just enough profits to

FIGURE 5.3   Bid-rent function with zero profit

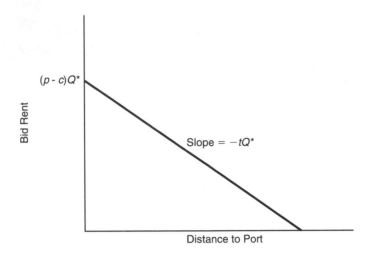

keep the firm in this particular line of business paying competitive returns to the inputs (other than land). The "perfection" of perfect competition acts to put firms on the bid-rent function that corresponds to zero economic profits.

Return now to Figure 5.3 and the bid-rent function

$$R = (p - c)Q^* - (tQ^*)x.$$

The position of this bid-rent function depends on several variables: the price of output (p), the average production cost (c), the transportation cost per mile per unit of output (t), and the level of the firm's output (Q^*). You should verify that the following statements are correct:

1. An increase in the price of output (p) shifts the bid-rent function up in parallel fashion.
2. An increase in the average production cost (c) shifts the bid-rent function down in parallel fashion.
3. A reduction in transportation cost (t) makes the bid-rent function flatter but does not change the intercept.
4. An increase in output per acre shifts the intercept of the bid-rent function up *and* makes the function steeper.

These results mean that landowners benefit when the price of output rises and lose when average production costs increase. Landowners reap the benefits of reductions in transportation costs per mile, where that benefit is greater at greater distances from the port in the center of the city. This case is depicted in Figure 5.4. Finally, an increase in output per acre could occur because of an increase in the productivity of the inputs. The increase in output increases the bid rent next to the port because the firm has more revenue (per acre). However, the increase in output (per acre) also means that the firm's transportation costs are greater because more output must be transported. As shown in Figure 5.5, there is some distance x' at which the old bid rent and the new bid rent are equal and beyond which the old bid rent is higher.

FIGURE 5.4 Effect of reduction in transportation costs on bid rent

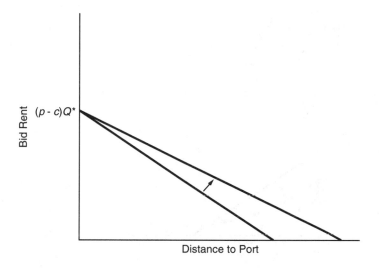

There is one more feature of bid-rent theory for firms that you should know. So far it has been assumed that the firm produces a given amount of output Q^* on an acre of land, and this quantity does not vary with distance from the port. This assumption is unrealistic because it means that land cannot be substituted for other inputs. There is always a fixed ratio of output to land. A more realistic model would assume that land and other inputs are substitutes, so that the ratio of output to land can vary. In particular, firms can change the amount of capital and labor per unit of land by building a taller building. Firms that face a higher land rent would then substitute

FIGURE 5.5 Effect of output increase on bid rent

FIGURE 5.6 Bid-rent function with input substitution

away from land and use more of other inputs to produce a given level of output, so the ratio of output to land is higher if land rent is higher (and as a result, buildings are taller). What does this modification of the model imply for the bid-rent function?

Figure 5.6 reproduces the linear bid-rent function (with zero economic profits) from Figure 5.3. Recall that the slope of this function is $\div tQ^*$, where Q^* is output per acre of land. As we have seen, the modified model leads to the conclusion that output per acre of land is itself a positive function of land rent. The higher is land rent, the higher is output per acre. Therefore, the slope of the bid-rent function $(-tQ)$ is steep near the port and gets flatter as distance from the port increases. This type of bid-rent function is shown as $R_v R_v$ in Figure 5.6. The equation for the bid-rent function (with zero economic profits) is still

$$R = (p - c)Q - (tQ)x,$$

but Q (output per acre) varies inversely with x. By the way, the intercept of this function $[(p - c)Q]$ is determined by finding the level of output per acre at distance $x = 0$. This solution requires knowledge of the production function for output, information that has not been given.

Bid-Rent Theory for Households

Now let us turn to the theory of bid rent for households. The concepts are similar to those used for firms. Suppose that the only attribute of land that matters to a household is distance to the downtown workplace. Greater distance to the workplace means that the household must spend more money and time to get to and from work. The household therefore bids less for land at greater distances so as to maintain its utility level. In particular, suppose that the time and money costs of being located 1 mile more distant from the workplace can be expressed a single dollar value t. For utility to remain constant as the household moves 1 mile, bid rent must adjust to make the marginal benefit of distance to the workplace equal to marginal cost.

The marginal benefit of moving 1 mile more distant is the *change* in bid rent times the amount of land occupied by the household. This is the amount of money that the household would save if its bid were accepted.

This basic condition can be expressed in equation form as

$$t = -\frac{\delta R}{\delta x} L,$$

where $\delta R/\delta x$ is the change in the bid rent as distance to the workplace x changes by 1 mile, and L is the amount of land occupied by the household. The negative sign appears on the right-hand side of the equation because $\delta R/\delta x$ is a negative number. The basic condition can be rewritten as

$$\frac{\delta R}{\delta x} = \frac{-t}{L}.$$

The *slope* of the bid-rent function is the -1 times the marginal cost of distance (t) divided by the amount of land occupied (L). For example, suppose that the annual cost of commuting 1 extra mile is $150. This is plausible given that the commuter must travel to work 250 days per year. A total of 500 miles is added to annual commuting. If the household occupies 1500 square feet of land, the slope of the bid-rent function is $150/1500, or 10 cents per square foot per mile. This may not sound like much, but convert it to dollars per acre. An acre contains 43,560 square feet, so bid rent changes by $4356 per acre per mile. And if the going interest rate is 10%, the value per acre that the household bids changes by $43,560 per mile.

Bid rent can also be a function of other variables, such as distance to other employment centers, location of shopping districts, the quality of the local public schools, distance from environmental disamenities, and a variety of other factors. But the basic point holds; there is a relationship between bid rent and location defined for a given utility level for a household (or profit level, in the case of a firm). For example, suppose that there is an environmental disamenity (e.g., air pollution) that is generated in the central business district. In this case households can avoid the disamenity by locating at greater distances from downtown. However, commuting costs still matter. The slope of the bid-rent function is now a combination of two effects: the increase in commuting cost and the decrease in the disamenity as distance to downtown increases. In equation form,

$$\frac{\delta R}{\delta x} = \frac{-t}{L} + \frac{\delta R}{\delta E}\frac{\delta E}{\delta x},$$

where $\delta E/\delta x$ is the change in the amount of the environmental disamenity as distance increases and $\delta R/\delta E$ is the effect of an additional amount of this disamenity on bid rent (per square foot). Both of these additional terms are negative numbers, so their effect is to make the slope of the bid rent function flatter than just $-t/L$. Indeed, if the effect of proximity to downtown on exposure to the disamenity is very large near downtown, the net effect of distance from downtown on bid rent could be positive over some range of distance. Over this range of distance households value the avoidance of the environmental disamenity more than they value the increase in commuting cost.

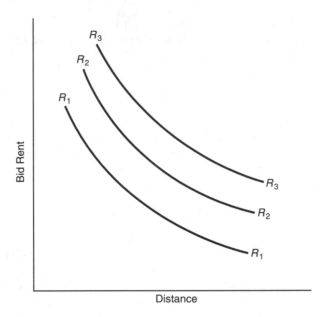

FIGURE 5.7 Bid-rent functions for a household

Figure 5.7 shows a family of bid-rent functions for a particular household. In this case it is assumed that bid rent at any given utility level declines with distance to downtown because the head of the household is employed in a downtown business, and no variable other than commuting cost matters. Bid rent function R_1R_1 corresponds to some utility level U_1. Bid rent function R_2R_2 is higher than R_1R_1 and therefore corresponds to a lower level of utility U_2.

The bid-rent functions shown in Figure 5.7 are drawn so that they become flatter as distance to downtown is increased. This shape is an immediate consequence of the result from above that $\delta R/\delta x = -t/L$. The slope ($\delta R/\delta x$) gets flatter as distance x increases because L (land occupied by the household) increases as distance increases. L increases as distance increases because the price of land (bid rent) declines with distance; as with any consumer good, the lower price causes the quantity to increase. Note that this result is similar to the bid-rent function for the firm that permits output per acre to vary with land rent.

It was mentioned that there are many different types of households in an urban area. Do different types of households have bid rent functions with different shapes? An answer to this question can be obtained by examining carefully the equilibrium condition

$$-\frac{\delta R}{\delta x} = \frac{t}{L}.$$

This condition says that the slope of the bid-rent function equals the ratio of commuting cost per mile (t) to land occupied by the household (L). How do households differ on these two determinants of the slope of their bid-rent functions? First consider a larger household with children versus a smaller household without children. It is likely that if the two households have the same income level, the larger household will wish to rent more land at any given land rent. The larger household has the greater demand for land, all other things being equal. Further, suppose that the larger and smaller households have the same commuting cost. (Both households have one worker who commutes, and both workers have the same value of time.) If all of these presumptions are true, the larger household will have the *flatter* bid rent function; t/L is smaller.

Alternatively, consider two types of households that differ only by income level. The households with the larger income will probably demand more land at any given land rent. Land can be presumed to be a normal good. However, households with larger incomes probably also have *higher commuting costs*. Why might this be? Recall that commuting involves the expenditure of both money and time. We can presume that monetary expenditures per mile do not vary much, if at all, with income. However, higher-income households place a higher value on time than do lower-income households. A person's time is the ultimate scarce resource, and people with more money regard the time spent commuting as having a higher monetary value. Therefore, both the numerator and the denominator in t/L increase with income. The bid-rent function for the higher-income households may be flatter, steeper, or have the same slope as the one for households with lower income. The answer depends upon whether the value of commuting time or land consumption increases more with increases in income. In particular, the result is proved in the appendix to this chapter that t/L decreases (gets flatter) as income rises if the income elasticity of demand for land is greater than the income elasticity of the cost of commuting, or if

$$\frac{\delta L}{\delta y}\frac{y}{L} > \frac{\delta t}{\delta y}\frac{y}{t},$$

where y is income. The bid-rent function gets steeper if the opposite condition holds. At this time there is no evidence to suggest that one of these elasticities is clearly larger, so there is no evidence to suggest that higher-income households have flatter (or steeper) bid-rent functions.

Finally, what about households with two commuters (as opposed to one)? Suppose that we are comparing households with equal income levels; each worker in the household with two commuters earns half the amount of the worker in the one-commuter household. The household with two commuters has a higher time cost of commuting and, let us suppose, the same demand for land as the household with one commuter. Therefore, the two-commuter household has the steeper bid-rent function; t/L is larger. However, this conclusion will not hold if the one-commuter household views the opportunity cost of the commuter's (i.e., worker's) time as being double the opportunity cost of time for each worker in the two-commuter household.

Bid rents by the various sectors in an urban area determine the uses to which land is put and the land rents—the market rents. The operation of the market based on bid rents is discussed below. For now you have learned to distinguish pure economic rent, land rent, and bid rent.

E. THE ROLE OF TRANSPORTATION INFRASTRUCTURE

One way to write a history of urban areas is to focus on the methods used to transport people and goods inside cities. Major changes in transportation are associated with major changes in the layout of an urban area. Historians usually emphasize the importance of the technical changes in long-distance transportation that began in the early nineteenth century when steam power was adapted for use in ships and railroad locomotives. Prior to that time people traveled over land on horseback or by wagon (stagecoach), or on foot. Goods moved by wagon over land and by sailing vessel over water. Roads were usually bad or nonexistent. Long-distance travel was very costly and was risky as well. The steam engine began to change all that.

Travel within urban areas until the 1850s was rudimentary. People "commuted" on foot, and goods moved by wagon. In fact, livestock also moved on foot. Telephones did not exist, so messages had to travel on foot. Streets were often narrow and became muddy quagmires when it rained. Something had to change or the urban transportation bottleneck would prevent cities from taking advantage of emerging economies of scale in production.

The first thing that was done in some of the world's major cities was to improve the street system. Streets needed to be widened, straightened, and paved. Paris underwent a massive facelift that became the inspiration for urban officials in many other places. The streets in Chicago were raised above the muck and mire. (This required raising the buildings, too.) Eventually, the people, horses, cattle, and hogs could walk around Chicago without sinking into mud.

The next step was to devise a system for moving people around an urban area at faster than walking speed. The first systems were horse-drawn trolley cars, which ran on rails embedded in the streets. This was an improvement over walking, but not much. The latter half of the nineteenth century saw a steady improvement in rail systems for the movement of people. The railroads concentrated on the movement of freight over long distances, but they also began to offer commuter service in large urban areas such as London, Paris, New York, Philadelphia, and Chicago. In those days the railroads had major terminals near the downtown areas anyway, so it was natural to provide passenger service in the morning and evening that would permit downtown workers to reside several miles from the workplace. Also, steam power was used for a few years on rail systems that moved people shorter distances within urban areas.

A major change in technology occurred in the 1890s when urban transit systems were converted to electric power. Electricity provided a more efficient and less noxious transit system and permitted urban areas to build subway systems. Anyone who has eaten a sandwich at a certain chain of sandwich shops knows that a certain John McDonald was the builder of New York's first subway system in the 1890s. As far as is known, the author of this book is not related to this important figure in urban history.

At the same time, rail systems were being built that facilitated the movement of goods within urban areas. The idea was to build a system of "beltway" rail lines and rail yards for the assembly and disassembly of trains to supplement the existing radial rail lines. Such a system meant that a factory could be located anywhere near a beltway rail line. The factory would have its own rail spur line, and when it had produced a carload of output to be shipped somewhere, a small work train could pick up the car and take it to a nearby rail yard. A train would then be assembled for a destination outside the urban area. The factory's output would not necessarily have to be moved to the downtown area first. Rail yards could be located at the periphery of the urban area. The construction of this type of system greatly expanded the area that could be used for manufacturing enterprises.

Rail systems dominated urban transportation until the 1920s. The development of the internal combustion engine and its widespread use after World War I changed the face of urban areas. The automobile provided remarkable freedom in choice of both trip origin and destination. People were no longer tied to the fixed routes of the urban rail system. Similarly, the truck provided an efficient vehicle for the movement of freight within urban areas that was not tied to existing rail lines. As more and more cars and trucks were put into use, the bottleneck once again became the urban street system. The field of traffic engineering was founded, and urban freeways, traffic control devices, and one-way streets were invented.

Street and bridge improvements were made on a wide scale in the 1920s. Many of the facilities constructed at that time are still in use, but urban highway construction reached its zenith in the late 1950s and early 1960s. A large portion of today's urban freeway systems in the United States were built at this time with the help of funds from the federal government under the Interstate Highway program. It became possible, in the absence of traffic congestion, to drive through an urban area at a speed of 65 miles per hour. The new radial and circumferential freeways opened up vast amounts of land to urban use. In some ways the nation is still in the process of adjusting to this boom in freeway construction that ended in the 1960s.

A model of urban location patterns must begin with a careful examination of the urban transportation system. People only have so much time in a day, and generally they do not particularly enjoy spending time commuting to work or making trips for other purposes. Some people can conduct business on the car phone, and others can really accomplish something while riding on the commuter train. But time spent in travel is simply not as enjoyable as time spent at home or as productive as time spent at work. The transportation system shapes the urban area as nothing else does.

F. THE BID-RENT AND LAND-USE NEXUS

The model of the urban land market presented in this section uses a simple characterization of how land uses and market land values are determined. Each urban site is allocated to the sector with the highest bid rent, and land value is just the discounted value of the stream of highest bid rents. As discussed above, the real world contains many types of business and household sectors. In this section we discuss how these sectors have different bid-rent functions. Then a simple three-sector model of the land market is presented; equilibrium land rent and land-use patterns are described. However, in the real world, land use is influenced by zoning regulations. In the next section we consider this complication to the basic competitive market model.

Different types of businesses may have very different bid-rent functions. Some businesses, such as financial institutions, law firms, and advertising agencies, have very high bid rents for downtown locations and relatively low bid rents for locations in the rest of the urban area. These businesses need the opportunities for immediate face-to-face communication with customers, suppliers, government agencies, and others that are offered by the downtown location. Some manufacturers also have this sort of bid-rent function. High-fashion clothing manufacturers and publishers need the immediacy of the downtown location. Other manufacturers, such as printers, bid for downtown locations but find that their bids are not high enough. Instead, they may locate on the fringe of the downtown area or nearby. They can serve the huge downtown demand for printed material without being located right in the downtown district. Or consider other types of manufacturers, such as food products, furniture, fabricated metals, instruments, machinery, and electrical equipment. There may be no particular need to locate factories and workshops for these industries in the downtown area. They bid for the land in industrial districts in various locations around an urban area. Locations near highways, rail lines, an industrial labor force, or a major airport may be advantageous for these kinds of firms. Indeed, suburban locations are increasingly popular choices for "light" industry. Finally, heavy industry such as primary metals, oil refining, transportation equipment (e.g., auto assembly), and chemicals usually require locations near water, rail, and highway transportation. The inputs and/or outputs are bulky and therefore require heavy-duty transportation facilities. Bid rent is determined accordingly. Different types of firms and the various clusters of employment they create in urban areas are discussed in Chapter 7.

The bid-rent function for the residential sector includes access to downtown employment, shopping, and various services. Residential bid rent may also depend upon access to other workplace locations, shopping, health services, and other attractions. Government services such as school, police and fire protection, and parks and recreation are also important. Negative factors include crime, environmental pollution, congestion, noise, and taxes (given a level of public services). Different types of households also exhibit different bid-rent functions. Single adults or couples without children may make relatively high bids for land located near the downtown area with its attractions, but make low bids for suburban locations where they would feel isolated. On the other hand, families with children will bid relatively more for the spaciousness and safety of suburban locations. Given that most employment is in fact not located downtown, bid rent for the same site varies across households because workplaces vary across households. Bid rent for a site by a household of a particular racial or ethnic group may depend upon who lives near the site. It is a fact of life in the United States that many white households will make low bids for sites located in all-black neighborhoods.

Clearly, there are many different bid-rent functions for households and businesses. How does the land market operate to allocate sites to the many types of possible users? Prior to the 1920s the allocation of land was largely left to the private market. The general laws pertaining to nuisances were used on a case-by-case basis to handle particular conflicts in land use, but there was no general policy to regulate the use of land. For simplicity suppose that there are three sectors in the urban economy: commercial and financial business, manufacturing, and households. Further assume that the bid rent for each sector is *only* a function of access to downtown.

In this case bid rent in each sector depends only on access to downtown, but the shapes of these functions are different. The commercial–financial sector places a very high value on the downtown location, and its bid rent drops off sharply as distance to downtown increases. Compared to the commercial–financial sector, manufacturing enterprises place a lower value on the downtown location, and bid-rent declines less as distance to downtown increases. Of the three, the residential bid-rent function includes the lowest bid for downtown land and the flattest slope with respect to distance to downtown. These three bid-rent functions are shown in Figure 5.8. A

FIGURE 5.8 Allocation of urban land according to bid rents

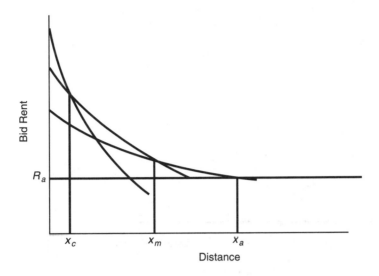

bid rent for the agricultural (nonurban) sector is also shown in Figure 5.8 at a constant level R_a.

The competitive market allocates land to the use with the highest bid rent, so land up to distance x_c in Figure 5.8 is allocated to the commercial–financial sector. Land between distances x_c and x_m is in manufacturing use, and the residential sector occupies land from distance x_m to distance x_a. Beyond distance x_a the land is devoted to agricultural use. Land use thus forms a set of concentric rings, and the equilibrium land rent function is a combination of the three bid-rent functions. Equilibrium land rent follows the commercial–financial bid rent up to distance x_c, moves along the manufacturing bid rent from x_c up to distance x_m, and is the residential bid rent from x_m to the fringe of the urban area at distance x_a.

Now recall our earlier discussion of bid-rent functions for different types of households. It was concluded, for instance, that larger households with children will have flatter bid-rent functions than those of smaller households without children. Bid-rent functions for these two types of households are depicted in Figure 5.9, and we can see that (as in Figure 5.8) the sector with the flatter bid-rent function will be located at the greater distances to the central point. Recall also that households with two commuters probably have steeper bid-rent functions than households with only one commuter, so "DINKS" (double income, no kids) will reside nearer downtown than will single-commuter households with kids. Finally, recall that higher income can make the slope of the bid-rent function flatter or steeper (or have no effect at all). Therefore, using this model based on commuting costs alone, we cannot conclude that households with higher incomes will live farther from (or closer to) downtown. The model omits the several other reasons why high-income households wish to live in the suburbs. Schools are better in the suburbs; crime is less in the suburbs; suburbs have new houses and the central city has old houses; and so on. These and other factors are discussed at length in the succeeding chapters.

FIGURE 5.9 Allocation of urban land according to bid rents

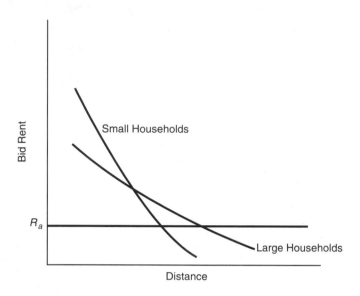

G. ZONING AND LAND USE

The first general zoning ordinance was adopted in New York City in 1916, and most urban areas had zoning laws by the end of the 1920s. The major exception is Houston, which as of 1995 did not have a zoning ordinance. (Voters in Houston defeated a proposed zoning ordinance in 1993.) How do zoning laws influence the allocation of land to the various possible uses?

Zoning laws do several things. They regulate the height and bulk of the buildings permitted on each site. They contain certain setback requirements so that buildings are not located "too close" to property boundaries. They often require that residential lots be of a certain minimum size. But first and foremost, zoning laws specify the basic use for each lot in a jurisdiction. Use can be specified in greater or lesser detail. Some zoning ordinances simply break private land use down into three categories: residential, commercial, and industrial. Other zoning ordinances specify two or more categories within each of these three basic sectors. Residential use might be (1) single-family detached houses and duplexes, (2) residential structures with up to six housing units, and (3) apartment buildings with more than six units. Commercial use might be broken down into (1) retail trade, (2) offices, and (3) wholesale trade. Industrial use is often split into two or more categories, depending on the extent of the possible nuisances created. The zoning ordinance then proceeds to allocate all privately owned land to one of these eight or more separate categories. Does this flurry of administrative activity have any sizable effect on the allocation of land?

The answer is: "Yes, it probably does." It is clear that at least in many suburban jurisdictions, single-family housing is the preferred use of land. Preferred by whom? Preferred by the current residents of the jurisdiction, and therefore preferred by the zoning officials. Suburban zoning officials often provide limited amounts of space for apartment housing even in the face of strong demand for apartments. Less obviously, they also often restrict commercial and industrial uses to areas adjacent to major highways and/or freight rail lines. This kind of decision for nonresidential uses would seem to follow the market, but there is evidence provided by McMillen and McDonald (1989) that zoning officials do not follow the market closely. Sometimes the unregulated market would have allocated more land (than did the zoning officials) for commercial and industrial use at locations away from the highways and rail lines. The role of the zoning official is to try to anticipate conflicts in land use and to plan accordingly in the interests of the existing residents. Indeed, some of these officials earn university degrees (in urban planning) which train them in such matters. Urban planners learn that commercial and industrial uses conflict with residential use, especially when the residential use involves middle (and higher)-class residents. They also learn that the "character" of residential neighborhoods should be maintained.

On the other side of the ledger, suburban officials worry about taxes and public spending on schools and other functions of local government. These matters are discussed at length in Chapter 10, but for now it is important to note that commercial and industrial land uses generally generate more tax revenue than they cost the local jurisdiction in expenses for public services. The main fact is that commercial and industrial land uses do not demand public schools, but that residential land use does. Zoning officials thus face a trade-off between the quality of the local environment and tax revenues. Shopping centers bring traffic, noise, and a lot of people who do not live in the community. They may also not be very attractive physically. Office buildings also bring in traffic, especially during the morning and afternoon rush hours. Industrial land use adds to traffic and, depending on the nature of the industry, can contribute to other environmental problems. Empirical studies such as that by Erickson and Wollover (1987) have investigated how communities respond to this trade-off. One finding is that communities with higher incomes tend to zone less land for commercial and industrial use—environmental quality is a normal good (demand increases as income rises).

Suppose that suburban jurisdictions do restrict the amount of land available for manufacturing use. Figure 5.10 depicts the same three bid-rent functions for the commercial–financial, manufacturing, and residential sectors as in Figure 5.8. Now the zoning officials have decreed that manufacturing shall not be located between distances x_1 and x_m; this land is zoned for residential use. We see immediately that there will be a discontinuity in the land rent function at distance x_1. Land rent drops abruptly from the manufacturing bid rent to the residential bid rent at this point. Effective restrictions on the use of land for manufacturing (or for apartments or commercial use) will create such discontinuities in the bids that are made for the same plot of land. This is what it means for zoning not to "follow the market."

What about land use in the older central cities? Has the adoption of zoning laws altered the allocation of land there? It is not clear that zoning has had any major impact in areas that were already built up prior to the adoption of the zoning ordinance. Use of the downtown area and most of the major industrial and commercial areas of central cities predates the zoning law. However, one minor impact often occurred. Prior to the zoning laws there was some tendency to mix light manufacturing and commercial uses in with residential use on the same block. Actual land use did not separate into the concentric rings implied in Figure 5.8. (The mixing of land uses

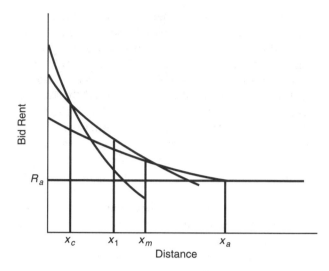

FIGURE 5.10 Zoning and land use

means that two sectors have very similar bid-rent functions.) Provided that these uses did not generate appreciable nuisances, this mixing of land uses might well have been of benefit to the residential population by providing ready access to retailing, services, and employment. Zoning ordinances usually ended this mixing of land uses over a period of years. Blocks were zoned exclusively for residential use, and conditions were set up for the elimination of "nonconforming" uses. Separate areas along the busier streets were zoned for commercial and industrial uses. Most of these areas were already being used by businesses, but the zoning laws excluded new residential use.

Suppose that the mixing of land uses can be depicted on a diagram such as Figure 5.11. In this figure the commercial–financial sector makes high bids for downtown locations as usual, but now the manufacturing and residential bid rent functions are identical. (The manufacturing sector here is really light manufacturing.) The market allocates the land between distance x_c and x_a to manufacturing and residential use on a random basis. Now the zoning officials come along and decree that only land between x_c and x_m shall be allocated to manufacturing. Over time the land uses are separated as ordered, but in this case the zoning ordinance has had no effect on the land rent function. There is no abrupt drop in land rent at distance x_m, the border between manufacturing and residential use as set by the ordinance.

McMillen and McDonald (1993) studied land use and land values in Chicago prior to the adoption of its first zoning ordinance in 1923. Their empirical results for 1921 showed that the mixing of small commercial and industrial uses with housing did not have a negative effect on residential land values. Indeed, the results suggest that close access to shopping and employment opportunities was of benefit to residents. One must remember that this result was obtained for 1921, a time when very few people owned automobiles. McMillen and McDonald (1993) concluded that the first Chicago zoning ordinance did not lead to an increase in residential land values.

The allocation of urban land is thus influenced both by the bid rents of the various sectors and by zoning. Zoning officials sometimes alter market allocations of land for apartment, commercial, and industrial uses. This is not to say that zoning of-

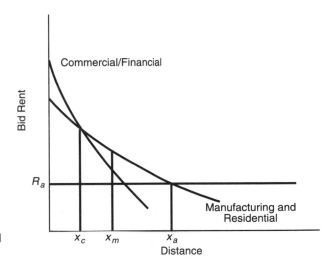

FIGURE 5.11 Bid rents and the mixing of land uses

ficials are completely unresponsive to market forces. Changes in zoning occur all of the time in response to requests from land owners. Requests for zoning changes are granted unless the requested change would lead to a conflict among land uses. It is fair to say that market forces operate through the zoning process and that zoning will occasionally alter market allocations.

H. THE INTENSITY OF LAND USE: POPULATION DENSITY

The intensity of land use is the amount of economic activity that takes place on a unit of land. An investigation of the location of economic activity must examine land-use intensity as well as the allocation of land to the various uses. There are many ways to measure land-use intensity, and this section and the next provide an introduction to these concepts. Population density is the topic of this section.

The most important measure of land-use intensity is population density. At the household level, population density can be defined as the number of people in the household divided by the land area occupied by the household. The general definition of population density is simply

$$\text{population} \div \text{land area.}$$

This definition can be used for land areas of any size, from individual lots and residential blocks to entire states and regions. One needs to measure the land area in question and the population that resides on that land. The U.S. Census of Population and Housing provides the necessary population data every 10 years. Population is enumerated at the block level, and these blocks are also aggregated into what are known as Census Tracts, census enumertion areas that contain approximately 4000 people. The Census of Population and Housing also provides a great deal of social and economic data at the level of the Census Tract. Breakdowns of the population by sex, household type, race, and age are provided. The economic data include the distribution of household income and the distributions of estimated house values and contract rents.

FIGURE 5.12   Gross population density function

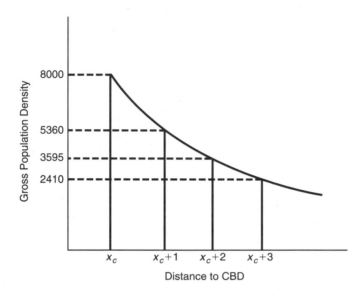

The population data from the Census, coupled with the measure of total land area of the Census Tract, generates the measure of land-use intensity known as *gross population density*, so called because the total land area of the Census Tract is used as the denominator. The density measure is population per unit of land, where *all* land uses are included in the measure of land area. Numerous empirical studies of gross population density have established that the typical pattern is as shown in Figure 5.12. Gross population density is rather low in and near the central business district because very little land is allocated to residential use there. Outside the central business area most of the privately owned land is allocated to residential use. Gross population density is greatest near the central business area and declines with distance to downtown in the nonlinear fashion shown in Figure 5.12; density declines rapidly near the center of the city and drops more gradually at greater distances from the center. This shape for the gross population density function can be expressed in mathematical form as the exponential function

$$D(x) = D(x_c)e^{-gx},$$

where the variables are defined as follows: $D(x)$ is gross population density as a function of x, distance to the edge of the central business district; $D(x_c)$ is gross population density at the edge of the central business district (this is the greatest value for density); the symbol e stands for the base of the natural logarithms, which is approximately 2.718; and the letter g stands for the value of the population density gradient, which is the *percentage* decline in density per unit of distance (i.e., per mile) from the central business district. This density function is defined for values of x equal to or greater than x_c. As the empirical studies have shown, gross population density inside of distance x_c is relatively low.

An understanding of the population density equation can be gained through numerical example. First, suppose that x_c is 1 mile. The central business area has a radius of 1 mile, which is fairly typical for an urban area of medium size, 250,000 to 500,000 population. Next, suppose that $D(x_c)$ is 8000 per square mile, or that gross density is 8000 per square mile at a distance of 1 mile from the center. Finally, assume that the gradient is 0.4, or that population density declines by 40% per mile. These values mean that gross population density at distance x to the edge of the central business district equals

$$D(x) = 8000 \times 2.718^{-0.4x}.$$

For example, population density at the edge of the central business district ($x = 0$) equals 8000 because 2.718 raised to the zero power is 1. At distance $x = 1$, $D(1)$ equals 5360 (because 2.718 raised to the -0.4 power equals 0.67). Other numerical values of $D(x)$ are displayed in Figure 5.12. The basic mathematics of this density function are discussed in the appendix to this book.

Why does gross population density decline with distance to the central business district? The basic model depicted in Figure 5.7 provides the answer. As we have seen, residential bid rent declines with distance to the central business district to compensate for commuting costs. Lower rents at greater distances mean that households use more land as distance increases. The basic law of demand says that when the price of a good declines, people purchase it in greater quantity. Land is no different in this regard. Holding other relevant factors constant (income and tastes), households that live where land rents are lower occupy more land. Lower land rent means that population density is lower.

This standard explanation for the decline in gross population density with distance to the center leaves one loose end. The argument really pertains to *net* rather than gross population density. Net population density is defined as population per unit of land that is allocated to residential use. For example, consider a square mile that houses 1000 people. Suppose that 40% of that square mile is in residential use; the rest is allocated to streets, commercial and industrial use, parks and public buildings, and so on. Gross population density is 1000 people per square mile, but net population density is 2500 people per square mile because the 1000 people actually live on 0.4 square mile of land.

There have been many empirical studies of urban population density based on the exponential function discussed above. If the natural logarithms (log to base e) of both sides of the equation are taken, the result is a linear equation

$$\ln D(x) = \ln D(x_c) - gx,$$

where ln stands for logarithm to base e. In many studies data are gathered for a sample of census tracts in an urban area and then the data are used to estimate this linear equation.

One such study by Johnson and Kau (1980) reports gross population density functions for a large number of urban areas in 1970. Some of their results are shown in Table 5.1. These results show that urban areas differ substantially in their population density patterns. The estimated central density is expressed in natural log form in Table 5.1 and then converted to actual population density per square mile. Central

| TABLE 5.1 | Estimated Gross Population Density Functions, 1970 | | |

Urban Area	*ln (central density)*	*Central Density*	*Gradient*
Akron	9.273	10,647	−0.202
Baltimore	9.767	17,448	−0.186
Birmingham	9.017	8,242	−0.190
Cincinnati	9.050	8,519	−0.162
Dayton	9.245	10,353	−0.179
Denver	9.624	15,123	−0.206
Detroit	9.714	17,001	−0.075
Flint	9.482	13,121	−0.386
Houston	9.209	9,987	−0.153
Jacksonville	9.205	9,947	−0.343
Louisville	8.619	5,536	−0.139
Nashville	9.078	8,760	−0.269
New Haven	9.791	17,872	−0.510
Omaha	8.845	6,940	−0.114
Philadelphia	10.612	40,619	−0.195
Phoenix	9.089	8,857	−0.134
Rochester	9.845	18,864	−0.327
Salt Lake City	8.883	7,208	−0.128
San Jose	8.910	7,406	−0.085
St. Louis	10.029	22,675	−0.170
Spokane	8.762	6,387	−0.256
Toledo	9.835	18,676	−0.317
Tucson	8.459	4,717	−0.146

Source: Table compiled from data obtained from Johnson and Kau (1980).

density varied from a low of 4717 people per square mile in Tucson to 40,619 in Philadelphia. Central densities were higher in the other older and larger urban areas, such as Baltimore, Detroit, and St. Louis. However, central densities were also quite high in some of the older urban areas that are not so large, such as Flint, New Haven, Rochester, and Toledo. Some of the newer urban areas in the west had low central densities. Included in this group are Phoenix, Salt Lake City, San Jose, Spokane, and Tucson.

The population density gradients estimated by Johnson and Kau (1980) varied from a very flat—7.5% per mile—in Detroit to a very steep—51.0% per mile—in New Haven. San Jose and Omaha also had relatively flat gradients, under 12% per mile. Steeper gradients were also found for Flint, Jacksonville, Rochester, and Toledo. These are among the smaller urban areas on the list.

Do empirical results such as those shown in Table 5.1 form a definite pattern? This question has been investigated by several researchers. The results of the studies have been summarized by McDonald (1989). It can be concluded that urban areas with larger populations have flatter gradients, older urban areas often have steeper gradients, and other variables are not consistent in their impact on the gradient. The fact that a larger urban population is associated with a flatter gradient needs some explanation. Some researchers argue that a larger urban population generates a greater decentralization of employment and hence of population. Others suggest that the supply of housing is more elastic at the urban fringe. Consequently, an increase in urban population means that population growth will be greater at the fringe. The observation that older urban areas have steeper gradients appears to require a model in which housing that was constructed in the past to accommodate high population densities lives on in the present. Some empirical evidence exists to support some other statements, but the results are rather weak statistically. These statements include:

- Employment concentration is associated with a steeper gradient.
- Substandard housing and black population in the central city are associated with a flatter gradient.

The central density also has been found to have systematic variations across urban areas. Central densities tend to be greater in larger urban areas and in older urban areas. One study by Edmonston and Guterbock (1984) found that central densities are high in smaller urban areas; central density declines with the size of the urban area up to a point, and then increases. These are the results that one would have expected.

Two of the most important findings about urban population density patterns are that both the central density and the gradient have become smaller over time. These are results that apply to virtually every urban area in the United States since the end of World War II (and probably before that). Population density functions for the Chicago urban area were estimated by McDonald (1979) and updated to 1990. Total population and the central density and gradient figures are shown in Table 5.2. The results show that the gradient has moved steadily closer to zero since 1880. The decline in the gradient was particularly rapid between 1880 and 1900 and for 1950–1970. These are periods of rapid change in the nature of the urban transportation system. The last two decades of the nineteenth century saw the introduction of reasonably modern public transit facilities that covered a wide area, and the period after World War II is, of course, the age of the auto (and the expressway). The central density increased up to 1910, declined substantially from 1910 to 1920, remained fairly constant up to 1950, and then dropped markedly after that. Immigration from Europe and from the farms in the United States meant that the population growth rate was particularly high prior to 1910, so central density increased. Central densities were roughly constant from 1920 to 1950 as the urban area expanded outward to accommodate the continued population growth. The introduction of the auto on a large scale, the expressway system, and the end of population growth in the urban area in the era after World War II were a three-pronged assault on the central density after 1950.

TABLE 5.2	Population Density Functions in the Chicago Urban Area		
Year	Central Density (thousands)	Gradient	Population (millions)
1870	44.2	−0.63	0.350
1880	86.9	−0.67	0.608
1900	88.7	−0.40	1.839
1910	99.3	−0.37	2.405
1920	79.5	−0.28	3.361
1930	83.2	−0.25	4.414
1940	78.7	−0.24	4.532
1950	74.8	−0.22	5.127
1960	54.2	−0.17	6.221
1970	41.2	−0.14	6.975[a]
1980	36.2	−0.13	7.102
1990	31.5	−0.12	7.260[a]

[a]*Population figure slightly smaller than shown in Table 1.3 because only the Illinois portion of the metropolitan area is included here.*

Source: Census of Population and Housing, U.S. Department of Commerce.

I. OTHER MEASURES OF THE INTENSITY OF LAND USE

The population density patterns are important, but there are several other measures of the intensity of land use that urban planners and economists employ. Additional measures for the residential sector are considered first, and then the commercial and industrial sectors are discussed.

Urban planners use physical measures of density such as housing units and residential floor space per unit of land area. The term *floor/area ratio* is used to refer to the ratio of floor space to land area. Some zoning ordinances regulate land per unit and the floor/area ratio directly. For example, the zoning ordinance in the City of Chicago contains the following residential zoning categories and regulations.

Category	Permitted Use	Floor/Area Ratio	Lot Area per Unit (ft²)
R-1	One-family detached	0.5	6250
R-2	Same as R-1	0.5	5000
R-3	One- and two-family	0.7	2500
R-4	R-3 plus apartments	1.2	900
R-5	Same as R-4	2.2	400
R-6	Same as R-4	4.4	200
R-7	Same as R-4	7.0	145
R-8	Same as R-4	10.0	115

The R-1 category requires a lot size of at least 6250 square feet (e.g., 50 feet by 125 feet) and limits the square footage of the house to 0.5 of the lot size (3125 for a lot of 6250 square feet). A one-story house can have 3125 square feet, or a two-story house can have 1562.5 square feet on each floor. If you want a larger house than that, you need to buy a larger lot. The categories run up to R-8, which permits an apartment building with floor space 10 times the size of the lot. In other words, a 20-story building can cover 50% of the lot, and a 40-story building can cover 25% of the lot.

Employment density and floor/area ratio are conventional measures of land-use intensity in the commercial and industrial sectors. These variables can be measured in net or gross terms. Recall that *net density* means that the land measure in the denominator is land used in that sector. *Gross density* measures are based on land in all uses. Data on these measures can be used to estimate exponential functions that describe their spatial patterns. Some examples of net density functions for Chicago in 1956 and 1970 are shown in Table 5.3. In 1956 the manufacturing sector in the city of Chicago had a central net density for floor area of 153,000 square feet per acre, and this density measure declined by 22.3% per mile. The net employment density function in manufacturing had a central density of 403 workers per acre, and the gradient was 28.2% per mile. Because the net employment density function was steeper than the floor space density function, these findings mean that the floor space per worker increased with distance to the central business district. From 1956 to 1970 the floor area density function in manufacturing changed to a lower central density and a flatter gradient. Older facilities near the downtown that were built at high densities were abandoned or torn down during this period in which the expressway system was opened. However, the net employment density function did not change between 1956 and 1970. This was a period in which manufacturing employment in the city of Chicago held fairly steady, and the net employment density function reflects that fact. Dramatic declines in manufacturing employment in the city of Chicago began immediately after 1970.

The results for the other employment sector shown in Table 5.3 is different from the manufacturing story. The other sector is the transportation, communication, and utility (TCU) sector. This sector is much smaller than the manufacturing sector; manufacturing employment in Cook County (the county that contains the city of Chicago) was 748,000 in 1963, and the TCU sector was only 137,000 at that same time. The decentralization of this sector from 1956 to 1970 is striking. The net floor area density gradient dropped from −29.2% per mile to −20.4% per mile, and the net employment density gradient changed from −25.3% to −13.1% per mile. Both measures of central density fell drastically.

Researchers who study net density must take care that the measure of economic activity (e.g., manufacturing employment) matches the measure of land area. For example, some employment in manufacturing firms is located in offices, which might be classified as commercial land use.

J. SUMMARY

A great deal of ground has been covered in this chapter (pun intended). You have learned that the economic sectors of the urban area have different bid-rent functions that express a willingness to pay for land at various locations. In a monocentric

TABLE 5.3 Net Floor Area and Net Employment Density in Chicago		
Year and Category	*Central Density*	*Gradient*
1956		
Manufacturing		
Net floor area	153,000 ft²/acre	−0.223
Net employment	403 per acre	−0.282
Transportation, communication, and utilities		
Net floor area	44,000 ft²/acre	−0.292
Net employment	52 per acre	−0.253
1970		
Manufacturing		
Net floor area	116,000 ft²/acre	−0.157
Net employment	437 per acre	−0.295
Transportation, communication, and utilities		
Net floor area	8,000 ft²/acre	−0.204
Net employment	12 per acre	−0.131

Source: Table compiled from data obtained from McDonald (1986).

city—a city with a single focal point—the bid rent declines with distance to that central point. The decline in bid rent depends on the costs of travel in the urban area, and great changes have taken place in the methods used to get around town. People used their feet in the small cities of 1800 that were discussed in Chapter 3. Urban residents graduated to horse-drawn vehicles, then steam-powered commuter trains, and then electric trains and streetcars. Modern subways were built in some urban areas, and commuter trains switched to diesel power. But most of all, we switched to the auto. Urban transportation is the topic of Chapter 8.

The bid-rent functions work to determine the use of land. The sector that makes the highest bid occupies the land unless some zoning law or other regulation prevents this outcome. Zoning laws primarily follow market forces but do exert an independent force on land use in some instances. Suburban zoning officials make decisions regarding commercial and industrial land use by considering the trade-off between environmental quality and the tax base that businesses can provide. Sometimes zoning decisions to restrict the amount of land available for commercial, manufacturing, or apartment use will create discontinuities in the land rent function whereby land zoned for these uses is more valuable than adjacent land zoned for single-family houses. Zoning in the older central cities eventually eliminated the mixing of residential land use with light commercial and industrial land use that had existed prior to the adoption of zoning.

The market also works to determine the intensity of land use. The theory of land-use intensity is presented in Chapters 6 and 7. In this chapter you learned how to measure the intensity of land use in the residential and business sectors. Population density is the most important measure of land-use intensity. Population density can be expressed in gross terms as population divided by land in all uses. Net population density is population divided by land only in residential use. Population density has its greatest value near the central business district (CBD) and declines with distance from the CBD at roughly a constant *percentage* rate. For example, gross population density in the Chicago urban area declined by 12% per mile in 1990. Other measures of land-use intensity include housing units per unit of land, floor space per unit of land (floor/area ratio), and employment per unit of land.

You are now ready to go on to Chapter 6, the chapter that puts into an economic model of a monocentric urban area many of the concepts developed to this point in the book.

APPENDIX TO CHAPTER 5

Income and the Slope of the Bid-Rent Function

Section E of the chapter includes an analysis of the effect of an increase in household income on the slope of the residential bid rent function. This appendix provides a proof of the statement that a higher income elasticity of commuting cost compared to the income elasticity of demand for land leads to a steeper bid-rent function as income rises.

Recall that the slope of the bid-rent function $R(x)$ is

$$\frac{\delta R}{\delta x} = \frac{-t}{L},$$

where x is the distance to the central business district, t the commuting cost per mile, and L the land rented by the household. Both t and L are positive functions of income (y), so

$$\frac{\delta R}{\delta x} = \frac{-t(y)}{L(y)}. \tag{A1}$$

The problem is to determine the *change* in $\delta R/\delta x$ as y increases.

Rewrite equation (A1) as

$$\frac{\delta R}{\delta x} = R' = -t(y)[L(y)]^{-1}.$$

Now use the product rule and the chain rule (from the appendix to the book) to determine the change in $\delta R/\delta x$ with respect to a change in y, or

$$\frac{\delta R'}{\delta y} = -t'(y)\,[L(y)]^{-1} + t(y)\,[L(y)]^{-2}L'(y), \tag{A2}$$

where $t'(y)$ and $L'(y)$ are $\delta t/\delta y$ and $\delta L/\delta y$. Factor $1/L(y)$ out of both terms of equation (A2) to obtain

$$\frac{\delta R'}{\delta y} = -\left(\frac{1}{L}\right)\left[t'(y) - \frac{L'(y)t}{L}\right]. \tag{A3}$$

The quantity t/y can be factored out of the terms inside the brackets to yield

$$\frac{\delta R'}{\delta y} = \frac{-t}{yL}\left[t'(y)\left(\frac{y}{t}\right) - L'(y)\left(\frac{t}{L}\right)\left(\frac{y}{t}\right)\right]$$

$$= \frac{-t}{yL}\left[\frac{\delta t}{\delta y}\left(\frac{y}{t}\right) - \frac{\delta L}{\delta y}\left(\frac{y}{L}\right)\right]. \tag{A4}$$

The sign of equation (A4) is determined by the two terms inside the brackets because (t/yL) is a positive number. And one can see immediately that $(\delta t/\delta y)(y/t)$ is the elasticity of commuting cost with respect to income, or

$$E_{ty} = \frac{\delta t/t}{\delta y/y}.$$

Also, $(\delta L/\delta y)(y/L)$ is just the elasticity of land demand with respect to income, or

$$E_{Ly} = \frac{\delta L/L}{\delta y/y}.$$

If E_{ty} is greater than E_{Ly}, then $\delta R'/\delta y$ is *negative*, and the bid rent function gets *steeper* (i.e., more negative). In other words, if the income elasticity of commuting cost is greater than the income elasticity of demand for land, the bid-rent function gets steeper as income rises. If E_{Ly} is greater than E_{ty}, then $\delta R'/\delta y$ is *positive*, and the bid-rent function gets flatter (its slope moves toward zero). An income elasticity of demand for land that is greater than the income elasticity of commuting cost means that the bid-rent function gets flatter as income rises.

EXERCISES

1. Return to the model of pure economic rent depicted in Figure 5.1. Recall that the market value V of an asset such as land that lasts forever is $V = R/r$, where R is the annual rent and r is the going interest rate. Let $R = \$10,000$ and $r = 0.05$. Now introduce an annual property tax that is a proportion t of the market value of the asset. In other words, the owner of the asset must now pay tax in the amount of tV each year, where the tax rate t is 0.03 (i.e., a 3% tax on market value). What is the market value of the asset now?

2. Suppose that a household resides in an urban area at a distance to downtown of 8 miles. The household occupies 3000 square feet of land, and at this distance land rent is \$1.50 per year per square foot. Land rent declines by \$0.05 per square foot as distance to downtown increases by 1 mile. A member of the household must travel downtown to work five days per week (50 weeks per year). The cost of this trip is \$4.00 per day, which includes both money cost and the time cost converted to money.
   (a) Assume that the marginal and average cost of distance from downtown are equal. What is the marginal cost of distance?
   (b) Is the household in locational equilibrium? How do you determine the answer to this question? If the household is not in locational equilibrium, which direction should it move to improve its welfare? (*Hint:* Compare the costs and benefits of moving 1 mile closer to downtown and of moving 1 mile away from downtown.)
   (c) What would the slope of the land-rent function have to be for the household to be in locational equilibrium?

3. Suppose that the gross population density function for an urban area is estimated to be

$$D(x) = 7500e^{-0.2x},$$

where x is distance to downtown.

a. In this case downtown has an area of zero, so the population density has what value at a distance of zero?

b. Fill in the following table

Distance	Gross Density
0	
1	
2	
4	
10	
	4000
	1514

[*Hint:* The easiest way to do this problem is to use a calculator with a natural log key (LN) and to convert the density function to natural log form.]

4. Consider an industry in a circular city. The industry produces a good for export, and the export point is the center of the city. The price of the good at the point of export is $10 per unit. Transportation costs within the city are 25 cents per mile per unit of the good, and other costs (labor and capital) are $5 per unit. Firms in the industry produce 100 units of the good per acre of land. The land market is perfectly competitive, which implies that the users of land bid enough to reduce their economic (excess) profits to zero.

a. Find the bid-rent function for the industry that corresponds to zero economic profits.

b. Assume that agricultural bid rent is $100 per acre at all locations. At what distance does agricultural bid rent equal the industry's bid rent?

5. Now add a second industry to the model in Exercise 4. This industry produces a good for export at a price of $20 per unit at the point of export, and transportation costs are $1 per unit of output. Other costs (labor and capital) are $10 per unit. Output is 75 units per acre.

a. Find the bid-rent function for this industry that corresponds to zero economic profits.

b. Where do the first (from Exercise 4) and second industries locate in the city?

6. Return to Figure 5.10, the depiction of the effect of zoning on land use and land rents. Suppose that in addition to zoning the land between x_1 and x_m for residential use, an Urban Growth Boundary of the Portland, Oregon type is established somewhere between x_m and x_a. What happens to land use and market rent?

REFERENCES

Edmonston, B. and T. Guterbock, 1984. "Is Suburbanization Slowing Down? Recent Trends in Population Deconcentration in U.S. Metropolitan Areas," *Social Forces*, Vol. 62, pp. 905–925.

Erickson, Rodney and E. Wollover, 1987. "Local Tax Burdens and the Supply of Business Sites in Suburban Communities," *Journal of Regional Science*, Vol. 27, pp. 25–38.

Johnson, S. and J. Kau, 1980. "Urban Spatial Structure: An Analysis with a Varying Coefficient Model," *Journal of Urban Economics*, Vol. 7, pp. 141–154.

McDonald, John, 1979. *Economic Analysis of an Urban Housing Market*. New York: Academic Press.

———, 1986. "The Intensity of Land Use in Urban Employment Sectors: Chicago 1956–1970," *Journal of Urban Economics*, Vol. 18, pp. 261–277.

———, 1989. "Econometric Studies of Urban Population Density: A Survey," *Journal of Urban Economics*, Vol. 26, pp. 361–385.

McMillen, Daniel and John McDonald, 1989. "Selectivity Bias in Urban Land Value Functions," *Land Economics*, Vol. 65, pp. 341–351.

———, 1993. "Could Zoning Have Increased Land Values in Chicago?" *Journal of Urban Economics*, Vol. 33, pp. 167–188.

Ricardo, David, 1821. *Principles of Political Economy and Taxation*. Reprinted in 1963 in London by Everyman Library.

CHAPTER

*Model of a Monocentric Urban Area

A. INTRODUCTION

A model of a simple urban area can now be constructed using elements introduced in Chapter 5. The focus of attention in the model is on the market for residential land, but the model also includes a market for nonresidential land, a market for the urban area's export product, a market for an all-purpose good consumed by residents of the urban area, and a market for labor in the urban area. All of these markets will be in equilibrium simultaneously. The model is set up so that the only feature of land that households care about is distance to the central workplace; the model is monocentric.

The first task is to set up the model and determine the properties of equilibrium in all five markets: the residential land market, the nonresidential land market, the market for the export product, the market for the imported good, and the labor market. Equilibrium in the model has several interesting implications, including the result that both residential land rent and population density decline with distance to the central business district. Also, total household income in the urban area is a multiple of household earnings in the export sector.

Next, the model is used to examine the effects of various changes in the urban economy. Three changes are examined in detail:

1. A decline in the agricultural land rent at the fringe of the urban area
2. An increase in population (and labor supply) in the urban area
3. A reduction in the cost of commuting within the urban area

In each case the implications for the pattern of land rent and population density are determined.

The model presented in this chapter is an adaptation of the method followed by Fujita (1989) in his comprehensive and mathematically rigorous text on the static monocentric urban model.

B. ASSUMPTIONS OF THE MODEL

In this section we set forth the assumptions of the model and illustrate the basic model of household behavior that is used. The exploration of the model of the household is a necessary preliminary step along the way to the presentation of the complete model in Section C.

It is assumed that the urban area produces a good for export and that the good can be sold for a given price on the open market. The nature of transportation costs within the urban area is such that this good is produced only in the central business district. The all-purpose consumption good is imported at the going price and is sold in retail stores that are also located in the central business district. The urban area's workers work in either the export industry or the retail stores. The number of households residing in the urban area is assumed to be fixed, and all of these households are identical.

Each household contains one worker, who travels to the central business district to work and to purchase the all-purpose consumption good. Therefore, each household makes the same number of trips to the central business district each year. The cost of an additional mile of distance from the central business district is a constant t, measured in units of money. Each worker in both industries makes the same wage W, and this is the entire income of the household. Hours of work are fixed.

The monocentric urban area is assumed to be circular. Transportation costs are equal in all directions. A fixed proportion of the space at each distance outside the central business district has been allocated to transportation facilities, so a fixed proportion of space is available for residential use at each distance. This last assumption implies that net and gross population density change together.

Households in the urban area maximize utility subject to the budget constraint in which wage income (W) equals the amounts spent on residential land rent, the all-purpose consumption good, and commuting. The household's utility level depends upon its amounts of land and the all-purpose consumption good. The amount spent on commuting neither adds to nor subtracts from utility.

The choice problem of the household can be depicted in Figure 6.1. The household has a set of indifference curves for the two goods, land and the all-purpose consumption good. It will be assumed that both goods are normal goods; an increase in income will increase the consumption of both goods. The budget constraint is defined by the equation

$$W - tx = G + RL,$$

where x is the distance from the edge of downtown, G the amount of the all-purpose consumption good, L the land consumption, and R the land rent. The slope of the budget constraint can be found to be $-R$ by writing

$$G = (W - tx) - RL.$$

At a given distance x_1, the household has $W - tx_1$ to spend on the two consumer goods. The relevant budget constraint is shown in Figure 6.1. Given this income and the prices of the two goods (1 and R_1), the household maximizes utility on indifference curve IC_1 by choosing point E.

FIGURE 6.1   Household equilibrium

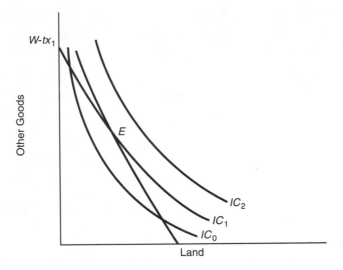

What if the household were located at some other distance x_2, where x_2 is greater than x_1? The theory of bid rent and equilibrium for the household both require that the household achieve the *same* level of utility at both distances. At distance x_2 the household has $W - tx_2$ to spend on the two consumer goods, an amount that is less than $W - tx_1$. Therefore, for the household to reach the same indifference curve as before (IC_1), land rent at distance x_2 must be less than at distance x_1. Figure 6.2a shows both of these budget constraints. The fact that R_2 must be less than R_1 means that the budget constraint at distance x_2 is flatter than the one at x_1. The household now chooses point E'' (rather than point E'). The household purchases more land and less of the all-purpose consumption good at the greater distance to downtown.

The information in Figure 6.2a can be translated into a demand curve for land, the curve that shows how land consumption varies with the land rent. (Land rent varies with distance to downtown, so land consumption varies with distance to downtown as well.) This demand curve for land is drawn in Figure 6.2b. But stop for a moment. This demand curve is a special demand curve. It is the demand for land while utility is held *constant*. The constant-utility demand curve is different from the normal demand curve in the following way. The normal demand curve is derived by changing the price of the good in question, and the utility level achieved by the household as the price changes is permitted to *vary*. A reduction in the price of a good increases the household's real income and will permit the household to reach a higher indifference curve. This effect of the increase in real income is built into the normal demand curve. However, the demand curve shown in the lower part of Figure 6.2b is a constant-utility demand curve because it has been derived from Figure 6.2a. In Figure 6.2a the household can obtain a lower land rent (R_2) only by increasing its distance from downtown and thereby increasing its commuting cost. This increase in commuting cost is, in effect, eliminating the increase in real income that might otherwise have been obtained with a lower land rent.

FIGURE 6.2 Household equilibrium at alternative locations

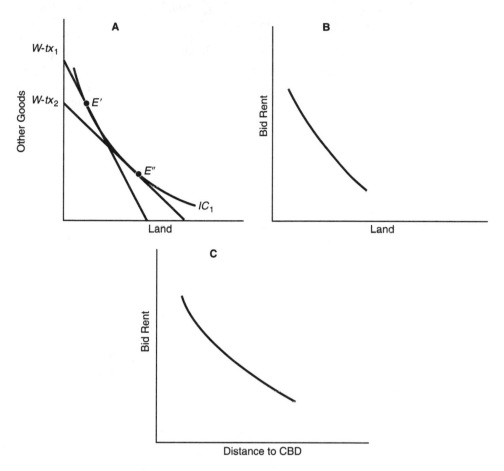

The information in Figure 6.2a can also be used to obtain the bid-rent curve that corresponds to the utility level along indifference curve IC_1. Figure 6.2c shows a graph of bid rent as a function of distance to downtown. Given utility level along IC_1, a level of bid rent can be found for any distance x. That bid rent is -1 times the slope of the budget constraint that pertains for distance x.

C. EQUILIBRIUM IN THE RESIDENTIAL LAND MARKET

Let us examine first the nature of equilibrium in the urban land market. We assume that the labor market is in equilibrium and that the size of the central business district is consistent with equilibrium in the other markets. These assumptions mean that the wage rate W is set. Also, the price of the all-purpose consumption good is fixed (at 1) and transportation costs are given.

A family of bid-rent curves identical to those presented in Chapter 5 and in Section B above can now be derived for the households in the urban area. Because they are identical in all respects, all households have the same bid-rent curves. All households make the same bid for land with equal attributes. These bid-rent curves are shown in Figure 6.3a. Bid-rent curves are denoted u_1, u_2, and u_3 for the utility levels to which each corresponds. Here utility level u_1 is less than utility level u_2, and u_2 is less than u_3. Figure 6.3a depicts household bid rent as a function of distance x to the central business district, but it also shows the radius of the central business district (x_c) and the bid-rent level for agriculture (R_a). The agricultural bid rent establishes the limit of the urban area, x_a, because competition in the land market allocates land to the use with the higher bid rent.

FIGURE 6.3

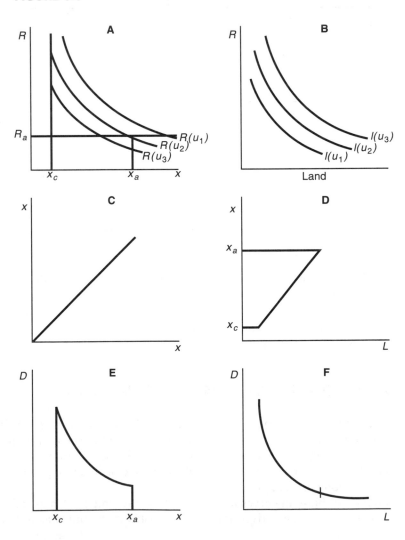

The household bid-rent function is the market equilibrium land rent between x_c and the distance x_a (where household bid rent falls to R_a). This result follows the bid-rent model of land-use allocation from Chapter 5. The population of the urban area resides between these distances. The number of households equals the number of workers who work in the central business district.

Given that the number of households that lives in the urban area equals the number of workers, the level of the bid rent function is determined. The number of households that lives in the urban area varies as we shift from one bid rent function to another. A higher level of bid rent at each distance means that the urban area contains more households, for two reasons. First, the size of the urban area expands as land is converted from agricultural use to residential use. Second, the higher bid rent means that households occupy less land at each location. The market squeezes more households into a given area. The equilibrium bid-rent function is the one for which the number of households accommodated between distances x_c and x_a (the edge of the urban area) is just equal to the actual number of households in the urban area. Suppose that bid rent function $R(u_2)$ is the equilibrium bid rent function, the one that is consistent with the number of households in the residential area being equal to the number of workers employed in the central business district.

Figure 6.3b shows the demand for land—the relationship between bid rent and the amount of land occupied by each household. As stated above, a higher bid rent means that less land is demanded. However, the demand for land $l(u_2)$ depicted in Figure 6.3b is the constant-utility demand curve introduced in Section B. It is the demand for land given that utility is held constant at the level (u_2) implied by bid-rent curve $R(u_2)$. There are other demand curves, $l(u_1)$ and $l(u_3)$, which correspond to utility levels u_1 and u_3. The demand curve $l(u_2)$ therefore depicts the amount of land occupied by households as they move down the bid-rent curve, because utility is held constant along $R(u_2)$.

The relationship between land occupied and distance can be derived easily. Figure 6.3c is called a *turning function*, and simply converts distance x from the horizontal axis to the vertical axis. Figure 6.3d thus relates land occupied (L) to distance x. The points on the line in Figure 6.3d are obtained by connecting the corresponding points on parts a, b, and c in the figure. As one moves away from the central business district (x increases), the household's bid rent falls and land demand increases, holding utility constant at u_2. Therefore, the function shown in part d has a positive slope: land per household increases with distance from the central business district.

Figure 6.3 has also been designed to show population density as a function of distance to the central business district. Population density is simply the inverse of land occupied per household. Suppose that households at some distance occupy 1500 square feet of land—1500 square feet per household. Household density then is 1 household per 1500 square feet, or 29 households per acre. Population density is household density times the number of people per household, denoted n. If $n = 3$, so that each household contains three members, the population density is 87 people per acre. In equation form, population density D is defined as

$$D(x) = \frac{n}{L(x),}$$

where both D and L are functions of distance x to the central business district.

Figure 6.3f is drawn to convert values of L into values of population density, n/L. Figure 6.3e graphs population density from Figure 6.3f as a function of x, distance to the central business district. Note that because L is an increasing function of x in Figure 6.3d, D is a decreasing function of x. This result that population density is a declining function of distance to the central business district is one of the most powerful theoretical results in urban economics. Many studies have shown that population density can be described accurately by the sort of nonlinear function depicted in Figure 6.3e. The nonlinear function becomes flatter as distance to the central business district increases. Population density drops off rapidly near the central business district but is flatter out in the suburbs and then drops off abruptly at the edge of the urban area.

D. THE LABOR MARKET

Now we must consider the labor market in the urban area. The demand for labor consists of two parts: the demand by the export industry and the demand of the retail trade sector. As mentioned previously, the supply of labor is fixed by the number of households who live in the urban area.

Figure 6.4 depicts the labor market. Given the price for the export product, assume that in the long run the export industry has a horizontal demand for labor, which is denoted D_e at wage rate W. (We are assuming constant returns to scale in the production of the export product.) The wage rate is thus set at W.

FIGURE 6.4 Labor market in an urban area

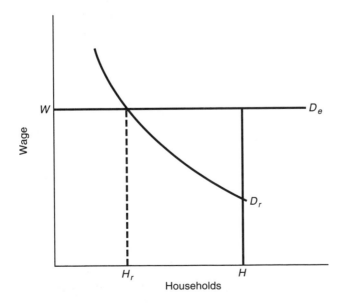

The demand for labor in retail trade depends on employment and earnings in the export industry. Added employment in the export industry will generate a local multiplier effect in retail trade, as well as additional imports of the all-purpose consumption good to the urban area. Suppose that the demand for labor in retail trade in Figure 6.4 is D_r, given the wage in the export sector and the total number of households in the urban area. The demand curve D_r slopes downward because a higher wage in retail trade means a higher price for the all-purpose consumption good and therefore a lower quantity demanded. Wage W must be paid to workers in retail trade. The fixed supply of labor means that H_r workers are employed in the retail sector, and the remainder are employed in the export sector. If employers attempted to shift more workers into the export sector (at wage W), there would be a shortage of workers in retail trade.

E. THE CENTRAL BUSINESS DISTRICT

The final piece of the model is the central business district. The employment sectors require land for their activities in the central business district. It would be simpler to assume that the employment sectors do not need land and therefore that the central business district is a dimensionless point. Would such an assumption be a helpful simplification or grossly inaccurate? We know that major urban areas have central business districts of nontrivial size in which few people reside, so a simple nonresidential land market will be included. Assume that each employee in both industries requires a fixed amount of land area l_e. This means that the total area of the central business district is $l_e H$, where H is the total number of workers and households. The radius x_c of the central business district is therefore written

$$x_c = \frac{\sqrt{l_e H}}{\pi}.$$

The requirement for land for the central business district establishes the distance at which residential land begins. Given that x_c has been determined, we return to the starting point of Figure 6.3a and select the bid-rent curve that is consistent with the number of households H that live in the urban area and have a member who works in the central business district. The model is now closed, but there are still a couple of loose ends.

For one thing, households pay rent on the land that they occupy, but whom do they pay? They do not pay each other because this form of income would have to be included in the model. Instead, it must have been assumed that all land rents are paid to owners who live somewhere else, not in the urban area. You may not particularly like this assumption, but it makes the model easier to understand. For another thing, the business sectors also pay rent on land and pay a competitive return to any other factors of production employed. Again it must have been assumed that these earnings have no impact on the local economy. The land and other factors (besides labor) in question are owned by people who live outside the urban area. Finally, it must be true that the amounts spent on commuting are also paid to someone outside the urban area. So this is an urban area that is owned lock, stock, and barrel by "foreign" investors.

These assumptions also ensure that the balance of payments for the urban area is indeed balanced. Some households in the urban area earn income by working in the export sector (the other households work in the retail trade sector), and all households consume the imported all-purpose consumption good. It must be true that the amount of money flowing into the local economy equals the money flowing out. The amount of money flowing in is PX, where P is the price of exports and X is the quantity produced. The amount of money flowing out is total residential land rents ($\Sigma\, RL$), plus expenditures on the imported all-purpose consumption good ($\Sigma\, G$) less the wages paid to local workers in retail trade (WH_r), plus the returns to the nonlabor factors of production (land and capital) used in the export sector (π_e), plus the amount spent on commuting ($\Sigma\, tx$). Therefore,

$$PX = \Sigma\, RL + \Sigma\, G - WH_r + \pi_e + \Sigma\, tx.$$

We also know that through the household budget constraint, each household must satisfy the condition that

$$W = RL + G + tx.$$

Therefore, for all households in the urban area,

$$WH = \Sigma\, RL + \Sigma\, G + \Sigma\, tx.$$

From these two conditions for PX and WH we know that

$$PX - \pi_e = W(H - H_r) = WH_e,$$

or that local export earnings $(PX - \pi_e)$ equal household incomes of workers in the export sector (WH_e). The number of workers in the export sector is simply $H_e = H - H_r$.

The addition of two more assumptions leads to an interesting implication of this model. Suppose that expenditures on the imported all-purpose consumption good are some constant fraction a of household income in the urban area, or that

$$G = a(WH).$$

Furthermore, assume that wages paid to local workers in the import industry are also some constant fraction b of sales; that is,

$$WH_r = bG.$$

These two assumptions imply that $WH_r = ab(WH)$.
We know that

$$WH = WH_e + WH_r,$$

and we now know that $WH_r = ab(WH)$. Therefore,

$$WH = WH_e + ab(WH)$$

and

$$WH = \frac{WH_e}{1 - ab}.$$

Recall that WH_e is local export earnings. Total income of households in the urban area (WH) is some multiple $[1/(1 - ab)]$ of local export earnings (WH_e). For example, suppose that households spend 50% of their incomes on the imported all-purpose consumption good ($a = 0.5$) and that 20% of the sales of this good are paid to local workers ($b = 0.2$). These figures imply that the export earnings multiplier is $1/0.9 = 1.11$. An increase in export earnings of $1 leads to additional earnings of 11 cents. Multiplier models applied to a local economy are discussed in more detail in Chapter 11.

F. MAKING PREDICTIONS WITH THE MODEL

In the preceding sections we have described the equilibrium spatial patterns in a simple version of an urban area. The features of equilibrium are useful to know, but the model can also be used to make predictions. In this section we examine the effects on equilibrium of changes in various exogenous variables. The model can be used for many possible exercises of this kind; the focus here is on (1) a decrease in the agricultural bid rent R_a, (2) an increase in population (number of households), and (3) a decrease in transportation cost per mile t. The effects of each of these changes are examined in turn.

Decrease in Agricultural Bid Rent

A decrease in agricultural bid rent is examined because the value of farmland actually did decrease significantly in the 1970s and 1980s, and because this case can be used to describe the workings of the model. The manipulation of the model is shown in Figure 6.5. Part a shows the reduction in R_a. This change permits the fixed number of households in the urban area to spread out more than before. The original bid-rent function is $R(u_2)$, but this function is no longer consistent with equilibrium. The intersection of $R(u_2)$ with the lower agricultural bid rent (R_a') supplies too much land to residential use given residential bid rents $R(u_2)$ and the fixed number of households. This surplus of residential land with the old bid-rent function means that the new equilibrium requires a shift to a lower residential bid-rent curve, $R(u_3)$. At the lower bid rents households occupy more space at each location, so the edge of the urban area has shifted outward from x_a to x_a'. Note that the intersection of R_a' with the lower bid-rent function $R(u_3)$ must be to the *right* of x_a to permit households to occupy more space. One loose end needs to be tied down. The urban employment sectors located in the central business district do not occupy more land because it has been assumed that there is a fixed amount of land needed per employee in both the export and retail trade sectors. A more complex model would relax this particular assumption.

The lowering of residential bid rent means that households have attained a higher level of utility at the constant wage rate W. The lowering of residential bid rents with a constant wage means that real income has gone up. (Households may also increase or decrease their purchases of the all-purpose consumption good, given a reduction in residential bid rent.) A higher level of utility means that the demand for land curve in Figure 6.5b shifts outward from $l(u_2)$ to $l(u_3)$. Recall that the demand

FIGURE 6.5

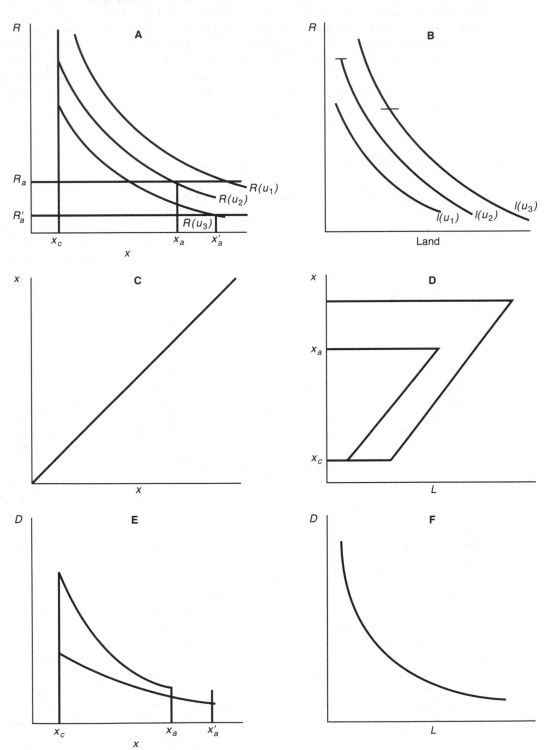

for land was drawn at a *given* level of utility. A higher level of utility means that more land is demanded at each rent. This shift is shown as movement from demand curve $l(u_2)$ to $l(u_3)$. The shift to a lower bid rent curve (and its higher level of utility) leads to a lowering of population density at all residential locations. Figure 6.5c is the turning function as before. Figure 6.5d shows that the amount of land occupied by a household has increased at each distance; the function that relates L to x has shifted to the right as shown. Finally, passing this new function relating L to x through the population density definition in Figure 6.5f to Figure 6.5e results in a downward shift in the population density function. Population density is now lower at each distance x inside the old boundary of the urban area. Of course, population density has increased in the area that has been converted from agricultural to urban residential use.

In summary, the lowering of agricultural bid rent results in:

1. A decrease in residential bid rent at all distances
2. An increase in the radius of the urban area
3. An increase in the utility level of households in the urban area
4. An increase in land occupied per household at each distance
5. A decrease in population density at all locations within the old boundaries of the urban area

Increase in Population

Next consider an increase in the number of households residing in the urban area. This means that the supply of labor has increased. Because the demand for labor in the model is perfectly elastic, employment expands by the increase in the number of households, and the wage rate W does not decline. In this instance, growth in the urban area is driven by an increase in supply of the labor input. The expansion of employment is split between export employment and retail trade employment to handle the increase in imports and the attendant retail sales. The central business district must expand to accommodate the increase in employment.

Household bid rent as a function of distance to the edge of downtown does not shift, but the increase in the number of households means that the demand for residential land has increased at all locations. The new equilibrium in the land market is on a higher bid-rent function (and a lower level of household utility, u_1 rather than u_2). The higher bid rent results in conversion of some land from agricultural use to urban residential use. Figure 6.6a shows the shift to the higher bid-rent function and the changes in the boundaries of the central business district and the urban fringe. The radius of the central business district increases from x_c to x_c'. The new bid-rent function is $R'(u_1)$, and the new radius of the urban area is x_a'.

Figure 6.6b depicts the shift in the utility-constant demand for land. Because household utility has declined in response to the increase in population, the utility-constant demand curve for land has shifted inward to $l(u_1)$ as shown. The higher bid-rent function in Figure 6.6a, combined with the lower demand for land in Figure 6.6b, results in the shift downward in the function in Figure 6.6d that relates distance to the central business district and land occupied per household. The decline in land occupied per household at each distance translates, via the population density definition in Figure 6.6f, to higher population densities at each distance in Figure 6.6e.

FIGURE 6.6

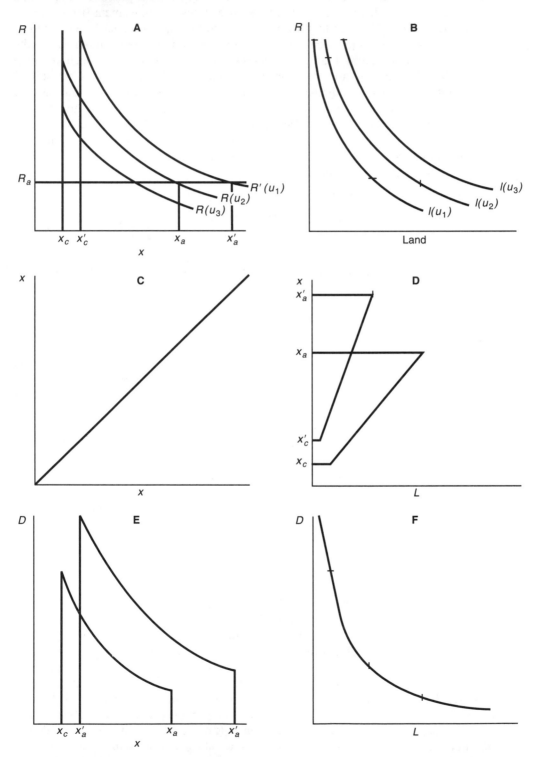

The increase in population thus means that:

1. The boundary of the central business district shifts outward to accommodate the increase in employment.
2. Equilibrium land rent in the residential sector increases.
3. The fringe of the urban area shifts outward.
4. The amount of land occupied by a household at a given location decreases; population density increases.

Decrease in Transportation Costs

Next consider what happens when there is a decrease in the transportation costs faced by households in the urban area. As Chapter 5 suggests, this is *the* case to study to gain insight into the long-run history of urban areas in the United States. Urban transportation costs repeatedly have been reduced significantly in the past 120 years or so. However, it is also true that urban populations have grown enormously in the past century. The version of the model that we have on hand assumes a fixed population as transportation costs decline, but this assumption will be relaxed at the end of this exercise. For the moment we proceed in the spirit of "one thing at a time."

The first effect of a reduction in transportation cost is to make all of the residential bid-rent functions *flatter*. Recall from Chapter 5 that the slope of a bid-rent curve is

$$\frac{\delta R}{\delta x} = \frac{-t}{L},$$

where t is marginal transportation cost. A reduction in t makes $\delta R/\delta x$ flatter (smaller in absolute value) *for a given amount of land occupied L*. In other words,

$$\frac{\delta(\delta R/\delta x)}{\delta t} = \frac{\delta R'}{\delta t} = \frac{-1}{L},$$

where R' is $\delta R/\delta x$. Households demand larger amounts of land at greater distances because land rent is lower, so the change in $\delta R/\delta x$ is smaller the greater is x. The flattening of bid-rent curves is shown in Figure 6.7a as a rotation of bid rent from $R(u_2)$ to $R'(u_2)$. If utility were to remain constant at u_2, the bid-rent function would be $R'(u_2)$. However, utility does *not* remain constant because households benefit from a reduction in transportation costs.

The reduction in transportation costs has a second effect: households now have more money to spend on consumer goods (land and the all-purpose consumer good). The increase in purchasing power caused by the reduction in transportation costs means that households can attain a higher level of utility. Bid rent at the higher utility level u_3 is $R'(u_3)$, as shown in Figure 6.7a. The figure also shows that households located at the edge of the central business district now pay lower land rents than before. These households pay no transportation costs, so their land rent must be lowered to cause their utilities to increase along with everyone else. The improvement in transportation has, in effect, reduced the demand for land near the central business district while it has increased the demand for land at greater distances from downtown. The old and the new bid-rent functions cross at distance x'; bid rent is now lower than before inside distance x' and greater than before outside distance x'.

FIGURE 6.7

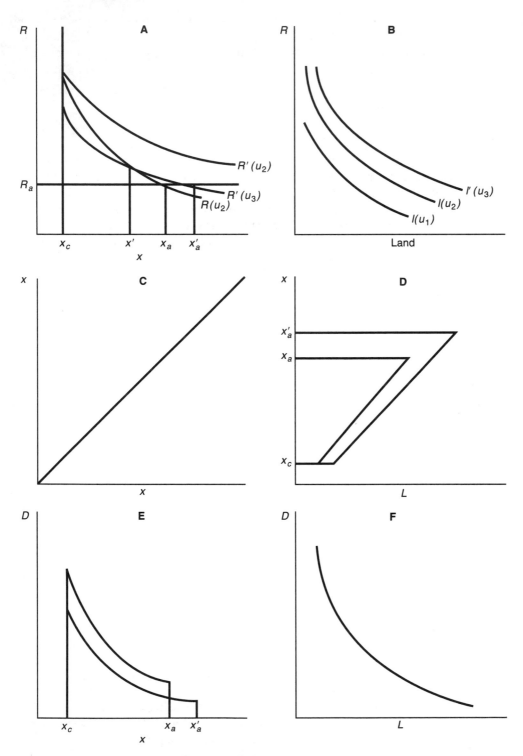

The higher utility level puts the household on a higher demand curve for land, $l'(u_3)$ in Figure 6.7b. The new bid-rent curve $R'(u_3)$ and land-demand curve $l'(u_3)$ imply a new curve relating land consumption to distance x in Figure 6.7d. As shown there, land consumption has increased at all distances even though households beyond distance x' now pay higher land rent. The urban area has spread out to distance x_a' to accommodate the increase in land consumption. The population density function in Figure 6.7e reflects these changes. Density is now lower because of the increase in the amount of land occupied by each household. The boundary of this urban area has shifted out. This is an essential implication of the model; a decline in marginal transportation costs leads to a spreading out of the residential population. Indeed, a large decline in commuting costs can lead to a sharp drop in population near the central business district and a large movement outward of the urban–rural boundary. Recall the cases of New York and Chicago during the 1970–1990 period as discussed in Chapter 1.

What is the process through which population density is reduced? The model implies that households now occupy larger residential lots at each location. Eventually, that is what happens, but the first part of the process involves vacating areas of the urban area so that they can be rebuilt at a lower density. This is a process that implies abandonment and demolition of older housing, a process that can take a very long time and be ugly to watch.

Urban areas have undergone both population growth and reductions in transportation costs, so the outcome in this typical case is a combination of the effects of these two changes. What can we say will happen in the model? We know that:

1. The boundary of the central business district will shift outward to accommodate the increase in employment.
2. The fringe of the urban area shifts outward because both population growth and reductions in transportation costs push the fringe out.

However, the effects on land rent and population density are ambiguous because the increase in population tends to increase these variables while the reduction in transportation cost reduces them. Whether the population density function rises or falls depends upon a "race" between population growth and reductions in transportation costs. Read the next sentence carefully. If population growth is rapid (slow) and transportation costs fall slowly (rapidly), the urban area will increase (decrease) in population density. The reader is supposed to read the sentence first ignoring the words in parentheses, and then to read the sentence again substituting each word in parentheses for the previous word. Economists often write sentences such as this to combine two opposite cases into one sentence. Why do we do this? It saves time and ink. Which reading of the sentence fits New York? Los Angeles?

G. SUMMARY

In this chapter we have presented a general equilibrium model of an urban area that includes simple versions of five markets: the market for residential land, the market for labor, the market for the export product of the urban area, the market for an imported all-purpose consumption good, and the market for land used by businesses in the central business district. All five markets are required to be in equilibrium. The model implies that residential land values and population densities decline with distance to the central business district. These are two of the most powerful results in theoretical urban economics.

The model was used to examine the effects of various exogenous changes: (1) a reduction in agricultural land rents, (2) an increase in population (and labor supply), and (3) a reduction in commuting costs. These results can be used to give reasonable predictions for urban areas that can be considered to be essentially monocentric in spatial configuration.

EXERCISES

The exercises for this chapter are more difficult than the exercises for the other chapters.

1. Assume the following:

   - The population and lot size are fixed.
   - All households occupy the same amount of land K.
   - All households must travel to and from the CBD once per day.
   - The marginal cost of travel is $\$t$ per mile; thus the marginal cost of distance to the CBD is $\$2t$.
   - Households are identical.
   - The number of households is P.
   - The CBD is a dimensionless point in the middle of a circular city.
   - All land is used for residential use.
   - The area of the city is PK.
   - Land rent at the edge of the city is zero.

     (a) Derive the land-rent function. This is the pattern of land rents that makes all households indifferent to all locations in the city. In particular, people who live at the edge of the city are just as well off as those who live right downtown.

     (b) Compare aggregate land rent and travel costs in the city. (*Hint:* The volume of a cone is $\frac{1}{3}bh$, where b is the area of the base and h is the height of the cone.)

     (c) What is the effect on land rent of a decline in the marginal transport cost?

     (d) If you answered part (c) correctly, you found that land rents generally declined in response to a fall in transport costs. How can this be? Are not improvements in transportation supposed to bring about *increases* in land rents and values?

2. The market for residential land in an urban area is described by the following set of equations:

   (1) $l_D(x) = BR(x)^\theta$ Individual household's demand curve for land at distance x

   (2) $L_D(x) = N(x)l_D(x)$ Market demand for land at distance x

   (3) $R'(x)l_D(x) + t = 0$ Condition for locational equilibrium of the household

   (4) $R(x^*) = R^*$ Land rent at edge of the city, x^*

   (5) $L_S(x) = 2\pi x$ Supply of land at distance x; circumference of circle

   (6) $L_S(x) = L_D(x)$ Market equilibrium at each distance x

It is further assumed that the total number of households in the urban area is fixed at N. The variables in the model are:

$l_D(x)$ = quantity of land demanded by a household

$R(x)$ = land rent at distance x

θ = price elasticity of demand for land

B = a constant

$N(x)$ = number of households located at distance x

$R'(x) = \delta R/\delta x$ = slope of rent function

t = commuting cost incurred by residing 1 mile farther from the CBD

The model incorporates the following assumptions:

- Households consume land, and consume less land per household where rent is higher [equation (1)].
- All households must commute to the central business district, a dimensionless point at which all employment is located.
- All land is consumed by households. No land is needed for transportation facilities [equation (5)].
- The market for land is perfectly competitive. In equilibrium the rent at each distance [$R(x)$] equates supply and demand in that annulus; $L_S(x) = L_D(x)$.

  Have you got all of that? Now here are the questions.

  (a) What is the meaning of equation (3)? Where does this equation come from?

  (b) Assuming that $\theta = -1$ (unitary price elasticity of demand for land), derive the land-rent gradient $R(x)$. This is actually a very simple question if you understand how to do it. If you find yourself performing an elaborate mathematical derivation, you are on the wrong track.

(c) Derive the population density gradient $N(x)/L(x)$.

(d) What happens to the distribution of population over space if t (marginal commuting cost) rises?

(e) How does this little mathematical model relate to the graphical model presented in Figure 6.3?

REFERENCE

Fujita, Masahisa, 1989. *Urban Economic Theory*. Cambridge: Cambridge University Press.

CHAPTER

7

Urban
Employment Centers

A. INTRODUCTION

The basic economic functions performed in urban areas were outlined in Chapter 4. Noyelle and Stanback (1983) defined the types of goods and services produced in urban areas according to the following classification system:

1. Agriculture, extractive, construction
2. Manufacturing
3. Distributive services
4. Complex of corporate activities
   a. Central administrative offices and auxiliary establishments
   b. Finance, insurance, and real estate
   c. Corporate services
5. Nonprofit services
6. Retailing
7. Consumer services
8. Government

The first task of this chapter is to discuss for each of these sectors the nature of its spatial pattern within an urban area. Taken together these spatial patterns produce the employment geography for an urban area, which includes distinctive features such as the central business district, the airport and its surrounding area, industrial zones, major shopping malls, and suburban office agglomerations. Changes in the geography of urban employment are discussed along the way. In addition to this section, you will enjoy reading the part of Hoover and Vernon's *Anatomy of a Metropolis* (1959), in which these topics are discussed for New York in the 1950s.

The agriculture, extractive, and construction sector is not given a detailed treatment because it does not really follow an overall coherent pattern. Agricultural activity in urban areas tends to be located at the urban fringe, of course. Extractive activity (mines, oil wells, quarries) has a location pattern determined by natural resources.

For example, there are oil wells in downtown Oklahoma City. Also, construction activity takes place in areas of physical growth, which usually are located in outer suburbs. (One exception is the downtown office building boom of the 1980s in many of the larger urban areas.)

In the second part of the chapter we examine the findings of recent research on employment centers in major urban areas. How are various types of employment centers identified? Are there distinct types of employment centers? How have these centers emerged, grown, and declined? This discussion is followed by sections on commercial and industrial real estate in urban areas that answer the following questions. What economic models can be used to analyze commercial and industrial real estate? How are market rents and values determined? How can one estimate the market value of commercial or industrial property? Until fairly recently urban economists have largely ignored the commercial and industrial real estate markets. Their focus of attention was housing, a topic that is covered in Chapter 9. However, a thorough understanding of the urban economy also calls for an understanding of commercial and industrial real estate as well.

B. SPATIAL PATTERNS FOR URBAN INDUSTRIES

Manufacturing

Most large urban areas in the United States began as trading centers, but by the late nineteenth century many had become centers of manufacturing. Manufacturing of that day was tied to water and rail transportation systems. Indeed, manufacturing was tied to water transport routes before the development of the rail network in the 1850–1890 era. Railroads freed manufacturing location decisions to a remarkable degree and in a manner not unlike the interstate highways in the 1960s and 1970s. For example, Inland Steel is a maker of basic steel that was founded around the turn of the century at a location in the Chicago urban area that is several miles removed from Lake Michigan and major waterways.

For our present purposes manufacturing can be divided into two basic categories: heavy and light. *Heavy manufacturing* involves the assembly of bulky raw materials or semifinished products for the manufacture of a bulky product. Included in this category are:

1. Primary metals (SIC 33)
2. Chemicals (SIC 28)
3. Petroleum and coal products (SIC 29)
4. Transportation equipment (SIC 37)
5. Paper and allied products (SIC 26)
6. Textile mill products (SIC 22)

Recall from Chapter 3 that Henderson (1986) found evidence of localization economies in primary metals, petroleum and coal products, paper and allied products, and textiles. He did not conduct a test for transportation equipment, so four out of five of the heavy manufacturing industries tested display localization economies. Heavy manufacturing to a considerable degree still occupies locations that are adjacent to water transportation and are also served by rail. The sharing of transportation facilities may be the source of the localization economies. These shared transportation facilities provide access to the raw materials that are important to these industries. But increasingly, some of these industries have reduced their intakes of raw materials and their reliance on water transportation. Railways and highways are sufficient to support auto assembly plants and auto parts manufacture (transportation equipment), minimills (steel), and chemical plants of various types, for example. Some of the old industrial districts in urban areas such as Pittsburgh, Detroit, Chicago, Cleveland, Buffalo, and New York City have been more than decimated—they have been virtually abandoned.

The rest of manufacturing can be called *light manufacturing*, and consists primarily of food products, apparel, printing and publishing, plastics, fabricated metal products, machinery (electrical and nonelectrical), and instruments. For these industries many of the location factors discussed in Chapter 3 come into play. Location choice within the urban area depends on access to the market for the product, which can be partly local in nature. Access to labor is important, as is access to intermediate inputs. Access to knowledge is especially important for many of these industries. After all, electrical machinery includes computers and their components. Silicon Valley, the area south of San Francisco that is the home of the nation's minicomputer industry, is perhaps the leading example of the importance of access to knowledge in a manufacturing industry. Access to knowledge is important in the high-fashion apparel business too. The actions of local governments can also influence the location choices of these industries within an urban area. The general quality of the neighborhood in which the facility is located can play a role. In addition, there is a factor that has not been discussed yet—room for expansion. Studies of industrial relocation show that relocation is most often prompted by running out of space. It is logical to conclude that the choice of location will depend in part on the availability of room for expansion.

Henderson's (1986) list of manufacturing industries that exhibit localization economies includes four in the above list of light manufacturing industries: food products, apparel, electrical machinery, and nonelectrical machinery. With examples such as the Silicon Valley phenomenon in the computer industry and the high-fashion apparel industry, it is clear that localization economies sometimes lead to clear clusters of an industry within an urban area. However, in other cases it seems that presence in the urban area is sufficient to reap the benefits of localization economies. However, this is only a conjecture that needs to be tested.

Some other clusters of light manufacturing have existed in the past, and some of those clusters continue to exist. Smaller firms in a variety of light manufacturing sectors have tended to cluster in the denser areas near the central business district, where there is ready access to space, labor, and a variety of business services. These are more properly considered to be economies of urbanization that exist in particular locations within the urban area.

Another type of cluster was formed by the printing and publishing industry in some urban areas. This industry is really two industries: printing and publishing. Printing tended to cluster near central business districts because much of the demand for printing was in the central business district. Many special printing jobs require rapid completion, so printers must be in close contact with their customers. The attraction of the central business district for printers has diminished in recent years, but many urban areas contain what was once a printers' district near downtown. For example, an area adjacent to the Chicago central business district called "Printers' Row" contains old-fashioned industrial loft buildings that have since been converted to a variety of other uses, including residential use. Publishing is the industry in which writers write, editors edit, and marketing departments sell. There is a sense in which this industry does not seem to be manufacturing, but that is how it is classified. For many years this industry responded to localization economies by being concentrated in the central business districts of a few major urban areas. Publishing is still big business in New York, of course. Some of the publishing houses have relocated to New Jersey and even to places such as San Diego. The publishing industry relies on sources of information, and much of that information is not easily interpreted without face-to-face contact. Publishing also relies on the talents of highly skilled people, so labor-market economies of localization are at work, too. Perhaps Henderson (1986) failed to find evidence of localization economies in printing and publishing because these two very different industries were lumped together.

The other sectors in the light manufacturing group correspond to one's image of the modern factory located in the suburbs. Larger firms in industries such as food products, machinery, plastics, fabricated metals, and instruments build factories that may be only one story (or two or three stories) in height. These facilities are surrounded by parking lots and, in some cases, by grass and trees. They are happy with convenient access to a highway, a good workforce nearby, a pleasant environment, and room to expand. Firms in some of these industries led the charge to the suburbs beginning in the 1950s. The completion of the expressway systems in urban areas accelerated the movement of these types of firms to the suburbs. Some of the smaller firms in these industries still require the external economies of locations near the central business district, but it is also true that those external economies of available space, labor supply and business services now can be found elsewhere in the urban area.

The impact of zoning can also be seen in the location patterns of light manufacturing, especially in suburban jurisdictions. Chapter 5 includes a discussion of the idea that suburbs can trade off the fiscal benefits of industrial land use and environmental quality. The amount of space made available to manufacturers depends upon how local officials view this trade-off. Given that a local jurisdiction has decided to make some land available for manufacturing use, there are clear patterns in the allocation of land. A detailed study of land-use allocations in zoning ordinances by McMillen and McDonald (1990) shows that land in suburban Chicago is more likely to have been allocated to manufacturing if it is:

- Near a limited-access highway
- Near a freight rail line
- Near a commuter rail line
- Closer to the major airport (O'Hare)
- At a greater distance from the village hall
- At a greater distance from downtown Chicago

This list includes very local effects and more regional patterns. Immediate access to highway and rail is important, and local officials evidently dislike zoning land for industry near the village hall, which is usually near the center of the village. Villages that are closer to O'Hare Airport provide more land for industry, as one would expect. This list also includes the tendency, holding all of these other factors constant, for land zoned for manufacturing to increase with distance to downtown Chicago. This result perhaps is evidence of a desire to put new manufacturing facilities on the outer fringe of the suburb. Finally, the study by McMillen and McDonald (1990) found that more land was zoned for manufacturing by older suburbs than by newer suburbs. As is explained below, newer suburbs are trying to attract commercial activity partly because of the lack of growth in manufacturing employment in recent years. Older suburbs were, at least at some time, trying to attract manufacturing activity.

The Distribution Sector

The Noyelle–Stanback (1983) distribution sector includes wholesale trade and transportation, communication, and utilities. McDonald (1992) prefers a narrower definition of the distribution sector: wholesale trade and trucking and warehousing. Clearly, this more narrowly defined distribution sector will usually locate near highways, rail lines, and airports. Some agglomerations of wholesale trade activity, such as fresh fruits and vegetables and meats, select a central location as a convenience to their customers. In some major urban areas there are agglomerations of wholesalers in apparel, furniture, and other durable goods so as to cater to the buyers from retail stores, many of whom come from outside the urban area. These agglomerations might be located downtown or near the airport. The airport is, of course, the center of the air transportation industry. Transportation services, such as travel agents, air freight companies, and other services, tend to cluster in the downtown area or at the airport.

The communication industry includes TV and radio broadcasters and the telephone company. TV and radio broadcasters often locate in the downtown district so as to maximize their access to the entire urban area. The telephone company has a central office and local offices to serve customers. The electric utility has power-generating facilities that resemble heavy manufacturing. Most power plants burn coal or oil and therefore must be located near the transportation facilities that are used to deliver the basic fuel. The transportation facilities include water routes, rail lines, and oil pipelines. Power plants often are located in the same districts as heavy manufacturing. The natural gas utility has a major facility located near the natural gas pipeline. Both utilities also have a network of facilities to serve the local population.

The story of the changes in location patterns in this sector is instructive. Transportation and wholesale trade were once concentrated in or near the downtowns of most urban areas. Many urban areas, and their downtowns, began life as ports. And remember those old railroad stations? Those railroad stations also came equipped with railroad yards, where trains were assembled and disassembled. Early trucking terminals were also located near the downtown areas. Wholesale trade was not usually located right in the downtown area, but used sites near the transportation facilities in the vicinity of downtown. Wholesale trade was much more centralized within an urban area than was retail trade. Finally, the earliest airports were located as close to downtown as possible. Airports require a lot of space, but LaGuardia in New York, National Airport in Washington, DC, Love Field in Dallas, and Midway Airport in Chicago are good examples of early airports that are located only a few miles from downtown.

As the urban areas grew along with the entire nation, the demand for the services of the distribution sector grew as well. The sites near the downtown area were not large enough to handle the demand, so new facilities had to be built on the periphery of the urban area. Rail yards became too small and congested. New rail yards were built at the periphery of the urban area. Later, even more rail yards were built at the new periphery of the urban area. The older, larger urban areas have a collection of rail yards that date from various times in their histories. Trucking terminals also became outdated, and new ones have been established at or near the periphery of the urban area. The particular process also has been stimulated partly by the deregulation of the trucking industry in the 1980s. Under the old regulations, trucking terminals had to be located inside the commercial trucking zone that had been set up by the Interstate Commerce Commission.

In like manner the air transportation industry outgrew the first set of airports. A second set of airports has been built, and these are located at what was the periphery of the urban area at the time of their construction. We now have Kennedy Airport and Newark Airport for New York, Dulles Airport in the vicinity of Washington, DC, Dallas–Fort Worth Airport, and O'Hare Airport in Chicago. The wholesale trade sector is attracted to these newer transportation facilities. Indeed, in some instances, a great deal of economic activity is attracted to the newer airports. Some urban areas have recently or are now facing the issue of where to build the *next* airport. New airports require an enormous amount of space, and that kind of space can only be found at rather great distances from the downtown area.

Complex of Corporate Activities

This sector consists of corporate offices, financial services, and business and professional services. All of this is office-based employment, and office buildings can vary from one to 100 stories in height. This is the sector that has been, and still is to a large degree, located downtown. Some parts of this sector, such as banks, insurance agents, and real estate brokers, have always located in residential areas because they are really providing services at the retail level. Beyond these functions, this sector was downtown employment because of the necessity for face-to-face contact. Indeed, the strength of the attraction of downtown was underestimated by some analysts. During the 1980s many of the downtown areas experienced unprecedented booms in the construction of office space. Employment in these sectors was growing rapidly and, contrary to the predictions of several people, the downtowns of major urban areas were the recipients of some of that growth. For example, employment in FIRE (finance, insurance, and real estate) almost doubled, from 3.6 million in 1970 to 6.7 million in 1990. Downtowns in places such as Baltimore and Cleveland have come back from the dead. Other places, such as Los Angeles and Phoenix, were thought by some people not to have downtowns. That thought turns out to have been wrong.

Downtown provides economies of agglomeration of all of the types discussed in Chapter 3.

The booming downtowns of the 1980s, with their yuppie (young urban professional) lawyers, accountants, and financial wheelers and dealers, got the attention of most people, including the author Tom Wolfe and the Marxists. Tom Wolfe wrote his remarkable novel *The Bonfire of the Vanities* about this time in New York. The novel concerns the misadventures of a Wall Street hotshot who wanders into the black ghetto by accident. Do you remember the Marxists from Chapter 2? They looked at many of the urban areas and saw a declining manufacturing base in the old industrial areas of the inner city along with booming suburbs and a booming downtown. To make matters worse, some of those yuppies were buying older residential properties in certain areas of the central city and, in some cases, evicting the poorer people from their homes. Here we have it—the Marxists have located what they think is the inevitable class struggle of capitalism, alive and well. The call to organize the poor and the lower-middle class of the inner cities has been issued and heard by some.

The growth of the complex of corporate activities has yielded growth for many downtowns, but even more spectacular is the creation of what journalist/author Joel Garreau has called *edge cities*. Garreau's 1991 book *Edge City* is both insightful and entertaining; you should put it on your reading list. Garreau points out that we built monocentric cities roughly between the years 1840 and 1920. Since then we have mainly been building suburbs, and the growth of suburbs has passed through three stages. First came the bedroom communities that permitted the downtown workers to live in a more pleasant setting. The next stage began in the late 1940s and brought shopping malls and industrial parks to the suburbs. The shopping malls grew to serve the rapidly growing suburban population, and the industrial parks attracted manufacturing plants that needed large amounts of relatively cheap land and ready access to highways. These developments changed the nature of suburbs, but there was still a heavy reliance on the economy of the central city. In the third stage corporate offices and many other activities have moved to suburban centers that Garreau calls edge cities. This stage began in the early 1970s, and it represents something entirely new. Just what is an edge city, and why is it so important?

Garreau does not use the terminology of Chapter 3, but clearly he means that an edge city is a large cluster of economic activity which includes a substantial amount of office-based employment and possesses economies of agglomeration. He calls them edge *cities* because of the existence of agglomeration economies. As you know, suburban shopping malls and industrial parks have agglomeration economies, too, but Garreau would contend that the agglomeration economies of the new edge city are far greater and more pervasive. Garreau contends that the agglomeration economies in edge cities rival those in the central business district. Economic growth is being created in edge cities. The primary physical manifestation of the economic growth of the American economy since the 1970s is the construction of edge cities near the edge of every major urban area in the nation. How are edge cities formed, and how do they work?

Garreau's book is a work of journalism rather than science. He interviewed hundreds of people who have been involved in creating edge cities, and he reported on their motivations and the guidelines that they used. First, it is clear that edge cities form at the intersections of major highways. Not every intersection has an edge city, but nearly every edge city has an intersection of major, limited-access highways. It is also clear that the highway intersection usually has reasonable access to an airport. A highway intersection may already have a shopping mall or an industrial park nearby, but often the precipitating event in the creation of an edge city is the decision of a major corporation to move some or all of its headquarters operation to that location. The headquarters operation might include the research and development facility, which employs people with high levels of education and training. The major corporation did not need agglomeration economies that are external to the firm. Firms such as IBM, AT&T, and Motorola brought much of their own supporting services with them. Their choice of location was driven by the convenience of their managers, scientists, and other critical personnel. Other large companies might then choose the same location largely for convenience in commuting. The crucial next phase in the creation of an edge city is the decision of smaller companies to locate in the vicinity. These firms might have some connection to the large corporation as supplier or consultant, but the critical difference is that they require extensive supporting services. Their agglomeration economies are external to the firm. Those supporting services include restaurants, hotels and conference facilities, office supply stores, lawyers, accountants, computer experts, financial services, engineering consultants, and a host of other activities. Once all of these kinds of enterprises are there, more new businesses are created because the supporting services are there.

Garreau has found that people really like edge cities. What are their reasons? Convenience in commuting for the important employees has already been mentioned. People regard commuting by public transportation as an unpleasant experience, so edge cities are based on the automobile. Edge cities have been created partly in response to the increase in the number of women who have entered the labor force in the past 25 years. What is more, people like the pleasant environment of the edge city. They like green grass and trees, and they like to live in suburban communities that have greenery as well. Garreau points out that edge cities cannot form unless some suburban housing already exists in the vicinity. An edge city is a nice compromise between the desires to live and work in a pleasant location and to have a productive career. The edge city corporate "campus" includes ball fields, picnic grounds, tennis courts, and jogging tracks. The nearby suburban communities provide good housing at decent prices and good public schools. An edge city and its surrounding residential areas provide safety, especially for women and children.

The big central city comes with dirt, crime, subways, stress, congestion, high taxes, and poor public schools. Edge cities are not immune to all of these problems (especially congestion), but for now they largely avoid most of them. Edge cities are subject to a certain amount of traffic congestion, but their developers have methods of ameliorating some of the problems. For one thing, they build parking garages. The construction of the first parking garage is an important event in the life of an edge city because a parking garage is a signal of the fact that the edge city has reached a certain size and status. Also, an edge city that has become large enough to create its own traffic jams will soon develop at an intensity of land use that permits a person to walk, rather than drive, to lunch and shopping. Lunch is particularly important in business communication (as in, "Let's do lunch.").

Edge cities are new and important features of modern urban areas, and we are just beginning to study them. Some of the empirical research on edge cities is discussed in the next section.

Retailing and Consumer Services

You already know that retailing and consumer services are of two types: convenience goods and shopping goods. Convenience goods and services follow residential location patterns closely, so little needs to be said about them because they are not major forces in the shaping of an urban area. Shopping goods are a different story. Once upon a time nearly everyone in an urban area went downtown to shop for clothing, jewelry, shoes, furniture, housewares, appliances, and most other things of a durable nature. Downtown shopping still exists in most urban areas (although not in Detroit, for example), but most shopping has shifted to the suburban shopping malls.

The rapid growth of residential suburbs in the 1950s brought convenience goods almost immediately, and branch stores of the downtown department stores soon followed. As suburban residential growth continued and as more highways were constructed, it became economically feasible to build huge suburban shopping malls. Huge shopping malls are designed to capture the shopping externalities that were discussed in Chapter 3. The shopping malls contain "anchor" department stores and a large variety of smaller stores that specialize in particular lines of business. These huge shopping malls are in competition with downtown *and* with the smaller shopping centers that were built in the 1950s and 1960s. In the process many downtown stores have folded, and many of the early suburban shopping centers have also been converted to other uses. All of this has been made possible by the automobile. A study by McDonald (1975) of retailing in Detroit in the early 1960s showed that for people who owned a car, the probability of shopping downtown declined sharply with distance from home to downtown. In contrast, most people who did not own a car shopped downtown, and that tendency did not decline with distance to downtown. Public transportation is centered on downtown, so those who do not own cars travel downtown to shop. The increase in auto ownership caused downtown shopping to decline.

The story for downtown is not entirely one of gloom and doom. The growth of downtown office-based employment of the 1980s has helped to create some opportunities for downtown retailers. Successful downtown retailers have changed to cater to the downtown worker. And some downtowns have been and still are tourist attractions. Included on a list of such downtowns are New York, Chicago, Boston, San Francisco, Washington, DC, Seattle, and perhaps a few others. Some other downtowns have been promoted as tourist attractions without much success. A particularly pathetic example of unsuccessful promotion is downtown Flint, Michigan. The film by the independent film maker Michael Moore entitled *Roger and Me* tells the story of the community after General Motors decided to close some its Flint plants. One response was to try to turn Flint into a tourist attraction by building a fancy downtown hotel, a "festival market" facility, and an indoor amusement park named Auto World. The hotel and the festival market facility have not been very successful, and Auto World closed within a few months of its opening.

Nonprofit Services and Government

Nonprofit services include health care, which is in fact very big business in the modern economy. The location patterns of hospitals and other health care facilities are important parts of the urban economy, and some big changes have occurred in recent years. Health care facilities are now organized according to a reasonably clear hierarchy. The offices of doctors and dentists in private practice and small health clinics are located in or near the residential areas that they serve. The next level of the hierarchy includes the smaller hospitals and larger clinics that serve an area but do not offer the full range of medical services that is available only in the large hospitals. Often, those large hospitals are attached to or affiliated with a medical school.

Major changes are taking place in the systems used to deliver health care. The use of health maintenance organizations and other forms of "managed care" is growing rapidly, even without any direction from the federal government. The old model of health care delivery was one in which doctors in independent private practice were affiliated with an independent, nonprofit hospital. Cases that could not be handled at that level were referred up the hierarchy to the large hospital with the staff of surgeons, cancer specialists, and medical researchers. The doctors and hospitals were reimbursed by private insurance companies of the basis of fees for services rendered. This system resulted in a rate of inflation in medical costs that spelled trouble. The average rate of inflation from 1970 to 1990 for all consumer goods and services was 6.1%, but the price of medical services increased by 7.9% per year. From 1980 to 1990 the rate of inflation as a whole averaged 4.6%, but the inflation of medical services was 7.8%.

The concern with the rising cost of medical care has prompted large employers to seek more efficient and cost-conscious providers, and the market has responded. A health maintenance organization (HMO) is a private company that operates for a profit. It hires salaried doctors and other medical professionals to provide care for a large group of people, such as the employees of a large firm. The contract drawn up between the HMO and the firm stipulates that the HMO is paid a certain amount to provide health care for the clients. The HMO is not paid on the basis of fees for services rendered. Cases that cannot be handled by the HMO staff are contracted out to the large hospitals. Clearly, this type of system gives the HMO a strong incentive to keep costs down.

The shift to managed care has meant that many of the old nonprofit hospitals in urban neighborhoods have been under a great deal of pressure. Many of the smaller hospitals have closed. In other cases they have been taken over by HMOs or other for-profit health care providers. Some of the doctors who were in private practice have gone to work for HMOs at a salary. These changes in the organization of health care have probably stimulated growth in large medical centers. The large hospitals, with their huge staffs and comprehensive set of services and medical education, have set up their own HMOs or managed care organizations. They have also set up contracts with HMOs to provide the specialized care that the cost-conscious HMO will not supply directly. The hypothesis is that the shift to managed care has created a more clearly defined hierarchy of medical institutions, and this change has been of benefit to the organizations at the top of the hierarchy. In addition, the public is demanding improvements in health care through public and private funding of medical research and development. The large hospital/medical school complexes are the recipients of most of this funding for research. These medical complexes are important parts of the urban economy.

Where are these major medical centers located in an urban area? Often they are located near the center of the urban area because that is where the hospital or medical school was founded. Major medical complexes are located adjacent to downtown in Chicago and New Orleans, for example. Others, such as the Mayo Clinic in the Minneapolis urban area, have sought a suburban location. Major medical complexes can be located in a variety of places within the urban area, and they will continue to exert major impacts on location patterns.

Government employment was 16.7% of all nonagricultural employment in 1990, so the location patterns of government are important to an urban area. Much of local government serves the population directly, so location patterns are driven by the location of the population. Other parts of local government, as well as state and federal government, often locate in downtown office buildings. Court houses have traditionally been part of downtown, and that tradition remains in force to a considerable degree. However, the growth of suburban counties has meant that there are now large centers of county government in the suburbs. In a few other cases major government employment centers exist for historic reasons. Some urban areas are centers of military employment, and the location of the naval base or other military post will influence location patterns. The analyst who seeks to understand location patterns in an urban area must take government into account.

C. EMPIRICAL STUDIES OF URBAN EMPLOYMENT CENTERS

Empirical researchers only recently have begun to recognize the importance of urban employment centers other than the central business district. Somewhat surprisingly, the central business district itself has been the subject of only a modest amount of research. Urban economics has tended to concentrate on distance to the central business district as a crucial variable in theoretical and empirical models of the spatial patterns of an urban area (as in Chapter 5), but the content of the CBD has been the subject of fewer studies. The reason for this relative lack of studies is a lack of data on employment *by place of work* enumerated for small geographic zones. This section begins with a brief look at the central business districts of Los Angeles and Chicago, and then the other employment centers in these urban areas are examined.

The Los Angeles urban area can be studied in detail because the data gathered in the 1980 census of population include information on the journey to work for 17% of households. These data were gathered by place of residence and then transformed to employment data by place of work. Giuliano and Small (1991) used the data to identify employment subcenters in the Los Angeles urban area, and their findings are discussed below. The first thing that they discovered is that the central business district was, by far, the most important center of employment. Downtown Los Angeles in 1980 had an employment level of 469,000 out of a total employment of 4.65 million in the entire urban area, so downtown contained 10.1% of total employment. The area that is traditionally used as the definition of the CBD is rather small and contained only 152,000 workers, but Giuliano and Small (1991) believe that an area of about 2.5 miles in radius is the better definition of the CBD. Clearly, a downtown that is 19.6 square miles in area is not a downtown made for walking. Here is clear evidence that some downtowns are spreading out, so travel within the downtown area is an emerging problem. Giuliano and Small (1991) examined downtown employment by industry and found a strong concentration in public employment and FIRE (finance, insurance, and real estate). Downtown contained about 20% of the urban area's employment in these two sectors, and downtown manufacturing employment was relatively low.

Data for the Chicago CBD permit an examination of the changes in downtown employment over time. These data are based on reports filed by employers to the state unemployment insurance system, and the reports are compiled by postal zip codes. This kind of data exists for all states, but Illinois makes a special effort to provide summary data for the public. Only employment in the private sector is included, but an estimate of public employment in the CBD is available from other sources. The Chicago CBD has also been spreading out over time. The definition that is used here is an area that is 4 miles long (in the north–south direction) and about 2 miles wide. The Chicago CBD is smaller than the Los Angeles CBD because Chicago is served by an extensive system of public transit and commuter rail lines that brings most of the workers downtown. Developers of downtown office buildings must provide reasonable proximity to the transit and commuter rail systems.

Data on employment by industry for the Chicago CBD are shown in Table 7.1. Private employment in downtown Chicago was 490,400 in 1979, a figure that was 18.8% of total private employment in the urban area. Note that as one would expect, downtown Chicago contains a larger proportion of total employment in the urban area than does downtown Los Angeles. Downtown employment had grown 6.4% to 521,600 in 1989, but downtown's share of total private employment had dropped to 17.4% because employment in the urban area had grown by 15.2% over the same period.

TABLE 7.1   Private Employment in Downtown Chicago

	1979		1989	
Industry	Workers (thousands)	Percent of Urban Area[a]	Workers (thousands)	Percent of Urban Area[a]
Total	490.4	18.8	512.6	17.4
Construction and mining	10.6	9.7	8.7	6.4
Manufacturing	73.0	9.1	52.4	8.0
Durable	21.1	4.1	13.8	3.6
Nondurable	51.9	18.2	38.6	14.1
Transportation	16.2	16.0	15.2	12.0
Communication and utilities	32.3	53.0	29.0	43.3
Wholesale trade	47.8	20.3	36.8	13.9
Retail trade	54.8	11.7	55.0	9.5
FIRE	103.0	47.9	128.6	46.3
Services	152.7	25.2	195.9	22.2

[a]*Defined as employment in industry in the CBD divided by employment in industry in the urban area.*
Source: Illinois Department of Employment Security.

Table 7.1 shows that downtown employment in the private sector is heavily concentrated in FIRE (finance, insurance, and real estate) and services. These two sectors made up 52.1% of downtown employment in 1979, and they had grown to 62.2% of downtown employment in 1989. Downtown employment in FIRE and services grew substantially over the decade, and (with the exception of retail trade) all of the other industries declined. During this period office space in the downtown area increased from 68 million square feet with an occupancy rate of 95% to 109 million square feet with an occupancy rate of 90% [McDonald (1991)]. Downtown contained 47.9% of all FIRE employment in the urban area in 1979, and that fraction dropped slightly to 46.3% in 1989. Employment in the service sector is more dispersed; 25.2% of service sector employment was located downtown in 1979, and this figure dropped to 22.2% in 1989. Communications and utilities is a small sector, but it is also heavily concentrated in the downtown area. In 1979, 53.0% of employment in this sector was located downtown, but this proportion had dropped to 43.3% in 1989. The major television stations are located downtown, as are the central offices of the telephone company and the electric and gas utilities. Local planning authorities estimated that downtown employment in the public sector was 112,000 in 1985, so total downtown employment in 1985 was approximately 618,000 in that year. Employment in downtown Chicago thus exceeded employment in downtown Los Angeles by about 30%.

Downtown employment in major urban areas is heavily concentrated in the FIRE, service, and public sectors, but what about other centers of employment in the urban area? An examination of other urban employment centers requires first that they be identified using some criteria. There is no standard set of criteria that everyone uses to identify employment centers. For example, Garreau (1991) defined an edge city as a place with at least 5 million square feet of office space, 600,000 square feet of retail space, and more workers than residents. Furthermore, Garreau required that the place was nothing like a city in 1960. Clearly, Garreau was focusing on newer concentrations of office-based employment. His definition misses other kinds of employment centers that concentrate in manufacturing, distribution, or transportation. Garreau's definition seems to run into trouble because he tried to establish boundaries for his edge cities. Sometimes his edge city is so dispersed that there are no clear boundaries, and in other cases the edge cities are so close together that it is not clear where one ends and the other begins. Using this definition he listed edge cities for 36 urban areas. The New York area contains 17 edge cities and four traditional downtowns. Four additional edge cities appeared to be emerging. The Los Angeles urban area was found to have 16 edge cities, two traditional downtowns, and nine more edge cities that seemed to be emerging. In contrast, the Chicago urban area is very simple. Garreau found only one traditional downtown and four edge cities. No more edge cities appeared to be emerging in the Chicago area.

Other researchers have recognized that most employment in an urban area is rather dispersed, and this fact will frustrate the attempt to delineate precise boundaries for employment centers. For example, Giuliano and Small (1991) showed that 68.0% of all employment in the Los Angeles urban area in 1980 was not located in identifiable employment centers. Instead of attempting to draw boundaries for employment centers, McDonald (1987) proposed that employment centers can be identified as peaks in gross employment density. The idea is that an employment center has a peak gross employment density that is greater than the employment density in the surrounding area. Gross employment density is used rather than net employment density because it is possible that a high level of net employment density simply reflects the fact that a small amount of land has been devoted to employment. Giuliano and Small (1991) agreed with this criterion and added the proviso that total employment in the vicinity must exceed 10,000. There seems to be agreement that a local peak in gross employment density serves as a reasonable criterion for establishing the location of an employment center.

Giuliano and Small (1991) used these criteria and identified 29 employment centers in the Los Angeles urban area outside the CBD in 1980. The largest of these centers is located about 10 miles west of downtown Los Angeles and had employment of 176,000. The next-largest centers are Santa Monica and Hollywood, and each had employment of about 65,000 in 1980. The center that ranked fourth, with employment of 59,000, is the Los Angeles Airport area. Giuliano and Small (1991) had data on employment by industry, so they classified the employment centers according to function as follows:

Economic Function	*Number of Centers*	*Important Industries*	
Specialized manufacturing	7	Manufacturing	73%
Mixed industrial	9	Manufacturing	45%
		Service	14%
		TCU	11%
Mixed service	8	Service	30%
		Retail	16%
		FIRE	15%
Specialized entertainment	2	Service	33%
		Entertainment	21%
Specialized service	3	Service	57%

Employment centers differ widely in economic function. Some are centers of manufacturing, while others perform specialized service functions such as health care and higher education. Others are diversified collections of industrial activities or service activities. The number of centers that specialize in a small collection of industries suggests that localization economies operate at this level. However, we do well to remember that 68% of employment in the Los Angeles urban area is not located downtown or in any of these centers.

Research on office rents in employment subcenters has just begun. An excellent study by Sivitanidou (1995) shows that office rent in the employment subcenters in the Los Angeles urban area varies systematically with the characteristics of the subcenter. Office rent declines with distance to the central business district, the nearest airport, and distance to the Pacific Ocean (i.e., distance to the beach). Office rent is higher if the subcenter has better access to freeways, lower crime, and more retail space. Holding other factors constant, office rents are also influenced by the degree of land-use regulation. A more severe limitation on the height of buildings (or on the permissible ratio of floor area to land area) leads to a higher office rent. The limitation on building height restricts the supply of office space in the subcenter, so office rents are higher.

McDonald and McMillen (1990) and McDonald and Prather (1993) have examined employment centers in the Illinois portion of the Chicago urban area. They made use of data from 1956, 1970, and 1980 so that changes in employment centers could be observed. McDonald and McMillen (1990) identified four zones as employment centers in 1956. All four were centers of manufacturing and related distribution activities, and all four were inside or close to the boundaries of the city of Chicago. The situation had changed by 1970. Two of the old industrial centers identified in 1956 had lost prominence, but two additional centers of manufacturing industry could be identified in the vicinity of O'Hare Airport. The airlines had moved their operations from Midway Airport to O'Hare in 1962, and the title of "world's busiest airport" had shifted accordingly.

As Garreau would probably say, something very different had happened by 1980. McDonald and Prather (1993) identified three employment centers for that year. The largest is the O'Hare Airport area, a center that specializes in transportation (of course), manufacturing, and wholesale trade. The O'Hare area is actually a spot with ready access to three modes of transportation: air, highway, and rail. The airport is located at the intersection of two major interstate highways, and the largest rail yard in the urban area is located just south of the airport. A huge agglomeration of economic activity surrounds the airport; employment within a 5-mile radius was approximately 250,000 in 1980. The other two employment centers are two of Garreau's edge cities. One is located in Schaumburg, a municipality that is located 26 miles northwest of the CBD (and about 8 miles northwest of O'Hare), near the intersection of two major highways. It is home to Woodfield Mall, the largest shopping mall in the urban area, and the main headquarters of Motorola, Inc. Garreau (1991) included Schaumburg on his list of edge cities. The other employment center is located 25 miles straight west of the CBD in DuPage County. The center, which includes the municipality of Naperville, is often called the Illinois Research and Development Corridor, running along a major highway. Garreau (1991) also identified this center as an edge city.

These last two employment centers are of a new type. They are based on access to the highway system, and neither has easy access to the freight rail or commuter rail systems. Both are located several miles from the boundaries of the city of Chicago. The Schaumburg employment center relies on employment in manufacturing (including the headquarters of Motorola), but the Illinois Research and Development Corridor does not. Employment in the service sector dominates this center. These two centers fit Garreau's specifications for an edge city very well indeed. Employment centers had existed in the Chicago urban area before 1980, but all of these earlier centers had been based on manufacturing employment and access to freight rail transportation.

This section has shown that the central business districts of major urban areas are dominated by employment in the FIRE (finance, insurance, and real estate), service, and public sectors. Employment in the CBD has grown as these sectors have grown, and that growth has caused the CBD to spread out over a wider area. The CBD in Los Angeles now has a diameter of 5 miles. Large urban areas probably have always had other centers of employment outside the CBD. Prior to the 1970s these other centers were most likely to be manufacturing centers that were partly based on access to the freight railroad system (and/or to the water transportation system). As Garreau (1991) pointed out in a popular book, a new type of urban employment center has emerged since the 1970s. Garreau called them edge cities because they seem to possess agglomeration economies that are external to the firms that are located there. They are based on immediate access to the highway system and on reasonable access to air transportation. Edge cities contain office-based employment in corporate headquarters, services, and FIRE (finance, insurance, and real estate). Edge cities do not have boundaries that can be clearly defined. It is better to think of edge cities as peaks in gross employment density. Suburban employment centers are an important new phenomenon, and urban economists currently are working to gain a better understanding of them.

*D. ECONOMIC ANALYSIS OF EMPLOYMENT DENSITY

Employment density has been used as an important indicator of the spatial patterns in an urban area in both Chapter 5 and in this chapter. This section presents an economic model of production on urban land that leads to some propositions concerning employment density. Land is at the heart of urban economics. The study of location patterns within an urban area requires that the production function introduced in the appendix to the book must be amended to include land.

   The usual production function used in economics considers output to be a function of labor and capital inputs. Output is measured as value added, so intermediate inputs are ignored. However, land is one of the basic inputs (along with labor and capital) that produces value added. The simplest approach might be to add land as an input in the usual production function, and write

$$Q = f(N, K, L),$$

where labor is N, capital is K, and land is L. However, this specification ignores the special relationship that land has with some of the capital. In particular, some capital is in the form of structures (buildings) that are constructed on the land. The rest of the capital consists of equipment (machines, computers, telephones, trucks, etc.) and inventories that can be moved around fairly easily. In fact, buildings and land are normally called real estate. There are separate markets for buildings and the land upon which the buildings are situated called real estate markets. Here we are interested in the markets for commercial and industrial real estate. Chapter 9 is concerned with residential real estate.

   This line of argument suggests that the basic inputs used by a firm are labor, equipment capital, structure capital, and land. Furthermore, structure capital and land can be grouped together and called real estate. Therefore, the production function will be written as

$$Q = f(R, N, E),$$

where R is real estate, E the equipment capital, and N the labor, as above. The input real estate is itself a function of structure capital and land, or

$$R = g(S, L).$$

Structure capital is S and L is land, as above. This production function for real estate requires that you stretch your imagination a bit and suppose that there is some commodity called real estate that is bought and sold in the real estate market. You must imagine that along an isoquant, there are various combinations of structure capital and land that produce the same amount of this thing called real estate. A couple of examples may help.

A simple case is real estate to be used for parking cars. You wish to provide parking for 250 cars. This can be done with a parking lot that is covered by asphalt— a lot of land and very little capital. Alternatively, a two-story parking garage can be built that uses a lot more capital and about 50% as much land. Or, a three-story parking garage can be built with even more capital and even less land. All three options provide parking for 250 cars. The story can be retold using office buildings that house office workers. There are alternative combinations of land and capital that will house the same number of workers. Taller buildings can also be built to conserve on the use of land in the retailing or in the manufacturing sectors as well. However, one suspects strongly that it is easier to substitute capital for land in office buildings than in manufacturing facilities or shopping centers. The world's tallest buildings are office buildings.

Now you are convinced that real estate is an input. Indeed, real estate is an input into everything! The production of all goods and services requires that the worker and his/her equipment (if any) be located somewhere. That somewhere could be on bare land, or it could be in a 100-story office building. A particularly convenient form for the production function is

$$Q = AR^\alpha E^\beta N^{1-\alpha-\beta}.$$

This function is known as the Cobb–Douglas production function, and the A term and the exponents in the equation are constant parameters of the function. This production function exhibits constant returns to scale because the exponents of the inputs sum to 1.0. To see this, suppose that all of the inputs are doubled and write

$$A(2R)^\alpha (2E)^\beta (2N)^{1-\alpha-\beta} = 2AR^\alpha E^\beta N^{1-\alpha-\beta} = 2Q.$$

The production function for real estate shall also be assumed to be a Cobb–Douglas function of the form

$$R = BS^\mu L^{1-\mu}.$$

We are now ready to explore the economics of land-use intensity. Recall from the appendix to the book that to be efficient in its use of inputs, the firm uses inputs so that the ratio of their prices equals the ratio of their marginal products. If you do not recall this proposition, this would be a good time to review the appendix to the book. The prices of the inputs are denoted as follows: w is the price of labor (N), q the price of equipment capital (E), r the price of structure capital (S), and v the price of land.

Consider first equipment capital and labor. The marginal product of equipment capital is

$$MP_E = \frac{\delta Q}{\delta E} = \beta AR^\alpha E^{\beta-1} N^{1-\alpha-\beta} = \frac{\beta Q}{E}.$$

Similarly, the marginal product of labor is

$$MP_N = \frac{\delta Q}{\delta N} = (1 - \alpha - \beta)AR^\alpha E^\beta N^{-\alpha-\beta} = \frac{(1 - \alpha - \beta)Q}{N}.$$

The ratio of the two marginal products can be found and set equal to the ratio of input prices as follows:

$$\frac{MP_E}{MP_N} = \left(\frac{\beta}{1 - \alpha - \beta}\right)\frac{N}{E} = \frac{q}{w}.$$

This equation can be rearranged to read

$$\frac{N}{E} = \left(\frac{1 - \alpha - \beta}{\beta}\right)\frac{q}{w}.$$

In short, the ratio of labor to equipment capital is a constant times the ratio of the price of equipment capital to the wage rate. This result has three important implications. The ratio of labor to equipment rises when the price of equipment rises, and it falls when the wage rises. In addition, the ratio of labor to equipment does *not* depend on the price of real estate, which depends on the prices of structure capital and land. We can say that the decision regarding the ratio of labor to equipment is *separable* from the real estate input.

The production function for real estate can be used to derive the equation for the ratio of structure capital to land. The marginal product of structure capital in the production of real estate is

$$\frac{\delta R}{\delta S} = \mu BS^{\mu-1}L^{1-\mu} = \frac{\mu R}{S}.$$

Similarly, the marginal product of land in the production of real estate is

$$\frac{\delta R}{\delta L} = (1 - \mu)\frac{R}{L}.$$

You should derive this result on your own. Setting the ratio of marginal products equal to the ratio of prices yields

$$\frac{(1 - \mu)R/L}{\mu R/S} = \left(\frac{1 - \mu}{\mu}\right)\frac{S}{L} = \frac{v}{r}.$$

The ratio of structure capital to land is essentially the height of the buildings and is a constant times the ratio of the price of land to the price of structure capital, or

$$\frac{S}{L} = \left(\frac{\mu}{1 - \mu}\right)\frac{v}{r}.$$

One can presume that the price of structure capital does not vary within an urban area, so the height of buildings depends directly on the price of land.

The next step is to derive an equation for employment density. To do this, first substitute the production function for real estate into the production function for output, or

$$Q = A(BS^{\mu}L^{1-\mu})^{\alpha}E^{\beta}N^{1-\alpha-\beta}$$

$$= AB^{\alpha}S^{\alpha\mu}L^{\alpha(1-\mu)}E^{\beta}N^{1-\alpha-\beta}.$$

The marginal product of land is

$$MP_{L} = \frac{\delta Q}{\delta L} = \alpha(1-\mu)AB^{\alpha}S^{\alpha\mu}L^{\alpha(1-\mu)-1}E^{\beta}N^{1-\alpha-\beta}$$

$$= \frac{\alpha(1-\mu)Q}{L}.$$

The ratio of the marginal product of land to the marginal product of labor is set equal to their price ratio, written

$$\frac{MP_{L}}{MP_{N}} = \frac{\alpha(1-\mu)Q/L}{(1-\alpha-\beta)Q/N} = \frac{v}{w}$$

or

$$\left[\frac{\alpha(1-\mu)}{1-\alpha-\beta}\right]\frac{N}{L} = \frac{v}{w}.$$

Net employment density can now be written as

$$\frac{N}{L} = \left[\frac{1-\alpha-\beta}{\alpha(1-\mu)}\right]\frac{v}{w} = Z\left(\frac{v}{w}\right),$$

where Z is the collection of constant parameters from the production function collected in the brackets. Note that this is an equation for net employment density because only land used in the production process in question is included in the analysis. The equation says that employment density is a constant times the ratio of the price of land to the wage rate. In natural logarithmic form the equation is

$$\ln\left(\frac{N}{L}\right) = \ln Z + \ln v - \ln w.$$

The equation for net employment density is important because it says that employment density will be high where land values are high. Recall the result from above that the ratio of structure capital to land (i.e., the height of the buildings) is also a direct function of the price of land. As you know from Chapters 5 and 6, land values are high where bid rents are high, and bid rents are high in places that have locational advantages for the bidder. Land values are high in the central business district because office-based firms find the agglomeration economies of this location advantageous. If Garreau (1991) is correct, edge cities also produce relatively high land values because of agglomeration economies. The appendix to this chapter presents a mathematical model of bid rent with this implication. These high land values produce high levels of net employment density compared to the surrounding areas. In addition, the theory in Chapter 5 says that the use of land will be determined by the market forces expressed through bid rent. The market will allocate land to the highest bidder, so much of the land in the central business district and in the edge cities will be allocated to commercial use (i.e., office buildings). In other words, gross employment density will also be at high levels in the CBD and the edge cities. Gross employment density can be defined as net employment density times the fraction of land devoted to employment use, or

$$\frac{N}{L}\left(\frac{L}{L_T}\right),$$

where N/L is the net employment density from above, L_T the total amount of land in the urban zone in question, and L/L_T the fraction of that land devoted to employment. Both parts of gross employment density are at high levels in the CBD and at the center of an edge city. This theory of employment density is the reason that Giuliano and Small (1991), McDonald and McMillen (1990), and McDonald and Prather (1993) used data on gross employment density to identify employment centers.

E. MARKETS FOR COMMERCIAL AND INDUSTRIAL REAL ESTATE

Most students have had some experience with the market for rental housing, and some have had experience with buying or selling residential property. Most of you are probably not very familiar with the markets for commercial and industrial property. There are markets for offices, retail space, industrial property, warehouses, restaurants, parking lots and garages, hotels and motels, auto service stations and repair shops, and other types of properties for business use. Each of these types of property can be rented or purchased, and each type of property has its own set of market procedures and institutions. Commercial and industrial real estate can be a fascinating subject, and I recommend that you take a course in real estate if you are considering this field. People with knowledge of urban economics can find interesting and rewarding careers in commercial and industrial real estate.

The purpose of this section is to provide a brief introduction to the markets for commercial and industrial real estate in urban areas. Commercial and industrial properties produce a stream of income, and the market value of such property is based on that stream of income. The first step in the analysis of the market for income–producing property is to look carefully at the income stream.

Leases for commercial and industrial property are usually very complicated documents, and the provisions in leases can vary a great deal. A fundamental distinction is the gross lease and the net lease. The *gross lease* is a lease in which the contract rent includes the tenant's share of all operating expenses of the building. The tenant pays only the contract rent, called *gross rent*, and the landlord is responsible for paying the property taxes, insurance, utilities, maintenance, replacement and repairs, and management fees. Alternatively, a *net lease* is a lease in which the contract rent does not include the operating expenses. Instead, operating expenses are passed through to the tenant as direct expense. The tenant pays *net rent* to the landlord. In addition, landlords have begun to use the term *effective rent* to refer to the rental income received after accounting for operating expenses and various concessions granted to the tenants. An oversupply of real estate of a particular type, such as office space in the early to mid-1990s, will lead to a proliferation of concessions to tenants to get them to sign a lease. The most popular concessions are months of free rent, extra allowances for finishing and decorating the space, moving allowances for tenants who are moving into the building, and payments to the new tenant's old landlord to cover part of the old lease. This last concession is called *lease assumption cost*. The value of a building is based on the actual stream of income that it generates, so concessions in leases must be taken into account. With this discussion of leases as background, the determination of the market value of income-producing property can be examined.

The job of a real estate appraiser is to estimate the market value, or most probable selling price, of a subject property. Appraisers usually estimate the value of income-producing property using the income capitalization approach. Capitalization means the conversion of expected future income into a current lump−sum amount. The general expression for the income capitalization approach is

$$V = \frac{I}{r},$$

where V is the estimated market value, I the expected future income, and r the capitalization rate. The appraiser must estimate both the expected future income and the capitalization rate. Each of these will be considered in turn.

The expected future income that is relevant to the determination of the market value of a property is called *net operating income*. Net operating income is closely related to the idea of effective rent, the net rent corrected for concessions to tenants. Refer to Table 7.2 to see how appraisers determine net operating income. The first step is to estimate the potential gross income (PGI) of the property. PGI is the total of gross rents that would be produced if the building were fully occupied and tenants paid the gross rent prevailing in the market for this type of real estate. The second step is to correct PGI for the vacancy rate that can be expected, yielding an amount called *effective gross income*. The third step is to deduct expected annual operating expenses and concessions to tenants from effective gross income. Operating expenses include fixed expenses, variable expenses, and reserves for the replacement of parts of the building that wear out. Fixed expenses include real estate taxes and insurance.

TABLE 7.2   Estimation of Net Operating Income

Potential gross income (PGI)
  Market rent per square foot times the total amount of space
    available for rental *plus* any other income generated by the
    building (parking fees, vending, etc.).
Effective gross income (EGI)
  PGI less vacancy allowance. Vacancy allowance is the expected
    amount of vacant space (in square feet) times the market rent per
    square foot.
Net operating income (NOI)
  EGI less
  Operating expenses
    Fixed expenses
    Variable expenses
    Reserves for replacement
  Tenant concessions (annualized basis)

Variable expenses consist of utilities, repairs, maintenance, and management fees. Tenant concessions that can be expected must be converted to an average annual figure. For example, a landlord might grant a tenant three months of free rent in the first year of a five-year lease, but the estimation of net operating income requires a figure for the average annual expense for tenant concessions. Net operating income is the bottom line of Table 7.2. Note that net operating income does *not* involve subtracting interest paid by the landlord on any loans taken to acquire the property. Also, income taxes paid by the landlord are not deducted. These two items count as part of the income generated by the property.

The other half of the process is the estimation of the capitalization rate for the type of property that is being studied. Professional appraisers generally use data on similar properties that have actually been sold recently to estimate the rate at which net operating income is being converted into market value. Suppose that the appraiser has a sample of properties for which the market value (V) is known and sufficient information exists to be able to construct a good estimate of expected net operating income (NOI). These data can be used to estimate the capitalization rate that is prevailing in the market via the equation

$$r* = \frac{NOI}{V}.$$

Alternatively, estimates of current market capitalization rates for various types of property are available from commercial real estate research services.

The final step in the appraisal is to divide the estimated NOI for the subject property by the capitalization rate that is prevailing in the market for this type of property; $V = NOI/r*$. The estimate of market value that is produced is the selling price of the property that can be expected under a normal sale to a typical buyer. The actual selling price can vary from this estimate because of special circumstances or because of simple randomness in the market. Special circumstances can arise when the seller must sell very quickly and cannot take the time needed to generate an offer that reflects full market value. Also, the contract for sale might include other considerations, such as financing to be provided by the seller at below-market interest rates. This sort of special financing usually will cause the selling price of the property to be above its appraised value. Finally, the appraised value is just an estimate of value. Not every conceivable factor that can influence selling price has been taken into account, so the actual selling price can vary from appraised value in a random fashion.

F. DISEQUILIBRIUM IN REAL ESTATE MARKETS

The appraisal of commercial and industrial real estate requires estimates of the expected rent and vacancy rate. It would be easy to obtain the needed estimates if the markets for real estate were always in long-run equilibrium (or close to it). The appraiser would simply use the current rents and vacancy rates as pretty good estimates of what can be expected in the long run. Unfortunately, there are times when some real estate markets depart from long-run equilibrium by a sizable amount and for a fairly long period of time. This section is an introduction to the short-run dynamics of office markets. Clapp (1993) has provided a survey of research on this topic.

Two important recent economic events in urban areas have been the boom in office building construction in the decade of the 1980s and the subsequent collapse of office rental markets in many urban areas. Large office buildings take several years to plan and construct, and this timing problem contributed to the condition of oversupply that has been evident in most large urban areas. Some recent research has focused on the dynamics of the market for office space. The theory that economists have used in explaining the office rental market includes the assumption that office rents reflect the degree to which the market's observed vacancy rate deviates from a long-run "natural" vacancy rate. This theory is presented first, and then an empirical example is discussed.

The basic proposition in the theory is that vacant space in a market has economic value because it permits a short-run response to unexpected increases in demand and reduces search costs for potential tenants. The market benefits from the existence of some (although not too much) unoccupied space. The standard theory includes the view that in the long run there is a natural, or optimal, vacancy rate at which the costs (to office building owners) and the benefits (to potential users) of additional vacant space are equal. A further proposition is that office rents be adjusted when the actual vacancy rate departs from this natural rate. As usually specified, the theory says that the adjustment in rent is lagged one year from the departure of the vacancy rate from its natural level. Rents are set this year based on vacancy rate data from last year.

The theory of the market can be explained diagrammatically. The market demand for office space is shown in Figure 7.1 as $D_1 D_1$, and the total stock of office

FIGURE 7.1 Supply and demand for office space

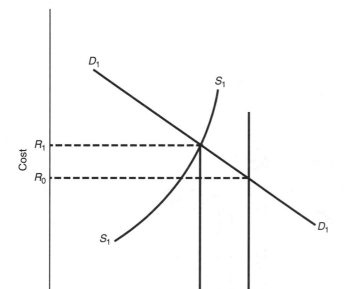

space in the short run is shown as fixed amount K_1. The stock is represented as a vertical line because in the short run, the total amount of space available cannot change significantly even if high rents motivate suppliers to build more office buildings. Despite the fact that the total stock is K_1, suppliers offer only the amounts represented by line $S_1 S_1$, as determined by the effective rent level. They do not offer the entire stock K_1 because of the aforementioned benefits of an inventory of vacant space. Supply schedule $S_1 S_1$ is expected to have a positive slope because higher effective rent is associated with a higher opportunity cost of leaving space vacant. In Figure 7.1 the short-run market equilibrium rent is R_1 and the quantity of occupied space is Q_1.

Suppose that the market depicted in Figure 7.1 is also in long-run equilibrium. At rent R_1 and occupancy level Q_1 the suppliers of office space are making a normal profit. This means that the vacancy rate equal to $(K_1 - Q_1)/K_1$ is also the normal vacancy rate. Note that the market rent R_1 exceeds the rent R_0 that would result in full occupancy if landlords chose not to hold any units vacant (i.e., if all office space available in the market, K_1, would be occupied). In effect, tenants are paying a premium of $(R_1 - R_0)$ per square foot for the privilege of having an inventory of vacant space on hand.

Now consider how the theory explains the market's response to a change in demand. Demand might rise because of economic growth or because of economic changes that emphasized office-based service employment over other types of employment. Figure 7.2 represents the reaction of the market depicted in Figure 7.1 when demand increases to $D_2 D_2$. Rents do not respond immediately to the change in demand because there is an inventory of vacant space that can be absorbed. The quantity of space occupied increases to Q_1', and the vacancy rate falls below the natural rate. Over time, however, the higher demand causes rents to increase to R_2 in response to the departure of vacancy from its natural rate. The change in rent is larger

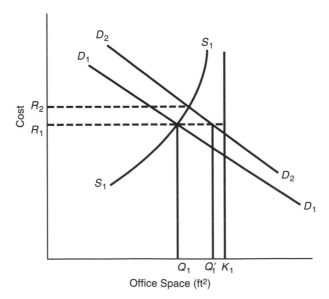

FIGURE 7.2 Supply and demand for office space

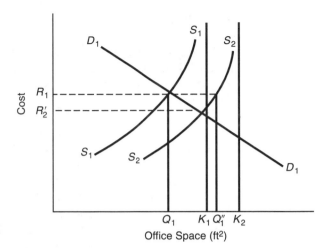

FIGURE 7.3 Supply and demand for office space

the greater the departure of the actual vacancy rate from its natural rate and the steeper the demand and supply curves.

The theory operates in similar fashion in response to a change on the supply side. Changes in supply in office markets cannot generally be timed to respond to current market conditions. In Figure 7.3 the total stock increases to K_2, perhaps because builders expect greater demand for office space in the future. The short-run supply curve shifts to $S_2 S_2$ as a portion of the new space is offered for use. The amount of space occupied shifts quickly to Q_1'', but at that level of occupancy the vacancy rate rises above its natural rate. Rent eventually adjusts downward to a short-run equilibrium at R_2'. Once again, the rent change relates to the departure of vacancy from the natural rate. Given the increase in supply, the size of the adjustment is determined by the slopes of the demand curve and the new short–run supply curve.

The standard theory is based on the assumption that the market initially is in long-run equilibrium, and therein lies a problem with using the theory to predict outcomes in actual markets. Return to Figure 7.2 and assume that rent has adjusted upward to R_2. Note that vacancy does not correspond to its long-run natural rate at this short-run equilibrium; it is below that optimal level. Because it can take several years for additional office buildings to be planned, financed, and constructed, it is reasonable to assume that there can be *further* increases in demand before supply can be increased sufficiently to restore vacancy to its natural rate. A further increase in demand will reduce the vacancy rate even more and, with a time lag, cause rents to rise even more. In this case it is the *change* in the vacancy rate (not its departure from the natural rate) that causes rent to rise above R_2. It was, in fact, a *change* in the vacancy rate (from its natural rate, as it happens) that had caused rent to increase from R_1 to R_2 in the first place. Therefore, a more general conclusion is that any change in rent results from a *change* in the vacancy rate.

Several recent studies have examined the relationship between vacancy rates and rents in the office market. For example, Shilling, Sirmans, and Corgel (1987) estimated a model based on the theory that

$$\delta R = a_1 \, \delta C - a_2 (V - V_n),$$

where δR is the change in gross rent, δC the change in operating expenses, V the actual vacancy rate, and V_n the natural vacancy rate. The theory says that the change in rent is zero if there are no changes in operating expenses and if the actual vacancy rate equals the natural rate. The natural vacancy rate is unknown, but if it is a constant, the equation can be estimated as

$$\delta R = a_2 V_n + a_1 \delta C - a_2 V,$$

with $a_2 V_n$ as the constant term in a linear equation. If this theory is correct, the natural vacancy rate can be computed as the estimated constant term $(a_2 V_n)$ divided by the coefficient of V (a_2). Shilling et al. (1987) estimated the model for 17 urban areas in the United States. They found that δC and V are both statistically significant determinants of the change in rent, and they also found that the estimated natural vacancy rate varied from 1.0% in one urban area to 23.9% in another. This extreme variation in the natural vacancy rate does not seem plausible.

The results of a study such as Shilling et al. (1987) become questionable, however, when we consider the theoretical argument, as presented above, that changing rents should relate to the *change* in the vacancy rate. Another difficulty with attempting to study office rents in recent years is the fact that true effective rents are usually not reported to those who gather the data. As discussed above, commercial leases can include a variety of concessions to tenants that will create an appreciable discrepancy between "stated" rent and effective rent. A reliable measure of effective rent is thus a critical ingredient in a study of the current rent/vacancy relationship.

The best available market data on effective rents are contained in a study by Webb and Fisher (1996) of effective rents in office buildings in downtown Chicago. This study includes three important features. First, the authors have gathered data on actual lease contracts signed during the 1985–1991 period. Second, they carefully computed effective rents by adjusting for lease features such as graduations in contract rents and the various types of concessions discussed above. Third, they then completed a statistical analysis of effective rent based on building characteristics. This procedure controls for the quality of the office space and thereby permits the estimation of year-to-year differences in effective rent for newly leased office space of standardized quality.

The Webb–Fisher data annual effective rent estimates can be combined with vacancy rate data provided by the Building Owners and Managers Association of Chicago in order to examine the relationship between vacancy and rent. The basic data for the analysis are shown in Table 7.3. The table shows that the vacancy rate in downtown Chicago was a relatively low 10.76% in 1984; it increased to 14.38% in 1987, dropped to 13.50% in 1988, and climbed steadily thereafter to 16.67% in 1991. Effective rent on new leases was a relatively high $9.45 per square foot per year in 1985; it dropped sharply to $5.40 in 1987, recovered to $7.05 in 1990, and then dropped again to $5.90 in 1991.

The theoretical discussion indicated that the change in effective rent is a function of the change in the vacancy rate. A simple regression of the change in effective rent (δR) on the lagged value of the change in the vacancy rate (δV_{-1}) produces the estimated equation

$$\delta R = 0.130 - 0.884 \delta V_{-1}.$$

	TABLE 7.3	**Vacancy Rates and Rents in the Downtown Chicago Office Market**	
Year	Vacancy Rate (%)	Effective Rent (per square foot)	Net Contract Rent (per square foot)
1984	10.76	—	—
1985	13.82	$9.45	$12.75
1986	14.32	6.60	10.90
1987	14.38	5.40	10.10
1988	13.50	5.50	7.75
1989	13.84	6.05	9.05
1990	15.72	7.05	10.80
1991	16.67	5.90	9.75

Source: Table compiled from data obtained from BOMA/Chicago and Webb and Fisher (1996).

This equation explains 74.8% of the variance of δR, and the coefficient of δV_{-1} is highly statistically significant, so there is a very strong relationship between the change in effective rent and the lagged value of the change in the vacancy rate in the market. The estimated equation says that an increase in the vacancy rate leads to a drop in effective rent on new leases of $0.88 one year later. It is evident that lease terms are negotiated after very careful attention has been paid to the previous changes in the vacancy rate.

The data in Table 7.3 can also be used to test the hypothesis that the change in rent is determined by the (lagged) level of the vacancy rate (V_{-1}). The estimated equation in this case is

$$\delta R = 5.447 - 0.423 V_{-1},$$

but this equation explains only 5.5% of the variance of δR, and the coefficient of V_{-1} is not statistically significant. This test rejects the hypothesis that changes in the effective rents are determined by the lagged level of the vacancy rate. It was suggested above that such would be the case if the market does not begin each period in long-run equilibrium; the timing of supply changes is not closely related to year-to-year changes in market conditions.

Webb and Fisher (1993) also provided data on net contract rents for the same office buildings and time periods as reported to a local Chicago firm that specializes in real estate market data. Net contract rents do not control for concessions, including free rent, tenant improvements, buyout allowances, and so on. A simple regression of change in contract rent (δCR) on the lagged change in the vacancy rate produces the result that

$$\delta CR = 0.020 - 0.637 \delta V_{-1}.$$

This equation explains 28.2% of the variance in δCR, and the coefficient of δV_{-1} is not statistically significant. While the time patterns for effective rent and net contract rent are similar, this regression result demonstrates the need to use effective rents rather than net rent as stated in the lease. Clearly, the various tenant concessions are sensitive to the market conditions as represented by the change in the vacancy rate.

The estimated equation $\delta R = 0.130 - 0.884 \delta V_{-1}$ can be used to forecast effective rents in downtown Chicago. The vacancy rate in the office market in downtown Chicago was 19.74% in 1992 and 21.3% in 1993. The increase in the vacancy rate from 15.72% in 1990 to 16.67% in 1991 implies a decline in effective rent of $0.71 to $5.19 in 1992. The subsequent jump in the vacancy rate to 19.74% in 1992 means that effective rent plummets in 1993 to $2.61 per square foot. The further increase in the vacancy rate to 21.3% in 1993 means a further drop in effective rent for 1994 to a predicted $1.36 per square foot. Participants in the market have indicated that these forecasts were pretty accurate. The office market was very weak, and landlords were signing leases that provided them with little or no return on their investments in the short run.

G. SUMMARY

In this chapter we have presented a discussion of the urban location patterns of various groups of industries. With its concentration of corporate offices, FIRE (finance, insurance, and real estate), services, and public employment, downtown remains an important feature of urban areas. Shopping malls and industrial areas are also important parts of the employment geography of an urban area. However, a relatively new phenomenon is the suburban employment center, based on corporate offices, FIRE, and services. Garreau (1991) has called these new types of centers edge cities, and there is evidence that they possess significant agglomeration economies. Giuliano and Small (1991) provided a complete catalog of employment centers in the Los Angeles urban area as of 1980.

A good criterion for identifying employment centers is a local peak in gross employment density. The chapter included a theoretical discussion of production on urban land that leads to the conclusion that the intensity of land use, measured as net employment density, is a direct function of land value. If employment centers are characterized by economies of agglomeration, bid rents in employment sectors should be high at those locations. High bid rents in employment sectors result in land being allocated to those sectors *and* in high land values and net employment densities. Employment centers with economies of agglomeration should therefore be characterized by high levels of gross employment density.

The chapter concluded with two sections on commercial and industrial real estate, one discussing the appraisal of income-producing property, and the final section examining the dynamics of the office market.

A Mathematical Model of Bid Rent

In Section D we stated the proposition that proximity to an employment center that possesses agglomeration economies will lead to higher land values and levels of employment density. The first step in that analysis is the proposition that proximity to such an employment center increases the bid rent offered by firms in the relevant industries. The purpose of this appendix is to develop a mathematical model of bid rent that has this implication. Your first reaction to this purpose might be something like: "Are you not doing it backwards? You are purposely setting up a model that has the implication you are seeking. Is it not better to set up a model using the best assumptions you can muster and see where it leads?" If you were to say all of that, you would be correct. However, economists do what is done in this appendix all of the time. The idea is to find one set of assumptions that leads to a particular conclusion. The next step is to determine whether these assumptions are correct.

Consider firms in a competitive industry in an urban area that produces a good or service that is sold for a price p^*. This price does not vary by location within the urban area. If the good or service is exported outside the urban area, the assumption of a constant output price is based on ubiquitous interurban transportation (e.g., trucking) at a constant price. If the good is consumed locally, a constant output price is justified by assuming that the consumers are highly mobile and eliminate any price differences.

The critical assumption in the model is on the production (supply) side. Assume that output (value added) is a function of two inputs, labor and land, *and* distance to a central point, or

$$Q = f(E,L,x),$$

where Q is the output, E the labor, L the land, and x the distance to the central point. The central point may be the central business district or one of Garreau's (1991) edge cities. It is assumed that greater distance to the central point reduces output, holding inputs constant. In other words, inputs are more productive if the firm is located closer to the central point. The central point is a center of information about markets and technology and provides legal, financial, and other services. Proximity to these intermediate inputs (purchased and unpurchased) makes the primary inputs more productive.

The production function can assume many forms. One convenient form with which you are familiar is the Cobb–Douglas function, which for this model shall be written

$$Q(x) = A(x)E^\alpha L^{1-\alpha}.$$

Here output is a function of x, distance to the central point, through a shift term $A(x)$. It is assumed that $\delta A(x)/\delta x < 0$, so that, holding the inputs constant,

$$\frac{\delta Q(x)}{\delta x} < 0$$

Now the bid-rent function can be derived. The firms are in a competitive industry, so it is assumed that each firm will make only a normal profit in the long run. Economic profits are zero, so a bid-rent function shall be derived for this level of profit. Recall from Chapter 4 that there is a bid-rent function for each level of profit, but in this case only one bid-rent function is relevant in the long run. If economic profits for a particular period of time are zero, total revenue minus total cost is zero:

$$p^*Q(x) = wE + v(x)L,$$

where w is the wage rate and v is the cost of using land for one time period. Note that v is assumed to be a function of x but w is not. The bid-rent function is derived by increasing distance to the central point, holding total revenue equal to total cost. This derivation is accomplished mathematically by considering a marginal change in x as follows:

$$p^* \left(\frac{\delta Q}{\delta x} \right) = L \left(\frac{\delta v}{\delta x} \right).$$

The firms therefore change their offer price for the use of land as distance to the central point increases according to

$$\frac{\delta v}{\delta x} = p^* \frac{(\delta Q/\delta x)}{L} < 0$$

Bid rent declines with distance to the central point because the productivity of the inputs declines with that distance (i.e., because $\delta Q/\delta x$ is less than zero from the discussion above).

The model in this appendix has demonstrated the following conclusion. If agglomeration economies at a central point enhance the productivity of the primary inputs, and if the effect of those agglomeration economies declines with distance to the central point, bid rent offered by the relevant industries also declines with distance to the central point. The industries that are relevant are, of course, the ones that benefit from the agglomeration economies. Is this a reasonable model? The model seems to be sensible in light of the discussion of agglomeration economies in Chapter 3, but the model needs to be tested empirically.

EXERCISES

1. Select an urban area of your choice and think about its downtown. What has happened to downtown retailing over the long run? Has downtown experienced much growth in office space since the 1970s? Does downtown have a business

association that tries to promote the use of downtown? If so, this group can be a useful source of information. Also, you can probably call up the local chamber of commerce to obtain some information on these questions. Also, think about the fringe, or outer ring, of downtown. What tends to locate just outside the downtown area proper? Does one find wholesale trade (e.g., fresh meat and produce) and light manufacturing along with old houses? What has been happening to these areas over time?

2. Select an urban area of your choice. Based on your knowledge of where things are, does it have employment subcenters? Where are they in relationship to downtown and to each other? Does the local airport create an agglomeration of employment that is large enough to be called an employment subcenter? Do the employment subcenters you have identified tend to specialize in any particular line of business? For example, is there an older manufacturing center, a newer center of corporate headquarters and research and development, a distribution center (trucking and warehousing), a health care center, and so on? Check Garreau (1991) to see if he included your urban area in his appendix where he lists the edge cities. How might you determine the locations of employment subcenters more systematically?

*3. Consider the economic model of employment density in Section D. Suppose that the production function for output is

$$Q = AR^\alpha E^\beta N^{1-\alpha-\beta}$$

and the production function for real estate is

$$R = BS^\mu L^{1-\mu}.$$

The parameter values are $\alpha = 0.2$, $\beta = 0.6$, and $\mu = 0.25$.

(a) Solve for the ratio of structure capital to land (S/L) as a function of their prices r and v.

(b) Solve for the ratio of employment to land (E/L)—employment density—as a function of their prices w and v.

(c) What interpretation can be attached to these results?

4. You have been given the task of estimating the market value of an office building, and you have been given the following information.

   • The building contains 150,000 square feet of rentable space, and the current market rent is $15 per square foot per year. The current vacancy rate is 10%.

   • Annual fixed expenses include real estate taxes of $350,000 and insurance of $250,000.

   • Annual operating expenses include repairs and maintenance of $100,000, utilities of $200,000, and a management fee of 5% of effective gross income. There are no tenant concessions.

   • The current capitalization rate for this type of building is 10%.

    (a) Estimate the potential gross income and the effective gross income. What assumptions are you making?

    (b) Compute the net operating income.

    (c) Estimate the market value of the building. What happens if the capitalization rate increases to 11%?

REFERENCES

Clapp, John, 1993. *Dynamics of Office Markets*. Washington, DC: The Urban Institute Press.

Garreau, Joel, 1991. *Edge City*. New York: Doubleday.

Giuliano, Genevieve and K. Small, 1991. "Subcenters in the Los Angeles Region," *Regional Science and Urban Economics*, Vol. 21, pp. 163–182.

Henderson, J. Vernon, 1986. "Efficiency of Resource Usage and City Size," *Journal of Urban Economics*, Vol. 19, pp. 47–70.

Hoover, Edgar and R. Vernon, 1959. *Anatomy of a Metropolis*. Cambridge, MA: Harvard University Press.

McDonald, John, 1975. "Some Causes of the Decline of Central Business District Retail Sales in Detroit," *Urban Studies*, Vol. 12, pp. 229–233.

———, 1987. "The Identification of Urban Employment Subcenters," *Journal of Urban Economics*, Vol. 21, pp. 242–258.

———, 1991. "Economic Update," *Chicago Office*, Vol. 1, pp. 6–9.

———, 1992. "Assessing the Development Status of Urban Areas," in E. Mills and J. McDonald, eds., *Sources of Metropolitan Growth*. New Brunswick, NJ: Center for Urban Policy Research, Rutgers University.

McDonald, John and D. McMillen, 1990. "Employment Subcenters and Land Values in a Polycentric Urban Area: The Case of Chicago," *Environment and Planning A*, Vol. 22, pp. 1561–1574.

McDonald, John and P. Prather, 1993. "Suburban Employment Centers: The Case of Chicago," *Urban Studies*, Vol. 31, pp. 201–218.

McMillen, Daniel and J. McDonald, 1990. "A Two-Limit Tobit Model of Suburban Land–Use Zoning," *Land Economics*, Vol. 66, pp. 272–282.

Noyelle, Thierry and Thomas Stanback, Jr., 1983. *The Economic Transformation of American Cities*. Totowa, NJ: Rowan & Allanheld.

Shilling, James, C. Sirmans, and J. Corgel, 1987. "Price Adjustment Process for Rental Office Space," *Journal of Urban Economics*, Vol. 22, pp. 90–100.

Sivitanidou, Rena, 1995. "Urban Spatial Variations in Office–Commercial Rents: The Role of Spatial Amenities and Commercial Zoning," *Journal of Urban Economics*, Vol. 38, pp. 23–49.

Webb, Brian and J. Fisher, 1996. "Development of an Effective Rent (Lease) Index for the Chicago CBD," *Journal of Urban Economics,* Vol. 39, pp. 1–19.

Wolfe, Tom, 1987. *The Bonfire of the Vanities*, New York: Farrar, Straus & Giroux.

CHAPTER

Urban
Transportation

A. INTRODUCTION

Transportation in an urban area is used to move both people and freight. Transportation is a service that is demanded by people because of a desire to pursue an activity at some other location. These activities include work, shopping, school, entertainment, and many more. Streets and highways, buses, rail rapid transit lines, and other facilities exist to transport people to their desired destinations. Freight transportation moves goods and services to a desired location. The movement of goods by rail or truck has been discussed in previous chapters, but other systems exist to transport natural gas, sewerage, electricity, telephone calls, water, and cable television signals. In other words, there are many demands for transportation and several transportation systems in an urban area. The focus of this chapter is largely on one type of trip, the trip to work by those employed outside the home. This choice is based on two reasons: (1) the trip to work is the most important trip the adult worker makes, and (2) trips to work are concentrated during the morning and afternoon rush hours, thus straining the capacity of the transportation system. Other types of trips are also made at rush hour (e.g., trips to school or for shopping and trips by trucks), and these are included in the discussion. However, the peaking of demand for transportation during the rush hours is driven primarily by the trips to and from work.

Much of the discussion in this chapter is devoted to the use of streets and roads by autos and trucks rather than public transportation or freight rail transportation. This focus is based on the overwhelming numbers of Americans who use the private auto (or truck or van) for the trip to work. Table 8.1 shows that, in 1990, 74.98% of trips to work in all metropolitan areas were made by a person driving alone. Another 13.23% of workers made the trip to work in a car pool, so 88.21% of all work trips were made by private automobile. All forms of public transportation accounted for 6.65% of trips to work, which was only slightly more than the 5.14% of work trips by miscellaneous methods (walking, motorcycle, and bicycle). These figures for 1990 represent some changes from 1980. In 1980, 66.9% of trips to work were by a person driving alone, and 18.5% made the trip in a car pool. All forms of public transportation represented 8.0% of work trips in 1980, so both carpooling and use of public

TABLE 8.1 Choice of Mode for Trips to Work, 1990						
	Total Workers Outside Home (thousands)	*Auto^a (%)*		*Public Transit (%)*		*Other^c (%)*
		Alone	*Car Pool*	*Rail*	*Bus and Other^b*	
All metro areas	89,146	74.98	13.23	2.61	4.04	5.14
CMSA^d						
New York	8,347	54.94	10.54	18.40	8.82	7.30
Los Angeles	6,623	74.38	15.88	.03	4.67	5.04
Chicago	3,760	68.88	12.21	6.70	7.23	4.98
San Francisco	3,089	70.77	13.47	2.91	6.70	6.15
Philadelphia	2,732	70.72	12.45	4.21	6.22	6.40
Washington, DC	2,151	64.81	16.23	6.88	7.16	4.92
Boston	2,088	71.89	10.54	5.60	5.32	6.65
Detroit	2,043	84.14	10.28	0.00	2.50	3.08
Dallas–Fort Worth	1,932	80.54	14.13	0.00	2.43	2.90
Houston	1,724	77.61	14.85	0.00	3.83	3.71

^a*Auto, truck, and van.*

^b*"Bus and other" includes bus, trolley, ferryboat, and taxi.*

^c*"Other" includes walking, motorcycle, bicycle, and any other.*

^d*"CMSA" stands for Consolidated Metropolitan Statistical Area.*

Source: Census of 1990, U.S. Bureau of the Census.

transit declined between 1980 and 1990. These trends should come as no surprise, since much of the employment growth during the decade was in the suburbs.

Not all metropolitan areas are alike, of course. Table 8.1 shows that only 54.94% of trips to work in the New York Consolidated Metropolitan Statistical Area were by workers driving alone. New York's subway and commuter rail systems provided transportation for 18.40% of the workers, and another 8.82% rode the bus, the Staten Island Ferry, or took a taxi. The use of public transportation by 27.22% of commuters in New York is, by far, the largest in the nation. Table 8.1 shows the top 10 urban areas in terms of employment, and the next-largest users of public transportation are the commuters of the Washington, DC (with 14.04%) and the Chicago (with 13.93%) metropolitan areas. Public transportation also has a sizable presence in San Francisco, Philadelphia, and Boston, but very little in Los Angeles, Detroit, Dallas–Fort Worth, and Houston. A subway system is under construction in Los Angeles, so the figures on commuting in Los Angeles should show some change in the 2000 census. Dallas–Fort Worth has what is perhaps the dubious distinction of having the largest percentage of auto commuters (94.67%, including carpoolers) among the top 10 urban areas. However, Detroit leads the pack with 84.14% of commuters who drive alone. Table 8.1 shows that there is more carpooling in Los Angeles, Washington, DC, Dallas–Fort Worth, and Houston than in the other top 10 urban areas. Can you think of any reasons for this outcome? One guess is that the absence of public transportation in Los Angeles, Dallas–Fort Worth, and Houston force more people to use car pools. Also, it may be that government workers in Washington, DC are strongly encouraged to carpool. [Note that "car pool" is now a thing, an activity (carpooling), a group of people (carpoolers, or maybe poolsters), and a verb (to carpool).] A cursory glance at the numbers in Table 8.1 certainly suggests that in most urban areas, carpooling makes the biggest contribution to reducing traffic. In any case, Table 8.1 provides ample justification for concentrating on autos and streets and highways.

The predominance of the auto for trips to work (and for most other purposes as well) is an overwhelming fact, but commuters will also tell you that traffic is getting worse. The recent book by Downs (1992) entitled *Stuck in Traffic* explains why traffic seems to be getting worse. The growth rate of population in the United States as a whole is not very great, but some urban areas, such as Los Angeles, Phoenix, Atlanta, and others in the sunbelt, have experienced big population increases. More population means more trips in the urban area. More important, employment, licensed drivers, and autos and trucks in use have all increased rapidly. In addition, those vehicles are driven more miles per year than before. According to Downs (1992, p. 13), population grew by 9.8% from 1980 to 1990, but the number of autos increased by 22.1%. In 1990 there were 76.5 registered vehicles per 100 people in the United States. These changes are coupled with a general failure to build new highways. Downs (1992, p. 11) notes that total highway mileage in the United States increased by only 0.6% from 1981 to 1989, a time period when autos and trucks increased by 24% and total vehicle miles driven jumped by 33.6%. Urban roads rather than high-performance highways are being built in the new suburbs but not at a rate that is fast enough to keep up with the drivers.

Traffic congestion is pretty bad and getting worse, so what can be done about it? This is the big question that is addressed in this chapter. However, you need to learn more about urban transportation before you can attempt to answer the question.

B. TRANSPORTATION AND URBAN LOCATION PATTERNS

The discussions so far in this book clearly suggest that transportation is a major force that shapes an urban area. The original cities in the United States began as ports, and the spatial patterns within those early cities around the port were determined by the rudimentary transportation methods of the early nineteenth century. The water and rail transportation revolution of the first half of the nineteenth century made large cities possible, and early rail systems also permitted cities to spread their growing populations over a wider area. Improvements in urban rail systems continued, but the shift to the truck and the automobile beginning roughly in 1920 was the truly revolutionary development in urban transportation.

As Table 8.1 shows, the system for moving people around an urban area is based mainly on the use of streets and highways by private automobiles. That system is supplemented by public transportation in the form of buses and, in a few larger urban areas, rail transit. The construction of commuter and freight rail lines once shaped urban areas. Now it is the highway system that shapes the urban area. However, urban areas have also been shaped by the change in the methods used to travel to destinations outside the urban area. The increased use of air transportation for both passengers and freight has made the airport a center of economic activity and has required the development of ground transportation facilities to serve the airport. The growth of trucking for interurban freight has meant a decline in demand for rail transportation. The construction of the highway system freed light manufacturers from locations near rail lines and permitted any location within reasonable proximity of a major highway to be a "point of export" for the urban area.

At the same time, it is not correct to regard urban highways and bus and transit systems as completely independent forces that act on an urban area. Transportation facilities are built in response to current or projected future demands. Sometimes transportation facilities have been built ahead of demand, but often, the construction of facilities is responding to demand forces that already exist. The construction of the urban expressway systems in the 1950s and 1960s was responding to a strong demand. Many people wished to live in suburban housing, but the lack of high-speed urban highways was preventing the fulfillment of this demand. Once those urban highways were constructed, the development of the suburbs was rapid. The era of massive urban highway construction is over. Now the construction of more urban highways is based more closely on existing demand—and costs, as well. The construction of public transportation facilities is also based on existing demand and careful projections of future demand. So it is true that urban transportation facilities are important in shaping an urban area and strongly influence land-use patterns and the total amount and spatial patterns of urban travel. But it is also true that changes in urban transportation facilities are determined partially by changes on the demand side. A broader perspective would recognize that urban transportation systems and urban land use and travel demands are interdependent and evolve together over time.

Another factor to consider in urban transportation is the independent influence of public policy that is formulated at the federal, state, and local levels. Large-scale highway or transit projects often become political issues in which many actors play a role. These actors may be motivated by a variety of goals, including political power. Some political actors are swayed by a particular constituency with a special interest. At other times local transportation policy is strongly influenced by budget and policy decisions that have been made by Congress and the president with little regard for local conditions and problems. Urban transportation policy would appear to be fertile ground for study by the conservative economists of the Chicago School of Political Economy, the people who enjoy uncovering the real motivations for particularly inefficient or inequitable policy decisions.

It was noted in the introduction to this chapter that both the demand and supply of transportation in an urban area are extremely complicated. Transportation analysts have made progress by breaking the general problem into smaller pieces and formulating models specific to each of those pieces. Models of the demand side are considered first.

C. DEMAND FOR TRANSPORTATION IN URBAN AREAS

One approach to the demand for transportation in an urban area would be to try to explain the total amount of travel demanded in an urban area in a period of time such as a typical weekday. The total amount of travel demanded would be measured as the total number of miles traveled during the day. The researcher might gather data on a sample of urban areas and suppose that total travel demand is a function of total population, average household income, age composition of the population, number of people who work, and perhaps some other variables. For example, one might wish to include variables that describe the location patterns of the urban area and the nature of the transportation system that is available. As a matter of fact, no one has used this approach to study the total demand for urban transportation. As Small (1992) discussed, several researchers have used this kind of approach to study the demand for public transportation in urban areas. But this aggregative approach has otherwise not been considered fruitful for the study of travel demand. The reasons are not difficult to determine, and they include the following:

1. It is not clear how to measure the "price" of travel in this context.
2. From a transportation planning standpoint, it is more important to know the demand for travel during the times of day when demand reaches its peaks.
3. Also from a transportation planning standpoint, one needs to know the locations of the peak demands.

The study of the demand for transportation is usually undertaken in an individual urban area. The urban area is broken down into a set of small geographic zones. It is assumed that the location patterns by geographic zone of houses, jobs, and shopping opportunities, as well as other possible trip destinations, are fixed. Travel demand analysis is then broken down into four steps. The first step is to study the generation of trips by a geographic zone during a particular time of day (e.g., the morning rush hour). Each zone is both an origin for trips and a destination for trips. The end of the first phase of the analysis yields models that explain (or predict) the number of trips that originate in a zone and the number of trips that have a zone as destination. Table 8.2 shows an urban area that consists of five geographic zones, each of which is both an origin and a destination of trips. The five zones as origins are displayed across the top of the table, and the fives zones as destinations are listed down the left-hand side of the table. The models from phase 1 of a transportation study will indicate the number of trips with zone A (and B, C, D, and E) as origin, and they will also predict how many trips will have each zone as a destination. The number of trips with zone A as origin during the morning rush hour, 100, is shown in the row labeled "column sum." The number of trips with zone A as destination, 90, is shown in the column labeled "row sum."

TABLE 8.2 Origins and Destinations of Trips in an Urban Area

Destination Zone	Origin Zone					Row Sum
	A	B	C	D	E	
A	T_{aa}	T_{ab}	T_{ac}	T_{ad}	T_{ae}	90
B	20 (15 auto)	T_{bb}	T_{bc}	T_{bd}	T_{be}	D_b
C	T_{ca}	T_{cb}	T_{cc}	T_{cd}	T_{ce}	D_c
D	T_{da}	T_{db}	T_{dc}	T_{dd}	T_{de}	D_d
E	T_{ea}	T_{eb}	T_{ec}	T_{ed}	T_{ee}	D_e
COLUMN SUM	100	O_b	O_c	O_d	O_e	ΣT

The second phase of a travel demand study, known as *trip distribution analysis*, is to fill in the elements of Table 8.2 by modeling how the trips from each origin are distributed to the various destinations. We know that there are 100 trips with zone A as origin, but how many of those trips are taken to each possible destination? The third step is to assign to a particular means of travel the trips that are taken from an origin zone to a destination zone. The means of travel are auto, bus, walking, and so on. This phase is known as *mode split analysis*. Given that 20 trips are taken from origin A to destination B, how many are taken by auto? The fourth and final step in the analysis is to assign the trips to a specific route in the transportation network. This step is known as *trip assignment*. Given that 15 trips are taken *by auto* from origin A to destination B, which routes will be used, and how many trips will be taken on each of these routes? Finally, a more complex analysis would involve all four of these steps for each *type* of trip: trips to work, trips for shopping, and truck trips. There would therefore be a table such as Table 8.2 and a set of demand models for each type of trip. Furthermore, the analysis might focus separately on the various particular times of day, such as the morning rush hour. The models that transportation economists have developed for each phase of the analysis are discussed in turn. The section concludes with a discussion of the concentration of demand in peak periods of the day.

Trip-Generation Models

Given that there are so many housing units located in zone A, how many trips to work will be generated by zone A? The answer depends upon several factors. Given the nature of the housing stock, what sorts of people will live in zone A, and what are their propensities to work? How accessible is zone A to employment? A study of trip generation will examine these questions. One approach is to formulate a model of bid rent for housing for each of several demographic groups and to assign them to housing and locations on the basis of their bids. Models of this type were discussed in Chapter 5. Also, how many trips will have zone A as destination? How many jobs are located in zone A? What sort of shopping opportunities are available in zone A, and how do they influence shopping trips? Data gathered on travel origins and destinations by type of trip, along with demographic and housing and commercial information on the zones, will permit the analyst to estimate models of trip generation along the lines suggested here. Transportation studies normally begin with a survey of travel behavior that can be used to estimate trip generation models. The Census of Population that is taken every 10 years includes (for a sample of households) information on the journey to work by each household member who is employed. This source is now widely used by local transportation planning agencies for statistical studies of travel demand for the journey to work.

Trip-Distribution Models

Given that the column and row totals in Table 8.2 are understood, how are the trips from zone A (B, C, D, and E) distributed among the possible destinations? Furthermore, how can it be assured that the trips distributed to a particular destination add up to the total number of trips to that destination? The model that is used to perform this complicated task is called the doubly constrained gravity model. The idea of a gravity model is explained first, and then the nature of the double constraint is examined.

The gravity model of spatial interaction says that the number of trips taken from origin i to destination j increases with the number of trips with origin at zone i and with the number of trips with zone j as destination. A greater number of trips originating in zone i will result in more trips being taken to zone j. A greater number of trips with zone j as destination will mean that this zone is more attractive as a destination and will therefore attract more trips from zone i. Also, the number of trips from i to j will depend on the cost of the trip, which is often measured as the distance from i to j. The simple "unconstrained" gravity model in mathematical form is

$$T_{ij} = \frac{O_i^\alpha D_j^\beta}{(d_{ij})^\tau},$$

where T_{ij} is the number of trips taken from i to j, O_i the number of trips with i as origin, D_j the number of trips with j as destination, and d_{ij} the distance (cost of travel) from i to j. The model is analogous to Newton's law of gravitational force between two bodies, especially if the distance variable appears in the denominator with an exponent of 2. In logarithmic form the model is

$$\log T_{ij} = \alpha \log O_i + \beta \log D_j + \tau \log d_{ij}.$$

In addition to urban travel, gravity models of this type are used to model spatial interactions of various kinds, such as population migration, air passenger travel, international trade, and financial flows. This simple model will usually yield a high level of explanatory power in statistical terms.

The unconstrained gravity model in the preceding paragraph provides no guarantee that the columns and rows in Table 8.2 will add up properly to the column and row totals. There are two types of constraints that must be satisfied simultaneously. First, the total number of trips with zone i as origin must be equal to the sum across destinations of the trips with zone i as origin. In other words, the numbers entered in the columns of Table 8.2 must add up to the column sums. Second, the total number of trips with zone j as destination must equal the sum across origins of trips with zone j as destination. The numbers entered in the rows of Table 8.2 must add to the row sums. Those who would forecast travel demand by origin and destination zone must make sure that their forecasts are consistent, and the doubly constrained gravity model provides that consistency. The doubly constrained gravity model is of the form

$$T_{ij} = \frac{ABO_i^\alpha D_j^\beta}{d_{ij}^\tau},$$

where A and B are balancing factors that ensure that the two constraints are satisfied. Computational procedures exist to find A and B, but these computations are not based on economic analysis and are too complex to be discussed here.

The gravity model is probably not part of the standard tool kit of economists in general, but it is an important method in urban and regional economics and in transportation planning. As Niedercorn and Bechdolt (1969) first demonstrated, the gravity model has a basis in conventional microeconomic theory. Consider the three variables in the model. First, the distance variable (d_{ij}) is a proxy for the cost of traveling from zone i to zone j, so this is just the price of the trip. Modern versions of the gravity model include careful measures of the price of the trip, which includes both money and time. Also, the more sophisticated models make the price of the trip a function of the amount of traffic that uses each particular route to capture the cost of traffic congestion. Second, the total number of trips with zone j as destination (D_j) is a measure of the "attractiveness" of that destination. Niedercorn and Bechdolt suggested that D_j is a measure of the utility one derives from traveling to zone j. Finally, the total number of trips with zone i as origin (O_i) measures the scale of the demand for T_{ij}. It plays a role that is similar to the total number of households in conventional market demand analysis.

There is one theoretical weakness in the gravity model interpreted as a microeconomic model of trip distribution. The only "price" term that appears in the gravity model is the price of travel from origin i to destination j. The price of traveling to any other destination is not included. You learned in basic microeconomic theory that the demand for a good is a function of its price, income, the nature of preferences, and *the prices of other goods*. The price of *every* other good is not relevant, but the prices of goods that are close substitutes and complements can be important influences on the demand for a particular good. Urban transportation researchers who use the gravity model have essentially ignored this problem, although some have formulated what they call an *intervening opportunities model*. Such a model modifies the demand for trips from i to j to account for opportunities that are encountered along the way from i to j. An item that ought to be on the future research agenda is an investigation of which *prices* of trips to *other* destinations are important enough to include in the model. One destination that immediately comes to mind in this context is the central business district.

Mode Split Analysis

Given that a certain number of trips is being taken from origin i to destination j, how are those trips divided among the modes of travel? One approach to this problem is to gather data on actual urban travel patterns as shown in Table 8.2, including the number of trips taken between each pair of origins and destinations by each mode of travel. One would then estimate a model of the proportion of trips made using each mode as a function of the features of each mode. For example, suppose that there are just two modes: private auto and bus. What proportion of trips is taken by private auto? One approach is to make this proportion a linear function of the difference in money costs and time costs between the private auto and the bus. The *differences* in costs are relevant because the choice under study is which mode to use, not whether to make the trip in the first place. In equation form,

$$P_{ija} = \frac{T_{ija}}{T_{ij}} = b_0 + b_1 (t_a - t_b) + b_2 (m_a - m_b),$$

where P_{ija} is the proportion of trips from i to j on mode a (auto), t_a and t_b the time costs of auto and bus, respectively, for trip from zone i to zone j, and m_a and m_b = money costs of auto and bus, respectively, for trip from zone i to zone j. The signs of both b_1 and b_2 are negative because increases in time or money costs for a mode reduce the proportion of travelers who make that choice. The constant term in the equation, b_0, should be 0.50 because if the two modes have equal time and money costs, the choice between them is arbitrary, like flipping a coin.

This linear model is easy to understand and to estimate, but it has one major difficulty. The dependent variable is a proportion that is, of course, a number that cannot be less than zero or greater than 1. The linear model is not restricted to the zero–one interval, so it can produce forecasts that are negative numbers or numbers that are greater than 1. The solution to this problem that has been adopted by transportation analysts is to specify a model of mode choice that is inherently restricted to the zero–one interval. The most popular version of such a model is called the *logistic transformation*, which is written

$$\ln \left(\frac{P_{ijk}}{1 - P_{ijk}} \right) = \alpha_0 + \alpha_1 (t_a - t_b) + \alpha_2 (m_a - m_b).$$

The dependent variable is the natural logarithm of P_{ijk} divided by $(1 - P_{ijk})$, and the model can be estimated as a linear function. How does this model restrict forecasts to the zero–one interval? To see this, first simplify the notation by writing

$$z = \alpha_0 + \alpha_1 (t_a - t_b) + \alpha_2 (m_a - m_b) \quad \text{and} \quad P_{ijk} = P.$$

Now we have

$$\ln \left(\frac{P}{1 - P} \right) = z.$$

The next step is to convert to the exponential form, which is

$$\left(\frac{P}{1 - P} \right) = e^z,$$

where e is the base of the natural logarithms. This equation is solved for P as follows:

$$P = e^z (1 - P),$$

$$P + Pe^z = e^z,$$

$$P = \frac{e^z}{1 + e^z}.$$

Clearly, P can never be zero or less because e raised to any exponent z is a positive number. P can never be 1 or more because e^z is divided by $1 + e^z$. The shape of the logistic function is shown in Figure 8.1. The proportion P approaches 1 as z goes to positive infinity, and P approaches zero as z goes to negative infinity. As shown in Figure 8.1, when $z = 0$, $P = 0.5$. To see this last result, set

$$P = 0.5 = \frac{e^z}{1 + e^z},$$

so

$$1 + e^z = 2e^z \quad \text{and} \quad 1 = e^z,$$

so that

$$z = 0.$$

The natural logarithm of e^z is z, and the natural log of 1 is zero.

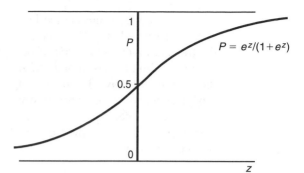

FIGURE 8.1 Logistic curve

Models of this type have been used extensively in transportation analysis, but actual applications of the model normally include more than two independent variables. For example, empirical findings have demonstrated that it is important to divide the time cost into its walking-, waiting-, and actual travel-time components. The proportion of people who choose the bus is strongly influenced by the amount of time spent walking to the bus stop and by the amount of time spent waiting for the bus to arrive and waiting to transfer from one bus to another. The studies show clearly that urban commuters are willing to pay more if the bus can be made more convenient by cutting down on walking and waiting time.

Route-Choice Analysis and the Value of Time

The final step in the analysis of urban travel demand is to model the choice of route given that a particular mode has been chosen. (Do you know the way from i to j?) In the model of mode choice discussed above it was assumed implicitly that there was only one route for each mode. The measures of time and money cost are taken from that one route. This procedure is accurate also if alternative routes for the same mode have identical costs. This is often a reasonable assumption. However, there are situations in which the routes that might be chosen have quite different time and money costs. For example, in some places auto drivers have a choice of using a tollway or a free road. The tollway has a higher money cost and, because of the toll, will usually enable the traveler to save some time compared to the free road. In other instances, bus riders may have a choice of an express bus with a higher fare that will drive on a limited-access highway versus the usual bus service on city streets with a lower fare. It is important for urban transportation policy to know how commuters make these choices.

Consider the choice of tollway versus free road. The same sort of logistic transformation model can be used in this situation, or

$$\ln\left(\frac{P_i}{P_f}\right) = \beta_0 + \beta_1(t_i - t_f) + \beta_2(m_i - m_f),$$

where P_i is the proportion taking the tollway and P_f is the proportion taking the free road. The signs of β_1 and β_2 are negative in this model as well because increases in the time or money cost of a route will reduce the proportion of people who choose it.

A model of route choice has the usual roles of explaining and forecasting the choice of route, but it also has another very important implication. Improvements in the transportation system are of benefit to people chiefly because of time saved. People are willing to pay money to save time in their urban travel, but how much are they willing to pay? If this willingness to pay were known, benefits expressed in monetary terms can be compared to construction and land costs. The model for route choice does indeed provide an estimate of the money value of travel time saved. Consider variations in the time- and money-cost differences in the model that leave the proportion who choose the tollway *constant*. In equation form

$$\delta \ln \left(\frac{P_i}{P_f} \right) = 0 = \beta_1 \delta \ (t_i - t_f) + \beta_2 \delta \ (m_i - m_f).$$

This equation says that the combinations of changes in time- and money-cost differences leave the commuters as a group indifferent to those combinations because the proportion who choose the tollway does not change. This equation can be rewritten as the value of a reduction in travel time, or

$$\frac{-\delta \ (m_i - m_f)}{\delta \ (t_i - t_f)} = \frac{\beta_1}{\beta_2},$$

which is a number greater than zero. The ratio of coefficients β_1/β_2 equals the value of a reduction in travel time because it is -1 times the change in money cost that just compensates for a reduction in travel time. If $\delta \ (t_i - t_f)$ is a negative number, $\delta(m_i - m_f)$ must be a positive number to keep constant the proportion who choose the tollway—hence the multiplication by -1.

Studies of mode choice also produce estimates of the value of travel time saved because mode-choice studies also produce the coefficients on time- and money-cost differences. However, the studies of route choice provide a cleaner look at the value of time saved because mode choice can be influenced by the features of modes of travel that are not easy to measure and include in the model. The choice of private auto versus bus involves the fact that the bus can be crowded with other people who are noisy. On the other hand, the traveler does not have to drive the bus. The choice of route for the same mode is not complicated by such factors.

A very large number of studies has produced estimates of the value of travel time saved. A book by Bruzelius (1979) provides a survey of some of those studies. The value of travel time saved for the trip to work has been estimated to be 20 to 100% of the after-tax wage rate of the commuter. The average of these estimates is approximately 50% of the after–tax wage. However, studies suggest that the value of commuting time saved does not rise proportionately with income. Also, there is evidence that commuters are willing to pay more to save time if they have longer commuting trips. In other words, the commuter who travels 45 minutes each way is willing to pay more to save 10 minutes than is the commuter who travels 30 minutes each way. This finding is consistent with the usual hypothesis in microeconomics of a declining marginal utility of a good, which is leisure time (or sleeping time) in this case. A longer commute means less time for leisure and therefore a higher value for additional leisure.

Concentration of Demand in Peak Periods

The discussion of urban travel demand concludes with a more detailed consideration of peak-load demand. As emphasized in Section A, the demand for urban travel is greatest in the morning and afternoon rush hours because most work trips occur during these times. Trips to school also peak during these times, but other types of trips (such as shopping, delivery, and trucking for freight) do not have peak demand periods that are as pronounced. Traffic in urban areas on weekday mornings normally starts to build between 6 and 7 A.M. and peaks between 8 and 9 A.M. Traffic drops off sharply after that because few workers have a starting time later than 9 A.M. The afternoon peak period starts building between 3 and 4 P.M., reaches the peak around 5 P.M., and drops off sharply as commuters reach their homes.

It was also noted in the introduction to this chapter that in recent decades the total amount of travel, especially by auto, has grown much more rapidly than has the road and highway system. One implication of this growth in demand is that the rush-hour period has become longer. It is clear that some people choose to leave for work early, and in some cases employers have altered their schedules to permit employees to try to "beat the traffic." Hill, Tittlemore, and Gendell (1973) showed that urban areas in the United States with lower highway capacities compared to traffic volumes have longer rush hours. Also, there is evidence that improvements in the urban transportation system lead to a shortening of the rush hour. For example, Sherret (1975) showed that the opening of a mass transit line in San Francisco diverted 8750 auto trips to transit during the rush hour but that additional auto trips were taken during the rush hour, so that peak-period traffic levels declined very little. It is clear that a model of urban travel demand should include the fact that for at least some people, the time of travel is flexible to some degree.

Two types of models have been developed to address the issue of flexible travel times. The older type of model is a set of conventional demand functions, with a demand function specified for each period during the day. Suppose that the task is to model the demand for travel between origin zone i and destination zone j. The model might break the day into six periods as follows;

1. Early portion of morning rush hour (6 to 7:30 A.M.),
2. Peak period of morning rush hour (7:30 to 9 A.M.),
3. Middle of day (9 A.M. to 3 P.M.),
4. Early portion of afternoon rush hour (3 to 4 P.M.),
5. Peak of afternoon rush hour (4 to 6:30 P.M.), and
6. Evening to early morning (6:30 P.M. to 6 A.M.).

Each period has its own demand function in which travel during that period is a function of the price during that period and the prices in the adjacent periods. In equation form,

$$T_{ijk} = f(P_k, P_{k-1}, P_{k+1}),$$

where the subscript k refers to the time period in question, P refers to the price of travel (time and money combined), and the subscripts $k-1$ and $k+1$ refer to the time periods before and after time period k. The adjacent time periods are viewed as substitutes for the time period in question, so reducing the price in either time period will reduce T_{ijk}. For example, an improvement in a highway will reduce travel times during the peak of the rush hour, increase traffic during the rush hour, and reduce traffic during the adjacent periods. More empirical research is needed to determine the magnitudes of these "cross-price" effects (i.e., the cross-elasticities of demand).

The second approach has been developed more recently, and it makes the time of departure for the trip a continuous variable. This type of model is discussed extensively in the urban transportation economics textbook by Small (1992). The model is based on the assumption that a cost is imposed on a person who arrives at a time other than the "desired" time. Work begins at 9 A.M. Early arrival means that there is some time spent at work that is neither as productive as regular working hours nor as pleasurable as leisure time at home. This cost of early arrival is a function of the amount of time spent in this state of limbo. The penalty for early arrival at work may not be very much, but the penalty for late arrival can be sizable. The worker can lose pay and, ultimately, be fired for lateness. The model assumes that this penalty for lateness is also a function of how late one arrives. In some cases it is reasonable to suppose that there is a lump-sum penalty for being late at all, and a further penalty that depends on the degree of lateness. *Schedule delay* is the general term that is used to refer to amount of time by which these early and late arrivals do not correspond to the desired time.

Here is the problem confronted by commuters in the schedule delay model. Commuters know the function that describes the cost of being early and being late. Commuters also know that the time spent to make the trip to work will be shorter if they avoid the peak of the rush hour. They can decide to go early, reduce travel time, and arrive early. Or they can decide to go late, reduce travel time, and arrive late. They make the choice of departure time based on a balancing of these two costs: the time cost of travel versus the cost of schedule delay. It would seem that more people decide to arrive at work early than choose to arrive late, so consider the choice of departure time for the early bird. Figure 8.2a shows the cost of the commuting trip as a function of departure time. The cost is converted into money by using the value of travel time as discussed above. The function labeled "trip cost" rises as departure time gets later because of peak-period traffic. The other curve in Figure 8.2a is labeled schedule delay cost, and this cost declines as departure time is later because a later departure time means less time spent at the workplace prior to the actual beginning of the workday. Of course, if departure time gets too late, the worker is late for work. This case is not depicted on Figure 8.2.

Figure 8.2b depicts the marginal cost and the marginal benefit for the early bird of increasing departure time by 1 minute. The marginal cost (MC) is the increase in travel time cost if one departs 1 minute later, and marginal benefit (MB) is the reduction in schedule delay cost from delaying departure by 1 minute. The commuter determines departure time by equating marginal cost and marginal benefit. Departure time H is the point at which the marginal cost of delaying departure is just equal to the marginal benefit of delaying departure. Shifts in the marginal cost or marginal benefit function will change the departure time. For example, suppose that new devices are installed to coordinate the timing of the traffic lights. This improvement will increase driving speed and therefore reduce the travel-time costs. As an exercise, use the model in Figure 8.2 to show how the commuter depicted will now depart later. (*Hint:* Be careful to show that the marginal cost of delaying departure *declines*.)

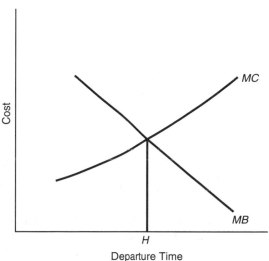

FIGURE 8.2 Optimal departure time

D. THE SUPPLY OF TRANSPORTATION IN URBAN AREAS

Trips taken by persons, as opposed to freight, are partly supplied by the very person who demands the trip. You supply the time needed to get to the desired destination. Private firms supply the auto and the gasoline that you use, and the government supplies the streets and highways (and traffic lights). There is a school of thought based on a famous article by Becker (1965) that argues that many, if not all, consumer goods have this feature. All goods and services require some time for their use, so all consumption decisions are also decisions regarding the allocation of time. This line of thinking leads to important insights into the demand for such things as dishwashers, frozen dinners, microwave ovens, and a host of other products that save time. In the case of urban transportation, the use of time by the traveler is central to the analysis. This discussion of supply begins with the short run and then turns to the long run. This section is devoted to the supply of travel by private vehicles on streets and highways. We examine public transportation in the following section.

Supply in the Short Run

As you know from basic microeconomics, the short run is the time period in which one of the basic inputs is fixed. In the case of auto and truck travel in urban areas, the fixed input is the capital stock supplied by the public sector: the streets and highways. The supply of travel in urban areas can be modeled using the production function, which is a standard tool in economics. To characterize what happens on urban highways as a production function, it is necessary first to identify the output of the highway. Quantity of highway travel Q is measured by a physical distance (i.e., total miles traveled). On a given highway it is normal to record traffic volume V, traffic density D, and average speed S. Traffic volume is measured in vehicles per unit of time (i.e., vehicles per hour passing a particular point), while traffic density is the number of vehicles per unit of distance if a photograph were to be taken of the highway. For example, the photo shows that there were 50 cars per mile. Average speed is measured in units of distance per unit of time (e.g., miles per hour). In common usage V is normally referred to as *flow*. However, actually it is speed that measures the miles of travel produced per unit of time by an individual driver. This measure of output, miles per hour, is the same as any output measure in the sense that it is a quantity of output per unit of time. General Motors produced 4 million cars last year (4 million cars per year). You produced 35 miles of travel in an hour by driving at an average speed of 35 mph.

   To establish the basic ideas, consider a road of fixed length and a time period of fixed duration. With no loss of generality, choose the units of distance and time such that both are 1 (1 mile and 1 hour). Assume that the highway is in a steady state over this unit of time, so that V, D, and S are constant. It is helpful to imagine that the highway has only one lane and is a circle 1 mile in circumference. Traffic density is the number of cars on the highway (i.e., the racetrack) at each point in time, so the total quantity of travel produced and consumed during 1 hour is

$$Q = DS = V.$$

Each car on the circular highway of unit length will pass a given point on the circle S times per hour; if $S = 35$ mph, each car passes the "finish line" 35 times per hour. If there are 50 cars on the highway, $35 \times 50 = 1750$ cars pass the finish line each hour, and 1750 miles are traveled per hour as well. The total quantity of travel Q is thus $DS = V$, which is the total number of vehicles that pass a given point on the circle each hour. This establishes the numerical identity between Q per unit of time and V. The assumption that the highway is a circle of unit length can be dropped. If a highway is in a steady state (with D, S, and V constant), the $V = DS$ cars that pass a given point per hour are all different cars.

   The key to converting this analysis into the conventional economics of production is to recognize that traffic density D is numerically equal to the time supplied by the driver and the vehicle, which is the variable input. Here it is assumed that the operating costs of the vehicle are a function of the amount of *time* the vehicle is in operation. The critical insight is that speed is the inverse of average variable cost *measured in units of time*. If speed is 35 mph, the average variable cost measured in units of driver and vehicle time is 0.0286 hour per mile. Recall that the output of the highway is volume. Thus average variable cost (*AVC*) in units of time is written

$$AVC = \frac{1}{S} = \frac{D}{V}.$$

Total variable costs (*VC*) in units of time are

$$VC = (AVC)V = D.$$

The total variable input measured in units of time is thus equal to traffic density. Go back to the example of the 1-mile circular road with 50 cars each traveling at 35 mph. The variable cost of producing the 1750 miles of travel in an hour is 50 hours of driver and vehicle time. This is the standard way to measure inputs—hours of labor and machine time. Variable cost can be converted to monetary units by using a value of driver time and the cost of operating a vehicle for an hour, but this conversion is not needed for the production function interpretation of the model. What is the shape of the short-run production function?

Highway engineers and other transportation researchers are familiar with the *fundamental diagram of traffic*, which relates traffic volume and traffic density for a given highway facility. Figure 8.3 shows that the traffic volume increases with traffic density up to the capacity of the facility and declines with further increases in density. The empirical relationship has been confirmed by numerous studies, one of which is discussed below. Given the definition of the variable input, the fundamental diagram of traffic (Figure 8.3) can be interpreted as a short-run production function in which output is related to the variable input. As shown in Figure 8.4, the average and marginal product curves for the variable input can be derived from this short-run production function. The average product of the variable input (driver and vehicle time) is simply average speed; $S = V/D$. The marginal product of the variable input

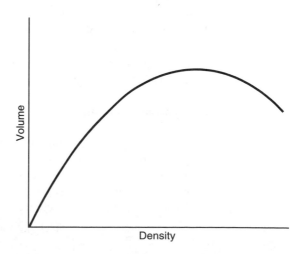

FIGURE 8.3 Fundamental diagram of traffic

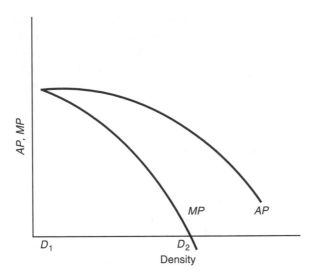

FIGURE 8.4 Average and marginal products of the variable input

falls to zero at the density corresponding to the capacity of the highway and is negative at higher densities.

Students of microeconomic theory learn this basic theory of production in the short run; as successive units of a variable input are added to a fixed input, the marginal product of the variable input starts to decline at some point and can possibly become negative if too much variable input is used. Students are also taught that no rational firm would hire units of the variable input with a negative marginal product. Those additional units of the variable input *reduce* total output. However, in the case of highway traffic, it is common to observe a highway operating in the region of negative marginal product. How is this possible? This situation arises because traffic flow is a classic example of a congestion externality in which there is no rational being present to prevent the addition of drivers and vehicles beyond the point at which marginal product is zero.

Traffic congestion is especially awful if the marginal product of the variable input is negative, but there is also the standard notion of traffic congestion. The normal idea of the traffic congestion externality corresponds to the portion of the short-run production function in which the average product of the variable input is declining and its marginal product is greater than zero. This portion of the short-run production function is shown in Figure 8.4 between traffic density levels D_1 and D_2. At low density levels (below D_1) the addition of more cars does not cause the average product (average speed) to fall, but beyond D_1 more cars on the highway will cause average speed to drop.

One study of traffic volume and density by Boardman and Lave (1977) estimated the short-run production function depicted in Figure 8.3 for a two−lane limited-access highway in the Washington, DC area on a day in 1968. Traffic volume is measured in vehicles in two lanes per hour, and density is vehicles per mile in the two lanes. The estimated function is

$$V = 2882 + 21.73D - 0.052D^2,$$

and the three regression coefficients are all highly statistically significant. The point at which volume reached its maximum can be found by computing

$$\frac{\delta V}{\delta D} = 21.73 - 0.104D = 0.$$

The solution for D is 209, which means that traffic volume was at a maximum when traffic density was 104.5 vehicles per lane per mile. At $D = 209$, $V = 5153$, or 2576.5 vehicles per lane per hour. This empirical estimate of the maximum traffic volume per lane per hour is greater than the 2000 figure that is often used as a rule of thumb by traffic experts. Traffic density of 104.5 vehicles per mile means that each vehicle is allocated 50.5 feet of roadway. If the average car is 20 feet long, the cars are separated by about 1.5 car lengths (30 feet). Average speed can also be computed at the point of maximum traffic volume. Recall that $S = V/D$, so $S = 24.7$ mph. So there you have it. If traffic density on the expressway is so high that cars are separated by less than 30 feet and if the average speed is less than 25 mph, you are probably in the region of negative marginal product. You are now better informed. Does this information make you feel better when you are in a traffic jam? You are invited to take some perverse pleasure in announcing these facts to your companions in the auto.

Why does average speed fall as traffic density rises? Traffic engineers have complex mathematical theories of road traffic flow that explain this phenomenon. One of those theories is called the "follow the leader" model. In this model drivers react to events that happen in front of them so as to avoid accidents. For example, if a driver in fairly heavy traffic slows down slightly, the following driver will slow down by *slightly more* than the first. The third driver will slow down even more, and so on. Those of you who have driven on an expressway in a major urban area have probably experienced a "rubbernecking" delay. Something worth observing, such as an accident on the other side of the highway, diverts the attention of drivers at some point. Drivers slow down slightly to look at the accident. Drivers in the chain of traffic overreact slightly to the driver in front, and at some point back in the chain of traffic, someone actually has to come to a complete stop. The impact of a rubbernecking delay on average speed is greater the higher is the density of traffic.

Another theory of road traffic flow is based on the safety rules that drivers are taught in driver's education. One is taught that the safe interval between cars on the expressway is larger at higher speeds. One fairly conservative rule of thumb is that the safe interval is one car length for each 10 mph. If people are following this rule, an increase in traffic density will reduce the interval between cars and cause speed to drop. Normal drivers are not like racing drivers (we hope); they will not drive at the speed limit in bumper-to-bumper traffic conditions.

In standard microeconomic theory the short-run production function is converted into a set of short-run cost curves, and this conversion can be done for highway traffic volume as well. Recall that average variable cost, in terms of time, is the inverse of average speed, which in turn is the average product of the variable input. Therefore, the average variable cost curve can be found as

$$AVC = \frac{1}{S} = \frac{1}{\text{average product}},$$

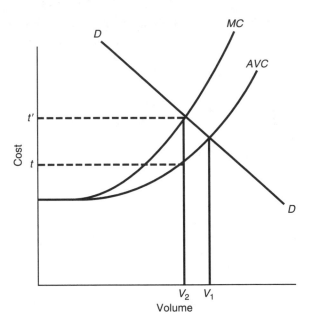

FIGURE 8.5 Cost and traffic volume

which is plotted as a function of output (traffic volume). This cost curve is shown in Figure 8.5. At low levels of traffic volume, average speed is constant (at the speed limit, presumably) and average cost is constant. As traffic volume rises, average speed falls and average cost rises. Marginal cost in the short run is defined as the change in total cost as output increases by 1 unit, or

$$MC = \frac{\delta VC}{\delta V} = \frac{\delta(AVC \times V)}{\delta V}.$$

This marginal change consists of two parts, so that

$$MC = AVC + V\left(\frac{\delta AVC}{\delta V}\right).$$

This is a crucial result; it says that the marginal cost of output (traffic volume) is equal to average variable cost *plus* the change in average cost with respect to traffic volume times the traffic volume. Average variable cost rises as traffic volume rises, and this increase in cost (arising from the drop in speed) is multiplied by the total traffic volume. This term is the difference between *AVC* and *MC*, or

$$MC - AVC = V\left(\frac{\delta AVC}{\delta V}\right).$$

The marginal cost curve is also plotted on Figure 8.5.

Now consider the external cost involved in traffic congestion. An external cost involves a cost that is imposed directly on others by, in this case, an individual traveler. An increase in traffic volume has a cost equal to the marginal cost shown above, but the individual traveler does not pay all of that cost. In fact, the individual traveler makes the trip at average variable cost (i.e., at the inverse of average speed). That is the cost that the traveler sees and is the price that the traveler uses to make the decision whether to travel on that highway at that time. The external cost is therefore the difference between marginal cost and average variable cost, or

$$\text{external cost} = V \left(\frac{\delta AVC}{\delta V} \right).$$

The external cost is the increase in cost imposed on each traveler ($\delta AVC/\delta V$) times the number of travelers (V).

Pricing in the Short Run

The demand for trips on the highway during the time period in question is also shown on Figure 8.5 as *DD*. Quantity demanded is expressed as a function of the cost of the trip that must be borne by the individual traveler, and that cost is expressed in units of time. Left to their own devices, travelers as a group will generate a traffic volume of V_1, where the demand curve intersects the average variable cost curve. At this point the marginal benefit of the trip, as measured by the height of the demand curve at V_1, is just equal to the cost borne by the last traveler, which is *AVC* at volume V_1.

You can see immediately that V_1 is an inefficient level of output because the *marginal cost* of the last unit of output exceeds its marginal benefit (*MB*). In fact, the marginal cost exceeds the marginal benefit by the size of the external cost, or

$$MC - MB = MC - AVC = V \left(\frac{\delta AVC}{\delta V} \right).$$

The efficient level of output in Figure 8.5 is V_2, where the marginal benefit of the output equals the marginal cost, which includes the externality. It is pretty obvious that the street and highway systems in urban areas are being used in this inefficient manner during the morning and afternoon rush hours. Is anything being done to cut back on traffic and use the system efficiently? The short answer is that virtually nothing is being done at this time. However, for many years urban economists have advocated the use of tolls to cut back on traffic congestion. A toll equal to the external cost *at efficient traffic volume* V_2 in Figure 8.5 would make the cost borne by the marginal traveler equal to the true marginal cost of the trip. This toll is shown as amount *tt'*, which is expressed in units of time. An actual toll would be collected as money, so the units of time have to be converted to monetary units. Toll *tt'* is an efficient toll provided that the travelers who are induced not to use the highway at the time in question do *not* create more traffic congestion at some other location, and provided that the collection of the toll can be accomplished costlessly.

Consider first the actual collection of tolls. Conventional toll booths create traffic jams of their own, so this method cannot be used. However, methods do exist that can probably be made to work well on a large scale. In one system, *automatic vehicle identification* (AVI), each vehicle carries an electronic transponder. An electronic transponder is a device that transmits an identifying signal automatically when it receives a signal from a device buried in the highway. Wire loops are buried in the pavement, and the transponder is activated and sends out the signal when the car passes over the wire loop. The signal is sent to a central computer that computes the appropriate toll and prints up a bill to be sent out every month. The computer knows the traffic volume and density at the time the car's transponder sent out its signal, so the toll can be computed correctly. The system will work only if drivers do not tamper with the transponder. Enforcement of the system can be done with the use of closed-circuit television cameras. As Downs (1992, pp. 53–54) discusses, the effectiveness of both the electronic transponder system and closed-circuit TV cameras has been demonstrated in Hong Kong. The imposition of congestion tolls without slowing the traffic is now technically feasible at some scale. Furthermore, it appears that the cost of the system itself is relatively modest compared to the gains in efficiency that are possible. Here is an example of the need for technology leading to its creation. In this case the need is for a method for low-cost monitoring of the use of a congestible public facility.

The more serious difficulty with the proposal for congestion tolls is the distinct possibility that not all (or most) of the urban street and highway system will be subjected to tolls. It may be relatively easy to impose a high-tech toll system on a few expressways, but expansion of the system to the bulk of the streets and secondary highways presents an enormous task that may prove to be too difficult and costly. Second, there is a strong tradition of free access to local streets and highways. In fact, at the moment it is against the law to charge tolls on the interstate highway system. Some of the major urban expressways are part of the interstate highway system, so that laws will have to be changed. More important, it is likely that the public will not stand for the imposition of tolls on local streets or secondary highways that provide immediate access to homes and businesses. What does all of this mean for congestion toll policy?

Suppose that only a portion of the urban highway network can be subjected to congestion tolls because of technical complexity and/or the tradition of free access to roads. Congestion toll policy must now be made under the constraint that some of the highway system cannot have a toll imposed. Does this constraint on policy mean that there are no gains to be made from a congestion pricing scheme? The answer to this question is "no," but the optimal congestion pricing scheme can be very different compared to the case in which tolls can be imposed on the entire highway system. The basic result is that if the drivers view the tollway and the free road as substitutes, traffic will be diverted to the free road. If this traffic diversion causes congestion on the free road, the optimal toll on the tollway is lower than the simple textbook toll shown in Figure 8.5. Indeed, in some cases the optimal toll on the tollway is far lower than the toll shown in Figure 8.5.

The problem is depicted in Figure 8.6, which displays the demand and short-run cost functions for two highways. These two highways are considered to be substitutes by rush-hour commuters. In the initial situation there is no toll on either highway, and initial traffic volumes are V_t and V_f. Both highways are being used inefficiently because the marginal cost of the last unit of traffic volume exceeds its marginal benefit as measured by the height of the demand curve at that volume. The efficient traffic volumes are V_t^* and V_f^*, respectively, because these are the volumes at which marginal benefit equals marginal cost. Now suppose that a toll can be imposed on the tollway but that the free road cannot have a toll. The imposition of the toll reduces volume on the tollway by two mechanisms. Some of those who no

FIGURE 8.6 Cost and traffic volume: two routes

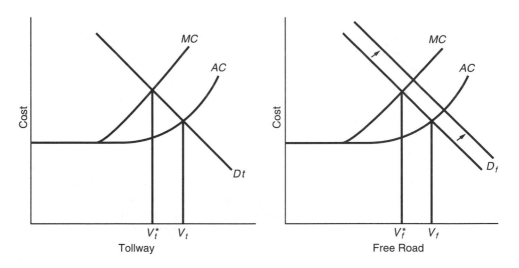

longer choose to travel on the tollway at this time do not travel at all or shift their trips to times during which the highways are not congested. This is the desired result. But the increase in the price of trips on the tollway also shifts outward the demand for trips on the free road. Traffic volume on the free road increases, which is a movement *away* from the efficient volume on this route and not the desired result. If *no* former tollway users switch to the free road (i.e., the two roads are not substitutes), the toll can be set at the level that will cause volume on the tollway to be V_t^*. However, those travelers who *do* switch to the free road are causing additional traffic congestion in the process, and this added congestion must be taken into account in setting the toll. The optimum toll is now less than the toll that pushes traffic volume on the tollway back to V_t^*.

How important is this problem of traffic diversion to substitute routes? First, it is known that some commuters will shift routes rather quickly. Commuters can be counted on to respond to incentives. There are no empirical studies of the exact situation depicted in Figure 8.6, but McDonald (1995) provided some fairly realistic numerical examples. One example sets up two routes with identical cost functions. The routes are assumed to be perfect substitutes. If optimum tolls can be imposed on both routes, that toll would be 23.4 cents per mile per vehicle. This is a fairly typical estimate of the optimum congestion toll on urban highways; if the commuter travels 10 miles each way for 240 days per year, the annual toll would be $1123.20. However, if a toll can be imposed on only one route, the computations show that the optimum level for this toll is only 6.2 cents per mile. The inability to cover half the system with tolls makes a very large difference in the size of the congestion toll that should be imposed.

It is fair to say that congestion tolls are not about to be imposed in the United States. However, Singapore and three cities in Norway already have some form of congestion pricing. Congestion pricing projects are being planned for several other cities around the world, and the U.S. Federal Highway Administration is funding a small number of demonstration projects to test the feasibility of congestion tolls in carefully controlled circumstances. In one of those projects a tollway is being inserted between the opposing sets of lanes of a freeway in southern California. This is a perfect example of the problem discussed above in which the tollway and free road are substitutes. In any event, congestion pricing is being taken somewhat seriously by transportation policymakers.

In the absence of congestion tolls, are there any other policy measures that can be used to reduce the inefficiency of traffic congestion? One suggestion is to use gasoline taxes because such a tax targets road use pretty well. However, the problem of traffic congestion is a problem of road use at particular times and in particular places. A gasoline tax is a pretty blunt instrument that will tax the guy who works the night shift just as much as it taxes the rush-hour commuter. It would also tax non-work trips that already tend to avoid the rush hours to some extent. Most important, the gasoline tax would not encourage people to shift their trips to times of day when congestion is less. Many advocates of a higher gas tax believe that we should cut back on our use of petroleum in general because we rely to a considerable degree on oil imports. Their arguments are about the balance-of-payments problem and national security and cannot be evaluated here.

Another suggestion is to impose taxes on parking in the central business district. The tax would be highest on those who arrive during the morning rush hour. The tax could thus be targeted to at least some of the people who are causing the traffic congestion problem, and it would encourage them to shift to public transit or car pools. The CBD parking tax has two relatively serious disadvantages, however. First, it misses the travelers who contribute to traffic congestion but do not have the CBD as their destination. In the dispersed urban area of today, that is a lot of people. Second, a parking tax does not tax commuters according to the number of miles they drive on the congested highway. Everyone who shows up at the parking garage between 7:30 and 9:30 A.M. and leaves between 3:30 and 6 P.M. would pay the same tax. Despite these objections, the CBD parking tax has some potential to have an impact on the traffic congestion problem.

Yet another suggestion is to draw people out of their cars by subsidizing public transit. A related suggestion is to subsidize companies to set up car pools. The idea is to reduce the cost of alternative methods of getting to work. Public transportation is discussed below, but for now it is important to realize that public transit fares are already heavily subsidized by federal, state, and local governments. Transit agencies generally do not cover all of their variable costs out of the fare box, and fixed (capital) costs are covered by general tax revenues. It is not clear how much further the general public is willing to subsidize public transportation. Programs to create car pools (or van pools) have met with some success. A study by Cervero (1989) shows that carpoolers tend to be workers with lower-level jobs who have longer commutes and quite regular work schedules. Workers who have more irregular schedules and travel patterns are not good candidates for carpooling. One aspect of the federal Intermodal Surface Transportation Efficiency Act (ISTEA) 1991 is to attempt to get large employers to increase the proportion of their workers who use car pools. However, experiments along these lines have so far met with limited success. So when all has been said and done, it is fair to say that commuters have little choice except to grimace and bear it and listen to the car radio.

Supply in the Long Run

In the long run the capital input embodied in the streets and highways is variable. The fact that the era of highway building of the 1950s and 1960s has reshaped urban areas has already been discussed. At this point the prospects for additions to the highway systems of most urban areas are few, but not zero. The emphasis in this chapter clearly is on the problem of traffic congestion and making more efficient use of our existing urban highway systems. This is a proper emphasis at this time, but there are still some possibilities for improvements in urban highways that can be of considerable benefit to the public. The analysis of highway improvements makes use of all of the concepts discussed so far in this chapter: models of demand, the value of reductions in travel time, production and cost functions under conditions of congestion, and pricing analysis.

Let us begin with a problem that is easy to study in theoretical terms. Suppose that we have a highway with the same short-run cost curves as in Figure 8.5, marginal cost and average variable cost. To this set of cost curves we shall add the average *fixed* cost curve and the average *total* cost curve. Using a value of time, all costs are now stated in money terms rather than in terms of commuters' time. This complete set of short-run cost curves is shown in Figure 8.7. The new idea is the average fixed cost, but this is just the fixed cost divided by the volume of traffic. The fixed cost is the cost of the land and capital embodied in the highway for the time period that is being depicted: for example, 1 hour. What is the cost per hour of the land and capital embodied in the highway? Suppose that the highway cost $100 million and the rate of interest is 6%. This means that the annual cost of the land and capital is $6 million. There are 8760 hours in a year, so the cost of land and capital for 1 hour in this example is $685. Here we have ignored the cost of maintenance to keep the highway functioning. The fixed cost per hour should include the annual maintenance cost divided by 8760. Also, if the highway depreciates over time, the hourly cost of capital should include a small amount to cover the eventual replacement of the facility.

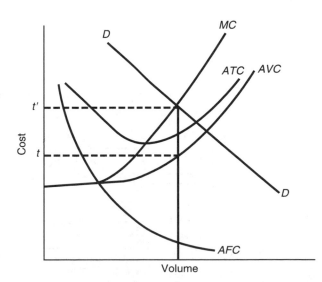

FIGURE 8.7 Cost and traffic volume

All of these ideas are built into the average fixed-cost curve in Figure 8.7. The average total cost is simply the sum of average fixed cost and average variable cost.

Now consider the efficient congestion toll that should be imposed in Figure 8.7. Given demand curve DD, that toll is amount tt', as before. An interesting comparison to make is between the congestion toll and average fixed cost. As depicted in Figure 8.7, the congestion toll tt' exceeds the average fixed cost because the toll is larger than the vertical difference between average total cost and average variable cost. In other words, the toll revenue collected over the time period exceeds the cost of the land and capital embodied in the highway. What is the significance of this outcome?

Suppose for the moment that demand curve DD is the demand curve for *every* time period during the year. Obviously, this is a silly assumption because it ignores the fact that demand peaks during the rush hour, but play along for now. Given this assumption, toll revenues in excess of fixed costs are being collected in every time period. This would appear to be a signal that the highway should be expanded. An expansion of the highway is shown in Figure 8.8. This expansion is carefully designed so that the congestion toll revenue that is collected in each time period is just equal to the fixed cost. This means that the price that each commuter pays (average variable cost plus toll) is exactly equal to the average total cost of each trip. In Figure 8.8 all of this happens at traffic volume V_2, where the congestion toll of t_2 just equals the average fixed cost. Note that the expanded highway has been designed so that traffic volume V_2 coincides with the *minimum* average total cost that is possible for that facility. We see that efficient use of this particular highway (i.e., price equals marginal cost) involves setting a congestion toll equal to average fixed cost.

Figure 8.8 depicts a nice result for efficiency in the short run, but suppose further that the facility that was built is also the highway that provides for the minimum average cost in the *long run* at traffic volume V_2. In other words, suppose that the long-run average cost curve passes through the minimum point of the short-run average total cost curve. This can happen only if the long-run average cost curve is tangent to the short-run average total cost curve at volume V_2 and is therefore a horizon-

FIGURE 8.8 Congestion toll equals average fixed cost

FIGURE 8.9 Optimum congestion toll in the long run

tal line. Figure 8.9 depicts the situation. (Consider the alternative. If the long-run average cost is not a horizontal line, it exceeds short-run average total cost in some range. This is a contradiction. Long-run average cost is, by definition, the minimum average cost for each level of output.)

A horizontal long-run average cost curve means that the production of trips is subject to *constant long-run marginal cost*. Figure 8.9 therefore depicts a situation in which the price paid by commuters is equal to long-run marginal cost as well as short-run marginal cost. The long-run marginal cost of a trip equals its marginal benefit, which is the usual condition for the optimal allocation of resources. Now we have another really nice result. If the production of trips is subject to constant marginal and average cost in the long run, the efficient highway facility in the long run will be the one where the collection of congestion tolls just equals the cost of the land and capital embodied in the highway. The commuters just pay for their highway through the congestion toll! Is that not nice of them?

Another way to state the result is that the efficient congestion toll is equal to average fixed costs. Average fixed costs are, of course,

$$AFC = \frac{\text{total fixed costs}}{\text{traffic volume}}.$$

Is the efficient congestion toll higher near the center of the urban area or in the suburbs? Fixed costs of a mile of highway near the downtown area are relatively high because land is more expensive and the highway requires more overpasses and intersections. On the other hand, the demand for travel is greater near downtown. The greater density of demand near downtown means that optimal traffic volume is larger near downtown. The outcome of these two opposing forces on the efficient congestion toll is ambiguous. Whether the toll is higher near downtown depends on whether the fixed cost or the demand effect dominates the computation. As discussed below, the real world is far more complex than the world depicted in Figure 8.9, but the general idea that proper congestion tolls could pay for the highways is intriguing.

FIGURE 8.10 Cost and traffic volume: two lanes, three lanes, and four lanes

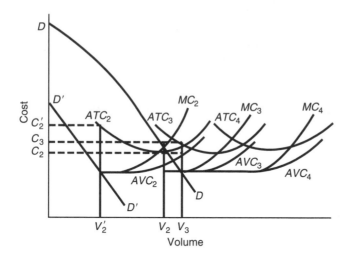

Now let us turn to a more realistic view of highway construction projects. An important category of highway improvements is the addition of a link in the highway system. This kind of project is usually very expensive because it involves the acquisition of land and the construction of bridges and underpasses. Under what conditions do the benefits of such a project exceed the costs? Furthermore, how large should the project be? Consider Figure 8.10, which depicts the short- and long-run cost curves for a particular highway facility. The short-run cost curves are now stated in money terms, but they are the same in essence as those depicted in Figure 8.5. The long-run average cost curve includes the costs that are variable in the short run *and* the capital costs of the highway scaled down to the time period under analysis. The time period under consideration in Figure 8.10 is *1 hour* during the peak demand period of a typical weekday. Therefore, the capital cost of the highway is the cost of that highway for 1 hour of its total lifetime.

In Figure 8.10 and in the real world, investment in a highway is lumpy. A limited number of investment options exists. It does not make sense to build a limited-access highway with only one lane in each direction, so that option is not depicted. Figure 8.10 depicts three options: a highway with two, three, or four lanes in each direction. Each of these three options has a set of short-run cost curves that includes the short-run average total-cost curve. This average total cost includes the fixed cost of land and highway capital, but the average fixed-cost curves have been omitted to reduce the clutter on the diagram. Average variable cost and marginal cost are the same concepts as in Figure 8.7. The long-run average cost curve consists of portions of the three short-run average total-cost curves, as shown. It is further assumed that the minimum points on each short-run average total-cost curve occur at the same level of cost.

Now consider the investment decision. Demand curve *DD* shows the marginal benefits of traffic volume, and the problem is to decide whether to build a highway link and, if the decision is to build, how many lanes to construct. Let us first suppose an ideal world in which congestion tolls can be imposed on all relevant portions of the system. If the two-lane tollway were to be constructed, efficient traffic volume for this facility would be V_2, and the average total cost would be C_2. Should a facility of at least this size be constructed? Clearly, the answer is "yes" because the total benefit of the output is the area under the demand curve up to volume V_2 and the total cost is the area equal to V_2 times C_2. There is another category of benefits that may exist as well. It is possible that the construction of the project will cause a reduction in traffic congestion on other parts of the street and highway system. Any reduction in variable costs experienced by commuters who still use those other parts of the system will count as benefits of the project in question.

Compare the result with demand curve DD in Figure 8.10 to the case if the demand curve instead is $D'D'$. In this case traffic volume V_2' is generated at an average cost of C_2'. Suppose that because traffic volume V_2' is rather low, the benefits to commuters who continue to use the other parts of the system are negligible. The total cost of these trips (V_2') exceeds the total benefits because the area under the demand curve up to V_2' is less than the total cost (C_2' times V_2'). No highway link should be built in this case.

Return to demand curve DD. The next question is whether the project should be three lanes instead of two. The question is now whether the *additional* benefits of the third lane exceed the additional costs. If the project has three lanes, traffic volume V_3 is generated at an average total cost of C_3. Traffic volume increases from V_2 to V_3. In this particular case no congestion toll is needed because, at volume V_3, no traffic congestion exists. The additional benefits created by the third lane consist of the area under the demand curve between V_2 and V_3, and any added benefits to commuters who continue to use other routes. However, the total cost of producing traffic volume V_3 is now V_3 times C_3. Average total cost of trips has increased from C_2 to C_3 because the three-lane facility will be rather underutilized with demand curve DD. The addition to total cost is C_3V_3 minus C_2V_2. The benefit of the additional traffic volume is the area under the demand curve from V_2 to V_3. The diagram has been drawn so that the *addition* to total costs exceeds the addition to benefits, and the third lane should be rejected. In this particular case the slight overutilization of the two-lane highway is better than underutilization of the three-lane highway. Note, however, that if the option to build the two-lane highway did not exist, the total benefits of building the three-lane highway (area under the demand curve up to V_3) exceed total costs (C_3 times V_3) and the three-lane project would be accepted. Still, the better choice is the two-lane highway.

The cost-benefit analysis of the expansion of the highway from two lanes to three lanes is usually done in another manner. The benefit side includes the value of the additional trips as above, but benefits also include the reduction in the cost of the trips taken by the original V_2 travelers. This benefit amounts to V_2 times the drop in the price paid by these drivers ($MC_2 - MC_3$ at volume V_2). Any benefits arising from reductions in traffic congestion on other routes would be added in as well. These benefits are then compared to the capital cost of the third lane scaled to the appropriate time period *plus* the loss of congestion toll revenue. The original V_2 drivers gain the toll revenue as part of the reduction in the price that they pay, and the public sector loses the toll revenue. The results of this computation are, of course, identical to the previous computation.

The analysis can be done over, assuming that a congestion toll cannot be imposed. As in Figure 8.5, equilibrium traffic volume is set where the demand curve intersects the average variable cost curve. The computations of total benefits and costs then proceed as before. In this case the traffic volume with the two-lane project is somewhat greater and average total costs are a bit higher. The total benefits of the two-lane project still exceed total costs. As an exercise, show these points on Figure 8.10. Traffic volume with the three-lane project does not change because no toll was imposed under a tollway regime. Therefore, the addition of the third lane adds less to equilibrium traffic volume than it would under a tollway regime. It is still true that the benefits of the added trips are less than the addition to cost, so the third lane is rejected. You complete the exercise by demonstrating this conclusion using Figure 8.10.

One final problem needs to be addressed. How do we proceed to perform the cost-benefit study in the presence of peak and off-peak demands? Return to Figure 8.10 and suppose that demand curve DD represents peak demand and that $D'D'$ is off-peak demand. It was shown that the benefits of the two-lane highway link exceed costs during the peak periods but that costs of this project exceed benefits during off-peak times. Suppose that there are 6 hours of peak demand and 18 hours of off-peak demand during each day. The solution to the problem is simply to compute the sum of the 24-hour net benefit (i.e., benefit minus cost) figures. The positive net benefits with demand curve DD count six times, and the negative net benefits with demand curve $D'D'$ count 18 times. Given the situation depicted in Figure 8.10, the positive net benefits during the rush hours actually do exceed the negative net benefits generated at other times of day. However, it is quite possible that the evaluation of a project such as that depicted in Figure 8.10 could go the other way.

Two additional points should be emphasized. The first point is that no congestion toll should be imposed in the off-peak periods because no congestion is generated at these times. It was previously emphasized that congestion tolls should vary with traffic conditions, and Figure 8.10 provides a simple example of this rule. Second, we should ask whether the congestion tolls collected during the peak periods are sufficient to pay for the land and capital embodied in the two-lane highway. In this case, clearly those tolls do not cover the fixed costs. The congestion tolls roughly cover the fixed costs incurred during the peak demand periods, but the absence of congestion tolls in the off-peak periods means that toll revenue will fall short of total fixed costs.

E. MASS TRANSPORTATION

Mass transportation is supplied using two basic technologies: internal combustion vehicles, which operate on the streets and highways (i.e., buses), and electric vehicles, which operate on fixed rail lines (e.g., commuter trains and subways). Both types of systems operate under conditions of economies of scale. However, because of those economies of scale, it is necessary to consider the costs of assembling the passengers at the points where they can be picked up and the costs of distributing the passengers to their final destinations after they leave the vehicles. The trip on mass transit is broken down into three parts: (1) the collection phase, (2) the line-haul trip, and (3) the distribution phase. This basic framework is used to discuss each of the mass transportation technologies.

Average costs of a complete trip on rail rapid transit were studied in detail by Meyer, Kain, and Wohl (1965) in their important book *The Urban Transportation Problem*. The title of the book refers to the fact that the real problem faced by urban transportation planners stems from the decentralization of urban areas. In essence, the problem is transporting workers to jobs at dispersed locations in the suburbs. Further, the problem is particularly acute for black and Hispanic workers who live in the central city and do not have the opportunity to reside in the suburbs. The problem is called *reverse commuting*. After 30 years this book is still important and quite relevant, even if the empirical evidence in the book is dated. But just why is reverse commuting such a problem?

Rail rapid transit systems are very good for moving large numbers of commuters to work in the CBD. Most of the urban areas listed in Table 8.1 that are the biggest users of rail rapid transit are those with large numbers of jobs in a fairly small CBD: New York, Chicago, Philadelphia, and Boston. These cities were developed to a significant extent with rail rapid transit systems already in place. There are very large economies of scale in the line-haul portion of the trip, and the CBD is the destination for a very large number of commuters. Rail rapid transit is even more efficient if the residential areas that are served have high population densities, as in New York, Chicago, Philadelphia, and Boston. A city with a high population density can support several rail rapid transit lines, so the distance that the commuter must travel to get to the transit station is relatively short. The costs of the collection phase of the trip are low. Because of the high employment density in the CBD, the costs of the distribution phase are also low.

Meyer et al. (1965) estimated that an hourly passenger volume of 20,000 on a line was needed to take reasonably full advantage of the economies of scale in line haul on rail rapid transit. At the time they wrote their book, only five cities had hourly passenger volumes at this level or greater: New York, Chicago, Philadelphia, Boston, and Washington, DC. The first four already had extensive rail rapid transit systems and downtown subways at the time. An extensive subway system has since been built in Washington, DC, and this system is discussed below.

Meyer et al. (1965) also studied the costs of bus systems. The usual city bus system has buses that run on the major streets and pick up and discharge passengers about every two blocks. Meyer, Kain, and Wohl pointed out that this sort of system is inefficient for transporting workers to the CBD because the line-haul phase of the trip is slow. Instead, they suggested a system that they called *bus rapid transit* or *integrated bus service*. The idea of bus rapid transit is to follow a route around a residential area until the bus is full of CBD workers and then to proceed directly downtown by the quickest route possible (e.g., on the expressway). They showed that a fleet of buses can provide service that is much less costly than rail rapid transit. The bus can follow a flexible route to pick up passengers, so the costs in the collection phase are cut substantially compared to the rail system. Economies of scale arise because if there are more passengers in an area to pick up, a single bus has to make many fewer stops to have a full load. Waiting time is also cut down by running buses more frequently. Meyer et al. (1965) also studied the possibility of having "feeder" buses pick up passengers who are delivered to the rail rapid transit stations. They estimated that this sort of system works about as well as bus rapid transit, especially in residential areas with high population densities. The idea of bus rapid transit proved to be persuasive, and most urban transit systems provide some service of this type.

The data from Meyer et al. (1965) cited above suggested that Washington, DC might have been a good candidate for a rail rapid transit system because potential passenger volume might have been in excess of 20,000 per hour. The current Washington, DC Metro system was completed in 1981 with a set of six major lines that run to the suburbs. As Mills and Hamilton (1994) point out, average ridership was 145,000 each way on the system, or an average of 24,167 per line. If the rush hour is approximately 2.5 hours in length, this works out to 9667 riders per hour, far below the target of 20,000 per hour. Mills and Hamilton (1994, p. 304) computed the capital and operating cost of the system as of 1981 and found that capital costs were about $13.30 per round trip and operating costs were $2.60 per round trip. They further estimate that the time costs for the commuter were about $2.50 per round trip, so the average total cost per round trip in 1981 was $18.40. If we add $13.60 and $2.60, we see that for the system to break even, the fare needed to be about $8.00 *each way*. Actual fares were, of course, much less. A bus rapid transit system could have provided much cheaper service. Indeed, Mills and Hamilton (1994) argue that a "system" based on commuting by private auto is probably cheaper. The Washington, DC Metro ranks pretty high in the annals of transportation policy mistakes. It is fair to say that some goal other than economic efficiency was being pursued. What do you think it was?

Thus far the discussion of mass transportation has concentrated on systems for moving commuters to jobs in the CBD. There is good reason for this focus. As Meyer et al. (1965) and others since have shown, the private auto is almost always the cheapest method for getting people to and from work for locations outside the CBD. The full costs include time, vehicle operation, roadway, parking, and pollution. There are some exceptions to this finding. For example, the rail rapid transit system provides service to O'Hare Airport in Chicago, a major destination for workers that is outside the CBD (see Chapter 7). This rapid transit line exists primarily to deliver workers to the CBD, but the trains must return to O'Hare anyway. A good use of those returning trains is to carry the workers to the O'Hare employment center. In a few other instances a bus system might be a feasible option for work trips to a major employment subcenter. Otherwise, the dispersed nature of residential locations and job locations makes the cost of a bus system high relative to private auto. Van pooling was mentioned above, and this is also a feasible option to the private auto for large employers. The key to making van pooling competitive with the private auto is to have a full van load of commuters who live in close proximity, who work for the same employer, and who have the same schedule. The results are a short collection phase and a very short distribution phase. But van pooling is not exactly mass transportation. There might be a valid argument for public subsidization of van pooling because it tends to reduce traffic congestion.

F. POLITICS AND TRANSPORTATION PROJECTS: A CASE STUDY

At the beginning of this chapter it was mentioned that proposed transportation projects can become hot political issues in an urban area. At any given time in most larger urban areas there is a proposed transportation project that is the subject of political debate and controversy. What is it in your urban area? In this final section we take a brief look at a proposed transportation project in Chicago that has been the subject of debate for several years.

The proposed project is a light-rail transit system for downtown Chicago. Most observers agree that the movement of people within the downtown area of Chicago and other large urban areas has become an increasingly important problem. Chicago's downtown area is large, about 5 miles long from north to south and 1.5 miles wide from east to west. Total employment in this area is approximately 600,000, and about 850,000 people enter the area on a typical weekday. There are about 1 million trips taken within the area per weekday. Some major businesses have resorted to private shuttle buses to transport their workers from commuter rail stations because of the shortage of mass transit and the difficulty the public transit buses have in moving through traffic.

Clearly, there is a need for a transportation system that connects commuter stations, parking facilities, and transit stations and bus lines with offices, shopping areas, cultural centers, hotels, and convention facilities. What is more, there is a need to connect offices with shopping areas, office areas with other office areas, hotels with cultural centers and convention facilities, and all of the other possible combinations. Indeed, one of the major reasons for the economic vitality of a place such as downtown Chicago is the relative ease with which face-to-face contacts can be made. The downtown area has been spreading out over time, so the demand for a downtown transportation system has increased. Chicago's original downtown was confined roughly to the famous Chicago "Loop," which is an elevated mass transit line around the central square mile.

A light-rail transit system for downtown Chicago was first proposed in the 1980s by a local community group, and this proposal has been studied in detail by the Chicago municipal authorities. The U.S. Department of Transportation has extensive requirements for the studies of proposed projects that involve the use of federal funds. Those requirements include a systematic examination of all reasonable alternatives. Those alternatives are described briefly below.

1. *Null alternative.*   The null alternative is required by the U.S. Department of Transportation's evaluation procedures, and serves as a baseline against which other policy options are compared. The basic idea is to estimate what will happen if nothing new is done. The null alternative includes the existing public bus lines that serve the downtown area.

2. *Transportation systems management alternative.*   This alternative involves some sizable operational and physical improvements in the bus system service. New bus stations would be added, new vehicles would be acquired, and better communications systems would be added, and some routes would be changed. Several steps would be taken to improve the management of traffic in the downtown area. The cost of this alternative is estimated at around $100 million.

3. *Bus-build alternative.* The objective of the bus-build alternative is to create a bus system that is nearly separate from general traffic by means of both at-grade and below-grade bus facilities. The studies indicate that this option provides very limited benefits at substantial cost and has therefore received no further consideration.

4. *Light-rail transit alternative.* This alternative involves a new type of transit system that makes use of railway tracks embedded in the streets. The vehicles are powered by electricity and are high-tech versions of the old trolley cars. The studies identify four corridors of high demand in the downtown area, so the plan includes four light-rail transit lines. The cost of the complete light-rail system is around $600 million.

5. *Grade-separated alternative.* This approach involves making use of existing railroad rights-of-way that exist below street level and constructing new elevated transit facilities. A grade-separated system could be implemented by extending rapid transit and commuter rail lines and/or by creating a new mode called automated guideway technology. Preliminary studies showed that this alternative is neither physically nor economically feasible.

The choices boil down to three: do nothing, improve the downtown bus system for a cost of $100 million, or build a light-rail system at a cost of $600 million. It turned out that the mayor of Chicago and many other local officials and downtown businesses are attracted to the light-rail transit project. They like the idea of nifty and attractive high-tech trolley cars moving people around downtown in an efficient manner. Light-rail transit is a popular idea; transportation experts seem to be subject to fads (as are we all). Light-rail systems had been built recently in several cities, including San Diego, Buffalo, Sacramento, San Jose, and Portland, Oregon, so Chicago perhaps is seeking to jump on this particular bandwagon.

Light-rail transit is a popular idea but it has what Gómez-Ibáñez (1985) calls the "dark side" to light rail. Light rail has sizable capital costs compared to the bus system that can serve as a substitute. In the case of the San Diego light-rail system, he found that the cost per rider of light-rail transit was about 2.7 times the cost of the bus system that it replaced. Note that the light-rail system for downtown Chicago costs about six times as much as the improved bus system (the transportation systems management alternative). But what are the benefits of these two alternatives?

Detailed studies have been conducted of the amount of time that travelers would save under the light-rail and bus project alternatives. Passengers on the light-rail transit system will travel at 3 miles per hour faster than they do on the current bus system. The study showed that the average trip inside downtown is 1.5 miles (3 miles per day). If the original average speed is 8 mph and improves to 11 mph, the typical person will reduce time spent traveling 3 miles from 22.5 minutes to 16.4 minutes, a saving of 6 minutes (0.1 hour) per day. Estimated ridership on the light-rail system is 50,000 per day (round trip), so the total amount of time saved per day is 5000 hours. The total amount of time saved per year would then be 1.25 million hours (5000 times 250 days). Recall that the value of time saved is about 50% of the after-tax wage rate. The average worker in downtown Chicago earns about $26,000 per year (or about $10 per hour after taxes), so the value of time saved might be about $5 per hour. The value of the time saved per year is therefore about $6.25 million. This annual benefit is 1.04% of the cost of the project of $600 million. That is, of course, a very poor rate of return. However, benefits to other travelers from reductions in traffic congestion have not been estimated.

The improved bus system (transportation systems management alternative) costs only $100 million, but it is estimated to save only about 40% of the time that is saved by the light−rail system. The value of the time saved is therefore about $2.5 million per year, for a rate of return of 2.5%. In short, neither project appears to be a good investment.

Despite the pessimistic cost-benefit analysis, plans for the light-rail transit system moved forward. The city of Chicago set up a special office to finalize plans and implement the project. The plan for financing the project is to split the cost equally among the local, state, and federal governments. With the support of many downtown interests, the local government set up a special real estate taxing district in the downtown area to cover its one-third share. Some grumbling could be heard among downtown property owners when this action was taken in 1991, but only weak organized opposition to the project has materialized at the local level. The Republican state legislature and governor of Illinois generally have supported the project, in part because they have opposed other projects that are favored by Chicago's Democratic mayor. For example, Republicans in state government are opposed to the mayor's plans to expand O'Hare Airport, and instead wish to build another airport in the suburbs. Under these circumstances, the political trade-off is to give the mayor the project that is of lesser importance.

What is the final disposition of the proposed light-rail transit system for downtown Chicago? The plans are complete, and both the local and federal governments are ready to start paying for its construction. However, the state of Illinois has been forced to pull the plug on the project because of its current (as of 1995) fiscal problems. The state has growing expenses for medical care for the poor (Medicaid), education, and criminal justice, and the political decision was made not to increase state taxes. One implication of this political situation is that many discretionary expenditure items must be postponed, perhaps never to be undertaken at all. In the case of the light-rail transit project, it would appear that the proper decision has been made for the "wrong" reasons.

G. SUMMARY

The chapter began by posing the "big question" of whether anything can be done about the time-consuming and wasteful traffic congestion, which is getting worse. You can now see that there are many little things that can be done. The battle must be fought on many fronts.

Consider first the demand side. There are several methods that can be used to encourage drivers to shift to time periods with less traffic congestion. Congestion tolls are the high-tech remedy that may never be implemented in a major fashion in the United States. Nevertheless, there may be specific places where a congestion toll can have the desired effect without creating too many traffic spillovers onto other routes. For example, congestion tolls on bridges seem to be workable. At a more practical level, CBD parking taxes, incentives for car pooling, and providing incentives to employers to stagger work hours all seem to be workable. Higher taxes on gasoline (or autos themselves) are alternatives that are less attractive because they do not target the problem very well. Indeed, Downs (1992, p. 69) argues that a higher tax on gasoline would cause drivers to switch to more fuel-efficient cars rather than to cut down on driving in the rush hour.

Even in an era of budgetary stringency, some improvements can be made on the supply side. There are bottlenecks out there that need to be widened. More advanced traffic control technology can be installed on major streets and minor highways. In the Chicago area a program known as "operation green light" has made life a bit easier. This project involved judicious widening of major streets and timing of stoplights.

Another tactic is to provide drivers with better information about their route choices. Drivers need to know if there are accidents or other causes of traffic tie-ups, and they need to know *immediately*. Traffic information services exist in the major urban areas, but these services can be improved. A related policy is to make sure that accidents and other impediments are removed *very* promptly. Helicopters might be used. An expansion of accident-prevention programs is also worth thinking about.

All of the partial remedies listed so far take our location patterns and mode choices as given. Clearly, these remedies will help, but the continued growth of population, employment, and vehicles will soon overcome the improvements these remedies have brought. Are there more fundamental changes in the nature of urban areas in the United States that can have a big impact on traffic congestion? Downs (1992) considers a variety of policies to increase population density, increase the concentration of jobs, and reduce the imbalances that exist between residential and employment locations. All of these suggestions will involve a substantial amount of planning, which is not likely to be very popular with Americans. Growth management policies may be feasible in some urban areas. Portland, Oregon, for example, has managed growth extensively—for an American urban area. But as Garreau would surely point out, if you impose too many regulations, Americans are likely to create another edge city that the regulations cannot yet reach. A dilemma is defined as a situation requiring a choice between equally undesirable alternatives. Are the choices highly intrusive growth management or increasingly bad traffic congestion? If they are, we truly face a dilemma. At this point we seem to be choosing traffic congestion—perhaps mainly by default.

EXERCISES

1. Suppose that a gravity model of trip distribution has been estimated as

$$T_{ij} = \frac{O_i^{0.5} D_j^{0.2}}{(d_{ij})^2}.$$

  (a) What is T_{ij} if $O_i = 100$, $D_j = 200$, and $d_{ij} = 5$ miles? What if the distance is 10 miles instead of 5 miles?

  (b) What happens to T_{ij} if both O_i and D_j double in size?

2. A model of mode split (with two modes) has been estimated as

$$\ln\left(\frac{P_{ija}}{1-P_{ija}}\right) = -8(t_a-t_b) - 2(m_a-m_b),$$

where mode a is auto and mode b is public transit, t (travel time) is measured in minutes, and m (money cost) is measured in cents.
   (a) At what values of t^a-t^b and m^a-m^b is the probability of using the auto equal to 0.5?
   (b) Draw the graph of P_{ija} as a function of $z = -8(t_a-t_b) - 2(m_a-m_b)$.
   (c) What is the value of reductions in commuting time implied by the estimated mode split function? What unit of measurement did you use to express the value of time?

3. You are supposed to be at your desk ready for work at 9:00 A.M. You cannot be late or you will be fired, but it is fine if you arrive early. You figure that each minute you spend at work before 9 A.M. costs you 3 cents. You also know that there is a function that describes the amount of time it will take you to get to work: that is

commute time = 15 minutes + 0.1 (departure time minus 8 A.M.)

+ 0.04 (departure time minus 8 A.M.)²

Departure time minus 8 A.M. is measured in minutes. Your value of reductions in commuting time is 5 cents per minute.
   (a) What is your optimal departure time?
   (b) How much time do you spend commuting?
   (c) When do you arrive at work?
   (d) What happens if you decide that time spent at work before 9 A.M. costs you 3.1 cents per minute instead of 3 cents?

4. Consider a circular road with one lane that is 2 miles in length. There are 80 cars on this "track" traveling 50 miles per hour—speed (S) is 50.
   (a) What is the traffic density (D)?
   (b) What is traffic volume (V)?
   (c) What units of measurement did you use?

5. Consider an urban highway that is subject to traffic congestion. The average cost of travel per mile on that highway is (in cents)

$$AC = 10 + 4V,$$

where V is traffic volume per hour, measured in hundreds of vehicles per hour. For example, if $V = 500$ cars per hour, $AC = 30$ cents per mile. Assume that the demand for traffic volume per hour (during rush hour) is

$$V = 46 - P,$$

where P is the "price" paid by the driver.
   (a) Assume that no congestion toll is imposed. Compute V and P.

(b) Assume that it is possible to impose the efficient congestion toll. Find the toll and the efficient levels of V, P, and AC.

6. The function that relates the inverse of speed ($1/S$) to traffic volume on a highway is

$$\frac{1}{S} = \frac{1}{60} + 0.0005V,$$

where the inverse of speed is measured in hours per mile. What would this equation be if expressed in minutes per mile? The demand for traffic volume on this road is

$$V = 6880 - 80 \text{ (travel time per mile)}.$$

Travel time per mile is measured in minutes.
(a) Find the equilibrium traffic volume in the absence of any congestion toll.
(b) Find the marginal cost function for traffic volume, where cost is expressed as travel time per mile in minutes.
(c) Find the optimal level of traffic volume.
(d) Find the optimal congestion toll, expressed in *minutes*. (Imagine that the congestion toll consists of sitting in the "penalty box" for this period of time. The toll can also be assessed in money terms, of course.)

REFERENCES

Becker, Gary, 1965. "A Theory of the Allocation of Time," *Economic Journal*, Vol. 75, pp. 493–517.

Boardman, Anthony and L. Lave, 1977. "Highway Congestion and Congestion Tolls," *Journal of Urban Economics*, Vol. 4, pp. 340–359.

Bruzelius, Nils, 1979. *The Value of Time*. London: Croom Helm.

Cervero, Robert, 1989. *America's Suburban Centers*. Boston: Allen & Unwin.

Downs, Anthony, 1992. *Stuck in Traffic: Coping with Peak-Hour Traffic Congestion*. Washington, DC: The Brookings Institution.

Gómez–Ibáñez, José, 1985. "A Dark Side to Light Rail," *Journal of the American Institute of Planners*, Vol. 51, pp. 337–351.

Hill, Donald, L. Tittemore, and D. Gendell, 1973. "Analysis of Urban Area Travel by Time of Day," *Highway Research Record*, Vol. 472, pp. 108–119.

McDonald, John, 1995. "Urban Highway Congestion: An Analysis of Second-Best Tolls," *Transportation*, Vol. 22, pp. 353–369.

Meyer, John, J. Kain, and M. Wohl, 1965. *The Urban Transportation Problem*. Cambridge, MA: Harvard University Press.

Mills, Edwin and B. Hamilton, 1994. *Urban Economics*, 5th ed. New York: HarperCollins.

Niedercorn, J. and B. Bechdolt, 1969. "An Economic Derivation of the 'Gravity Law' of Spatial Interaction," *Journal of Regional Science*, Vol. 9, pp. 273–282.

Sherret, Alistair, 1975. "Immediate Travel Impacts of Transbay BART," Report TM 15-3-75, Peat, Marwick, Mitchell & Co., for U.S. Department of Transportation.

Small, Kenneth, 1992. *Urban Transportation Economics*. Chur, Switzerland: Harwood Academic Publishers.

Housing in Urban Areas

A. INTRODUCTION

Housing bulks large in the household budget, and it occupies more space in urban areas than anything else. According to the *Economic Report of the President*, in 1990 housing expenditures, including the imputed rent of owner-occupied houses, were $547.5 billion, 14.6% of all personal consumption expenditures. The costs of household operation (electricity, gas, insurance, etc.) were $215.0 billion, another 5.7% of total consumption. Furniture and other household equipment added another $172.1 billion (4.6% of total consumption). All together, the expenses related to the home amounted to 24.9% of all consumption expenditures. Neidercorn and Hearle (1963) examined studies of land use in 48 urban areas and found that, on average, 29.6% of all land and 39.0% of developed land in an urban area is devoted to residential use. A sizable part of the spatial pattern of an urban area is the spatial pattern of its housing stock.

Table 9.1 offers a snapshot of housing in the 322 metropolitan areas in 1991. There were 79 million housing units at that time. Of those 79 million units: 8.0% were vacant, 56.8% were owner-occupied, 35.3% were occupied by renters, 41.5% were located in central cities and 58.5% in suburbs, and 61.6% of occupied units were owner-occupied and 63.4% of owner-occupied units had mortgage loans.

Table 9.1 provides data for owner-occupied and rental units located in both central cities and suburbs. The median size of units in central cities was 1671 square feet, and the median size in the suburbs was 1778 square feet. Owner-occupied units were larger than rental units in both locations. The median cost for units in the central cities was $458 per month, and the figure for the suburbs was $554. Rental units cost almost as much, on average, as owner-occupied units in both locations. Very few housing units were crowded, where crowded is defined as more than 1.5 persons per room. More units lacked plumbing for exclusive use than were crowded, but the numbers are still pretty small. In central cities 1.8% of the units lacked plumbing for exclusive use, while 2.2% of suburban units had this deficiency. Vacant units were the most likely to have this plumbing deficiency in both locations. More troubling is the fact that 13.4% of households in central cities reported that crime was a problem

TABLE 9.1 Housing in Metropolitan Areas, 1991							
	Central Cities				*Suburbs*		
		Occupied				*Occupied*	
	Total	*Own*	*Rent*	*Vacant*	*Total*	*Own*	*Rent*	*Vacant*
Units (mils)	32.8	14.4	15.3	3.1	46.2	30.5	12.6	3.2
Square feet (median)	1671	1770	1264	1374	1778	1863	1298	1365
Cost/month (median)	$458	$474	$451	—	$554	$573	$536	—
Mortgage	—	61.2%	—	—	—	64.5%	—	—
Crowded[a]	0.9%	0.1%	1.7%	—	0.3%	0.2%	0.8%	—
No plumbing, exclusive use[b]	1.8%	1.7%	2.3%	4.1%	2.2%	1.9%	2.2%	7.7%
Crime problem	13.4%	10.7%	18.7%	—	4.2%	3.1%	7.9%	—
Cost/income (median)	24%	19%	29%	—	22%	19%	28%	—
Cost > 30% of income	36%	23%	48%	—	30%	24%	45%	—

[a]*"Crowded" is defined as persons per room exceeds 1.5.*

[b]*Unit does not have plumbing for exclusive use.*

Source: American Housing Survey, U.S. Department of Housing and Urban Development, 1993.

in their neighborhoods (compared to 4.2% of households in the suburbs). These results show that housing units in urban areas in the United States are large on average, and that few have the basic problems of crowding or lack of plumbing. However, the average cost of housing is rather high, $5500 per year in central cities and $6650 per year in the suburbs.

The problem of cost is shown further in Table 9.1. One measure that is used is the ratio of monthly housing cost to monthly income for the household. In the data reported in Table 9.1 all forms of cash income before taxes are included in the definition of income. Welfare payments are counted as well as wages, business income, retirement income, and so on. The survey shows that the median for the ratio of housing cost to income was 24% for households in central cities and 22% for households in the suburbs. However, the median ratio was only 19% for households that owned their homes and 29% (central city) or 28% (suburbs) for renters. Renters clearly are paying a higher percentage of their incomes for housing than are homeowners, and this fact is underscored by the last line in Table 9.1. This line shows the percentage of households who spent more than 30% of their incomes on housing. Almost half of renters fall into this category; 48% of central city renters and 45% of suburban renters spent at least 30% of their incomes on housing. The 30% figure is generally used to define a problem with *affordability* of housing. The message in Table 9.1 is now pretty clear. Urban Americans generally have a housing stock of fairly high quality, but housing has a high cost both in absolute terms and relative to income. The apparent high cost of housing relative to income is particularly evident among renters in urban areas.

Be that as it may, the idea of affordability as determined by some ratio of housing cost to current income is a slippery concept that should be used with caution. For one thing, the demand for housing is more properly considered to be a function of income averaged over a period of years rather than just current income. A household's current income can fluctuate around a longer-run average. It is likely that one would always observe some percentage of households with a ratio of housing costs to current income in excess of some figure (such as 30%) even though there is no problem with affordability because no household exceeds the 30% figure in the longer run. For another thing, some households may simply freely choose to spend a high percentage of income (in the longer run) on housing. So long as the children are receiving adequate care and no laws are being broken, why should anyone else care? Indeed, spending a lot of money on housing may have positive external effects on the neighborhood!

The real social problem behind the idea of affordability needs to be defined more precisely. The social problem arises when households with lower incomes over the longer run *must* spend a high fraction of that income on housing to obtain a decent, minimal domicile. The cost of a decent house or apartment is high relative to their ability to pay in the long run. The nature and extent of the problem depends, of course, on the standard for decent housing that is used. Also, local governments play a role in determining the ratio of housing costs to income for low-income households. Nearly all municipal governments in urban areas have ordinances called building codes and housing codes that impose minimal requirements on the housing that can be offered for sale or rent in that jurisdiction. Zoning ordinances often impose minimum lot sizes and other requirements that affect housing. All of these laws can mean that the minimal housing unit set by law costs more than some households with low incomes would choose to spend if left to their own devices. In short, some households would choose to live in housing of relatively low quality, but the municipal government will not permit them to make this choice because of concern for the health and safety of the public and/or an interest in the overall quality of the neighborhood. These matters are examined more fully below as part of the discussion of housing policy.

Housing is a big part of people's lives and a big part of an urban area, but it is also unique among consumer goods in other respects. Housing is potentially *very* durable. A useful life for a house routinely is 70 years, and many last far longer than that. With careful maintenance and periodic modernization, a well-built house can last indefinitely. But misuse and lack of maintenance can also shorten the life of a house. The high degree of durability means that the market for housing is dominated by existing housing units. New construction adds, at most, about 2% to the nation's existing stock of housing in a year, although the housing stock grows more rapidly in urban areas with high growth rates. Housing is also immovable. (Even mobile homes are not moved very much.) When one selects a particular housing unit, a choice of residential location has been made as well. The neighborhood surrounding the house contains neighbors, schools, and many other things that people care about. The analysis of the market for housing in an urban area cannot be divorced from neighborhood factors. Finally, houses and apartments are very complicated commodities that contain numerous features that have value for the consumer. The housing market is a market that is characterized by complicated, highly durable units each of which is located in a neighborhood with many attributes. This statement makes it sound as if each housing unit is unique, and there is considerable truth in that thought. However, it is also true that the housing market functions. Every day houses and apartment buildings are bought and sold, and housing units are rented. How do the actors in the housing market simplify things so that transactions can be made on a routine basis?

B. APPRAISAL AND THE DETERMINATION OF HOUSING VALUES

One good way to understand the housing market is to examine the process through which a house is sold. This section provides a brief overview of the functioning of the housing market. The appendix to this chapter provides a lengthier discussion of the details on the operation of the market for housing. This appendix is an introduction to the law and institutions that govern the housing market. A course in real estate is recommended for those who are interested in learning more about real estate markets. The appraisal of house value is part of the sale process.

The owner who decides to sell a house typically will contact a real estate broker, a person who operates a business that specializes in selling houses. A listing contract is drawn up between the seller and the broker. This contract stipulates the price that the seller is willing to accept, the fee that the broker will receive when the house is sold, and the time limit on the contract. The broker's commission is usually 6% of the sale price and is paid by the seller. It is important to remember that the real estate broker is working on behalf of the *seller*. The broker employs real estate agents who engage in marketing activities designed to sell the house.

Potential buyers contact the broker or his or her agents. If a potential buyer wishes to make an offer to the seller, a contract for sale is drawn up. This contract stipulates the price to be paid, the date at which ownership will be transferred and payments made, and several other terms and conditions for the sale. The potential buyer signs the proposed contract, and the agent presents the contract to the seller. The seller can sign the contract, thereby accepting the offer, or draw up another proposed contract that is a counterproposal. Because contracts for the sale of real estate are rather complex documents with many provisions, there are many opportunities for the parties to bargain. Eventually, the buyer and the seller agree on a set of terms, and the contract for sale is signed by both parties.

The most important term in the contract for sale, the price, is determined by the bargaining process. The original listing contract included a price that the seller was willing to accept, and this figure was probably based on the broker's comparative market analysis of the property (plus a little more added on, perhaps). The broker is familiar with the current market prices for houses in the area, so the seller will normally defer to the broker's expertise. The buyer may base an offer on information provided by the broker, or he may hire someone else to perform a comparative market analysis that can serve as the basis for an offer. Recall that the broker is working for the seller and is paid a commission that is larger, the higher is the selling price.

In most cases the next step is the arrangement of financing by the buyer. The typical buyer must arrange for a home loan from a financial institution such as a savings and loan association or a bank. Conventional home loans usually require a down payment of 20% of the purchase price, so a loan of 80% of the price is a standard financing package. However, some government home loan programs permit the buyer to make a down payment that is far less than 20% of the price.

The basic contract for a home loan, a mortgage contract, stipulates that if the buyer fails to make the required payments on the loan, the financial institution can *foreclose*. Foreclosure means that the financial institution has assumed ownership of the property for the purpose of selling it to recover the amount loaned. Before the financial institution offers a loan to a buyer, a formal appraisal of the value of the property is conducted. An appraisal is an estimate of the market value of the property if it were to be sold under normal conditions. The appraisal will tell the financial institution whether the price as set by the buyer and seller is reasonable and therefore whether the financial institution will be able to recover its money if a foreclosure becomes necessary. The appraisal is performed by an appraiser, a professional who specializes in this kind of work. The basic idea is to gather data on three houses that have been sold recently that are also comparable to the subject house. The selling price of each "comparable" is adjusted up or down for any differences between it and the subject house. For example, if the comparable property is larger than the subject house by 100 square feet, the price of the comparable is adjusted *downward* by the market value of 100 square feet to make it more identical to the subject property. The techniques used in appraisal are discussed in the appendix to this chapter.

The last step in the process of selling the house is the closing. At the closing the deed, the document that is evidence of legal title is transferred from the seller to the buyer. The buyer's lender pays the seller, and the buyer writes a check for his or her part of the price (and any other expenses). The buyer also signs the mortgage contract. The seller pays off the balance on any loans that were outstanding on the property and walks away with the selling price minus the final loan payment and any expenses (including the broker's commission).

C. STATISTICAL MODELS OF HOUSE VALUES

Suppose that you work as an appraiser of residential property and the files in your office contain data on hundreds of sales. Suppose also that you had a statistics course in college. Your job is to estimate the market value of a subject house given its location and the attributes of the house and lot. Most likely it would occur to you that the data base in your office could be used to estimate a statistical model of house prices that would make your job easier. You know the attributes, locations, and selling prices of many properties. You might also have data on the important features of the neighborhood in which each house is located. All of this information can then be used to estimate an equation that can be used to predict the price of a subject house.

The statistical model of house prices estimated using such a data base is called a *hedonic model*, a term derived from the word *hedonism*, which is the idea that one should pursue pleasure. The idea is that a house consists of numerous components which add to one's pleasure, and that each of these components has a price. The market price of the house is the sum of the market prices of its components. Consider a very simple model of house value in which the components are the size of the house (interior square feet), the size of the lot (exterior square feet), and the proximity to employment. The market value of houses (V) can be specified as a linear equation

$$V = a_0 + a_1 F + a_2 L + a_3 x + e,$$

where F is the number of square feet of interior space, L the number of square feet of exterior space, x the distance to employment, and e is a random error term. The coefficient a_1 is the market value of an additional square foot of interior space, a_2 the market value of a square foot of exterior space, and a_3 the reduction in value that is associated with greater distance from employment. The random error term reflects the fact that the three variables do not completely account for variations in the value of houses. Each house in the data base has its own individual error term, which is a collection of other influences on value that are not included in the equation.

Suppose you use the multiple regression program that came with the computer in your office to estimate the foregoing linear model of house prices. You have just finished this task when a client walks in the door and asks you to appraise a house with 1500 square feet of interior space on a lot that is 50 by 100 feet and located 5 miles from the CBD. It takes you about 2 minutes to compute an estimate of market value V^* as

$$V^* = a_0 + a_1(1500) + a_2(5000) + a_3(5).$$

Appraisers are not permitted to perform appraisals in this manner. They must follow the procedure discussed in the appendix to this chapter. However, hedonic models are useful tools for appraisers because they indicate the market value of particular attributes. For example, suppose that the subject property and the comparable properties used for appraisal purposes differ in the amount of interior space they provide. The estimated coefficient a_1 tells you the magnitude of the adjustment to the price of the comparable property that is needed in the standard appraisal. Another use of hedonic models is for property tax assessment. The task of the county tax assessor is to determine an assessed value for every house in the county. Many assessors estimate a hedonic model based on a sample of houses and then use it to "predict" the market value of all the houses in the county. Assessed value is then based on this predicted market value.

Scores of hedonic studies of house prices have been published in academic and professional journals. A study is deemed worthy of publication if it adds something to our knowledge of the determinants of housing values, but they all include a fairly standard list of variables. Most hedonic studies of house prices use an exponential function rather than a linear function of the form

$$V = \exp(a_0 + a_1 F + \cdots + a_n X + e),$$

where $\exp(\cdot)$ means that the base of the natural logarithms is taken to the power shown in parentheses. The natural log of the price is then the dependent variable in a linear hedonic model of the form

$$\ln V = a_0 + a_1 F + \cdots + a_n X + e.$$

This log-linear equation usually fits the data better than does the conventional linear equation in which V is the dependent variable. Recalling the discussion from Chapter 5, the coefficients in the log-linear model (a_1 to a_n) indicate the *percentage* change in V associated with a change in the independent variable.

A typical example of such a study is one by Do, Wilbur, and Short (1994) of houses in one part of San Diego that were sold during the period January 1991 to September 1992. Data were provided by the local realtors' multiple listing service

TABLE 9.2	Hedonic Model of House Values (Dependent Variable Is Natural Log of Selling Price)	
Variable	*Mean*	*Percentage Price Effect*
Age	22.6 years	−0.22% per year
Time on market	78 days	−0.009% per day
Interior space	1529 ft²	3.07% per 100 ft²
Garage spaces	1.77	5.93% per space
Fireplace	0.77	2.84% per fireplace
Good view	0.29	3.37%
Lot size	8148 ft²	0.61% per 1000 ft²
Time trend		−0.49% per month from 1/91 to 9/92
Distance from church	634 ft	+0.006 per 100 ft
Distance from church squared		−0.00035 per (100 ft)²
Constant term		11.521
R^2		0.76

Source: Table compiled from data obtained from Do, Wilbur, and Short (1994, p. 131).

(MLS) for 469 sales. The results obtained by Do et al. (1994) are shown in Table 9.2. The mean selling price for the houses in the sample was $185,368. The average house in the sample had 1529 square feet of interior space and 8148 square feet of exterior space and was 22.6 years old. The results show that the selling price of a house was 0.22% lower for each year since it was built, and was 0.009% lower for each day it was on the market. Each 100 square feet of interior space added 3.1%, each garage space 6%, and each fireplace added 2.8% to value. A house with what was judged to be a "good view" sold for 3.4% more. An added 1000 square feet of land boosted the price by only 0.61%, perhaps because the lots in this area of San Diego are quite large. A time trend result indicates that the price fell by 0.49% per month from January 1991 to September 1992. This was a time of recession in the California economy. These coefficients can be helpful to appraisers, who must make adjustments to the selling price of comparable properties.

The original contribution of the study by Do et al. (1994) is to measure the effect on selling price of proximity to a church. The effect of distance from the nearest church is specified as a quadratic function because the researchers hypothesized that proximity to a church may have a negative (percentage) effect on selling price, but that the effect in percentage terms gets smaller as distance to the church increases. The empirical findings are consistent with this idea; the coefficient of distance from the church is positive and the coefficient of distance squared is negative. The results *fail to reject* the hypothesis. Figure 9.1 shows the effect of distance from the church graphically; the slope of the curve shown in Figure 9.1 is the change in the natural logarithm of selling price for a change in distance (D) of 100 feet, which equals

FIGURE 9.1 Effect on house value of proximity to a church

Distance to Church · 850 ft

$$\frac{\delta \ln V}{\delta D} = 0.006 - 0.0007\ D.$$

(Recall the rule from the appendix to the book that if $Y = aX + bX^2$, then $\delta Y/\delta X = a + 2bX$.) The effect of additional distance from the church falls to zero where $\delta \ln V/\delta D = 0$ (i.e., where $D = 850$ feet). The study thus does establish the existence of a negative external effect of a nearby church that probably arises from traffic, parking problems, and other factors associated with church activities. A house located 850 feet from a church sold for about 3% more than a house located only 100 feet from a church. This result is found by setting distance alternatively equal to 100 and 850, and noting the difference in the natural logarithm of selling price implied.

D. HOUSING PRICES, NEIGHBORHOOD CHARACTERISTICS, AND RACIAL SEGREGATION

In the preceding section we established that the price of a house reflects the attributes of the house and lot and the characteristics of the neighborhood in which the house is located. The price is established through the process of negotiation between buyer and seller, but there is no sale unless the buyer makes a bid. Buyers base their bids on many factors, and the purpose of this section is to discuss the neighborhood characteristics that influence bids. This section also introduces the idea that different types of households may make different bids for the same property. Not everyone places the same value on a given bundle of attributes and neighborhood characteristics. As in Chapter 5, the household with the highest bid occupies the property. If there are systematic differences in the bids made by different types of households, there will be clustering of households of particular types.

What neighborhood factors have been found to influence the selling price of a house? No doubt the following list is not complete, but its length gives you some idea of how many variables seem to matter to people. These variables have been found to have a statistically significant impact on the selling price of houses in at least one study:

1. Quality of local school (positive effect)
2. Crime rate in area (negative effect)
3. Property tax rate (negative effect)
4. Neighborhood income, size of houses in neighborhood, etc. (positive effect)
5. Air pollution (negative effect)
6. Airport noise (negative effect)
7. Proximity to contaminated areas (negative effect)
8. Proximity of nuclear power plant (negative effect)
9. Proximity to a park (positive effect)
10. Industrial noise (negative effect)
11. Heavy traffic on street (negative effect)
12. Location in a floodplain (negative effect)
13. Distance to employment (negative effect)
14. Distance to shopping (negative effect)
15. Distance to airport (negative effect)
16. Rating of the quality of houses next door and on the block (positive effect)
17. Within walking distance of public transit or commuter rail station (positive effect)
18. Adjacent to rail line, highway, or transit line (negative effect)
19. Proximity to highway interchange (positive effect)
20. Proximity to a church (negative effect)
21. Existence of zoning or restrictive covenants versus their absence (positive effect)
22. Previous price increase in neighborhood, to capture expectation of future price increases (positive effect)

This is a pretty bewildering list of variables. Each variable makes sense individually, but how can a person possibly take all of these factors into account in formulating a bid for a house, or for that matter, in doing an empirical study of house values? It is fair to say that researchers in the field are busy making the list longer rather than shorter. The typical study will gather data on selling prices, include several attributes of the house and lot, and measure a few neighborhood characteristics. The focus of the study will usually be on some neighborhood characteristic that has not previously been studied, and the results of the study will be published because a statistically significant result has been obtained for that new variable. This procedure for research settles few issues because no one ever includes *all* of the neighborhood characteristics that have been found to be statistically significant in previous studies. If all of these variables were included, would the addition of another variable add to the explanatory power of the model? This question is difficult to answer, but perhaps it would not.

The individual household obviously cannot take all of these factors into account at once. A sensible procedure is to restrict the search to areas with reasonable access to work where it is known that many potential neighborhood problems do not exist. The household probably specifies a desired set of characteristics in the housing unit itself and a price range, and the real estate agent identifies units that meet these criteria. If a subject house meets the basic criteria, the household will take a look at the neighborhood characteristics that are regarded as most important (e.g., school quality, access to shopping, and the like).

It is worthwhile to understand how the appraiser deals with this problem of the large number of potentially relevant neighborhood characteristics. The appraiser first seeks comparable properties that are in the same neighborhood as the subject property. If comparables must be used from another neighborhood, the appraiser estimates the difference in value attributable to location by use of paired observations from the two neighborhoods. In either case, the appraiser does not need to know anything about the various neighborhood characteristics to do the job. The appraiser relies on the market to do the job for him and whatever the market says will be used.

The foregoing list of neighborhood characteristics is very long, but it leaves out the one characteristic that has captured more attention among researchers, and probably among the general public also, than any other. That characteristic is the racial composition of the neighborhood. There is a large and growing body of evidence to support the notion that the demand for housing expressed by white households is influenced by the racial composition of the area in which the house is located. In particular, the importance of the black residential population on white demand has emerged in several studies. It appears that white demand is reduced both by the percentage black population in the area immediately surrounding a house and by proximity to the closest predominantly black neighborhood. Both of these effects arise from racial prejudice, an aversion to an individual member of a racial group regardless of the attributes of that person. Furthermore, there is evidence of discriminatory behavior against blacks that takes the form of exclusion and price discrimination on the part of housing sellers. The purpose of this section is to review some recent studies of these phenomena.

King and Mieszkowski (1973) first pointed out that it is important to separate the effects of demand and supply factors on racial price differences. If prejudice on the part of white households is the only racial factor operating, the aversion of whites for blacks will lead to supply adjustment, which brings about lower housing prices for blacks than for whites who avoid blacks. However, if housing suppliers discriminate against blacks by limiting access as black demand grows, for example, we may find that blacks pay more than whites for equivalent housing while white demand for housing in some areas is reduced by racial prejudice. To untangle these various effects, King and Mieszkowski (1973), in their study of rents in New Haven during 1968–1969, examined the rents paid by white and black households in two types of areas, the black interior and the racial boundary, compared to rents paid by whites in the white interior. The results of estimating the hedonic equation show that white rents in the boundary areas were 7% lower than rents in the white interior. Rents paid by blacks in the boundary areas were equal to white interior rents, so there was a 7% difference between white and black rents in the boundary area. This is their estimate of the effect of racial prejudice, the aversion of whites for blacks. Both white and black rents in the black interior were about 9% higher than white interior rents, suggesting limitations on the expansion of the black residential areas during a period of demand growth.

The study by King and Mieszkowski has been followed by a few more studies that separate the depressing effect of black neighbors on white housing demand from the effect of supply restrictions imposed on blacks. One influential study of housing prices in Chicago for 1968–1972 by Berry (1976) found that prices were lower in white areas near black and Latino areas than in white areas that were removed from the racial borders. However, Berry (1976) also found that prices were lowest of all in the traditional black and Latino neighborhoods. Prices in the zones of recent black and Latino expansion were about equal to prices in the white border areas. In contrast to the King–Mieszkowski study, the race of the individual household is unknown. What can account for the pattern in Berry's (1976) results?

Berry argued that in the 1950s and early 1960s, the black and Latino populations were expanding rapidly, but that the stock of housing available to these groups was expanding slowly because of racial discrimination on the part of white sellers, which was no doubt partly created by the racial prejudice of their neighbors. At this point it is appropriate to recall the image of Martin Luther King leading housing integration marches in Chicago in the summer of 1965. Those marches yielded angry reactions from whites in Chicago.

According to Berry (1976), the situation had changed considerably by the end of the 1960s. Berry (1976) pointed out that 482,000 new housing units were built in the Chicago urban area during the 1960s, but the number of households increased by only 285,000. As a result, 128,000 units were transferred from white to black occupancy and 63,000 units were demolished. The number of black households in the city of Chicago increased by 80,000, while the number of white households declined by 119,000. The Latino population increased by 35,000 households. Berry argued that these massive changes in the racial geography of the city, as the whites relinquished neighborhood after neighborhood to blacks and Latinos, resulted in substantially lower prices for blacks and Latinos than whites in their traditional neighborhoods. This combination of results suggested to Berry that, in effect, the model of white prejudice was operating and that there were no barriers to a rapid increase in the aggregate supply of housing available to blacks and Latinos. The timing of Berry's study is important, because he examined the housing market just after completion of the expressway system in Chicago. Whites were moving to the suburbs in large numbers as new suburban housing was being built. The general effects of new construction are discussed in more detail below.

Smith (1981) strongly questioned Berry's conclusion that blacks and Latinos paid less for housing than did whites. Smith's (1981) study of Chicago housing prices in 1972 found that prices were lower in traditional black areas and zones of recent black expansion than in white interior areas. Also, prices were lowest in the black–white border areas. However, Smith attributes these seeming racial price effects to differences in crucial neighborhood characteristics that Berry failed to take into account properly. In particular, black areas had significantly higher crime rates and levels of air pollution. Smith's general conclusion is that blacks paid less for housing because they purchased housing in inferior neighborhoods. The discussion of racial segregation below suggests that black households do not necessarily prefer the option of lower prices and inferior neighborhoods. Smith even questioned the conclusion that after controlling properly for other neighborhood characteristics, prices are really lower in the black–white border areas.

If the empirical evidence on racial differences in housing prices and rents is somewhat ambiguous, the segregation of the races is not. A recent book by sociologists Douglas Massey and Nancy Denton (1993) with the title *American Apartheid* documents the degree of segregation in urban areas in America. One measure of segregation is the percentage of blacks who would have to move to achieve an equal percentage of blacks in all census tracts. (Blacks who hypothetically move are hypothetically replaced by whites who move.) This index of segregation as reported by Massey and Denton (1993, p. 64) for the top 10 urban areas (as of 1990) for 1970 and 1980 is as follows:

	Segregation Index for:	
	1970	*1980*
New York	81.0	82.0
Los Angeles	91.0	81.1
Chicago	91.9	87.8
San Francisco	80.1	71.7
Philadelphia	79.5	78.8
Washington, DC	81.1	70.1
Boston	81.2	77.6
Detroit	88.4	86.7
Dallas–Ft. Worth	86.9	77.1
Houston	78.1	69.5

The average segregation index for 1970 for these 10 urban areas was 83.9, and the average had fallen somewhat to 78.2 in 1980. The greatest declines in the segregation index occurred in the sunbelt urban areas of Los Angeles, San Francisco, Washington, DC, Dallas–Fort Worth, and Houston. The five largest urban areas of the northeast had little change in segregation over this decade.

What are the causes of racial segregation? The study of racial segregation is more within the province of urban sociology than urban economics, and Schwab (1992, Chap. 12) provides a good introduction to the topic. A list of the factors that cause racial segregation would include:

1. Segregation by social and economic status, caused by tastes for social linkages
2. Segregation related to ethnic group, which may in part stem from the timing of arrival of immigrants to the urban area
3. Segregation caused by active discrimination against certain racial groups
4. Segregation caused by prejudice against certain racial groups

The first two causes on this list bring about voluntary segregation of groups, but the last two involuntarily segregate the victims of discrimination and prejudice. The studies reviewed by Massey and Denton (1993) indicate that voluntary segregation can explain very little of the high degree of segregation of the black population in urban areas. A study by Miller and Quigley (1990) of the San Francisco urban area found that almost none of the racial segregation in both 1970 and 1980 could be attributed to segregation by type of household (household composition and income).

Segregation through prejudice often involves a process called neighborhood *tipping*. Consider an all-white neighborhood that is adjacent to a black neighborhood. Houses are put up for sale on a regular basis because people change jobs, retire, and so on. The process begins when a black household buys a house in the adjacent all-white neighborhood. The purchase may have been made because of demand growth in the black portion of the housing market. This household may be subjected to racial discrimination and antisocial behavior, or maybe nothing happens. White households continue to buy houses in the neighborhood because they are not influenced by the presence of one black household. However, soon more black households buy homes in the formerly all-white neighborhood. Now some potential white buyers "avoid" this area, and more and more of the houses that are put on the market are sold to black households. What we really mean is that potential white buyers make lower bids than do potential black buyers *because of the presence of blacks in the area*. The *tipping point* is defined as the percentage of houses in the neighborhood occupied by black households at which potential white buyers begin to avoid the area for racial reasons (i.e., make lower bids than potential black buyers). If a neighborhood has crossed the tipping point, transition to a neighborhood that is largely occupied by black households will occur. Some white households may remain, and some white households may purchase homes in the area, but their numbers will not be great enough to prevent the racial transition.

E. THE FILTERING MODEL OF THE HOUSING MARKET

The discussion of racial prejudice, discrimination, and segregation included the idea that new houses were built in the suburbs for white households, and this led to an expansion of the residential areas occupied by minority households, especially black households. Housing researchers have observed that this kind of mechanism is at work in any housing market that includes a variety of both household and housing types. The filtering model of the housing market has been devised to take both types—households and housing units—into account.

The presentation of the model will begin by ignoring location and neighborhood characteristics. This assumption is relaxed later. As a beginning, suppose that all housing units can be arrayed in a hierarchy from best to worst. The array goes from the fanciest mansion to the run-down, single-room apartment. Further suppose that households are arrayed in order of the amount of housing that they demand. Households with higher incomes demand more housing, so the order of the household in the array will be strongly correlated with income. The housing market assigns each household to a housing unit and determines prices for the various units. Now let us simplify the picture by grouping the households and their assigned housing units according to the quality level of the housing unit. For concreteness, suppose that the housing units are grouped into the top, middle, and bottom thirds. We now have set up a model with markets for three general types of housing units: high-quality units, medium-quality units, and low-quality units. These three markets are interrelated because they are markets for goods that are, to some degree, substitutes.

FIGURE 9.2 Filtering model of the housing market

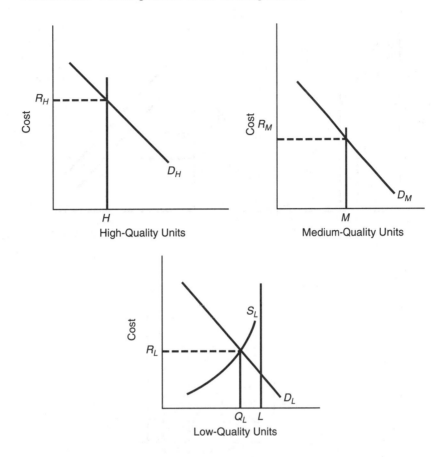

The basic three-market model is depicted in Figure 9.2. The initial demand functions for high-, medium-, and low-quality units are denoted D_H, D_M, and D_L. The supply of high-quality units initially is H, the M units of medium-quality units are supplied. These supplies are fixed (for the moment), and it is assumed that there are no vacant units in these two markets. The number of low-quality units in the market is L, but the short-run supply curve is S_L, to reflect the fact that the number of units actually offered in the market depends on the housing rent. The supply of low-quality housing is thus depicted in the same manner as was used in Chapter 7 to portray the supply of office space. Given the market demands, the initial equilibrium housing rents are R_H, R_M, and R_L. In addition, the number of vacant units of low-quality housing is $L - Q_L$.

The model in Figure 9.2 has many uses. Perhaps the standard exercise is to introduce an increase in the supply of high-quality units. Why might this supply increase occur? One possible reason is a reduction in the cost of building these units.

FIGURE 9.3   Filtering model of the housing market

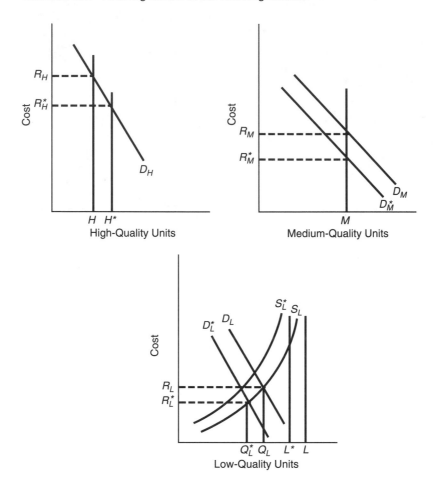

The increase in the supply of high-quality units is shown in Figure 9.3 as a shift from H to H^*. Given that the demand for high-quality units has not changed, the housing rent must decline from R to R^* so that the additional units will be occupied. Who occupies those units? The obvious candidates are households who occupy medium-quality units. Since high- and medium-quality units are substitutes, the demand curve for medium-quality units shifts to the left (decreases) as the rent in high-quality units falls. In Figure 9.3 the demand for medium-quality units shifts to the left by the increase in high-quality units. The decline in rent in high-quality units must be enough to shift D_M to D_M^*. Some households who occupy units of medium quality move up to high-quality units. What happens next? Housing rents in units of medium quality fall and cause the demand for low-quality units to decrease. Some households who occupy low-quality units move into the vacated medium-quality units. Housing rents in medium-quality units fall to R_M^*. Finally, housing rents in low-quality units fall to R_L^*, and there is an increase in the number of vacant low-quality units equal to the increase in high-quality units.

Note carefully what has happened. The increase in high-quality units has set off a series of changes in which all housing rents declined and some households "filtered" up in the quality hierarchy. In fact, the number of households who moved up in quality is, in this case, equal to two times the original increase in high-quality units. This appears to be a good thing for everyone, but what can go wrong? For one thing, the process is initiated by an increase in supply of high-quality units *relative to demand*. The filtering process will not occur if new construction at the top end only matches the growth in high-income households. Furthermore, the results are altered if the number of households can expand in response to lower housing rents. Suppose that some of the households who live in medium-quality units can split into two households. One of these households moves into a vacant high-quality unit and the other household stays put. This can mean that the demand for medium-quality units does not decline at all, and the housing rent for these units does not decline. No occupants of low-quality units move up in quality. This is an extreme example, but the creation of new households from the same population tends to choke off the filtering process.

Next consider the market for low-quality units. The housing rent has declined and the vacancy rate has increased. Do the suppliers of low-quality housing react to these changes? Eventually they will because a high vacancy rate will mean that some units will be vacant for lengths of time that are too great to make them economically feasible. A unit is no longer economically feasible if the housing rents cannot cover the variables costs of operating the unit as housing. This is the usual decision to shut down a business. Clearly, units will be withdrawn from the housing stock, but just exactly how does that happen? If there is a good alternative use for the land under the unit, the owner will demolish the housing and convert to another use, such as commercial, parking lot, and so on. The withdrawal of units from the low-quality stock will shift supply to the left (to L^* and S_L^*) and cause housing rents to rise at this end of the market. This reduction in supply and increase in housing rents can be a good thing because they ensure that the remaining low-quality units are now economically feasible. The occupants of low-quality housing must pay the higher housing rents, of course.

One more feature of housing needs to be added to the model. Housing is durable, but it is not infinitely durable. Some households move up in housing quality, but the units that they occupy may not remain at the original quality level. Medium-quality units eventually may become low-quality units, and high-quality units can become units of medium quality. The improvement in housing quality generated by the filtering mechanism may well not be permanent. Indeed, note that the rents paid for both high- and medium-quality units have declined. These declines in rents will probably lead landlords to cut back on maintenance expenditures, which will eventually lead to a decline in the quality of some units. Some high-quality units will be turned into medium-quality units, and some medium-quality units will be turned into low-quality units. The entire housing market may eventually return to the original price and quantity for each level of quality.

So far the model has generated reductions in the stock of low-quality housing by demolition, but a drive around older central cities will demonstrate that many units are removed from the stock simply by being abandoned. The owner walks away from the building and leaves no forwarding address for the property tax collector and the building inspector. Abandonment can be a good choice for the owner. The abandonment of a property means that the housing rents cannot cover variable costs *and* that the value of the land, less any demolition costs, is zero (or less). Given that the value of land in some inner-city areas has collapsed virtually to zero, abandonments can be expected to result from increases in the supply of high- or medium-quality housing.

Abandonment may be a good decision for the owner, but it is often a disastrous decision for the society. Abandoned units cost something to demolish, and usually the municipal government must pay that cost. Before the demolition can be accomplished, the abandoned unit can be a source of negative external effects in its neighborhood. Abandoned units hurt the appearance of a neighborhood, are fire hazards, and can be places of criminal activity. Abandoned units are red flags which say that the neighborhood is in trouble. It appears that abandonment can beget more abandonment as many factors interact to reduce the quality of the neighborhood further unless the city government can keep on top of the problem with timely demolition. Central cities sometimes have lost the race against abandonment, but in some cases the city is its own worst enemy. A study by White (1986) showed that the most important factor in housing abandonment in New York City during the late 1970s was a high property tax bill compared to the rents the building can earn. The property tax bills loomed large as a percentage of rent because the city had failed to adjust assessed values downward as rents declined. Landlords were pushed over the edge by high property tax bills. The economics of the property tax are discussed in Chapter 10.

Now let us put location into the filtering model. The fact is that most of the newer and high-quality housing is in the suburbs, and most of the low-quality housing is the old housing located in the inner city. Mieszkowski and Mills (1993) argue that the filtering model provides a primary reason for the movement of population to the suburbs and for the concentration of low-income households in central cities. They call the model the natural evolution theory. The construction of the expressways in the 1950s and 1960s, coupled with federal policies that encouraged new construction and homeownership (discussed below), opened the flood gates for movement of (mostly white) middle-class people to the suburbs. As we have already seen, the movement of employment to the suburbs in great numbers came later. Rising real incomes, at least up to the 1970s, stimulated new construction as well. In this kind of housing market in the suburbs, the filtering mechanism worked and neighborhood after neighborhood was relinquished to the growing minority populations. The old minority neighborhoods increasingly became areas of abandonment. A good research project would be to examine the data on census tracts in an urban area with which you are familiar for the years 1950, 1970, and 1990. Do you see evidence of the filtering process at work? How has the racial geography of the urban area changed over these 40 years? As a supplement to the data work, ask someone over the age of 60 who has always lived in the urban area where the "old neighborhood" is. Find out where that person lives now.

It is true that the old housing in the central cities eventually wears out and must be demolished and replaced even in the absence of the construction of high-quality units. However, the construction of high-quality units in the suburbs in excess of the growth of the number of households ultimately leads to demolition (or abandonment)

FIGURE 9.4 Filtering model of the housing market

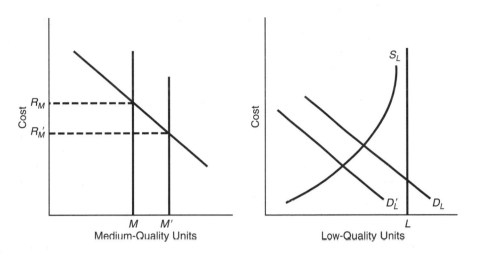

of some units in the inner city *without replacement*. Vast areas of some of the older central cities, such as New York, Detroit, Chicago, Milwaukee, St. Louis, and others, are vacant and awaiting redevelopment. Furthermore, the central city has lost middle-class households and their tax base in the process. The loss of tax base, in both the residential and nonresidential categories, puts pressure on the budget of governments in the central city.

The model of filtering as in Figure 9.2 has other uses. For example, one aspect of housing policy in the United States is the subsidization of the construction of housing units that fall within the medium-quality category. In Figure 9.4 an increase in the quantity of medium-quality units from M to M' causes housing rents to fall to R'_M and the demand for low-quality units to drop as people move up in quality to these new units. Here it is being assumed that the market for high-quality units is not affected by this increase in medium-quality units. The impacts on the market for low-quality units include reduced housing rents and increased vacancies and, ultimately, removals of units from the stock and restoration of the rent level. The construction of medium-quality units on a large scale might very well lead to the abandonment of areas that contain the old low-quality units unless that construction is managed to preserve those neighborhoods.

F. HOUSING POLICY IN THE UNITED STATES

The housing market is the one market for a consumer good that is subjected to more policy initiatives than any other. The main actor is the federal government, but local governments are deeply involved in administering federal programs and in creating their own programs, such as rent controls. We include in this section a brief history of federal housing policy since the first program was begun in 1934. Federal policy is of two basic types: policies designed to enable middle-class households to own their own homes, and policies aimed at upgrading the housing of lower-income households. Before the details of various programs are discussed, it is worthwhile to consider the reasons why society has singled out housing as a good that people are encouraged to consume.

As you might have guessed, economists of the conservative school of thought have serious doubts about the wisdom of policies designed to increase the consumption of housing. As discussed in Chapter 2, conservatives will acknowledge that there is a poverty problem and that there is a good case for cash transfer payments to the poor, couched in a system with strong incentives to work. If low-income households have a decent amount of cash, they can decide how to spend it. There is no particular reason to encourage housing consumption. To the conservative economist the housing market appears to be a competitive market that does not need intervention by the government. Furthermore, as Milton Friedman would say, attempts by the government to "do good" in the housing market will probably end up with the opposite result. How do the advocates of housing policy respond?

Several theoretical arguments are made. The housing market contains both positive and negative externalities in neighborhoods. The quality of one housing unit can have either positive or negative effects on the value of neighboring units and the living conditions of the neighbors. As discussed above, abandoned housing units are unsightly, create fire hazards, and attract crime. At the other extreme, a neighborhood filled with nice, well-maintained houses (and filled with decent people) creates a strong positive effect. Some economists and housing advocates go further and argue that there are additional serious imperfections in the housing market that arise from racial discrimination. Racial discrimination circumscribes the choices that minority households have in the housing market, and this reduction in choices limits the ability to minorities to consume good housing and to reside in locations that are easily accessible to suburban workplaces. In addition, many argue that there is overt discrimination in the markets for mortgage loans and housing insurance that limits the ability of minority households to maintain and upgrade the housing stock in their racially segregated neighborhoods. Recent detailed empirical research by economists at the Federal Reserve Bank of Boston [Munnell et al. (1992)] has documented what appears to be discrimination in the mortgage market. They have found that black households are rejected for mortgages at a higher rate than are white households, even after the effects of a large number of variables (income, employment stability, credit rating, etc.) are included.

Others advocates of housing policy go even further and argue that housing is a *merit good*, a good that society views as more important than allowed for by individual choices. A merit good is a good that creates benefits for the community as a whole, and housing, health, recreation, and education are often mentioned as being in this category. It is fair to say that conservative economists take a very dim view of the idea of merit goods. They see the idea of merit goods as a vague justification for all sorts of ill-considered interventions into the private economy. Because of this criticism, the use of the term *merit good* has fallen into disuse. Nevertheless, the idea of a merit good is based on externalities. The question is whether the externalities in the housing market are strong enough to justify intervention and, if they are, what sort of intervention is indicated. The answers to these questions are much in dispute among economists and the public at large.

One point that is more persuasive pertains to the support of housing for lower-income households. As discussed in the introduction to this chapter, in accordance with a general negative externality argument, cities have housing codes and building codes that establish minimum standards for housing units. These codes come under the police power of local government to protect the health, safety, and welfare of the public, but they mean that some households have great difficulty affording housing at the minimum standard. The minimum rent implied by the housing and building codes exceeds the amount that some households would choose to pay of their own accord. For example, some poor single men would choose to live in shabby single-room occupancy hotels or rooming houses, but local governments regard such buildings as unsafe and have forced them to close down. Housing subsidies can then be viewed as a method of compensating the low-income households for being forced to make an allocation of their incomes not of their own choosing (or to be homeless). With these points in mind, let us now turn to the actual policies.

Housing Policies for the Middle Class

Middle-class Americans are encouraged to own their homes through two long-standing policies: federal mortgage insurance and federal income tax deductions for mortgage interest payments and local property taxes. The Federal Housing Administration (FHA) was established in 1934 to provide mortgage lenders with a guarantee that the default of a borrower will not cost them money. Prior to the creation of FHA, most home loans had high down payments and were of rather short duration by today's standards—5 to 15 years. Those loans required repayment in full at the end of the term of the loan, which meant that the household usually had to obtain another loan to repay the first loan. This kind of loan is called *nonamortizing* because the monthly payments do not include an amount that reduces the principal of the loan to zero by the end of the term. During the early years of the Great Depression, which began in 1929, many households lost their homes because they could not qualify for the new loan that was needed to pay off the old loan. High unemployment and declining wages meant that monthly incomes were insufficient to make the loan payments. Other households simply defaulted on their existing home loans because of the drop in income, and the decline in the market value of the house caused by the depression left the lender unable to recover the principal amount.

Policymakers at the FHA decided that a good solution to these problems was to create a mortgage loan instrument that had a long term of 25 to 30 years that would also be fully amortizing. A loan that is fully amortizing eliminates the need to find new financing. If the loan is to be fully amortizing, the longer term for the loan will reduce the size of the monthly payment needed to pay back the loan. Furthermore, policymakers wanted to encourage ownership of homes by having lower down payments. FHA officials reasoned that lenders would not agree to low down payments and long terms for the home loan unless there was a guarantee. FHA loans were thus formulated as loans with maximum 30-year terms, low down payments, full amortization, and mortgage insurance that is purchased by the borrower. The insurance premium can be paid in a lump sum at the beginning, or it can be included in the loan amount and thus paid over the term of the loan. FHA loans are limited in their amount, so expensive houses cannot be bought under the FHA program. However, the FHA loan guarantee program demonstrated that loans of this type were feasible, and private lenders soon began to offer the same type of loan (but with higher down-payment requirements) to any borrower. The conventional home loan is for 25 to 30 years, is fully amortizing, and requires a down payment of 20%. It is fair to say that once the Great Depression and World War II era had ended, the creation of this new type of home loan enabled many households to become owners of homes in the sub-urbs. Many may wonder today about the wisdom of encouraging suburban home-ownership, but clearly the FHA program has been highly successful in addressing the problems as they existed in the 1930s. The appendix to this chapter contains a finan-cial analysis of the fully amortizing loan.

The other major housing program aimed at the middle (and upper) class is the favorable treatment of owner-occupied housing in the federal income tax. The own-ers of homes are permitted to deduct from income their expenses for mortgage inter-est and state and local taxes. They are not permitted to deduct loan payments that re-duce principal—only the interest payments are deductible. American taxpayers also get to avoid paying the capital gains tax on the increase in the value of their homes under fairly broad conditions. No capital gains tax is paid if the homeowner pur-chases another house of equal or greater value within 2 years. Furthermore, the homeowner receives a one-time capital gains exclusion (up to a limit of $125,000) if he or she is over the age 55 when the house is sold. This favorable treatment of capi-tal gains is an incentive to "invest" in one's home rather than other assets.

The economic impact of these tax provisions can be examined through the use of a framework developed by King and Fullerton (1984) to study the taxation of in-come from capital. In this case the income is the implicit (or imputed) housing rents that are created by an investment in an owner-occupied house. Obviously, the house generates a flow of housing services that has market value. Note that the homeowner does not report imputed rent on the owner-occupied house on the federal tax form but may deduct interest and property taxes, which are two of the main expenses incurred in producing housing services. (Imputed rent is reported in Italy, and it used to be re-ported in Sweden and the United Kingdom.) The King–Fullerton framework uses two basic concepts: (1) the marginal effective tax rate, and (2) the cost of capital.

The marginal effective tax rate is defined as

$$t = \frac{p - s}{p},$$

where p is the homeowner's before-tax real rate of return on the marginal investment (net of depreciation), and s is the after-tax real rate of return to the saver who sup-plied the financing for the investment. The simple difference $p - s$ is known as the *tax wedge*. The real rate of return p is in the form of imputed net rents. This equation for marginal effective tax rate can be written $t = 1 - s/p$. The assumption used in the King–Fullerton model is that p is equal to some constant such as 10%, so

$$t = 1 - 10s.$$

The before-tax real rate of return is held constant so that differences in tax provisions can be compared at a given real rate of return for housing investment. The finding that a change in tax regimes lowers the effective tax rate will, of course, provide an incentive for greater investment in housing capital.

The saver who supplied the financing for the house earns a real rate of return after taxes of

$$s = i(1 - m_L) - \pi - w,$$

where i is the nominal discount rate, m_L the saver's marginal tax rate, π the expected rate of inflation, and w the marginal personal tax rate on wealth. All of these variables that determine s, with the exception of i, are known. The trick now is to estimate i.

King and Fullerton (1984) assume that investors in housing invest up to the point at which p is equal to the cost of capital net of depreciation. Assuming that one knows the nominal discount rate, the cost of capital varies with the details of the tax code. The cost of capital net of depreciation can be written

$$c = (1 - A)(i - \pi + \phi) + (1 - B)w + z(\pi - \Omega),$$

with the additional terms in the equation defined as follows: A is the present value of tax allowances for owner-occupied housing (e.g., mortgage interest deduction), ϕ the tax rate on imputed rental income, B the present value of tax allowances that offset the wealth tax (i.e., income tax deduction for property taxes), Ω the real rate of depreciation, and z the tax rate on capital gains.

Consider this equation for the cost of capital net of depreciation very carefully. It says that the cost of capital net of depreciation includes the real discount rate $(i - \pi)$ and the tax rate on imputed net income ϕ, all multiplied by the factor $(1 - A)$ to reflect tax benefits provided to owner-occupied housing. The cost of capital also includes the wealth tax rate w (with offset factor B) and the tax rate on nominal capital gains after depreciation has been allowed $[z(\pi - \Omega)]$. This last term assumes that the house appreciates in value at the same rate as the expected inflation rate π.

The King–Fullerton procedure assumes that $c = p = 10\%$, and solves for i, the nominal discount rate. The value for i is then inserted into the equation for s, the real after-tax rate of return to the saver who supplied the housing finance. Actually, all of this can be performed in one operation. Consider the simple tax regime in which A, ϕ, B, and z are all equal to zero and where savers are not subject to the wealth tax rate w (homeowners are subject to the wealth tax). This is, in fact, the system that exists in Canada, and the cost of capital net of depreciation is just

$$c = 0.1 = i - \pi + w,$$

which means that $i = 0.1 + \pi - w$. The result for the effective tax rate is

$$t = 1 - 10\,[(0.1 + \pi - w)\,(1 - m_L) - \pi].$$

For example, suppose that π (expected inflation) is 0.05, w (property tax rate) is 0.02, and m_L (marginal tax rate for savers) is 0.30. For this example, suppose that the house is financed entirely by debt (i.e., by borrowing from people who face a marginal tax rate on their savings of 0.30). The marginal effective tax rate is 0.59 if the house is financed by debt. The interpretation is that 59% of the imputed return to a marginal investment in owner-occupied housing is taxed away.

The system in the United States permits tax deductions for interest and property taxes (i.e., $A = B$), so with 100% debt finance,

$$c = 0.1 = (1 - A)(i + w) - \pi.$$

In this case

$$t = 1 - 10 \left[\frac{0.1 + \pi}{1 - A}(1 - m_L) - w(1 - m_L) - \pi \right].$$

The only difference is that $0.1 + \pi$ is divided by $(1 - A)$, but the effective tax rate is changed dramatically. If $A = m_L = 0.30$ and the other numerical values remain unchanged, t falls to 0.14! Now the imputed rent of owner-occupied housing is taxed very lightly, which provides a strong incentive to invest compared to the Canadian system without the favorable tax deductions. In addition, the research reported in the book edited by Jorgenson and Landau (1993) shows that owner-occupied housing in the United States has a very low effective tax rate compared to other forms of private investment. Analogous computations for regular corporate investment show that the effective tax rate in 1990 was in the range 30 to 45%, compared to an estimated effective tax rate on owner-occupied housing of 11%. How can one invest in more owner-occupied housing? The usual procedure is to build more of it in the suburbs.

Housing Policies for Lower-Income Households

The goal of housing policy in the United States is, as stated in the Housing Act of 1949, to "provide a decent, safe, and sanitary living environment . . . for every American." The pursuit of this goal has spawned an array of federal programs, and the purpose of this section is to review briefly the history of federal low-income housing programs. Housing programs, or programs targeted at any other consumer good, can be classified as programs that function on the supply side or on the demand side of the market. For example, in the case of food, the government could produce the food and then give it away to poor households (supply-side program), or it could give the poor households food stamps that are spent on food (demand-side program). The general theme of this brief discussion is that federal policy began by supplying housing for low-income households directly and has, over the decades, gradually shifted to subsidies that operate on the demand side. Table 9.3 has been constructed to show the numbers of housing units in urban areas that are covered by the various housing programs in 1991.

TABLE 9.3   Subsidized Housing Units in Urban Areas, 1991 (Thousands of Units)

	Central Cities		Suburbs		Total
	Occupied Rental	*Vacant Rental*	*Occupied Rental*	*Vacant Rental*	*Rental Units*
No subsidy	12,540	1,353	11,175	1,036	26,104
Rent controlled	874	82	201	23	1,180
Public housing	1,247	80	434	21	1,782
Federally subsidized rental unit	745	49	518	16	1,328
State or locally subsidized rental unit	323	19	174	—	516
Income verification required	238	—	121	—	359
Not reported	173	21	152	18	364

Source: American Housing Survey, U.S. Department of Housing and Urban Development, 1993.

The first federal program was begun under the Housing Act of 1937, which created federally funded public housing. Under this program local governments were authorized to set up public housing authorities that would receive federal funds to build public housing. The federal government set up the eligibility criteria for residents of public housing, who then paid a low rent to the local public housing authority. The program was expanded under the Housing Act of 1949, the law that also created the urban renewal program. The 1949 act authorized the construction of 800,000 units of public housing. The urban renewal program set up local urban renewal authorities that received federal funds for the purchase of slum properties. Under the urban renewal program the local urban renewal authority demolished the slum buildings, assembled land into usable parcels, and then sold the land at below-market prices to housing developers. Sometimes that land was turned over to the local public housing authority for the construction of public housing, but most of the land parcels were sold to private developers that built a variety of types of housing. Table 9.3 shows that as of 1991, there were 1.782 million public housing units in urban areas in the United States and that 74% of those units were in central cities. Public housing makes up 2.2% of the 79 million housing units in urban areas.

Housing policy branched out in the 1960s to encourage the construction of housing for low-income households by private developers. Also, a small program of rent supplement for low-income households was created in 1965. Another new program in 1965 permitted public housing authorities to lease existing private housing units and subsidize low-income households to live in them. The 1960 Census of Population and Housing showed that 17% of housing units were either dilapidated or deteriorating, that 12% were overcrowded, and that affordability was a problem. Furthermore, the baby-boom generation would soon form their own families and overwhelm the limited housing stock unless the nation acted to meet its housing needs. Analysts at the U.S. Department of Housing and Urban Development (HUD) estimated that 26 million units would be needed between 1969 and 1978, and set a goal of 6 million subsidized units. The Housing Act of 1968 adopted this goal and created programs whereby below-market interest rates were offered to apartment developers to enable them to offer below-market rents to low and moderate-income tenants. Another part of the 1968 Act offered below-market interest rates to eligible home buyers under the FHA mortgage insurance program. During the 1970–1973 period 1.7 million subsidized units were added to the stock of housing. There were problems with the implementation and costs of these new programs, and after he had won a landslide election victory in 1972, President Nixon called for a thorough review of housing policy.

The result of this review was the 1974 Housing and Community Development Act, which included the Section 8 low-income rental assistance program, a revision of the programs that were created in 1965 and mentioned above. This program had separate elements for new construction, substantial rehabilitation, and existing housing. Under the new construction and substantial rehabilitation parts of the program, private and nonprofit developers obtained their own FHA-insured financing, and HUD entered into a long-term contract of 20 to 30 years to subsidize the difference between fair-market rent and 25% (30% after 1981) of the tenant's income. At this time some of these long-term contracts are expiring, and controversy surrounds the issue of whether those contracts should be extended. The Section 8 program for new housing was eliminated in 1983 because the program was too expensive. According to the U.S. Department of Housing and Urban Development (1982), the annual subsidy per unit was over $6000.

In contrast to all of the programs described so far, the Section 8 program for existing housing is a demand-side program. An eligible tenant obtains a rent certificate from the local housing authority and then shops for suitable housing that meets the quality standards and a rent limit set by HUD. The local housing authority retained some control over location and assisted with lease negotiation. The actual payments go directly from the local housing authority to the landlord. The tenant pays rent that is no more than 30% of income.

Table 9.3 shows that as of 1991, there were 2.2 million subsidized housing units of various types in urban areas in the United States. There were 1.328 million federally subsidized rental units (i.e., Section 8 units) and 516,000 units subsidized by state or local governments. Verification of tenant income was required in another 359,000 units because these units fall under the 1968 Housing Act program that provided low-interest loans to developers. About 62% of these units are located in central cities, but 829,000 subsidized units are located in the suburbs. Subsidized rental units, together with public housing, made up 5.0% of the total housing stock and 12.6% of the rental housing in urban areas in 1991. Some 16.7% of the rental housing in central cities is either public housing or subsidized rental units. Therefore, while publicly subsidized housing makes up a small fraction of the total urban housing market, it plays a significant role in the rental housing market in central cities.

The other program shown on Table 9.3 is rental units that operate under rent controls put in place by local governments. As of 1991, 1.18 million units were under rent control, the vast majority (81%) in central cities. The largest number of rent-controlled apartments is in New York City, which has had rent control since World War II, but more recently, Boston, Washington, DC, Los Angeles, San Francisco, and many other places that experienced rapid increases in rents have instituted rent controls. Economists generally take a dim view of rent controls that remain in place for any extended length of time. Rent controls that are truly effective discourage maintenance and can ultimately lead to the withdrawal of units from the housing stock. Rent control is discussed in detail in Section H.

Despite all of these programs aimed at providing housing for lower-income households or controlling rents, there is a serious problem of housing affordability among households in poverty. In 1991 there were 9.059 million units in urban areas occupied by households with incomes below the poverty level. The official poverty level of income depends on the size of the family; for a family of four in 1990 it was $13,359. Of those urban households in poverty, 78% had housing costs that exceeded 30% of their incomes. The median ratio of housing costs to income was 56%; half of the urban households in poverty spent more than 56% of their incomes on housing, and half spent less than 56%. In other words, if a family of four with an income of $13,000 (in 1990) spent 56% of that income on housing rent, only $5720 was left for all other purposes. The failure of wages and labor productivity to grow since 1973 (as discussed in more detail in Chapter 11), coupled with increases in housing rents, has created a severe housing problem among the low-income population in urban areas.

G. THE DEMAND FOR HOUSING AND DEMAND-SIDE HOUSING POLICIES

Rent certificates became a significant part of federal housing policy in the 1974 Housing and Community Development Act, but the idea of demand-side subsidies was not new. Such a program was discussed and rejected in the formulation of the Housing Act of 1937, and they were reconsidered and rejected during the congressional discussions that led up to the Housing Act of 1949. In 1968 the President's Committee on Urban Housing argued in favor of demand-side programs and recommended that the government undertake an experiment to determine the feasibility of such programs. Advocates of demand-side programs argued that

1. Housing provided directly or indirectly by the public sector is more expensive than private-sector housing.
2. Demand-side subsidies are more equitable because the same amount of money can be used to serve more households.
3. Demand-side subsidies give households freedom to choose their own housing and location.

Opponents of demand-side subsidies include housing suppliers who argue in their own self-interest, but there are other opponents who make theoretical arguments in favor of supply-side programs. Some argue that the best way to make sure that the low-income households actually improve their housing is for the public sector to have housing built for them. For example, Friedman and Weinberg (1982) noted that low-income minority households largely failed to participate in the experiments that tested the effects of housing vouchers similar to the Section 8 existing housing program. Others point out that once built, public housing and other units that are directly subsidized cannot be removed or canceled. A program of demand-side subsidies is just money, and Congress can take away the money at any time. Advocates of supply-side policies also point out that increasing demand for housing through the use of demand-side subsidies might cause an increase in housing rents for all low- and moderate-income households.

Theory of Housing Demand and Demand Subsidies

Before we examine research on the effects of demand-side subsidies, it is helpful to think through various policy options using the basic economics of housing demand. Consider a household with a relatively low income. The household allocates its income to housing or to other consumption goods. To keep the theory simple we assume that expenditures on all other goods can be lumped together. The household has preferences for housing and other goods that can be depicted on the standard indifference curve diagram shown in Figure 9.5. Indifference curves are labeled IC_1, IC_2, and so on. Housing is assumed to be a commodity that can be measured in standard units of housing services. The combinations of housing and other goods that are on the same indifference curve yield equal levels of utility for the household. As explained in the appendix to this book, the slope of the indifference curve is the rate at which the household is willing to trade one commodity (housing) for the other (expendi-

FIGURE 9.5 Household choices of housing and other goods

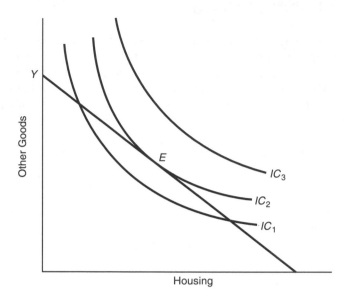

tures on other goods) and stay at the same level of utility. The household has a family of indifference curves; indifference curves farther to the northeast on the diagram pertain to higher levels of utility.

Now let us add the household's budget constraint to the model. The household has a particular level of income Y and faces a price per standardized unit of housing services of R. The "price" of expenditures on all other goods is \$1, of course. These pieces of information determine the position of the budget constraint. Write the budget constraint as

$$Y = RH + G,$$

where H is the number of units of housing services purchased and G is expenditures on other goods. This equation can be manipulated to yield

$$G = Y - RH,$$

so the budget constraint in Figure 9.5 has an intercept of Y and a slope of $-R$.

Given its preferences as represented by the indifference curves and its budget constraint, the household selects the combination of housing services and other goods represented by point E in Figure 9.5. At this point the slope of the budget constraint $(-R)$ is equal to the slope of indifference curve IC_2, the highest indifference curve that is attainable.

The household depicted in Figure 9.5 may well be spending a rather high proportion of its income on housing, or it may not. The household is simply doing the best it can with what it has. Now let us suppose that the municipal officials enact building and housing codes that, in effect, require a low-income household to consume some minimum quantity of housing services (or move elsewhere). If that minimum is less than the amount of housing services shown on Figure 9.5, nothing has

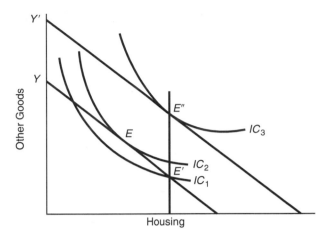

FIGURE 9.6 Effects of a minimum housing standard

happened. However, suppose that the household is required to increase its consumption of housing. Figure 9.6 shows the result. The household moves from point E to point E', consumes more housing and less other goods, and suffers a loss of utility as shown from a move from indifference curve IC_2 to IC_1. Now here we have something that might be called a housing affordability problem. On its own, the household chooses to purchase less than the minimum amount of housing deemed suitable by the local government. The policy of forcing the household to consume the minimum amount of housing reduces its utility. One solution to this problem would be to give the household additional income until its consumption of housing freely chosen equals the minimum required by the local government. This option is shown on Figure 9.6 as the move of the budget constraint from Y to Y'. To its delight, the household now achieves the utility level on indifference curve IC_3 at point E''. Comparing points E and E'', the household has increased its consumption of housing and other goods as well. However, a general income subsidy may be an expensive method for the government to induce the household to increase its housing consumption.

The same apparatus can be used to examine the effects of the Section 8 existing housing program—the rent certificate program. The rules of the program specify that the participating household pays 30% of its income on housing, and the government pays the difference between the actual rent and the household's contribution. Actual rent cannot exceed some estimated fair market rent for a dwelling of the required level of quality. This program tells the household that it will not be spending more than 30% of its income on housing. The new budget constraint for the household is shown in Figure 9.7 as line YAB; the AB portion of the constraint is horizontal up to housing consumption level H^* because the household never has to spend more than $0.3Y$ on housing. Obviously, the household maximizes utility by choosing point B. The government has paid a subsidy to the landlord equal to distance CB because the cost of H^* units of housing services is, in Figure 9.7, equal to $0.3Y + CB$ (and the household paid $0.3Y$).

Is this a cheaper method than an income subsidy for inducing the household to increase its consumption of housing to H^*? It is if the situation is as depicted in Figure 9.8a. In this figure an income subsidy of DC is needed to induce the household to increase housing consumption of H^* (compared to the smaller rent certificate BC).

FIGURE 9.7 A rent certificate program

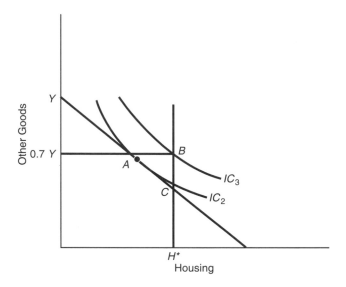

However, in Figure 9.8b the household has a different set of preferences, and the required income subsidy of DC is smaller than the rent certificate BC. What is the difference between Figure 9.8a and b? In the first case the household has a relatively low income elasticity of demand for housing, and in the second case the income elasticity is higher. Which figure depicts the more likely outcome? Note that Figure 9.8b depicts the case in which the household responds to an income subsidy by increasing its expenditures on other goods by only a small amount. In other words, the income elasticity of demand for all other goods as a group (food, clothing, appliances, entertainment, etc.) must be rather low. This is not likely, especially for low-income households. Indeed, numerous empirical studies indicate otherwise. Figure 9.8a therefore depicts the real case, and the rent certificate program is the cheaper method for inducing the household to increase housing consumption to H^*.

In response to the recommendation of the President's Committee on Urban Housing, the 1970 Housing and Urban Development Act directed HUD to carry out a major experimental study of demand-side housing allowances. Two issues were of immediate concern. First, if low-income households were given housing allowances (also called *housing vouchers*) that reduced the housing rent that they pay, how much improvement in their housing standards would result? In short, what are the price and income elasticities of demand for housing? Second, if all low-income households received housing allowances, will housing rents rise (and by how much)?

The empirical literature on the demand for housing at the time did not provide clear answers to the question of price and income elasticities of demand for housing. The estimation of price elasticity is particularly problematic because there is no market "price" for a unit of housing services. The prices that are observed in the market are actually household expenditures on housing (either the market price of a house or the housing rent; i.e., price times quantity). The estimation of income elasticity was

FIGURE 9.8 Rent certificate or income subsidy

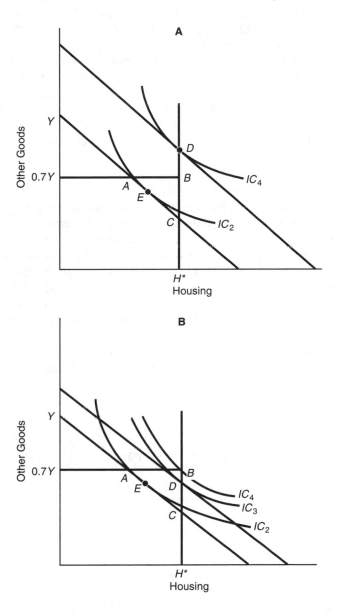

not so problematic, although clearly the relevant income concept is permanent (or longer-run) income rather than just current income. Short-run fluctuations in current income cannot be expected to have a major impact on housing expenditures because it is costly to move and adjust one's housing consumption bundle.

The Housing Allowance Demand Experiment was designed to address these methodological problems. As discussed by Friedman and Weinberg (1982), the experiment enrolled about 1200 families in housing allowance programs in each of two sites (Pittsburgh and Phoenix) during a three-year period beginning in 1974. The experiment also included 500 families in each site as control groups. The experiment tested two types of programs. One program reduced the rent paid by the household by a fixed percentage, such as 30%. The other type of program was similar to the Section 8 existing housing rent certificate program that is discussed above. The crucial experimental variable is the size of the subsidy received by the households. The experiment was designed so that the experimenters could manipulate the price of a unit of housing services or the amount of the rent certificate and observe the results of price changes. For example, suppose that the members of the experimental group received a rent subsidy of 30%, so the price of a unit of housing services is 70% of its market price.

The effects of this rent subsidy can be depicted graphically. Figure 9.9 shows the same initial household equilibrium at point E as does Figure 9.5. The rent subsidy reduces the price of a unit of housing services by 30%, so the budget constraint rotates to line YE'. The consumption of housing services has increased for two reasons. First, the price of housing relative to other goods has been reduced. The budget constraint has become flatter, and this change in slope pushes the household to consume more housing and less of other goods. The effect of the change in *relative prices* is called the *substitution effect*. Second, the rent subsidy has caused the household to have a higher income in real terms. The household's money income (Y) has not increased, but the amount it must pay for its bundle of consumer goods has been reduced. This increase in real income generally causes an increase in the consumption of all goods, including housing, and this effect is known as the *income effect*.

Following the analysis in Figure 9.9, suppose that the demand for housing H can specified for a household as

$$H = AY^b p_h^c,$$

or

$$\ln H = \ln A + b \ln Y + c \ln p_h,$$

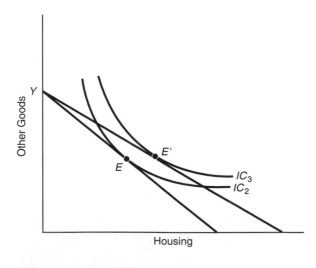

FIGURE 9.9 Rent subsidy program

where H is units of housing services, Y the household's permanent income, and p_h the price of a unit of housing services. The coefficients b and c are the income and price elasticities of demand. To see this, write the change in H as

$$\delta H = (bAY^{b-1}p_h^c)\delta Y + (cAY^b p_h^{c-1})\delta p_h = \frac{bH}{Y}\,\delta Y + \frac{cH}{p_h}\,\delta p_h\,.$$

Therefore, income elasticity can be derived as

$$\frac{\delta H}{\delta Y} = \frac{bH}{Y},$$

so

$$e_y = \frac{\delta H}{\delta Y}\left(\frac{Y}{H}\right) = b.$$

Similarly, price elasticity of demand can be found from

$$\frac{\delta H}{\delta p_h} = \frac{cH}{p_h},$$

so that

$$e_d = \frac{\delta H}{\delta p_h}\left(\frac{p_h}{H}\right) = c.$$

The variables H and p_h are not directly observable. Housing expenditures E are $p_h H$, so $\ln E = \ln p_h + \ln H = \ln(p_h H)$, and

$$\ln E = \ln A + b \ln Y + (1+c)\ln p_h.$$

The experimental housing allowance reduces p_h to $(1-a)p_h$, where a is the subsidy amount (ranging from 0.2 to 0.6 for the various experimental groups and zero for the control group). Substitution of $(1-a)p_h$ for p_h yields

$$\ln[(1-a)p_h H] = \ln A + b \ln Y + (1+c)\ln[(1-a)p_h],$$

or

$$\ln(1-a) + \ln E = \ln A + (1+c)\ln p_h + b \ln Y + (1+c)\ln(1-a).$$

Subtraction of $\ln(1-a)$ yields the equation

$$\ln E = [\ln A + (1+c)\ln p_h] + b \ln Y + c \ln(1-a).$$

The variable p_h is still not observable, but it can plausibly be assumed to be constant within the same housing market (e.g., within the same neighborhood). The equation can therefore be estimated with $\ln Y$, $\ln(1-a)$, and neighborhood control variables included. The coefficient of $\ln(1-a)$ is the elasticity of demand for housing services.

Friedman and Weinberg (1982, p. 32) reported that the price elasticities estimated for low-income households in Pittsburgh and Phoenix are -0.18 and -0.23, respectively. These estimates mean that a 30% reduction in the price of housing leads to an increase in housing consumption of about 6%. In other words, a program that reduces housing rents by 30% will increase the quantity of housing by only 6%, and expenditures on housing out of the household's own income decrease. The elasticity of the change in expenditures on housing that result from a price change can be written

$$\frac{\delta E}{\delta p_h}\left(\frac{p_h}{E}\right) = \frac{p_h}{E}\frac{\delta(p_h H)}{\delta p_h} = \frac{p_h}{p_h H}\left[H + p_h\left(\frac{\delta H}{\delta p_h}\right)\right]$$

$$= 1 + \frac{\delta H}{\delta p_h}\left(\frac{p_h}{H}\right) = 1 + e_d,$$

where e_d is the price elasticity of demand. If demand is inelastic ($0 > e_d > -1$), expenditures increase when the price increases. If the price of housing is *cut*, housing expenditures *fall* by $(1 + e_d)$. If the price of housing is cut by 30% and e_d is -0.2, expenditures on housing fall by $0.3 \times 0.8 = 0.24$, or 24%. The estimated income elasticities (based on income averaged over three years) are 0.33 for Pittsburgh and 0.44 for Phoenix. These responses are less than overwhelming, but they are based only on a three-year experiment. Perhaps the responses would have been larger if the program had been permanent. However, it is plausible to argue that most households in the experiment were already living in housing that is more or less acceptable and that the real housing problem is one of affordability. A reduction in housing rent mainly enabled households to save money on their housing so that other goods and services could be purchased, although a small improvement in housing quality was also observed.

While the housing allowance experiments were under way, other housing economists were making progress on estimating housing demand functions using nonexperimental data. One particularly good study by Polinsky and Ellwood (1979) specified the demand for housing as

$$\ln H = \beta_0 + \beta_1 \ln Y + \beta_2 \ln p_h + \beta_3 \ln p_o,$$

where p_o is the price of all other goods besides housing. We know from basic demand theory that $\beta_1 + \beta_2 + \beta_3 = 0$ because doubling income and all prices leaves the quantity demanded unchanged. Doubling each variable means, for example $\ln 2Y = \ln 2 + \ln Y$, or adding $\ln 2$ to $\ln Y$, $\ln p_h$, and $\ln p_o$, so the result follows. The demand function can now be written as

$$\ln H = \beta_0 + \beta_1 \ln Y + \beta_2 \ln p_h - (\beta_1 + \beta_2) \ln p_o.$$

Housing expenditures divided by the price of other goods can be found as

$$\ln\left(\frac{p_h H}{p_o}\right) = \beta_0 + \beta_1 \ln Y + (\beta_2 + 1) \ln p_h - (\beta_1 + \beta_2 + 1) \ln p_o,$$

or

$$\ln\left(\frac{E}{p_o}\right) = \beta_0 + \beta_1 \ln\left(\frac{Y}{p_o}\right) + (\beta_2 + 1) \ln\left(\frac{p_h}{p_o}\right).$$

Housing expenditures and income are observable. The price of other goods is the index of consumer prices (excluding the price of housing) for the metropolitan area in which the household is located, and the price of housing is predicted using a model in which the price of land and the price of construction determine the price of a unit of housing. Note that the coefficient of $\ln(p_h/p_o)$ is the price elasticity of demand plus 1.

Polinsky and Ellwood (1979) estimated the model using a sample of 10,054 households in 31 urban areas that purchased housing through the FHA mortgage guarantee program. Their estimate of β_1 (income elasticity) is 0.57; and their estimate of $\beta_2 + 1$ is 0.28, so the estimated price elasticity of demand is -0.72. Polinsky and Ellwood (1979) think that their estimate of income elasticity is a bit low because the FHA program has an upper limit on the size of the loan that can be insured. Some people with high incomes who wish to be part of the FHA program must therefore reduce the amount that they otherwise might spend on housing. Their final estimate of income elasticity is therefore adjusted upward to 0.80. These estimates pertain to the general population, and price and income elasticities can be different for different groups. However, there is general agreement that the demand is inelastic with respect to price and that income elasticity is less than 1.

The federally sponsored housing research of the 1970s also included two tests of housing allowances that were designed to determine whether housing rents would be driven up by a general housing allowance program. Two sites were chosen— Green Bay, Wisconsin and South Bend, Indiana—and housing allowances were made available to any household that qualified on the basis of income and family size. The results of these field tests were as follows:

1. Participation of eligible households was rather low, with only about 40 to 45% of those eligible enrolled.
2. Participating households increased their housing consumption by small amounts (as in the Pittsburgh and Phoenix experiments).
3. Housing rents in the two markets did not rise.

Because the participation in the Green Bay and South Bend projects was rather low, these results probably cannot be generalized to all housing allowance programs. Surely there are situations in which inundating a local housing market with housing allowances would lead to increases in housing rents.

H. RENT CONTROL

Table 9.3 shows that as of 1991, there were 1.2 million housing units in the United States under some form of rent control, or about 4.5% of the total stock of rental housing. Rent control has existed in New York City since World War II, and many other large and small cities have instituted rent control programs since the 1970s. The list of cities includes Los Angeles, Washington, D.C., Boston, San Francisco, Cambridge (Massachusetts), and many smaller cities and towns in California, New Jersey, Connecticut, Massachusetts, and New York. Rent control programs come in many forms. Some programs froze rents, while other programs permitted rent increases according to some formula based on general inflation or increases in landlord expenses. Some early rent control programs controlled rents on all rental units, but more recent programs exempt new construction and/or units of very high quality. In addition, some programs permit rent to adjust to the market when the unit is vacated. The purpose of this section is use basic microeconomic theory to examine some of these programs. Most economists agree that the old-fashioned rent controls discouraged new construction, caused abandonment, reduced maintenance and mobility, created mismatches between tenants and housing units, caused rental units to be converted to owner-occupied housing, stimulated black markets and other methods for getting around the controls, and potentially led to greater racial discrimination. However, one prominent urban economist [Arnott (1995)] has a mildly dissenting view. Arnott believes that a well-designed version of the newer form of rent control (with exemptions for new construction, rent adjustments for inflation and verifiable increases in expenses, and regulations regarding maintenance) can be beneficial.

The conventional analysis of old-fashioned rent control uses a simple supply and demand model, as shown in Figure 9.10. In this model all housing units are identical. The current supply of units is S and the current demand for units is D. As always, supply and demand are functions of the real price of the good, the opportunity cost in terms of other goods. Rent is frozen on all units in *nominal* terms at the current level R_1. Consider first what happens when the costs of supplying housing rise in nominal terms but the rent is still frozen in nominal terms. The result is a reduction in the real rent that is permitted to R_2. (The supply and demand curves do not shift. Why?) This reduction in real rent creates a shortage of housing units in this market by both increasing quantity demanded and reducing quantity supplied. In the short run the quantity of units supplied will not change much because housing is very durable, but in the longer run some rental units will be removed from the rental stock. Some units will be converted to owner-occupied units and others eventually will be demolished because the full cost of owning and operating the units cannot be covered. If the elasticity of supply is large enough and the reduction in real rent is great enough, the stock of rental housing in this city could disappear entirely!

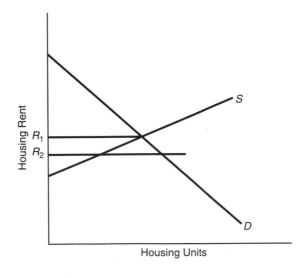

FIGURE 9.10 Old-fashioned rent control

Rent control has an impact on the distribution of income. The winners in the game are those tenants who continue to live in the remaining rental housing stock—their rents in real terms have declined. Landlords of those remaining units suffer a loss of real income, and the real market value of rental units also drops. Some tenants are displaced by the withdrawals of units from the rental housing stock, and they must pay the cost of searching for and moving into a new unit in some other city. Rent control as depicted in Figure 9.10 has some other interesting effects. Rent control will cut down on the mobility of tenants because the existing tenants know that the shortage of rent-controlled units means that many households are out there waiting for the chance to get a low rent. Tenants know that if they move out, there is a slim chance that they will be able to rent another unit that is under rent control. Rent control therefore leads to anomalous situations such as retired couples (or widows) living in large apartments while families with children are unable to find a rent-controlled unit. In addition, when a rent-controlled unit does become vacant, the lucky new tenant may find that it was necessary to pay additional fees to secure the unit. Such a fee is sometimes called *key money* or a *finder's fee*. Under some rent control laws such fees are illegal, but they exist nonetheless. In other cases the long list of households desiring to move into a rent-controlled unit may enable the landlord to screen tenants heavily on the basis of income level, race, and so on.

This basic model is consistent with evidence from some cities that have introduced rent controls. For example, Santa Monica and four other cities in California introduced rent controls in 1979 that prohibited rent increases when the apartment turns over. Newspaper accounts describe how a new tenant must pay a big finder's fee—or the vacated apartment goes to a relative of the landlord. Many units have been boarded up and withdrawn from the market. Tenants in some buildings are paying maintenance expenses. In response to such stories the state of California has just (in 1995) enacted a law that prevents cities from prohibiting rent increases when a unit turns over.

Now let us change the game and impose what Arnott (1995) calls "second-generation" rent control. This program permits landlords to raise rents because of general inflation and verifiable increases in costs, and newly constructed units are exempt from controls. In this case the problems arising in Figure 9.10 from a decline in real rent cannot occur. Let us, instead, examine the effects of an increase in the demand for rental units. In Figure 9.11 demand has increased from D_1 to D_2. An uncontrolled market will respond with an increase in quantity from H_1 to H_2 and an increase in rent on all units from R_1 to R_2. With old-fashioned rent control the market will not respond to this increase in demand, and a shortage of units exists. With second-generation rent control the rent on the old units will remain at R_1 but the quantity supplied will increase to H_3 and rent on new units will be R_3 because with this program demand has actually increased to D_3. New units have been built without the redistribution of income from the old tenants to the old landlords that would accompany the uncontrolled market response. Furthermore, more new units have been built and rents in new units have increased more compared to the uncontrolled market. Why does this happen? Without rent control the quantity of housing units demanded by the *old* tenants falls, but with rent control these old tenants continue to demand quantity H_1.

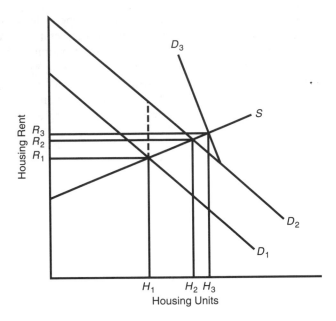

FIGURE 9.11 Second-generation rent control

Fallis and Smith (1984) provided empirical evidence for the Los Angeles housing market that rents in the uncontrolled portion of the market increased more with rent control than they would have without rent control.

Second-generation rent control has some of the problems of old-fashioned rent control. Tenant mobility can still be reduced, and mismatches between tenants and units therefore can be created with the passage of time. In addition, the nature of any adjustment of rent with unit turnover presents a dilemma. Do we permit real rents to adjust upward at that time, thereby giving the landlord an incentive to get rid of the current tenant? Or do we prohibit the adjustment and create the black market, the waiting lists, and the key money payments?

The harmful effects of old-fashioned rent control, as depicted in Figure 9.10, are not in dispute, but the jury is still out on second-generation rent control programs. Some of these programs have prevented income redistribution from tenants to landlords while encouraging new construction.

I. SUMMARY

In this chapter we have examined both the workings of the private market for housing in urban areas and the history of housing policy in the United States. The main points made in the chapter can be outlined as follows.

1. Housing is the biggest part of the household's budget for many people, and it is the largest use of land in urban areas as well.

2. Housing is a complicated commodity that is very durable and immovable.

3. The housing market has its own set of institutions for recording ownership, buying and selling, and borrowing money to purchase a house. The urban economist needs

to understand these institutions and the role that they play in determining the market value of residential property. This chapter includes a brief introduction to residential real estate transactions, and more details are provided in the appendix to this chapter. Students interested in pursuing these topics in greater depth and/or interested in a career in real estate should take a course in real estate.

4. A useful model of the urban housing market is based on the idea of filtering. The housing stock can be arrayed in order of quality, with households arrayed in order of their demand for housing. The housing market assigns households to housing units and determines housing prices and rents. An increase in the supply of housing at or near the top of the quality hierarchy, for example, provides opportunities for households to improve the quality of their housing by filtering up.

5. There is clear evidence of racial prejudice and discrimination in urban housing markets. The level of segregation of the black population from other groups is far higher than can be attributed reasonably to voluntary segregation. During the period of the 1950s to the 1970s when the black population in urban areas was growing very rapidly, housing rents were often observed to be higher for black households than for white households. However, at this time housing rents in black neighborhoods may actually be lower than rents in white neighborhoods largely because black neighborhoods have fewer amenities and higher crime rates.

6. Housing policy in the United States has encouraged the ownership of homes by the middle class and has attempted to improve the housing occupied by low-income households. The policies of home mortgage guarantees and income tax incentives for homeowners have been successful in promoting the ownership of homes. Furthermore, the quality of the housing units occupied by the vast majority of urban Americans is quite good. However, urban households with low incomes have a serious problem with the affordability of urban housing. Federal housing policy has failed to make much progress on the affordability issue, but the idea of demand-side subsidies (i.e., housing allowances) holds some promise. So far demand-side housing subsidies are a small program that must compete with many other programs for federal funds. The empirical studies suggest that when a low-income household is given a housing allowance, it reduces expenditures of its own income on housing in order to have more money to spend on other things. Given the high cost of housing relative to income among low-income households, this is an altogether reasonable choice.

7. Rent control exists in several local housing markets around the country, especially in New York and California. The old form of rent control, which froze rents in nominal terms, clearly was harmful on many counts. New construction and maintenance were discouraged, and units were abandoned. However, newer forms of rent control, which Arnott (1995) calls second-generation programs, have been designed to permit landlords of existing units reasonable increases in rents and to encourage construction by exempting new units. These provisions tend to mitigate some, but not all, of the adverse effects of rent control.

APPENDIX TO CHAPTER 9

Housing Markets and Home Loans

A. HOW A HOUSE IS SOLD

This appendix is an introduction to the law of real estate and the institutions that are used to engage in the sale of residential real estate. A basic course in real estate will provide you with much more depth on the topics that are covered here, but this appendix will at least give you some familiarity with some of the peculiar terminology that is used in the real estate business.

The process of selling a house begins when the owner decides to sell. The owner is selling the physical property (the house and the lot) *and* the legal rights of ownership. There are many forms of real property ownership, or estates, that are recognized in law. A fundamental distinction is between ownership by one party (estates in severalty) and more than one party (concurrent estates). The term *estates in severalty* designates a single owner because that owner's estate is *severed* from those of others. Estates in severalty can be of indefinite duration (freehold estates) or of definite duration set by private contract (leasehold estate). The most common leasehold estate is the rental of an apartment. Freehold estates can be "of inheritance" or "not of inheritance." Freehold estates of inheritance means that the owner has the legal right to transfer ownership as he or she sees fit (e.g., by sale or will), and a freehold estate that is not of inheritance does not include this right. An example of the latter is the life estate, wherein the owner possesses the rights to the property during his or her lifetime, but upon the death of the owner the estate passes to some other owner as stipulated in the private contract that set up the life estate.

The most common form of freehold estate of inheritance is called *fee simple absolute estate*, the form of ownership that provides the maximum legal rights of ownership that are consistent with the laws of the land. Those legal rights include the aforementioned right to transfer ownership as one sees fit (the right of disposition), the right of exclusive possession and control, and the right of quiet enjoyment. These legal rights apply regardless of the physical nature of the property involved. The right of exclusive possession and control means that the owner can control entry to the property, collect damages in case of trespass, and use the property as collateral for loans. The right of quiet enjoyment has nothing to do with an absence of noise; it means that the owner is legally protected from unfounded claims about the validity of the title to the property. The owner with a fee simple absolute estate is still subject to restrictions imposed by government: zoning laws, building codes, taxes, and eminent domain. Under the power of eminent domain, the government (usually a local government) has the right to force the sale of property for just compensation if the property is needed for a public purpose. The term *fee simple* is a legal term that combines *fee*, which is an inheritance in legal terminology, and *simple*, which means unconditional.

The owner decides to sell the residential property and the accompanying fee simple absolute estate. Legal title to the physical property and the legal rights are evidenced by a *deed* that is in the possession of the owner. A copy of the deed is on file with the county's recorder of deeds. The next step ordinarily is for the owner to draw up a listing contract with a real estate broker, a person who operates a business that specializes in selling real estate. The listing contract will stipulate the price that the owner is willing to accept, the fee that the broker will receive if the property is sold, and a time period for the listing contract. There are different types of listing contracts, but the one used most often in residential real estate is the exclusive right of sale listing. With this type of listing the broker is due the commission if the property is sold during the time period of the contract *regardless of who sells the property*. This type of listing is used by brokers who are members of multiple listing services (MLS) because, under MLS agreements, the brokers share listings. If another broker sells the house, the entire commission is paid to the listing broker, who, by prior agreement, splits the commission with the selling broker. The normal commission is a stated percentage of the selling price of the property. A commission of 6% is common, but the commission rate is always subject to negotiation prior to the signing of the listing contract. Under the listing contract the broker promises to market the property through the appropriate media and to employ real estate agents who show the property to potential buyers and help negotiate a contract for sale.

The contract for sale is often called the most important document in real estate. Contracts in real estate are governed by the state's general law of contracts. Legally binding contracts all have the following features:

1. The parties to the contract are legally competent to act (e.g., the seller actually owns the property).
2. The parties have legal objectives.
3. There is an offer and an acceptance.
4. There is value given or a promise made by each party. This is called a *statement of consideration*, and legally binding contracts impose obligations on both parties. In this case the seller promises to deliver the property upon payment of a sum of money, and the buyer promises to deliver the money.
5. There must be no defects to mutual agreement (e.g., no one is under duress).

In addition, contracts in real estate must be in writing and must include a legal description of the property (i.e., its location in precise terms).

Contracts for the sale of real estate are fairly complicated documents and normally include the following additional provisions: (1) date of the closing, (2) financing terms for the buyer, (3) condition of building and its equipment, (4) brokerage commission, (5) earnest-money deposit, and (6) remedies for breach of contract. The contract states a date upon which the actual transfer of ownership will take place (date of closing). By that date the buyer must have acquired the financing as stated in the contract. For example, the contract states that the buyer will obtain a loan for 80% of the purchase price of the property at an interest rate of 9% or less. If the buyer, after reasonable effort, is unable to obtain the financing as stated, the contract for sale says that the sale is void. The buyer puts up earnest money when the contract for sale is signed. The earnest money is usually a small percentage of the purchase price (e.g., 1%), and this money is held by the broker in a separate bank account until the date of closing.

How do the buyer and seller arrive at the purchase price that is then written in the sale contract? This is the crucial question. The determination of the price begins with the listing contract, where the seller states the price that is acceptable. The *listing price* is set in discussions with the real estate broker. The broker's real estate agent will conduct a comparative market analysis to determine the price at which the house is likely to sell. The real estate agent is familiar with the market in the immediate neighborhood and knows the prices at which houses are selling. However, the houses that have been sold recently may differ from the subject house in some respects (e.g., size of the house, size of the lot, and appearance of the neighborhood). The real estate agent will make adjustments to those prices to make them pertain more accurately to the subject house. This process is described below. The broker will take the real estate agent's estimate of selling price and boost it a little as a bargaining tactic. Remember that the broker is the *seller's* agent. The seller can take the broker's recommendation for listing price or can insist on some other price. It is fair to say that sellers sometimes insist on an unrealistically high listing price—at first. Hope springs eternal.

The buyer enters the picture by contacting a real estate agent. The agent will assist the buyer in finding the house that meets his or her needs and also fits within the buyer's budget. Once the buyer has found a house, an offer is made by writing up a proposed contract for sale. But how does the buyer determine the price that is offered? Naturally, the buyer discusses the offer with the real estate agent (who, you will recall, is working for the seller). The broker and real estate agent do not get paid unless there is a sale, so they have a strong incentive to get the two parties together. However, since the commission is usually a percentage of the selling price, they also get paid more the higher the price. Under these circumstances, it is advisable for the buyer to seek additional advice from another professional in the business. The buyer's attorney often plays this role. If the buyer is making a particularly large purchase, a buyer's real estate agent may be hired to carry out the search and handle the negotiations. These advisors may conduct their own comparative market analysis to help determine the offer price.

The price that is agreed upon is, of course, the present discounted value of the stream of housing services that the housing unit will provide. In equation form, the selling price is determined in the usual present-value formula, written

$$V = \frac{R_1}{1+r} + \frac{R_2}{(1+r)^2} + \frac{R_3}{(1+r)^3} + \cdots + \frac{R_n}{(1+r)^n},$$

where R_1 to R_n is the stream of implicit housing rents, r the discount rate, and n the number of years remaining in the economic life of the house. It is not assumed that the rent stream is a constant. Indeed, because a house deteriorates over time, the rent in real terms (corrected for general inflation) should fall. By the way, if the projected rent stream is stated in real terms, the discount rate also should be corrected for inflation. Current nominal interest rates include the rate of inflation that is expected. The real discount rate is the nominal rate minus that expected inflation rate—whatever that may be.

Once the sale contract has been signed, the buyer arranges for financing with some lender. The lender is usually a financial institution, such as a savings and loan company or a bank, that specializes in home loans. The lending institution will make its own independent assessment of the market value of the property because the buyer may default on the loan. If default occurs, the lender recovers the value of the loan by forcing the sale of the property (foreclosure), so the lender needs to know the price at which the property can be sold. The lender normally will require a professional appraisal of the market value of the property. The government regulations that apply to lending institutions also require that appraisals be performed in most instances. In addition, the seller, the buyer, or both might have engaged the services of a professional appraiser in the process of determining the listing or offer price.

How are appraisals performed? The task is to estimate the market value of the property, assuming that the property is being sold by a "normal" seller to a "normal" buyer under "normal" market conditions. The professional appraiser has extensive training and, if the appraisal is done properly, makes use of procedures that are actually quite scientific. The appraisal process for a residential property is very standardized; in fact, the appraiser fills out a standard form that meets the requirements of government agencies. The standard appraisal of a house is based primarily on a sales comparison approach that is supplemented by two other methods, the income capitalization and cost-less-depreciation methods. The *income capitalization method* is similar to the method used for commercial properties that was described in Chapter 7, except that a market rent for the house must be estimated from rental market data. The *cost-less-depreciation* method begins with the cost of reproducing the structure today. Standard sources on construction costs, such as Marshall and Swift's *Residential Cost Handbook*, are used to determine this cost, and then allowances are made for the depreciation of the structure's value. An estimate of the value of the land is added on. Let us focus on the sales comparison approach because this is the method that all parties to the transaction primarily rely upon.

The formal, professional appraisal process requires that three actual sales of comparable properties be used. Detailed data on the subject property and the three "comparables" are gathered, and the use of the data is described below and in Table A9.1. The basic idea in appraisal is to adjust the actual selling price of the comparable property so that the adjustments make the comparable property as close as identical to the subject property as is possible. After the price of the comparable property has been adjusted, the adjusted selling price is an estimate of the market value of the subject property. The critical step is the *selection* of comparable properties so that the adjustments to their selling prices do not have to be very large and, therefore, less subject to error.

The sequence of adjustments to the selling prices that appraisers follow is shown in Table A9.1. The first adjustment that must be considered is called *conditions of sale*. The sale-comparable property may not be a conventional arm's-length transaction. For example, transactions involving members of the same family may not really be a fair market price. The appraiser should select only comparables that are straightforward arm's-length sales. The next adjustment is made to account for the effect of any special financing arrangements. For example, suppose that the seller

TABLE A9.1 Sales Comparison Approach to Appraisal

	Comparable Sales			Subject Property
	No. 1	*No. 2*	*No. 3*	
Sale price	$125,000	$130,000	$140,000	
Price per square foot				
Data source	MLS	MLS	MLS	
Adjustment for:				
Conditions of sale				
Financing concessions				
Date of sale				
Location				
Site/view				
Design				
Quality of construction				
Age				
Condition				
Rooms				
Bathrooms				
Gross living area				
Basement				
Heating/cooling				
Garage/carport				
Porch/patio				
Pool				
Fireplaces				
Other				
Total adjustment				
Indicated Value of subject property				

loans some of the purchase price to the buyer at an interest rate that is below the rate that prevails in the market. This sort of concession will tend to boost the selling price of the house, so the effect on the price of a financing concession must be *subtracted* from the actual selling price. Remember that the idea is to estimate the market value of the subject property under normal selling conditions. The third possible adjustment is for the date of sale of the comparable property. If the comparable was sold six months ago and it is known that prices are increasing over time, the price must be adjusted upward by a percentage to reflect the price increase. This price adjustment should be based, if possible, on data for the immediate neighborhood of the comparable property. Price trends can be quite different in different parts of the same urban area. At this point we have an estimate of the price of the comparable property if it were to be sold today under normal selling conditions.

Now the task is to adjust the price of the comparable property to match the subject property. The first adjustment that must be made is for location. If the comparable and the subject properties are located in the same immediate neighborhood, no location adjustment is needed. However, if the comparable property is located in a different local school district or is located in what is clearly another neighborhood, a location adjustment should be made. The location adjustment is made by finding two actual sales: one near the subject property and one near the comparable property. If the appraiser is lucky, these two sales are identical properties *except for the location factor*. The difference in their sales prices is computed in percentage terms, and that percentage is used to adjust the price of the comparable property. If it is required, the location adjustment is obviously a critical step. The appraiser hopes that comparable properties can be found that are all in the same neighborhood as the subject property.

Now come the adjustments for the actual physical characteristics of the comparable and subject properties. Table A9.1 lists the factors that are taken into account. Again, the appraiser hopes to find comparables that are *very* similar to the subject property on these features. An adjustment must be made if the comparable and the subject properties are not identical on a feature. For example, suppose that the comparable is 10 years older than the subject property. It is known that houses in the market in question decline in value as they age by 0.5% per year, so the price of the comparable must be *increased* by 5.1% because it is the older property. The appraiser has this knowledge because of previous comparisons of value that have been made. As another example, suppose that the subject property does not have central air conditioning but that the comparable property does have this feature. From previous comparisons, the appraiser knows that central air conditioning adds about 12% to the value of houses of this type. This means that the sales price of the comparable must be *reduced* by 12% to make it match the subject property. The sum of all of the adjustments is computed, and the indicated value of the subject property is shown at the bottom of the table.

The final step in the sales comparison approach is to use the sample of three "indicated values" to estimate the market value of the subject property. The usual approach is to compute the mean of the three indicated values. However, there are times when more weight might be put on one of the comparable properties. For example, if the comparable property is the house directly across the street from the subject property, substantially more weight should be placed on this indicated value. However, the appraiser must not put 100% of the weight on the comparable from across the street because that would mean relying on a sample of one. The vagaries of negotiating a sale price may have made this sale somewhat unusual in a way that has not been measured. The other two comparables provide additional information that should be used. Indeed, you may be asking, "Why three comparables? Why not five, or ten, or twenty?" Three is the number required for professional appraisals by convention, but why not a bigger sample indeed?

The work of the appraiser is sent along to the lending institution and, assuming that the subject property is really worth about as much as the price agreed to by the seller and the buyer, the application for the loan is approved. The last step in the process of selling the house is the closing. The lender's agent makes sure that all the details are in order. The deed has been prepared, and the seller has obtained a title insurance policy to guard against any possible legal defects in title. The mortgage contract has been prepared for the buyer's signature, and a check has been prepared by the lender for the seller. The lender's agent prepares the closing statement, which is a comprehensive list of debits and credits for both the seller and the buyer. The lender has made payment to satisfy any remaining balance that the seller has on a home loan, and a statement of satisfaction of the old mortgage has been obtained. When the transaction has been completed, the buyer and seller will probably find that the costs of making the transaction (broker's commission, lawyers' fees, loan fees, document preparation, title search and title insurance, etc.) are about 10% of the value of the property. The real estate market has high transactions costs.

B. FINANCIAL ANALYSIS OF MORTGAGE AMORTIZATION

The home loan obtained by the typical buyer includes the feature that it is fully amortizing, which means that the loan payments that are made each month both pay the interest on the loan and retire the debt itself. Another application of the same idea is the computation of the annual cost of capital, which includes opportunity cost of the funds tied up in the capital *and* the depreciation of the capital itself.

Two preliminary steps are needed before the relevant formula can be derived. The first idea is the present value of a one-time payment that is made at the *end* of year n. A one-time payment made at some point (end of year n) in the future is called a *reversion*. Suppose that the payment is $1; its present value ($PV$) is

$$PV = \frac{1}{(1+r)^n},$$

where r is the discount rate. A series of reversions is called an *annuity*, and the present value of an annuity of $1 per year for n years in duration can be written

$$PV_a(n) = \frac{1}{1+r} + \frac{1}{(1+r)^2} + \cdots + \frac{1}{(1+r)^n},$$

where it is assumed that each reversion is paid at the end of the year.

There is a standard financial formula for the present value of an annuity, and it is found as follows. First multiply both sides of the equation for present value by $(1+r)$, or

$$(1+r)PV_a(n) = 1 + \frac{1}{1+r} + \cdots + \frac{1}{(1+r)^{n-1}}.$$

Subtraction of the present value equation from this equation yields

$$(1+r)PV_a(n) - PV_a(n) = 1 - \frac{1}{(1+r)^n},$$

so that

$$PV_a(n) = \frac{1 - [1/(1+r)^n]}{r}.$$

This is the present value of an annuity of $1 per year for n years. Note that if n is infinitely large, then $PV_a(n)$ simply is $1/r$. However, if n is some number of finite size, the term $[-1/(1+r)^n]$ adjusts the present value down from $1/r$.

Now we are ready to consider the mortgage loan that is fully amortizing. We seek the constant annual payment that will pay the interest and retire the debt. Suppose that the original loan amount is $1. In this case the constant annual payment is called the *mortgage constant* because it is the payment that is needed for each dollar of the loan. The mortgage constant is also called the *capitalization rate* because the annual payments include the return on the investment and the recapture of capital by the end of n years, assuming that the useful life of the capital is n years. In this case the present value of the annuity in question is $1 because the stream of payments must have a present value equal to the original loan amount of $1; therefore,

$$PV_a(n) = 1 = \frac{R}{1+r} + \frac{R}{(1+r)^2} + \cdots + \frac{R}{(1+r)^n},$$

where R is the constant annual payment that is made at the end of each year. The borrower is borrowing $1 in the first year and pays the interest on a loan of $1 for 1 year at the end of the year. However, that payment of R also includes an amount that goes to retire the debt.

The trick is to solve for R, the annual payment. Once again, multiply by $(1+r)$ to obtain

$$(1+r)PV_a(n) = 1 + r = R + \frac{R}{1+r} + \cdots + \frac{R}{(1+r)^{n-1}}.$$

Subtraction yields

$$1 + r - 1 = r = R - \frac{R}{(1+r)^n} = R\left[1 - \frac{1}{(1+r)^n}\right].$$

The solution for R is

$$R = \frac{r}{1 - [1/(1+r)^n]}.$$

The formula for the mortgage constant is the inverse of the formula for the present value of an annuity of $1 per year for n years at interest rate r. If the loan is of infinite duration (or the capital is of infinite life), $R = r$. The annual payment per dollar of loan is just equal to the discount rate, which is the opportunity cost of the capital. However, if the loan is of some finite duration n, the annual payment must be increased above r to amortize the loan.

Consider a simple example in which you borrow $1 for 3 years at an interest rate of 5% and make annual payments at the end of each year. In this case the term $1/(1+r)^n$ is

$$\frac{1}{(1.05)^3} = 0.8638.$$

The annual payment is

$$R = \frac{0.05}{1 - 0.8638} = \frac{0.05}{0.1362} = 0.3671.$$

The annual payment is 36.71 cents on the $1 loan. (If you borrow $1000, the annual payment is $367.10.) At the end of the first year you make that payment, which consists of an interest payment of 5 cents and a payment that goes to retiring the debt of 31.71 cents. In the second year you are borrowing only $1 - 0.3171 = 0.6829$ dollars. At the end of the second year you make the same payment of 36.71 cents, of which $0.05 \times 68.29 = 3.41$ cents is interest and 33.30 cents goes to retire the debt. In the third year you are borrowing 34.99 cents because the loan has been reduced from 68.29 cents to this amount. The payment of 36.71 cents at the end of the third year consists of $0.05 \times 34.99 = 1.75$ cents in interest and 34.96 cents to retire the remaining debt of 34.99 cents. The computation is off by 0.03 cent because of rounding errors.

Financial calculators or financial tables exist to enable you to compute the mortgage constant for a loan of any length and any interest rate. Also, mortgage payments are normally made on a monthly basis rather than on an annual basis. In this case you are borrowing the money for one month at a time and paying an interest rate of $r/12$ at the end of each month. The formula for the monthly mortgage constant is

$$R = \frac{r/12}{1 - [1/(1 + r/12)^{12n}]}.$$

The formula for the present value of an annuity of $1 can be used to determine the balance that remains on the loan at any time during the term of the loan. The trick is to realize that the remaining loan balance B is the present value of the remaining payments, or

$$B = \frac{R}{1 + r} + \frac{R}{(1 + r)^2} + \cdots + \frac{R}{(1 + r)^m},$$

where m is the number of years that remain on the term of the loan. The annual payment R is known, so

$$\frac{B}{R} = PV_a(m),$$

where $PV_a(m)$ is the present value of a $1 annuity that extends for m years at interest rate r. The remaining loan balance is simply the annual payment R times this factor. Recall that the mortgage constant is the inverse of the present value factor, so

$$B = \frac{R}{R_m},$$

where R_m is the mortgage constant for a loan of $1 for m years at interest rate r.

Return to the numerical example of the $1 loan at 5% interest for 3 years. The mortgage constant is 36.71 cents. Now consider the remaining loan balance after 1 year. We already know that the remaining loan balance is 68.29 cents after the first payment has been made. In this case the computation of R_m is

$$R_m = \frac{r}{1 - [1/(1+r)^2]} = \frac{0.05}{1 - 1/1.1025} = 0.5376.$$

The remaining loan balance is therefore

$$B = \frac{R}{R_m} = \frac{36.71}{53.76} = 0.6828 \text{ dollar.}$$

As an exercise, compute the remaining loan balance after 2 years. Did you get 34.99 cents (or close to it)?

One additional financial formula that is very useful and related to the mortgage constant is the sinking fund factor. The sinking fund factor is the amount that must be set aside at the end of each year to yield a certain amount at the end of year n, given an interest rate r. For example, you know that you must replace your roof at the end of 10 years, and you want to know how much should be set aside each year to pay for the new roof at that time. The amount that is set aside each year will earn interest at rate r per year. The sinking fund factor is derived assuming that the goal at the end of n years is $1. The future value (FV) of the accumulated money is to be $1, so

$$FV = 1 = A + A(1+r) + \cdots + A(1+r)^{n-1},$$

where A is the amount set aside at the *end* of each year. Because of the timing, the last amount set aside earns no interest, and that the first amount set aside earns interest for $n-1$ years. The solution for A proceeds as before; multiply both sides of the equation by $(1+r)$ to get

$$(1+r)FV = 1 + r = A(1+r) + A(1+r)^2 + \cdots + A(1+r)^n.$$

Subtraction yields

$$(1+r)FV - FV = r = A(1+r)^n - A = A[(1+r)^n - 1].$$

Therefore, the sinking fund factor is

$$A = \frac{r}{(1+r)^n - 1}.$$

Suppose that you need $1 at the end of 3 years and that the interest rate is 5%. How much do you need to set aside at the end of each year? You know that 33.33 cents at the end of each year will more than do the job because you will earn interest on the first two payments. In this case

$$A = \frac{0.05}{(1.05)^3 - 1} = \frac{0.05}{0.1576} = 0.3173,$$

or 31.73 cents per year.

EXERCISES

1. This project is to perform what the real estate agents call a comparative market analysis. Select a subject property (e.g., a single-family house) for which you wish to obtain an estimate of market value. The idea is to find three houses that have been sold recently that are very similar to the subject house. You can visit a local real estate agency and ask for the "closing book," the book that records the recent sales in the vicinity. Many real estate offices now obtain this information for a particular area from a centralized computer. Find your three comparables and make the adjustments to their market prices so as to make them as close to identical to the subject property as possible. This project may take you some time and legwork, but it can be a very valuable exercise.

2. Gather data on a group of census tracts for an urban area of your choice for the years 1950, 1970, and 1990. Be sure that the definitions of the census tracts are identical in the two years so that you can compare the data over time. Examine the data on housing: the number of units (both owned and rented), the number of units built in various time periods, the median contract rents and estimated market values, the number of vacant units, and so on. Do you see evidence of filtering down in this sample of census tracts? What kind of evidence would suggest that filtering has taken place? Do you see evidence of redevelopment in these tracts? For example, how many newer units were there as of 1990? If you can, ask someone over the age of 60 who has always lived in the urban area to tell you where his or her "old neighborhood" is. Where does this person live now?

3. For the urban area of your choice, determine the extent of racial segregation in 1980 (or 1990, if possible). What are the borders of the submarket that is occupied by the black population? Are housing prices and rents generally higher or lower in the black submarket than in areas occupied by the white population? Are there areas that can be identified as Latino or Asian submarkets?

4. Use the model of filtering in the housing market depicted in Figure 9.2 to determine the effects of:

    (a) Demolition of some high-quality housing.

    (b) Demolition of some low-quality housing.

5. Consider the King–Fullerton analysis of the taxation of income from capital as applied to owner-occupied housing. Use the same model and numerical magnitudes as in the text. What would happen to the effective tax rate on implicit rent if the income tax rate in the United States were increased from 30% to 40%?

6. Suppose that the demand for housing by low-income households is

$$H = AY^b\, p_h^c,$$

    where b is the income elasticity of demand and c is the price elasticity of demand. Let $A = 0.0333$, $b = 1$, and $c = -0.5$.

    (a) If Y is $15,000 and the price of a unit of housing is $100, how much housing is purchased, and what is the level of housing expenditures?

(b) Now let income increase to $20,000, with all other data constant. How much housing is purchased, and what is the level of housing expenditures?

(c) Assume that income returns to $15,000. What happens to housing purchased and housing expenditures if the price of housing is reduced by 30% (to $70)?

7. Compute the market value of a rental house given the following assumptions:

- The annual rent is $6000.
- The annual expenses (taxes, maintenance, etc.) are $4000.
- The annual maintenance expenses permit the house to last forever.
- The discount rate is 5%.

(a) Compute the market value of this house.

(b) Now compute the market value of the same house assuming that the buyer will sell it after 3 years for $40,000. Assume that the house is purchased at the beginning of year 1, rents are received at the end of years 1, 2, and 3, and the house is sold at the end of year 3.

(c) What is the current value of the house if its price at the end of year 3 is expected to be $50,000 instead of $40,000?

REFERENCES

Arnott, Richard, 1995. "Time for Revision on Rent Control?" *Journal of Economic Perspectives*, Vol. 9, pp. 99–120.

Berry, Brian, 1976. "Ghetto Expansion and Single-Family Housing Prices: Chicago, 1968–1972," *Journal of Urban Economics*, Vol. 3, pp. 297 323.

Do, A. Quang, R. Wilbur, and J. Short, 1994. "An Empirical Examination of the Externalities of Neighborhood Churches on Housing Values," *Journal of Real Estate and Urban Economics*, Vol. 9, pp. 127–136.

Fallis, George and L. Smith, 1984. "Uncontrolled Prices in a Controlled Market: The Case of Rent Controls," *American Economic Review*, Vol. 74, pp. 193–200.

Friedman, Joseph and D. Weinberg, 1982. *The Economics of Housing Vouchers*. New York: Academic Press.

Jorgenson, Dale and R. Landau, eds., 1993. *Tax Reform and the Cost of Capital*. Washington, DC: The Brookings Institution.

King, A. Thomas and P. Mieszkowski, 1973. "Racial Discrimination, Segregation, and the Price of Housing," *Journal of Political Economy*, Vol. 81, pp. 590–606.

King, Mervyn and D. Fullerton, eds., 1984. *The Taxation of Income from Capital: A Comparative Study of the United States, United Kingdom, Sweden and West Germany*. Chicago: The University of Chicago Press.

Massey, Douglas and N. Denton, 1993. *American Apartheid*, Cambridge, MA: Harvard University Press.

Mieszkowski, Peter and E. Mills, 1993. "The Causes of Metropolitan Suburbanization," *Journal of Economic Perspectives*, Vol. 7, No. 3, pp. 135–147.

Miller, V. P. and J. Quigley, 1990. "Segregation by Racial and Demographic Group: Evidence from the San Francisco Bay Area," *Urban Studies*, Vol. 27, pp. 3–21.

Munnell, Alice, L. Browne, J. McEneaney, and G. Tootel, 1992. "Mortgage Lending in Boston: Interpreting the HMDA Data," Working Paper 92-7. Boston: Federal Reserve Bank of Boston.

Niedercorn, John and E. Hearle, 1963. "Recent Land-Use Trends in Forty-Eight Large American Cities," RM-3663-1-FF. Santa Monica, CA: Rand Corporation.

Polinsky, A. Mitchell and D. Ellwood, 1979. "An Empirical Reconciliation of Micro and Grouped Estimates of the Demand for Housing," *Review of Economics and Statistics*, Vol. 61, pp. 199–205.

Schwab, William, 1992. *The Sociology of Cities*. Englewood Cliffs, NJ: Prentice Hall.

Smith, Barton, 1981. "A Study of Racial Discrimination in Housing," in J. V. Henderson, ed., *Research in Urban Economics*, Vol. 1. Greenwich, CT: JAI Press.

U.S. Department of Housing and Urban Development, 1982. "HUD Subsidized Housing Overview," in *Major Themes and Additional Budget Details: 1983 Budget of the United States Government*. Washington, DC: U.S. Government Printing Office.

White, Michelle, 1986. "Property Taxes and Urban Housing Abandonment," *Journal of Urban Economics*, Vol. 20, pp. 312–330.

CHAPTER

10

The Public Sector in Urban Areas

A. INTRODUCTION

The public sector performs many functions in urban areas. These many roles are carried out by a variety of governmental institutions. One goal of this chapter is to provide you with the ability to understand the complex system that is local government in the United States. Another goal of the chapter is to explore the effects that the local public sector has on the spatial patterns of the urban area. The field of local public finance is itself a large and diverse subject that could be (and is, in some colleges) a separate course. We cannot cover all aspects of local public finance in this chapter but concentrate on those general aspects of the local public sector that influence spatial patterns. Transportation facilities were discussed in Chapter 8. We begin with a general discussion of the functions of local government and then turn to some official data to get an idea of the magnitudes of local taxation and spending. The next step is to examine the economic theories that have been advanced to try to explain the outcomes that we observe.

Two prominent theories stand side by side in the field of local public finance. One theory is based on the idea that people in an urban area can change their residential locations easily and express their demands for local public services by "voting with their feet." They set up local governmental jurisdictions to satisfy these demands, and people join the "club" that most closely matches their preferences. The other theory is based on the notion that residents are not particularly mobile and/or cannot change local jurisdictions very easily. In this theory jurisdictions contain a variety of people, and decisions regarding the local public sector are made through the political process of setting up interest groups, running candidates, voting, and so on. Clearly, both of these theories contain a great deal of truth and have implications for urban spatial patterns. One important task of this chapter is to determine which theory is applicable in different situations.

A critical feature of local government is its system for raising revenues. Local governments rely largely on the local real estate tax, but they also charge fees for various services and receive revenues from the state and federal governments. The first order of business on the revenue side is to examine the role of the real estate tax in the two theories mentioned in the preceding paragraph. Then the other sources of funds are discussed.

Local governments do much more than tax and spend. They also regulate our lives to a considerable degree. They pass building codes, zoning ordinances, and many other laws. They enforce laws, and they plan for the future. Chapter 5 included an examination of some of these functions.

B. THE ROLES OF THE URBAN PUBLIC SECTOR

You have probably already learned that mainstream economists put the economic functions of government into three categories. The public sector has programs to (1) allocate resources to public goods and services, (2) redistribute income in accordance with the decisions made by the society, and (3) promote economic stability and growth. This three-way categorization was invented by the eminent public finance economist Richard Musgrave (1959), and he called them the *allocation branch*, the *distribution branch*, and the *stabilization branch*. Musgrave's system comes straight from the standard microeconomic and macroeconomic theory courses. In microeconomic theory you learn the principles of efficient allocation of resources, including the principles that apply to goods and services that include external costs or benefits or are public. Goods and services that are public have two features; they are consumed jointly by a large number of people, and it is costly to exclude people from enjoying them. In microeconomics you also learned that the society may decide that there should be a policy regarding the distribution of income. In theory the efficient use of resources and the distribution of income can be separate considerations, but nearly all policies in the real world have impacts on both resource allocation and income distribution. In macroeconomics you learned about the business of macroeconomic policies aimed at reducing unemployment, promoting price stability, and providing for future growth.

You may also have already learned that the various levels of government in a federal system, such as we have in the United States, will logically assume different roles within Musgrave's three-part system. The federal system of government in the United States is the result of over 200 years of experience; it goes back to the founding of the country. The original 13 colonies were separate entities that originally looked first to England. Once they had decided that there was mutual interest in setting up a separate nation, it was necessary to devise a central government that carefully preserved the powers of the individual states. The first attempt to create a central government, under the Articles of Confederation, did not work well. The federal government under this system did not have enough power to carry out its basic functions, including the power to tax and to provide for the common defense. The United States as we know it was created by the adoption of the Constitution, which (as amended) defines the powers of the federal government and leaves to the states the power over matters that are not mentioned. It may be difficult to believe, but all expansions of the role of the federal government had to have been consistent with the Constitution. Under the Constitution a great deal of power resides with the state governments. A major responsibility of state governments is to set up the system of local government in the state. Local governments, even the cities of New York, Los Angeles, and Chicago, are creatures of their state governments.

From adoption of the Constitution the duties of the federal government have included the sole power to regulate the money supply, international trade, and interstate commerce. These powers have grown into the responsibility for promoting the economic stability of the nation, which was formally stated in the Employment Act of 1946. In the 1950s and 1960s the macroeconomic policy agenda was expanded to include economic growth as well, and the Employment Act was amended in 1978 by the Full Employment and Balanced Growth Act. However, most states and many local governments have undertaken the job of trying to promote growth and stability in their economies. There is nothing in the Constitution that prevents them from promoting their own economies, and this topic is discussed extensively in Chapter 14. For now we shall set aside the topic of the role of local government in fostering economic stability and growth.

We also think of policies regarding income distribution as the province of the federal government. As a practical matter, this is largely true. The largest income redistribution programs are Social Security (income for the elderly) and Medicare (medical care for the elderly). However, the basic welfare programs for nonelderly people are Aid to Families with Dependent Children (AFDC) and Medicaid (medical care for the poor). These programs are run by the states, and the benefit levels are set by the states. The federal government set up the programs and covers roughly half of their cost, but the fact that the programs are run by the states has resulted in widely different benefit levels from state to state. It might appeal to one's sense of logic to have income distribution programs be entirely a federal responsibility, but the fact is that these programs are a joint responsibility of the states and the federal government. Indeed, there are many (especially among members of the Republican Party) who think that the current welfare system is a failure and that the states should be more in control of income distribution policy.

Is income distribution policy a local responsibility? Prior to the Great Depression of the 1930s, public welfare was one of the roles of local government (and private charities). At this point, however, very few people would argue that local governments should set up and finance their own income redistribution programs beyond temporary emergency relief. People can move and easily overwhelm a program set up at the local level. Nevertheless, local governments do set up limited public welfare programs (e.g., homeless shelters and general assistance), and they operate income distribution programs such as AFDC, food stamps, public housing, and Medicaid.

This discussion leaves the allocation of resources to public goods and services as the primary function of local government.

These public goods and services include:

- Education
- Hospitals and health care
- Transportation (streets, highways, public transportation)
- Public safety (police, fire protection, public health)

- Parks and recreation
- Community development and planning
- Water, sewerage, and solid waste management (garbage)
- Other parts of local infrastructure

By far the largest of these functions is the provision of public education. All states have created a system of school districts to provide free high school education, and most have also set up a system of local junior college districts to provide two years of college at low cost to qualified students. Many local junior colleges also provide a wide variety of adult education courses at low cost. [The provision of four-year colleges and universities with graduate programs is a responsibility that the states assume themselves, with notable exceptions (e.g., City University of New York).] The quantity and quality of the goods and services delivered by local governments vary enormously. Some local governments do not provide all the items on the list above. For example, local governments in some rural areas do not provide fire protection except by voluntary subscription. In these cases the property owner is not compelled to pay taxes for a fire department but can join a fire protection club if he or she wishes. The reason for this seemingly odd system is that an isolated building that is on fire will not cause a problem for neighboring property. Fire protection becomes a public service when the possibility of external costs arises. My burning house setting your house on fire is perhaps the ultimate negative externality. After saving lives, the first job of the fire department is to prevent the spread of a fire to other properties. We are concerned with local governments in urban areas, so the case of the rural fire department is not relevant.

   With one exception, it is pretty clear that each of the items on the list above is best considered a public good or service in urban areas. That one item is education, the largest item. Is it not true that the individual student benefits from education? How much spillover benefit to other members of the community could there be? It is clear that education is regarded as a public good in the United States, and it is worthwhile to review the arguments briefly. First, the consumer of education up to grade 12 is a child, a person who largely is not held responsible for making major decisions. The decision maker is not the consumer of the education services (the child) but the parents. The *states* have decided that school attendance is compulsory up to age 16 to protect children from irresponsible parents (and from their own immature judgments). In addition, there are spillover benefits to other members of the society. The current and future families of the student benefit from the student's education in many ways, from enhanced earning power to increased ability to handle family matters. The larger local community also benefits from a more educated citizenry. People with more education tend to have a better understanding of public issues and create fewer social problems such as delinquency and crime. People with more education are less apt to be unemployed or need public assistance. A more educated citizenry creates a greater demand for more and better information (newspapers, books, etc.), and information has some public goods features. These are powerful arguments for considering education, perhaps up to twelfth grade, to be a good with a substantial public component.

   A more difficult issue to decide is whether education for children should be *provided directly* by government agencies (i.e., public schools). Conservative economists, and many others, argue that we should separate the notion of education as a good with substantial public benefits from the idea that the education should be in a public school. They think that education for children should be subsidized by the public sector but that the parents should have wider choice to send children to a variety of schools (provided that those schools meet certain standards). The conservatives advocate the public provision of education *vouchers*, certificates worth a certain amount of money when spent at the school of the parents' choice. As the discussion in Chapter 2 would tell you, conservatives argue their case on the basis of personal freedom. They think of the local public school system as sort of a monopolist, and point out that a voucher system would create competition among providers of education, which would promote the more efficient provision of educational services as well. As we shall see in the next section, the theory of the local public sector in which people "vote with the feet" tends to undermine this argument. Nevertheless, the idea of education voucher programs has become more popular in recent years, and this topic has become one of the biggest issues in local public economics.

A brief overview of local government expenditures and revenues is provided in Table 10.1. Data are presented for two fiscal years, 1966–1967 and 1986–1987. Expenditures per capita increased in real terms over those 20 years from $1017 to $1680 (in 1987 dollars), an increase of 65.2%. During this same period personal income per capita increased from $11,062 to $15,159 (in 1987 dollars), for an increase

TABLE 10.1 Local Government Expenditures and Revenues: All Local Governments		
	1966–1967	*1986–1987*
Direct general expenditures (%)		
Education	48.0	42.3
Health and welfare	12.4	12.9
Transportation	8.7	7.2
Public safety	8.0	9.8
Environment and housing[a]	9.8	11.0
Administration	3.6	5.4
Interest and misc.	9.5	11.4
Per capita direct general expenditures	$299 ($1017 in 1987 dollars)	$1680
General revenue (%)		
Local sources	65.3	62.0
Real estate tax	43.2	28.3
Other taxes	6.7	10.1
Charges and misc.	15.4	23.6
Intergovernmental	34.7	38.0
State	31.7	33.3
Federal	3.0	p 4.7

[a]*Includes parks and recreation, housing and community development, sewerage, and other sanitation.*

Source: Census of Governments (1967, 1987), U.S. Department of Commerce.

of 37.0%. Therefore, expenditures per capita by local governments grew by an average of 2.5% per year compared to the growth of personal income per capita of 1.57% per year. Table 10.1 shows that the particular categories of spending that grew most rapidly were public safety (police, fire, and correctional facilities), environment and housing, administration (including the courts and general administration), and interest and miscellaneous expenditures. The proportions of local expenditures for these functions increased, and the fraction devoted to public schools dropped from 48.0% to 42.3%. However, this decline in the proportion spent on schools still involved an increase in expenditures per capita from $488 to $711 (1987 dollars), an increase of 45.7% (average increase of 1.88% per year). Clearly local governments have increased their expenditures on public safety and the courts, and had to pay higher interest rates on their borrowed funds. They also spent more on community development and general administrative functions.

Sources of general revenue are also shown in Table 10.1. In 1966–1967 local governments obtained 65.3% of general revenue from local sources. The largest local source was the real estate (property) tax, which accounted for 43.2% of all general revenue. Funds received from state government contributed 31.7% of general revenue. In 1986–1987 local governments were still raising 62.0% of general revenue from local sources, but now the real estate (property) tax was only 28.3% of general revenue. Other taxes had increased from 6.7% to 10.1% of general revenue, and charges and fees jumped from 15.4% to 23.6% of the total. The proportion of revenue received from intergovernmental sources increased by 3.3%, with both state and federal sources exhibiting increases. Clearly, the biggest change on the revenue side is the reduction in the reliance on the real estate (property) tax and the increased use of charges and fees. The real estate tax was still the largest single source of revenue raised from local sources in 1986–1987, but intergovernmental grants from the state had become the largest source of funds for local governments around the nation.

Table 10.1 pertains to all local governments in the nation, including governments in rural areas as well as urban areas. The Census of Governments can be used to show the expenditures and revenues for all units of local government in any county in the nation. Two counties have been chosen for display in Table 10.2. These two counties are the central county in the Chicago urban area (Cook County, Illinois) and a suburban county adjacent to Cook County (DuPage County, Illinois). Local governments in Cook County spent $1696 per capita in 1986–1987 compared to $1475 in DuPage County. Cook County spent 39.3% of those funds on education ($666 per capita), while DuPage County used 50.8% of its expenditures for education ($749 per capita). Compared to DuPage County, local governments in Cook County spent greater proportions of their budgets on health and welfare programs, transportation (including the public transportation system in Chicago), public safety, and environment and housing programs. It would appear that the greater demand for such services in Cook County compared to DuPage County has a detrimental effect on spending for schools. A similar conclusion was reached by Luce and Summers (1987) in a study of local government in the Philadelphia urban area; spending on schools in the city of Philadelphia had to compete with heavy demands for other public services.

The revenue picture for Cook and DuPage counties is also shown in Table 10.2. Local governments in the suburban county raised 81.0% of total general revenue

TABLE 10.2 Local Government Expenditures and Revenues, 1986–1987	DuPage County	Cook County
Direct general expenditures (%)		
Education	50.8	39.3
Health and welfare	3.7	5.5
Transportation	7.1	10.5
Public safety	9.5	13.3
Environment and housing[a]	12.0	14.7
Administration	5.9	5.3
Interest	4.5	6.2
Other	6.6	5.2
Direct general expenditures per capita	$1475	$1696
General revenue (%)		
Local sources	81.0	66.6
Real estate tax	48.4	34.2
Other taxes	10.1	16.9
Charges and misc.	22.5	15.5
Intergovernmental	19.0	33.4
State	14.4	25.7
Federal	4.6	7.7

[a]*Includes parks and recreation, housing and community development, sewerage, and other sanitation.*

Source: Census of Governments (1987), U.S. Department of Commerce.

from local sources in 1986–1987. Reliance on the real estate (property) tax was a heavy 48.4% of the total. The state of Illinois provided only 14.4% of the revenue used by governments in DuPage County. This last figure compares with a national average of 33.3% (Table 10.1) and 25.7% for Cook County. Local governments in Cook County raised 66.6% of their general revenue from local sources, and 34.2% of the total was from the real estate (property) tax. Cook County governments made greater use of other taxes (particularly the local sales tax), and made lesser use of charges and fees than did DuPage County or local governments in general (Table 10.1).

We turn now to economic theories that are designed to shed some light on local government expenditure decisions.

C. THE TIEBOUT MODEL OF URBAN PUBLIC FINANCE

The Tiebout, or "vote with the feet," theory of urban public finance was invented by Charles Tiebout (1956) in a celebrated paper entitled "A Pure Theory of Local Expenditures." Tiebout did not intend to set out a complete theory of how resource allocation decisions are made by local governments, but his theory has become a very influential tool for studying those decisions. Tiebout's article was written in response to the classic articles by Paul Samuelson (1954, 1955) on the pure theory of public expenditures. In those articles Samuelson defined a public good as a collective consumption good; one individual's consumption of the good does not subtract from any other individual's consumption of the good. If X is the total amount of a public good supplied, X_i is the amount consumed by individual i, and X_j is the amount consumed by individual j, and so on, then

$$X = X_i = X_j = \cdots = X_n,$$

where there are n individuals in the society in question. This definition is in sharp contrast to the normal private good Y, where the total amount consumed is the sum of the amounts consumed by the individuals:

$$Y = Y_i + Y_j + \cdots + Y_n.$$

If Y is hamburgers, every one I eat cannot be eaten by anyone else.

Samuelson's definition of a public good really includes two criteria: (1) the good is jointly consumed, and (2) there is no easy method available for excluding people from consuming the good. Consider a football game played in a stadium that seats 60,000 people. This good is consumed jointly by those in attendance, but it is easy to exclude people—just build a fence around the stadium and sell tickets. Now suppose that the game is being televised. Anyone with a television set can tune into the game for free. But wait! Suppose that the game is being carried on television with a scrambled signal, and only those who pay for a signal unscrambler can watch. Technology can change a public good into a jointly consumed private good. Indeed, there is a strong incentive for the invention of technologies to do just that.

Samuelson's point is that for a public good, the optimal amount is found where the marginal cost of the good equals the *sum* of the marginal benefits of the good's consumers. Should the United States purchase another aircraft carrier for the Navy? That decision depends on the cost of the carrier versus the sum of the amounts that each of us is willing to pay for it.

Consider Figure 10.1, which depicts the demand curves for a public good by three individuals: person A, person B, and person C. Samuelson says that to find the total demand for the public good, we should add the individual demand curves *vertically* to find out how much the three people as a group would be willing to pay for the public good at each possible quantity. This total demand curve is shown in the bottom right of Figure 10.1. An economically efficient quantity of the public good is set by equating the marginal cost of the good to its marginal benefit, which is the height of the total demand curve. At quantity X^* the marginal cost of the public good is equal to the marginal benefit of the good to the group, the amount that the *group* is willing to pay for another unit of the good, which is MB^* in Figure 10.1. Note that all members of the group then consume the same amount of the public good, X^*, and that the marginal benefit of the public good to each person is shown by the height of the individual demand curves at X^*. For example, person A consumes quantity X^* and has a marginal benefit for the public good of MB_a^* at that quantity.

For Samuelson there is one fundamental implication that follows from this theorem. Individuals have no incentive to reveal how much they are really willing to pay for more of a public good. They have an incentive to try to be "free riders," peo-

FIGURE 10.1   Optimal provision of a public good

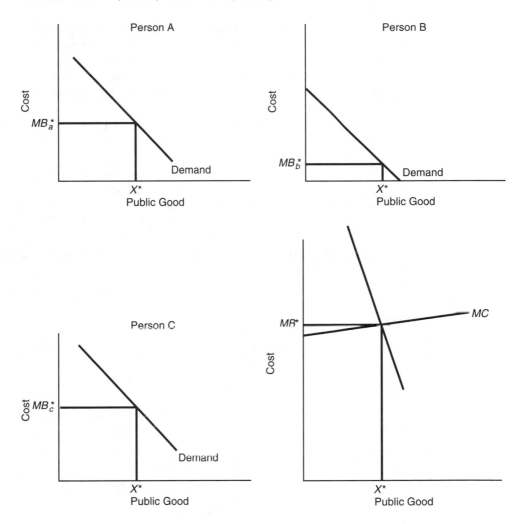

ple who do not pay but benefit from the public good anyway. (The demand curves depicted in Figure 10.1 are the true demand curves, but individuals have no incentive to reveal what these demand curves are.) This lack of incentive to reveal demand means that the private market is not capable of supplying an efficient level of a public good. People may be willing to pay a private firm some amount of money to supply a public good (i.e., voluntary contributions), but contributions will not be enough to generate an efficient level of output (where marginal cost equals sum of marginal benefits). This lack of incentive to reveal preferences also means that the public provision of a public good is problematic. The public sector has the power to tax, so it does not have to rely on voluntary contributions. Resource allocation decisions in the public sector regarding public goods are made through the political process, but there is still no method available to induce consumers to reveal their true preferences. An efficient outcome is far from assured. Mainstream and conservative economists agree on this point.

Tiebout took this unsettling result as his starting point and wondered if there is a mechanism that could force consumers to reveal their true preferences for public goods, could supply those public goods in the same sense that the private market supplies goods, and could levy a tax on consumers equal to the value of benefits received. His answer created a revolution in the way mainstream and conservative economists think about local public finance.

Tiebout (1956) instructed us to consider the class of public goods that are local in nature. His local public goods benefit only those people who live in the particular local jurisdiction that supplies the public goods in question. There are no spillovers to other people in other jurisdictions. His model further assumes that consumer-voters are freely mobile and will move to the local jurisdiction with the supplies of local public goods that best match their preferences. The consumer-voters are not constrained in their movements by other factors such as employment location. The consumer-voters have complete knowledge of the spending and taxation policies of the local jurisdictions, and there is a large number of these jurisdictions offering a range of choices. Let each of those jurisdictions be operating at the minimum of average cost for the combination of public goods chosen, and assume that the households in a jurisdiction each pay an amount in local taxes equal to total expenditures divided by the number of households. Given all these assumptions, which Tiebout admits are unrealistic, consumer-voters will reside in the jurisdiction that best matches their preferences for local public goods. They will each pay a local tax for a marginal unit of the public good equal to its marginal benefit.

To see this last result, return to the public good X defined above. Suppose that there are three consumer-voters in the local jurisdiction, and that each unit of X costs p. Suppose that the quantity of X is set at X^*. These facts are shown in Figure 10.2, a set of diagrams that is similar to Figure 10.1. The total amount of taxes collected is pX^*, and each household pays $pX^*/3$. In effect, each household pays a "tax price" of $p/3$ for each unit of X. Each household that chooses to locate in this jurisdiction has a marginal benefit for the public good (at quantity X^*) equal to its "tax price," or

$$MB_i = \frac{p}{3}$$

for each household i among the three households. Other households for whom this condition is not true at the quantity X^* choose to locate elsewhere. This is true because quantity X^* is not the amount that these other households would choose at the tax price of $p/3$. These other households would set up their own local jurisdictions so that tax price for the public good *will* equal marginal benefit.

The condition for the efficient provision of the public good is marginal cost equal to the sum of the marginal benefits,

$$\Sigma\, MB_i = MC.$$

In Figure 10.2 the summation runs over the households from 1 to 3. Because all households in the jurisdiction face the same "tax price" for a marginal unit of the public good of $p/3$, the sum of the marginal benefits is just $3(MB)$, where MB is the marginal benefit for each household. Therefore,

FIGURE 10.2 Equilibrium in the Tiebout model

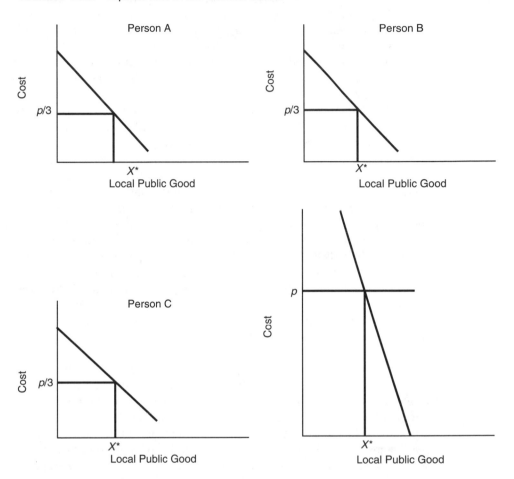

$$\Sigma\, MB_i = MB^* = 3(MB) = 3\frac{(p)}{3} = p = MC.$$

This idealized interpretation of how local governments operate produces an efficient level of the local public good. Under this kind of local government, decisions regarding local public goods are made unanimously. Everyone who has chosen to live in a particular jurisdiction has the same marginal benefit for the local public good, so there are no disagreements (at least on resource allocation matters).

Tiebout has thus responded to Samuelson's (1954, p. 388) contention that "no decentralized pricing system can serve to determine optimally these levels of collective consumption." For Tiebout local public goods are being provided by a system that is, in effect, a decentralized pricing system. His system works if households can sort themselves according to the amount of the local public good demanded. Remember the football game that is being played in a stadium in front of 60,000 spectators? This good is jointly consumed, but the consumers pay for the good by buying tickets.

There are no free riders. Those who are unwilling to pay the price of a ticket do not go to the game. This example resembles the Tiebout model in that he has, in effect, turned a local public good into a private good that is consumed jointly. The local head tax is the price of admission.

Tiebout recognized that the system he described is not a perfect allocator of resources because the real world does not match all his assumptions. One obvious problem with the Tiebout model as presented thus far is that local taxes are equal for each household in a jurisdiction. The tax system implicitly in use is a type of "head tax." Each household has one head of the household, and that person has one head. Taxes are not assessed in that manner in the real world, of course. In fact, the real estate tax is the largest local tax, and it is assessed on the value of real estate property. This method of taxation creates an obvious problem for the operation of the Tiebout model. People can try to be free riders. Suppose that a group of people wishes to set up a local jurisdiction with a high level of a local public good, but also suppose that their only means of collecting taxes is through a real estate tax. These people know that, once the jurisdiction is set up, other people will want to build cheap houses and move into the jurisdiction so as to benefit from the public good and pay little in taxes. This line of thinking will lead the members of the original group to think, "Why should I reveal my true preferences for this public good? My better course of action would be to become a free rider in some other jurisdiction." We are back to Samuelson's problem—people will not reveal their true preferences for public goods, and they will be undersupplied by local governments.

The solution to this problem was devised by Bruce Hamilton (1975). He proposed that when the group sets up its local jurisdiction, it can prevent free riders by imposing a requirement that each household own a certain minimum amount of real estate. Local jurisdictions cannot impose a precise minimum requirement for real estate (land plus buildings), but it *can* impose a minimum lot size in a zoning ordinance and require that houses meet quality requirements set out in a building code. If the real estate tax were only a tax on the quantity of land, setting a minimum lot size would create a perfect Tiebout mechanism. The minimum lot size would also become the maximum lot size because those people who want larger lots and the same level of the public good would set up their own jurisdiction (with a larger minimum lot size). The Hamilton (1975) mechanism requires that households must sort themselves along two dimensions—amount of the local public good demanded, and lot size— rather than just one. Furthermore, the Hamilton mechanism is not perfect because a minimum lot size requirement does not impose complete uniformity in real estate value, which is the base of the real estate tax. Zoning ordinances are adopted for a variety of reasons, including protection of health and safety of the public, maintenance of community character, and planning for growth. Nevertheless, it surely is true that local officials in the suburbs of large urban areas recognize the use of zoning as a method for ensuring some minimum real estate tax payment. Zoning ordinances were discussed at some length in Chapter 5.

Hamilton (1975) provided the Tiebout mechanism with a more realistic method for collecting taxes, but there are other problems that cause the real world to depart from the Tiebout theory. It may be true that households are neither as mobile nor as informed as Tiebout assumed. In my view these criticisms are not compelling. Households in the United States are highly mobile, and they pay close attention to the quality of local public services, especially schools. It would appear that racial discrimination is the most serious limitation on household mobility in large urban areas in the United States. The problem is particularly serious because minority households are primarily confined to the central city in the major urban areas. The problem of the central city in the Tiebout model is discussed below. The Tiebout model also requires that there be a large number of local jurisdictions to provide for the efficient sorting of households. There may not be enough local jurisdictions to match everyone's preferences precisely, but there certainly is a large number of jurisdictions in any major urban area. Tiebout's assumption is not obviously wrong on this count.

Formal efficiency in the Tiebout model also required that there be no spillovers of benefits from one jurisdiction to others. If there are significant spillovers, the solution is to set up jurisdictions that are large enough to contain the spillovers. We should set up public transportation districts, environmental protection districts, mosquito abatement districts, and so on. In fact, we do just that. In many cases county governments provide some of these services that cover a wider area. In other instances, special governmental units are created for these purposes. However, the creation of such larger districts reduces the number of choices available to households. Suppose that I do not care for the options available in the two mosquito abatement districts in my urban area. My choices are to move to another urban area (not a sensible option) or to engage in political activity to get my mosquito abatement district to conform more closely to my preferences. The latter option is the subject of the next section.

The criticisms of the Tiebout model discussed in the preceding paragraph have some substance, but in my mind the two most important limitations of the Tiebout model are (1) the existence of the large central city, and (2) the fact that the real estate tax is collected on commercial and industrial real estate.

Major urban areas are not simply collections of small jurisdictions; they all contain a major central city. Given the trend toward suburbanization, the major central city has a diminished importance in the local economy, but it still provides local public services to a large number of people with diverse preferences, real estate holdings, and income levels. Residents of the central city are provided with roughly the same level of public services. Indeed, the mayor can count on hearing complaints when people perceive that they are *not* receiving that level of services. The connection between local taxes paid and the quality of public services received may not be very close in the central city. The real estate tax is a tax rather than the charge for benefits received as envisioned by Tiebout and Hamilton. For this reason, resource allocation decisions by central city governments are based primarily on the political process that is discussed in the next section.

The other major problem with the Tiebout–Hamilton model is the existence of nonresidential real estate. This is a major omission indeed. Commercial or industrial real estate normally generates a fiscal surplus for the jurisdiction in which it is located—the taxes and fees paid exceed the cost of providing the services needed by these types of real estate. For example, one study by Bernhard and Stott (1977) of revenues and costs by type of land use for Milwaukee in 1975 showed that commercial and industrial properties contributed 32% of local revenues but represented only 14% of local expenditures. Households paid 68% of local revenues but created 86% of the costs. What is more, households with children in the public schools paid 31%

of the revenues but were the source of 61% of the costs. Households without children in public school provided 37% of the revenue and imposed only 25% of the costs. One might argue that households without children in public school potentially are users of these schools but clearly commercial and industrial properties are not. (The owners of nonresidential properties may use public schools, of course. But they also pay residential real estate taxes.)

How do commercial and industrial real estate change the Tiebout–Hamilton story? As Hamilton suggests, the crafting of the zoning ordinance for the local jurisdiction is a critical part of the model. Now the local zoning officials must decide on the amount of land to be allocated to commercial and industrial activities. Given that these activities provide a fiscal surplus, the basic idea is that there is a trade-off between environmental quality and tax base. Communities that value environmental quality highly will zone little land for commercial or industrial use. Following state law, most local jurisdictions must impose the same real estate tax rate on all classes of property. In some cases local jurisdictions are permitted to impose different real estate tax rates on different classes of property. Permission to charge different real estate tax rates usually means that local officials decide that commercial and industrial property will face higher tax rates than residential property, which will create an even larger fiscal surplus from these uses of land. Even if the real estate tax rate must be uniform over classes of property, the addition of commercial and industrial property to the model means that the local officials in a Tiebout–Hamilton jurisdiction now face a more complex set of decisions. We can imagine that they must simultaneously determine the level of local public goods, set the allocation of land to the various uses, set minimum lot size, and set the real estate tax rate—all to match the preferences of the households whom they intend to attract to their "club." They must do all of this while recognizing that the location decisions of commercial and industrial activities are probably sensitive to the real estate tax rate. Furthermore, the requirement that commercial and industrial real estate must pay a real estate "tax price" for public goods that exceeds the value of the marginal benefit of those goods means that the outcome is no longer an efficient allocation of resources. The exception to this conclusion occurs if the tax price faced by commercial and industrial real estate exceeds the marginal benefit of public goods by the amount of the external cost imposed by these activities on the rest of the jurisdiction. The tax price could be an efficient price after all, but this is not likely to be the case because the local jurisdiction also wants to use the fiscal surplus generated to fund local public goods for its households. Efficient pricing of external costs is not the only motive, and may not even be a very important motive, for taxing commercial and industrial real estate at rates that exceed the marginal benefits of public goods.

Is the addition of commercial and industrial property an important consideration? The answer clearly is "yes." Local jurisdictions vary widely in the amount of commercial and industrial real estate they contain, and it is clear that they respond to the size of the fiscal surplus that is generated. As an example we examine a study of 30 elementary school districts in DuPage County, Illinois in 1990 [McDonald et al. (1991)]. DuPage County is a suburban county located in the Chicago urban area, and it generally contains middle-class households who value good schools. These 30 school districts vary enormously in the proportion of the tax base that is residential and in the assessed value of real estate per pupil. The district with the most commer-

TABLE 10.3	Mean Expenditure per Pupil by DuPage County Grade School Districts, 1990			
	Percent Residential Tax Base			
Total Assessed Value per Pupil	*Low^a* *(49.0%)*	*Medium* *(73.4%)*	*High* *(90.0%)*	*All*
Low^a	$3859^b	3720	3701	3724
($106,900)	(1)	(4)	(5)	(10)
Medium	4772	4447	4096	4404
($153,400)	(3)	(3)	(4)	(10)
High	5346	4243	6146	5095
($273,500)	(6)	3 (3)	(1)	(10)
All	5025	4095	4104	4408
	(10)	(10)	(10)	(30)

^aFigure in parentheses is the median for the group.
^bFigure in parentheses is the number of school districts in the group.
Source: McDonald et al. (1991).

cial and industrial property had only 30.2% of its tax base as residential property. At the other extreme, 91.2% of tax base of another district was residential. The median for the group of 30 districts was 73.4% residential tax base. Table 10.3 shows the relationships between expenditure per elementary school pupil and two variables: the percentage of the tax base that is residential and the total assessed value per pupil. Spending per pupil clearly rises with assessed value per pupil, as one would expect. However, spending per pupil falls with the percentage of the tax base that is residential. The 10 districts with the lowest percentage residential in the tax base spent an average of $5025 per pupil, while the other 20 districts spent an average of $4100 per pupil. The former group of districts clearly perceive a lower tax price for schools because of the presence of commercial and industrial property.

The point can be made more precisely by using the data shown in Table 10.3 to estimate a multiple regression model. A simple linear equation fitted to the data is

$$E = 4600 - 12.79R + 3.68AV.$$

where E is the expenditures per pupil, R the percentage of the tax base that is residential, and AV the total assessed value per pupil (thousands of dollars). This equation explains statistically 57% of the variance of expenditures per pupil. The equation says that expenditures per pupil fall by $12.79 if the percentage of the tax base that is residential increases by 1% and rise by $3.68 if the assessed value per pupil is $1000 greater.

Econometric studies of the demand for local public services have confirmed the existence of the wealth and tax price effects, and as suggested by the data in Table 10.3, the wealth effect is usually the stronger of the two. One reason for this result is that residents do not view the business tax base as immobile. One particularly interesting study by Ladd (1975) confirmed this idea. Ladd studied school expenditures in the Boston metropolitan area in 1970. Her results show that these spending decisions are based on the assumption that commercial and industrial property will exhibit some mobility in response to increases in property tax rates. Her adjusted measure of the *perceived* residential share of the tax base is $1 - aC - bI$, where C is the actual percentage commercial, I is the actual percentage industrial, and a and b are parameters representing the shares of the commercial and industrial tax bases that are perceived not to burden local residents. If a and b are both 1, none of the business tax burden falls on residents. Ladd estimated a to be 0.79 and b to be 0.45, which means that voters did not act as if commercial and industrial property taxes had no cost to residents. Given these estimates of a and b, residents apparently believed that the industrial tax base was more sensitive to tax rates than was the commercial tax base because increases in the commercial tax base reduce the perceived residential share by more than increases in the industrial tax base. Nevertheless, Ladd's results show that the existence of commercial and industrial property does reduce the resident's perceived tax price and contributes to higher expenditures.

Where do the chief criticisms of the Tiebout–Hamilton model leave us? Clearly, a Tiebout mechanism for the efficient provision of local public goods is not at work in the large central cities. But what about the suburbs? Clearly, the Tiebout–Hamilton mechanism is at work here. However, the addition of commercial and industrial property to the real estate base makes the problem that must be solved by officials in a local jurisdiction much more complex and probably destroys the efficiency of the outcome. Local officials can try to attract commercial and industrial activity in order to "oversupply" their jurisdictions with local public goods. Does this actually happen? Research needs to be done on this question because nearly all of the studies of the Tiebout model have ignored commercial and industrial property.

D. THE MEDIAN VOTER MODEL

If the Tiebout mechanism is working perfectly, the residents of a jurisdiction all want the same level of local public goods and the same real estate tax rate. If the Tiebout mechanism is not working very well, the residents have diverse views about these matters. Local spending and taxation policies must be decided by a political process in which diverse points of view are included. The actual method in a representative democracy is to elect a mayor and members of the city council (or officials of other local governmental jurisdictions) and to delegate to them the responsibility for setting local policy. If a majority of voters does not like their decisions, the voters can elect someone else in the next election. People vote for a candidate for many reasons, and a candidate can embody a complex bundle of opinions, intentions, and abilities. What is more, many people do not vote at all. Does this mean that they are satisfied with the way things are, or does it mean that they perceive that their votes are meaningless? All of these complexities are more properly the subject matter of political science, but economists and political scientists have ventured into this briar patch and proposed a simple model of voting and local public finance. Called the *median voter model*, it does provide considerable explanatory power at the local level.

The basic conclusion of the median voter model is that decisions regarding local spending and taxation will mimic the preferences of the median voter, the person who is right in the middle of the range of opinions on these matters. The median voter model bears a strong resemblance to the principle of median location that was presented in Chapter 3. The pizza parlor selects a location in physical space next to the median customer. The winning local candidate selects a location in political space next to the median voter. A leading book on this theory by Enelow and Hinich (1984) is entitled *The Spatial Theory of Voting*. Let us see how the model works in a simple case.

Suppose that the decision at hand is the provision of a single local public good. As we assumed in Section C, suppose that this local public good can be purchased by the local jurisdiction at a constant cost of p and that each household pays an equal share of that cost. As before, each household faces the tax price of p/n, where n is the total number of households in the local jurisdiction. In the Tiebout model, given this tax price, everyone in the jurisdiction prefers the same quantity of the local public good; they all equate marginal benefit to the tax price at the same quantity. In the median voter model, the quantity of the local public good demanded by households at tax price p/n varies. Suppose that those quantities demanded at some given price p/n are as shown in Figure 10.3 for voters A through G. Ignore points D' and G' for now. (Note that this diagram resembles Figure 3.3.)

Figure 10.3 depicts the preferences of the voters. Now let us suppose that an election is held between two candidates and that those candidates are running on a platform that includes only a single plank: how much of the local public good to provide. Candidate M is a crafty politician and proposes the quantity of the local public good that matches the preferences of voter D, the median voter. Candidate L proposes a quantity that matches the preferences of voter C. The election is held, and candidate M wins by a vote of 4 to 3. Voters D, E, F, and G vote for candidate M because he is closer to their preferences than is candidate L. Alternatively, suppose that the M's opponent is candidate H, who proposes a quantity that matches the preferences of voter E. Now candidate M wins by a vote of 4 to 3 because he now gets the votes of voters A, B, and C (in addition to the vote of voter D). What if both candidates propose the quantity that coincides with the preferences of voter D? In this case the preferences of the median voter prevail again, and it does not matter who wins. The quantity of the public provided in Figure 10.3 is D.

The outcome of the median voter model is not sensitive to extreme points of view. Suppose that voter G "moves" to point G'. Voter D is still the median voter, and candidate M still wins. However, this result reveals an important aspect of the median voter model. There is nothing to guarantee that the level of the local public good (X^*) provided will be the efficient level in the usual sense (i.e., where $\Sigma MB_i = p$, where index i runs from voter A to voter G). The move of voter G to G' means that he or she has an increased marginal benefit (demand) for the local public good at its current level D (ΣMB_i increases), but the political process does not respond by increasing the quantity provided. This result is similar to the outcome in the

FIGURE 10.3 The median voter model

Quantity of Local Public Good at Tax Price p/n

principle of median location model in Chapter 3. (However, remember that the decision of the pizza parlor not to change location is also efficient.) The quantity will increase only if the demand of the median voter increases. If voter D moves to point D', that crafty politician M will follow. No one else has any influence unless he or she becomes the median voter. For example, if voter C (instead of voter D) were to shift his or her demand to point D', candidate M would follow.

You can now see that the median voter model offers the very specific prediction that resource allocation decisions regarding local public goods will follow the median voter, and no one else. The only problem is to identify the median voter! Just who is that person? One approach that is often used is to assume that preferences for the local public good follow household income, so that the median voter has the median household income. This assumption will introduce inaccuracy if preferences for the local public good also depend upon other variables, such as age and number of children. Numerous empirical studies of various types of local public goods have been done, and Inman (1979) summarized the results. Inman's summary is that the elasticity of demand for total local public expenditures with respect to median income varies from 0.34 to 0.89. The income elasticities of demand for specific public goods, such as education, police and fire, and public works, generally fall in this range. However, the income elasticity of demand for parks and recreation is larger, falling in the range 0.99 to 1.32. Another prediction of the median voter model is that the preferences of other voters, who are clearly located far from the median, do not influence the outcome. For example, the preferences of the very poor or the very rich should not matter. Inman (1978) tested this implication and found two things. First, the median voter is more accurately portrayed as a homeowner with the median income *and* a child in the local public schools. Second, the budget that was chosen depended not only on the preferences of this median voter but also on the number of renters, elderly, and families with children in private schools. In short, voters who are not the median voter also exert some influence. The median voter model is too simple to capture the whole story.

The median voter model obviously is a gross simplification of political reality, but it does have considerable explanatory power in matters of local public finance. It may be that local issues are primarily decisions over taxes and spending largely unclouded by political ideology or other complicating factors. The median voter model also sometimes has value at the national level as well. I am writing this chapter on January 3, 1995, the day before the Republicans take over the U.S. Congress. They won an important electoral victory in November 1994 by promising to cut federal spending, taxes, and balance the budget. It would appear that the median voter changed to prefer less federal spending and that the Republican congressional candidates realized what the winning platform would be. At least this is an intriguing hypothesis.

E. THE REAL ESTATE TAX

Recall from Table 10.1 that 28.3% of the revenue raised by local governments in 1986–1987 was through the real estate tax. Real estate tax collections were 45.6% of all revenues raised from local sources. All other taxes (sales, income, and licenses) accounted for only 16.3% of locally raised revenue in 1986–1987. The real estate tax is, by far, the most important tax that is levied by local government. Who actually pays this tax? What are its effects on location patterns? These are critical questions and the topics of this section.

Mechanics of the Real Estate Tax

The first step in answering these questions is to understand the mechanics of the real estate tax. There are two independent parts of the system. The first half of the process is the determination of the size of the tax base for each property owner and for a jurisdiction as a whole. This task is usually undertaken by an official called the county tax assessor. This office of county government has the job of determining the *assessed value* of each parcel of real estate in the county. The assessed value by state law is set as some percentage of fair market value. This percentage is known as the *assessment ratio*, and figures of 0.33 or 0.50 are fairly common. The county assessor uses standard techniques of real estate appraisal to obtain an estimated market value and then applies the assessment ratio to this figure. Many counties revise assessments every year, but others do it less frequently. When the assessor has completed the job, the property owners are notified of their assessed values. This notification is *not* a tax bill, but the time to protest is when one's assessment notice arrives. County assessors provide for a time period in which the property owner can challenge the assessor's judgment. It is possible to have one's assessed value reduced, but it usually requires proof that the assessor was inconsistent in assessing the property in question. This proof normally consists of evidence that other, identical properties were assessed for lower amounts.

Once the time for appeals has passed, the assessor then sends notice to each local jurisdiction of the size of its tax base for the next fiscal year. A county contains several municipalities, school districts, park districts, and other types of local governments. The boundaries of these jurisdictions normally do not coincide, so the assessor must figure out the size of the tax base for each local governmental jurisdiction by keeping track of which jurisdictions contain each parcel of real estate. An example may astound you. Local government in Illinois is more complicated than in most places. I reside in the following local jurisdictions:

- School district 90 (elementary)
- Village of River Forest
- Village of River Forest Library District
- River Forest Park District
- Triton Community College District
- Consolidated High School District 200
- Des Plaines Valley Mosquito Abatement District
- Metropolitan Water Reclamation District of Greater Chicago
- General Assistance, River Forest
- Township of River Forest
- Consolidated Election Commission
- Suburban TB Sanitarium

- Forest Preserve District of Cook County
- County of Cook
- Cook County Health Facilities District

The county assessor keeps track of all of this for each real estate parcel in the county.

The second half of the process starts with the determination of the amount of revenue to be raised by each unit of local government. Each jurisdiction starts by determining its expenditure level and the amount of revenue that will be received from other sources in the coming fiscal year. The other revenue sources vary by type of jurisdiction. For example, school districts will receive funds from the state through the state's school aid formula and (perhaps) from the federal government through grants for various programs. Municipalities receive funds from the state and federal governments for a variety of purposes, and they also levy several charges and fees. The difference between proposed spending and anticipated revenues from other sources is the amount of the real estate tax levy. Each local jurisdiction then determines its official real estate tax rate by dividing its tax levy by the total assessed value in the jurisdiction, or

$$\text{official tax rate} = \text{tax levy} \div \text{total assessed value.}$$

The official tax rate is usually expressed in mills (tenths of a cent) per $100 of assessed value. One therefore often hears the term *mill rate* in reference to the real estate tax. The county assessor then takes the official tax rates for all the local jurisdictions and computes the tax bill for each parcel of real estate in the county. Recall that the county assessor knows *all* of the local jurisdictions in which a particular parcel of real estate is located. The county assessor uses all of the official tax rates that apply to each property and sends out the real estate tax bills to the property owners. These bills list each unit of government to which the property owner pays taxes, but payment is simply made to the county assessor. The assessor's office then sends the money to the local jurisdictions. The property tax bill also shows the total of the official tax rates for the parcel of real estate. For example, the official real estate tax rate that I paid to the total of 15 different local jurisdictions listed above was 10,645 mills in 1993. In other words, I paid $10.645 per $100 of assessed value.

I have told you my official tax rate. At 10.645% this tax rate sounds very high, but this number really is meaningless. The meaningful figure is the real estate tax as a percentage of the market value of the property. In my case I estimate that this "real" tax rate is approximately 2.15%, which is a fairly standard rate. The real tax rate is figured as

$$\text{real tax rate} = (\text{tax bill/assessed value}) \times (\text{actual assessment ratio}).$$

The actual assessment ratio is the assessed value divided by the appraised value of the property. The actual assessment ratio may differ from the assessor's official assessment ratio if the assessor's office uses an inaccurate appraisal of the property in question. In my case you can determine that I have estimated my actual assessment ratio to be 20.2% (i.e., 2.15/10.645).

Let us end this discussion of the mechanics of the real estate tax by examining an actual real estate tax bill. My wife owns a vacant lot in Lubbock, Texas that has an assessed value of $1470 (14.7 hundreds). Her tax bill for 1994 is as follows:

Taxing Unit	Tax Rate (mills per $100)	Taxes
Lubbock School District	14.75	$21.68
City of Lubbock	6.40	9.41
Water District	0.084	0.12
Lubbock County Hospital	1.0499	1.54
Lubbock County	1.7117	2.52

Yes, her real estate tax bill was $35.27. She estimates that the vacant lot is worth about $3500, so the real tax rate is 1.008%. That is a very low tax rate.

Economic Effects of the Real Estate Tax

Now we can consider the economic effects of the local real estate tax. The tax is levied on residential, commercial, and industrial property. The previous discussion showed that the economically meaningful way to specify the tax is as a percentage of market value. We first consider the tax on residential property. Residential property includes rental units as well as owner-occupied housing. The tax is levied on the owners of the property, but is the tax shifted forward to tenants? What is the real incidence of the tax? The answer to the question requires an economic model of the housing market. One sort of model of the urban housing (or residential land) market has been introduced in this book in Chapters 5, 6, and 9. This model emphasizes the location patterns of housing and population in an urban area, but a simpler model can be used that does the job. We shall use a model that can be formulated as supply and demand curves.

Consider the market for housing in a local jurisdiction. The demand for housing is a demand for the services of housing in a given time period. The price that is paid for these services is housing rent, an amount that a tenant pays to the landlord or that the homeowner implicitly pays to himself. Assume that the number of households in the local jurisdiction is fixed (an assumption that will be changed later). These households have a demand for housing services, and this demand curve is shown in Figure 10.4a. On the other hand, the supply of housing is best considered to be a function of the market value of houses. The supply of housing cannot be altered a great deal in the short run, but in the long run housing units can be added to or subtracted from the stock of housing. The addition or subtraction of units depends on the market value of those units. In this model we shall use the notion that the stock of housing consists of a large number of units of standardized quality. Both an increase in the quantity and in the quality of houses increases the supply of "housing" as defined here. It shall also be assumed that the quantity of housing services supplied by a given stock of housing is proportional to the size of the stock. The supply of housing as a function of the value of a standardized unit of housing is shown in Figure 10.4b. The demand and supply curves are on different diagrams, so how do we get them together?

The crux of the model is the relationship between housing rent and market value. The market value of a unit of housing is the present discounted value of the stream of rents that the unit will generate. If those rents are expected to be constant at R per year and the real estate tax as a percentage of market value is t, the market value V is

$$V = \Sigma_i \frac{R - tV}{(1 + r)^i},$$

where r is the rate of discount and i is the number of years into the future. In this discussion the rate of discount will be assumed to be fixed by the preferences of the public for future income versus current income. This is known as the *rate of time preference*. If the housing unit lasts forever (i goes to infinity), the equation for market value simplifies to

$$V = \frac{R - tV}{r},$$

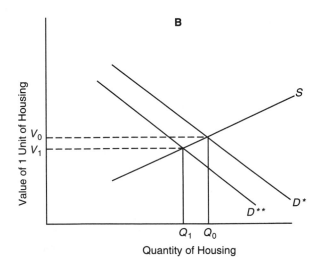

FIGURE 10.4 The real estate tax and the housing market

which becomes

$$V = \frac{R}{r+t}.$$

The term $r+t$ is known as the *capitalization rate* (or "cap" rate), the rate that converts gross (before tax) annual housing rent into market value.

Now return to the model in Figure 10.4. Given that the quantity housing services consumed (in the top half of the diagram) is proportional to the quantity of standardized housing units supplied, we can define a unit of housing services so that the two are numerically identical. The two diagrams can therefore be read vertically. We are now ready to perform two conversions. First convert the supply of housing units in the lower half of the diagram into a long-run supply of housing services in the upper half. This conversion is accomplished, at a given quantity, by multiplying V on supply curve S by $r+t$ to obtain the corresponding value of R. This supply curve is denoted S^*. The other conversion needed to translate demand in the upper half of the diagram into long-run demand in the lower half. This conversion is done, at a given quantity, by dividing R by $r+t$ to obtain the appropriate V. This long-run demand curve is labeled D^* in Figure 10.4b. Equilibrium quantity, housing rent, and value are denoted Q_0, R_0, and V_0. Recall that $V_0 = R_0/(r+t)$.

Now we are ready to play the game of increasing the real estate tax rate in the local jurisdiction. An increase in the real estate tax rate does not change the position of the demand curve for housing services in Figure 10.4a, nor does it shift the supply curve of standardized units of housing in the lower half of the diagram. Demand is still the same function of gross housing rent, and supply is still a function of market value. A change in the real estate tax rate *changes the capitalization rate $r+t$*. A higher value for t means that we must redo the conversions that were performed in the preceding paragraph. First consider the supply curve. At a given quantity we now multiply V on supply curve S by a larger capitalization rate $r+t'$ and obtain the supply curve in the upper half of the diagram denoted S^{**}. Similarly, the new demand curve for the lower half of the diagram is found by dividing R on demand curve D by the larger number $r+t'$. This shifts the demand curve down to D^{**}. Note that the new equilibrium values for quantity, housing rent, and value are Q_1, R_1, and V_1.

The effects of an increase in the property tax can now be seen clearly. The quantity of housing (measured as standardized housing units) has declined, housing rent has increased, and the value of a unit of housing has decreased. In other words, the rents paid by tenants (per unit of housing services) have gone up *and* property values for owners have gone down. Another important conclusion is that the size of the tax base is sensitive to the tax rate. An increase in the tax rate reduced both the quantity of the housing stock and the value of each unit. The tax base is VQ, and both terms in this product have declined along supply curve S. The general conclusion regarding tax incidence is that the real estate tax is paid by both tenants and owners. This is a general result, but some special cases are of interest.

First, consider the possibility that the supply of housing is highly elastic. This would be the case if property owners can move their capital (in the long run, of course) to avoid suffering a capital loss that would mean making a rate of return on capital that is below the rate that is available in other locations. Examine Figure 10.5,

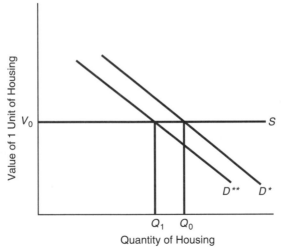

FIGURE 10.5 The real estate tax and the housing market

which depicts the housing market as in Figure 10.4. The supply curve in the lower half of the diagram is horizontal because if a unit of housing is not worth V_0 in this urban area, it will be moved to some other location where it is worth V_0. This movement can occur over time as the quality of units declines in the urban area depicted in the diagram and new units are built elsewhere. Supply curve S is translated to the upper half of the diagram by multiplying V_0 by $r + t$, so this supply curve is also horizontal. The demand curves in Figure 10.5 are the same as in Figure 10.4.

Now increase the real estate tax rate from t to t'. The supply curve in the upper half of Figure 10.5 shifts upward, and the demand curve in the lower half shifts downward as before. The market value of housing units remains at V_0, but the housing rent rises from $R_0 = (r + t)V_0$ to $R_1 = (r + t')V_0$. The quantity of housing units (and services) declines from Q_0 to Q_1. In this case only the consumers of housing services pay the real estate tax increase. The property owners escape the increase in the tax by being able to move capital around freely. Many people think that tenants pay the entire real estate tax. Figure 10.5 shows the conditions under which this claim is true. The tenants pay the tax if they are immobile and the capital is mobile.

An alternative case is created if we assume that households are mobile to some extent but that capital is not mobile. In the extreme case households are perfectly mobile and housing rent cannot rise in response to an increase in the real estate tax. Housing rent is pegged at R_0, but the value of a unit of housing will fall from $V_0 = R_0/(r + t)$ to $V_1 = R_0/(r + t')$. The immobile capital pays the tax and loses value as a result, but the mobile housing consumers escape the tax increase. As an exercise, draw a set of diagrams to depict this case. In drawing your diagrams, assume that the demand curve for housing services in the urban area is horizontal but that the supply curve has a positive slope as in Figure 10.4.

So far we have considered an isolated increase in the real estate tax. The tax was increased in one local jurisdiction, while all other locations held their tax rates constant. Furthermore, the tax rate was increased without any increase in spending on local public goods. The conclusions of the model are valid if these assumptions are correct. Suppose instead that the real estate tax is a tax on all capital (and land) in the economy and that the tax is increased everywhere. Mieszkowski (1972) posed this version of the model and reached the conclusion that if the total supply of capital is fixed, the owners of capital will bear the entire burden of the increase in the tax in the form of a reduction in its market value. The reason is that there is no place for capital to hide to escape the increase in the tax. The imposition of this increase in the tax on all capital will have no impact on the allocation of resources.

The expenditure side of the local public sector should also be considered. In a Tiebout world with only residential property, an increase in the real estate tax in a local jurisdiction presumably is matched by an increase in local public goods of equal value, so the simultaneous and equal increases in the tax and public goods will have no effect on housing rents, values, or quantity of housing units. However, consider the more realistic case in which the real estate tax is increased on residential, commercial, and industrial property to provide residents with more of the local public good. These changes mean that residential property gains benefits of the local public good that exceed the increase in taxes but that commercial and industrial property simply are taxed more heavily. The effects on the commercial and industrial sectors can be depicted in Figure 10.4. If Figure 10.4 applies, the increase in the tax rate is at least partly capitalized into lower market values for commercial and industrial property. The tenants who occupy those properties also bear a portion of the increase in the tax.

The story is different on the residential side. Residential property receives a benefit that exceeds the increase in the tax, so residential property values increase. To see this implication, suppose that the market value of a unit of housing is now

$$V = \frac{R - tV + bV}{r}$$

where bV represents the value of the local public goods provided to the housing unit in question. These benefits are expressed as a constant times the value of the housing unit, so

$$V = \frac{R}{r + t - b}.$$

The assumption is that both t and b increase but that the increase in b is greater than the increase in t. This means that $r + t - b$ *declines*. A decline in $r + t - b$ is the same thing as cutting the tax rate in Figure 10.4, so the implications can be found by running the model in reverse; use the shift in supply in the upper half of the diagram from S^{**} to S^* and the shift in demand in the lower half of the diagram from D^{**} to D^*. Market value per unit increases, housing rent per unit declines, and the quantity of units increases. In effect, the ability to impose a tax on commercial and industrial property is of benefit to both housing consumers and the owners of housing units.

An extensive literature, beginning with Oates (1969), has established that higher real estate tax rates, holding public expenditures constant, reduce housing values. Similarly, an increase in public expenditures (especially on schools), holding the tax rate constant, will increase the value of a house. The effect of real estate taxes on commercial and industrial property has been the subject of very few empirical studies. One study by Wheaton (1984) found that differences across local jurisdictions in property taxes paid per square foot had no effect on gross rents in office buildings in metropolitan Boston. This finding means that none of the burden of the tax was being shifted forward from real estate capital and land onto tenants. Another study of office buildings in downtown Chicago [McDonald (1993)] found that 45% of the real estate tax was being shifted forward to tenants in the form of higher gross rents and that 55% of the tax was being absorbed by the owners of the real estate. More empirical studies of the commercial and industrial sectors are needed.

This discussion of the real estate tax has been rather lengthy, but we can now return to the questions raised at the beginning of this section. Who pays the real estate tax? If we ignore the expenditure side, Mieszkowski (1972) suggested that if the real estate tax is a uniform tax on all capital and land and if both are in fixed supply, the owners of capital and land pay the tax. Clearly, the real estate tax is not uniform. The model depicted in Figure 10.4 shows that an increase in the real estate tax on housing in one jurisdiction is paid by both owners and housing consumers. Similarly, a decrease in the tax rate in one jurisdiction is of benefit to both. If the national average real estate tax rate is taken as the starting point for these changes, housing consumers pay a portion of the local real estate tax that is above the national average and reap a benefit if the local real estate tax is below the national average. The analysis of the real estate tax on commercial and industrial property reaches the same conclusions. If the expenditure side of the local public sector is added to the model, it is possible that relatively high real estate taxes on housing are matched by better local public services. In this Tiebout-type case the higher real estate tax is just a payment for better public services. However, this argument cannot be made in the case of commercial and industrial property. A higher real estate tax on these types of property is truly a tax, and the model in Figure 10.4 applies.

What is the impact of the real estate tax on location patterns within an urban area? One can presume that both residents and capital are, in the long run, mobile within an urban area. It is perilous for a local jurisdiction to raise its real estate tax rate to a level appreciably above the average for the urban area. Highly elastic demand and supply curves in Figure 10.4 mean that an increase in the tax rate leads to large changes in the quantity of housing located in the local jurisdiction. Indeed, you can show with the model in Figure 10.4 that sufficiently large demand and supply elasticities will mean that an increase in the tax rate will cause the local jurisdiction to cease to exist. Local officials and local voters must be cognizant of the fact that a high real estate tax rate, which is not offset by a high level of local public goods, will alter location patterns within the urban area to their detriment. The study by Ladd (1975) showed that they *are* aware of this fact and try to behave accordingly.

F. INTERGOVERNMENTAL GRANTS

The other chief source of revenue for local governments is grants from higher levels of government. State governments provide funds primarily for education, but they also fund a variety of other activities, such as community development and highways and other transportation facilities. The federal government provides funds primarily for housing, transportation, community development, job training, and education. The provision of federal funds for income redistribution—direct support of the poor and the elderly—is not considered here.

Some of these funds are awarded to local governments automatically through complex distribution formulas. Other programs require that the local government prepare an application that documents eligibility and need. The larger units of local government employ sizable staffs of people to keep track of the distribution formulas and prepare these applications. Larger local governments also employ lobbyists in the state capital and in Washington, DC to try to influence the rules and regulations of the funding programs. Why do the state and federal governments provide funds to local governments? What are the economic arguments for this kind of federalism? The matter of income redistribution policy has already been discussed, so the question here pertains to resource allocation policies.

The largest intergovernmental grants are provided by states for elementary and secondary education, so let us begin there. Education is the responsibility of the state government, and it has delegated this responsibility to local school districts. Clearly, not all local school districts have the same ability to provide an education for their children, but clearly the society is also committed to some degree of equality of educational opportunity. State school aid tries to make up for the differences of school districts in their tax bases (per pupil). It does not succeed. School districts within the same state can have enormous differences in spending per pupil because spending is still based to a considerable degree on the local tax base. The crafting of a school-aid formula that tends to equalize educational opportunity is a tricky business.

Grant formulas can be categorized in two ways: categorical or noncategorical grants, and lump-sum or matching grants. Categorical grants are for specific purposes such as education, while noncategorical grants can be used for a variety of purposes. These grants can be awarded as a lump sum, or they may require that the local jurisdiction put up matching funds. In other words, they can be awarded on the basis of need or on the basis of local effort to raise revenue. Indeed, some grant programs use both criteria at the same time. For example, a state's school-aid formula can provide a certain amount of funds per pupil as a function of the tax base per pupil, where districts with lower tax bases per pupil receive more funds. This formula can also contain a part that rewards the local district for imposing a higher real estate tax rate as well. This is done because a lump-sum grant provides little incentive for the local school district to use its own resources, limited as they are. Indeed, a lump-sum grant

may induce the school district to give all property owners a tax cut with no net increase in spending on schools. Empirical studies reviewed by Inman (1979) show
that this is not what happens, but the studies also show that a matching provision
tends to stimulate total spending on the service in question more than does a lump-
sum grant. These propositions regarding lump-sum and matching grants can be
demonstrated theoretically.

To begin the theoretical demonstration, suppose that the preferences of the people in a local jurisdiction for the local public good and private goods can be depicted
as the indifference curves in Figure 10.6. Given the income levels of the households
in the jurisdiction, the community has a budget constraint of *AB*. With no intergovernmental grants, the local jurisdiction chooses a combination of private goods and
the local public good designated by point *E*. Local taxes are imposed to raise the
money for the local public good.

Now consider the effects of alternative intergovernmental grant programs. The
simplest type of grant is the lump-sum grant. The local jurisdiction is simply given
amount *G* shown in Figure 10.6. This grant can either be categorical or noncategorical. In other words, the rules may state that amount *G* must be spent on the local public good in question (categorical), or amount *G* can be spent on anything (noncategorical). Suppose first that the grant *G* is noncategorical. In this case the
community's budget constraint shifts up to *A′B′*, and point *E′* is chosen. Note that the
community, with the increase in income of *G*, has decided to increase its consumption of both the local public good and private goods. Some fraction of the grant
amount *G* is spent on increasing the consumption of the local public good and the remainder is used to cut local taxes. Indeed, the local jurisdiction could have decided to
use all of the grant for tax cuts, or it could have decided to *increase* spending on the
local public good by the entire amount of the grant and give no tax cut. We would expect that the actual outcome would fall between these two extremes.

FIGURE 10.6 Effects of a lump-sum grant

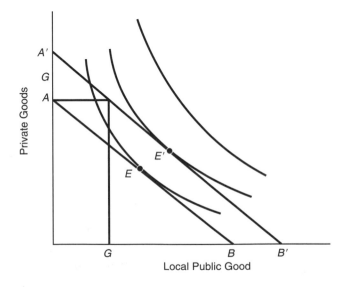

Now suppose that the lump-sum grant is categorical. The rules state that the grant money received must be spent on the local public good in question and records must be kept to document this use. However, the federal or state government cannot require that the local jurisdiction must *increase* its spending on the local public good in question by the amount of the grant. The only effective requirement is that at least amount G must be spent on the local public good. In Figure 10.6 the local jurisdiction would have spent that much on the local public good even in the absence of the grant program. Therefore, the categorical lump-sum grant has the same effect as the noncategorical lump-sum grant.

The only case in which the effects of the two types of lump-sum grants differ occurs when the local jurisdiction, left completely to its own devices, would have spent less than amount G on the local public good *with the grant program in place*. Now the categorical grant rules force the local jurisdiction to increase this spending up to G. This case is shown in Figure 10.7, where the local jurisdiction starts with a low level of spending on the local public good (less than amount G) and prefers to take the entire grant as a tax cut. The rules of the grant program prohibit this move, spending on the local public good increases to G, and the local jurisdiction reaches a lower level of utility than it reaches if the grant were noncategorical.

Public finance economists argue that except for the case shown in Figure 10.7, a categorical or noncategorical lump-sum grant is economically identical to an increase in income for the members of the local jurisdiction. In Figure 10.6 the grant shifts the budget constraint up, but an identical upward shift can be induced by an increase in the income of the households in the local jurisdiction. If this hypothesis is correct, the grant money would be spent just as if it were an increase in disposable income for the households. However, several studies show that an increase in household income of \$1 will increase spending on local public goods by \$0.05 to \$0.10, but a \$1 increase in lump-sum grants will increase local public goods spending by \$0.25 to \$0.50. This result is known as the "flypaper effect" because grant money

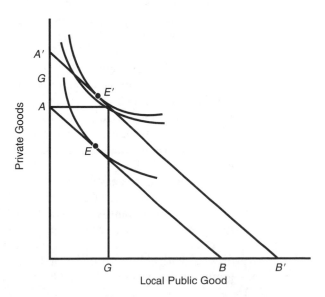

FIGURE 10.7 Effects of a categorical grant

tends to stick where it hits—in the public sector. Somehow the households in the local jurisdiction do not view lump-sum grants as equivalent to ordinary income. What is going on here?

One possibility is that the studies are flawed. For example, the analysis in Figure 10.7 shows that a categorical lump-sum grant will increase spending on the local public good but a general increase in income will not. Some lump-sum categorical grants may be provided for things that the local jurisdiction simply will not purchase with its own money. In the absence of the grant program, local demand is zero. This sort of argument may explain some of the flypaper effect, but there are several studies that seem to be without methodological flaws.

Suppose that the flypaper effect is real. What can explain it? The leading argument is that the nature of the political process leads to incorrect perceptions by local voters. There is reason to believe that local public officials are interested in having a larger budget. Local officials like to give tax cuts too, but they have some tendency to prefer to keep a good part of a lump-sum grant in the public sector. If local officials can control the public agenda, decisions on taxes can be kept separate from decisions on the use of grant moneys. The basic idea is that local officials have some monopoly power that stems from a lack of complete information on the part of the local voters.

Next we turn to grants that require matching funds from the local jurisdiction. Most categorical grants require matching funds from the local jurisdiction. Many state and federal categorical grant programs specify a local matching rate m, which specifies the amount of money the local jurisdiction must spend for every dollar received from the grant program. For example, if $m = 1$, the local jurisdiction must put up \$1 for every dollar received. The local jurisdiction pays one-half of the cost of the local public good. In general, the share of the cost of the local public good paid by the local jurisdiction is $m/(1 + m)$. From the point of view of the local jurisdiction, the price of an additional dollar spent on the local public good is $m/(1 + m)$. If $m = 0.5$, the local jurisdiction sees that an increase in spending on the local public good of \$1 costs only \$0.33 because the grant program matches every local dollar with two dollars.

The matching grant program can be depicted graphically. In Figure 10.8 the grant program provides a one-for-one match of local funds, so the price of the local public good facing the local jurisdiction has been reduced from \$1 to \$0.50. The community's budget constraint has shifted from AB to AB', and the local jurisdiction chooses point E'. In the diagram the matching grant program has caused increases in consumption of both the local public good and private goods. However, because the consumption of private goods has increased, the case depicted in Figure 10.8 includes a local tax cut in response to the matching grant program. Even a matching grant cannot force the local jurisdiction to spend the entire grant on an increase in the local public good.

However, it is easy to show that the matching grant increases spending on the local public good more than does an equivalent lump-sum grant. The dollar amount of the matching grant is distance CE'. [How do we know this? Distance DE' is the total amount spent on the local public good. Amount DF is paid by the local jurisdiction, and the grant is the (equal) amount FE'. We know that $FE' = CE'$ because the original budget line AB makes a 45° angle with the axes.] Suppose that a lump-sum grant equal to amount CE' had been given instead. This grant enables the local juris-

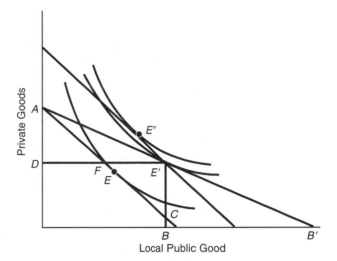

FIGURE 10.8 Effects of a matching grant

diction to reach point E' if it so chooses. But remember that a lump-sum grant does not change the "price" at which the local public good can be purchased. The slope of the community's budget constraint with the lump-sum grant is -1, and the budget constraint passes through point E'. This means that the local jurisdiction can actually reach a higher indifference curve by choosing point E'' rather than point E'. Point E'' means less spending on the local public good with the equivalent lump-sum grant, compared to point E' with the matching grant. The lump-sum grant has a positive *income effect* on the local public good, but the matching grant has both an income effect and a *substitution effect* because the "price" of the local public good has been reduced by the rules of the program. Those of you who have had a course in microeconomic theory at the intermediate level will recall that the substitution effect always acts to increase consumption of the good that experiences the decline in relative price.

What types of grant programs are used by states to fund local public schools? The first grant programs were lump-sum categorical grants of a certain uniform dollar amount per pupil. The idea was to ensure a minimum level of education across the state, so this kind of grant is called *foundation aid*. The effects of this kind of grant program are shown in Figures 10.6 and 10.7. Now most states use some version of a foundation aid grant formula that is based on the amount of taxable real state per pupil. A general formula for this kind of grant program is

$$G = \frac{B - r(V - V^*)}{B} \quad \begin{array}{l} \text{for } V > V^* \\ \text{for } V \leq V^*, \end{array}$$

where G is the grant per pupil, B the basic per-pupil grant, V the property tax base per pupil in the school district, V^* a threshold property tax base per pupil, and r a rate set by law. In this program, if the tax base per pupil in the school district is less than or equal to V^*, the grant per pupil is B. If the tax base per pupil is greater than V^*, the grant per pupil is reduced by $r(V - V^*)$. Note that this kind of grant program is still a lump-sum grant because the grant does not depend on the tax rate that is imposed by the local jurisdiction. There is no matching provision in the formula. Wealthier school districts receive smaller per-pupil grants from the state, but there is no assurance that this kind of grant program will equalize spending per pupil.

Despite the careful crafting of state school-aid formulas, the wide disparities in school expenditures per pupil remain. Some argue that these disparities violate the provisions in state constitutions for equal protection under the law and that education is the responsibility of the state. Lawsuits have been filed in most states; some of those cases have been won, some have been lost, and some are still pending. The plaintiffs (those who brought the lawsuits) who challenged the system for funding public schools won their most significant victory in California in 1974. In that case, *Serrano* v. *Priest*, the plaintiff claimed that unequal funding for schools based on the local property tax violated the equal-protection clause in the California Constitution. The courts agreed and ordered that the state devise a system that keeps spending per pupil equal across districts (or within $100 per pupil). The equalization of spending across districts in California required a dramatic increase in the amount of state spending on schools, a topic that is discussed below. Cases in other states have led to changes in the system, but they have not equalized spending per pupil. Equality of spending per pupil may be a desirable goal for society to pursue, but the U.S. Constitution, state constitutions, and current laws do not require it. In fact, the U.S. Supreme Court ruled in the case of *San Antonio Independent School District* v. *Rodriguez* that the equal-protection clause in the U.S. Constitution does not apply to education because education is not mentioned in the Constitution. This means that plaintiffs cannot win suits based on unequal spending on education across states. Sizable differences in spending per pupil will continue to exist within the same urban area (except in California), and these differences will continue to have impacts on the location choices of households and on the market value of housing.

State and federal funding programs for other local public expenditures, such as transportation, community development, and job training, can be justified on the grounds that each of these has substantial spillover effects outside the local jurisdiction. Programs that have sizable spillover benefits will be underfunded by local jurisdictions, so higher levels of government should subsidize these programs to some degree to induce local governments to do more. As discussed in Chapter 8, most major urban transportation projects are funded jointly by local, state, and federal revenues (matching grants) and are also usually subjected to reasonably comprehensive cost-benefit and environmental impact studies. Other programs, such as community development and job training, are not analyzed as rigorously.

G. THE SPECIAL CASE OF CALIFORNIA

California is the first state to equalize spending per pupil in its public school districts. What is the nature of the system of local public finance that made this happen?

The 1974 court case *Serrano* v. *Priest* was noted in the preceding section. This is the case that ordered California to devise a system of financing local public schools so as to equalize spending per pupil. In response the state of California established a limit on spending by local school districts. The state also limited the rate at which spending could be increased but allowed the districts with low spending per pupil to increase spending at a more rapid rate than districts with high spending. Spending differences narrowed over time during the 1970s.

The full equalization of spending per pupil across school districts was accomplished in the wake of the taxpayer revolt in California. In 1978 the voters of California enacted Proposition 13, a law that imposes strict limits on local real estate taxes. The law rolled back existing real estate taxes by over 50%, placed a 2% limit on annual reassessments (except at time of sale), and required that any other tax increase must be approved by a two-thirds vote. School districts are allowed a real estate tax of 1% of market value. Note that the real estate tax bill can increase only very slowly if the property is not sold to another owner but that the assessment will "catch up" to the appreciation in market value when ownership changes. This feature is known as the "welcome stranger" tax increase.

How did Proposition 13 affect school spending? After the passage of Proposition 13, the state made an offer that school districts could not refuse. The state said that if the school district has the maximum permissible real estate tax (i.e., 1%), the state would pay the difference between the local revenue and the maximum amount of spending per pupil permitted by the state. All of the school districts accepted the offer, and it meant that all districts moved up to the state limit on spending per pupil. The state is now in complete control of the public school spending in California.

The passage of Proposition 13 left local governments, including school districts, with very limited ability to raise taxes to finance infrastructure projects. Infrastructure needs to accommodate population growth can require more funds than are available through local taxes and intergovernmental grants. School districts need to build schools, and municipalities need to build public roads, fire stations, police stations, parks, jails, sewer mains, and so on. This problem was addressed in 1982 by passage of the Mello–Roos Community Facility Act, which permits local governments to set up special community facility districts. These special districts can issue tax-exempt bonds that are supported by special taxes levied on *new* properties in the special district. The new facilities are needed to accommodate the growth of population, so only the new properties must pay to support the bonds. Many local municipalities, counties, and school districts have used this method of financing public facilities. As one would expect, the special tax on new houses has a strongly negative effect on their market prices. One study by Quang Do and Sirmans (1994) found that an annual Mello–Roos payment of $705 per year for 25 years reduced the value of a house by $13,500 compared to neighboring properties in the same jurisdiction that were not subject to this tax.

Proposition 13 and the *Serrano* v. *Priest* decision have had a major impact on the financing of local public goods and services. Table 10.4 has been prepared to highlight the change. This table compares the sources of general revenue for all local governments in the United States and in California for 1966–1967 and 1986–1987. The earlier year is prior to passage of Proposition 13 and also prior to the *Serrano* v. *Priest* decision. The later year is eight years after the passage of Proposition 13. Table 10.4 shows that local governments in California in 1966–1967 obtained revenues in a manner that is very similar to the average for local governments nationwide. Local sources accounted for about 65% of general revenue, and the real estate tax was over four-tenths of local revenue. The state's share of local revenues was about one-third.

TABLE 10.4 Sources of General Revenue by Local Governments, United States and California (Percent)

	1966–1967		1986–1987	
	All Local Gov't.	*California Local Gov't.*	*All Local Gov't.*	*California Local Gov't.*
Local sources	65.3	65.1	62.0	52.8
Real estate tax	43.2	45.1	28.3	19.4
Other taxes	6.7	5.8	10.1	9.1
Charges and misc.	15.4	14.3	23.6	24.3
Intergovernmental	34.7	34.9	38.0	47.2
State	31.7	32.9	33.3	43.9
Federal	3.0	2.0	4.7	3.3

Source: Census of Governments (1967, 1987), U.S. Department of Commerce.

Now look at the figures for 1986–1987. As we saw in Section B, local governments around the nation shifted away from the real estate tax toward other taxes and charges and miscellaneous local revenue sources. The share of revenue raised through the local real estate tax dropped from 43.2% in 1966–1967 to 28.3% in 1986–1987. But look at California! The share of local revenues obtained through the local real estate tax dropped from 45.1% to 19.4% over this same period. Local governments in California increased their reliance on other taxes and charges and miscellaneous revenue sources as well, but the share of revenue that came from the state jumped from 32.9% to 43.9%. Almost half of local revenues (47.2%) for California local governments in 1986–1987 came from intergovernmental sources. This increase in intergovernmental funds can be attributed largely to the system for funding the California public schools that is described above.

H. SUMMARY

This chapter has covered a great deal of material on the local public sector. The major points that were made are as follows.

1. The chief function of local government is to allocate resources to local public goods and services. Income redistribution and economic stabilization and growth are secondary functions.

2. The most important local public service is elementary and secondary education, but local governments provide many other goods and services.

3. There are two economic–political models of how public resource allocation decisions are made at the local level. One is the Tiebout model, which emphasizes the role of household mobility in enabling local jurisdictions to be set up that provide local public goods to match the preferences of households who choose to live there. The other theory, the median voter model, is a theory of voting that is based on the presumption that a local jurisdiction will contain households with different views regarding resource allocation decisions. The Tiebout model is a useful tool for under-

standing how local jurisdictions function in the suburbs. The median voter model is the realistic approach for studying the large central city's government.

4. The real estate tax is the most important local tax. Variations in this tax rate (as a percentage of the market value of property) within an urban area can have sizable effects on location patterns. A local jurisdiction with a real estate tax rate that is close to the average for the urban area will not suffer adverse consequences. A substantial increase in the tax rate relative to the average can cause housing rents to rise, housing values to fall, and capital to migrate to other locations. Similarly, a cut in the real estate tax rate relative to the average can have the opposite effects. Real estate tax incentives are used widely to stimulate local economic development. A discussion of real estate tax incentives for local economic development is included in Chapter 14.

5. The other major source of revenue for local governments is intergovernmental transfers. The largest grant program is the support for local schools provided by the states. State school-aid formulas are designed to offset part of the disparities in the tax bases of school districts. Sizable disparities in expenditures per pupil still exist, except in California. California has implemented a program that equalizes spending per pupil across school districts. The program has resulted in a major increase in the funding of local schools by the state.

EXERCISES

1. Look up your county in the Census of Governments for 1992. (If the 1992 issue is not available, use the 1987 issue.) Construct a table similar to Table 9.1 for that year. Now look up the same county in an earlier Census of Governments, such as 1967 or 1972. What changes have occurred in the size, the composition, and the financing of local government in this county?

2. A local jurisdiction is (à la Tiebout) populated with 125 households who have identical demands for a local public good G that can be expressed as

$$G = 100 - 0.5p,$$

where p is the price per unit of the public good. Each unit of the public good costs $5000, and each household pays pG in taxes.

   (a) What is the price for a household per unit of the public good?

   (b) What is the optimal amount of the public good for this jurisdiction?

   (c) How much will each household pay in taxes?

3. Return to Exercise 2 and assume that the jurisdiction now includes the same 125 households *and* 175 households whose demand for the public good is

$$G = 50 - 0.5p.$$

Suppose that the decision regarding the amount of public good to be supplied is determined by the median voter model.

   (a) How much of the public good will be supplied and at what price per unit?

   (b) How much will each household pay in taxes?

4. Suppose that the demand for housing in an urban area can be expressed as

$$R = 10,000 - Q,$$

where R is annual rent and Q is quantity of housing units. The supply of housing is a function of the market value, V, of a unit, or

$$V = 50,000 + 2.5Q.$$

Assume that the real rate of discount is 6% and that the annual property tax is 2% of the value of a unit.

(a) What are the market equilibrium quantity, annual rent, and market value?

(b) Assume that the annual property tax is increased to 4% of market value. What happens to quantity, annual rent, and market value? How much of the increase in the tax is borne by the consumers of housing (tenants), and how much is borne by the owners of the housing?

(c) Perform the graphical analysis mentioned in the text, in which the supply of housing is fixed and the households are perfectly mobile across urban areas. What is the effect of reducing the property tax rate? Show using your diagrams.

5. There are two types of matching grants. The one presented in the text is actually an *open-ended* grant because there is no limit to the amount of money that will be provided by the grant program as long as the local government allocates the required matching funds. The other type of matching grant is called *closed-ended* because there is a limit to the amount of the grant. For example, suppose that the matching grant program has a matching rate of $1 for $1 but that the maximum amount of the grant is $1 million.

(a) Along the lines of Figure 10.8, draw the budget constraint for the local community under this closed-ended grant program.

(b) Compare the effects of these two types of matching grants on the amount spent for the local public good. Assume that both programs have a matching rate of $1 to $1 but that the closed-ended grant program has a maximum grant of $1 million.

6. As this chapter is being written the U.S. Congress is considering a basic change in the welfare system, Aid to Families with Dependent Children. The proposed change is from a matching federal grant (1:1 with state funds) to a block grant (a lump-sum categorical grant). What do you expect the impact of this change might be on the benefit levels provided to welfare recipients? See Chapter 16 for a further discussion of the welfare system.

REFERENCES

Bernhard, A. and B. Stott, 1977. "Milwaukee Revenue Cost Analysis," *Urban Land*, Vol. 36, No. 11, pp. 16–18.

Do, A. Quang and C. Sirmans, 1994. "Residential Property Tax Capitalization: Evidence from California," *National Tax Journal*, Vol. 47, pp. 341–348.

Enelow, James and M. Hinich, 1984. *The Spatial Theory of Voting.* New York: Cambridge University Press.

Hamilton, Bruce, 1975. "Zoning and Property Taxation in a System of Local Governments," *Urban Studies*, Vol. 12, pp. 205–211.

Inman, Robert, 1978. "Testing Political Economy's 'As If' Proposition: Is the Median Voter Really Decisive?" *Public Choice*, Vol. 33, pp. 45–65.

———, 1979. "Fiscal Performance of Local Governments: An Interpretive Review," in P. Mieszkowski and M. Straszheim, eds., *Current Issues in Urban Economics.* Baltimore: Johns Hopkins University Press.

Ladd, Helen, 1975. "Local Education Expenditures, Fiscal Capacity, and the Composition of the Property Tax Base," *National Tax Journal*, Vol. 28, pp. 145–158.

Luce, Thomas and A. Summers, 1987. *Local Fiscal Issues in the Philadelphia Metropolitan Area.* Philadelphia: University of Pennsylvania Press.

McDonald, John, 1993. "Incidence of the Property Tax on Commercial Real Estate: The Case of Downtown Chicago," *National Tax Journal*, Vol. 46, pp. 109–120.

McDonald, John, C. Orlebeke, A. Sen, and W. Wiewel, 1991. "Real Estate Development and Property Taxes in DuPage County," Center for Urban Economic Development, University of Illinois at Chicago.

Mieszkowski, Peter, 1972. "The Property Tax: An Excise Tax or a Profits Tax?" *Journal of Public Economics*, Vol. 1, pp. 73–92.

Musgrave, Richard, 1959. *The Theory of Public Finance.* New York: McGraw-Hill.

Oates, Wallace, 1969. "The Effects of Property Taxes and Local Public Spending on Property Values: An Empirical Study of Tax Capitalization and the Tiebout Hypothesis," *Journal of Political Economy*, Vol. 77, pp. 957–970.

Samuelson, Paul, 1954. "The Pure Theory of Public Expenditures," *Review of Economics and Statistics*, Vol. 36, pp. 387–389.

———, 1955. "Diagrammatic Exposition of the Pure Theory of Public Expenditures," *Review of Economics and Statistics*, Vol. 37, pp. 350–356.

Tiebout, Charles, 1956. "A Pure Theory of Local Expenditures," *Journal of Political Economy*, Vol. 64, pp. 416–424.

Wheaton, William, 1984. "The Incidence of Inter-jurisdictional Differences in Commercial Property Taxes," *National Tax Journal*, Vol. 37, pp. 515–527.

C H A P T E R

11

Models of Metropolitan Economic Growth

A. INTRODUCTION

Economic growth is a topic that is central to the entire discipline of economics. Adam Smith thought about it deeply in the book that many will argue founded economics in 1776, *An Inquiry into the Nature and Causes of the Wealth of Nations*. In the first years of the nineteenth century, Parson Malthus worried what would happen when the growth of population outstripped the growth of food and other necessities of life. Modern thinking about economic growth at the national level started just after World War II when the field of economic development was founded. This field in economics concentrates on the problems of economic growth in less-developed countries, such as India, China, and Mexico. More recently, urban planners and public officials in the United States have decided to use the term *economic development* to refer to the study of the problems of growth of state and local economies in the United States. You should be aware that different people will use the term *economic development* in these two senses. An economist with gray hair will probably be referring to places such as India, while a younger person with a background in state and local policy studies will probably mean places such as Cleveland.

The hope that less-developed countries might be placed on a growth path that would increase significantly their standards of living stimulated economic theorists in the 1950s to devise models that can explain national economic growth. The most famous contributor to the theory of economic growth is Robert Solow, who received the Nobel Prize in 1987 for his analysis of economic growth. It is fair to say that nearly all of the subsequent research on economic growth either augments Solow's model or is an attempt to criticize and replace Solow's basic framework. Solow used a fundamental idea from microeconomics: the production function, a function that relates inputs to potential outputs at the level of the firm (or industry). But Solow was frying bigger fish; he asserted that there exists a production function for an entire national economy that relates real gross domestic product (GDP) to capital and labor inputs and an autonomous growth factor that might be called "technological change." This production function can be written

$$Y = AF(K,L).$$

Here Y is real GDP for a year, K an index of the capital input, L the labor input, A the autonomous growth factor, and F a function of K and L. The appendix to this book includes an introductory discussion of functions of this type, and you should review the material in this appendix as needed as you read this chapter.

At this point you should recall that GDP is *value added* by the primary inputs capital and labor. One way to measure GDP is to measure "final" output: consumption, investment, government purchases of goods and services, and net exports. The other way to measure GDP is to compute the value added by firms at each step of the production process. Auto companies purchase steel from steel companies, glass from glass manufacturers, mufflers from muffler firms, and so on, and then add value to these intermediate inputs by assembling them into automobiles. The auto companies hire labor and use their own plants and equipment to add the value.

What did Solow say about this basic production function? He stated that the growth in GDP stems from the growth in the capital input, the growth of the labor input, and the growth of the autonomous factor. In other words, growth in GDP has two basic causes: growth in the basic inputs and growth in output relative to the growth in the basic inputs. He also pointed out that growth in GDP per worker is generated by growth in capital per worker in the economy and by growth in the autonomous factor. Since Solow wrote in 1950s much of the debate has centered on just what is included in the autonomous factor. This question is discussed at length in this and the next three chapters in the context of urban areas.

Public officials, urban and regional planners, economists, and the public in general are concerned about the rate of economic growth in their state and local economies. State and local governments have been trying to increase the rate of economic growth through a wide variety of policies. Does your local government have an office of economic development or similar department? What are your local officials doing to stimulate the local economy? Chances are that they are doing something. Despite the widespread use of economic growth policies at the state and local level, research on the determinants of state and local economic growth has lagged far behind policy formulation and implementation. State and local officials are using policies that have unknown effects. For example, some 37 states have an enterprise zone program, a program that designates certain areas for some state and local tax breaks and subsidies. What are the effects of these enterprise zone programs in various types of locations? At this point we simply are not sure. The purpose of this part of the book is to help you to understand the various models of economic growth that can be used to examine an urban area, to learn what is known empirically about the determinants of local economic growth, and to gain a perspective on local economic development policy. We shall begin with what was once a popular model for the local economy, economic base analysis, and then turn to models of the Solow type. In later sections of the chapter we add more local economic growth models to the mix.

B. ECONOMIC BASE ANALYSIS

The first economic model used to study the local economy, *economic base analysis*, was invented in the late 1930s. Given when it was invented, it is not surprising that economic base analysis is similar to Keynesian multiplier models. This would be a good time to review the basics of the *Keynesian multiplier*. We suppose that there is a national economy (with no government, for simplicity) that is suffering from unemployment. The GDP of the nation is written using the final output approach as

$$Y = C + I,$$

where C is consumption spending and I is investment spending. This is really just an accounting identity which says that all final output is either consumption or investment. The GDP of the nation is also the income earned by the primary inputs, capital and labor. Consequently, there is the behavioral relationship for consumption spending, written as a linear function,

$$C = a + bY.$$

Here the propensity to consume is b, the fraction of additional income that is spent on consumption. The consumption function implies that there is also a function for saving, or nonconsumption. By another accounting identity, $C + S = Y$, where S is saving. This identity and the consumption function imply that

$$S = Y - C,$$

or that

$$S = (1 - b)Y - a.$$

The propensity to save is $1 - b$, or 1 minus the proportion of additional income that is spent on consumption.

A critical insight supplied by Keynes is that income that is not spent on consumption is spent on investment goods. The critical purpose of the financial sector is to channel savings by households to those firms and households who make investments. Investment spending is regarded in the simple multiplier model as being *exogenous*, determined outside the model. Because $I = S$,

$$I = (1 - b)Y - a,$$

or

$$Y = \frac{a + I}{1 - b}.$$

An increase in I of $1 will increase Y by $1/(1 - b)$; this is the Keynesian multiplier. It says that an increase in investment spending will increase Y by the inverse of the propensity to save, which is $1 - b$. If the propensity of consume is $\frac{3}{4}$, the propensity to save is $\frac{1}{4}$, and the multiplier is 4.

Before we go on to the economic base model, note that this simple Keynesian model has no foreign trade sector. Also, note that the exogenous category of spending is investment. You should also recall from your study of macroeconomics that the multiplier works to increase real output (GDP) only when the economy is operating as less than full employment. If the economy is at full employment, an increase in investment spending cannot increase GDP in real terms.

The economic base model for urban areas focuses attention on trade with the rest of the economy. One good way to focus on exports and imports is to add them to the basic Keynesian model. For this purpose, assume that exports are exogenous (as investment is exogenous) and that imports are a function of income (as consumption is a function of income). The import function can be specified as

$$M = c + dY,$$

where d is the propensity to spend an increase in income on imports. We now have two "leakages" of spending in the local economy, saving and imports. In this model gross "urban" product is

$$Y = C + I + X - M,$$

where X is exports. Assume that the spending on imports is for consumption activity. Consequently, total output of the local economy includes exports, but we must net out imports from C, consumption spending. As defined here, C includes some imports.

Instead of $S = I$ as in the simpler model without trade, the relevant condition is that $S + M = I + X$, or that "leakages" equal exogenous spending. In this model imports do not have to equal exports. Why not? Because, if you decide to import more than you export, you pay by having less savings at a given level of investment.

Substitution of the behavioral equations for C and M into the income equation above produces

$$Y = (a + bY) - (c + dY) + I + X,$$

or

$$Y = \frac{a - c + I + X}{1 - b + d}.$$

In this case an exogenous increase in investment or exports of $1 increases local income by $1/(1 - b + d)$. This is the multiplier for a model with trade. For example, if $b = 0.75$ (as before), but $d = 0.25$, the multiplier is 2. Recall that the multiplier was 4 when there were no imports ($d = 0$).

Now suppose that we add a government to the model. We will suppose that the government spends amount G in the local economy and collects taxes according to a proportional income tax at rate t, or that taxes collected from the local economy are

$$T = tY.$$

Consumption spending is now regarded as a function of disposable income, which equals income minus taxes [i.e., $(1 - t)Y$]. The consumption function is now

$$C = a + b(1 - t)Y,$$

the saving function of income after taxes is

$$S = (1 - t)Y - C = -a + (1 - b)(1 - t)Y,$$

and the import function is now

$$M = c + d(1 - t)Y.$$

All government spending in the local economy will be assumed to be exogenous and for the services of local labor.

With government in the model the definition of total local expenditure and income is

$$Y = C + I + G + X - M.$$

Given that $Y = C + S + T$, this equation can be manipulated to yield

$$S + T + M = I + G + X,$$

or that the total "leakages" of saving, taxes, and imports equal the total of exogenous spending.

Substitution for S, T, and M in the equation above produces

$$(1 - b)(1 - t)Y - a + tY + c + d(1 - t)Y = I + G + X,$$

or

$$Y = \frac{a - c + I + G + X}{1 - b + bt + d - dt}.$$

Now the local multiplier is $1/(1 - b + bt + d - dt)$, an increase in spending for investment, government, or exports will increase local income by this amount. If $b = 0.75$ and $d = 0.25$ as before, and $t = 0.3$ (30% tax rate), the local multiplier is 1.54. In other words, an increase in exports of $1 will increase local income by $1.54. A local multiplier inherently is not very large because the leakages, including saving, imports, and taxes, are sizable fractions of additional income in a local economy.

Now let us turn to the economic base model. The local economy is partitioned into two parts, the sector that produces goods and services for export outside the urban area and the sector that produces for local use. This partition of the local economy can be based on income or employment—employment is probably the more popular choice because of better data availability. The fundamental equation for total employment T is

$$T = B + L,$$

where B is basic (export) employment and L is employment for the production of locally consumed goods and services. As in the Keynesian model, employment in the export sector is exogenous. A behavioral relationship is specified as

$$L = a + bT;$$

employment in the local sector is a function of total employment just as consumption is a function of income. The propensity to employ additional workers in the local sector for each additional worker is b. Substitution for L in the total employment equation yields the basic result that

$$T = \frac{a + B}{1 - b}.$$

This equation implies that an increase in basic (export) employment of 1 will increase total local employment by $1/(1 - b)$. This is the local multiplier.

In some cases it is assumed that $a = 0$, so that

$$L = bT.$$

In other words,

$$b = \frac{L}{T}$$

and

$$1 - b = 1 - \frac{L}{T} = \frac{T-L}{T} = \frac{B}{T}$$

In short, the local multiplier is just T/B, the ratio of total to basic (export) employment. This method for estimating the local multiplier simply requires an estimate of basic (export) employment. Total employment for a local economy is provided by standard government data sources.

This final economic base model is indeed very simple—too simple. Using the Keynesian multiplier model, we found that multipliers for a local economy are likely to be pretty low because of savings, imports, and taxes. Suppose that we take the earlier multiplier of 1.54. The economic base model produces a multiplier of $T/B = 1.54$, or $B = 0.65T$. Basic (export) employment must be 65% of total employment! Clearly something is wrong here. Employment in local economies does not consist of 65% export employment and 35% local services or anything even close to those proportions. Export employment is much smaller than 65% of the total. The problem stems from the assumption that $a = 0$ in the equation $L = a + bT$. If $a = 0$, the average and marginal propensities to employ workers in the local sector are equal. If a is greater than zero, the average propensity is greater than the marginal propensity. We want the marginal propensity for purposes of estimating the multiplier; but there is no justification for assuming that the marginal and average propensities are equal.

Let us take one final look at the algebra of the model. We know that the local multiplier is $1/(1 - b)$ and that $L = a + bT$. The crucial quantity is b, which equals

$$b = \frac{L-a}{T} = \frac{L}{T} - \frac{a}{T.}$$

Substitution into the multiplier equation yields

$$\frac{1}{1-b} = \frac{1}{1 - (L/T) + (a/T).}$$

We know that $1 - (L/T) = B/T$, so

$$\frac{1}{1-b} = \frac{1}{(B/T) + (a/T)}$$

$$= \frac{T}{B+a}.$$

As before, if $a = 0$, the multiplier is T/B. But if a is greater than zero, the multiplier is smaller than T/B. The greater is a, the smaller is the local (marginal) multiplier. The use of the simple economic base model with a local multiplier of T/B is *not* recommended.

There are two further problems with this sort of model as a model of the economic growth of an urban area. First, as indicated above, Keynesian multiplier models (and economic base models) presume that there is unemployment. Total output is surely constrained by the supply of inputs, but this kind of model has nothing to say about the supply side. Even more important, the model emphasizes exports (and other exogenous spending) as the engine of growth. That is fine as far as it goes, but it does not go very far. Why does an urban area have a demand for its exports? What causes that demand to increase or decrease? The model is silent on these vital questions. The other models of urban economic growth provide some answers. In truth, the economic base model is an adaptation of the Keynesian multiplier model, which was expressly intended as a tool for short-run analysis. Economic growth is ultimately a long-run business. These are harsh criticisms, but I do not mean to suggest that we should ignore that fact that exports and imports are very important aspects of an urban economy. An alternative model with exports and imports is proposed in Section F.

C. NEOCLASSICAL GROWTH THEORY

Solow's model of economic growth is called *neoclassical* because it is based on a production function for the economy in which it is possible to substitute capital for labor continuously, holding output constant. This idea of continuous substitution between inputs in production, holding output constant (and between consumer goods along an indifference curve), was devised in what is known as the neoclassical period of economics, from about 1870 to 1914. Suppose that we begin with a particular neoclassical production function, the familiar *Cobb–Douglas function*, which is written

$$Y = AK^\alpha L^{1-\alpha}.$$

From Chapter 7 you know that because the exponents sum to 1, the production function has constant returns to scale. To see this again, multiply both inputs by 2. The implications are as follows:

$$A(2K)^\alpha(2L)^{1-\alpha} = A \cdot 2^{\alpha+1-\alpha}K^\alpha L^{1-\alpha} = 2Y.$$

Doubling both inputs doubles output. Another important property is output per worker (average product), which is also called *productivity*, or

$$\frac{Y}{L} = A\left(\frac{K}{L}\right)^\alpha.$$

Output per worker is a function of the autonomous growth factor and capital per worker. The growth in productivity thus depends upon the growth in the autonomous growth factor and in capital per worker.

The basic equation for growth can be easily derived from the general form of the aggregate production function. If

$$Y = AF(K,L),$$

then from the mathematics covered in the appendix to this book, the change in output can be written

$$\delta Y = \delta A\, F(K,L) + MP_K \delta K + MP_L\, \delta L.$$

Here MP_K and MP_L are the marginal products of capital and labor. This equation can be converted to percentage change form by dividing by Y, or

$$\frac{\delta Y}{Y} = \frac{\delta A}{A} + MP_K\left(\frac{K}{Y}\right)\frac{\delta K}{K} + MP_L\left(\frac{L}{Y}\right)\frac{\delta L}{L}.$$

Since MP_K is just $\delta Y/\delta K$, $MP_K(K/Y)$ is the elasticity of output with respect to the capital input, which is $(\delta Y/Y)/(\delta K/K)$. Similarly, MP_L is $\delta Y/\delta L$, and $MP_L(L/Y)$ is the elasticity of output with respect to the labor input. The basic growth equation can be written

$$\frac{\delta Y}{Y} = \frac{\delta A}{A} + E_K\left(\frac{\delta K}{K}\right) + E_L\left(\frac{\delta L}{L}\right),$$

with E_K and E_L denoting the elasticities of output with respect to capital and labor. This equation says that the growth rate of GDP equals the growth rate of the autonomous growth factor plus the growth rates of the two basic inputs weighted by the proper elasticities of output.

If we use the Cobb–Douglas production function, the elasticity of output with respect to capital is α (the exponent of capital in the Cobb–Douglas function) and the elasticity of output with respect to labor is $1 - \alpha$ (the exponent of labor). To see this, consider the change in output with respect to a change in K using the power-function rule, or

$$\frac{\delta Y}{\delta K} = \alpha A K^{\alpha-1}L^{1-\alpha} = \alpha A\left(\frac{L}{K}\right)^{1-\alpha}.$$

The marginal product of K is determined by the ratio of labor to capital (L/K). Multiplication by K/Y will convert the equation to elasticity form:

$$E_K = \frac{\delta Y}{\delta K}\left(\frac{K}{Y}\right) = \frac{\alpha A K^\alpha L^{1-\alpha}}{Y} = \alpha.$$

The proof for the labor input follows the same method. Finally, suppose that each input is paid its marginal product, as would be the case with perfectly competitive markets for the two inputs. Denote the payment to each unit of capital as r, and denote the wage paid to labor as w. These assumptions mean that

$$\alpha = \frac{rK}{Y}$$

and

$$1 - \alpha = \frac{wL}{Y}.$$

The elasticities of output are the shares of total output paid to each input. With constant returns to scale these elasticities just sum to 1, and the total output is exhausted by the payments to the two inputs.

Now you understand the basic mechanics of neoclassical growth theory. Before we turn to its use in the explanation of growth in urban areas, you need to understand how the model has been used to examine growth at the national level. Use of the model at the national level did not proceed smoothly and a heated controversy ensued.

D. EXPLANATIONS OF U.S. ECONOMIC GROWTH

It is helpful first to examine some empirical estimates of the sources of economic growth at the national level. Substantial progress has been made in quantifying the sources of national growth, so those who seek to understand economic growth at the urban or regional level must have an understanding of this work.

One of the articles for which Robert Solow received the Nobel Prize is a study of the sources of U.S. economic growth from 1909 to 1949 [Solow (1957)]. In that study 87.5% of the increase in gross output per labor-hour was attributed to technical change in the broadest sense (the autonomous growth factor), and the remaining 12.5% was attributed to increased use of capital. Solow used the phrase *technical change* to refer to the autonomous growth factor. Solow's 1957 paper is justifiably famous, but it had at least one unintended consequence. Taken by itself, Solow's paper leaves the false impression that economists have no coherent explanation for economic growth. Indeed, one still hears the basic result of this paper cited in conversation and in popular literature today. Solow's study led Edward F. Denison to produce his first study (1962) of the sources of economic growth in which technical change is still regarded as the main source of growth.

In contrast to these studies, Dale Jorgenson and Zvi Griliches (1967), in a controversial paper, claimed that they measured the quantities of output and inputs with greater accuracy and found that disembodied (or residual) technical change contributed very little to growth. Their chief innovation was to devise methods for measuring the changes in the *quality* of the capital and labor inputs. This study set off a heated exchange between Denison and Jorgenson and Griliches that was published in the *Survey of Current Business* in 1969 and 1972. Denison's comments on the original Jorgenson–Griliches paper induced some revisions in the estimation methods; the revised estimates of the sources of U.S. economic growth for 1950–1962 published by Jorgenson and Griliches (1972) are as follows:

Capital		1.71% per annum
Capital stock	1.30	
Quality change	0.30	
Utilization	0.11	
Labor		0.71%
Labor stock	0.37	
Quality change	0.44	
Utilization	−0.10	
Autonomous growth factor		1.03%
Growth of gross private domestic product		3.47%

In these estimates technical change (autonomous growth factor) accounts for 30% of the growth in gross private domestic product and 33% of the growth in real output per worker. The growth in the measured capital stock accounts for a somewhat larger proportion of total growth over this period, and the changes in capital and labor quality (as measured by the change in the distributions of capital and labor toward more highly priced input forms) are significant contributors to growth.

Denison has continued to study the sources of U.S. economic growth and his latest estimates (1985) for the 1929–1982 period are:

Labor	34%
Education per worker	13%
Capital	17%
Advances in knowledge	26%
Improvements in resource allocation	8%
Economies of scale	8%
Other factors	−6%
	100%

The proportion of growth attributed to advances in knowledge is 26%, which agrees fairly well with the earlier Jorgenson–Griliches estimates, but Denison attributes a smaller fraction of growth to capital than do Jorgenson and Griliches.

A major study by Jorgenson, Gollop, and Fraumeni (1987) is the best empirical study of the sources of national growth over the period 1948 to 1979 from both the theoretical and empirical standpoints. Their perspective on economic growth emphasizes the contribution of the mobilization of resources within individual industries using a neoclassical framework. The explanatory force of this perspective is powerful at the sector level. For 46 of the 51 industrial sectors included in their study, the contributions of intermediate, capital, and labor inputs were the predominant source of the growth of output. Technical change (the autonomous growth factor) accounts for the major portion of growth in output in only five industries.

For the nation as a whole, Jorgenson et al. (1987) found that capital (both quantity and quality increases) accounted for 45.6% of the 3.42% annual average growth in aggregate output from 1948 to 1979. Labor (both quantity and quality) accounted for 30.7% of growth, and the autonomous growth factor explained 23.7% of total growth. Improvements in the quality of capital were associated with only about one-fourth of the growth that can be attributed to capital, but the growth in the quality of labor accounted for almost 50% of the growth attributed to the labor input. In short, the sheer quantity of capital is very important to growth, and improvements in the quality of labor and technical change (the autonomous growth factor) make big contributions as well.

One message to urban economics is clear from this brief examination of empirical studies of economic growth. Understanding economic growth is a complicated matter. No study as comprehensive as the Jorgenson et al. (1987) has been done at the urban or regional level. Indeed, given the data requirements, there is little prospect that such a study can be done for urban areas anytime soon. Another message from these studies is pretty clear. Economic growth policy at the national level can focus first on investment in capital goods and then on labor quality and technical change.

Despite the sophisticated work of Solow, Denison, Jorgenson, Gollop, Fraumeni, and many others, there is still much that we do not understand about economic growth. For Americans the unsolved mystery is the slowdown in productivity growth that has occurred since 1973. As defined above, productivity is real GDP divided by the total amount of labor employed in its production. According to various issues of the *Economic Report of the President*, from 1948 to 1973 productivity in the U.S. economy grew by an average of 2.5% per year, but from 1973 to 1991 the average growth rate for productivity was only 0.7% per year. This sharp drop in productivity growth has been translated into stagnant household incomes and wages. The median household income in real terms increased by 2.7% per year from 1948 to 1973, but from 1973 to 1989 (the peak year) the annual average increase was only 0.5%. This stagnation of household income took place during a period when the percentage of the population over the age of 16 who were employed increased from 58% to 63%. During this same period, 1973 to 1989, the average hourly earnings in the private sector declined in 1982 dollars from $8.55 to $7.64, an average annual decline of 0.7%. (However, there is evidence that fringe benefits grew by more than enough to make up for this decline in hourly pay. Total hourly compensation grew from $10.45 to $11.89 over this period, an average annual increase of 0.8%, a figure that is line with the productivity growth rate.)

Why did the productivity growth rate drop? There are many causes, and there is no overall consensus. One expert in empirical macroeconomics, Robert Gordon (1993, pp. 363–372), shows that slower growth in capital explains only a small part of the slowdown in productivity growth. Many economists cite a decline in the average quality of workers because of the increase in the labor force participation of teenagers and women since 1973. Others claim that the nation has failed to invest enough in public capital, the infrastructure. Still others point out that we are running out of raw materials; it costs more to recover the same amount of oil, natural gas, and other natural resources. The impacts of increases in governmental rules and regulations, particularly environmental and safety rules, are blamed by some. These impacts seem to be concentrated in particular industries, such as electric power generation. All of these arguments have merit, but at this point we do not know enough to determine how much of the decline in productivity growth can be attributed to each. Paul Krugman, a prominent member of the younger generation of economists, puts it (perhaps a bit too pessimistically) as follows (1990, p. 15): "So we really don't know why productivity growth ground to a near-halt. That makes it hard to answer the other question: What can we do to speed it up?" This kind of situation creates the opportunity for a lot of people to make a lot of suggestions, many of which have very little research to back them up. The discussion of economic growth policy is deferred to Chapter 14, where both national and local economic growth policies are considered.

E. NEOCLASSICAL MODELS OF METROPOLITAN GROWTH

The basic neoclassical model has been used to study economic growth at the metropolitan level. In this section we outline the methods for such a study and review some of the empirical findings. Growth models for urban areas concentrate attention on the growth rates of capital and labor, which depend critically on migration from or to other parts of the nation. A good example of the model was developed by Ghali, Akiyama, and Fujiwara (1978). They applied the model of the states of the United States, but the same principles can be used to study urban areas or regions. Their study is described in detail here because it represents a direct and reasonably convincing application of the basic neoclassical growth model. The fledgling researcher (such as you) often can learn how to do research by studying in some detail how someone else did it.

Consider again a one-sector model in which the relationship between aggregate output and inputs for an urban area is expressed as a Cobb–Douglas production function

$$Y_{it} = A e^{rt} K_{it}^{\alpha} L_{it}^{1-\alpha},$$

where the subscript i refers to the urban area and t refers to year t. Recall that α and $1 - \alpha$ are the elasticities of output with respect to K and L. The term e refers to the base of the natural logarithms, and the parameter r is the rate of technical change. Parameter r is a decimal, such as 0.04, which means 4% per year. Ghali et al. (1978) assumed that output elasticities and the rate of technical change are the same in all urban areas, but this assumption might not be tenable in some applications of the model. However, the model allows for differences across urban areas in the marginal products of capital and labor because, as was shown above in Section C, marginal products are determined by the capital/labor ratio in the urban area.

If factor markets are competitive, the wage (w) will equal the value of the marginal product of labor, and the rental rate of capital (r) will equal the marginal product of capital in equilibrium. Thus

$$w_{it} = P_t \left(\frac{\delta Y}{\delta L} \right)_{it}$$

and

$$r_{it} = P_t \left(\frac{\delta Y}{\delta K} \right)_{it},$$

where P_t is the price of output, which is assumed to be the same in all urban areas. It is clear that the capital/labor ratio determines interurban factor price differentials. The factor prices above and the ratio of capital to labor will change over time if the rates of growth of the two inputs differ.

It is conventional to assume that capital and labor move from urban area to urban area in response to factor price differentials. Thus the rate of growth of labor in an urban area is the natural increase in the labor force plus a component that is a function of the difference between the wage in the urban area in question and average for all other urban areas. Similarly, the rate of growth of capital in an urban area is the "natural" increase in capital derived from saving and investment within the urban area plus interurban capital movement that is a function of the difference between the rental price of capital in that urban area and the average rental price for all other urban areas. It is also conventional to assume that labor and capital do not respond instantly to such price differentials. A "partial adjustment" mechanism is assumed; labor and capital respond to price differentials, but not enough so that the price differential is eliminated in one year.

The movement of labor and capital in response to factor price differentials should, in the long run, eliminate those factor price differentials. Urban areas (or states or regions) with high ratios of labor to capital presumably have low wages and high rental prices of capital. Labor migrates away from and capital migrates to such areas. Similarly, urban areas with high ratios of capital to labor have low rental prices of capital and high wages. If capital responds more rapidly than labor to factor price differentials, the lower-wage regions will grow more rapidly than higher-wage regions. In the end wages in all urban areas (or states or regions) converge to the national average, except for wage differences related to amenities associated with living in particular places. For example, places with good weather will have lower measured wages as compensation. The hypothesis of the convergence of wages (and per capita income) across regions of the United States has been the subject of a great deal of research. For the most part, researchers have observed a long-run convergence of per capita incomes across regions, but there are enough exceptions to this result to suggest that more complicated forces are at work. Borts and Stein, in an influential book that was published in 1964, found that there have been time periods when growth was higher in states with high wages. Also, there have been times when both wages and the rental price of capital were relatively high in the same state. Borts and Stein (1964) set out to devise a neoclassical growth model for states that can explain this more complicated set of empirical findings. Their model is discussed below.

The model proposed by Ghali, Akiyama, and Fujiwara (1978) includes one other determinant of factor movements. Specifically, they suggest that growth rate *differentials* may carry information on the probability of gaining employment at the prevailing wage and on other factors that might influence the migration of labor and capital. Input growth equations can be written

$$L_{it}^* = \beta_0 + \beta_1 \left(\frac{w_i}{w}\right)_{t-1} + \beta_2 (g_i)_{t-1}$$

and

$$K_{it}^* = \beta_3 + \beta_4 \left(\frac{r_i}{r}\right)_{t-1} + \beta_6 (g_i)_{t-1},$$

where L^* and K^* are the growth rates of L and K, w and r the national average wage rate and rental rate on capital, and $(g_i)_{t-1}$ the growth rate differential for urban area i relative to the national average growth rate (expressed as a percentage of the national growth rate). In equation form

$$(g_i)_{t-1} = \left(\frac{Y_i^* - Y^*}{Y^*}\right)_{t-1},$$

where Y_i^* and Y^* are the growth rates for urban area i and the national average. Growth of labor and capital for urban areas is discussed in detail in Chapter 13.

The study by Ghali et al. (1978) estimated the model for 1958–1963 using the states of the United States as observations, and they also estimated the basic growth accounting equation

$$Y^*_{it} = r + \alpha K^*_{it} + (1 - \alpha)L^*_{it}.$$

The growth rate $\dot{Y}^*_{it}$ is the estimated rate of growth of gross state product, and the rate of growth of capital was approximated as the rate of growth of nonwage income. (Note that this measure of capital growth leaves out capital that is owned by the public sector—the public infrastructure. This is a potentially serious omission.) The equations estimated by multiple regression analysis are:

$$Y^*_i = 0.013 + 0.457K^*_i + 0.769L^*_i, \qquad R^2 = 0.486$$

$$L^*_i = 0.017 + 0.031\left(\frac{w_i}{w}\right)_{t-1} + 0.020(g_i)_{t-1} \qquad R^2 = 0.620$$

$$K^*_i = 0.050 + 0.024\left(\frac{r_i}{r}\right)_{t-1} + 0.009(g_i)_{t-1} \qquad R^2 = 0.583.$$

All estimated coefficients are statistically significant at conventional levels. The term R^2 refers to the percentage of the variance of the dependent variable accounted for by the independent variables included in the regression analysis. Note that the equation for the growth of output suggests increasing returns to scale $(0.457 + 0.769 = 1.226)$. However, the figure 1.226 is not statistically significantly different from 1.0. This model is dynamic; the rates of growth of inputs influence the rate of growth of output in the state during the same period. This rate of growth of output affects the rate of growth of inputs in the following period, leading to further changes in the rate of growth of output. The hypothesis that the rate of growth conveys information about future employment prospects has been confirmed.

The results of the Ghali et al. model indicate that interstate disparities in the *level* of output per worker are quite persistent over time (out 15 years), but the wide disparities in the rates of growth of output and output per worker narrow quite rapidly. The model thus generates long-run convergence of *growth rates*, but if the levels of output per worker are compared, little convergence will be found as long as the initial levels of output per worker differ.

Recent research by John Crihfield and Martin Panggabean (1995) has used a model very similar to that of Ghali et al. (1978) to study growth and per capita income convergence in metropolitan areas. They also seek to test for the effects of investment in human capital and public infrastructure at the metropolitan level, factors that were omitted by Ghali et al. Their model is estimated for 288 metropolitan areas in the United States for the period 1963–1977. They specify a production function for a metropolitan area at time t as the Cobb–Douglas function

$$Y_t = A_t K_t^\alpha H_t^\beta L_t^{1-\alpha-\beta},$$

where K includes both public- and private-sector capital, and H is human capital. The growth rate of the autonomous growth factor, A, is assumed to exogenous to an urban area, but the growth rates of labor and private capital are functions of several variables. Output is measured as the total personal income for the metropolitan area, K is measured as the share of local income invested in private- and public-sector capital, and H is approximated by the percentage of residents over age 25 with at least 12 years of schooling. The production function is converted to a growth equation for per capita income. Their empirical results for the parameters in the production function are that $\alpha = 0.113$, $\beta = 0.204$, and $1 - \alpha - \beta = 0.683$. Crihfield and Panggabean (1995) acknowledge that the estimate of α, which is also supposed to be capital's share in total income, is low compared to studies at the national level. The share of capital is actually about 0.25. This inaccuracy may be the result of an imperfect measure of capital. Otherwise, the results appear to be quite reasonable. Note particularly that the measure of the quality of the labor input is a significant factor. Crihfield and Panggabean also found that metropolitan areas with higher per capita incomes in 1960 had lower growth rates. This result supports the hypothesis that per capita incomes of metropolitan areas are converging over time, in line with the neoclassical model.

Other research uses the neoclassical framework to examine employment growth (instead of output growth) at the metropolitan level. These studies are discussed in Chapter 12.

F. NEOCLASSICAL EXPORT BASE MODELS OF URBAN GROWTH

In this section we examine a two-sector neoclassical model of urban growth in which one sector produces a product for export and the other sector produces a good only for local consumption. We call this model a *neoclassical export base model*. This type of model is more complex than the one-sector models discussed above, but the greater complexity also yields a richer set of possible outcomes that can be explained by the model. For more advanced students, a mathematical version of this model is presented in the appendix to this chapter.

Borts and Stein (1964) developed the model presented in this section. They turned to a more complex neoclassical model because the one-sector model was unable to account for some empirical findings for states of the United States. There have been periods in which high-wage states grew more rapidly than low-wage states. At times, regions may have returns to labor and capital that are both above the national average and other regions where both returns are below the national average; and the former regions may grow more rapidly than the latter. It is clear that even though it is over 30 years old, the book by Borts and Stein (1964) is one of the best works on regional growth. It may also be true that it is not well understood. For example, Clark, Gertler, and Whiteman (1986, p. 41) stated that "any reading of Borts and Stein (1964) would show that their own neoclassical production function models lacked much empirical validity." They note that (1986, p. 258) "taking changes over three intervals (1919–29, 1929–48 and 1948–53), Borts and Stein (1964) measured the growth of capital, expecting it to grow fastest in low-wage states. In fact, this occurred only in one period (1929–48), casting some doubt on this aspect of the simple model they had chosen to test."

Richardson (1973, p. 221) argued: "However, it must be recognized that some of these findings, particularly that both capital and wages increased more rapidly in high wage areas in the first and third periods, are compatible with views of the regional growth process that are not extensions of but are quite contradictory to the neoclassical approach." In fact, Borts and Stein (1964) took the findings referred to in these quotations as the starting point for their more sophisticated investigation. Borts and Stein (1964, p. 20) state: "We have found that neoclassical price theory, suitably developed, provides the explanation of interstate differences in growth rates." Instead, it seems that the critics of neoclassical theory are prepared to discard it because its simplest version failed to explain some important facts about state growth rates.

The model developed by Borts and Stein is a conventional two-sector model of growth for an individual state. If the economy of the state is disaggregated to two sectors, the growth rate in the real wage does not depend solely on the growth in the autonomous growth factor and the capital/labor ratio (as in the one-sector model). An increase in the ratio of capital to labor in a state may not lead to a rise in the ratio of capital to labor in each of the two sectors; a reallocation of output may occur in favor of the commodity produced by the relatively capital-intensive sector. This reallocation of output releases a relatively large amount of labor from the labor-intensive sector. This labor is employed in the capital-intensive sector, but these workers who shift sectors now require a greater amount of capital per worker than before. For the wage to rise, capital accumulation must raise the ratio of capital to labor in both output sectors. This requires that capital accumulation be accompanied by an increase in the relative price of output in the sector that is relatively labor intensive. If, during capital accumulation, the relative output prices remain unchanged, the factor proportions do not change in either sector. All that happens is a reallocation of output in favor of the sector that is relatively capital intensive; the wage does not increase. The empirical evidence presented by Borts and Stein confirmed their view of the growth process. Reallocation in favor of the labor-intensive services sector occurred in the group of states that underwent the greatest growth of capital relative to labor (during the period 1929–1953). This reallocation produced the observed increase in the marginal product of labor (i.e., wage rate) in those states.

The neoclassical economic base model as developed by Borts and Stein assumes that all markets within the urban area are perfectly competitive, capital is perfectly mobile and hence can be imported at the going price, and the growth rate of labor in the urban area is a given. This last assumption means that labor does *not* respond to wage rate differentials across urban areas, an assumption that empirical evidence has shown is not tenable. An exogenous growth in labor will cause the urban area to grow in the Borts–Stein model. Some of the critical results of the model pertain to the impacts of a change in the *price* of the export product. An increase in this price represents an increase in the demand for exports. A fundamental result of the model is that an increase in the price of exports will increase the wage rate. The wage increases because the increase in the price of the export product leads to importation of capital at its going (national) price. If the price of the exported output rises but the price of capital does not increase, the wage rate in the export sector must increase. This increase in the wage is transmitted to the local sector.

G. A SYNTHESIS OF MAINSTREAM ECONOMICS: PRELIMINARY VERSION

The Keynesian model in Section B and the two-sector neoclassical model in Sections F are two types of mainstream economic models. The Keynesian model generates growth through increases on the demand side, while the neoclassical model relies on growth of supply—labor in particular. It is useful to depict both models on a diagram for a local labor market.

Consider Figure 11.1, which shows the local market for labor. There is only one kind of labor in the market, and therefore everyone makes the same wage rate. The Keynesian model, in labor market terms, presumes that curve AA is the supply curve of labor. The supply is perfectly elastic at the current wage rate (at least in the relevant range of supplies). The demand for labor is curve BB. A given level of aggregate demand $(C + I + G + X - M)$ requires an amount of labor L_0 at the current wage. The supplies of labor and all other inputs are perfectly elastic in the relevant range, so that employment in the local economy can grow only if demand increases. An increase in aggregate demand that increases the demand for labor to $B'B'$ will increase employment to L_1.

The two-sector neoclassical growth model has a perfectly elastic *demand* for labor because more exports can be sold at the prevailing price, capital can be freely imported at the prevailing price, and the local industries produce under constant returns to scale. The wage equals the value of the marginal product of labor in the export industry. The value of the marginal product is the price of output times the marginal product of labor. The price of output is taken as a constant, and the marginal product of labor can always be adjusted and kept constant by importing the appropriate amount of capital. Therefore, in Figure 11.2 the horizontal line AA is the demand for labor in the local economy. The supply of labor from the current residents is curve

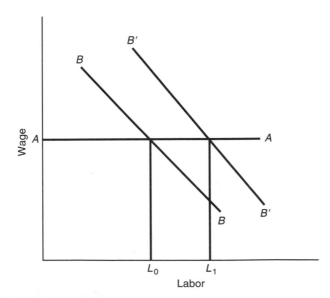

FIGURE 11.1 The labor market in an urban area

FIGURE 11.2 The labor market in an urban area

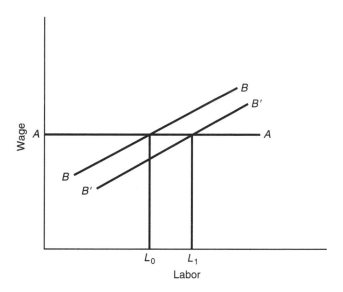

BB, so equilibrium employment is L_0. With a perfectly elastic demand for labor (and other inputs), growth occurs when the supply of labor increases. If the labor supply increases to curve *B'B'*, by natural population growth or by net in-migration, employment increases to L_1.

Few economists are prepared to believe that either labor supply curves or demand curves are perfectly elastic at the level of an entire metropolitan area. There may be limitations on the ability of an urban area to sell its export good at a constant price. If nothing else, an expansion of exports will require that the good be transported greater distances and incur greater transportation costs. The price received by exporters will have to be reduced to offset the increase in transportation costs as more distant markets are penetrated. Similarly, even Keynes believed in the perfectly elastic supply of labor only under conditions of high unemployment.

A synthesis of the two mainstream economic models is shown in Figure 11.3. The demand for labor is labeled *DD*, the supply of labor is *SS*, the current wage is W_0 and the employment level is L_0. Employment growth can be generated by either an increase in demand (to *D'D'*), or an increase in supply (to *S'S'*). An increase in the demand for exports will generate an increase in demand for labor directly and indirectly through the local multiplier effect. Note that an increase in demand causes both employment and the wage to increase; part of the potential employment increase is choked off by a wage increase.

An increase in labor supply increases employment and decreases the wage. The decrease in the wage depends on the elasticity of demand for labor, of course. If Borts and Stein (1964) are correct in asserting that the demand for labor in a local economy is highly elastic, employment will increase and the wage will not decline very much. Assuming that the increase in employment increases aggregate demand in the local economy, there will be an increase in the demand for local good (and im-

FIGURE 11.3 The labor market in an urban area

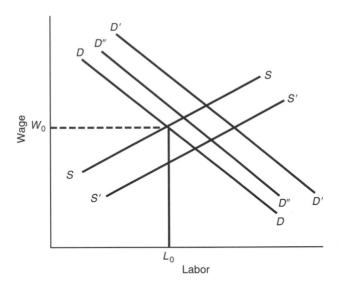

ports, as well). This further increase in the demand for labor to produce local goods is shown as $D''D''$ in Figure 11.3. These increases in employment can then stimulate further increases in labor supply through migration, and the process can start again.

An early study by Muth (1971) found that an increase in migration to an urban area (in the 1950s) caused a direct increase in employment in that urban area equal to the increase in migration and that the direct increase in employment induced migration of about two-thirds of that employment increase. In equation form,

$$\delta E = \alpha M$$

and

$$M = \beta(\delta E) + \theta,$$

where δE is the change in employment, M is migration, and α, β, and θ are coefficients. Muth's (1971) estimates are that $\alpha = 1$ and $\beta = 0.67$. The two equations can be solved for δE, or

$$\delta E = \frac{\alpha\theta}{1 - \alpha\beta} = \frac{\theta}{1 - 0.67} = 3\theta.$$

This result means that an increase in migration of 1 (brought about by increasing θ by 1) will lead directly and indirectly to an increase in employment of 3. The indirect effect includes further in-migration that is induced by the increases in employment. Note that for Muth's (1971) model to be stable, it must be true that $\alpha\beta$ is less than 1.0. Muth's (1971) estimate of the effect of net in-migration will be examined again in Chapter 13.

The simple synthesis of mainstream economic models is called "preliminary" because the impacts of changes in the autonomous growth factor have been ignored.

The details of the autonomous growth factor are considered in Chapter 12 and then another synthesis of models is offered.

H. INPUT–OUTPUT ANALYSIS

So far in this chapter we have introduced the export base and the basic one- and two-sector neoclassical models of urban economic growth. These models come straight from the Keynesian and neoclassical models of mainstream economics, and it is probably true that most researchers of urban economic growth are not happy with these tools. The search is on for models that will explain more of the variety and detail of urban growth and decline. The purpose of the remainder of this chapter is to provide an account of the leading models that either supplement, or are intended to replace, the models that have been discussed thusfar.

The first model included here is an expanded version of the Keynesian multiplier model discussed at the beginning of the chapter. The *input–output model* was invented by Wassily Leontief of Harvard in the 1930s, and he received the Nobel prize for his stunning accomplishment [Leontief (1951)]. The model is called "input–output" because it explicitly includes all of the intermediate goods and services that are used in the production of final goods and services. Recall that the Keynesian model and the neoclassical growth model are both models of *value added* only. Leontief rightly believes that much of the detail—and reality—of the economy is omitted by the concentration on value added. Leontief took a direct approach to the problem and in so doing, invented a brilliant scheme for keeping track of an economy. Input–output analysis is a valuable accounting system but can also be used to make projections and examine impacts of policy in the short run. As with the Keynesian multiplier models, its value is not primarily as a method for analyzing long-run growth. Nevertheless, it is included because it clarifies one's thinking about any economy, including an urban economy.

The basic data for the input–output model are provided by a transactions table, a simplified example of which is shown in Table 11.1. This table is drawn up to resemble an urban economy, so the model presented here is intended to be at least somewhat realistic. Notice first that the local economy consists of four sectors: manufacturing, services, trade, and households. Across the top of the table the columns carry the labels of the sectors to which output is *sold*. Output is sold to the four local sectors, and there are exports to buyers outside the urban area. Down the left-hand side of the table are listed the sectors that supply *inputs* to the production activity that is carried on in the urban area. The manufacturing, service, and trade sectors are listed here as suppliers of intermediate inputs. The other inputs used in local production include the services of local labor, capital, and land. These inputs create the *value added* by the local economy. To simplify the model we assume that local labor, capital, and land are all owned by local households. This means that the income earned by these basic factors of production will accrue entirely to the local economy. The last input used in local production is imports from outside the urban area. Imports are shown as the fifth line in the table.

	TABLE 11.1 Transactions Table for a Local Economy					
	Output Sold to:					
				Final Demand		*Gross*
Inputs Supplied by:	*Manufacturing*	*Services*	*Trade*	*Households*	*Exports*	*Output*
Manufacturing	6	4	10	0	20	40
Services	5	8	2	25	10	50
Trade	0	0	0	30	0	30
Local labor, capital, land	14	33	8	0	0	55
Imports	15	5	10	0	—	30
Total inputs	40	50	30	55	30	

Let us pause for a moment to consider each of the three basic production sectors of this economy. Manufacturers produce a wide variety of goods; a good deal of local manufacturing output is exported, and some is also purchased by local manufacturing, service, and trade firms. Some manufacturers produce parts and equipment used by other local businesses, but in this model it is assumed that manufacturers do not sell directly to households. Instead, manufactured products are sold to households by firms in the trade sector. Indeed, this is all the local trade sector does in this model—sell to local households. The service sector in an urban area is a very large and diverse collection of activities, including health care (14% of the economy!), business services (accountants, lawyers, computer firms, financial services, etc.), and other sorts of personal services. Services are purchased by local businesses and households, and some services are also exported. For example, financial services supplied by firms in an urban area can be performed for clients who live elsewhere, and some medical services can be provided for patients who come to the urban area for that purpose.

Local residents supply the labor, capital, and land used by the three production sectors. The production of services is assumed to require a great deal of labor and some land and capital as well. Manufacturing uses labor and factories, which require capital and land. The trade sector purchases goods from local suppliers and from firms outside the urban area and requires a relatively small amount of local labor, capital, and land compared to the total sales volume. Goods and services that are imported are presumed to be imported by firms, and households then purchase some of those imports from local service and trade firms. The other imports are used as intermediate inputs into local production.

Now return to Table 11.1. The numbers in each column represent the dollar amounts of the *inputs* used in the sector shown at the top of the column. In particular, manufacturing in the urban area used $6 worth of manufactured goods (made locally); $5 in local services; $14 in local labor, capital, and land; and $15 worth of imports. The total value of the inputs in the local manufacturing sector is therefore $40. Note that manufacturing is assumed to use a good deal of imported products—parts, equipment, and so on. Similarly, the local service sector bought $4 from local manufacturers, $8 from the local service sector itself, $33 from local households (labor, capital, and land), and $5 in imports. What was purchased by the local trade sector?

Consider the column labeled "households." This column does not represent inputs into a production process, but rather, lists final consumption activity. Households bought nothing from local manufacturers (as mentioned above), purchased $25 in services, and spent $30 with the local trade sector. In this model there is no saving; households spend all of their incomes. The model could be expanded to include saving and investment. Next, the column for exports shows the amounts sold to customers outside the urban area by the manufacturing and services sectors.

The final column is called "gross output." Gross output is the dollar value of *total sales* for a sector. For example, the local manufacturing sector had sales of $40. This is *not* value added (which was $14) but the value of *sales*. This entry of $40 is the sum of the figures in the first row, the row that shows the sales by local manufacturers to the various sectors. The $40 is also equal to the total value of the inputs purchased by the local manufacturing sector. Total purchases of inputs equal total sales because profits are included in the payments to local households. Note that the local service sector had a grand total of $50 in sales, distributed across the sectors as shown in the second row of the table. The local trade sector had $30 in sales, all of which were to local households.

The last column also lists a gross output figure for households. This figure of $55 is really the total income earned by households in the urban area from the sale of the services of labor, capital, and land. Total income is also equal to total value added in the local economy; hence the local gross domestic product was $55. Finally, total exports were $30, which equals the total imports shown in the fifth row. The fourth and fifth columns together constitute the final demands for goods and services. The accounts in Table 11.1 are all in balance. Table 11.1 shows why input–output analysis is highly useful as an accounting system.

The accounts shown in Table 11.1 can be converted into a model of the local economy. The first step is to compute the input coefficients for each sector. An input coefficient is the proportion of the total value of inputs spent on one particular input. For example, the local manufacturing sector purchased $6 from the local manufacturing sector out of a total of $40. The input coefficient is thus $6/40 = 0.15$. The remaining input coefficients for manufacturing are 0.125 for services, 0.35 for local value added (labor, capital, and land), and 0.375 for imports. These proportions add up to 1.0, and together they are the "recipe" for the goods manufactured locally. At this point it is necessary to make some behavioral assumptions. It will be assumed that the prices of all goods and services in this economy are constant. It is further assumed that the goods and services in the economy are produced under constant returns to scale and that input proportions do not change as the scale of production is changed. Therefore, if we wish to increase local manufacturing output by $1, we will need $0.125 in manufactured goods, $0.125 in services, $0.35 is value added, and $0.375 in imported goods and services. The increase in output of $1 is the same thing as an increase in 1 unit of output because the price of output is constant. The input coefficients have been computed for each sector and are shown in Table 11.2.

The input coefficients shown in Table 11.2 can be used to set up a system of equations to represent the local economy. We shall use the following notation: M is the gross output in manufacturing, S the gross output in services, T the gross output in trade, Y the total income (value added) in the local economy, X_m the exports of manufactured goods, and X_s the exports of services. Now pay close attention. Read-

TABLE 11.2 Input Coefficients for a Local Economy

	Manufacturing	Services	Trade	Households
Manufacturing	0.150	0.080	0.333	0.000
Services	0.125	0.160	0.067	0.455
Trade	0.000	0.000	0.000	0.545
Value added	0.350	0.660	0.267	0.000
Imports	0.375	0.100	0.333	0.000

ing across Table 11.2, we know that the gross output in manufacturing is 0.15 of the gross output in manufacturing, plus 0.08 of the gross output of services, plus 0.333 of the gross output in the trade sector, plus exports of manufactured goods. In equation form,

$$M = 0.150M + 0.080S + 0.333T + X_m,$$

$$S = 0.125M + 0.160S + 0.067T + 0.455Y + X_s,$$

$$T = 0.545Y,$$

and

$$Y = 0.350M + 0.660S + 0.267T.$$

The usual assumption is to take exports as exogenous variables, so this system of four equations can be solved for the four unknowns (M, S, T, and Y) in terms of the two export variables.

Finding the solution even to this simple system of four equations is not easy, so the usual technique is to convert the model to matrix form and use a computer to find the solution. Real input–output models can contain hundreds of sectors, so use of the computer to solve them is mandatory. After moving all the endogenous variables to the left-hand side, the model in matrix form is

$$\begin{bmatrix} 0.850 & -0.080 & -0.333 & 0.000 \\ -0.125 & 0.840 & -0.067 & -0.455 \\ 0.000 & 0.000 & 1.000 & -0.545 \\ -0.350 & -0.660 & -0.267 & 1.000 \end{bmatrix} \begin{bmatrix} M \\ S \\ T \\ Y \end{bmatrix} = \begin{bmatrix} X_m \\ X_s \\ 0 \\ 0 \end{bmatrix}.$$

The system of equations can be solved by successive substitution to eliminate variables (otherwise known as brute force), and the solutions are:

$$M = 1.613X_m + 0.772 X_s,$$

$$S = 3.236X_s + 1.141X_m,$$

$$Y = 2.413X_s + 1.542X_m,$$

and

$$T = 0.5455Y.$$

These solutions provide various multipliers associated with an increase in exports. An increase in manufacturing exports of $1 will increase gross manufacturing output by $1.61, gross output in services by $1.14, local income (value added) by $1.54, and gross sales in trade by $0.84. The multipliers associated with service exports are 0.77 on manufacturing output, 3.24 on output of services themselves, 2.41 on income, and 1.32 on gross sales in trade. In this model, exports of services have the larger effect on local income because there is more "local content" in services; value added is 66% of service gross output, but only 35% of gross output in manufacturing, and the two income multipliers are 2.41 and 1.54. Recall that total income is 55 and total exports are 30, so the ratio of income to exports is 1.83. This figure is just the weighted average of the two export multipliers, where the service sector export multiplier of 2.41 gets half the weight of the manufacturing export multiplier of 1.54. (Manufacturing exports are 20 and service exports are 10.)

Input–output analysis as a model of the economy in the short run has provided some useful results. It has shown that different types of exports have different multiplier effects on the local economy. It also shows the full increases in output in all the sectors of the local economy that are needed to respond to increased exports. The solutions to the model above tell us that to expand manufacturing exports by $1, the local economy needs to produce $1.61 worth of manufactures and $0.77 in services. An added dollar of service exports requires $3.24 in services and $1.14 in manufactured goods. Coupled with information on potential supplies in various sectors, the input–output model can thus be used to determine whether the local economy has the capacity to handle the requirements of a large increase in exports.

The model can also be used to estimate changes in imports used in each sector. From Table 11.2, the equation for imports is

$$I = 0.375M + 0.100S + 0.333T.$$

Hence knowledge of the changes in M, S, and T produces a projection of the change in imports. The total change in imports should equal the change in exports, of course. As an exercise, you can confirm that a $1 increase in manufactured exports generates a $1 increase in total imports.

Input–output models have become a popular analytical tool for local economic development officials. Several types of studies are conducted with the help of such a model. For one thing, the table of input coefficients can tell local officials whether the local economy supplies a lot or a little of the intermediate inputs needed by the export industries. If local suppliers appear to be weak, the next step is to find out why and consider whether the intermediate suppliers can be strengthened. On the other hand, if the suppliers of intermediate inputs are abundant, perhaps more of the export product can be attracted to the local economy. One can imagine the advertisements in industry trade journals that say, "We have the suppliers that you need right here in Ourtown." Another, less obvious use of the model is to examine the impacts on the local economy of a change in technology, changes in the input coefficients. We run the model with a given set of export demands and the old input coefficients, and then we rerun the model with the same export demands and a new set of input coefficients. What happens? Is local income increased? What are the changes in output requirements?

As one might suppose, the usual use of the model is to make projections that show the impact of a particular exogenous change in final demands. For example, the Chicago input–output model recently has been used to estimate the effects of a proposed theme park and legal gambling casino to be located near downtown. So many tourists are expected to visit these attractions each year, and to spend money at hotels, restaurants, museums, and so on. What will be the increases in output and employment in the various sectors of the Chicago economy? The input–output model provides a set of answers that is internally consistent. All of the rows and columns add up properly; no fudging is required to make all the changes in all of the sectors balance. Indeed, the model does all of this automatically. Clearly, Leontief deserved his Nobel Prize.

The input–output model is a useful and popular tool, but there are some limitations that one must bear in mind. The biggest problem with the framework is the requirement for data. The transactions table needs data on transactions. For each sector we need to know how much of the intermediate inputs were purchased locally versus imported. The task of collection of original survey data is costly, so model builders turn to cheaper alternatives. One approach is to use data that exist (only for manufacturing) at the U.S. Bureau of the Census on the identities of suppliers and customers for a sample of establishments from around the nation. The sample of establishments includes enough observations from major metropolitan areas to permit the estimation of input coefficients. Another approach is to adapt the national input–output table for the local economy. It is assumed that the local sector has the same input requirements as does the industry at the national level. These input requirements are divided between local suppliers and imports based on the relative size of the relevant local sectors. For example, if a local industry needs computer chips for its product but there are no local producers, we can conclude that the computer chips are imported. These alternatives to original survey research usually work fairly well in the sense that the input–output model that is generated is capable of replicating past data on the local economy with reasonable accuracy.

A more serious problem with input–output models for a local economy is the stability of the input coefficients. The input coefficients must, of necessity, be derived from data on the past record of the local economy. However, input coefficients can change suddenly when a local sector decides to import an intermediate input rather than to purchase it locally (or purchase it locally rather than import it, for that matter). Input coefficients are rather stable over time in the national input–output model, but the national model does not have to include trade among urban areas and regions. This problem may be particularly acute in an industry that is undergoing rapid technical change or growth, and such an industry may just be the kind of industry with which the local analyst in concerned. Input coefficients can be unstable because of price changes as well. The basic input–output model explicitly assumes that all prices are constant, but a change in relative input prices should lead to some substitution effects. Input–output models are not designed to handle this kind of problem easily, although changes in the input coefficients can be made. Changes in input coefficients must also be made when there is technical change. These problems mean that the model needs to be updated periodically.

Recall that the input–output model is also based on the assumption of constant returns to scale for the local industries. The projections of the model are inaccurate if there are increasing (or decreasing) returns to scale. A related point is that the model is also inaccurate if there are agglomeration economies of the types discussed in Chapter 3. Localization economies essentially are economies of scale for the industry, and urbanization economies are economies that stem from the size of the local economy as a whole. Input–output models do not account for these phenomena.

Finally, as I have emphasized, input–output analysis is a short-run tool. It is useful for making projections and performing impact analyses that are of short duration. It is not really a tool for the analysis of long-run growth because the model really has no supply side. The model presumes that the needed supplies of labor, capital, land, and intermediate products will be forthcoming when there is an exogenous increase in final demand. It may be perfectly reasonable to assume all of this in the short run, but the long run is a different story, as the neoclassical growth model tells us.

I. ECONOMIC HISTORY AND URBAN GROWTH AND DEVELOPMENT

Now we turn from the world of formal models to the more informal and eclectic field of economic history. Economic history is an important tool for understanding urban economies. The best modern economic historians combine analyses of the institutions and historical context of the urban area and its region, economic analysis, and political economy to provide a convincing narrative of what happened and why. This explanation may also have considerable relevance for current economic development policy. Two excellent examples of economic history as applied to an American city or region are discussed in this section. William Cronon's *Nature's Metropolis* is the story of Chicago and the midwest in the nineteenth century, and *Old South, New South* by Gavin Wright tells the story of the transformation of the southern economy since the 1930s. Wright's book does not deal specifically with urban areas in the south, but the connections between the region and its urban areas are pretty obvious. Both of these books are outstanding works of scholarship written for a pretty wide general audience, and I strongly recommend that you read them. If you are assigned to do a book report or book review in one of your courses, these would make good choices.

William Cronon's book (1991) is a chronicle of the intimate connections between the growth and development of Chicago and the rest of the midwest. The book contains rich descriptions of the lumber industry of the midwest, the development of the grain trade and futures markets, the meatpacking industry, the coming of the railroad, and much more. As such, it provides the historical background needed to understand the evolution of Chicago's economic functions in the larger economy. This brief discussion cannot do this great book justice—only basic themes and a few examples can be covered here.

Chicago essentially did not exist before the state of Illinois announced in 1833 that it was going to build a canal that would connect the Chicago River to the Illinois River about 20 miles to the southwest. Why was this important? First, it represented the most convenient connection between the waterway systems of the Great Lakes and the Mississippi River. The Chicago River is a very short river that flows into

Lake Michigan, and the Illinois River is a long, wide, and fairly deep river that flows southwest to the Mississippi. Second, the Erie Canal had opened in 1825. This human-made waterway permitted freight to move from New York City to the Great Lakes system and hence to Chicago. The connection at Chicago would permit freight to move between New York and the great midwestern hinterland, which was largely vacant in 1833. The announcement of the construction of the Illinois and Michigan Canal created a boom in land values in the muddy place called Chicago the likes of which has not been seen since. Chicago suddenly had become the chief transshipment point for much of the continent. Because of the economic turbulence of the late 1830s and early 1840s, the canal itself was not completed until 1848. The state of Illinois in fact defaulted on its original canal bonds. Nevertheless, the city of Chicago had been created.

Chicago got its start shipping agricultural products that could be transported from the nearby farms even without the canal in place. But the place really took off when the canal opened in 1848 and when the construction of the railway network centered on Chicago was begun at roughly the same time. Agricultural products could be shipped in from a wider hinterland, and various products needed by farmers could be supplied from Chicago. One of those products needed by the farmers of the midwest was lumber. The original lumber industry of the midwest harvested wood in northern Wisconsin and Michigan, shipped the rough lumber to Chicago by water, produced the more finished lumber in Chicago, and then shipped the lumber to its final users by rail and water. The owners of the lumber firms often hired their lumberjacks and other workers for the season in Chicago. Lumber was cut down in the winter so that it could slide on snow to nearby rivers. In the spring the logs moved down river to the sawmills, and then the ships transported the sawn lumber to Chicago. Chicago was the Mecca for the lumber firms because its market for lumber was so large that the lumber buyer in Chicago could purchase an entire shipload of lumber for cash right at the dock on the Chicago River. The buyer then moved the lumber a short distance up the Chicago River to the lumber district, where the lumber wholesalers maintained their inventories. The lumber district was served both by rail and water transportation. So this is another example of how Chicago was "nature's metropolis," a metropolis created by the natural resources of the great midwestern region.

Another instructive story, already mentioned in Chapter 5, is the saga of cattle, hogs, and meatpacking. The business of packing meat began in Chicago in its earliest years, but the business really boomed during the Civil War. In 1865 the various stockyards and meatpackers in Chicago decided to create the Union Stockyards, a stockyards large enough to serve the entire industry. Prior to 1865 the stockyards and meat packing plants were scattered throughout the city. One might add that cattle and hogs (alive or dead) do not make very good neighbors. This facility was located at the southwestern edge of the city, where good access to both rail and transportation was provided. The meatpacking plants soon followed to this location. Then, in the early 1870s, the hunters cleared most of the western plains of the bison. This hunting, which was unrivaled in its savagery, permitted the cattle ranchers to take over large expanses of territory from Texas to Montana. The construction of railroads connected these far-flung places to the market for livestock in Chicago. We are all familiar with the fabled cattle drives from Texas to places in Kansas such as Abilene and Dodge City. Perhaps we tend to forget that from there the cattle were transported to Chicago by rail, or they were fattened up on corn on farms in Iowa or Illinois and then shipped to Chicago. Here we have it again. An entire complex of industries was created in Chicago by the natural resources of the midwest.

One final example tells the other side of the story. Chicago, with its excellent transportation connections to a wide area, was a natural site for manufacturers and wholesalers who catered to the farmers and the residents of the smaller towns. All of this was not lost on Cyrus McCormick, who invented the mechanical reaper in the 1830s and opened a factory in Chicago in the 1840s. Another entrepreneur of great renown was Montgomery Ward, who figured out that a mail-order business could eliminate the middle man and make money. His business was greatly enhanced by the introduction of rural free delivery by the U.S. Post Office. A couple of guys named Sears and Roebuck soon followed. All three companies still have their headquarters in the Chicago area.

Cronon's book (1991) demonstrates that Chicago was, to some degree, a special case of a special place. However, perhaps the more important point is that Cronon's methods of historical and economic scholarship can be applied to many other urban areas around the nation (and world, for that matter). Indeed, Cronon stopped his story in 1893. Chicago's story in the twentieth century is awaiting another Cronon.

Now let us move forward in time and look to the south. The south is the region of the nation that has attracted the greatest attention of the economic historians. The reason is obvious; as a region the economy of the south was, until quite recently, very different from the rest of the nation. It is to the south that we must look for the best regional economic history. The best of the best is a book by Gavin Wright (1986) entitled *Old South, New South*.

The relevant part of Wright's analysis is his account of how and why the south was transformed from an economic backwater in 1930 to an integral part of the economy of the nation in 1980. Wright's analysis is that the economy of the south in 1930 was based on a low-wage labor market and an associated cultural isolation. Political power was used to maintain an economy based on low-wage labor. The abolition of slavery had not eliminated the historical legacy of separateness, which continued until modern times. However, because the south lost the Civil War and could not set up its own national government, during the twentieth century it increasingly came under the political jurisdiction of the larger nation. It was subject to the laws and policies of the New Deal of the 1930s as well as the market forces and technologies of the nation. In Wright's view, the critical economic event was the imposition of national wage and labor standards beginning in the 1930s. These actions eventually eliminated the stake that southern property owners had in keeping a separate labor market. Decisions were made to invite in flows of capital and labor, and the distinct "southern economy" has largely disappeared.

Once change was under way, several factors as summarized by Wright (1986, pp. 239–240) contributed to southern economic development:

1. Market incentives brought capital and skilled and educated labor to the south, particularly to its urban areas.
2. Federal spending (defense spending in particular) that the south once shunned was now sought.

3. Favorable climate and other amenities worked in the south's favor (especially after the invention of air conditioning).

4. The south invented state and local economic development policies such as industrial revenue bonds, long-term tax exemptions, and active local economic development corporations.

5. The south had a relatively clean slate in terms of absence of labor unions, entrenched bureaucracies, and restrictive legislation—a good "business climate."

6. A shift was made from relatively high to relatively low taxes on business.

Does Wright the economic historian provide a formula for policy for other places at other times? Perhaps some of these elements are relevant, but we must remember the context in which these policies were adopted and generated successful outcomes.

Another facet of the work of economic historians is the explanation of economic growth in part using the notion of strategic industries. A strategic industry is one whose growth induces growth of a complex of industries and thus creates a substantially new economy. Growth is thought of as being induced by backward linkages to suppliers and forward linkages to customers. These industries generate rapid changes in technology in complex combinations and sequences. The standard example from economic history is the English cotton textile industry of the late eighteenth century, as described in rich detail by Landes (1969). Other examples abound in the literature; railroads and machine tools in the United States in the nineteenth century and chemicals in nineteenth-century Germany are good examples. Examples in urban areas in the United States include autos in Detroit, steel in Pittsburgh, financial services in New York, microelectronics in Silicon Valley in northern California, and risk management financial services in Chicago.

The issues regarding strategic industries for those concerned with the growth of particular urban areas are:

1. Can strategic industries be identified?
2. Are there any local policies that can foster the growth of strategic industries?

It would seem that both of these questions can be answered in the affirmative, at least at a broad level. Economic analysis of an urban economy should be able to identify the key export sectors and to determine if any of these sectors also induces growth in other sectors through market or technological linkages. Once these sectors are identified, it should be possible to determine if there are public policies that inhibit growth or if such sectors have special needs for public services, infrastructure, particular labor skills, and other important inputs. At the very least, it should be possible to devise public policies that do not stand in the way of progress. For example, Ferguson and Ladd (1988) have argued that this was the essential contribution of state policy to the "Massachusetts miracle" of the 1980s. However, it is fair to say that not much research has been done that validates the cost-effectiveness for urban areas or states of targeting programs to strategic industries. Also, there is little evidence that local governments are really very capable of identifying an emerging strategic industry. It may be easy to identify an industry that *once was* a strategic industry. The problem is to identify industries with appreciable potential for further growth and then to foster that growth. There really is little evidence at this time to suggest that local governments can pursue such a course successfully. Indeed, the *na-*

tional debate over industrial policy seems to have subsided with the general conclusion that the public sector is probably not very effective at targeting industries as strategic industries.

This guarded conclusion regarding local public policy does not, however, suggest that researchers should abandon work that uncovers the historic roots of a local economy. Also, methods for improving the studies that are done of the local economy should be pursued. Some of these methods are discussed below.

J. THE PRODUCT CYCLE AND URBAN GROWTH

Another important perspective on urban and regional growth has been derived from the field of economic history. Currently, it is known as the product cycle model, or long-wave model, or product-profit cycle. Its adherents include scholars such as Norton and Rees (1979), Markusen (1985), Markusen, Hall, and Glasmeier (1986), and Booth (1986). Norton and Rees (1979) provided an early description of the regional shift in manufacturing in the United States during 1966–1977. Booth (1986) has provided a succinct statement of the model, and this section follows his presentation.

Historical studies have established the existence of industrial life cycles. New industries experience a period of rapid growth after an initial phase of incubation, and as a consequence of competition from still newer industries, they eventually face a retardation of growth or absolute decline. The existence of industrial life cycles may be related to Schumpeter's (1942) concept of competition involving a constant struggle in the marketplace between entrepreneurs to gain a monopoly position in a new commodity, a new technology, a new source of supply, or a new type of organization. Any competitive edge gained in this struggle is ultimately eliminated by competition from even newer innovations in the market. The private-enterprise economy thus involves a constantly changing mix of products, technologies, sources of supply, and forms of business organization. New industries emerge periodically to replace older industries as growth leaders in the economy. For awhile these industries may be the strategic industries that were discussed above. The early stages of the industrial life cycle exhibit rapid technical change, requiring flexible, labor-intensive production processes. The later stages involve a stabilizing of technology, saturation of product markets, and increasing concern with cutting unit production costs through the attainment of scale economies.

There may be a connection between industrial life cycles and urban growth and decline. The growth of an urban area or a region is stimulated by the presence of industries in the rapid-growth phase of their life cycles and retarded by the presence of industries in the slow growth or decline phase. Indeed, firms that are intent on cutting production costs may relocate from large urban areas with high costs of labor and real estate. An urban area with an appropriate mix of growing and stable industries will not experience a period of decline in its growth rate, but the scholars mentioned above believe that urban areas with aging industries suffer through relatively lengthy periods of time without developing substantial amounts of economic activity in new, growth industries. If this is true, there must be barriers to the formation of new industries in urban areas with a mature industrial base.

Generally, it is true that new industries are formed by new businesses. Only rarely do existing large firms in already established industries become the driving force for the creation of entirely new industries. Consequently, Booth (1986) states that the central issue is whether there are impediments to new business formation in older urban areas with mature industries. One factor is that firms in mature industries focus on management rather than entrepreneurship because their central problem is achieving scale economies and cutting costs. Such firms train managers, not entrepreneurs who would be capable of starting new firms in the area. Such firms provide (seemingly) secure, well-paying jobs for capable people, so the push to become an entrepreneur may be absent. Also, the presence of large mature firms in an urban area could place a limit on the availability of venture capital for new businesses. Mature enterprises provide stable and secure returns on investment compared to startup companies.

However, once employment opportunities begin to decline in mature industries in an urban area, the prospects for the formation of new businesses begin to change. Managerial opportunities in mature firms begin to disappear, and those with business skills who do not migrate to other regions will start to turn to the formation of new businesses. Also, capital and labor will be attracted to new firms as opportunities in the mature sectors decline. But the adherents to the product-cycle model suggest that the fundamental problem is that a lengthy period is often required before new businesses that manage to survive grow to the point where they become major employers. In the meantime, an older urban area with mature industries in a state of decline will experience slow economic growth and social problems associated with inadequate employment opportunities. Eventually, new industries will emerge and the growth rate will recover, but the time lapse between the growth phase of one wave and another could be lengthy.

An auxiliary part of the story is that large, mature firms do not engage in the development of new products and technologies at the rate required to keep the urban area growing evenly. Booth (1986) hypothesizes that the bureaucratic form of management in large firms is partly designed to inhibit product and process innovation because there is a strong desire to control the activities of the employees. Whether this is true, empirical evidence summarized by Scherer (1980) suggests that very large corporations are only infrequently the source of major new innovations. Although there are exceptions, large firms have not felt a strong pressure to innovate until their traditional business activity is seriously threatened, and the time lapse between feeling this pressure and developing major new sources of economic activity will be lengthy.

The product-cycle story is certainly plausible, and daily reports in the newspapers seem to validate the idea that large firms have difficulty being truly innovative. However, there are problems with the model at this point:

1. The empirical evidence in support of the model is weak and subject to alternative interpretation.
2. The model provides very limited policy prescriptions for lagging urban areas (besides the suggestion to "wait").

The empirical evidence in support of the model begins with the observations that much of the growth in newer science-based industries has been in southern and western urban areas and that the New England area seemed to have entered a new long wave in the late 1970s and 1980s. However, these developments might also be explained by the presence of specific human and nonhuman capital, factor costs, emerging agglomeration economies, and federal government procurement policies. In my opinion, more sharply focused empirical tests are needed.

Booth (1986) conducted an empirical study of new incorporations by state from 1950 to 1982 and found that incorporations per thousand population were higher in the eastern segment of the old industrial belt (Massachusetts, Rhode Island, Connecticut, New York, New Jersey, and Pennsylvania) than in the rest of the nation in general and in the western segment of the old industrial belt in particular. Booth (1986) also found that incorporations were positively related to lagged population growth in the state. Other factors that were examined but were not significant are the state's tax effort, unionization of the workforce, the unemployment rate, and defense procurement expenditures per capita. Booth (1986) interprets his basic result as supporting the long-wave hypothesis because the rate of incorporations was highest in the oldest industrial region of the nation, controlling for population growth. The problem with this interpretation is that a significant coefficient on a dummy variable indicating a region in a regression model does not indicate very well the underlying cause of the result. The result is certainly suggestive, and further research needs to be done to determine the underlying reasons for the pattern observed. We know that incorporations were higher in the oldest part of the industrial belt, but we really do not know why.

Markusen (1985) has modified the product-cycle model to consider profits (as well as output and employment) and oligopoly as key elements in the historical development of an industry. Markusen's version of the model is called the profit-cycle model. The profit-cycle model has five characteristic stages:

1. Zero profit, corresponding to the initial birth and design stage of the industry.
2. Super profit, corresponding to the era of excess profit from an innovative edge.
3. Normal profit, corresponding to the stage of open entry and movement toward market saturation.
4. Normal plus or normal minus profit, corresponding to the postsaturation stage in which the industry becomes an oligopoly or excessively competitive.
5. Negative profit, corresponding to the obsolescence stage.

The industry is spatially concentrated in the first two stages and begins to disperse in the third stage. The presence of oligopoly will retard dispersal in the fourth stage and may accelerate dispersal and disinvestment in the fifth stage.

Markusen (1985) conducted 18 case studies of U.S. industries over the period 1947 to 1977 to test the profit-cycle model. These case studies are of six producer goods industries, six consumer goods industries, and six resource-based industries. Markusen claims that the case studies lend strong support to the model. In the producer goods industries, the rapidly innovating industries of computers and semiconductors displayed increasing employment shares in the top states, while the more mature industries (two textile industries, steel and aluminum) dispersed continuously. Oligopoly played a role in the steel and aluminum industries—production remained more spatially concentrated than would have been the case under competitive conditions.

The consumer goods sectors examined are pharmaceuticals, women's clothing (suits and dresses), auto assembly and parts, brewing, and shoes. All of these sectors show the expected geographical agglomeration and dispersion tendencies. In two mature sectors (apparel and shoes), oligopoly never appeared (according to Markusen) and dispersal occurred soon after innovation subsided. Oligopolies, and organized labor in autos, in the other sectors slowed dispersal. Because their location patterns are more constrained by resource supplies, the resource-oriented sectors display a more varied pattern with respect to the profit-cycle model, as one might expect.

The profit-cycle model is a useful method for organizing information about industries, and it can be quite useful to know the stage of the cycle for a particular industry at a particular time. However, there are two fundamental difficulties with the profit-cycle model. First, it is not really a theory. It is a tautological method for organizing information about industries. New industries are born somewhere and then disperse once the basic innovations have been made. They either become oligopolies or they do not. Eventually, products developed by someone else displace some (or all) of the demand for the original products. All of this is true essentially by definition. The model seems to make only one testable hypothesis that can be refuted; oligopoly slows down the dispersal of the industry in stage 3. Otherwise, the model cannot really be subjected to empirical testing that can lead to its rejection. Recall the discussion in Chapter 2 of Baran and Sweezy's *Monopoly Capital* (1966). Their basic method was to label a large part of the output of the economy "economic surplus." They can give a label to anything they wish — that does not make a testable hypothesis. This point has been recognized by others; Seninger (1985) has developed a more sophisticated theoretical treatment of the product cycle model that does generate refutable hypotheses (but does no empirical testing). Second, the profit-cycle model has no policy implications at the urban or regional level. Evidently, the important thing for an urban area is to be the site of major product innovation, but the model is silent on how products are born. Others are silent on this point as well, but the profit-cycle model has no alternative policy handle.

Markusen, Hall, and Glasmeier (1986) continued research using the profit-cycle framework in an examination of high-technology manufacturing industries. High-tech industry was defined as 100 as industries with relatively high concentrations of technical personnel such as engineers, computer scientists, scientists, and mathematicians. Markusen et al. used the stages of the profit-cycle framework to organize descriptive data on the high-tech industries. They charted employment change, market power, and geographic concentration and dispersal.

Next they conducted statistical tests based on standard location theory hypotheses. Regression analyses were performed on metropolitan area high-tech employment in 1977 and employment change from 1972 to 1977. A summary of these results is shown in Table 11.3. High-tech employment in 1977 was positively affected by favorable climate, more educational options, freeway density, availability of business services, and defense spending. High housing prices had a negative effect. The results for employment change are similar. What is interesting about these results is the insignificance of some traditional location factors, such as the average wage rate in manufacturing and unionization. Also, university research and development in the metropolitan area had no impact. Thus it is probable that high-tech industries are influenced by a different set of location factors than are other manufacturing industries.

TABLE 11.3	Factors Associated with Urban Area High-Tech Jobs[a]	
	Jobs in 1977	*Job Change, 1972–1977*
Labor		
Wage rate (manufacturing)		
Unionization rate		
Unemployment rate		
Amenities		
Climate	+	+
Housing price	−	
Education options	+	+
Access		
Freeway density	+	
Airway access		
Agglomeration		
Fortune 500 headquarters		
Business services	+	+
University R&D		
Sociopolitical		
Defense spending	+	+
Percent black population		−
R^2	0.52	0.45

[a] $+ (-)$ *indicates variable is statistically significant at the 95% level.*

Source: Table compiled from data obtained from Markusen, Hall, and Glasmeier (1986).

The importance of highly trained and educated workers to these industries suggests as much. The regression study by Markusen et al. (1986) is a useful attempt at specifying these determinants of location patterns. It is also revealing for the product/profit-cycle framework that one of its leading adherents (Markusen) turned to a more mainstream economics model of location to gain a clearer picture of high-tech location patterns.

K. CUMULATIVE CAUSATION MODELS

In numerous publications since the late 1960s, the distinguished regional economist Harry Richardson has written that the main rival to the neoclassical model is the class of models known as *cumulative causation models*. In this section we present Richardson's view in one of its most recent forms [Richardson (1985)]. Richardson (1985, p. 10) asserts that the main difference between naive versions of the neoclassical model and the cumulative causation model is that the latter allows for increasing returns to scale. As a result of increasing returns to scale, both capital and labor can flow in the same direction rather than in opposite directions. Growth-rate differentials may persist over time and may even widen. One neoclassical reaction to this contention is that a neoclassical model does not have to become very complicated to permit increasing returns to scale.

The first statement of a cumulative causation model was by Myrdal (1957), who argued that a few leading regions or urban areas in underdeveloped countries will exploit initial advantages. The growth will be self-sustaining if, for example, there are scale economies to be exploited in the leading regions. Linkages between growing areas and lagging areas will be both favorable (spread effects) and unfavorable (backwash effects), but the latter will tend to dominate.

A simple version of the model can be based on the idea that the growth rate of labor productivity T is a function of the growth in output Y^*, or

$$T = e + fY^*,$$

where f is a positive coefficient. Efficiency wages (money wages deflated by an index of productivity) will therefore be inversely related to the growth of labor productivity, or

$$W^* = g - hT.$$

Lower growth in efficiency wages leads to greater output growth, as in

$$Y^* = m - pW^*.$$

Substitution of the first two equations into the third, with the addition of a time index, yields

$$Y^*_{t+1} = m + p(eh - g) + fhpY^*_t.$$

One condition for cumulative growth is that $fhp > 1$, in which case a higher growth rate in period t leads to an even higher growth rate in period $t + 1$. This particular hypothesis has not been tested for regions, states, or urban areas of the United States.

The concept of cumulative causation has been used by Pred (1966) in a historical study of the growth of urban areas in the United States from 1800 to 1914. Pred (1966) argued that some urban areas had initial advantages of location that were already evident in the early nineteenth century and that those initial conditions produced a cumulative growth process in places such as New York, Chicago, and Philadelphia. Pred's hypothesis begins with an invention or innovation that creates a new product. The entrepreneurs associated with the new product will choose as a site for new production activity the city or cities that already have the initial advantage in such things as transportation facilities, access to resources, and availability of business services and labor force. This new industry will generate demands for more of all of these things and may therefore create additional opportunities to take advantage of localization and urbanization economies. Furthermore, the growth of the new industry may lead to additional innovations in that industry or in other industries to which it is related. Pred (1966) studied the location patterns of inventions and innovations in manufacturing during the period 1860–1900. He found that (1966, p. 111) "patents were disproportionately concentrated in the swiftly enmerging metropolises."

Another scholar who finds the cumulative causation approach appealing is Paul Krugman (1991), although he finds the idea most applicable to an individual industry in an urban area. An initial advantage in the industry can be turned into cumulative growth by labor force, intermediate input, or technological spillovers. Empirical tests of these ideas are reviewed in Chapter 12.

A good example of this cumulative growth process began with Cyrus Mc-Cormick's invention of the mechanical reaper, a machine that harvested wheat. McCormick actually invented his first reaper in Virginia and gave its first successful demonstration in 1831. He started his enterprise in Virginia and continued to make improvements in the machine and, in 1845, moved the company to Cincinnati, Ohio to be closer to the growing agricultural areas of the midwest. However, by 1847 it was clear that Chicago would become the economic center of the great midwestern agricultural region, and McCormick moved the McCormick Reaper Works to Chicago in that year. Thus began the long and continuing association of Chicago and the agricultural machinery industry. The McCormick Reaper Works became International Harvester (and recently, Navistar), a company that developed a huge array of farm and construction machinery products.

It is not clear that the simple model of cumulative causation discussed above is very useful for the study of entire modern urban areas or regions in the United States (as opposed to individual industries within an urban area). Indeed, Borts and Stein (1964) would say that the idea that Myrdal's model could be applied to the regions of the United States should have died out when they published their book in 1964. The next chapter focuses on a detailed presentation of static and dynamic agglomeration economics couched in the neoclassical growth framework. This augmented neoclassical growth model clearly includes the possibility of growth at the industry level in an urban area that is cumulative. The empirical evidence pertaining to this possibility is discussed in detail.

A model of cumulative causation has been tested and found to be quite useful in another urban context by Bradford and Kelejian (1973). They tested the hypothesis that economic decline of a central city can be a cumulative process. They found that middle-class families were more likely to live in the suburbs if the central city had a higher proportion of poor people residing there 10 years ago and if the fiscal situation in the central city was less favorable for the middle class (i.e., higher taxes and the lower quality of public services). The flight of some of the middle class from central cities causes both of these variables to move in favor of causing more middle-class families to move to the suburbs. I view this scenario as the central city mayor's nightmare. My simple characterization of the mayor of an older central city is that he or she wakes up in the morning and says, "What can we do today to prevent or reverse cumulative decline?"

L. DISEQUILIBRIUM DYNAMICS

One of the most sustained and technical attacks on neoclassical theory in recent years is the work of the economic geographer Gordon Clark and his associates. They have compiled their views and empirical findings in Clark, Gertler, and Whiteman (1986). Their basic point is simple enough: Urban or regional economies (or any other economic unit, for that matter) evolve historically, and a theory of disequilibrium dynamics is needed to understand that history. One can agree with both the latter and the former propositions, or just with the former. It may be that neoclassical theory of equilibrium is sufficient to comprehend the process of urban growth well enough for one's purposes. Instead, Clark et al. (1986, p. 2) state: "Our goal is to show that the actual means and institutions of economic adjustment, the strategies and decisions concerning economic fluctuation and change are very important in determining the long-run fortunes of different regions."

To pursue this goal, they first present a characterization of the economic landscape that emphasizes how uncertainty is channeled and distributed, and they suggest how industries and firms secure and manage a labor supply in the face of economic fluctuations and uncertainties. Finally, they use these devices to show the implications on location for patterns of change and fluctuation in regional employment. One point of this exercise is to show that employment patterns in a region can be understood within the context of the "wider form of economic organization" (1986, p. 20).

What is their characterization of the economic landscape? What is the "wider form of economic organization"? Do they have empirical tests that confirm the explanatory power of their approach?

The nature of the contemporary economic landscape in the United States is described at some length, but their characterization is familiar to you, a person who presumably has read Chapter 2 of this book. Corporations have the power to construct locational hierarchies that place the various types of production activities at different places. This creates a spatial division of labor with several characteristics:

1. Variable demands are allocated to a periphery of small firms.
2. There is a separation of technical, control, and management functions.
3. An increasing specialization and division of labor is implemented.
4. A "dual" labor market emerges with a spatial component added. (In simple terms, a dual labor market is one in which there are "good" jobs and "bad" jobs. Access to the good jobs is restricted, in this case by spatial separation.)

They state that (1986, p. 23) "Corporations construct locational hierarchies which are aimed at achieving a particular distribution of economic uncertainty between labor and capital. In this way, spatial inequalities become a normal working order of the economy and no longer a sign of its failure or demise." This is a spatial version of a combination of John Kenneth Galbraith's *The New Industrial State* (1967) and contemporary Western Marxist economics (which includes the notion of a dual labor market). I gather that these authors are Marxists because they rarely, if ever, refer to the liberal Democrat Galbraith.

Clark et al. emphasize that this spatial division of labor characterizes only certain sectors, such as electronics, plastics, and many high-tech industries. But these sectors are important because they constitute the most recent round of capital investment and employment growth in manufacturing. In the book they present a wide variety of empirical investigations related to various versions of their dynamic adjustment framework. They show adjustment patterns in metropolitan labor markets and labor contracts, wages and prices, labor migration, and capital growth. Their empirical work is discussed in Chapter 13, which focuses on urban input growth and dynamic adjustments in inputs.

M. SUMMARY

In this chapter we have introduced three basic models of economic growth that can be applied to urban areas. The first is a simple Keynesian multiplier model with exports and imports, which is also called the economic base model. This model is really a model of short-run impacts of changes in exports (and other changes), and it is not really a model of long-run growth. However, its emphasis on exports and imports is on target. Other more complex models presented in this book also emphasize exports and imports.

The second model discussed in this chapter is the one-sector neoclassical growth model developed by Robert Solow. This model ignores exports and imports; instead, it concentrates on the growth of inputs and technical change. This model has been applied extensively to the analysis of economic growth at the national level. However, a complete explanation for the national slowdown in the growth of labor productivity since 1973 remains elusive. The one-sector model has also been applied to the economic growth of states and urban areas. However, those applications have not yielded results that are fully satisfactory.

The failure of the one-sector neoclassical growth model to explain some important empirical findings for states led Borts and Stein (1964) to develop a two-sector neoclassical growth model. In this model the local economy produces a good for export and another good only for local consumption. The export good faces a perfectly elastic demand curve, and capital can be imported freely at the national price. Under these circumstances the growth of the local economy is determined by the growth rate of the labor force, increases in the demand for exports, and by technical change. An increase in the demand for exports means that the price of exports rises. An increase in the price of the export good will increase the wage in the local economy.

The Keynesian and two-sector neoclassical growth models can be combined into a more general mainstream economic model that acknowledges the importance of both the demand and supply sides. An even more general synthesis of models is discussed at the end of Chapter 12.

In addition, in this chapter we surveyed several other approaches to urban economic growth. The mechanics of input–output analysis have been presented to clarify our thinking about the structure of a local economy and to emphasize the intermediate inputs as well as value added. The eclectic works of urban and regional economic history have been discussed briefly to point out the importance of historical factors in the development of an area. Urban areas in the south had very different histories compared to urban areas in the northeast or midwest. This distinction used to matter a great deal. Does it still matter for purposes of understanding the local economy? One should not rule out the importance of history.

Three additional frameworks were discussed: the product cycle framework, cumulative causation models, and disequilibrium dynamics. In my opinion, these approaches to understanding urban growth have yet to demonstrate that they offer a serious challenge to mainstream economic models. Scholars are continuing to use these frameworks. At this point they are in the stages of formulating more formal economic models and conducting empirical investigations. It might be useful for you to reread Section A of Chapter 1 on research progress in applied fields in economics.

Up until now we have not taken a systematic look at the autonomous growth factor, what Solow called technological change. This is our task in Chapter 12.

It is useful to present more formally the Borts–Stein model of state economic growth because it can be adapted to contemporary urban areas. The keys to the model are the equations for the growth of wage payments and payments to capital. These equations can be used to study, for example, the effects of a change in export prices, which leads to a movement of capital between states. It is assumed that the economy of the state produces two goods: X, a capital-intensive export good, and Y, a labor-intensive domestic good (consumed within the state). Capital K and labor L are freely mobile between the two industries. The economy consumes three goods, X, Y and M, an imported good that is not produced in the state. C_x denotes domestic consumption of X. The relevant prices are P_x, P_y, P_m, W (wage), P_k (purchase price of a unit of capital), and r (rate of return for capital). It is assumed that the labor force is growing at a fixed percentage rate L^*. The asterisk denotes the rate of growth for the variable in question. The price of X is fixed in the national market, as are the import prices of M and K and the rate of return of capital. The wage rate and the price of Y are determined inside the model.

The production functions for X and Y are assumed to be Cobb–Douglas with constant returns to scale. Export production is assumed to be capital intensive relative to domestic goods production. The two production functions can be written

$$X = A K_x^\alpha L_x^{1-\alpha}$$

and

$$Y = B K_y^\beta L_y^{1-\beta}.$$

The assumption about capital intensity in the two industries means that α is greater than β. The wages in these two sectors equal their respective values of the marginal products of labor, or

$$W_x = P_x \left[(1-\alpha) A \left(\frac{K}{L} \right)_x^\alpha \right]$$

and

$$W_y = P_y \left[(1-\beta) B \left(\frac{K}{L} \right)_y^\beta \right].$$

Wages in the two sectors are equal, or $W_x = W_y = W$.

Full employment of capital and labor in the state means that

$$L_x + L_y = L$$

and

$$K_x + K_y = K.$$

The return on capital in both sectors must equal the borrowing rate set in the national market, or

$$rP_K = P_x \text{ (marginal product of } K \text{ in } X)$$

$$P_y \text{ (marginal product of } K \text{ in } Y).$$

The total product of a state equals the value of the final goods and services produced:

$$Z = XP_x + YP_y.$$

The expenditure of the total product is divided between savings and the consumption of the three types of goods in given proportions. Assuming no income payments to foreign owners of capital,

$$Z = S + C_x + MP_m + YP_y,$$

$$C_x P_x = cZ,$$

$$YP_y = eZ,$$

and

$$S = sZ,$$

where S is saving. The other terms have already been defined. Note that $MP_m = (1 - c - e - s)Z$.

The growth rate of labor is assumed to be exogenous, or

$$\frac{\delta L/\delta t}{L} = L^*,$$

where t is time. The growth rate of capital is defined as the ratio of investment to the capital stock, or

$$\frac{\delta K/\delta t}{K} = K^* = \frac{I}{K},$$

where I is net investment. The proportion of the labor force employed in the export sector is defined as L_x/L.

Total income Z is the sum of the wage bill WL and the payments to capital $rP_k K$, or

$$Z = WL + rP_k K,$$

where

$$WL = W(L_x + L_y)$$

and

$$rP_k K = rP_k(K_x + K_y).$$

Borts and Stein showed that in the absence of technical change and exogenous disturbances such as a change in the price of exports, the state's economy will grow in a balanced fashion determined by the rate of growth of labor, L^*. In this case $L^* = K^* = I^* = S^* = Z^*$. To see this result, recall that the price of exports (P_x) is fixed, as are the prices of capital and imports. The state can freely import capital to match the growth in its labor force. The state will expand its export production along a perfectly elastic demand curve. Because of this, the wage rate will remain constant because it will be determined by the wage in the export sector. The additional workers in the export sector will call forth production of the domestic good Y, and factor prices are constant in this industry as well. Output proportions remain constant as the state's economy grows. The growth in the labor force thus calls for an equal growth rate for capital (and investment and saving) and total output. In short, in this economy with capital freely imported at a constant price and with perfectly elastic export demand, the growth rate is set by the growth rate of the other input, labor.

The critical results pertain to the impacts of a change in the price of the export product, P_x. An increase in P_x represents an increase in the demand for exports, so this is where the idea of the *neoclassical export base model* originates. The fundamental result of the model is that

$$W^* = \frac{P^*_x}{1 - \alpha}.$$

This equation says that the growth rate of the wage rate equals the growth rate of the price of the export product divided by $1 - \alpha$, which is the share of income going to labor in the export sector.

To see this result, we need to solve the model for the equation that relates W^* to P^*_x. Return to the production function for X and solve for the marginal product of K_x, or

$$\frac{\delta X}{\delta K_x} = \alpha A K_x^{\alpha - 1} L_x^{1 - \alpha} = \frac{\alpha X}{K_x}.$$

Now set the value of the marginal product of capital equal to its price, as in

$$P_x \frac{\alpha X}{K_x} = rP_k,$$

and solve for K_x, so that

$$K_x = \alpha X \frac{P_x}{rP_k}.$$

The demand for capital is thus a function of the quantity of output, the price of output, and the price of capital. Similarly, find the marginal product of labor in X, set the value of the marginal product of labor equal to the wage, and solve for L_x as follows:

$$\frac{\delta X}{\delta L_x} = (1 - \alpha)A K_x^{\alpha} L_x^{-\alpha} = \frac{(1 - \alpha)X}{L_x},$$

$$P_x \frac{(1 - \alpha)X}{L_x} = W,$$

and

$$L_x = (1 - \alpha)X\frac{P_x}{W}.$$

The demand for labor is thus a function of the output level, the price of output, and the wage rate.

Now substitute these equations for K_x and L_x into the production function, or

$$X = A(\alpha X \frac{P_x}{rP_k})^\alpha [(1-\alpha)X \frac{P_x}{W}]^{1-\alpha}.$$

Note that X on the right-hand side of the equation has exponents α and $1-\alpha$, so X appears on both sides of the equation and cancels out. We wish to solve the equation for W. After some manipulation, we have

$$W^{1-\alpha} = A\alpha^\alpha (1-\alpha)^{1-\alpha} P_x (rP_k)^{-\alpha}.$$

Let E stand for the collection of constant terms:

$$E = A\alpha^\alpha (1-\alpha)^{1-\alpha}.$$

Therefore, the final equation for W is

$$W = [EP_x (rP_k)^{-\alpha}]^{1/1-\alpha}.$$

This equation can be solved for P_x, and the result is that

$$P_x = \frac{1}{E}(rP_k)^\alpha W^{1-\alpha}.$$

This equation says that the supply price (i.e., marginal cost) of the good is a Cobb–Douglas function of the input prices. In short, a Cobb–Douglas production function generates a Cobb–Douglas function for supply price. However, we must remember that in the Borts–Stein model, P_x is an exogenous variable that helps to determine W (and not the other way around).

The computation of the derivative of W with respect to P_x is a bit messy, but straightforward using the chain rule. Define the terms inside the brackets as J, so $W = J^{1/1-\alpha}$. Therefore,

$$\frac{dW}{dP_x} = \frac{dW}{dJ}\left(\frac{dJ}{dP_x}\right)$$

$$= \left(\frac{1}{1-\alpha}\right)\frac{J^{\alpha/1-\alpha}J}{P_x} = \frac{(1/1-\alpha)W}{P_x}.$$

Conversion to elasticity form gives us the percentage change in the wage resulting for a 1% change in P_x, or

$$\frac{dW}{dP_x}\left(\frac{P_x}{W}\right) = \frac{1}{1-\alpha}.$$

This is the result we sought. It says that a 1% increase in the price of the export good will increase the wage rate by the inverse of the share of labor. If the share of labor is 0.75, the increase in the wage rate will be 1.33%. Assuming that the labor market in the urban area is perfectly competitive, this increase in the wage rate will be transmitted to workers in the domestic good industry as well.

EXERCISES

1. You are the economist for the Department of Economic Development of Ruston, Pennsylvania. You know that employment in export industries is 25,000 and that total employment in the urban area is 60,000. You receive word that Volkswagen has decided to locate a plant in your community and that they plan to hire 3000 workers.

   (a) Can you use the information in the question to predict the effect of the increase in export employment on total employment in the urban area? How would you go about generating such a forecast?

   (b) Make a careful listing of the assumptions that you made in making your forecast so that you make clear the potential weaknesses in that forecast.

2. You have estimated a Keynesian model for Ruston as follows:

$$C = 100 + 0.9\,(1 - t)Y$$

$$T = tY = 0.3Y$$

$$M = 0.23\,(1 - t)Y$$

$$I = 150$$

$$G = 200$$

$$X = 300$$

Remember that imports (M) are part of total consumption spending (C) and that disposable income is $Y - tY$, where t is the tax rate.

   (a) Compute equilibrium income (Y) and taxes (T), imports (M), consumption (C), and saving.

   (b) What is the multiplier for Ruston?

   (c) What happens to Y, T, M, and C if exports increase by 100?

   (d) Return to the original value for exports. What happens if the propensity to consume out of disposable income falls from 0.9 to 0.8?

3. Suppose that the growth rate of gross urban product for an urban area is

$$y = 0.25k + 0.75l + t$$

$$k = \frac{s}{v} + j$$

$$l = n + m,$$

where y is the growth rate of GUP, k the growth rate of capital, l the growth rate of labor, t the rate of technical change, s the saving rate, v the capital/output ratio, j the rate of in-migration of capital, n the natural rate of growth of labor in urban area, m the rate of in-migration of labor.

   (a) Assume that $s = 0.1$, $v = 4$, $j = 0.05$, $n = 0.02$, $m = 0.03$, and $t = 0.03$. Calculate y.

   (b) Calculate the percentage of growth in y that can be attributed to
   1. Labor force growth

   a. Natural growth
   b. Migration
2. Capital growth
   a. Natural growth through local saving
   b. Migration of capital
3. Technical change.

4. Suppose that the aggregate production function for an urban area is

$$Y = Ae^{rt}L^{\alpha}K^{\beta},$$

where Y is the output, r the rate of technical change, t the time, L the labor input, K the capital input, and α and β are the elasticities of output with respect to labor and capital. Assume that $r = 0.02$, $\alpha = 0.75$, and $\beta = 0.25$.
   (a) Prove that α and β are the elasticities of output with respect to labor and capital.
   (b) Derive the basic growth equation in Section C for this model.
   (c) What is the rate of growth of this economy if labor grows at 1% per year and capital grows at 2% per year? What is the rate of growth of the wage rate under these conditions (assuming that labor is paid its marginal product)?

5. Consider Muth's famous "chicken or egg" model of urban growth. It is written that

$$\delta E = \alpha M$$

$$M = \beta(\delta E) + \theta,$$

where E is employment in the urban area, M is migration into the urban area, and θ is an exogenous amount of in-migration.
   (a) Why might migration increase when the change in employment (δE) increases?
   (b) Suppose that $\alpha = 0.5$ and $\beta = 0.4$. What is the change in employment (δE) when θ changes by 1?
   (c) For the model to be "stable," it must be true that $\alpha\beta$ is less than 1.0. Why? What is meant by stability here?

6. Assume the following input–output table for a local economy:

	Purchasing Industry		Final Demand	Gross Output
	A	B		
Producing A	10	50	40	100
Industry B	30	10	30	70
Value added	60	10		
Total inputs	100	70	70	170

Assume that value added is entirely attirbutable to local labor and capital inputs.
   (a) What are the direct input (technical) coefficients?
   (b) What is gross output, and how are the figures obtained?

(c) Write the model in equation form as shown in Section H.

(d) Assume that final demand is now $A = 50$ and $B = 30$. Recalculate the entire table. What is the multiplier implied by these results?

(e) You will note that final demand does not include separate entries for exports outside the urban area. Does this urban area export anything? How do you know?

7. Return to the local economy depicted in Table 11.1. Suppose that exports double (manufactures increase to 40 and services increase to 20).

   (a) Recalculate the entire table.

   (b) Does the size of the local economy double?

8. Find out if there are any books on the economic history of the urban area of your choice. Most of the older, large urban areas have rather extensive bibliographies. Select one of these books. Does the author of this book use a conceptual framework that resembles one of those covered in Chapter 11? If so, what is it? Is some other conceptual framework used? If so, what is it? If there is no conceptual framework used, which one would you suggest? Why?

REFERENCES

Baran, Paul and Paul Sweezy, 1966. *Monopoly Capital*. New York: Monthly Review Press.

Booth, Douglas, 1986. "Long Waves and Uneven Regional Growth," *Southern Economic Journal*, Vol. 53, pp. 495–518.

Borts, George and Jerome Stein, 1964. *Economic Growth in a Free Market*. New York: Columbia University Press.

Bradford, David and H. Kelejian, 1973. "An Econometric Model of Flight to the Suburbs," *Journal of Political Economy*, Vol. 81, pp. 566–589.

Clark, Gordon, M. Gertler, and J. Whiteman, 1986. *Regional Dynamics*. Boston: Allen & Unwin.

Crihfield, John and M. Panggabean, 1995. "Growth and Convergence in U.S. Cities," *Journal of Urban Economics*, Vol. 38, pp. 138–165.

Cronon, William, 1991. *Nature's Metropolis*. New York: W.W. Norton.

Dension, Edward, 1962. *The Sources of Economic Growth in the United States*. Washington, DC: Committee for Economic Development.

———, 1985. *Trends in American Economic Growth*. Washington, DC: The Brookings Institution.

Ferguson, Ronald and H. Ladd, 1988. "Massachusetts," in R. Fosler, ed., *The New Economic Role of the States*. New York: Oxford University Press.

Galbraith, John K., 1967. *The New Industrial State*. Boston: Houghton Mifflin.

Ghali, Mohab, M. Akiyama, and J. Fujiwara, 1978. "Factor Mobility and Regional Growth," *Review of Economics and Statistics*, Vol. 60, pp. 78–84.

Gordon, Robert, 1993. *Macroeconomics*, 6th ed. New York: HarperCollins.

Jorgenson, Dale and Zvi Griliches, 1967. "The Explanation of Productivity Change," *Review of Economic Studies*, Vol. 34, pp. 249–283.

————, 1972. "Issues in Growth Accounting: A Reply to Edward F. Dension," *Survey of Current Business*, Vol. 52, pp. 65–94.

Jorgenson, Dale, F. Gollop, and B. Fraumeni, 1987. *Productivity and U.S. Economic Growth*. Cambridge, MA: Harvard University Press.

Krugman, Paul, 1990. *The Age of Diminished Expectations*. Cambridge, MA: MIT Press.

————, 1991. *Geography and Trade*. Cambridge, MA: MIT Press.

Landes, David, 1969. *The Unbound Prometheus: Technological Change and Industrial Development in Western Europe from 1750 to the Present*. Cambridge: Cambridge University Press.

Leontief, Wassily, 1951. *The Structure of the American Economy 1919–1939,* 2nd ed. Fair Lawn, NJ: Oxford University Press.

Markusen, Ann, 1985. *Profit Cycles, Oligopoly and Regional Development*. Cambridge: Cambridge University Press.

Markusen, Ann, P. Hall, and A. Glasmeier, 1986. *High Tech America*. Boston: Allen & Unwin.

Muth, Richard, 1971. "Migration: Chicken or Egg?" *Southern Economic Journal*, Vol. 37, pp. 295–306.

Myrdal, Gunnar, 1957. *Economic Theory and Underdeveloped Regions*. London: Gerald Duckworth.

Norton, Robert and J. Rees, 1979. "The Product Cycle and the Spatial Deconcentration of American Manufacturing," *Regional Studies*, Vol. 13, pp. 141–151.

Pred, Allen, 1966. *The Spatial Dynamics of U.S. Urban Growth*. Cambridge, MA: MIT Press.

Richardson, Harry, 1973. *Regional Growth Theory*. New York: Wiley.

————, 1985. "Regional Development Theories," in H. Richardson and J. Turek, eds., *Economic Prospects for the Northeast*. Philadelphia: Temple University Press.

Scherer, Frederick, 1980. *Industrial Market Structure and Economic Performance*. Chicago: Rand McNally.

Schumpeter, Joseph, 1942. *Capitalism, Socialism and Democracy*. New York: Harper & Row.

Seninger, S., 1985. "Employment Cycles and Process Innovation in Regional Structural Change," *Journal of Regional Science*, Vol. 25, pp. 259–272.

Solow, Robert, 1957. "Technical Change and the Aggregate Production Function," *Review of Economics and Statistics*, Vol. 39, pp. 312–320.

Wright, Gavin, 1986. *Old South, New South*. New York: Basic Books.

12

Agglomeration Economies, Technical Change, and Urban Growth

A. INTRODUCTION

The basic neoclassical growth model was discussed in Chapter 11, and the survey of the variety of approaches to the study of economic growth in that chapter has made us sensitive to input–output relationships, product cycles, the possibility of cumulative causation, and disequilibrium dynamics. The discussion of the neoclassical models in Chapter 11 introduced the autonomous growth factor but included no detailed discussion of this factor for urban areas. The time has come to correct this deficiency. Agglomeration economies were discussed in Chapter 3 as creating cost advantages for firms in an industry that is concentrated in a particular urban area (localization economies) or that is located in larger urban areas (urbanization economies). The role of technical change was emphasized in Chapter 11 as a factor of considerable importance in determining the national growth rate. What are the contributions of these kinds of factors to urban growth? Just how do these factors work in an urban area to generate growth? In recent years these questions have engaged some of the very best researchers.

These questions have also engaged some of the best researchers in earlier years. Benjamin Chinitz, one of the researchers in the New York Metropolitan Area Study of the 1950s, went on to study Pittsburgh in the early 1960s. The contrast between these two urban areas led Chinitz (1961), in a classic paper, to ask, "How does the growth of one industry in an area affect the area's suitability as a location for other industries?" How might industrial diversity foster growth? Chinitz supplied hypotheses that remain fresh today. He suggested that competitive industries, as opposed to oligopolistic industries, have more entrepreneurs, people who are willing and able to take the risk of starting a new business. An urban area full of competitive industries is likely to create new businesses and more growth. A similar point was made about the supply of capital. The presence of competitive industries means that financial institutions that supply loans to businesses must be prepared to deal with smaller borrowers and, therefore, be more receptive to the entrepreneur. A more diversified local economy will have a more diversified demand for labor and will therefore call forth a greater supply of labor, especially among women. All of these factors suggest that an urban economy with competitive and diversified industry will grow more rapidly than one with oligopolistic and undiversified industry. These ideas, and others, have been tested empirically and largely confirmed in recent research. That research is reviewed in this chapter. The chapter concludes with two industry case studies of agglomeration economies: the automobile industry in Detroit and the semiconductor industry in the San Francisco metropolitan area (Silicon Valley).

B. THE NEOCLASSICAL PRODUCTION FUNCTION REVISITED

Let us return to the basic concept of the production function, but following the two-sector neoclassical model in Chapter 11, we shall assume that a particular production function pertains to an *industry* in an urban area. We shall not assume that a single production function can be used for an entire urban area. For example, suppose that a production function can be specified for the manufacturing sector of an urban area as follows:

$$Q = A(z,t)F(K,L).$$

Here z is a collection of factors that create agglomeration economies, t the level of technology, and $F(K,L)$ the function of capital and labor, as usual. However, it will now be assumed that $F(K,L)$ can exhibit economies of scale for the local industry. In fact, most of the empirical studies of manufacturing industries in urban areas indicate that economies of scale exist at the industry level for some industries. The study by Henderson (1986) was discussed at length in Chapter 3. Such economies of scale are external to the individual firm in the urban area but are internal to the industry. This is precisely what is meant by localization economies, so localization economies are not being included in the collection of factors called z.

There is a critical distinction between agglomeration economies and technical progress. Technical progress means that a *firm* that adopts the new technology can produce more output with the same amounts of capital and labor inputs. Technical progress, when implemented, is internal to the individual firm. Agglomeration economies are, by definition, external to the individual firm in an urban area. However, it may be that some agglomeration economies act by *increasing* the rate of technical change for firms in a particular urban area. There may be agglomeration economies in the invention and development of new technologies, and there may be agglomeration economies in the adoption of new technologies. Other agglomeration economies, such as economies of scale in transportation facilities, create lower costs that are passed along to individual firms.

Now is a good time to review the theory of agglomeration economies that was presented in Chapter 3. Figure 12.1 reproduces Figure 3.7 for an industry in an urban area. The average and marginal cost curves for the industry have negative slopes because of localization economies (i.e., economies of scale at the industry level in the urban area). The demand curve DD intersects the average cost curve AC at output level Q, the equilibrium level of output. Ignore cost curves AC' and MC' for now. Because of localization economies, the local industry is larger than it would be if the industry operates with constant average costs.

With Figure 12.1 in mind, it is possible to classify the different types of agglomeration economies. One distinction is between agglomeration economies that are *static* and those that are *dynamic*. Static agglomeration economies mean that the *level* of some agglomerative factor is associated with some *level* of industry output. In the production function for the local industry,

$$Q = A(z,t)F(K,L),$$

the level of z creates a level for $A(z,t)$ and thus for output. For example, a larger urban area has better and cheaper air transportation (the z factor). This creates a one-time increase in $A(z,t)$ and a one-time shift downward in the industry's cost curves in Figure 12.1. In contrast, a dynamic agglomeration economy means that the *level* of the agglomerative factor is associated with an *increase* in industry output that *continues* through time. For example, a larger urban area has more inventive inventors, who in turn create a continuous stream of technical change that is larger than in smaller urban areas. The size of the urban area (the z factor) causes technology (the t factor) to increase continuously.

The other essential distinction is, of course, between localization and urbanization economies. Both types can be static or dynamic. We now see that Figure 12.1 is depicting a static localization economy. For example, economies of scale in the production of some intermediate input means that the size of the local industry in question is associated with a one-time reduction in average cost. Figure 12.1 also depicts a static urbanization economy because the positions of the average and marginal cost

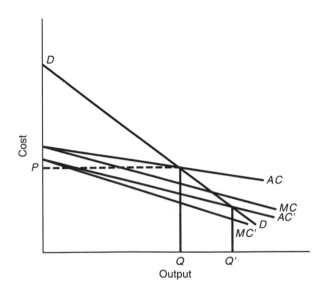

FIGURE 12.1 Cost and output for an urban industry

curves for the industry are based on an assumption about the size of the urban area. With static urbanization economies, an increase in the size of the urban area will shift the average and marginal cost curves down to AC' and MC'. The industry experiences a one-time increase in output to Q'.

What about dynamic agglomeration economies? Dynamic agglomeration economies mean that the level of the agglomerative factor creates continuous reductions in costs for the industry. The effect of a dynamic urbanization economy is depicted in Figure 12.2. The size of the urban area is given, but the dynamic urbanization economy shifts the average and marginal cost curves down again and again. The output of the industry grows from Q to Q' in the first year, for Q' to Q'' in the second year, and so on. Figure 12.2 can also be used to depict a dynamic localization economy. In this case the *size* of the industry itself causes the average and marginal cost curves to shift down again and again. What is more, the resulting growth of the industry means that the size of the industry is larger in the next time period, which will influence the size of the next shift downward in the cost curves. For example, a larger local industry may generate a more rapid rate of technical change (changes in t). This idea of dynamic localization economies is closely related to the notion of cumulative causation that was discussed in Chapter 11.

One final distinction needs to be made concerning dynamic agglomeration economies. Figure 12.2 shows that they lead to continuous increases in the output of the industry, but it does not indicate whether a higher level of an agglomeration factor is associated with increases in output that are larger in absolute or percentage terms. Turn to Figure 12.3, which depicts the same industry in two different urban areas. In Figure 12.3a the industry is relatively small. The dynamic localization economy leads to small absolute increases in the output of the industry, but these in-

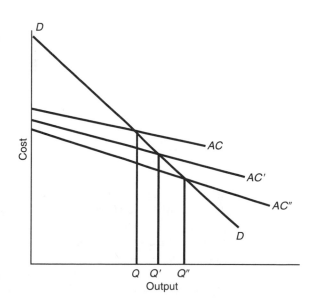

FIGURE 12.2 Dynamic agglomeration economies

FIGURE 12.3 Dynamic agglomeration economies

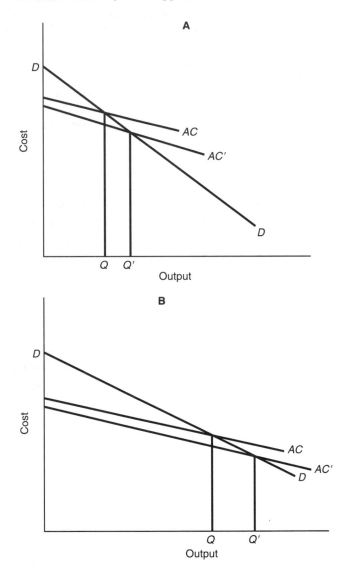

creases are large in percentage terms. In Figure 12.3b the industry is relatively large. The dynamic localization economy produces fairly large increases in the level of output, but those increases are small in percentage terms. Thus this particular dynamic localization economy produces a larger absolute continuous increase in output but not an increase in the rate of growth of output. Figure 12.3 has been drawn to show this case because the empirical results discussed below are consistent with this story. However, another diagram could have been drawn showing a dynamic localization economy that results in a higher rate of growth of output—the larger the local industry, the larger is the rate of growth.

The expanded neoclassical production can be used to obtain a growth equation that is similar to the growth equation in Chapter 11, or

$$\frac{\delta Q}{Q} = \frac{\delta A}{A} + E_K \frac{\delta K}{K} + E_L \frac{\delta L}{L},$$

where E_K and E_L are the elasticities of output with respect to capital and labor. It is now assumed that these two elasticities may add up to a number that is greater than 1.0 (increasing returns to scale for the industry, i.e., static localization economies). The crucial term in the equation is $\delta A/A$. How are the other types of agglomeration economies specified?

The answer can be found by writing down an equation for the total change in A (δA_T) alone. For simplicity assume for the moment that there is only one z factor, so

$$\delta A_T = \left(\frac{\delta A}{\delta z}\right)\delta z + \delta A(z,Q) + \left(\frac{\delta A}{\delta t}\right)\delta t(z,Q,\delta z,\delta Q).$$

This equation includes the following: $(\delta A/\delta z)\delta z$ is a static urbanization economy; $\delta A(z,Q)$ represents dynamic urbanization and localization economics because δA is written as a function of the *levels* of z and Q (industry output); and $(\delta A/\delta t)\delta t(z,Q,\delta z,\delta Q)$ represents the effects of both static and dynamic urbanization and localization economies on the level of technology because δt is made a function of both the levels and changes in z and Q. These three terms are referred to in the succeeding discussion.

Now we understand the mechanics of a growth equation that includes agglomeration economies and technical change. What we need now is insight into the actual market and nonmarket processes that might be at work.

C. DYNAMIC AGGLOMERATION ECONOMIES

What can create dynamic agglomeration economies in urban areas? Most of the leading scholars of this topic seem to agree at least on one thing. At the heart of dynamic agglomeration economies are the production and use of knowledge. Krugman (1991) is an exception to this statement; he thinks that knowledge is an important part of the story but that dynamic agglomeration economies can be associated with labor market and intermediate input markets effects as well. In this section we review the arguments that are made in favor of putting knowledge at the center of the story, and in the following section we examine the empirical studies that have been done to test hypotheses.

Something of a revolution has been going on in economic growth theory in the past 10 years. External economies arising from knowledge spillovers are thought to be critical to the productivity level or the rate of economic growth of a nation. This point of view has been stated by several leading scholars, including Romer (1986), Lucas (1988), and Porter (1990). If knowledge spillovers are important, it is logical to think that the spillovers are more important in urban areas, where people and firms are in close proximity. This point of view harks back to an earlier book by Jane Jacobs, *The Economy of Cities*, that was published in 1969. Her book is insightful and easy to read, and you should add it to your reading list. (I have thoughtfully compiled your reading list in the preface to this book.)

The general idea of knowledge spillovers is too vague to generate hypotheses that can be tested. More details about how knowledge spillovers work are needed, and it turns out that there are three somewhat different theories that all fall into the category of knowledge spillovers. These three theories are set out nicely in a recent article by Glaeser, Kallal, Scheinkman, and Shleifer (1992) in the *Journal of Political Economy*, a leading journal that usually publishes very technical articles. However, this article is quite readable by someone who is majoring in economics and who has familiarity with multiple regression analysis. Glaeser et al. (1992) point out that the theories of dynamic agglomeration economies based on knowledge spillovers differ along two dimensions. First, do knowledge spillovers come primarily from firms within one's own industry or from firms in other industries? Second, what is the impact of market structure (competition versus oligopoly) on knowledge spillovers? We shall consider these two questions in turn.

The first theory argues that the knowledge spillovers occur largely within a local industry. This is one form of localization economies. In Chapter 3 you learned that static localization economies can stem from economies of scale and specialization among the suppliers of intermediate inputs and services and from specialization and better training of workers. You also learned that firms can learn about the most efficient production process from other firms in an urban area. However, these ideas were presented as static, not dynamic, cost advantages. As discussed above, a dynamic theory must posit a mechanism for *continued* reductions in costs for firms in an urban area. The knowledge spillover idea is that a greater concentration of firms in a particular industry in an urban area will cause there to be a greater rate of new product development, improvements in existing products, and improvements in the methods for producing those products. The rate of innovation will be more rapid because there are more highly trained people around who are thinking about how to improve the industry. An idea created by one person will stimulate another, and another, and so on. Ten isolated innovators are less productive than 10 innovators located in the same urban area. There will also be a rapid transmission of all of this new knowledge to firms if they are located in close proximity. The information is transmitted in several ways: through highly trained workers who move from firm to firm, through business meetings and conferences, through industrial spying, through copying of a competitor's product, and through more formal education and training programs that exist in the urban area to serve the industry. In short, dynamic localization economies act to increase the rate of technical change, so Q (the output level in the urban area) appears in the technical change term $(\delta A/\delta t)\delta t(z,Q,\delta z,\delta Q)$.

At this point you may ask about the modern technologies for the transmission of information. Is it not true that information can be transmitted easily around the nation (indeed, the world) on the internet? Do innovators and imitators have to be located in the same urban area? In some cases, clearly they do not. But there are other cases, perhaps the most important cases, where proximity is needed. Edwin Mills (1992) has called this situation the one of transmitting *ambiguous information*. Mills (1992, p. 11) offers the definition that "ambiguous information is information that requires an interactive and convergent set of exchanges before the final exchange can be consummated." Consider a few examples. An industrial buyer and a seller of a specialized piece of electronic equipment will need to hold a series of meetings between specialists in design, production, marketing, and other departments before the contract is signed. A second example occurs within one firm. The development of a new product requires that a great deal of information be exchanged between the R&D people, production people, marketing specialists, legal experts, and others. A third example is the research seminar. Such seminars occur in universities, but they also are held by one firm for its own employees or by an industry, professional, or trade association for a wider audience. The seminar speaker presents some new ideas to fellow specialists, but often the most valuable part of the seminar is the discussion that ensues. Thoughts can be offered, and new ideas are sometimes generated. This kind of exchange of ambiguous information, with its frequent generation of new ideas, can take place in any field of endeavor that relies on ideas.

Does the idea of the exchange of ambiguous information apply to localization economies? Clearly, it does. An industry that is undergoing change is an industry that is generating new ideas. Those 10 innovators who live in close proximity are more productive than if they are isolated precisely because they communicate in the interactive way that Mills describes. However, the concept of the exchange of ambiguous information can also apply to a sector of the economy that is broader than an industry. Indeed, the first example offered by Mills (1992, p. 11) is that of a customer and a supplier, not of firms in the same narrow industry. This argument means that the urbanization factor z appears in the terms $\delta A(z,Q)$ and $(\delta A/\delta t)\delta t(z,Q,\delta z,\delta Q)$.

Jane Jacobs (1969) stressed that knowledge spillovers take place across different industries and lines of work. She argued that diversity of industry in an urban area is more stimulating for the production of new ideas than is the greater size of an individual industry. In fact, some industries are born because the firms in one particular industry perceive the need for new products or services and act to develop them. For example, in the nineteenth century grain and cotton merchants saw the need for better systems for making financial transactions. The financial services industry was born, including the futures and options industry. The futures and options industry is concentrated in Chicago, and the exchanges compete over the development of new products for the management of risk (a localization economy). For Jacobs, it is diversity rather than uniformity that produces the new products and the new technologies. For her the essential function of urban areas is the creation of "new work." The knowledge spillover is wider than an individual industry but not as wide as the entire urban economy.

Now let us turn to the second dimension along which these theories differ. The effect of market structure on technical change has been debated in the literature of industrial organization economics for many years. Does monopoly (or oligopoly) foster technical change because only they can afford the costs of R&D? Or do competitive industries generate technical change because the competitors are always seeking to gain a competitive edge? Some of the most influential books on economics in modern times have grappled with this issue, and it is worthwhile to do a brief tour of this literature.

Joseph Schumpeter's 1942 book *Capitalism, Socialism and Democracy* has been a big seller and a staple of college reading lists since the 1940s. Schumpeter has been justifiably renowned for what he called the process of creative destruction inherent in the capitalist economy. Schumpeter's (1942, p. 32) summary of this process states that "possibilities of gains to be reaped by producing new things or by producing old things more cheaply are constantly materializing and calling for new investments. These new products and new methods compete with the old products and old methods not on equal terms but at a decisive advantage that may mean death to the latter. This is how 'progress' comes about in a capitalist society." These concepts are taught in today's schools of business administration (along with the related product-cycle framework). But with good reason, those schools rarely teach the second half of Schumpeter's story—that capitalism was being killed by its own success. I shall tell the entire story here because you should know it and because it may have been the case that Schumpeter made his arguments to fit his end result. Economists no longer take the second part of Schumpeter's story seriously.

Schumpeter recognized that modern capitalism produces industrial enterprises that operate at a very large scale and have some monopoly power but that this monopoly power is not of great concern because of the "perennial gale of creative destruction." Indeed, those large firms are the ones with the wherewithal to turn the process of creating new products and new processes into a routine function. In short, Schumpeter believed that the existence of large firms would increase the rate of product and process innovation. He did not stop there but went on to state that the people who made the innovations would be employees of large firms. In this process the class of entrepreneurs and small business owners are largely wiped out. As firms become larger and larger, ownership is divorced from control. The owners of these firms lose their entrepreneurial function, and the firms are operated by professional managers. In addition, the success of the large firms will drive many smaller firms out of business. Few people are vitally concerned with the sanctity of private property and freedom of private contracting. With fewer people left to defend the institution of private property, its opponents win the day. The opponents include intellectuals, who will persuade the mass of workers through the written and spoken word that socialism will improve the conditions of the working class and that the grossly unequal income distribution produced by capitalism is not needed to ensure economic progress. Capitalism thus destroys its own institutional framework and sets the stage for the socialistic takeover of those large firms.

What a prophesy! Schumpeter thought that the balance of forces he described would lead to the advent of socialism in the United States in about 50 years from the time he wrote his book (in 1947). Clearly, his prophesy was wrong! By the way, Schumpeter died in 1950, shortly after he reiterated his prophesy at the American Economic Association meetings.

John Kenneth Galbraith, the most popular interpreter of the U.S. economy of the 1950s, also wrote that oligopoly would foster technical change. *American Capitalism*, which was published in 1956, was his first best-seller and is a major work of political economy written with Galbraithian flair. His point of departure was to note the oligopolistic nature of many modern industries, especially in manufacturing. He argued that oligopoly is the natural outcome in industries in which firms have sizable economies of scale. Entry into such industries is easy only when they are new; as the industries mature the surviving firms gather both economies of scale and experience. Latecomers face barriers to entry that are all but insurmountable. Galbraith saw that firms in oligopolistic industries usually do not engage in price competition, but instead, compete using advertising, product differentiation (if feasible), and technical change. He contended that these firms charge excessive prices and engage in wasteful advertising and product differentiation but that they also produce socially beneficial technical progress. In this regard Galbraith's model is similar to Schumpeter's framework. Large firms in oligopolized industries can afford the expense of technical change and have the market power to reap its benefits. As Galbraith (1956, p. 88) put it, "the net of all this is that there must be some element of monopoly in an industry if it is to be progressive." He concluded that we must learn to live with oligopoly, warts and all. He saw no connection between oligopoly and socialism.

Modern economists who study technical change argue that Schumpeter and Galbraith may have a point because compared to a firm in a competitive industry, a large firm in an oligopolized industry is able to reap more of the immediate benefits of technical change and therefore has a greater incentive to invest in R&D. The lack of property rights may slow down the pace of innovation. Oligopolies may be good for growth because they are more able to "internalize the externality" of a new discovery. On the other hand, it may also be true that the ability to appropriate the benefits of a new discovery are determined by many other factors as well. In contrast to Schumpeter and Galbraith, Jacobs (1969) and Porter (1990) believe that competition will foster innovation. Jacobs argues that monopolies limit alternative methods and products, and Porter believes that stiff competition leads to the creation and adoption of innovations.

Industrial organization economists study the economics of technical change without giving much consideration to the spatial dimension. It is generally agreed that both the development and the adoption of new technology depends on (1) appropriability (ability to capture the benefits), (2) market structure, and (3) technological opportunity. In fact, recent research by Levin, Cohen, and Mowery (1985) indicates that R&D spending depends primarily on appropriability and technological opportunity and not on market concentration. The adoption of new technologies, however, is probably stimulated by competitive markets. Note that appropriability is a matter that can be considered to be separate from market structure, an idea that eluded Schumpeter and Galbraith. These conclusions are based on studies of specific industries at the national level and have not really been seen as applicable to matters of urban growth.

A geographer, Edward Malecki, has done several studies of specific industries in urban areas. His survey article (1983) indicates that the adoption of new technologies tends to be associated with larger firms, lower-cost innovations, more flexible management, and more complete information. There is no apparent association with the size of the urban area. In addition, there is evidence both supportive of and contrary to the notion that large firms adopt innovations earliest. In short, what is known about technological change from the industrial organization literature is generally too specific to an industry to provide general implications for urban growth theory and policy.

The bottom line on the market structure argument is that the nature of the market structure for the industry in an urban area may be a separate dynamic localization economy. The equation for δA_T should therefore be revised to read

$$\delta A_T = \frac{\delta A}{\delta z}\,\delta z + \delta A(z,Q) + \frac{\delta A}{\delta t}\,\delta t(z,Q,m,\delta z,\delta Q),$$

where m stands for market structure.

D. EMPIRICAL STUDIES OF STATIC AND DYNAMIC AGGLOMERATION ECONOMIES

There are two types of empirical studies that seek to test for the presence of static and dynamic agglomeration economies in urban areas. Studies of the first type estimate a version of the growth equation for output:

$$\frac{\delta Q}{Q} = \frac{\delta A}{A} + E_K \frac{\delta K}{K} + E_L \frac{\delta L}{L}.$$

These studies are confined to the aggregate manufacturing sector in urban areas because only the industries in this sector have the required data for output (value added). These studies also require data on growth in capital and labor. In particular, the researcher must construct estimates of the urban area's capital stock in manufacturing for each year of the study. Mullen and Williams (1987) and Fogarty and Garofalo (1988) have been pioneers in this laborious task, and the interested reader can consult their articles for the details. The labor input used in the studies is simply labor-hours of work. No attempt is made to adjust the measure of the labor input for changes in the educational level of the workers. The second type of study adapts the neoclassical growth model to examine employment growth rather than output growth. Employment growth is easily observed; it is reported annually by county for very detailed industry categories. Consequently, employment data can be used to study urban industry growth in narrowly defined industries.

A study by Beeson (1990) using capital data provided by Fogarty and Garofalo decomposed the growth in manufacturing output in 45 large metropolitan areas into the three constituent parts of the basic growth accounting equation above. Her goal was to discover the reasons for the slowdown in manufacturing output growth in the large metropolitan areas, particularly those in the old manufacturing belt of the northeast. Some investigators have suggested that agglomeration economies have declined in importance. The study included the 45 largest metropolitan areas in terms of manufacturing value added, and covered the period 1959 to 1978. She was also able to perform the same decomposition of output growth for the rest of the nation, the parts of the country outside the 45 largest metropolitan areas.

Some of Beeson's (1990) results are shown in Table 12.1. The table shows that the rate of output growth slowed down dramatically from the 1959–1965 period to the 1973–1978 period both in the 45 largest metropolitan areas and in the rest of the nation. Furthermore, the biggest culprit in the slowdown of output growth is technical change (the $\delta A/A$ factor). Technical change was causing output in the large metropolitan areas to grow by 4.01% per year in the period 1959–1965, but its contribution to growth was only 0.44% per year from 1973–1978. Mullen and Williams (1987) found essentially the same result in a study of 30 large urban areas over the same period. Beeson also found that the productivity growth rate suffered a similar drop outside the largest metropolitan areas. Table 12.1 reveals that the output growth rate was consistently higher outside the largest metropolitan areas. More rapid growth in capital and labor outside the largest urban areas accounts primarily for the higher growth rate in output. This finding was especially pronounced for the large metropolitan areas in the manufacturing belt in the northeast, but these metropolitan

TABLE 12.1 Sources of Growth in Manufacturing Output		
	Large Urban Areas in:	
Manufacturing Belt (n = 20)	*Other Regions (n = 25)*	*Outside Large Urban Areas*
1959–1965		
Real value added	4.50	6.09	6.32
Capital	−0.19	1.03	1.28
Labor	0.47	2.21	1.13
Productivity	4.21	2.85	3.91
1965–1973		
Real value added	2.20	3.28	5.02
Capital	0.48	1.22	1.96
Labor	−0.37	1.42	1.63
Productivity	2.08	0.64	1.45
1973–1978		
Real value added	−0.17	4.19	2.67
Capital	0.24	1.02	1.68
Labor	−1.12	2.57	0.53
Productivity	0.72	0.61	0.46

Source: Table compiled from data obtained from Beeson (1990, pp. 80–83).

areas also lost their productivity growth advantage that had existed in the 1959–1965 period. Beeson's study does not reveal the underlying causes for the decline in the productivity performance of manufacturing in the large metropolitan areas of the northeast. The other studies reviewed in this section shed some light on these causes.

Now we turn to the studies that use the production function equation to test hypotheses regarding static and dynamic agglomeration economies. The first study, by Fogarty and Garofalo (1988), examines manufacturing output (value added) in 13 urban areas over the period 1957 to 1977. Their study is based on the production function

$$Q = A(z,t)F(K,L),$$

and they permit increasing returns to scale with respect to the capital and labor inputs. They hypothesize that the z variables, the factors that create agglomeration economies, include (1) population of the urban area, (2) age of the urban area (1977 minus the year the central reached population of 50,000), (3) the central density of manufacturing employment in 1963, and (4) the gradient of manufacturing employment density in 1963. Note that they are testing for *static* urbanization economies and localization economies for the manufacturing sector as a whole and that they are not testing a market-structure hypothesis. In addition to testing for a standard static urbanization effect (the size of the urban area), they are testing whether the age of the urban area and the spatial pattern of manufacturing have impacts on productivity. These are static urbanization and localization economies, respectively.

The equation estimated is

$$\ln Q = a_0 + a_1 t + b_0 \ln K + b_1 \ln L \ln K + b_2 \ln L$$
$$+ c_1 z_1 + \cdot \cdot \cdot + c_n z_n,$$

where t is time (1957 = 0), and $z_1, \ldots, z_n$ are the factors that create agglomeration economies. They also tested variables that indicate the time periods 1965–1972 and 1973–1977. All of the variables enter the estimated equation with statistically significant coefficients, and the results are as follows:

1. Urban area population is positively related to output up to a population level of 2.9 million but has a negative effect thereafter.
2. Age of the urban area has a strong negative effect on productivity.
3. Central density of manufacturing employment in 1963 has a positive effect on productivity.
4. The steeper manufacturing employment density gradient has a positive effect on productivity up to a gradient of 50% per mile but has a negative effect at steeper gradient levels.

The results also indicate that the manufacturing sector in an urban area is subject to increasing returns to scale; at the mean values of K and L, the sum of their output elasticities is 1.19. Finally, as other productivity studies find, there is evidence of a slowdown in productivity growth after 1973.

Together these results provide intriguing confirmation of several ideas about static agglomeration economies. The result for economies of scale indicates the presence of economies external to the firm but internal to the manufacturing sector as a whole. However, given that the manufacturing sector is such a broad definition of an industry, it is questionable whether the Fogarty–Garofalo findings should really be called evidence of static localization economies. Rather, the result suggests something that falls between static localization economies and static urbanization economies such as interindustry linkages as discussed in Chapter 3. The findings pertaining to the size of the urban area indicate the presence of urbanization economies up to a point (2.9 million) but that further growth in the population of the urban area detracts from productivity in manufacturing. Finally, the findings regarding the spatial structure of the manufacturing sector are quite interesting. The results say that a greater spatial concentration (higher central density, and steeper density gradient— up to a point) contributes to productivity. Are static localization economies stronger when the industry is spatially concentrated in the urban area? The results are pointing in that direction.

Fogarty and Garofalo (1988) use their estimated equation to provide an explanation for the changes in productivity in the 13 urban areas over the period 1957–1977. The observed average growth rate for the 13 urban areas over the period was 3.35% per year. Excluding the increasing returns to scale, growth of capital and labor provided accounted for 1.17% of that growth. Productivity growth accounted for the remaining growth. Increasing returns to scale added 0.44% to the growth rate, and population growth added a very small 0.13% to growth. However, on average the decentralization of the urban areas (lower central density and flatter density gradient) *reduced* productivity growth by an estimated 1.22%. The remaining 2.83% is growth not related to the static agglomeration economies included in the analysis. In summary, the Fogarty–Garofalo study does not test for dynamic agglomeration economies but finds strong evidence of static localization economies. The particularly interesting finding is that the spatial pattern of local manufacturing is a static localization economy.

A second study of this type, by Mullen and Williams (1990), examined productivity growth in the entire manufacturing sector in 24 urban areas over the period 1958 to 1977. Productivity growth was estimated as

$$\frac{\delta Q}{Q} - \alpha \frac{\delta K}{K} - \beta \frac{\delta L}{L},$$

where α and β are the factor shares. They then used their estimate of productivity growth as the dependent variable. They found that productivity *growth* was positively influenced by faster growth in manufacturing output and by urbanization economies (population level in the urban area). These findings are very important. The finding that productivity growth is related to output *growth* is a finding of a *static* localization economy. Return to Figure 12.1. An increase in demand (outward shift in the demand curve) will increase both output and productivity along the given average cost curve (AC). On the other hand, the finding that the level of population positively influenced the rate of output growth is evidence of a *dynamic* urbanization economy.

In the Mullen Williams (1990) results, productivity growth was negatively related to the population growth rate and the rate of growth of the manufacturing capital stock in the most recent period (1974–1978). They think that the positive effect of the output growth rate on productivity growth is caused by use of more modern capital, which embodies later technology. We learned in Chapter 11 that Jorgenson and Griliches and others argue that new technology often comes embodied in new capital of higher quality. Mullen and Williams (1990) have found some indirect confirmation of this idea for urban areas. However, the negative effect of capital growth in the last four years of the study period may be caused by the energy crisis of that period or by the increase in environmental regulations that were instituted at that time. Also, rapid population *growth* seems to cause diseconomies, perhaps because of congestion and other effects (which may be only temporary).

Next we come to the studies of employment growth in specific industries in urban areas. Two influential studies were published in 1992; one by Glaeser, Kallal, Scheinkman, and Shleifer and the other by O'hUallachain and Satterthwaite. These two studies seemingly reach sharply different conclusions regarding the presence of dynamic localization economies, so they must be examined in detail to determine the sources of the different results. It turns out that the two studies have reasonably consistent results concerning localization economies. They find that localization economies are rarely strong enough to increase the *growth rate* of employment in a local industry but that some larger absolute increases in employment are often generated. Recall Figure 12.3 and the discussion surrounding it.

It must be remembered that studying employment growth is not the same thing as studying output growth. Employment data are available for all industries in an urban area, but output data are available only for manufacturing. Glaeser et al. (1992) and O'hUallachain and Satterthwaite (1992) did not wish to restrict their studies to manufacturing. It is helpful first to consider the neoclassical model for *employment* demand in an industry in an urban area. That model says that employment demand depends on the wage rate, the rental price of capital, demand for output, the level of technology, and agglomeration economies. Holding the other factors constant, an increase in the wage rate reduces employment because of both the substitution effect (toward the capital input) and the output effect (resulting from a higher marginal cost and price of output). An increase in the price of capital may increase or decrease employment because the substitution effect operates to increase employment but the output effect works to reduce employment. An increase in demand increases output and employment, of course. Finally, technical change and agglomeration economies can increase or decrease employment. An improvement in technology or an increase in an agglomeration economy (e.g., an increase in the size of the urban area) will mean that the same output can be produced with fewer labor (and capital) inputs. If output remains constant, employment falls. However, output will not remain constant because of the reduction in cost and output price brought about by the increase in productivity. If demand is responsive to the reduction in price, output may increase enough to generate more employment. In short, it is possible that employment can either rise or fall as output rises.

A study by this author [McDonald (1992)] examined employment growth in entire manufacturing sector in 263 urban areas for the period 1983–1986. This study found that changes in the local wage rate and in local demand are important factors in manufacturing employment change. The model that was estimated followed closely the theoretical discussion in the preceding paragraph, and the following elasticities of employment change were found.

Variable	Effect of 1% Increase on Percentage Employment Change
Wage rate in urban area	−0.71
Population of urban area	0.84
Real income per capita in urban area	0.81
Share of employment in declining industries	−0.18
Federal procurement	0.04

All of these variables attained high levels of statistical significance. The elasticity of demand for labor in manufacturing is estimated to be −0.71. Employment is responsive to increases in local demand—population and real income per capita have elasticities of slightly over 0.8. Employment growth is lower the greater is the share of local employment in the declining parts of the manufacturing sector at the national level. The declining industries are food products, tobacco, textile mills, apparel, chemicals, petroleum and coal products, leather products, and primary metals. Federal procurement has a positive effect on employment, as expected. This study also tested for the presence of dynamic localization economies for employment in the manufacturing sector as a whole, with the result that the employment level in the base year had no effect on employment growth in the subsequent three-year period.

Now we are ready to examine the study by Glaeser et al. (1992). They studied employment growth from 1956 to 1987 in the six largest industries at the two-digit SIC code level in the 170 largest urban areas. The two-digit SIC code system is described in Chapter 4. The six largest industries were selected because they wanted to focus on industries that represent specialties for the urban area and because they wished to avoid small industries that may have volatile growth records. They assume that there are national markets for labor and capital, so they assume that the changes in the wage rate and the rental rate of capital were the same for all the industries and urban areas. This assumption concerning the wage rate clearly is incorrect and may have had a serious effect on the empirical results. They also assume that technical change in an industry consists of a national rate of change and local dynamic agglomeration economies.

Assuming that changes in input prices can be ignored and that there is technical change that occurs at the national rate for the industry, the growth in employment depends upon demand growth and dynamic agglomeration economies. Their measures of dynamic agglomeration economies are:

1. Employment in the industry in the urban area in 1956
2. Average size of establishments in the local industry relative to the nation
3. Urban area's other top five industries' share of total employment in the urban area
4. The location quotient for the industry in the urban area

The first variable tests for dynamic localization economies as a function of the size of the local industry, and the second is aimed at the market-structure hypothesis. The third variable tests for Jacobs's idea that diversity in the local economy enhances growth, a form of dynamic urbanization economy. Finally, the location quotient (share of industry in local economy divided by the industry's share in the national economy) tests whether a high degree of specialization in the industry fosters growth. This seems to be a combination of a dynamic localization effect and a dynamic urbanization effect. The study includes a variable for demand growth—employment growth in the industry at the national level (excluding the urban area in question). They also included variables for the wage level in the industry in 1956 and for location of the urban area in the south.

The findings of the study are as follows:

Variable	Sign of Effect on Employment Growth
Employment growth in industry in the United States	+
Wage level in 1956	Not significant
Employment in industry in urban area in 1956	−
Location in south	+
Location quotient	−
Average size of establishment (relative to nation)	−
Employment share of other top five industries	−

Note that the employment level in the industry in 1956, the initial year, had a negative effect on the employment growth rate. The estimated coefficient is highly statistically significant but not very large in its effect. The estimated coefficient says that if the initial employment level in the local industry was 10,000 larger, the growth from 1956 to 1987 was 4% less than it otherwise would have been. The effect is only -0.13% per year. This result no doubt reflects the fact that many of the older urban areas of the northeast lost a sizable amount of employment in their largest industries during the 1970s and 1980s. Pittsburgh lost most of its steel industry because of competition from foreigners and domestic minimills. Chicago suffered a sharp drop in meatpacking (food products). Employment in the apparel manufacturing business dropped in New York. The empirical result certainly suggests that the reasons for the concentration of those basic industries in a few urban areas seem to have evaporated. However, there is one problem with this statistical finding. Employment growth would be negatively related to the employment level if the wage rate tended to increase more in these large local industries. In fact, Glaeser et al. (1992, p. 1147) include evidence that this is precisely what happened. Wage increases were positively related to the urban area's employment level in the industry in 1956. This is not a new story; there is evidence to suggest that wages in some of the basic industries in northern urban areas were pushed up in the 1950s and 1960s and that the loss of jobs can be attributed partly to this factor. As discussed above, McDonald (1992) tested and confirmed the importance of changes in local wages. Recall also that greater localization economies do not necessarily lead to an increase in employment. The positive effect on output must be large enough to cause employment to expand. Finally, recall from Figure 12.3 that greater localization economies may not be associated with a larger percentage increase in the industry but only with a larger absolute increase in the industry.

The other findings of Glaeser et al. (1992) provide confirmation that both diversity and competition in local industry foster growth. Employment growth was greater the less specialized was the local economy in the industry in question and in the other top five industries. Employment growth was greater the smaller were the establishments in the industry compared to average establishment size for the industry in the nation. These are *dynamic* agglomeration economies as defined in Section B. The hypotheses of Benjamin Chinitz (1961) and Jane Jacobs (1969) come out looking good. As discussed above, the finding regarding the presence of localization "diseconomies" can be questioned.

Another influential study of urban employment growth was completed by Breandon O'hUallachain and Mark Satterthwaite (1992). They also examined individual industries, but their selection criterion was different from that used by Glaeser et al. (1992). They selected 37 industries that grew rapidly during the period of their study, 1977–1984. Nine of the industries are in manufacturing, and the rest are wholesale trade, six industries in transportation and communications, four industries in FIRE (finance, insurance, and real estate), and 17 services. Data were collected from the urban areas in which the industry existed in 1977 and in which growth occurred. A regression model was estimated for each of the 37 industries.

For each industry they postulated the model

$$E_1 - E_0 = aE_0^\alpha L^\beta \exp(bX + cZ + \epsilon).$$

where E_1 and E_0 are employment in the industry in 1977 and 1984, L is the size of the labor force in the urban area, X is a group of variables that describe economic development incentive programs in the urban area, Z is a group of variables that describe the urban area, ϵ is a random error term, and exp stands for e, the base of the natural logarithms (here e is raised to the power $bX + cZ + \epsilon$).

Taking the natural log of both sides of the equation produces the equation that was estimated:

$$\ln(E_1 - E_0) = \ln a + \alpha \ln E_0 + \beta \ln L + bX + cZ + \epsilon.$$

This equation requires that $E_1 - E_0$ be positive, of course, because the logarithm of a negative number or zero does not exist. This dependent variable, the log of the absolute change in employment, was chosen rather than the percentage change in employment because some urban areas with very small initial levels of employment for an industry can experience huge percentage increases that are really indicative of nothing in particular.

The O'hUallachain–Satterthwaite model has an interesting implication concerning dynamic localization economies. As in Glaeser et al. (1992), base-year employment in the industry is included in the model to test for localization economies. The model can be written in percentage growth terms as

$$\frac{E_1 - E_0}{E_0} = a E_0^{\alpha - 1} L^\beta \exp(bX + cZ + c),$$

which means that the employment growth rate is higher the greater is E_0 if α is greater than 1.0. If α is less than 1.0 and greater than zero, the employment growth rate is lower when E_0 is greater. If α is positive, an increase in E_0 means that the absolute growth $(E_1 - E_0)$ is larger. But $\alpha = 1$ is the dividing line between a localization economy that increases the growth rate of employment in the industry and a weaker localization economy that increases employment but not its growth rate. Once again, refer to Figure 12.3. If α exceeds 1, employment in a growing industry becomes concentrated in the urban areas with the largest initial levels of employment. If α is less than 1, employment growth in the industry will be more dispersed across urban areas.

A summary of the results obtained by O'hUallachain and Satterthwaite is shown in Table 12.2. A large number of variables were tested for the 37 industries, but only a few results stand out. First, the initial employment level had a statistically significant and positive effect in 33 of the 37 industries. No other variable even comes close to this overwhelming result. A more detailed discussion of this finding is provided below. The size of the labor force in the urban area produced the expected result in 17 industries, which is strong confirmation of dynamic urbanization economies for a variety of industries. The average size of the firms in the local industry had a negative effect in 17 industries, a result that is in full agreement with the Glaeser et al. (1992) findings. A more competitive market structure seems to foster growth in a variety of industries. High wages and unions deterred employment growth in some industries (14 and 9, respectively), while labor quality (college graduates) stimulated some growth in nine industries. The last variable to show any consistent result was a measure of market strength, total income in the urban area di-

TABLE 12.2 Summary of Factors Contributing to Employment Growth in Selected Industries, 1977–1984

Variable	Sign Expected	Number of Industries with Significant Coefficient and Expected Sign
Localization economies	+	33 of 37
Urbanization economies	+	17
Scale of firms	−	17
Income/employment in 1977	+	7
Income growth	+	2
Wage rate	−	14
Unions	−	9
Labor quality (college grad)	+	9
Good climate	+	1
Recreation	+	2
Electricity price	−	2
Percent black population	?	−
Corporate tax rate	−	1
Personal tax rate	−	4
Local government expenditures	+	1
Education effort	+	0
Industrial revenue bonds	+	1
Defense contracts	+	3
Airport access	+	3
Enterprise zones	+	3
University R&D parks	+	6

Source: Table compiled from data obtained from O'hUallachain and Satterthwaite (1992).

vided by employment in the industry in the base year (1977). This variable had the expected positive effect in seven industries. The large collection of other variables that was included had no consistent effects. These variables include various local amenity and policy variables. Notable is the absence of effects for public policy: taxes, education, industrial revenue bonds, and enterprise zones. University R&D parks did have the expected positive effect in six industries. It would seem that at least with some of these policy variables, the policy has been instituted in response to unfavorable changes in the local economy. If such is the case, it will be difficult to identify a positive effect of policy.

Let us now return to the findings regarding dynamic localization economies. Recall from the previous discussion that a coefficient of 1.0 for base-year employment is the dividing line between a strong dynamic localization economy that increases the local employment growth *rate* in the industry and a weaker localization economy that lowers this employment growth rate but increases the employment level. Of the 33 statistically significant and positive effects, the average is 0.75 and only five exceed 1.0. Of these five, only three are statistically significantly greater than 1.0:

Industry	Localization Effect
Wholesale trade	1.19
Legal services	1.14
Accounting services	1.18

In these industries a higher base-year employment level is associated with a higher employment growth rate. These three industries centralized as they grew. The other industries did not. In short, O'hUallachain and Satterthwaite (1992) found very few instances in which the effect of the localization economy is so strong that it increases the growth rate of employment. Their finding is thus almost completely consistent with the findings of Glaeser et al. (1992), who found that base-year employment had a slight negative effect on the employment growth rate.

O'hUallachain and Satterthwaite (1992) also estimated their model for the manufacturing sector as a whole in urban areas. In these results employment growth was associated with the "weaker form" of dynamic localization economies (with a coefficient of 0.56), and positively affected by good climate, enterprise zones, and university R&D parks. No other variables attained statistical significance. These results for the policy variables are more encouraging for policymakers, of course.

We have taken a good deal of time and energy to review some important recent studies of dynamic agglomeration economies. Empirical findings can always be subjected to further study, but some fairly clear results have already emerged. Dynamic localization economies exist in growing industries but not in a form that is strong enough to cause the rate of employment growth in a local industry to increase. Dynamic urbanization economies also exist in some industries. Fogarty and Garofalo (1988) found a small static urbanization effect in total manufacturing up to a population level of 2.9 million. Mullen and Williams (1990) found evidence of dynamic urbanization economies in the manufacturing sector, and O'hUallachain and Satterthwaite (1992) found the presence of dynamic urbanization economies in 14 of 37 growth industries. Curiously, Glaeser et al. (1992) did not test for urbanization economies by using a simple measure of the size of the urban area. Both Glaeser et al. (1992) and O'hUallachain and Satterthwaite (1992) confirmed the hypothesis that a more competitive local industry (in terms of smaller firms) generates more employment growth, and Glaeser et al. (1992) found that diversity in the local economy also contributes to employment growth in an industry. Fogarty and Garofalo (1988) found that the spatial pattern of the manufacturing sector can influence its growth—a very neat connection between the two basic topics (urban location patterns and urban growth) in this book.

E. IDENTIFICATION OF INDUSTRIES WITH DYNAMIC AGGLOMERATION ECONOMIES

Is it possible to identify the industries that are experiencing dynamic agglomeration economies? This kind of information has high value for many people in a local economy. Those who hope to work in or those who supply inputs for such an industry have an obvious interest in this knowledge. Officials who plan public infrastructure programs or education and job training programs need this information. Public officials who are trying to promote the growth of the local economy are also keenly interested in knowing about these areas of strength. Unfortunately, there is no foolproof method for identifying industries that will continue to grow as a result of dynamic agglomeration economies.

The research reported in the preceding section does provide some suggestions that one might follow. Recent employment growth is a good clue, but the industry should also already be large enough to generate its own dynamic localization economies. Smaller firms also lead to more rapid growth. A more diverse local economy also helps, but this factor does not help one pick the industries with dynamic agglomeration economies within a given local economy.

How much recent growth is indicative of dynamic agglomeration economies? The more the better, one might suppose. However, there is one immediate problem. Some urban areas, such as Los Angeles (see Chapter 1), have been growing rapidly in nearly all categories, whereas many other urban areas are not growing very rapidly as a whole. An urban area that is growing rapidly overall may indeed have dynamic agglomeration economies operating in a large number of sectors, but it is likely that those sectors are growing more rapidly than "average" in some sense. An economy that is growing rapidly as a whole will pull along industries that are not dynamic generators of growth, and it is reasonable to suppose that such industries perform no better than the average for the local economy. What is more, an urban area that is not growing rapidly as a whole (e.g., New York and Chicago) may contain dynamic industries. How can such industries be identified in that sort of environment?

A technique exists that puts these thoughts into numerical terms. The method, known as *shift-share analysis*, divides the growth of an industry in an urban area into components that are helpful in identifying dynamic agglomeration economies. In the conventional form of shift-share analysis, the percentage change in employment in a particular industry i in a local economy can be written down as

$$\frac{\delta e_i}{e_i} \equiv \frac{\delta US}{US} + \left(\frac{\delta US_i}{US_i} - \frac{\delta US}{US}\right) + \left(\frac{\delta e_i}{e_i} - \frac{\delta US_i}{US_i}\right),$$

where US is the total employment in the United States, US_i the employment in the United States in industry i, and e_i the employment in the local economy in industry i. As always, δUS means "change in" employment in the United States. Employment growth in the local industry has been divided into three parts: the part attributable to total employment growth in the nation, the part attributable to the fact that national employment growth in the particular industry was more rapid (or slower) than the nation as a whole, and a third part that compares the employment growth in the local industry to that industry's national growth rate. This last term is normally called the *competitive position* of the local industry because it is a direct comparison of the industry's growth locally and nationally. The method is called shift-share analysis because the first term in the equation can be called the (national) share term, and the sum of the two other terms represents a shift relative to the overall national growth rate.

The critical term for purposes of identifying local industries with dynamic agglomeration economies is the third term, the competitive position. If an industry is growing more rapidly in the local economy than in the national economy, perhaps it is exhibiting dynamic agglomeration economies. The word *perhaps* is used because this is a very weak criterion. In fact, nearly all industries in the Los Angeles urban area grew more rapidly than their national counterparts during the 1980s. Does this mean that nearly all industries in Los Angeles had dynamic agglomeration economies? Clearly, one cannot reach that conclusion. Conventional shift-share analysis does not appear to provide a very discriminating criterion.

Let us not give up on the idea of shift-share analysis just yet. One problem with the conventional form of shift-share analysis is that the growth rate of the local economy as a whole does not appear in the formula. Many industries in Los Angeles grew rapidly simply because they were located in Los Angeles and the rising tide lifted all the boats. McDonald's version of shift-share analysis is

$$\frac{\delta e_i}{e_i} \equiv \frac{\delta E}{E} + \left(\frac{\delta US}{US} - \frac{\delta E}{E}\right) + \left(\frac{\delta US_i}{US_i} - \frac{\delta US}{US}\right)$$
$$+ \left(\frac{\delta e_i}{e_i} - \frac{\delta US_i}{US_i}\right).$$

The new notation is E, which denotes total employment in the local economy. McDonald's share term is $\delta E/E$, the percentage change in total employment in the local economy. The rest of the formula represents the shift relative to $\delta E/E$. The competitive position is now defined to be

$$\frac{\delta e_i}{e_i} - \frac{\delta US_i}{US_i} + \left(\frac{\delta US}{US} - \frac{\delta E}{E}\right).$$

The competitive position in conventional shift-share analysis has now been adjusted by the difference between the national and local growth rates in total employment. For example, suppose that an industry in Los Angeles grew by 15% and that its national counterpart grew by 8%. However, suppose that total employment in the United States grew by 5% compared to 10% in Los Angeles. The conventional shift-share method would say that the local industry has a competitive position of +7%. On the other hand, McDonald's shift-share method says that the competitive position is +2%, because 5% of that growth was more rapid general growth in the local economy. One can say that the local industry grew by 2% more than might have been expected given the identity of the industry and the fact that it is located in Los Angeles.

To repeat, there is no foolproof method for identifying industries in the local economy that may be exhibiting dynamic agglomeration economies. McDonald's competitive position is a tool that may prove to be useful. It is used in Chapter 14 in the discussion of local economic development policy.

F. A SYNTHESIS OF MAINSTREAM ECONOMICS: LATER VERSION

Recall that Chapter 11 includes a preliminary synthesis of Keynesian and neoclassical models of urban growth. In this section we update that synthesis to take into account what has been learned about agglomeration economies. This synthesis is called a later version because no version of a model is the final version. Actually, Figures 12.1, 12.2, and 12.3 present the synthesis of mainstream economics as it pertains to the level and growth of *output* of an industry in an urban area. In this section we examine employment and employment growth in a particular industry in an urban area. Recall that the model depicted in Figure 11.3 is the market for labor for an entire urban area.

Figure 12.4 depicts the initial demand curve for labor by the industry as *DD* and the supply curve is *SS*. The labor supply curve is drawn with a positive slope, indicating that the industry can recruit more workers only by increasing the wage rate a bit. The industry is only a part of a larger labor market in the urban area, so it faces a fairly elastic labor supply curve.

The market demand for labor by the industry is a bit complicated because of the static localization economy. Individual firms in the local industry operate under constant returns to scale, but the local industry operates under increasing returns to scale. The market demand for labor in the long run is the value of the marginal product of labor *as seen by the firms*, which is less than the value of the marginal product of labor for the industry as a whole. The individual firm presumes that given the price of capital services and the wage rate, it can expand at constant marginal cost (i.e., at a constant marginal product of labor). Therefore, the firms in the industry think that the marginal product of labor is a constant MP^*. The value of the marginal product is the price of output times MP^*, but the price of output for the industry is given by the de-

FIGURE 12.4 Dynamic localization economies

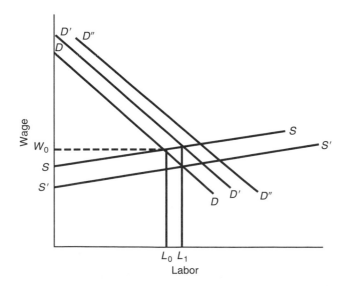

mand curve for output. The price of output falls as the industry output and employment expand, and this declining output price is incorporated into demand curve *DD*.

The initial wage rate and employment level are W_0 and L_0. The empirical results found in the study by Glaeser et al. (1992) and O'hUallachain and Satterthwaite (1992) indicate the presence of dynamic localization economies. The dynamic localization economies *increase* the productivity of the inputs, leading to reductions in cost and market price and an increase in output as in Figure 12.2. The empirical evidence indicates that the output effect outweighs the productivity effect for a local industry, so the labor demand *increases* rather than decreases when labor productivity increases. The demand for labor shifts to $D'D'$ in the next time period. This means that at employment level L_0, reductions in costs are generated by the industry that cause output and employment to rise in the next time period. The increase in the size of the industry (to employment level L_1 and its corresponding output level) generates a further increase in productivity that reduces costs and market price again. This further shift in the demand curve for labor (to $D''D''$) results in an employment increase to L_2. In Figure 12.4 this series of increases in employment is declining in percentage terms but increasing in absolute terms.

An increase in the supply of labor, shown as a shift from SS to $S'S'$, will increase employment and reduce wages as usual. However, the presence of dynamic localization economies means that the employment and output increases will lead to even larger improvements in productivity than would otherwise occur at that time. The demand curve for labor is constantly shifting outward, but an increase in labor supply will cause a one-time jump in labor demand that will have further dynamic effects. At this point there is no empirical evidence to support this chain of events.

G. TWO CASE STUDIES

The models and econometric results reviewed in this chapter may appear to be lifeless to some readers, so it is useful to examine some case studies that highlight some static and dynamic agglomeration economies. Two cases have been chosen because of their importance for both the U.S. economy and their home urban areas. The first case is the automobile industry and Detroit, and the second is the semiconductor industry and metropolitan San Francisco. The first case is the story of events that took place almost 100 years ago, while the second case is from the recent past. It is clear that both of these cases are quite exceptional. They represent extreme examples of the exploitation of agglomeration economies. But extreme examples have their uses in that they demonstrate the existence of particular phenomena, including in these cases the phenomenon of dynamic localization economies.

Detroit and the Automobile Industry

The first American automobile producer was not located in Detroit. The Duryea Company of Springfield, Massachusetts was the first to begin production of a gasoline powered car in the United States in 1896. Olds, the first Detroit producer, began in 1899, but by 1904 42% of American autos were being produced in the Detroit area. By 1914 Detroit was making 78% of a vastly expanded auto industry output. What accounts for this concentration of the industry in one urban area?

Jackson (1988) argues that Detroit possessed concentrations of crucial industries, skilled workers, available local venture capital, and entrepreneurs. He argues that this combination of factors, combined with strong consumer demand, created the critical mass that resulted in continued innovation that other urban areas simply could not match. In short, Jackson thinks that a dynamic localization economy was at work that operated through the rate of technical change. But what are the details of this argument?

The critical antecedent industry was the shipbuilding industry. It was here that the internal combustion gasoline engine was developed into a practical engine for powering boats. This kind of engine, rather than the steam engines that were used for ocean vessels, was designed to be used on the rivers and lakes in and around the Michigan area. The gasoline engine rather than steam or electric engines turned out to be the best engine for the auto. Several early Detroit automobile entrepreneurs had backgrounds in the boat engine business. Olds produced them, Leland made parts for them, and Dodge and Ford repaired them. Other industries that were present in Michigan supported the auto industry, examples being the carriage industry, steel, wheelwrights, and the machine tool industry. The firms and workers in these industries had the skills to produce the components needed for the auto. Another important factor was the availability of financing for the fledgling auto companies. Considerable fortunes had been made in lumber, mining, food processing, and other industries. What is more, the investors in Detroit were willing to learn about the potential of the auto industry. All of this created what Jackson (1988, p. 95) calls "an innovative contagion, in which the development of ideas, products, and markets acquires its own momentum and energy, continuing until the industry matures."

A good deal of the story of the early Detroit auto industry can be told through the life of one person, Henry Ford. Ford's story is included in a massive history of the auto industry by David Halberstam titled *The Reckoning* (1986). Halberstam's book is fascinating and I recommend that you read it—after the school term is over and when you have plenty of spare time. Henry Ford was born on a farm in Michigan in 1863. As a boy he grew to hate farming and to love tinkering with machines. In 1879, at the age of 16, he walked to Detroit to look for some interesting work. At the time Detroit was full of small foundries, machine shops, boat builders, and carriage makers. He worked in a machine shop for a while, and later worked repairing boat engines for a company called Detroit Dry Docks. He returned to the farm in 1886 in response to an offer from his father, but by 1891 he was back in Detroit. His reading of technical magazines had convinced him that important new inventions were imminent.

He told his wife that he intended to invent the horseless carriage, but before he could do that he needed to learn more about electricity. He took a job with Detroit Edison (the local electric power company) as an engineer to support his family and his tinkering and inventing activities. He had his first experimental car on the street by 1896. The vehicle was really a four-wheel bicycle with an engine. He followed up with a better car, and in 1899 he started his first car company. At this time dozens of engineers and inventors were starting car companies in Detroit. Ford's company folded within 18 months, but he continued to improve his experimental models. With Henry Ford at the wheel, one of his improved models won an important auto race in 1901 in nearby Grosse Pointe. This bit of notoriety moved him ahead of many of his competitors.

Ford was ready to start another auto company in 1903. At this point he was 40 years old, and he knew just about everything there was to know about the car business at that time. Furthermore, he had the vision that the future of the business was to build a car that was cheap enough to be marketed on a massive scale to the farmers and artisans of the day. In 1903 cars were expensive, and only the well-to-do bought them. There were only about 800 cars in Detroit at the time, and many of Ford's financial backers were quite dubious about his plan. Nevertheless, Ford's new company was successful from the beginning. The company made money, and some of the money was ploughed back into additional design work.

The year 1908 stands as a landmark year in industrial and urban economic history. In that year Henry Ford introduced the Model T Ford. The Model T was reliable, durable, and compact. It benefited from recent improvements in steel technology that permitted steel parts to be both lighter and stronger. Ford realized immediately the implications of improvements in steel for the auto industry. Ford's Model T was very successful from the beginning. In 1908 Ford had a 9.4% share of the American market. But now the nature of the story changes. Up until 1908 Ford had been only a part of the Detroit auto industry and its dynamic localization economies.

When the Model T was introduced in 1908, Ford began the process of creating economies of scale for his company. He did this by inventing the assembly line. At first assembly lines were developed for various parts of the Model T: motors, transmissions, and so on. Then, in 1914, the first moving assembly line was introduced. The chassis of the Model T was pulled along by a conveyer belt that was fashioned after the system used by Chicago meatpackers to "disassemble" cattle into cuts of beef. These improvements in production methods permitted Ford to cut the price of the Model T from $780 in 1910 to $360 in 1914. Halberstam (1986, p. 81) informs us that in 1914, Ford produced 268,000 cars with 13,000 employees while the other 299 U.S. automakers produced 287,000 cars with 66,000 employees. Ford's share of the market (in terms of cars produced) had increased from 9.4% in 1908 to 48% in 1914. The chief source of this tremendous growth in the Ford Motor Company was economies of scale that were *internal to the firm*. As Mr. Ford once put it, "I invented the modern age."

Ford did not stop with the Model T assembly line. Beginning in 1918 he created his River Rouge complex, which eventually became a fully integrated manufacturing facility that took iron ore in at one end and shipped cars out the other end. "The Rouge" began as a boat factory in 1918, added a pig iron plant in 1920, branched out to tractors, auto engines, and a steel plant in 1925, and then became the plant for the Model A Ford that was introduced in 1928. The Rouge employed 75,000 workers, was 1.5 miles long by 0.75 mile wide, and had 23 major buildings and 93 miles of railroad track. The glass for the Model A was even made there. At the Rouge it took 4 days to produce a complete car from raw materials. Halberstam (1986) thinks that Henry Ford invented "just-in-time" inventory and production methods.

So there we have it. The early years of the auto industry in Detroit were characterized by dynamic localization economies as dozens of little firms and their inventor-owners created several products and an industry. They were assisted also by static localization economies in the labor market, capital market, and the markets for intermediate inputs. However, after 1908 the story changes as Ford made his drive for mass production through the development and use of huge economies of scale at the firm level. As you know, huge economies of scale create cities, too. But Ford's internalization of scale economies means that they are not externalities. It was noted above that in 1914, Detroit had a 78% share of American auto production. Ford had 62% of Detroit's share. The tremendous growth of the Detroit auto industry was therefore a combination of static and dynamic localization economies *and* the exploitation of theretofore unimagined economies of scale by Ford Motor Company.

Silicon Valley and the Semiconductor Industry

The transistor was invented on December 23, 1947 at the Bell Laboratories in Murray Hill, New Jersey. Many people have come to regard the transistor as the major invention of the twentieth century. In 1956, its three inventors, John Bardeen, Walter Brattain, and William Shockley, received the Nobel Prize for physics for this major scientific and technological breakthrough, but just what is the transistor, and why is it so important? You need to understand just a little bit of the science and technology to understand the origins of the Silicon Valley industry agglomeration. My source for the information is the book by Braun and Macdonald (1982), which is a nice nontechnical history of the semiconductor industry up to the beginning of the 1980s.

The transistor is a device that uses semiconductor material to amplify or switch an electrical signal. The *New York Times* of July 1, 1948 described it as follows: "The working parts of the device consist solely of two fine wires that run down to a pinhead of solid semi-conductive material soldered to a metal base. The substance on the metal base amplifies the current carried to it by one wire and the other wire carries away the amplified current." Scientists at Bell Labs, MIT, Purdue, and other centers of scientific research had been experimenting with semiconductor materials since the 1930s for a variety of purposes. The article in the *New York Times* reported on the demonstration at Bell Labs of a transistor radio, a radio that contained none of the standard vacuum tubes but instead used solid-state amplifiers. But what is a semiconductor?

A semiconductor is a substance that conducts electricity poorly at low (room) temperatures but will conduct electricity if minute quantities of certain substances (called impurities) are added, or if heat, light, or voltage is applied. In other words, a semiconductor is an insulator of electric current in its normal state, but it can become a conductor of electricity that can be *modulated*, or controlled, by one of these alterations in its state. For example, the addition of the proper impurity alters the configuration of the electrons in the semiconductor so that electricity is conducted. The elements germanium and silicon were two of the semiconductor materials that were under basic scientific study before and during World War II. Both are strong and hard substances that seemed to have promising semiconductor properties.

The first transistor that was invented at Bell Labs in 1947 was in fact a germanium crystal with two wires attached. Bardeen and Brattain discovered that the application of a small positive electric charge greatly increased the capacity of germanium to carry current. This meant that an amplifier could be achieved by the close spacing of two conducting wires on a germanium crystal. By the way, the term *transistor* is a combination of the two words transfer and resistor to indicate that current is transferred across a resistor. The Bardeen–Brattain transistor is called a point contact transistor. A much more practical transistor, called the junction transistor, was invented by William Shockley and was first constructed in 1951, also at Bell Labs. Shockley's idea is to make a sandwich of two types of semiconductors to create the needed reconfiguration of electrons. Limited application of both types of transistors began in the early 1950s, but the reliability of the early devices was not very good. Bell decided to publish the findings from the lab, hold symposiums, and license the technologies widely in the hope that other firms would help to improve the devices. The benefits of a practical transistor for the telephone business were obvious, but Bell also hoped to enhance its reputation and avoid charges that it was a monopoly. Indeed, the first practical application of the junction transistor was made in hearing aids by another company, Raytheon. But in the early and mid-1950s the world was far away from today's world with powerful computers, communication satellites, electronic calculators, and other miniature electronic devices of almost every conceivable sort.

Several companies, including Raytheon, RCA, General Electric, Philco, and Texas Instruments, began working on the transistor right after a Bell symposium in 1952. In 1954 Texas Instruments announced that it had succeeded in making a silicon junction transistor. Silicon had the ability to work at much higher temperatures than germanium, so this transistor was of great interest to the military. By 1957 there were 26 firms that were making some 600 different types of transistors commercially. It turned out that relatively small groups of physicists who were trained in solid-state physics could develop new transistors for various purposes. These people soon learned that the knowledge gained by working for one company could be quite valuable for another company. Frequent movement of semiconductor experts from one company to another became routine. For California's Silicon Valley the most important move of this kind was the decision by William Shockley in 1954 to leave Bell Labs and start his own company in Palo Alto, Shockley's home town. Shockley Semiconductor Laboratory was established in 1955, and because of his great reputation, Shockley was able to hire some of the best young semiconductor experts away from older firms in the East.

Shockley's company was only moderately successful, but in 1957 eight of his men decided to leave and create their own company, Fairchild Semiconductor. The influence of Fairchild has been felt throughout the entire semiconductor industry, and its influence in Silicon Valley is incomparable. Braun and Macdonald (1982, p. 126) noted that by the early 1970s some 41 companies had been founded by former Fairchild employees. Most of these companies are (or were) in Silicon Valley. These companies include industry giants such as Intel and National Semiconductor. But before we get ahead of ourselves with the story of Silicon Valley, we need a little more technical information.

The next great breakthrough was the invention of the integrated circuit in 1959 at Texas Instruments in Dallas. An integrated circuit is a device in which the functions of a number of components are performed inside a single chip of semiconductor material. The first simple integrated circuit was invented at Texas Instruments, but the device was first put into production at Fairchild Semiconductor in 1960. In the early 1960s the entire output of integrated circuits was purchased by the federal government, but numerous private commercial uses for such devices were introduced within a few years.

The experience of Fairchild and other firms with integrated-circuit technologies led to the major breakthrough that has created the world as we now know it. In 1968, three men, Robert Noyce, Gordon Moore, and Andrew Grove, left Fairchild to start a new firm, a little outfit called Intel (also located in Silicon Valley, of course). Does your personal computer have an "Intel inside"? Chances are pretty high that it does. Intel's work on an electronic calculator for a Japanese firm led in 1969 to the invention of the microprocessor, a silicon chip that is programmable. The world's first microprocessor was announced on November 15, 1971. At the time it was called a "micro-programmable computer on a chip." This chip could be combined with more ordinary chips and input–output devices to create a complete microprocessor. Between 1972 and 1982 the 120 chipmaking companies grew to over 3000 firms that offer an enormous variety of high-technology products and services for the private market.

Now we can address the question of why Silicon Valley became the center of the semiconductor industry and its explosive growth. It would seem that there might have been other candidates. What about Dallas, with Texas Instruments? How about New Jersey (near Bell Labs) or Boston or somewhere else? Sure, Shockley started his own company in Silicon Valley, and his company spawned Fairchild Semiconductor, but what else was involved? We will probably never know with certainty, but several factors have been suggested by various experts.

One fairly conventional account of these factors has been provided by Henton and Waldhorn (1988). The role of the federal government was supportive by providing the market for integrated circuits in the 1960s and by providing funds for solid-state physics research and graduate students at various universities. They give a great deal of credit to the growth of the commercial market beginning in the late 1960s, and the availability of venture capital was critical in the creation of new firms. Venture capitalists must have intimate knowledge of the industry because they play an important organizing and planning role in the early years of a company. However, these factors do not tell us why Silicon Valley was uniquely successful. Henton and Waldhorn (1988) also mention the role of Stanford University and electrical engineering professors Fred Terman and John Linvill. They recruited the brightest graduate students and trained them to work in the semiconductor industry, and in 1951 Terman was instrumental in establishing the first university-based research and industrial park at Stanford. These factors tell us something about how Silicon Valley grew through export demand and the exploitation of agglomeration economies. It is clear that venture capital and the training of solid-state physicists and electrical engineers at Stanford are, at least, static localization economies. They may even lead to dynamic localization economies, but this point is not clear.

Braun and Macdonald (1982) provide a more detailed account of how growth took place in Silicon Valley. To Henton and Waldhorn's list of factors they add suppliers of intermediate inputs and good weather, but their main argument concerns the benefits one firm gains from proximity to the others. Information about the latest technological and commercial developments is vital. The latest information is extremely valuable, but its value lasts only for a short time. Under these conditions it behooves one to be located as close to sources of information as possible. Information is not shared on a formal basis but is transmitted through informal contacts. A certain establishment called the Waggonwheel Bar, which is located only a block from Intel, Raytheon, and Fairchild, was known as the fountainhead of the industry because this was where the semiconductor men socialized, exchanged information, and hired employees. As mentioned above, often the hiring involved "stealing" key people from other firms. The inducements usually included both high salaries and stock options because the success of a firm in the semiconductor industry usually depends on the expertise of a few key people. The industry is one with an extremely rapid rate of technical change, and it is clear that the density of firms and the highly competitive environment in Silicon Valley enhanced that rate of technical change. A reasonable hypothesis is one of dynamic localization economies operating through the rate of technical change that were related to the size of the local industry and its competitive market structure. It is pretty clear that early in the 1960s, these dynamic localization economies began to function in Silicon Valley.

H. SUMMARY

The empirical study of static and dynamic agglomeration economies has really just begun. Nevertheless, as recounted in Section E, some findings are emerging that confirm the existence of agglomeration economies that have enhanced growth in urban areas. The size of the local industry (localization economies) seems to matter, but dynamic localization economies may not be as strong as some have thought, except in some fairly unusual cases such as the early auto industry in Detroit and the semiconductor industry in Silicon Valley. Urbanization economies have an influence in some industries, but urbanization economies also may not be as pervasive as some have suggested. A more competitive urban industry, as measured by smaller size of the firms, grows more rapidly. This is a very important recent finding that adds greatly to our knowledge. Also, the evidence points toward diversity in the local economy as a contributor to the growth of an industry. In brief, what we think we know at the moment is that an industry in an urban area will grow more rapidly if it produces a product that is in demand, is competitive, is already of some size in the urban area, is located in a larger urban area (but not too large), and is surrounded by a diverse collection of industries. This is not conjecture but the results of solid, time-consuming empirical research. Hard work—there is no substitute for it.

EXERCISES

1. Suppose that the growth rate of an industry in an urban area has been found to be a function of:

   • The growth rate of labor, with a coefficient of 0.75
   • The growth rate of capital, with a coefficient of 0.4

- The employment level in the industry
- The rate of growth of employment in the urban area
- The number of flights daily departing from the local airport

Is growth in this local industry subject to:

- Static localization economies?
- Dynamic localization economies?
- Static urbanization economies?
- Dynamic urbanization economies?

In each case, how do you know?

2. You conduct a study of a growth industry in a large number of urban areas and find that

$$\ln(E_1 - E_0) = 0.44 + 0.62\ln E_0 + 0.48\text{Pop} + \cdots,$$

where E_0 is employment in the industry in 1979, E_1 is employment in 1989, Pop is the population of the urban area, and $\cdots$ stands for other variables that have been included in the study.
   (a) Is this industry subject to dynamic localization economies? Why? What is the magnitude of the effect, if any?
   (b) Do these results tell us whether the industry is subject to static localization economies? Why or why not?
   (c) Is this industry subject to dynamic urbanization economies? How do you know?

3. Assume that the nation and an urban area have the following employment figures in the base-year:

	Industry A	Industry B	Industry C
United States	1000	2000	500
Urban area	100	100	100

Assume national growth rates of A (10%), B (5%), and C (30%), and assume local growth rate of A (5%), B (10%), and C (25%).
   (a) Use conventional shift-share analysis to compute, for each industry, the three components of growth: the part attributable to total employment growth in the nation, the part attributable to national employment growth in the industry was faster (or slower) than total national growth, and the competitive position of the local industry.
   (b) Use McDonald's version of shift-share analysis to compute the four components of growth for each industry shown in the text. Does the nature of the results change compared to conventional shift-share analysis?

REFERENCES

Beeson, Patricia, 1990. "Sources of the Decline in Manufacturing in Large Metropolitan Areas," *Journal of Urban Economics*, Vol. 28, pp. 71–86.

Braun, Ernest and S. Macdonald, 1982. *Revolution in Miniature: The History and Impact of Semiconductor Electronics*, 2nd ed. Cambridge: Cambridge University Press.

Chinitz, Benjamin, 1961. "Contrasts in Agglomeration: New York and Pittsburgh," *American Economic Review, Papers and Proceedings*, Vol. 51, pp. 279–289.

Fogarty, Michael and G. Garofalo, 1988. "Urban Spatial Structure and Productivity Growth in the Manufacturing Sector of Cities," *Journal of Urban Economics*, Vol. 23, pp. 60–70.

Galbraith, John K., 1956. *American Capitalism*. Boston: Houghton Mifflin.

Glaeser, Edward, H. Kallal, J. Scheinkman, and A. Shleifer, 1992. "Growth in Cities," *Journal of Political Economy*, Vol. 100, pp. 1126–1154.

Halberstam, David, 1986. *The Reckoning*. New York: William Morrow.

Henderson, J. Vernon, 1986. "Efficiency of Resource Usage and City Size," *Journal of Urban Economics*, Vol. 19, pp. 47–70.

Henton, Douglas and S. Waldhorn, 1988. "The Megastate Economy," in S. Fosler, ed., *The New Economic Role of American States*. New York: Oxford University Press.

Jackson, John, 1988. "Michigan," in S. Fosler, ed., *The New Economic Role of American States*. New York: Oxford University Press.

Jacobs, Jane, 1969. *The Economy of Cities*. New York: Vintage Press.

Krugman, Paul, 1991. *Geography and Trade*. Cambridge, MA: MIT Press.

Levin, Richard, W. Cohen, and D. Mowery, 1985. "R&D, Appropriability, Opportunity and Market Structure," *American Economic Review, Papers and Proceedings*, Vol. 75, pp. 20–24.

Lucas, Robert, 1988. "On the Mechanics of Economic Development," *Journal of Monetary Economics*, Vol. 22, pp. 3–42.

Malecki, Edward, 1983. "Technology and Regional Development: A Survey," *International Regional Science Review*, Vol. 8, pp. 89–125.

McDonald, John, 1992. "Assessing the Development Status of Metropolitan Areas," in E. Mills and J. McDonald, eds., *Sources of Metropolitan Growth*. New Brunswick, NJ: Rutgers University Press.

Mills, Edwin, 1992. "Sectoral Clustering and Metropolitan Development," in E. Mills and J. McDonald, eds., *Sources of Metropolitan Growth*. New Brunswick, NJ: Rutgers University Press.

Mullen, John and M. Williams, 1987. "Technical Progress in Urban Manufacturing: North–South Comparisons," *Journal of Urban Economics*, Vol. 21, pp. 194–208.

————, 1990. "Explaining Total Factor Productivity Differentials in Urban Manufacturing," *Journal of Urban Economics*, Vol. 28, pp. 103–123.

O'hUallachain, Breandon and M. Satterthwaite, 1992. "Sectoral Growth Patterns at the Metropolitan Level: An Evaluation of Economic Development Incentives," *Journal of Urban Economics*, Vol. 31, pp. 25–58.

Porter, Michael, 1990. *The Competitive Advantage of Nations*. New York: Free Press.

Romer, Paul, 1986. "Increasing Returns and Long-Run Growth," *Journal of Political Economy*, Vol. 94, pp. 1002–1037.

Schumpeter, Joseph, 1942. *Capitalism, Socialism and Democracy*. New York: Harper & Brothers. 2nd ed., 1947.

CHAPTER

$\boxed{13}$

Labor, Capital, and Urban Growth

A. INTRODUCTION

The factors that contribute to economic growth at the national level were discussed in Chapter 11. Most economic growth can now be attributed to growth in the quantity and quality of labor and capital, rather than to Solow's (1957) "residual." In this chapter we examine the growth of labor and capital in urban areas. Labor is considered first; the chapter begins with a discussion of the theory of human capital and then looks at education and training as sources of investment in human capital. The problems of urban public education in the United States are included in the discussion. We then turn to the migration of labor as a source of growth or decline for urban areas. The migration of labor is found both to respond to economic opportunity and to create economic opportunities in the destination urban areas.

The growth of capital in urban areas is broken down into public and private capital. The urban public infrastructure of highways and roads, buildings, water and sewer systems, and other items is examined first. It is found that investment in public infrastructure began to decline as a percentage of GNP just prior to the time that productivity growth in the United States dropped in 1973. Causation cannot be proved in this case, but the circumstantial evidence is suggestive. Finally, we take a look at the growth of private capital in urban areas. The situation is far more complex than that depicted by Borts and Stein (1964), who assumed that capital was freely mobile into an urban area at a price equal to the national cost of capital. There can be a surfeit of capital embodied in office buildings at the same time that entrepreneurs are having trouble finding financing for promising new ventures. The possible causes of such anomalies in the allocation of capital are examined.

B. HUMAN CAPITAL THEORY

The improvements in our overall standard of living depend in part upon investments that we have made in ourselves. Back in 1961, Theodore Schultz (1961) argued that those investments take several forms:

1. Formal education at the elementary, secondary, and higher levels
2. On-the-job training
3. Adult education (both formal and informal)
4. Health services
5. Migration in response to economic opportunity

Each of these activities contains a sizable element of giving up something in the current time period in order to enhance the potential for future earnings. The investment element of education and training is pretty obvious, but health services and migration may not seem to be human capital investments. Health services can be broadly conceived as expenditures that improve the life expectancy, strength, and vigor of people. A great deal of health expenditures are made during a person's last few months of life, but other health programs and medical procedures prevent disease or permit younger people to live more productive lives. Migration can also be viewed as a form of investment inasmuch as the migrant bears the cost of moving to a new location in exchange for benefits that usually take the form of higher earnings. This section is a brief review of the theory of investment in human capital.

An investment consists of costs paid in the present in return for expected future benefits. Human capital investments involve costs that fall into three general categories: (1) direct expenses (tuition, moving expenses for migration, etc.), (2) forgone earnings during the investment period, and (3) psychic costs (the challenge of learning, the loss of old attachments in migration). The costs vary from person to person and by type of human capital investment. These variations are discussed below. The benefits of human capital investments are of two types: (1) increased earnings, and (2) psychic benefits. The psychic benefits of human capital investment can arise from a more pleasant job (e.g., no heavy lifting), from feeling better through better health, and from education that permits one to enjoy more that life has to offer. All of these cost and benefit factors can make the human capital investment decision complicated in practice, but the outline of the basic theory is very simple.

Suppose that all of the costs and benefits of human capital investment somehow can be measured in terms of money. The decision is whether to make a proposed investment in human capital. If no investment is made, the individual continues to live life as is and receives a stream of benefits $b_0, b_1, \ldots, b_n$, where 0 is the current period and $1, \ldots, n$ are future periods. If the investment in human capital is made, the individual must pay a cost in the current period of C_0. The payment of this cost reduces benefits received in the current period to $B_0 = b_0 - C_0$. The investment results in a new stream of benefits beginning with B_1 and extending to B_n. The investment is made if the discounted present value of the new benefit stream exceeds that of the old benefit stream. In equation form, the investment is made if

$$B_0 + \frac{B_1}{1+r} + \cdots + \frac{B_n}{(1+r)^n}$$

$$> b_0 + \frac{b_1}{1+r} + \cdots + \frac{b_n}{(1+r)^n}.$$

The discount rate is r, and it is a subjective rate that the individual applies to future benefits. Subtraction of terms for the same time period yields the investment criterion

$$\frac{B_1 - b_1}{1 + r} + \cdot \cdot \cdot + \frac{B_n - b_n}{(1 + r)^n} > C_0.$$

This inequality says that the investment is made if the present value of the increases in benefits (e.g., increases in earnings) exceed the cost. Note that the model implicitly has the person making the decision every year. In year 0 the person decides to go to college. In year 1 the person decides whether to continue to attend college, and so on.

This basic model of human capital investment has some important implications. People who are "impatient" have high discount rates and are therefore less apt to make an investment. Holding other factors constant, younger people are more likely to invest in human capital because they have longer lives to reap the benefits of the investment. Investment will increase if the costs of making the investment fall. Finally, more investment will be made if the benefits increase. We consider each implication in turn.

Who has high discount rates and who has low discount rates? An answer to this question may require psychological explanations, but it is known that people do differ in the degree to which they are oriented toward the future. It may stem from the nature of the parenting one receives. One of the virtues of the middle class is its willingness to postpone gratification, and this is something that must be taught to children. Children do not automatically perceive the benefits of doing well in school. Decisions made by teenagers can close off options for the future, and a very important part of being a parent is to make children aware of the implications of their decisions. A related point is life expectancy. Younger people are more likely to make investments in human capital, but only if they have long life expectancies. One observation is that widespread school attendance at the elementary and secondary levels did not occur until life expectancies for the average person had improved in the latter half of the nineteenth century. In the current era consider the life expectancy of a male minority teenager who is a member of the urban underclass. His chances of surviving beyond the age of 30 are lower than for other groups, and his decisions probably reflect this realization.

The propensity to invest in human capital is inversely related to the cost of the investment. Cost can be influenced by many factors. Monetary costs obviously can be influenced by scholarships, health insurance payments (in the case of investment in health services), and other subsidies. But forgone earnings and psychic costs should not be ignored. For example, limitations on child labor reduce the forgone earnings of attending school. The availability of illegal activities (e.g., drug dealing) increases forgone earnings for those so inclined. More stringent law enforcement and higher penalties for breaking the law reduce forgone earnings for those who would pursue illegal activity. Psychic costs of education and job training can be reduced by making education and training institutions more friendly and in tune with the wishes of the students. Psychic costs can be reduced by giving all students high grades, too. Psychic costs of migration are reduced if you already know people in the place to which you migrate.

Benefits have their monetary and psychic sides as well. Some people go to college just to enhance their earning power, but that reason does not explain fully why some people choose to major in history, English, and other fields (economics?) in the liberal arts that do not necessarily offer sizable monetary gain. For some people being an educated person is, to some degree, a reward in itself. Indeed, this is the "product" that liberal arts colleges are selling. If you want a real chance to make big money after graduating from a liberal arts college, you probably must go on to get an MBA degree, go to law school or medical school, get a Ph.D. in computer science, and so on.

As you can see, the basic model of human capital investment is a very flexible analytical framework that can be applied to a wide variety of situations. There is one big potential pitfall with a model that is so flexible. We run the risk of making our "explanations" of behavior tautological. A tautology is the needless repetition of an idea in different words. Consider the following conversation.

Person A says, "It's too bad that Sam decided not to go to college. He is so smart, but he just doesn't care about the future."

Person B says, "I learned in my economics class that Sam doesn't care about the future because he has a high discount rate." Person B has offered only a restatement of the idea expressed by person A, not an explanation of Sam's behavior. Person B has offered no hypothesis that can be tested and found to be *wrong*. A third person joins the conversation.

Person C says, "People who are left-handed are killed in accidents more often than right-handed people, and so they also tend to have lower life expectancies. Sam is left-handed, so that is why he decided not to go to college." Person C's hypothesis cannot be tested with just one observation (Sam), of course, but the idea can be tested (and possibly found to be wrong) using data on a large number of people. Holding other factors constant, are left-handers less likely to attend college?

In the next two sections we use the human capital framework to discuss investment in education and training and in interurban migration.

C. EDUCATION AND TRAINING

The studies of national economic growth discussed in Chapter 11 indicated that about 13% of economic growth in recent years can be attributed to improvements in the level of education and training of the workforce. Denison (1985) estimated that 20% of the growth in output per worker over the period 1929–1982 was associated with the increase in the general education level of workers. Education contributes to economic growth, but do investments in education offer high returns to individuals and to an entire urban area?

Labor economists and others have studied the monetary returns of education to individuals extensively since the early 1960s. The standard method in these studies is to find the discount rate at which the present value of the stream of monetary benefits is just equal to the monetary cost and forgone earnings, or find r^* such that

$$\frac{B_1 - b_1}{1 + r^*} + \cdots + \frac{B_n - b_n}{(1 + r^*)^n} = C_0.$$

Becker's (1975, p. 155) classic study of human capital includes a rate of return to a four-year college education for white males in 1939 that was estimated to have been about 14.5%. This figure is a rate of return in real terms (corrected for inflation). Becker's estimate for the 1949 cohort is 13%, which reflects the fact that federal income taxes had increased and hence the after-tax returns had dropped. White men of that era who invested in college earned high rates of return. The return for college dropouts was estimated to have been 9.5% for white males in 1939 and 8% in 1949. In other words, the men who attended college but did not graduate earned a return on their costs that was, on average, 9.5% (8%). These are still substantial real rates of return. Becker also estimated rates of return for nonwhite men for both the south and the north for 1939; the rate of return in the south was 12.3%, while the return in the north was 8.3%.

Another standard method for looking at the monetary returns to education is to plot the age–earnings profiles for people at various levels of education. Figure 13.1 shows the age–earnings profiles for men who worked full time during 1992. Eight different education levels are shown, from those with fewer than nine years to those with a professional degree. Two patterns are immediately obvious from this figure; men of a given age with greater education levels earn more, and earnings rise with age to a peak that occurs when the man is in his late 40s or 50s. The figure also reveals that the biggest jumps in earnings for men occur between the associate degree (two years) and the bachelor's degree (four year), and between the master's degree and the professional degree (i.e., doctors and lawyers). For example, men at age 40–44 earned $37,292 with the associate degree and $52,119 with the bachelor's degree. Men in this age group with a master's degree earned $53,537, but those with a professional degree earned $99,585. As a point of comparison, high school graduates earned $32,194. Men in this same age group who had not attended high school earned $18,949, and high school dropouts earned $23,337. It is not for nothing that they say, "Stay in school."

Figure 13.1 disguises the fact that earnings vary a great deal by race and ethnic group. For example, average full-time earnings for men in the 25–34 age group in 1992 were:

	Whites	*Blacks*	*Hispanics*
Less than 9 years	$15,433	—	$14,992
High school dropout	19,918	$14,524	16,350
High school graduate	25,143	19,306	22,009
Some college	28,773	23,986	25,869
Associate degree	29,725	28,209	28,077
Bachelor's degree	38,558	27,922	30,945
Master's degree	46,348	—	—
Professional degree	54,950	—	—

Note that the sample size for blacks and Hispanics with advanced degrees is too small to provide reliable estimates. The earnings of black men lag behind those of whites by a substantial amount with the exception of one category of education; blacks with the associate degree earn 95% of the amount earned by whites. The black

FIGURE 13.1 Age–earnings profiles for men: year-round full-time workers in 1992

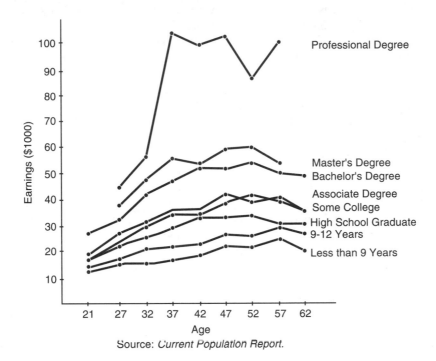

Source: *Current Population Report.*

man with the associate degree earned almost twice as much as a high school dropout. The earnings of Hispanic men lag behind the earnings of whites at each level of education, but the discrepancies are smaller than between blacks and whites. Hispanics also show a high payoff to the associate degree. The associate degree that is offered by junior and community colleges can qualify one for many jobs that require fairly advanced technical training. Junior colleges are crucial institutions that enable workers to upgrade their skills to match the changing demands in the modern economy. However, it is somewhat puzzling that the associate degree does not offer such a high payoff for white men. Junior colleges now attract about 50% of all high school graduates who go on to college, and they are just beginning to attract the attention of human capital and labor market researchers.

Age–earnings profiles for women who worked full time in 1992 are shown in Figure 13.2. The profiles for women at each education level are much flatter than those for men. For example, the woman high school graduate of age 25–29 earned $18,136, and the peak earnings for high school graduates was only $21,445 for the group at age 45–49. Also, the payoff to each additional amount of education is generally lower for women than for men. Full-time earnings for women vary by racial and ethnic group as well, but these variations are smaller than those for men. Full-time average earnings for women in the 25–34 age group in 1992 were:

	Whites	*Blacks*	*Hispanics*
Less than 9 years	$13,285	—	—
High school dropout	14,987	$14,265	—
High school graduate	19,272	17,491	$18,638
Some college	21,907	19,442	20,700
Associate degree	24,324	21,050	—
Bachelor's degree	29,063	27,121	28,949
Master's degree	35,067	—	—
Professional degree	45,810	—	—

Note that the average full-time earnings for Hispanic women are almost equal to the earnings of white women and that the earnings of black women average 86.5 to 95.2% of the earnings of white women. Also, for all three groups, the bachelor's degree adds about $10,000 in comparison to the earnings of high school graduates.

The data examined so far show that there are strong economic incentives to pursue more education, but do these incentives vary over time? In fact, there have been substantial variations over time in the payoff to education. A full exploration of this point would take the discussion into the realm of labor economics rather than urban economics, but a few numbers can illustrate the idea. Some readers may recall that during the 1970s, the payoff to education had dropped compared to previous

FIGURE 13.2   Age–earnings profiles for women: year-round full time
workers in 1992

Source: *Current Population Report.*

time periods and there was talk of the "overeducated" American. You will be happy to know that the return to higher education came back with a vengeance in the 1980s and early 1990s. One useful comparison is ratio of the full-time earnings of holders of bachelor's degrees to the earnings of high school graduates. These figures for males and females in the 25–34 age group (taken from various issues of the *Current Population Reports*) are as follows:

	Males	*Females*
1970	1.38	1.42
1975	1.16	1.29
1980	1.19	1.29
1985	1.27	1.35
1990	1.48	1.59

The dip to the payoff to the college degree is clearly evident, but the recovery of the 1980s made the payoff to the degree even higher in 1990 than it was in 1970. It is no secret that the decade of the 1980s was a good decade for many college-educated workers.

Another technique that is used to study the relationships between earnings, schooling, age and experience, race, and other factors is to estimate a multiple regression model with earnings of individual workers as the dependent variable. Labor economists have been busy estimating earnings functions since the 1960s, and they now use a standard functional form. A study of the earnings of male adults in 1978 by Henderson (1982) can serve to illustrate the method and present a fairly typical set of results. The basic hypotheses are that earnings depend on education and work experience. Work experience is valuable because the worker acquires training that is specific to the job or profession while he or she is on the job. Some firms offer formal programs of on-the-job training, while others provide for training that takes place in more informal settings. It is also true that a worker becomes more productive by doing the job and figuring out how to be more productive in the process. One of Becker's (1975) seminal contributions to the theory of human capital is to make the distinction between general training and specific training. General training is training that increases a worker's productivity in many firms, while specific training increases one's productivity more in one firm than in the others. General training is associated with formal education; educational institutions are useful for imparting knowledge that is of a general nature—knowledge that can be used in many settings. Some firms offer general training as well, but they prefer not to provide workers with training that will enhance their earning power in general. Instead, firms prefer to offer specific training to workers so that those workers become more productive only if they stay with the firm that provided the training.

Let us now see how these ideas have been applied in the study by Henderson (1982). It is possible to measure the worker's amount of formal education (i.e., general training), but it is extremely difficult to measure the amount of specific training that has been acquired on the job. Empirical studies of earnings usually use total work experience as a reasonable substitute for the worker's amount of on-the-job training. However, many studies of earnings do not have a measure of actual years of (relevant) work experience. Often, they know only the age of the worker and the years of formal education. This is the case in Henderson's (1982) study of adult men, and he followed the conventional procedure in such a case. He assumed that the amount of work experience of adult men is equal to the man's age minus his years of formal education minus six. In other words, he assumed that the worker entered school at age 6, went to school for the number of years indicated, and then worked without interruption since he left school. These assumptions are reasonable for most adult men. However, we know that some men (especially blacks and Hispanics) suffer from extended periods of unemployment or periods in which they are not in the labor force. Henderson's (1982) study, as well as many others, ignore the possibility that minority workers at a particular age and education level may have less work experience than white workers. There is one more complication. The age–earnings profiles shown in Figure 13.1 show that earnings for adult men peak at an age of 45 to 55. It is apparent that age/experience does not continue to enhance earnings over one's entire working life; the effect is not linear.

With all of this as preface, what did Henderson (1982) find? The dependent variable in the analysis was the natural logarithm of earnings after taxes in 1977 for males who were fully employed at the time of the survey (March 1978). His regression model included many control variables for some personal characteristics, occupation, and the nature of the urban area in which the worker lived, and he found that

$$\ln(\text{earnings}) = 7.879 + 0.047(\text{education})$$

$$+0.032\,(\text{age} - \text{education} - 6) - 0.00058(\text{age} - \text{education} - 6)^2$$

$$-0.116(\text{black}) + \text{other effects,}$$

where age $-$ education $-$ 6 is the measure of work experience. The equation says that the payoff to one more year of education was an increase in earnings of 4.7% and that black workers earned 11.6% less than comparable whites. The payoff to experience declined in percentage terms as the worker gained more experience. The marginal effect of experience so measured at various amounts of experience is $\delta \ln E/\delta(\text{age} - \text{education} - 6) = 0.032 - 0.00116\,(\text{age} - \text{education} - 6)$, or:

Age $-$ Education $-$ 6	Effect on Earnings of One More Year (%)
0	3.2
2	3.0
5	2.6
10	2.0
20	0.9
27.6	0.0

Henderson (1982) also found that some of the characteristics of the urban area influenced earnings. The size of the urban area—the population level—had a positive effect on earnings that diminished slightly as the size of the urban area increased. The average housing price in the urban area had a positive effect on earnings, with an elasticity of 0.17; a 1% higher housing price was associated with earnings that were 0.17% higher. The murder rate in the urban area (per 100,000 population) also had a positive effect on earnings, and workers who lived in the central city earned 7.1% less than their suburban counterparts. These variations in earnings appear to be compensating the workers for various good and bad features of urban areas. This idea is discussed at more length below in Section D.

The last few paragraphs and Figures 13.1 and 13.2 contain many data on earnings and education levels, but one must take care in drawing implications from these data. The data only show the average earnings of people at various education levels. The data do *not* tell us that the average person at a particular education level can earn a certain greater amount if he or she acquired the additional education. First, many people with lower levels of education are not capable of pursuing higher levels of education. Furthermore, some did not pursue more education because they knew that, for them, the payoff was not sufficient to justify the cost. The other way to make the point is that part of the payoff to more education is a payoff to a person's basic intellectual ability. How much of the payoff of a college degree can be attributed strictly to the degree, and how much stems from the fact that college graduates have higher native ability and motivation than many other people? Labor economists and other researchers have wrestled with this question from the very beginning of the human capital "revolution," but they have not come up with a decisive answer. Surely the answer depends on the field of endeavor. In some fields one can be self-taught. Remember that Abraham Lincoln taught the law to himself. Other fields require years of formal instruction. We prefer to have a doctor who has actually attended medical school. In recent years several fields that people learned on their own or through experience have become curricula in institutions of higher education. Charlie Chaplin did not attend film school. Walter Cronkite did not major in TV and radio.

Despite this caveat, it is illuminating to take a brief look at the educational attainment figures for adults in the United States. Table 13.1 displays data on educational attainment for adults aged 25 and over for 1993 by age and race. In that year 19.8% of adults did not have a high school diploma, 35.4% had the high school diploma (and no additional formal education), and 21.9% had a college degree (7.4% with advanced degrees). Educational attainment varies somewhat by age group. As you probably would have guessed, more older adults who are still of working age

TABLE 13.1	Educational Attainment of Adults (Age 25 and Over), 1993 (Percent)					
	Less than High School	*High School*	*Some College*	*Assoc. Degree*	*BA/BS*	*Advanced Degree*
All	19.8	35.4	16.6	6.4	14.5	7.4
Age						
25–34	13.1	35.9	19.2	7.9	18.6	5.2
35–44	11.4	34.0	19.6	8.3	17.6	9.1
45–54	15.3	35.8	17.1	6.5	14.1	11.2
55–64	25.7	37.9	13.3	4.4	10.9	7.7
White	18.5	35.6	16.8	6.5	14.9	7.7
Black	29.6	36.3	16.7	5.3	8.8	3.4
Hispanic	46.9	26.8	12.8	4.5	6.4	2.6

Source: Statistical Abstract of the United States, 1994.

(aged 55–64) had not graduated from high school and fewer in this group had graduated from college. However, the variations in educational attainment across the younger age groups (25–34, 35–44, and 45–54) were not very large. For example, 23.8% of the youngest group (25–34) had graduated from college compared to 26.7% for the 35–44 age group and 25.3% for the 45–54 age group. Only 18.4% of the 55–64 group had graduated from college.

The variations in educational attainment by race are far more telling. Table 13.1 shows that in 1993 18.5% of white adults had not graduated from high school, but the figures for black and Hispanic adults are 29.6% and 46.9%, respectively. Among whites 22.6% had graduated from college, but only 12.2% of black and 9.0% of Hispanic adults had graduated. Educational attainment for the two main minority groups in the United States has a great deal of room for improvement.

One of the most perplexing problems is the tendency of students to drop out of high school. Some data on dropouts are shown in Table 13.2. This table shows dropout percentages by age group and race. A dropout is a person who is not enrolled in regular school and who has not completed 12 years of education or received a general equivalency degree (GED). The proportions of young people who dropped out of high school clearly have declined since 1970, but the figures show that a sizable problem still exists. Concentrate on the groups that are aged 18 to 21. The dropout percentage in 1990 was 14.0% for whites and 16.0% for blacks, but the Hispanic dropout figure was 32.9%. These figures do not tell us what policies should be adopted, but they do say something about the dimension of the dropout problem.

What does the evidence concerning the monetary returns to education mean for an urban economy? Clearly, it means that an urban area with a more highly educated labor force will have higher output and income levels. It also means that improvements in education will lead to output and income growth. The evidence also presents an urban area with a challenge and a dilemma. We know that a sizable fraction of students in many of the public school systems in the large central cities are failing

TABLE 13.2 High School Dropouts: Percentage of Population Group				
	1970	*1980*	*1990*	*1992*
Total dropouts				
Age 18–21	16.4	15.8	13.4	12.8
Age 22–24	18.7	15.2	13.8	12.5
White				
Age 18–21	14.3	14.7	13.1	12.3
Age 22–24	16.3	14.0	14.0	12.1
Black				
Age 18–21	30.5	23.0	16.0	16.9
Age 22–24	37.8	24.0	13.5	15.6
Hispanic				
Age 18–21	n.a.	40.3	32.9	30.7
Age 22–24	n.a.	40.6	42.8	38.1

Source: Statistical Abstract of the United States, 1994.

to graduate from high school. Many of those high school dropouts are black and Hispanic. Table 13.2 showed that the dropout problem was particularly acute among Hispanics. We have seen that the minority high school graduate earns substantially more than the high school dropout, especially among males, but how much will it cost to increase the graduation rate? We have also seen that there are very large returns to the associate degree among black and Hispanic men. If the goal is to increase aggregate income in the minority population, the more efficient choice might be to concentrate on getting high school graduates through junior college rather than focusing on reducing the high school dropout rate. Alternatively, the more equitable choice is to concentrate on increasing the high school graduation rate because dropouts have the lowest income levels. If resources for education programs were unlimited, we could pursue all good programs at once. A more realistic view is that difficult choices must be made. One of the roles of the economist is to point out the nature of these choices so that the discussion over policy can be clearer.

In recent years serious concerns have been raised about the quality of education in America in general. Stories abound of the large numbers of high school graduates who do not know when the Civil War took place. It is claimed that one-third of adults are functionally illiterate. In 1983, the National Commission on Excellence in Education published *A Nation at Risk*, a report that depicted American education in stark terms. Criticisms abound of American education at virtually every level, from preschool programs to graduate schools. (Some place the blame for failures of American businesses on MBA programs, for example.) What on earth is an urban area supposed to do? Many people would start with the elementary and secondary schools in the inner city, which are producing people who are clearly poorly educated. We can let the MBAs and the firms that hire them fend for themselves, but the level of educational attainment of many black and Hispanic students in inner cities truly represents a huge problem for society. The implications for earnings of failing to graduate from high school have been spelled out in this section. Do we know what to do to improve public education in the inner cities?

One strategy that evidently does not work is to exhort everyone to "stay in school." If you enter high school reading at the fourth-grade level, it is probably pointless for you to remain in a conventional high school program. You may scrape through ninth grade, but things will only get worse. Most likely it is true that people who drop out of high school when they reach their sixteenth birthday were in the process of dropping out for a considerable period of time. So why do many students reach high school unable to cope with a normal (or even watered-down) high school program? We have a pretty good idea. It begins with parents who cannot or will not support children in their attempts to learn. Parents who are overwhelmed by their own economic and social problems have little energy left over to provide the necessary environment and encouragement. For example, the mobility of low-income households is notoriously high in some inner cities. Many children are forced to change schools frequently; a student turnover rate in inner city schools of 40% per year is fairly common. The next step is to place such children together in a school that is not particularly well funded. Finally, locate that school in a neighborhood where there are very few positive role models of people who have attained some measure of success through schooling. That ought to do it. We know pretty well what to do—change all of the factors that have just been mentioned. How can this be accomplished? It turns out that we know what to do, at least on a limited scale. A series of studies by Rosenbaum (1993) and his associates has shown that taking minority children and their welfare mothers out of public housing in Chicago and placing them in subsidized housing in white suburbs actually has significantly improved the educational attainment of the children compared to others who remained in the city schools. This project is discussed in more detail in Chapter 16. Racial and economic integration seems to work. A comprehensive strategy for improving the human capital of an urban area includes school integration. What *else* can we do, you might ask?

Murnane and Levy (1992) provide a summary of what is known and advocate a policy of systemic school reform that is backed up with support from the federal government. For Murnane and Levy, reform of our system of schooling involves:

1. Creating standards for student performance in crucial subjects such as math and reading and creating valid methods for assessing progress in meeting those standards,

2. Creating incentives for students (especially high school students) to work harder in school and take more demanding subjects,

3. Forging better connections between school and work,

4. Creating better teachers by drawing in more of the better college graduates and giving them better training, and

5. Reforming the system for financing of the public schools by reducing the reliance on the local property tax. (As discussed in Chapter 10, the state of California now has a system that essentially equalizes spending per pupil across school districts.)

The federal government can support these reforms by supporting high-quality schooling for disadvantaged children, helping to recruit and train talented teachers, and assisting with the development of educational standards and assessment techniques.

Murnane and Levy (1992) see an important role for parental choice in school reform as well, but they are quite skeptical of proposals for school vouchers. The matter of school vouchers to support students to attend any school of their (or their parents') choice was introduced in Chapter 10. Murnane and Levy answered those who advocate such a broad voucher program. They argued that permitting parental choice within the public school system would improve accountability and might improve student achievement as well. However, they think that vouchers that can be used at any school would probably increase the inequalities that already exist in the education system. Schools will naturally wish to take good students and avoid the ones who are problems. They acknowledged that private schools in general do produce achievement results that are a bit better than results in public schools. But they worried that schools that are in a market-like system will send the message that the parents wish to hear — that their student is doing well (even if he or she is not). They are far from convinced that schools that make their living by attracting students and their vouchers will actually produce better achievement results. They also pointed out that any voucher system must be structured so that disadvantaged or disabled students cannot be left out and so that fraud is controlled. For example, certain disadvantaged students might be given vouchers that are worth a good deal more to the school than the vouchers presented by other students. Their view is that there is a very small constituency for such a voucher system, but they could be wrong on this score.

D. ECONOMICS OF MIGRATION

Americans are a mobile group of people. Greenwood (1981) showed that every year about 3.5% of the population moved between states, an additional 3.0% or so moved across county boundaries within the same state, and about 12% moved within the same county. In other words, about 18% of the population moved in any given year. The most mobile group is young adults; about 9% of those aged 20–24 moved between states in any year. Migration has been studied from many perspectives; our focus is on labor migration as a source of economic growth and development of urban areas.

The first thing that you need to understand about migration is the distinction between gross and net migration. The change in the population of an urban area can be written as

$$\text{change in population} = \text{births} - \text{deaths} + \text{in-migration}$$

$$- \text{out-migration.}$$

Births minus deaths is called the *natural increase* in the population, while in-migration minus out-migration is *net migration. Gross migration* refers both to the amount of in-migration and the amount of out-migration. Normally, these gross migration flows are large compared to the amount of net migration. The natural rate of population growth varies from place to place, but migration flows are the main source of rapid population growth for an urban area. An urban area such as Los Angeles that experienced very rapid population growth had very large amounts of in-migration, sizable amounts of out-migration, and natural population growth as well. An urban area with little population growth, on the other hand, has negative net migration that roughly offsets the natural increase in the population. Negative net migration can involve large or small gross migration flows as long as the out-migration exceeds the in-migration.

The next thing to understand about migration is that the in-migrants are probably different from out-migrants in some way. People who move to the Chicago urban area include young college graduates who come to work in the financial or business service sector and young adults from Puerto Rico and Mexico who seek better economic opportunity. People who move away include retirees, factory workers who have lost their jobs, and students who are going away to college. In recent decades those who moved away have exceeded those who moved in. A good exercise would be to look up the data on migration for the urban area in which you live. The data from the 1990 Census is a good place to start.

The decision to migrate can be formulated in the human capital investment framework. The classic paper on this topic is by Sjaastad (1962); the migrant incurs monetary (including forgone earnings) and psychic costs in order to gain a stream of monetary rewards and/or nonmonetary gains in the new location. The relevant benefits and costs are different for different types of migrants. The migrants who are moving primarily for labor market reasons should follow the basic monetary human capital model; moving is prompted by gains in earnings and reduced by higher costs of moving. The cost of moving is, for one thing, associated with distance, so migration is more likely to be for shorter distances. The benefits and costs of moving are influenced by the familiarity that the migrant has with the destination. For this reason, migrants often move to places where they have relatives or acquaintances. In addition, younger workers have more to gain from moving, and people who have a greater orientation toward the future (i.e., people with more education) are more likely to move. Numerous studies, many of which were reviewed by Greenwood (1981), have tested these and other hypotheses. Greenwood's (1981) study combined gross migration flows with economic growth in urban areas, so it is discussed in detail below.

Before we turn to Greenwood's (1981) model, there is a third thing that you need to understand about migration—or rather, about studies of migration. There are two schools of thought about migration within the United States or within any advanced national economy in which the population may move about freely. One school of thought is based on the idea that urban labor markets are generally in equilibrium most of the time. People are always migrating for a wide variety of reasons, and the net advantages to migration that open up tend to be closed fairly quickly by shifts in the flows of migrants. Equilibrium wage rates for identical workers can vary substantially from place to place because of amenities and disamenities that people value. People who work in large urban areas are paid more because they face higher housing prices and longer commuting times, for example. People who work in places with nice weather get paid less than people who work in Minneapolis. Indeed, there is a substantial body of research on the quality of life in urban areas that is based on the assumption that variations in wage rates (and housing rents, as well) capture the values of amenities as they exist in various urban areas.

An influential study by Roback (1982) found that wage rates increased with the size of an urban area, the crime rate, heating degree days, snowfall, and the number of cloudy days. Also, she found that wages were higher in urban areas that had grown more rapidly in the previous decade. In Roback's results the effects of education, occupation, industry, race, and other personal characteristics were taken into account. As another example, Blomquist, Berger, and Hoehn (1988) found that (holding these same personal factors constant) wages varied from urban area to urban area in statistically significant fashion with variations in:

- Precipitation (negative effect)
- Heating degree days (negative effect)
- Cooling degree days (negative effect)
- Windspeed (positive effect)
- Violent crime in the urban area (positive effect)
- Teacher/pupil ratio (negative effect)
- Air pollution (negative effect)
- Landfill waste in county (positive effect)
- Superfund hazardous waste sites in county (positive effect)

Note that the results generally are in accordance with intuition in that amenities (disamenities) were associated with lower (higher) wages. The exceptions are precipitation, heating degree days, and air pollution; more rain, colder weather, and more pollution were linked to lower wages. If labor markets and "markets" for amenities are in equilibrium across urban areas, migration patterns will not be related to differences in wage rates.

The other school of thought in migration studies presumes that disequilibrium prevails most of the time and that differences in wage rates and unemployment rates can therefore be used to predict migration patterns. All of the early research on migration was based on the presumption of disequilibrium; research that made use of a model of equilibrium began in the 1970s. Evans (1990) has reviewed the various studies and the logic that stands behind them and concluded that the persistence of net migration in clear patterns is inconsistent with the presumption of equilibrium. Evans (1990) also concluded that urban area wage differentials, especially for occupations of lower skill, are too large to be consistent with equilibrium. Therefore, for purposes of this section it is presumed that there is disequilibrium in labor markets sufficient to cause migrants to respond to wages and/or other simple measures of opportunity in the labor market.

The basic model that Greenwood (1981) used originated with Muth (1971) in a paper entitled, "Migration: Chicken or Egg?" Migration should be in the direction of those urban areas with the most employment growth. But the migrants will create demand for goods and services produced locally and cause employment to rise. Muth (1971) argued that migration and employment growth are mutually dependent; employment growth causes migration *and* migration causes employment growth. His study of net migration to urban areas in the 1950s suggested that 60 to 70% of additional jobs in an urban area were taken by migrants and that each net in-migrant generated one additional job (which had a 60 to 70% chance of being taken by another migrant). Muth's estimate that of 60 to 70% of new jobs taken by in-migrants is in rough agreement with Bartik's (1991) estimate of 77%. [See Chapter 14 for a discussion of Bartik's (1991) work.]

Greenwood (1981) built on the models of Borts and Stein (1964) (described in Chapter 11) and Muth (1971) and developed a more comprehensive model of gross migration of the labor force, employment growth, and unemployment for urban areas. Table 13.3 shows a simplified version of Greenwood's model for urban areas for 1960–1970. The top half of Table 13.3 shows the results for four migration equations; the migration measures cover the five-year period from 1965 to 1970, and are (1) rate of gross out-migration to other urban areas, (2) rate of gross out-migration to non-urban areas, (3) rate of gross in-migration from other urban areas, and (4) rate of gross in-migration from nonurban areas. Note first that each rate of gross migration was positively related to its opposite variable (e.g., the rate of out-migration to other urban areas was positively related to the rate of in-migration from other urban areas). Most studies of gross migration have found that these opposite migration flows are positively related.

Beyond this relationship between opposing gross flows, gross migration for the most part responded to economic variables as expected. Income growth had a positive effect on out-migration to other urban areas (as was not expected), a negative effect on out-migration to nonurban areas, and positive effects on both in-migration flows. Employment growth had one negative effect on out-migration and one positive effect on in-migration. The per capita income level in 1960 had a positive effect on both out-migration to other urban areas and in-migration from nonurban areas. The level of unemployment in 1960 had negative effects on out-migration to other urban areas and on both measures of in-migration. The size of the labor force in 1960 (a measure of the size of the urban area) had a positive effect on out-migration to nonur-

TABLE 13.3 Greenwood's Model of Migration and Urban Growth, 1960–1970

	Dependent Variables: Rates of:			
	Out-migration to urban areas	Out-migration to nonurban areas	In-migration from urban areas	In-migration from nonurban areas
Out-migration to urban areas			+	
Out-migration to nonurban areas				+
In-migration from urban areas	+			
In-migration from nonurban areas		+		.
Income growth	$+^a$	−	+	+
Employment growth	−			+
Unemployment change	$-^a$	+	−	−
Income, 1960	$+^a$			+
Unemployment, 1960	$-^a$		−	−
Labor force, 1960		+		−
Education, 1960	$-^a$	$-^a$		
Age, 1960	−	−		

	Growth Rates of:			
	Manufacturing Employment	Government Employment	Other Employment	Unemployment
Out-migration	−	−	−	−
In-migration	+	+	+	
Natural population growth	+	+	+	+
Unemployment in 1960				−
Manufacturing employment in 1960	−			
Government employment in 1960		−		
Other employment in 1960			−	

^{a}*Sign not as expected. Regression models include control variables for region.*
Source: Table compiled from data obtained from Greenwood (1981, p. 173).

ban areas. Finally, both education and age were negatively related to both measures in out-migration. The asterisks in Table 13.3 indicate that the sign of the effect was opposite to that expected. The good news is that all of the statistically significant coefficients in the equations for in-migration have the expected sign and the equation for out-migration to nonurban areas has only one "incorrect" sign. However, the equation for out-migration to other urban areas has five of eight "incorrect" signs. Clearly, the in-migrants to urban areas were responding to economic opportunities as represented by income and employment growth, declining unemployment rates, and low unemployment rates. The model of out-migration to nonurban areas also says that people responded to economic factors in the urban area of origin. However, the model of out-migration to other urban areas is not satisfactory.

The bottom half of Table 13.3 summarizes the Greenwood (1981) model for the employment growth rates of three broad industry categories (manufacturing, government employment, and all other employment) and for changes in the rate of unemployment. The models are quite simple and easy to interpret. The employment growth rate in each industry category was negatively related to out-migration, positively related to in-migration and natural population growth (births minus deaths), and negatively related to the initial employment level in the industry category. All of these results are as expected, including the results relating to the initial level of employment. Recall from Chapter 12 that O'hUallachain and Satterthwaite (1992) found the same kind of result for most of the industries that they studied. The results for the change in the unemployment rate also make sense. Out-migration reduced the increase in unemployment, natural population increases increased the rise in unemployment, and the level of the unemployment rate in 1960 held back increases in unemployment.

All in all, the Greenwood (1981) study of gross migration of the labor force and employment growth in urban areas tells us that migrants, especially in-migrants, responded to measures of economic opportunity and also generated employment growth. The ability to attract the labor force is a prime mover in the growth of employment on a broad front, and the labor force can be attracted by conventional economic incentives such as income growth, employment growth, reductions in the unemployment rate, high income levels, and low unemployment levels. These findings are important as we consider the question of an overall economic growth strategy for an urban area in Chapter 14.

E. PUBLIC CAPITAL

The consideration of capital as an input into the economic growth of an urban area must include the capital that is provided by the public sector. It is clear that the returns to investments in urban public infrastructure can be of considerable magnitude, but in an era of budget stringency at the federal level, those investments must be chosen wisely. Urban transportation facilities have already been discussed in Chapter 8. In this section we take a brief look at the problems of maintenance and more efficient use of, as well as new investment in, urban infrastructure in general.

Perhaps the most relevant measure of the public infrastructure is the value of the public capital stock as a percentage of gross national product. Data on the public capital stock for various years are available from the U.S. Department of Commerce. Of the total public capital stock of $2180 billion in 1990, 86% was owned by state and local governments and 14% was owned by the federal government. The largest components of the infrastructure owned by state and local governments are highways and streets (37%), and public buildings: schools, hospitals, office buildings, police and fire stations, courthouses, and so on (31%). The state and local infrastructure also includes water and sewer systems (16%), other structures such as airports and transit facilities (8%), and equipment (7%).

The data on public capital tell an important story—the public infrastructure as a percentage of GNP has declined steadily since 1970. In 1970 the ratio of public infrastructure of all kinds to GNP was 0.489, but by 1990 that ratio had dropped to 0.406, a drop of 0.083. Much of that drop can be attributed to the decline in the ratio of state and local highway and street infrastructure to GNP from 0.178 to 0.130, but other infrastructure categories such as public buildings and flood control projects exhibit declines as well. The failure to build new urban highways was discussed in Chapter 8. The failure of public infrastructure to grow with the economy stems from a decline in gross investment in infrastructure that began in the late 1960s. According to data in Winston and Bosworth (1992), gross investment in public capital peaked in 1969 at 3.9% of GNP and dropped steadily throughout the 1970s and early 1980s to 2.0% of GNP in the years 1982–1985. Since then it increased slightly as a percentage of GNP to 2.2% in 1991. Winston and Bosworth (1992) showed that spending on one critical component of infrastructure, highways and streets, increased sharply in the 1950s and 1960s to a peak level of $36 billion (1990 dollars) in 1969 and then fell to $19 billion in 1981. Spending on this category had recovered to $30 billion in 1990, so there has been an effort in recent years at least to maintain the existing highway and street systems and to make some new investments.

Some of the spending in recent years has been to replace portions of the urban highway systems that were built in the late 1950s and 1960s. These highways have useful lives of 25 to 30 years in northern urban areas, and after that they must be replaced from the dirt up. They reach a point at which putting patches on the patches does no good. I live in the Chicago urban area and have watched as most of the expressway system has been rebuilt. Winston and Bosworth (1992) explained that the most important reason for falling infrastructure investment, especially in highways and roads, is a lack of revenues dedicated to the purpose. Highway construction is financed primarily by taxes on gasoline. The federal tax on gasoline remained at 4 cents per gallon from 1960 to 1982, which meant that the real federal gas tax dropped from 4 cents per gallon to 1.3 cents per gallon. The federal gas tax has since been raised twice and is now 14 cents per gallon. State taxes on gas also remained flat in nominal terms from 1960 to 1980 at about 9 cents per gallon. Since then the average state tax has increased to approximately 16 cents per gallon. It seems that the sharp increase in gasoline prices in the 1970s caused by the Organization of Petroleum Exporting Countries (OPEC) deterred governments from increasing gas taxes. The price of gasoline dropped in the 1980s; government officials evidently felt that gas taxes could be increased in an era of declining pump prices. The recovery of spending on highways and roads was the result. Much of that increase in spending was financed by rising gas taxes that increased the monies in the federal and state highway trust funds. Grants from the U.S. Department of Transportation, the U.S. Department of Housing and Urban Development (under community block grants), and state governments also played a role.

There is no doubt that some investments in urban public infrastructure yield high returns. The Congressional Budget Office (1988) has examined a large number of cost-benefit studies and concluded that:

1. Investments used to maintain the urban highway systems yield 30 to 40% per year.
2. Certain urban highway expansion projects yield 10 to 20% per year.
3. Investments in major airports and the system for controlling air traffic can reduce congestion and yield high returns.

4. Investments in most waterway projects and public transit systems in smaller cities, however, yield low returns.

Much of the investment in urban public infrastructure has been, and most likely will continue to be, financed by the federal government. Under these circumstances federal officials have the responsibility of choosing from among applications for investment projects that are proposed by states and/or local governments. The federal infrastructure programs require that cost-benefit analyses and environmental impact statements must be performed so that allocation decisions can be based on economic criteria. Political factors have played, and no doubt will continue to play, a role in deciding who gets what in public infrastructure funds. Nevertheless, let us suppose for the moment that a federal agency attempts to allocate its limited budget for infrastructure projects in such a way as to maximize the return to investment. How should the agency proceed?

The agency faces what is called the *capital budgeting problem*. The agency has required that all applicants use the same methods in their cost-benefit analyses and has discovered that the proposed projects that have benefits in excess of costs will far exceed the available budget. Which projects should be selected? At this point the agency must realize that the relevant opportunity cost is the best project that must be rejected, not the costs of resources used in the projects. For example, suppose that the agency has a budget of $100 and that the following applications have been received:

Project	Cost	*Present Value of Benefits*	$B - C$	B/C
V	50	75	25	1.50
W	25	40	15	1.60
X	100	140	40	1.40
Y	25	35	10	1.40
Z	75	112	37	1.49

This is a group of outstanding projects; all have sizable net benefits (benefits minus costs), and the benefit/cost ratio is at least 1.4 for all of them. First, suppose that projects are chosen on the basis of the size of the net benefits. Project X has the largest net benefit (40), but its cost of 100 will consume the entire budget. Clearly, the agency can do better by, for example, selecting projects V, W, and Y at a cost of 100 and net benefits of $25 + 15 + 10 = 50$. The procedure of selecting projects on the basis of the absolute size of the net benefits does not work.

Next, suppose that projects are selected in order of their benefit/cost ratios. Project W, with a benefit/cost (B/C) ratio of 1.60, is chosen first. The next-best project by this criterion is V, with a B/C value of 1.50. The third-best project is project Z, with a B/C value of 1.47. However, project Z costs 75 and, given that projects W and V have already been selected, the agency cannot afford project Z. The agency skips over project Z and selects the next-best project that it can afford, project Y. The agency has selected projects W, V, and Y, and these choices produce net benefits of 50. By now you may have figured out that there is a better option. The combination of projects Z and W costs 100 and yields net benefits of 52. The point is that the simple rule of selecting projects in order of their benefit/cost ratios does not always work either. The correct procedure is to consider all projects at once and maximize net benefits for the given capital budget.

Now let us turn to the problem faced by local officials. Different pots of federal money exist for different purposes: mass transit, highways, sewers, community development, housing, and so on. Consider applications for money from just one of those pots. Federal programs normally require that the state and/or local government provide a portion of the funds for a project. Suppose that the cost of a project for the local government is $m\%$ of its actual cost and the federal government's share is $1-m$. The local government has an incentive to propose any project for which benefits exceed its costs, or

$$B > mC.$$

This criterion will include a lot of proposed projects that should not be funded because total project costs exceed benefits, but local officials do not have an incentive to worry about total costs. The allocation decisions must be made at the federal level.

Given that local government is paying $m\%$ of the costs, will the federal officials make the correct choices by maximizing benefits minus *federal* costs? They will make the correct choices provided that all local governments pay the same share of the costs *and* provided that it is worthwhile to spend the entire capital budget of the federal agency. To see this, suppose that in the numerical example above, local governments pay 25% of the costs of each project. Assume that the cost figures above now refer to the costs paid by the federal agency. The total cost of the projects is now 133 (100 paid by the feds and 33 paid by the locals), and the benefits are the same as before. The project set Z and W is still the best choice, and net benefits are $152 - 133 = 19$. Furthermore, both projects Z and W have positive net benefits. The total cost of project Z is 100 compared to benefits of 112, and the total cost of project W is 33 compared to benefits of 40. However, suppose that the local share is 33% of the costs. Now the total cost of the two projects, Z and W, is 150. The total benefits are still 152, but project Z should not be selected because its net benefits are negative. The cost of project Z is now 112.5 (75 paid by the feds and 37.5 paid by the locals). The federal agency should, in this case, resist the urge to spend the money and save it for a better project. In fact, there is a better project. Project V has benefits of 75 and a cost of 75. However, project V also should not be chosen because it produces no net benefits.

Do we have any idea about the amount of the urban infrastructure projects for which benefits clearly exceed costs? We have no answer to this question, but Winston and Bosworth (1992) attempted to estimate infrastructure investment needs by two methods. In the first method they computed the amount of infrastructure needed to maintain the ratio of core infrastructure capital to GNP. Core infrastructure consists of highways and streets, water and sewer systems, and other structures (mainly mass transit and airports). The ratio of core infrastructure to GNP in 1990 was 0.22. If GNP grows by 2.5% per year, net additions to core infrastructure need to be 0.55% of GNP (0.22 times 2.5%). Spending needed to maintain the current infrastructure was estimated at 0.60% of GNP, so 1.15% of GNP needs to be spent on core infrastructure to maintain the ratio of 0.22. The 1.15% of GNP translates into $63 billion in 1990 dollars; actual spending on core infrastructure in that year was $55 billion, so this goal can be achieved with a fairly modest increase in spending. Winston and

Bosworth (1992, p. 279) estimated that spending on core infrastructure would have to be increased by $33 billion per year (in 1990 dollars) to reach the goal of a ratio of core infrastructure to GNP of 0.25, the ratio that existed in 1970.

The second method that Winston and Bosworth (1992) used for estimating infrastructure needs was based on a review of the detailed studies of needed highways and bridges, water and sewer systems, mass transit, and airport and air traffic control systems. The federal agency that is responsible for each of these infrastructure programs has conducted the relevant studies as part of their regular duties. Winston and Bosworth (1992) found that the greatest needs, as indicated by the federal agencies, are for investments to reduce traffic congestion on urban highways and air traffic congestion at large airports. Studies by the U.S. Department of Transportation indicate that goals for reduction in these two forms of congestion can probably be met with an increase in spending on core infrastructure that is roughly equal to the $33 billion that was mentioned in the preceding paragraph. However, this estimate ignores the fact that the existing highway and airport facilities are being used inefficiently. The inefficiencies of traffic congestion were discussed at length in Chapter 8. A similar analysis could be developed for airports.

The difficulties of implementing congestion pricing on urban highways were discussed thoroughly in Chapter 8. The conclusion reached is that some congestion pricing of urban highways is better than none at all but that a failure to cover a major portion of the urban highway system with tolls will cause traffic diversion that will reduce substantially the efficiency gains of the toll system. On the other hand, the implementation of congestion pricing at major airports could be accomplished relatively easily because all the airplanes pay a landing fee. That fee could be made a function of the number of takeoffs and landings that occur during the same time period during the day. Efficient peak-load landing fees would reduce congestion (and the amount of time and fuel wasted) by shifting some of the flights to less congested times of day or, perhaps, to less congested airports. Morrison and Winston (1989) estimated that optimal runway pricing would yield annual gains in welfare equal to $3.8 billion (in 1988 dollars). Morrison and Winston (1989) also reported that several major airports have too little capacity. They recommended that additional runways are needed at a number of airports that serve the large urban areas and that there are other methods for enhancing capacity that are not being used. They estimated that a program of airport expansion could generate annual net benefits of $11 billion.

The implications of this discussion of infrastructure for urban area economic growth are pretty clear:

1. Urban areas cannot expect dramatic increases in federal funding for infrastructure projects, but some increase would be reasonable.

2. Urban areas should get busy on the congestion and capacity problems at their commercial airports. They should be seeking federal support for airport projects, and these projects should tend to win approval because sizable gains in welfare can be documented.

3. Urban areas should be looking at making improvements in their urban highway systems, and they should be trying to find opportunities for the use of congestion tolls and/or other methods for making more efficient use of existing facilities.

4. According to Small, Winston, and Evans (1989), urban areas should review and alter the design standards used in urban highways to make them more durable as less costly to maintain.

These modest steps are likely to have a high payoff for the urban area.

F. PRIVATE CAPITAL

At last we come to private capital investment. The estimates of the contribution of private capital to economic growth vary, but they all agree that its contribution is substantial. One reason for the variation in estimates is the fact that advances in knowledge often come embodied in new capital, so we have difficulty figuring out whether to attribute economic growth to capital or to improvements in technology. This theoretical dispute should not divert us from the fact that capital is essential. Indeed, it is even more important to attract investment if that new investment embodies new technologies. In the long run, increases in capital per worker will increase worker productivity and earnings.

There are several ways to look at capital and investment. One method is to look at the categories of investment in the GNP accounts. Private investment consists of:

1. Capital consumption allowances (depreciation)
2. Nonresidential structures (e.g., industrial buildings, office buildings, stores, etc.)
3. Producers' durable equipment
4. The change in business inventories
5. Residential structures.

Gross private domestic investment in 1990 had the following composition (in billions):

	Gross private domestic investment	$799.5
less	Capital consumption allowance	602.8
	Net private domestic investment	196.7
	Nonresidential structures	51.4
	Producers' durable equipment	55.5
	Residential structures	83.5
	Changes in business inventories	6.3

Gross private domestic investment was 14.5% of GNP in 1990, but *net* private domestic investment, the amount that the capital stock really increased, was only 3.6% of GNP in that year. However, some of the investment that went for capital consumption represents improvements in the quality of the capital stock because old capital that is worn out is being replaced by new capital. Net investment had been a larger fraction of GNP earlier in the decade; the figure for net investment was 5.8% of GNP in 1985. Also note that 45.6% of net investment in 1990 was in residential structures and increases in business inventories. There is nothing wrong with these investments, but worker productivity depends upon investment in nonresidential structures and producers' durable equipment. These investments amounted only to a net investment of 1.9% of GNP in 1990. These two categories of private business investment had been 3.4% of GNP in 1985. However, either figure is far below the amounts that are invested in other leading economies, such as Japan and Germany. Macroeconomists have studied this problem extensively, and many of them believe that our low levels of net investment stem from crowding out by the federal government's persistent increases in borrowing to finance its budget deficit and from a federal tax system that encourages private borrowing rather than saving.

Not only is net investment in the United States low by international standards, but the allocation of that investment in the 1980s was clearly inefficient. The story is overbuilding of commercial real estate in general and office space in particular. Much of that overbuilt office space is located in the downtowns of major urban areas and in some of the suburban employment centers—the edge cities. The problem of inefficient timing of commercial real estate investment was examined theoretically in Chapter 7. In this section we provide a narrative discussion of the problem. At the same time too much was being invested in commercial real estate, one suspects that too little was being invested in more productive capital assets. This proposition is also examined. These discussions are important for urban areas because major private investments are made in major urban areas. What determines how much investment of various types is made in an urban area?

Before we attempt to answer this question, it is useful to introduce another method for looking at capital and investment that builds on the idea of the product cycle. Investments of different types are made by firms in different phases of the product cycle. Firms that are just in the process of developing a new product make what are often fairly small investments in research and development and prototype versions of the products. The entrepreneur needs funds to make investments of these kinds, and the risk attached to such investments may be very high. Venture capital is one source of investment funds for these enterprises. Venture capital is provided by specialized venture capital institutions which usually take an equity share in the business and take an active role in the management of the firms that they finance. In the next phase of the product cycle the firm needs more sizable amounts of financing to take the new product to the larger market. The firm may go the equity markets and issue shares of stock at this point. Finally, the more mature firm that is now growing at a slower pace may require financing for continued expansion into new markets or for investments in plant and equipment to reduce costs. However, often the mature firm will be able to finance at least some of its required investment out of retained earnings. The more mature firms will also probably have ready access to bank loans, bond financing, and equity financing.

Let us examine empirical evidence on these three types of firms in reverse order. Manufacturing in the United States is, for the most part, composed of mature firms. Clark, Gertler, and Whiteman (1986) examined capital accumulation in total manufacturing (and in four individual manufacturing industries) at the state level from 1954 to 1976. They made investment a function of past profit levels, changes in profits, and the preexisting capital stock. This is a standard formulation that was used to study investment at the national level in the 1940s and 1950s. This emphasis on internal liquidity (past profits and changes in profits) has a long history in investment modeling. Recently, Fazzari, Hubbard, and Petersen (1988) have developed a more formal model based on asymmetric information about investment prospects to justify this emphasis on internal liquidity. If you know more about the prospects for an investment than your banker (or the bond market) knows, and if you are running a successful business, the easiest way to finance investment is to make enough profits to pay for it. This way you do not have to deal with people who want to charge too much or who just will not be cooperative.

The empirical results obtained by Clark et al. (1986) are moderately successful; the three variables are statistically significant with the hypothesized signs in about one-half of the regression equations estimated (positive signs for past profits and changes in profits, and a negative sign on preexisting capital). Further empirical tests revealed that capital accumulation rates were usually influenced by lagged profit rates (positive sign) and wage rates (negative sign). Finally, the capital/labor ratio was found to be influenced in many cases by past changes in the profit rate (negative sign), past changes in wages (positive sign), and past productivity changes (positive sign). These results are generally consistent with a neoclassical production function for manufacturing of the type introduced in Chapter 11.

Clark et al. (1986, pp. 250–251) drew from these empirical results some conclusions for public policy concerned with stimulating growth in declining regions. They believed that their results support the use of public capital funds and risk pools to overcome capital constraints often faced by small, growing firms. Many others have reached the same conclusion concerning policy, although one might question whether manufacturing is the sector in which firms generally face capital constraints on growth.

Another study of investment in manufacturing was conducted by Hodge (1981) using annual data over the period 1963–1972 on four manufacturing industries for 42 urban areas. The industries are furniture, apparel, rubber and plastics, and electronics. Furniture and apparel are very mature industries, whereas rubber and plastics (especially plastics) and electronics are industries that have more firms in the phase of rapid growth. The data are old, but the choice of industries provides a useful perspective. The dependent variable in Hodge's (1981) analysis is gross investment in the urban area for each industry as a percentage of the existing capital stock: I/K. The empirical results obtained by Hodge (1981) are as follows:

Variable	Furniture	Apparel	Rubber and Plastics	Electronics
GNP level	+	+		+
GNP growth	+	+		
Output price	+	+		+
Capital price	−			
Interest rate				−
Local wage	−	+	−	
Property tax	−	−		
State corporate tax	−			
Electric price			−	
Spatial demand			+	
Suppliers' index			+	

The first thing to note is that national variables (GNP level, GNP growth, price of output at the national level, the price of capital or the interest rate) drove investment at the local level in three of the industries: furniture, apparel, and electronics. Local prices or taxes had some negative effects in three industries. A higher local wage rate in the industry reduced investment in two industries (furniture and rubber and plastics) but increased investment in apparel. Either sign is possible on theoretical grounds; a higher wage means that costs are higher and output (and investment) is lower, or a higher wage results in a substitution of capital for labor that dominates the output effect. Higher local property taxes and state corporate taxes reduced investment in the furniture industry, and the property tax had the same effect in the apparel industry. The price of electricity had a negative effect on investment in rubber and plastics. Finally, indexes of strong demand nearby and nearby suppliers of inputs increased investment in rubber and plastics.

The results indicate that local cost conditions were especially important in the furniture industry, one of the mature industries. Also, the local property tax had a negative impact on investment in the apparel industry, the other mature industry. The rubber and plastics industry was particularly sensitive to location patterns, on both the demand and supply sides. This industry was also sensitive to local wages and electricity prices. Rubber and plastics was a growth industry but one that was sensitive to transportation costs and input prices. In contrast, the electronics industry was a growth industry that was not sensitive to any local variables; investment in this industry was driven by national economic factors. The message from this study is not crystal clear—few empirical studies provide crystal-clear results. However, there was some tendency for local investment in mature industries to be sensitive to local costs as well as national economic conditions. The study also shows that local investment in at least one growth industry, rubber and plastics, was sensitive to local cost conditions and transportation costs. Finally, local investment in the other growth industry (electronics) showed no sensitivity to local costs or transportation costs and was driven by national economic trends.

Many other studies have examined the decision of where to locate an investment; these studies have been reviewed in detail by Bartik (1991, pp. 216–232). Bartik's main interest was in discovering whether state and/or local taxes had an impact on investment. His review uncovered nine studies that examined business investment location decisions at the level of the urban area, and in six of those nine studies some measure of state and/or local taxes had a statistically significant negative effect on investment. All but two of those studies concentrated on manufacturing, albeit some of the manufacturing industries were in the "high-tech" category. Bartik's (1991) summary of the studies is that investment decisions at the level of the urban area are moderately sensitive to state and/or local taxes, which are one component of local costs. The evidence therefore suggests that it is prudent to keep state and local taxes and other costs in line with other locations, because some more mature manufacturing industries (and perhaps some others) are sensitive to local costs.

Now we come to investments financed by venture capital. Venture capital is used to finance the risky investments that are needed to take a new product through the development and initial marketing stages. The sources and uses of venture capital funds has been studied extensively by Florida and Smith (1992). Their research has led them to the following conclusions:

1. Venture capital is supplied by venture capital institutions that are located mainly in New York, northern California (Silicon Valley), and Boston's high-tech beltway (Route 128). Venture capital also originates in Chicago, Texas, and a few other places.

2. Venture capital flowed primarily to established centers of high technology, such as Silicon Valley in California and Route 128 around Boston. Venture capital flows from New York, Chicago, Texas, and other supply sources to these established centers.

3. Venture capital alone cannot create a high-tech industrial base where there was none. Investors in the high-tech centers were linked to other sources of venture capital by coinvestment arrangements of various types.

4. Venture capital is an important element in high-tech agglomerations, but it is not a cure-all for declining areas.

In short, venture capital was used primarily to finance new ventures in the computer industry, both hardware and software. It had not really gained widespread use as of the time the Florida–Smith research was done in the late 1980s. Florida and Smith (1992) warned against the use of venture capital programs as a "quick fix" for the local economy. Their advice is to develop an overall economic growth and development strategy. That overall strategy may or may not include a venture capital program. The business of an overall economic development strategy is the topic of Chapter 14.

Finally, we come to the peculiar case of investment in commercial real estate in general and office space in particular. Perhaps lenders were willing to lend for real estate projects because the collateral for the loan was the building itself, a real asset that could always be seized and sold for recovery of a loan in default. What many lenders discovered to their great displeasure was that when office vacancy rates topped 20%, the market value of some commercial buildings had dropped to levels that were far below the amount of the loan. How could this gross overinvestment in urban office space in the late 1980s have happened?

Many have ruminated over this question. Table 13.4 shows vacancy rates in the downtown and suburban office markets for selected urban areas from 1988 to 1992. Downtown vacancy rates were at or well over 20% in places such as Atlanta, Denver, Los Angeles, Chicago, and Cleveland. Some of the urban areas listed actually had higher vacancy rates in 1992 than they did in 1988, even though many of those vacancy rates in 1988 were very high by historic standards. What was going on here? (The low vacancy rate in downtown Phoenix may be caused by rapid growth in some particular sectors of the local economy, but this has not been investigated.)

Edwin Mills (1995) tried to provide some answers. He cited an estimate by Birch et al. (1990) that 43% of all of the office space ever built in the United States was built in the 1980s. Contracts for the construction of office space increased from 1976, reaching a peak in 1981. There was a small decline in contracts from 1981 to 1983 and then a further boom from 1983 to 1986. The amount of contracts then declined until 1989, and then the bottom dropped out completely. Office development therefore began to slow down in 1986, and contracts dropped by 75% over the subsequent six years. This kind of decline qualifies as a depression in this particular sector. What caused the depression in the office market? First, Mills (1995) noted that the office employment growth slowed substantially after 1985, and by 1990 and 1991 of-

TABLE 13.4	Office Vacancy Rates for Selected Downtown and Suburban Office Markets (Percent)				
	1988	1989	1990	1991	1992
Atlanta					
Downtown	18.98	18.26	19.58	20.83	25.28
Suburbs	20.10	21.92	19.31	19.22	16.99
Miami					
Downtown	30.00	24.00	25.00	27.00	27.00
Suburbs	25.50	24.30	21.60	22.60	23.60
Dallas					
Downtown	37.25	31.53	26.15	19.61	13.59
Suburbs	25.40	26.64	28.76	30.16	32.80
Denver					
Downtown	30.53	27.09	25.57	26.30	24.95
Suburbs	27.40	25.40	20.80	22.40	20.20
Phoenix					
Downtown	4.80	6.70	4.20	5.60	7.20
Suburbs	NA	NA	28.00	25.00	25.90
Los Angeles					
Downtown	NA	NA	26.60	24.40	21.50
Suburbs	16.80	15.00	17.00	20.00	21.00
Kansas City					
Downtown	24.79	18.38	17.14	22.72	21.06
Suburbs	17.66	15.21	13.13	14.06	12.13
Milwaukee					
Downtown	12.46	22.55	24.00	16.90	19.90
Suburbs	16.47	20.25	19.10	17.80	17.70
Chicago					
Downtown	13.02	13.12	16.39	17.21	20.03
Suburbs	21.35	20.90	21.85	22.53	21.60
Cleveland					
Downtown	10.72	9.96	15.38	23.42	23.04
Suburbs	15.10	18.80	19.40	18.80	16.60
Indianapolis					
Downtown	21.40	19.80	19.20	19.90	20.70
Suburbs	22.60	20.60	23.30	23.40	21.30
Boston					
Downtown	12.00	12.00	16.00	20.00	18.00
Suburbs	16.00	20.00	23.00	28.00	22.00

Source: Table compiled from data obtained from Building Owners and Managers Association International (1994).

fice employment was actually declining slightly. Evidently, the demands for the services provided by office workers stopped growing as rapidly as had been the case in the first half of the 1980s. Mills suggested that a level of saturation had been reached by about 1987 or 1988 in sectors such as accounting, law, FIRE, business consulting, public relations, advertising, and so on. For example, employment in FIRE grew at an annual rate of 4.2% from 1982 to 1987, but the growth rate was only 0.9% from 1987 to 1990. But if the growth rate of office employment was slowing down, why did they continue to build office buildings? Several hypotheses have been advanced:

1. It takes a long time to plan and construct office buildings, and it takes a long time to adjust to a change in the trend in demand.
2. The deregulation of financial institutions in 1981 permitted depository institutions to make bad loans while keeping deposits insured by an agency of the federal government.
3. The change in the federal tax law in 1981 permitted real estate investors to take highly accelerated depreciation allowances that could offset other sources of income. Real estate investments were being made for their use as tax shelters rather than for income purposes. The federal income tax was changed again in 1986 to eliminate the worst of the abuses, but there were many buildings on the drawing boards and under contract that evidently could not be stopped.

Mills (1995) pointed out that there is certainly an element of truth in each of these arguments, but they fail to explain the huge overinvestment in office buildings compared to other commercial real estate ventures, such as shopping centers and rental housing. Both of these industries have suffered large downturns as well, but they adjusted fairly quickly and vacancy rates did not rise nearly as far as in the office market. Mills (1995) is forced to conclude that office developers and those who financed them simply did a horrible job of investment analysis. The boom was expected to continue even though it could not be sustained. We awakened in 1990 to discover that we had 13 billion square feet of office space and that 1.56 billion square feet of it (about 12%) was excess capacity that would not all be needed until sometime after the year 2000. What will private investors do next? It might be prudent to assume that the allocation of investment over the next decade will not necessarily be particularly efficient.

Despite, or perhaps partly because of, this oversupply of office space, there may be some reason for optimism. Mills (1995) offered the view that the growth of office employment may have already resumed. The greatly expanded use of computer technology may mean that a wide variety of new services can be performed at low cost. The increased productivity of the service sector, caused largely by the computer revolution, may mean that we will soon be consuming more services and causing even more people to be employed in offices. Also, the oversupply of office space should be viewed as a potential asset that has been provided for an urban area. All of that office space is being offered for low rents, so there may be opportunities to start new businesses or expand old ones that otherwise might not be possible. The owners of the office space are working desperately to market the space, and there is no reason why the local public economic development officials should not help them.

In this section we have examined private investment. We have found that the United States has a low level of investment and that the allocation of that investment in the 1980s was not rational. Most urban areas probably would have been better off if more of the investment that was made had been in producers' durable equipment rather than in nonresidential structures. Given the findings of Florida and Smith (1992) that venture capital for new businesses flowed mainly to the established centers of high technology in northern California and Massachusetts, one suspects that there were a lot of small businesses out there with good potential that were starved for capital. Further, the empirical findings of Clark et al. (1986) suggested that many businesses in manufacturing rely on retained earnings to finance investments. Given these vagaries of the private capital market and the penchant of the federal government to keep changing the laws under which investments are made, some local program for lending to new and growing businesses would seem to make sense. This idea is discussed more fully in Chapter 14.

G. SUMMARY

In this chapter we have presented rather extended discussions of two main sources of economic growth: labor and capital. An urban area can grow by increasing both the quality and the size of its labor force. Investment in human capital is a joint enterprise of the individual citizen and the state and local governments. The returns to education increased in the 1980s in part because the wages of workers with lower levels of education fell in real terms while the earnings of college graduates increased. Returns to technical training increased in some other fields, such as computers and various technical jobs in health care, for example. At the same time, many young people who attended schools in the inner city have been left behind by their lack of education.

The discussion of capital was divided into its public and private components. Investments in urban public infrastructure slowed markedly beginning roughly in 1970. Part of that decline in investment made sense because the interstate highway system (including urban highway systems) had been completed and a new generation of airports had been built to handle jet aircraft. However, there is now widespread concern that we have underinvested in urban infrastructure and that much needs to be done as quickly as possible. There is no doubt that some urban infrastructure projects have a high payoff; projects to keep the urban infrastructure functioning, to make marginal improvements in urban highway systems, and to expand airports all are highly productive. However, there is also no doubt that the demand for infrastructure projects will exceed the supply. Urban areas must be prepared to propose the infrastructure projects that will do the most good.

The final topic of the chapter was private investment and capital. Given the record of the 1980s of low levels of total investment and overinvestment in commercial real estate, it is difficult to accept the presumption that the American capital markets consistently do a good job of allocating capital to its most productive uses. This point of view is heresy in departments of finance, but the point is visible to residents of urban areas. Better analysis of the demand for office space clearly was needed, and it is fair to say that a great deal of effort is being expended to improve our understanding of commercial real estate markets. It is also fair to say that we do not have a complete understanding of the factors that bring business investments to an urban area. Most studies have concentrated on the manufacturing sector, and some investments in mature manufacturing industries responded to a variety of local cost factors (e.g., wages, taxes, etc.). On the other hand, investments in high-growth industries responded to agglomeration economies. Venture capital flowed in sizable amounts to the agglomerations of high-tech computer firms in California's Silicon Valley and

Boston's Route 128 area despite the fact that these were, by conventional measures, locations with very high costs. But what about financing for firms in industries that are not quite so "hot?" Are there worthwhile investments out there that are not being funded? Our overall low levels of net investment, coupled with the overinvestment in commercial real estate, suggest that such was the case in the 1980s. Perhaps the sharp drop in commercial real estate investments in the 1990s has meant that worthy ventures are being supported. Let us hope so. At the same time, an economic growth and development strategy for an urban area might usefully include programs to support emerging enterprises. This matter is a topic for Chapter 14.

EXERCISES

1. Suppose there is a training program that will increase a trainee's earnings by $1000 per year before taxes and by $750 per year after taxes. The actual cost of the program is $5000 per trainee, and the trainee must forgo two months of earnings equal to $2000 per month before taxes ($1500 after taxes). Assume that the increase in earnings created by the training program lasts forever and that the trainee has a time horizon that is infinite.

   (a) Assume that the trainee does not pay tuition because the training is a public program. What is the (private) rate of return to the trainee? What is the rate of return of the program for society? (*Hint:* The rate of return for society takes into account all the costs and benefits of the program. Earnings that are part of costs or benefits are counted *before* taxes.)

   (b) Suppose now that the trainee must pay $5000 in tuition and that her discount rate is 6%. Assuming purely monetary motivation, will the person enroll in the training program?

2. Following the data depicted in Figure 13.1, suppose that the average male high-school graduate earns about $4000 per year more (after taxes) than does the man who never attended high school from age 19 to age 25 and then earns $7000 (after taxes) per year more from age 26 to retirement (approximately an infinite time horizon). Assume that in order to attend high school, the person must forgo earnings of $12,500 per year. High school charges no tuition to the student but costs the taxpayers $7000 per year per student. Assume a discount rate of 5%.

   Is earning a high school diploma a good investment for the individual man? What are the present value of benefits and costs, where the present is the year when one would enter high school?

3. Use the 1990 Census of Population to examine the amounts of gross in-migration and net in-migration to the urban area of your choice. What are the main origins of migrants to this urban area? Does this urban area tend to attract in-migrants with high or low levels of education?

4. Return to the capital budgeting problem discussed in Section E. Assume that the present value of the benefits of project Z is now 108 (rather than 112). Given that the total budget is 100, how does this change the selection of the optimal set of projects?

REFERENCES

Bartik, Timothy, 1991. *Who Benefits from State and Local Economic Development Policies?* Kalamazoo, MI: W.E. Upjohn Institute.

Becker, Gary, 1975. *Human Capital*, 2nd ed. New York: National Bureau of Economic Research and Columbia University Press.

Birch, David, et al., 1990. *America's Future Office Space Needs*. Washington, DC: National Association of Industrial and Office Parks.

Blomquist, Glenn, M. Berger, and J. Hoehn, 1988. "New Estimates of Quality of Life in Urban Areas," *American Economic Review*, Vol. 78, pp. 89–107.

Borts, George and J. Stein, 1964. *Economic Growth in a Free Market*. New York: Columbia University Press.

Building Owners and Managers Association International, 1994. *The Commercial Real Estate Compendium*. Washington, DC: BOMA International.

Clark, Gordon, M. Gertler, and J. Whiteman, 1986. *Regional Dynamics*. Boston: Allen & Unwin.

Congressional Budget Office, 1988. "New Directions for the Nation's Public Works." Washington, DC: CBO.

Denison, Edward, 1985. *Trends in American Economic Growth*. Washington, DC: The Brookings Institution.

Evans, Alan, 1990. "The Assumption of Equilibrium in the Analysis of Migration and Interregional Differences: A Review of Some Recent Research," *Journal of Regional Science*, Vol. 30, pp. 515–531.

Fazzari, Steven, G. Hubbard, and B. Petersen, 1988. "Investment, Financing Decisions, and Tax Policy," *American Economic Review, Papers and Proceedings*, Vol. 78, pp. 200–205.

Florida, Richard and D. Smith, 1992. "Venture Capital's Role in Economic Development: An Empirical Analysis," in E. Mills and J. McDonald, eds., *Sources of Metropolitan Growth*. New Brunswick, NJ: Rutgers University Press.

Greenwood, Michael, 1981. *Migration and Economic Growth in the United States*. New York: Academic Press.

Henderson, J. Vernon, 1982. "Evaluating Consumer Amenities and Interregional Welfare Differences," *Journal of Urban Economics*, Vol. 11, pp. 32–59.

Hodge, James, 1981. "A Study of Regional Investment Decisions," in J. Henderson, ed., *Research in Urban Economics*. Greenwich, CT: JAI Press.

Mills, Edwin, 1995. "Crisis and Recovery in Office Markets," *Journal of Real Estate Finance and Economics*, Vol. 10, pp. 49–62.

Morrison, Steven and C. Winston, 1989. "Enhancing the Performance of the Deregulated Air Transportation System," *Brookings Papers on Economic Activity: Microeconomics*, pp. 61–123.

Murnane, Richard and F. Levy, 1992. "Education and Training," in H. Aaron and C. Schultze, eds., *Setting Domestic Priorities*. Washington, DC: The Brookings Institution.

Muth, Richard, 1971. "Migration: Chicken or Egg?" *Southern Economic Journal*, Vol. 37, pp. 295–306.

National Commission on Excellence in Education, 1983. *A Nation at Risk*. Washington, DC: U.S. Department of Education.

O'hUallachain, Breandon and M. Satterthwaite, 1992. "Sectoral Growth Patterns at the Metropolitan Level: An Evaluation of Economic Development Incentives," *Journal of Urban Economics*, Vol. 31, pp. 25–58.

Roback, Jennifer, 1982. "Wages, Rents and the Quality of Life," *Journal of Political Economy*, Vol. 90, pp. 1257–1278.

Rosenbaum, James, 1993. "Closing the Gap: Does Residential Integration Improve the Employment and Education of Low-Income Blacks?" in L. Joseph, ed., *Affordable Housing and Public Policy*. Champaign, IL: University of Illinois Press.

Schultz, Theodore, 1961. "Investment in Human Capital," *American Economic Review*, Vol. 51, pp. 1–17.

Sjaastad, Larry, 1962. "The Costs and Returns of Human Migration," *Journal of Political Economy*, Vol. 70, No. 5, Part 2, pp. 80–93.

Small, Kenneth, C. Winston and C. Evans, 1989. *Road Work: A New Highway Pricing and Investment Policy*. Washington, DC: The Brookings Institution.

Solow, Robert, 1957. "Technical Change and the Aggregate Production Function," *Review of Economics and Statistics*, Vol. 39, pp. 312–320.

Winston, Clifford and B. Bosworth, 1992. "Public Infrastructure," in H. Aaron and C. Schultze, eds., *Setting Domestic Priorities*. Washington, DC: The Brookings Institution.

14

Economic Development Policies for Urban Areas

A. INTRODUCTION

It is quite likely that some of you, the readers of this book, one day will be engaged in the formulation, implementation, and evaluation of economic development policy at the state or local level. To perform this role well, you will need to think about and formulate basic objectives, set measurable goals that are consistent with these basic objectives, devise overall economic development strategies and supporting policies, and conduct evaluations of the results. This chapter takes you through this policy process for local economic development in a systematic fashion. The chapter concludes with a brief discussion of local economic development policy in practice.

B. THE GOALS OF ECONOMIC DEVELOPMENT POLICY

The first task in formulating a policy for economic development is to think well about the goals that the community wishes to pursue. In this section we pause to think about basic goals. The usual statements that are made by state and local public officials boil the goals down to two things: jobs and tax base. There may be nothing wrong with jobs and tax base as goals, but what is the logic that supports them? What about consumption and leisure time as goals? For whom are these jobs being created? What about efficient use of resources, equitable distribution of income, and personal freedom? The discipline of economics provides a coherent framework that can be used to formulate the goals for an economic system.

Throughout the book the goal of policy has been the one derived from the mainstream economist's notion of Pareto optimality. A Pareto-optimal (i.e., efficient) allocation of resources is one in which it is not possible to increase the welfare of one person unless the welfare of another person is reduced. The goal of policy is to move toward a Pareto-optimal allocation of resources by identifying policies that increase the welfare of someone without reducing the welfare of anyone else. In the language of cost-benefit analysis, the value of benefits exceeds the value of the costs, and those upon whom costs are imposed receive compensation or side payments so as to restore them to their original levels of utility. However, in practice, often it is not possible to compensate fully those upon whom costs are imposed. If the value of benefits exceeds costs but compensation is not paid to keep everyone at or above their initial levels of utility, the policy or project in question is said to offer a *potential* Pareto improvement in the allocation of resources. Clearly, the use of the potential Pareto improvement criterion by itself can be dangerous; for example, it would signal approval of a project that taxes the poor to provide some large benefit for the rich.

It was pointed out in Chapter 2 that mainstream economists also acknowledge that even an efficient economy can produce a distribution of income that is highly unequal. Society may wish to alter that distribution through a variety of policy measures. Equity in the distribution of the fruits of the economy is a goal that is separate from the goal of Pareto optimality. These are the goals of the mainstream economist: efficient use of resources in the sense of Pareto, and an equitable distribution of income in accordance with society's notion of equity.

Can these goals be used to formulate policies for economic growth and development? The essence of a policy to promote economic growth and development is that the society must give up something now to gain a return later. A condition for Pareto optimality exists in this problem of *intertemporal* (now versus later) choice. To focus just on Pareto optimality, suppose that the economy consists of just one farmer. (An economy with only one person has no income distribution problem, of course.)

The lonely farmer can allocate his time to working in his field, or he can devote his time to clearing more ground for cultivation. If he clears one acre for cultivation, he can grow more food and fiber next year and in all the succeeding years. It is assumed that each succeeding acre of newly cleared land adds less to output because the farmer has only a limited amount of time to work in any given year; investment is assumed to have a declining marginal product. The time devoted to clearing land subtracts from this year's food and fiber production. The farmer can grow more food and fiber this year by working harder in his field. In this model land is, in effect, unlimited. The farmer's time is the scarce resource that must be allocated between producing for now and investing for the future.

Let us suppose that the farmer can clear an additional unit of land in one week. The farmer gives up δQ units of output for use this year and gains δq units of output in all future years. Once cleared, the land produces a stream of output forever, so the rate of return in terms of output is $\delta q/\delta Q$. This trade-off between current and future output is shown as line qQ in Figure 14.1.

How does the farmer evaluate this trade-off in terms of his own utility? We must assume that the farmer's utility depends upon the quantity of output produced and consumed in the current year and in the future, or

$$U = U(Q,q),$$

where Q is the current output and q is future output. It is assumed that the farmer has indifference curves for current and future output of the usual sort, with a declining marginal rate of substitution of one output for the other, as discussed in the appendix to the book. The decision to spend one more week clearing land means that the farmer must give up utility in the current period. The gain in utility terms is the sum of the subsequent increases in utility for all future periods. This willingness to give

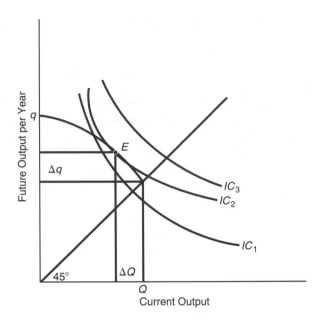

FIGURE 14.1 Choice of current versus future output

up current output for future output is shown by a set of indifference curves in Figure 14.1. These indifference curves are labeled IC_1, IC_2, and so on.

The farmer chooses point E on his highest possible indifference curve, as shown in Figure 14.1. The condition for efficient use of the farmer's time says that the rate of return to investment ($\delta q / \delta Q$) equals the marginal rate of substitution of output in future years to output in the current year.

Suppose that the farmer's utility function is the same in each year and that all of his remaining n years count equally in his mind. In the absence of investment in the clearing of land, his output, consumption, and utility would be the same every year. He would therefore go ahead and clear the next unit of land as long as

$$\frac{\delta q}{\delta Q} > \frac{1}{n}.$$

If the farmer is 30 years old and his life expectancy is 70 years, he clears the next unit of land if $\delta q / \delta Q$ is greater than or equal to 0.025 (i.e., the rate of return to investment is 2.5%). Note that the required rate of return is higher the shorter is the farmer's life expectancy. If he expects to live only one more year, the condition for investment is $\delta q / \delta Q > 1$.

How does this condition for efficient investment translate to a market economy with many people? Now the farmer is not self-sufficient. A crop is produced and sold in the market, and consumer goods are purchased with the income earned. The farmer's utility is a function of income, but the optimality condition is still the same:

$$\frac{\delta y}{\delta Y} = \text{MRS of future for current income,}$$

where y is the permanent gain in income earned by giving up Y income in the current year. What makes this model different is that the economy consists of many producers who are facing the same decision. They have the choice of allocating their time to investment or to current production for sale, but they also have the option of producing for sale and lending part of the income to someone else who wishes to make an investment but not suffer the drop in consumption in the current year. Such a person is willing to pay interest on the loan because the loan enables him or her to consume more in the future and consume no less in the present year. The borrower may be a person with such excellent investment opportunities that attempting to invest in all of them would quickly use up all of current income. Suppose that the loan is one year in duration but the borrower has the ability to borrow again next year. A market for these loans is formed; borrowers demand loans and lenders supply loans. Figure 14.2 shows the competitive market for loans. The demand for loans is a declining function of the interest rate that must be paid, and the supply of loans is an increasing function of the interest rate that is received. An interest rate on one-year loans is set at r^*.

Now return to the farmer's original problem. The farmer can invest and earn a return of $\delta y/\delta Y$, or he can lend money and earn a return of r^*. The optimality condition for the individual farmer is now

$$\frac{\delta y}{\delta Y} = r^* = \text{MRS of future for current income.}$$

The return on investment in clearing land (or whatever the real investments are) must be equal to the interest rate that can be earned on loans. If this equality does not hold, the farmer can reallocate his current income and earn a higher rate of return. The same thing holds for the borrower. This person borrows money as long as the return on the real investment exceeds the interest rate that must be paid on the loan. Under these conditions, all members of the economy equate their marginal rates of substitution to the same r^*. Everyone has the same marginal rate of substitution of future for current income. The economy is adding to capital, so both capital per person and output per person are also growing.

In this market economy everyone begins with some endowment of resources that can be used to produce income for current consumption or for investment in im-

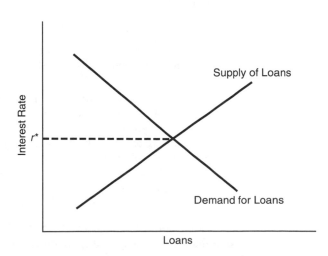

FIGURE 14.2
Market for loans

proving those resources for future use. In the end everyone has the same rate of return to investment and the same marginal rate of substitution of future for current income. It is therefore not possible to make someone better off unless someone else is made worse off. For example, suppose that we ordered person A to invest 1 unit less and person B to invest 1 unit more. Remember that we assume that the marginal product of investment declines, so this means that person A must give up more future income than person B gains. Person A gives up a return of $r*$ or more, and person B gains a return of $r*$ or less. We do not wish to make person A unhappy, so we order person B to compensate A for the loss. But this makes B worse off because the additional return earned on the investment is not enough to compensate A. Our competitive market economy is at a Pareto optimal allocation of resources. An optimal amount of resources available in the current year is being used to invest in the expansion of resources and output in the future. In this economy, there is no need for government to alter that allocation of resources.

What can go wrong with the market allocation? The market outcome can be inefficient for all the usual reasons: (1) monopoly and oligopoly, (2) public goods, (3) externalities (e.g., agglomeration economies), and (4) failure of actors to have perfect information about current and future tastes, technologies, and prices. Item (4) points to an important feature of investment; its returns usually are risky. Risk-averse investors require a higher expected rate of return on risky investment than on investments with certain outcomes. However, what is very risky for the individual investor may not be very risky at all for society. Suppose that a new product is developed and a large number of firms consider entering the market. For the individual firm the prospects may be very risky because some firms may lose out in the competition. However, for the society, the total investment made in the entire industry produces a return with little risk. The individual firm cannot diversify its investment into all of the other firms that are entering the industry. Individual risk-averse firms will require a rate of return that is too high from the point of view of society, so there is justification for subsidizing investment in this case.

Setting Pareto optimality as a goal has yielded an extensive list of reasons to formulate an economic growth and development policy. These reasons include the following:

1. Investment in industries that are monopolized should be increased.
2. Some public goods involve investment, not simply current expenditures for currently consumed goods and services. The public capital stock includes everything from airports to zoos.
3. The presence of externalities creates the usual problems. A good example is the presence of localization economies, where the firms in the urban area do not invest the efficient amount on their own. Another critical example is expenditures on research and development. The patent and copyright systems provide incentives for inventors and innovators in many areas, but the creation of basic knowledge (for example) usually cannot be patented or copyrighted.
4. The distinction between social risk and the risk faced by an individual firm can mean that investment in something such as a new product should be subsidized.

Next consider the goal of equity. Establishing equity as a goal means that we must decide on a way to add together the utility levels of the members of the society.

We need to know whether the society is better off if we reduce person A's utility as we increase person B's utility, so we must assume that these changes can be measured and compared. A general form of a *social welfare function* is

$$W = W(U_1, U_2, \ldots, U_m),$$

where there are m people in the society. This social welfare function will tell us how much, for example, U_1 can be reduced as U_2 is increased in order to leave social welfare constant. One form of the social welfare function is the classical utilitarian or Benthamite welfare function, written as the sum

$$W = U_1 + U_2 + \cdots + U_m.$$

A slightly more general form would attach different weights to the utilities of different people, or

$$W = a_1 U_1 + a_2 U_2 + \cdots + a_m U_m,$$

where the weights $a_1, \ldots, a_m$ are positive numbers. For example, McDonald (1987) proposed that criminals have lower weights and victims of crime have higher weights.

The field of pure economic theory includes an extensive literature on optimal economic growth that has been summarized by Solow (1970). In this literature the goal of the economy is to maximize the stream of consumption per capita over time. This is a pure case of the classical social welfare function in which all members of society count equally. A reallocation of consumption that leaves the per capita amount constant has no impact on social welfare under this assumption. What this social welfare function is really doing is separating efficiency matters from distributional matters. The idea is that we will figure out how to maximize our consumption possibilities, and then later we can worry about the distribution of the goods. Others argue that it is not really possible in practice to separate efficiency and distribution, so some kind of equity goal must be built in from the beginning. Reasonable people are in disagreement over this issue.

A social welfare function that attempts to address this issue was proposed by the moral philosopher John Rawls (1971); what is now known as the Rawlsian social welfare function is

$$W(U_1, U_2, \ldots, U_m) = \min\{U_1, U_2, \ldots, U_m\}.$$

This function says that social welfare is not improved unless the utility of the person with the lowest level of utility is increased. How does Rawls justify this proposed social welfare function? He thinks that this is the social welfare function that the members of society would agree upon in what he calls the *original position*. The original position refers to the hypothetical time when people come together to make up the rules for a society without specific knowledge of their positions within that society. They do not know whether they will be rich or poor, intelligent or dull. Rawls thinks that a rational person would not agree "in advance" to a classical social welfare function that would permit society to reduce his or her welfare to enhance the welfare of someone else. Instead, the rational person adopts what is called the *maximin rule*, which ranks alternatives by their worst outcomes. This is a rule for pessimists, those who presume that the worst is likely to happen. This extremely high degree of aversion to risk is not consistent with existing empirical evidence about choice under uncertainty. Few mainstream economists advocate the use of the Rawlsian social welfare function with the maximin rule. In addition, the rational person in Rawls's initial position would set up a society with liberty and equal rights for all and equal opportunities for all to attain positions and offices. Note that for Rawls, the social contract does not require equal *outcomes* but rather, equal rights, liberties, and opportunities coupled with the maximin rule.

You might be wondering why a chapter on local economic development policy has ventured into moral philosophy. It so happens that one of the most thoughtful practitioners of local economic development, the late Robert Mier, wrote a book entitled *Social Justice and Local Development Policy* (1993) in which a Rawlsian view is adopted. As commissioner of economic development for the city of Chicago in the 1980s, Mier tried to be consistent in favoring policies and processes for policy formulation that tended to increase the welfare of those with the least. As you can imagine, it was not easy to stick to this principle. His book recounts his experiences as a public official in the administration of Mayor Harold Washington of Chicago, and the policies he attempted to implement are discussed below.

Mainstream economics offers two goals: Pareto optimality (efficiency) in resource allocation, and equity. In contrast, conservative economists such as Milton Friedman offer the goals of freedom and liberty, but Friedman also advocates a policy of income redistribution, for reasons discussed in Chapter 2. His proposal for a policy of income redistribution, the negative income tax, is consistent with freedom and liberty for those who receive the transfer payments and those who pay for them. Conservatives naturally take a dim view of policies that interfere with the operation of the market, but they do acknowledge the need for public investments in urban infrastructure and other public goods. Marxists must surely approach local economic development policy with mixed emotions. They wish to see the urban proletariat get organized and eventually overthrow the capitalist class and establish a socialist state. However, when the proletariat gets organized, it may succeed in winning some real concessions from its capitalist masters that, in effect, prevent the revolution from happening. This process is what is known as being *co-opted*. Real Marxists worry a great deal about co-optation, but non-Marxist urban community organizers worry about winning real concessions.

C. THE GOALS OF LOCAL ECONOMIC DEVELOPMENT

The theoretical literature in economics on optimal growth pertains almost exclusively to the national economy. The location of people and economic activity is ignored. Yet it must be stated frankly at the outset that much of local economic development policy is designed to alter the location of certain kinds of economic activity. An urban area can build a nice, modern airport that provides economies of scale and makes a lot of people more efficient, but the people of that urban area also are aiming to attract economic activity that otherwise would be located elsewhere. Local economic development policy inherently has an impact both on efficiency and distribution. What is more, we can expect that policymakers at the local level are really only concerned with the welfare of their constituents, the residents of their area. They are probably not particularly interested in policies that are designed to attract migrants to the urban area unless benefits to residents are generated. The empirical evidence reviewed in Chapters 11 and 13 [Muth (1971) and Greenwood (1981)] indicates that migration to an urban area does lead to employment gains for residents through the stimulation of demand for local goods and services. The evidence thus runs contrary to the more popular view that in-migrants take jobs away from local workers.

A consideration of local economic development policy is also complicated by the fact that there are many actors in the drama but that probably there is no one in authority who is responsible for designing policies for the urban area as a whole. Large central cities have their economic development officials and programs, and most counties and larger suburban municipalities have economic development programs. States are engaged in economic development programs in a big way as well. With a small number of notable exceptions (e.g., Minneapolis–St. Paul), real metropolitan government does not exist in the United States. Urban areas are economic units, but they do not have a government that just encompasses that unit. In this situation perhaps we look to the states as the makers of economic development policy that can come closest to matching the interests of a large urban area. The state level for making policy also has the advantage that the interests of all people who live in the state are (we hope) being taken into account. State officials would probably think twice about a policy that simply shifts economic activity from one part of the state to another. In any case, the structure of government in the United States is a serious complication that influences local economic development policy. This complication is discussed at more length in the final section of this chapter.

Now let us get down to business. What do state and local officials want from economic development policy, and why do they want it? How do those goals stack up against the general goals of efficiency and equity?

The goal of expanding the tax base has been discussed extensively in Chapter 10. Local public officials are interested in attracting commercial and industrial property as long as the benefits of the expansion of the tax base are greater than any diminution of the quality of the local environment. The added tax base permits the local government to provide better public services for the residents and/or impose lower taxes or charges or other user fees on local residents. The expansion of the tax base may create benefits for all local residents, rich and poor alike. If the effort to expand the tax base is successful, local officials and legislators (as agents for the local residents) must decide how those benefits shall be used: tax cuts, increased spending on public schools, more police protection, and so on. Pursuit of the goal of an expanded tax base can largely be considered an effort to redistribute benefits from other communities to one's own. Whether the efficiency of the larger economy is improved in the process is incidental and depends on the specific means that are used to attract the tax base. Specific policies are discussed in the next section.

Now consider the goal of expanding employment in the local economy. The pursuit of this goal by an entire urban area can possibly lead to a shift in the demand for labor in the local economy that is large enough to increase wage rates for everyone who works there. However, a general increase in wage rates usually is not the motivating idea. Rather, local officials wish to expand employment opportunities because sizable numbers of local residents are unemployed, underemployed, or not seeking work because they are discouraged about their chances. Unemployment means that the worker is actively seeking work but is unable to find work at the current wage rate. Unemployment is a serious problem in most large central cities, but underemployment may be an even greater problem. A person who is underemployed is employed but is working at less than his or her capacity. Some part-time workers wish to work on a full-time basis. Many others work in jobs that do not make full use of their skills and abilities and get paid less than they might be able to earn if better jobs were available. Finally, discouraged workers are workers who would be drawn into the labor market if they thought that jobs were available to them. Official data are collected on unemployment and part-time workers, but we do not really know how many people fall into the underemployed and discouraged worker categories. However, it is reasonable to presume that a substantial number of people who earn very low wages are underemployed. These are people who work and cannot lift themselves out of poverty but if given the chance are capable of holding better jobs with higher pay.

Local economic development officials must be careful to distinguish short-run economic fluctuations and long-run economic growth and development. The local rates of unemployment and underemployment may be high temporarily because the national economy is in recession. The local economy must rely upon recovery of the national economy to bring local employment up to the level that is consistent with what is regarded as full employment at the national level. At this time macroeconomic policymakers at the Federal Reserve Bank regard national full employment to be an unemployment rate in the range 5.5 to 6.5%. A lower level of unemployment is believed to cause an *accelerating* rate of inflation. However, a national unemployment rate of 5.5 to 6.5% can still mean that some local economies, especially central cities, have serious economic problems and high levels of poverty, unemployment, and underemployment.

The goal of enhancing employment opportunities for unemployed, underemployed, and discouraged workers has merit on both efficiency and equity grounds. Unemployed and underemployed resources are wasted resources. Putting an unemployed or discouraged worker to work adds to society's available output at an opportunity cost that is the value of the worker's "leisure time." An apparent benefit is the reduction in unemployment compensation or welfare payments that were being paid to the unemployed person, but we shall see precisely how to figure the benefits. Suppose that a job is found for the unemployed worker at a wage rate of $6.00 per hour and that the worker values his or her own leisure time at $2.50 per hour. Assume that the unemployed worker had been receiving $350 per month in welfare payments. The worker now earns an income of $960 per month (i.e., four weeks). Previously, monthly income had been $350, and the leisure time that is given up to work was worth $400 per month. The worker is now better off by $210 per month, and the rest of society is better off by $350 per month from the reduction in welfare benefits. The benefits therefore total $560 per month. Another way to think of it is that, while unemployed, the worker was producing leisure time that was worth $400 per month. Employment at a wage of $6.00 per hour produces output worth $960 per month, for a net gain of $560. In this case, society chooses to distribute this net gain by reducing the welfare payment to zero. This distributional scheme results in a gain of $210 for the worker and $350 for the rest of society.

The case of the underemployed worker is essentially the same. Society gives up the value of whatever the underemployed worker had been producing but gains the value of his or her new output. The new output is assumed to be more valuable than the old output. Assuming that the worker is paid the value of the marginal product, the net gain to society accrues entirely to the individual worker.

In addition to the direct employment effect, the increase in employment, output, and income may have a multiplier effect on the local economy that will result in putting more unemployed, underemployed, or discouraged workers to work. The computation of multiplier benefits is the same as for the direct employment benefits above. Multiplier models and economic base models were discussed in Chapter 11.

The policies that put unemployed, underemployed, or discouraged workers to work (either directly or through the multiplier effect) also has distributional consequences that most people favor. At least some of the benefits accrue to the worker who is the target of the policy, and it is probable that this person has a low income. The exception would be proposals to make welfare recipients work at wages that are so low that they really experience no gain. This analysis suggests that one criterion for judging proposals to change the welfare system is whether both the welfare recipients and the rest of society benefit from the changes.

In the preceding section we introduced two very different social welfare functions that society might wish to use to evaluate distributional changes. The weighted classical social welfare function adds together the (weighted) utility levels of all members of the society, while the Rawlsian social welfare function evaluates a change on the basis of whether it benefits the person with the lowest level of utility. These two different ways of specifying the goal can lead to very different policies. Even if the weighted classical social welfare function that is used puts heavy weights on the utility levels of those people with low incomes, it is possible that a policy would be chosen that increases primarily the utility levels of higher-income people. This outcome would not be selected with the Rawlsian social welfare function.

Consider a concrete example that is not unlike the choices that economic development officials sometimes must make. Suppose that the city has an amount of money available to subsidize the redevelopment of one of two sites. In this example possible multiplier effects are ignored. One site will be used by the developer of an office building, which will be used by lawyers, accountants, and management consultants. Because of localization economies, the incomes of these professionals will be enhanced somewhat. The office building will also provide some jobs for local unemployed or underemployed janitors, low-level clerks, and some other lower-income people. The other site will be used by a manufacturer in food processing. The manufacturer hires semiskilled workers who are roughly at the same level as the janitor or low-level clerk. An evaluation of these alternatives based on the Rawlsian social welfare function would examine only the benefits experienced by the lower-income workers. Who hires more lower-income workers — the manufacturer or the firms that occupy the office building? How much are these workers paid? Use of the weighted classical social welfare function would include the benefits to other workers and to the owners of the firms and real estate properties involved.

D. LOCAL ECONOMIC DEVELOPMENT: STRATEGIES AND POLICIES

A *strategy* is a plan for reaching a goal, and *policies* are the individual actions or elements that support the strategy. Local economic development policymakers have invented alternative methods for defining strategy, and these are discussed first. We then turn to an examination of policies.

Strategies for Local Economic Development

Strategies are discussed in various ways, but local economic development officials will most often classify strategies as business attraction, business retention, or local business growth. This can be a useful way to organize one's thoughts; a distinct set of activities is used to support each of these strategies. The three strategies also reflect an evolution in the thinking of many local economic development officials. Serious efforts at local economic development probably began in the 1940s and 1950s with the efforts of southern states and localities to attract manufacturing plants from the older manufacturing areas of the northeast. Those efforts, which were based on publicizing low wages, lack of unions, low taxes, supporting infrastructure, southern hospitality, and warm weather, met with considerable success in some places. The idea of business attraction caught on, and many states and local governments copied the southern strategy. However, many of the state and local governments that followed this strategy found little success or found that businesses were demanding large subsidies. The strategy of business attraction has been given the mildly derogatory term "smokestack chasing" because of these problems.

Beginning in the 1950s and 1960s states and local governments in the industrial northeast realized that they were losing businesses to the suburbs and to the sunbelt. Large companies were closing their old plants in the older central cities and opening new plants in other locations. Smaller companies that were growing were running out of space and moving out. As Hoover and Vernon (1959) discussed, the New York Metropolitan Region Study of the late 1950s devoted a good deal of attention to this phenomenon. The strategy of business retention was devised to prevent these plant closings if possible. The idea is to discover and address the problems that the company is having with its current site. Is more land needed? Is there a problem with crime and security? Are real estate taxes a problem? The city can help the company find more land, improve police services, and grant a real estate tax break for plant expansion. Perhaps most important, the city can show that it cares about the business and wants to keep the lines of communication open. Business retention efforts have met with some success, but often state and local officials found that there was really nothing that they could do to prevent an old plant from closing. Besides, they found that they were responding to emergency situations involving the impending closing of a plant rather than formulating a coherent strategy for the local economy.

After experience with business attraction and retention efforts, state and local officials realized that their most productive strategy might well be to concentrate on the businesses that are actually located in their communities and are not planning to move away. The strategy of local business growth has evolved into a comprehensive economic growth and development strategy that includes support for new enterprises, and the policies that are used to support this strategy are discussed below. It is fair to say that states and localities still devote some efforts to business attraction and that business retention still receives high priority, but the modern program for local economic development is a comprehensive economic growth and development strategy.

There is a second method for classifying economic development strategies that makes the distinction between a sectoral strategy and an area strategy. The idea of a sectoral strategy is to identify the industries, or groups of industries, that can be promoted to achieve the goals that have been articulated. For example, employment gains are possible in industries that are subject to localization economies. Also, additional investment is called for in industries that are subject to monopolization or represent low social risk compared to individual risk. Then policies are designed to support the growth of the "target" industries. An area strategy targets a particular geographic area because the residents of that area are in particular need. Then the idea is to design policies that will improve the economic prospects for these residents. The enterprise zone program that exists in most states is a package of policies aimed at particular small areas that are in economic distress. In 1994 the federal government started a program called "Empowerment Zones" to provide federal tax incentives and other benefits for businesses and workers located in certain parts of six particular central cities. Sectoral and area strategies may or may not be complementary. An industry with a high potential for growth may have no interest in locating in an impoverished neighborhood and hiring low-income residents. An area strategy may imply policies aimed at a simple redistribution of existing economic activity, such as commercial and retail development. Firms attracted to such developments will tend to hire some local residents and will at least enhance the shopping in the area.

Policies for Local Economic Development

We already know from Chapters 11 to 13 that the sources of urban economic growth fall into the following general categories:

- Export demand
- Import replacement
- Private capital
- Public capital (infrastructure)
- Labor (primarily through in-migration)
- Education and training
- Technical change
- Entrepreneurship
- Amenities
- Agglomeration economies (static and dynamic)

Now is a good time to review briefly what we know about each of these sources of growth.

Export Demand and Import Replacement

The models presented in Chapter 11 emphasized export demand as a source of urban growth. The Keynesian models are driven by the quantity of exports, while the two-sector neoclassical models are driven by the price of exports. Either way, exports are important. Furthermore, the economic functions of an urban economy in the larger economy were discussed in Chapter 4. The task of local economic development policy is to identify export sectors that have the potential for further growth. This analytical task is discussed below.

The Keynesian models in Chapter 11 also included imports into the urban area. In those models there is a propensity to import that helps to determine both the level of local income and the size of the local income multiplier. In particular, recall that the local income multiplier from Chapter 11 is

$$\frac{1}{1 - b + bt + d - dt},$$

where b is the propensity to consume, t the tax rate, and d the propensity to import. Clearly, a reduction in the propensity to import will *increase* the multiplier. The importation of goods and services also plays an important role in the input–output model of a local economy (Chapter 11, Section H). In that model the local economy imports *inputs* into local production processes. Close examination of the input–output model showed that the local multiplier is greater for the sector with the greater "local content" in its output.

The task for local economic development policy then is to identify points where greater use of local inputs is possible. Clearly, this task requires a great deal of data on the use of local and imported inputs by various industries. One reasonably simple method for approaching this task is to concentrate on the local labor content of goods and services. Data on total sales and payments of wages and salaries are generally available by industry for local economies (e.g., in *County Business Patterns*), so this approach is feasible. However, concentration on labor content omits other local inputs (capital, land, intermediate inputs). A complete input–output model is needed to consider all of the possibilities for import substitution for inputs.

Capital

The empirical evidence reviewed in Chapters 11 and 13 showed that the growth of capital is instrumental in the growth of both national and local economies. The discussion in Chapter 13 also showed that the U.S. economy has had a low level of investment in private capital in recent years and that this investment sometimes has not been allocated to its best use. In addition, both the level and best allocation of public-sector investments are continuing sources of controversy.

The federal government must take the lead in formulating policies designed to increase the overall level of private investment, and federal policies can also influence greatly the allocation of private invesment to alternative uses (such as commercial real estate versus capital equipment). Decisions about federal tax policy regarding depreciation allowances, capital gains, small-business loan programs, and investment tax credits can have important consequences for local economies. At the same time, the growth of the local economy can depend upon local programs that pertain to private capital. As discussed in Chapter 10, the local real estate tax is an obvious policy handle. Most states and major municipalities also have business loan programs that provide some financing, for example, to newer or smaller businesses. It appears that local economic development officials need to have a more comprehensive view of private capital and its potential to further local economic growth.

Decisions regarding investment in public capital are made by all three levels of government: federal, state, and local. A good deal of the investment in public capital in urban areas is funded partly by the federal government. Examples include public transit, airports, highways, sewer lines, and many other important items. At this point sizable investments are needed to maintain the existing capital stock. Chapter 13 included a review of the issues and concluded that the most productive investments are to be found in maintenance of existing facilities, selected highway projects, and airports.

Labor

The growth of the labor force is a primary determinant of the growth of an economy. The primary source of labor force growth for an urban area is in-migration of population, and the studies of migration discussed in Chapter 13 showed that a greater in-migration increases the demand for labor and stimulates more in-migration. One can conclude that a local economy with unemployed, underemployed, and discouraged workers should not fear the in-migration of population. Studies by Bartik (1991, 1994) reveal that households at the lower end of the income distribution are the primary beneficiaries of employment growth. These studies are discussed in detail below.

Education and Training

The importance of education and training has emerged consistently in studies of the sources of economic growth. Indeed, the recent data show that the returns to higher education have increased in the United States because the real earnings of workers with a high school education or less have declined and real earnings of those with college experience have increased. However, it is probable that the fraction of the labor force that has graduated from college (about 25%) will not be increasing appreciably. The society faces the huge task of providing better education and training for the other 75% of the labor force. It is fair to say that improvements are needed at every level from preschool to junior college and adult job training programs.

Local governments are the primary providers of education from preschool to junior college, and they are also responsible for providing the job training programs that are funded by the federal government. The policy issues in the field of education and training are many and varied and cannot be covered fully in a book on urban economics. Should more education be provided by the private sector through voucher programs? This issue was discussed in Chapter 13. How can high schools, junior colleges, and adult job training programs be connected to employers more effectively? How can elementary and secondary education be improved so that disadvantaged and minority groups in the society are better prepared for the job market? These are issues that will not go away soon, and they are the basic stuff of local economic development policy.

Technical Change

Technical change can take the form of new, improved products, better production processes, and diffusion of new technologies to a larger number of producers. Historically, the formulation of policies to enhance technical change has been within the purview of the federal government. The federal government supports a great deal of basic and applied research, and it provides assistance to small businesses to help with the adoption of new technologies. However, dissatisfaction with the rate of technical change in the United States since the 1970s has prompted many state and local governments to introduce their own policies designed to improve the rate of technical change. For example, many state and local governments operate technology assistance centers for business. Some states, including Michigan, support research efforts that are connected to one of the state's industries. Recall that the study by O'hUallachain and Satterthwaite (1992) tested for the effects of university R&D parks on local industry growth and found that this variable did contribute to growth in six of 37 industries. At this point we have no studies of the cost-effectiveness of these kinds of state and local efforts. (Agricultural states have, of course, for many years funded agricultural research through their state universities.)

Entrepreneurship

The creation of new business ventures requires entrepreneurship, the undertaking of risky business activities. Entrepreneurship calls for the ability to assess market opportunities and to organize an enterprise that is capable of seizing those opportunities. Entrepreneurship has recently become a part of the curriculum of schools of business administration as well as a field of academic research. Some of the skills needed to assess opportunities and organize a business can be taught, and students now have the opportunity to major (or minor) in the field of entrepreneurship in some MBA programs (and in a few undergraduate programs, too).

Many state and local governments have sought to encourage entrepreneurs by providing what are called *business incubators*. A business incubator is a facility that provides some institutional support for the fledgling business, such as cheap office or lab space, secretarial assistance, and telecommunications equipment. As the name indicates, the idea is that the business will thrive in the incubator and eventually move out and be on its own. Sometimes business incubators are supported through a university, and the hope is that professors and other researchers associated with the university will transform their scientific and technological discoveries into marketable products. Some business incubators have been quite successful, while others have languished. A great deal of anecdotal information exists, but at this time, there is no comprehensive study that demonstrates the factors involved in creating a successful business incubator.

Amenities

Most local economic development specialists believe that local environmental, cultural, public goods, and social amenities are important to the success of a local economy. Amenities are becoming increasingly important because, so the argument goes, many industries have become less tied down by the traditional location factors of access to raw materials, intermediate inputs, and markets. A high level of "quality of life" in an urban area permits its firms to recruit critical personnel more easily. Recall that this is thought to have been a factor in the success of Silicon Valley. However, we have no solid estimates of the effects of various types of amenities on local growth.

The study of growth in 37 industries by O'hUallachain and Satterthwaite (1992) found that two measures of local amenities, good climate and recreation facilities, had essentially no effect. Would it be worthwhile for an urban area to create a first-rate symphony orchestra? The answer is (in my view) undoubtedly in the affirmative, but we have no idea whether the growth rate of the local economy would be increased.

Agglomeration Economies

Chapter 12 is a reasonably comprehensive review of what is known about urban agglomeration economies. In that chapter it was concluded that:

1. Static localization economies (i.e., scale economies for individual industries in an urban area) exist in several industries, but more testing is needed in nonmanufacturing sectors.

2. Dynamic localization economies clearly have been quite strong in a few cases, such as in Silicon Valley, and O'hUallachain and Satterthwaite (1992) found evidence of a weaker form of dynamic localization economies in a large number of growth industries.

3. Both static and dynamic urbanization economies have been found to exist in some studies, but the results are not as conclusive as with localization economies.

4. A more competitive local industry tends to grow more rapidly, other things equal.

5. Diversity in the local economy contributes to the growth of particular industries.

A comprehensive strategy for state or local economic development recognizes all of these sources of growth and selects individual policies that clearly have the potential to make a contribution to the basic goals as expressed through an economic development strategy. Numerous policies exist to enhance each of these sources of growth, and several examples for each source of growth are listed in Table 14.1.

The choice of the package of policies depends, of course, on the statement of goals and selection of the economic development strategy. For example, suppose that the basic goal is simply to increase the per capita income of the residents of an urban area, and suppose that the strategy chosen is to support growth without attempting to select target industries or areas. Given this goal and this strategy, the local officials might select these policies:

- Export demand   General national/international ad campaign
                            Tourism bureau

- Import replacement   General ad campaign to buy locally

- Capital (private)   Loan programs to which any business may apply
                            Real estate tax incentives for new business property
                            Land assembly assistance

- Capital (public)   Infrastructure replacement, maintenance, and development

- Labor   Improve amenities (see below)
                            General ad campaign to sell the area as a fine place to live

- Labor quality   Improve basic education

- Technical change   Research grant program to which any business or university researcher can apply

- Entrepreneurship   Entrepreneurship education programs
    Small-business assistance centers
    Business incubators

- Amenities   Provide good public services with low tax rates
    Promote local culture, education, recreation

- Agglomeration economies   Concentrate on urbanization economies

TABLE 14.1 Sources of Economic Growth and Examples of Growth Policies

Sources of Growth	*Policies*
1. Export demand	Export promotion offices, ads, etc.
	Assistance for businesses to enter export markets
	Convention and tourism bureau
	Create new products (see source 7)
2. Import replacement	General campaign to buy local goods
	Public purchasing to local firms
	Identify imports and target industries
3. Capital (private)	Direct loans (revolving loan funds)
	Industrial revenue bonds
	Venture capital funds
	Loans from public pension funds
	Real estate tax incentives
	Assistance with real estate planning
	Land assembly and sale at low price
4. Capital (public)	Infrastructure replacement, maintenance, and development
5. Labor	Campaign to sell area as a good place to live
6. Education and training	Basic education
	Higher education
	Vocational education
	Job training programs (Job Training Partnership Act)
7. Technical change	
a. New products	Support basic R&D
	Public/private industrial research centers
	University research
b. New production processes	Support applied R&D
	Public/private industrial labs
c. Diffusion of new technology	Business technology assistance centers
8. Entrepreneurship	Entrepreneurship education programs
	Small business assistance centers
	Business incubator facilities
9. Amenities	Promotion of local cultural, educational, recreational facilities
	Provision of high-quality basic public services with low taxes
10. Agglomeration economies	
a. Urbanization economies	Infrastructure: transportation, etc.
	All of the above to promote growth of the urban economy in general
b. Localization economies	All of the above targeted at particular industries

This policy package makes no particular attempt to worry about the distribution of income, and it avoids the selection of target industries. Because it avoids the selection of target industries, there are many policy options listed in Table 14.1 that cannot be included. Only so much can be done to promote exports or replace imports without targeting specific export industries or imports, thereby targeting the export promotion or import substitution campaign. Some types of programs to support the growth of private capital require that particular industries be identified. Loan programs work better if the lending officers can specialize in particular industries, for example. The enhancement of labor quality beyond basic education requires that some choices be made concerning the type of education or training programs to be offered. Programs to increase technical change must normally have an industry or group of industries in mind. Industrial research centers and business technology assistance centers must focus on particular research topics and types of assistance. Entrepreneurship programs can be of a general nature up to a point, but learning how to be an entrepreneur in a sophisticated line of business requires teachers with specialized knowledge. Finally, we have learned that both static and dynamic localization economies exist in many lines of business. Programs to exploit possible localization economies require first that the industries be identified. Many local economic development officials therefore think that some industry targeting is necessary to make effective use of their limited resources.

An example of a different economic development program is outlined by Mier (1993). Mier was the top economic development official for the city of Chicago during the period 1983–1989. It has already been noted that he advocated a Rawlsian social welfare function for the evaluation of economic development strategies and policies. He opposed programs unless he could see that benefits would accrue to the lower-income and minority residents of Chicago. He also believed strongly that a coherent policy required the identification of target industries and that policies for those target industries should always emphasize jobs for the needy. He fought against economic development strategies that emphasized downtown office growth in the financial and services sectors on the grounds that suburbanites held most of the jobs and few benefits "trickled down" to the needy. He saw one role of the city's department of economic development as supporting grass-roots community organizations across the city that would then exercise some influence over policy decisions. Together with other city officials, he drew up a strategic plan known as "Chicago Works Together." The basic strategy was to promote "balanced growth" (i.e., not just downtown growth) and neighborhood development, to create job opportunities for lower-income Chicagoans, and to provide for greater public participation in the formulation of specific policies. Mier envisioned both sectoral and area development strategies. The policies that were used to pursue this agenda included:

1. Local preference in public-sector hiring and buying
2. Selection of target industries for support with loan programs, technical assistance centers, export promotion, and other programs
3. Neighborhood planning
4. Skilled labor force development related to target industries
5. Job retention efforts, especially in manufacturing
6. Infrastructure investment related to job development

7. Linked development

8. Planned manufacturing districts

The last two policies require some explanation. Under Mier's leadership, the city of Chicago attempted to extract from developers and firms in highly successful areas such as downtown and the O'Hare Airport area promises to create links to the lower-income areas of Chicago in exchange for the city's support. For example, if a developer needs a zoning change and some infrastructure improvements for a downtown site, the city bargains for goals in hiring city residents or requires that the developer also help to develop another site in one of the target neighborhoods. Planned manufacturing districts are designed to slow down the conversion of land zoned for industry to commercial or residential use. Under ordinary circumstances the owner of property zoned for industry can apply for a change in zoning on the basis of a plan for redevelopment to another use and that application normally will be approved by the zoning board. Mier believed that this process caused what he called industrial displacement, which resulted in a loss of manufacturing jobs in the city. The worst-case scenario is one in which a factory that employs city residents at good pay is displaced by condominiums and shopping areas for high-income people who work downtown. Under the planned manufacturing district ordinance industrial properties in such a designated district can be converted to other uses only if they are first marketed for manufacturing use in good faith and if the new uses do not affect industry negatively.

Under Mier's guidance, target industries were selected based on their historic locations in Chicago's industrial areas outside of downtown and on the fact that they hire semiskilled workers at reasonably good pay. Task forces were set up to study the prospects for job growth in the steel and apparel industries. Once it had been possible for a semiskilled worker to find a job easily in these and other manufacturing industries in Chicago. Indeed, such job prospects were a big reason for the massive migration of black workers from the south in the 1940s, 1950s, and 1960s. Industrial employment had been a way out of poverty for many, but that avenue had largely been closed by the massive loss of manufacturing jobs in the city. Manufacturing employment in the city of Chicago had dropped almost continuously from 668,000 in 1947 to 277,000 in 1982. Mier's task forces were set up to find out what could be done in the steel and apparel industries, two large industries that had been especially hard hit by employment declines. The task forces concluded that there are some smaller subsectors in both industries that represent opportunities for employment growth.

This section has outlined two very different economic development strategies. One attempts to promote economic growth in general and avoids the targeting of industries. The other promotes economic growth that can have obvious tangible benefits for lower-income households in a large central city and attempts to target both industries and areas accordingly. How effective are these (and other) strategies? The matter of evaluation of both strategy and individual policies is taken up later in this chapter.

E. THE SELECTION OF TARGET INDUSTRIES

Many, if not most states and large municipalities with economic development programs have attempted to focus their efforts through the selection of target industries. It is difficult to resist the temptation to select target industries because, once selected, those industries give guidance to decisions about policy—from selection of trade journals for ad campaigns to worker training programs to the focus of business assistance centers. But what is the theory behind the selection of target industries? After all, some have questioned the usefulness of target industries because forecasts for individual industries for an urban area are subject to large errors. Furthermore, focusing attention on a short list of industries may cause policymakers to neglect the more basic conditions for general economic growth and development. Policymakers must be sensitive to these problems. With these points made, it still may be that the industries that represent the economic future of the urban area can be identified and targeted. This section looks at the question of industry targeting for two urban areas, Philadelphia and Des Moines.

This chapter and previous discussions in this book have supplied the theoretical argument for target industries. Target industries are industries for which the level of investment supplied by the private market falls short of the efficient level. As we have seen, the private market fails to be efficient in the presence of monopoly, public goods, externalities, and information gaps. We have seen that both static and dynamic localization economies are important categories of externalities in the context of local economic development. Also, while this topic is in need of research, a difference between individual risk and social risk can exist for some types of investments. Individual firms may be applying a discount rate to the future returns of some investments that is too high from society's point of view.

Philadelphia

One well-known study of target industries for the Philadelphia urban area by Stull and Madden (1990) suggests that the objective of economic development policies should be to eliminate impediments to and promote the growth of the industries that are well suited to the Philadelphia environment. This statement of objectives is somewhat vague because it mentions two types of target industries: (1) industries that are growing slowly because of some local constraints and falling short of their potential, and (2) industries that are growing rapidly that might be induced to grow even more rapidly. In the end, Stull and Madden (1990) opt for the latter group of industries because it is difficult to identify industries that are growing slowly simply because of some local impediment (as opposed to slow growth for fundamental reasons). Their method then is to identify industries or sectors that have shown rapid growth in recent years and have additional potential for growth. They are sensitive to the product-cycle model, which implies that an industry with rapid growth in the past may pass into a phase of slow growth. Such industries should be avoided as targets because probably they will not respond to policy initiatives. A more detailed examination of the Stull–Madden (1990) study is useful.

The book begins with an examination of manufacturing in the Philadelphia urban area by Richard Bernstein (1990). An industry is defined by the three-digit SIC codes. The list of potential target industries is created using a single criterion: employment in the industry grew from 1978 to 1986. Out of 136 manufacturing industries, 31 qualified on this criterion. Twelve of the industries were eliminated because they are in printing and publishing or construction materials, two sectors that produced almost entirely for the local market. Three more can be eliminated because they employed fewer than 1000 workers in 1986. Eight industries are members of the high-technology group, and include: pharmaceuticals, ordnance, computers, communications equipment, electronic components, aircraft and parts, optical instruments, and medical instruments. Some of these industries may be good candidates for being target industries, although Stull and Madden (1990) think that the growth of all except pharmaceuticals and medical instruments was tied to federal defense spending. They rightly conclude that reliance on federal defense spending can no longer serve as a basis for local economic growth.

The remaining eight industries include five in metal products and machinery: hand tools, structural metal products, refrigeration machinery, miscellaneous non-electrical machinery, and railroad equipment. The other three are miscellaneous food products, miscellaneous textile products, and miscellaneous plastic products. These eight, plus pharmaceuticals and medical instruments, represent a list of potential target manufacturing industries. The 10 industries employed 55,400 workers in the Philadelphia urban area in 1986, so this group of industries clearly is large enough to matter a great deal to the Philadelphia economy. Stull and Madden (1990) conclude that attention should focus on the industries in this group that are characterized by small establishments and customized products or rapid changes in technology. They do not say it, but these criteria may also be reasonable proxies for localization economies. However, it is fair to say that Stull and Madden (1990) think that manufacturing generally represents very limited opportunities for future growth in Philadelphia. They look elsewhere for sources of substantial growth.

The large producer services sector appears to be a good place to look for target industries. Stull and Madden (1990) include in this sector finance, insurance, and real estate (FIRE), business services, legal services and other professional services, and administrative and auxiliary establishments. They argue that these industries may represent good opportunities because their services sometimes are exported outside the urban area, the jobs usually offer good pay, and a solid producer services sector can attract firms in other industries. Their analytical procedure is to compare the industries in the producer services sector in Philadelphia with their counterparts in the other 19 largest urban areas in the United States. Using location quotient analysis, they find that Philadelphia is somewhat less concentrated in this sector than are the other urban areas but that insurance and legal services are clearly sources of strength and growth. They also find that Philadelphia appears to be importing an unusually large amount of its computer programming and data processing services, so a program of import replacement might be pursued in this industry. Otherwise, they conclude that the producer services in the Philadelphia urban area are sufficiently strong and comprehensive to represent attractions for firms that require these services.

Another critical service sector is health care. Erwin Blackstone and Kathleen Carr-Possai (1990) examined this sector in Philadelphia and found it to be a strong export sector. Leading medical schools and teaching hospitals make Philadelphia one of the nation's leading centers of medical education, research, and training. Philadelphia ranks second among the 20 largest urban areas in the fraction of total employment engaged in health care. Blackstone and Carr-Possai point out that some hospitals will close or be consolidated as the provision of health services shifts to other entities, and Philadelphia's concentration in hospitals makes it especially vulnerable to this change in the organization of medical practice. Nevertheless, they argue that a good economic development strategy would include the continued strengthening of Philadelphia's health education sector.

The final sector that was examined in the Stull–Madden volume (1990) is research and development. Stull and Madden wish to call attention to the idea that Philadelphia's opportunities for growth may be in activities that are in the early stages of the product cycle. A special survey was conducted that revealed that Philadelphia has a concentration of R&D activity in the medical/biology field, aerospace, chemicals, and electronics/computers. The R&D in the medical/biology field is particularly extensive and includes activity in pharmaceuticals, biology/biotechnology, medical research, and medicine. This R&D activity fits in both with the pharmaceutical and medical instruments industries and the medical education and training sector. Stull and Madden (1990) conclude that the best target sector for Philadelphia is its vast and diverse health care complex, which includes related manufacturing, R&D, and education and training providers. Given that the demand for more and better health care shows no signs of slowing down, why not?

Des Moines

The economy of Des Moines was studied in some detail in Chapter 4 using the idea of industry clusters. In that examination it was found that manufacturing employment in Des Moines had declined by 13.1% during the period 1980–1987, compared to a national decline of 10.2%. This kind of lackluster performance suggested that manufacturing does not represent a very good opportunity for growth in the Des Moines economy. That judgment is too hasty because there may be individual manufacturing industries, or clusters of industries, in Des Moines that benefit from localization economies. We have already seen [Henderson (1986)] that some individual manufacturing industries do indeed display localization economies. The question is whether such industries can be identified in Des Moines. The method of shift-share analysis was proposed in Chapter 12 as a device that might be useful for the identification of industries that may possess localization economies. That method is used here to examine the manufacturing sector in Des Moines.

The study of manufacturing in Des Moines is shown in Table 14.2. The table includes industries that had at least 500 employees in either 1980 or 1987. The employment level for each industry in Des Moines in 1987 is shown, along with the percentage changes in employment and pay per employee in the industry for both Des Moines and the United States as a whole. For example, employment in the food products industry in Des Moines in 1987 was 3580. Employment in the industry in Des Moines had grown by 21.1% from 1980 to 1987 compared to a decline of 6.1% in the nation. Pay per employee in nominal terms (not corrected for inflation) increased by 25.8% in Des Moines and 37.8% in the nation over this same period. Table 14.2 shows that Des Moines has two other large manufacturing industries: printing and publishing and nonelectrial machinery. Four of the nine industries in Des Moines lost more than 30% of their employment during the period 1980–1987, but three others show substantial employment gains. The manufacturing sector in Des Moines represents what might be called a "mixed bag," so it is worthwhile to proceed with some further analysis.

TABLE 14.2 Shift-Share Analysis of Manufacturing Employment in Des Moines, 1980–1987

Industry	Employment in 1987 in DM	Employment Change (%) 1980–1987		Wage Change (%) 1980–1987		Competitive Position	
		DM	US	DM	US	Basic	Adj.
Food products	3580	21.1	−6.1	25.8	37.8	29.9	21.4
Paper products	987	3.4	−4.4	71.3	53.0	10.5	23.3
Printing and publishing	6661	3.8	19.1	48.7	50.0	−12.6	−13.5
Chemicals	477	−30.4	−12.0	45.5	53.3	−15.7	−21.2
Stone, clay, and glass	371	−55.0	−14.1	61.7	48.5	−38.2	−29.0
Fabricated metals	872	−52.9	−13.7	63.1	48.8	−36.5	−26.5
Machinery, nonelectricals	3595	−32.9	−23.4	49.5	50.0	−6.8	−7.1
Transportation equipment	948	47.2	−1.7	65.9	54.3	51.6	59.7
Misc. manufacturing	785	38.9	−11.4	29.6	51.6	53.0	37.6

The first technique is to compute the competitive position (*CP*) as defined in Chapter 12, or

$$CP = \frac{\delta e_i}{e_i} - \frac{\delta US_i}{US_i} + \left(\frac{\delta US}{US} - \frac{\delta E}{E} \right),$$

where e_i is employment in industry i in the local economy, US_i is employment in the same industry in the United States, and US and E are total employment in the United States and in the local economy. This equation says that the competitive position for an industry is the difference between the growth rate of the industry in the local economy and in the reference economy (the nation) *plus* the adjustment for the extent to which the reference economy as a whole grew faster than the local economy. In this case employment in the nation grew by 14.2% from 1980 to 1987 and employment in Des Moines grew by 11.5%, so the adjustment is +2.7%. The competitive positions so defined are shown in Table 14.2 under the heading "competitive position, basic." Three manufacturing industries in Des Moines have strongly positive competitive positions: food products, transportation equipment, and miscellaneous manufacturing. The food products industry has a sizable presence in Des Moines and is discussed further below. The other two industries each had fewer than 1000 employees in 1987, so the large percentage increases in employment from 1980 to 1987 were not very large in absolute terms. Industries that are so small do not make good target industries, but they should be watched to see if the growth continues.

Two other industries in Des Moines, paper products and printing and publishing, experienced modest employment growth during the period 1980–1987. Paper products is a small industry in Des Moines, but it shows a positive competitive position and deserves to be watched for further developments. Printing and publishing is the largest manufacturing industry in Des Moines, but its modest employment growth of 3.8% over the period compares unfavorably with the national growth of 19.1%. The competitive position in printing and publishing is −12.6% over these seven years. The other three industries listed in Table 14.2 have a small presence in Des Moines and strongly negative competitive positions.

This brief look at manufacturing in Des Moines has identified one possible target industry: food products. You may recall from Chapter 3 that food products is one of the industries that exhibited static localization economies in the Henderson (1986) study. In other words, there are economies of scale at the industry level in an urban area. It is not known whether there are dynamic agglomeration economies associated with this industry. More insight can be gained from a closer look at the industry in Des Moines. The total food products employment of 3580 in Des Moines in 1987 consisted of 1150 workers in meat products, 571 in dairy products (down from 701 in 1980), and the rest scattered across the remaining categories of food products. Furthermore, County Business Patterns shows that Des Moines has one major meatpacking plant that experienced a substantial increase in employment from 1980 to 1987. We do not know exactly how large the employment increase was in this plant, but we do know that it went from a size class of 250–499 workers to 500–999 over the seven years. The employment increase in food products in Des Moines was 624 over this period, so it is quite possible that much of the increase in the industry took place in this one plant. No doubt a knowledgeable resident of Des Moines can tell us the identity of this plant. Further investigation is needed to determine whether the growth in employment in meatpacking was the result of localization economies or simply scale economies at the plant level. If the latter, there is no particular justification for making the industry the target of public economic development efforts.

Table 14.2 contains one final column that makes use of the data on pay per employee that is provided in County Business Patterns. Recall from Chapter 12 that employment growth in an industry can be influenced by the growth of the wage rate. The study by McDonald (1992), for example, found that the elasticity of demand for labor in manufacturing with respect to the wage rate was -0.7. We would expect that employment growth in an industry would be lower the greater is the increase in the wage rate, but the shift-share computations introduced so far fail to take this factor into account. Shift-share analysis measures the performance of an industry in the local economy compared to the nation, so a correction is needed for the change in the local wage rate compared to the national average wage rate in the industry. The comparative wage change figures are shown in Table 14.2. For example, the wage in food products in Des Moines increased by 25.8% over the period 1980–1987, and the national average wage change in the industry was 37.8%. These are nominal wage changes (not corrected for inflation). The consumer price index increased by 37.9% over this period, so the real wage did not change at the national level and dropped by 12.1% in Des Moines. We therefore expect that employment would have increased more in Des Moines simply because of the drop in the wage rate relative to the national wage. If we apply an elasticity of demand for labor of -0.7, employment in the industry in Des Moines actually increased by 8.5% more than if its wage had not dropped relative to the national wage. We therefore adjust the Des Moines competitive position *down* by 8.5% to reflect the employment growth that occurred because of the local wage change relative to the nation. The final column in Table 14.2 shows these adjusted competitive positions for the manufacturing industries in Des Moines. These adjustments for the wage effect do not change dramatically how we evaluate these industries, but note the paper products industry. In this industry the wage rate increased by 71.3% in Des Moines compared to a 53% increase in the nation. This 18.3% increase in the wage relative to the nation means that this industry had more strength in Des Moines than we had thought previously. An adjustment of $+12.8$ (18.3×0.7) is made to the competitive position.

In this section we have examined the problem of the selection of target industries through the use of Philadelphia and Des Moines as examples. Target industry selection is obviously a risky business, but careful study of the recent trends in the local economy should cut down on the risk.

F. EVALUATION OF ECONOMIC DEVELOPMENT STRATEGIES AND POLICIES

Now we come to the most difficult part of the topic of local economic development—evaluation. As economists we seek to discover the results produced by economic development strategies and policies that would not have occurred otherwise. It is fair to say that the quality of evaluation research in this field is generally pretty low and that experimentation with policies has far outstripped our meager efforts at evaluation. It is also true that state and local officials often have shown a disinterest in evaluation research. Indeed, some officials who are responsible for operating particular programs are interested largely in self-serving evaluation efforts. Competent and unbiased evaluation efforts are something of a rarity in the field. The improvement of evaluation efforts is an important issue that the readers of this book will face in their careers. This section is a basic introduction to evaluation research in the context of local economic development policy.

Evaluation of strategy and policies must begin with the goals that are being pursued. A misunderstanding about goals leads to evaluation that is not on target. For example, many critics of local economic development policies point out that the main result is to shift the location of some economic activity. This result may have been the goal of policy, so the critics are complaining about the goal rather than the policies themselves. This chapter began with a lengthy discussion of the basic goals of economic policy: to improve efficiency and to create a more equitable distribution of income. These goals are adopted here as the standards against which to judge local economic development efforts. All strategies and their attendant policies will affect both efficiency and equity, so evaluation work should try to measure both. In this chapter we also discussed the more immediate goals of increasing the local tax base and the local employment level. At the very least, evaluation research should be directed at the measurement of these variables.

The evaluation researcher can contemplate making an evaluation of the overall economic development strategy and/or the individual policies that make up the implementation of that strategy. As a practical matter it is usually, but not always, easier to evaluate the impacts of a particular policy rather than to determine the total effects of an overall strategy. Indeed, one approach to the evaluation of an overall strategy is to perform an evaluation of each policy and sum the effects. This approach has the advantage that it will tell us (we hope) which policy elements of the strategy had the largest effects on the desired outcomes. This information can then be used to allocate more effectively the resources available for economic development. Let us turn to the evaluation of individual economic development policies.

Economists use two basic methods for policy evaluation; they estimate economic models using nonexperimental data, and they use experimental (or "quasi-experimental") data. Both of these methods were introduced in Chapter 9 in the discussion of housing policy. The estimation of an economic model using non-experimental data means that the data that are used have been generated by the normal operation of the economy. For example, data gathered by the Federal Housing Administration were used to estimate the price and income elasticities of demand for housing. These estimated elasticities can then be used to perform an economic evaluation of housing policies. Alternatively, the U.S. Department of Housing and Urban Development ran two experiments in which low-income households were given housing allowances and other households were members of the "control" group. Data were gathered during the experiments to determine the effects of the policy.

Both techniques can be used to evaluate local economic development policies, but the experimental method is used only rarely. The use of nonexperimental data has already been illustrated in the study by O'hUallachain and Satterthwaite (1992) that was discussed in Chapter 12. They tested for the effects of policies such as enterprise zones, research parks, and industrial revenue bond programs on employment growth in growth industries. You may recall that both enterprise zone programs and research parks had positive effects on employment growth in manufacturing as a whole. The research strategy is to gather data on a large number of local economies and to measure and test for the statistical significance of the many factors that may contribute to growth in employment and tax base. In the experimental method individual firms or workers are selected for participation in a program or to be members of the control group, and data on both groups are collected for several years of participation in the program.

A survey of nonexperimental evaluation research on local economic development policies up through 1990 has been provided by Timothy Bartik in his 1991 book, *Who Benefits from State and Local Economic Development Policies?* This book is an excellent source of information on this topic and would make a good required text for a course on economic development policy. Tax incentives are the local policies that have been studied most extensively. Newman and Sullivan (1988) have also done a survey of research on this topic. The surveys of research on tax effects find that local taxes have strong effects within an urban area but that the effects are much weaker across urban areas. Bartik (1991, p. 40) found that 7 of 10 studies of intraurban growth found statistically significant local tax effects. The average size of the local tax effect is an elasticity of -1.92 (i.e., if a small suburban jurisdiction reduces its local real estate tax on business by 10%, in the long run business activity will increase by an average of 19%). Bartik's (1991) survey of interarea studies shows that 24 of 30 found a statistically significant tax effect, controlling for the amount of public services. The average size of these effects is an elasticity of -0.33, so a state or urban area that cuts its taxes on business by 10% (holding public services constant) can expect an increase of about 3% in business activity. Capital and labor resources are highly mobile within an urban area but much less mobile across states or urban areas, so these empirical findings make sense.

Bartik (1991) also surveyed research on a variety of other economic development programs. Six of the studies surveyed were of state enterprise zones, a program that is of recent vintage. The first proposal for enterprise zones was made in 1978 by Sir Geoffrey Howe, a Conservative member of the British House of Commons who later served as a minister in the government of Prime Minister Margaret Thatcher. Stuart Butler, a researcher with the Heritage Foundation, introduced the idea in the United States in 1979. Jack Kemp, the former conservative Republican congressman and former Secretary of Housing and Urban Development, immediately became a strong advocate for enterprise zone programs. The basic idea of an enterprise zone program is to provide incentives in the form of tax breaks and regulatory relief to businesses located in depressed parts of urban areas. Kemp and his congressional colleagues did not succeed in creating a federal program in the 1980s, although a new federal program called "Empowerment Zones" was created in 1994 and is just being implemented as this book is being written. However, the enterprise zone idea was received enthusiastically by many state and local public officials, and an enterprise zone program in some form was begun in 37 states in the 1980s.

The enterprise zone programs in the states differ widely. Some states have a small number of zones, and others have many zones. As Erickson (1992) discusses, the criteria for the designation of enterprise zones can be generous or stringent and are usually based on unemployment and/or poverty. Economic development incentives in enterprise zone programs fall into three general categories: investment incentives (e.g., tax rate reductions or tax credits), labor incentives (e.g., tax credits for jobs created, job training tax credits, incentives for hiring zone residents), and financing programs (e.g., investment fund linked to zone location). Indeed, some state enterprise zone programs approximate a comprehensive economic development strategy for a small, depressed area within a larger urban area.

Bartik (1991) and James (1991) conducted careful surveys of the evaluation research on state enterprise zone programs. They found that the evaluations have not been convincing one way or another because the programs were not designed from the beginning for effective evaluation and because little high quality research has been done. A few studies have used the "before and after" method, and others have used surveys of zone businesses. Bartik (1991) and James (1991) concluded that the best feasible evaluation method would make use of "comparison areas" to determine the impacts of an enterprise zone program. The "before and after" method, which looks for discontinuities in economic trends, may attribute an effect to the enterprise zone program when in fact a broader economic force is at work. Surveys of zone businesses, which are usually conducted after a program has been in operation, fail to gather information from businesses that failed or moved away in the interim. Also, these surveys usually do not include businesses that are *not* located in enterprise zones.

The first study of a state enterprise zone program that compared enterprise zones with comparable areas that did not participate in the program was conducted for the Illinois program by McDonald (1993). The use of regression analysis controlled for other factors that influence economic growth in both types of areas. The Illinois enterprise zone program includes a sales tax exemption on building supplies, a state income tax credit for investment in machinery, equipment, or buildings, and a local property tax abatement. The program also includes a tax credit for each job created in a zone if certified dislocated or disadvantaged workers are hired to fill them and a loan program was set up for zone businesses. Clearly, the program promotes investment in buildings. As one local enterprise zone administrator put it, "The enterprise zone program is mainly a bricks and mortar program."

What were the goals of the Illinois enterprise zone program? The Illinois law that created the program states that the goal is to stimulate business growth and retention in depressed areas of the state. The original statement of the program's goals and regulations from the state agency responsible for implementing the program included the goal of causing some investment to be made in enterprise zones rather than elsewhere in the state. Thus the program had, as one of its original objectives, the stimulation of economic activity in depressed areas of Illinois even if that would have meant a reduction in economic growth in other areas of the state. Enterprise zones were designated in all of the largest urban areas in the state, including 12 enterprise zones in Cook County (the central county in the Chicago urban area).

The research performed by McDonald (1993) showed that the enterprise zone program had no statistically significant effect on total employment in the zones, but that the program stimulated growth in the distribution sector (wholesale trade and transportation) during the period 1983–1987 by about 25% beyond what it would have been. The evidence strongly suggests that the enterprise zones attracted economic activity in this sector that they would not otherwise have attracted in the absence of the program. Two other findings are worth noting. First, the enterprise zone program tended to be targeted at depressed areas. Therefore, a failure to control for past employment growth performance (including decline) may lead to the incorrect impression that the enterprise zone program had a negative impact on employment growth. This is a case of a "treatment" being given to a nonrandom group of subjects. One must take special care in evaluating programs with this characteristic. Second, the distribution sector was characterized by fairly rapid growth during the period under study and by sizable demands for investment in real estate capital. The enterprise zone incentives appear to be targeted at industries with these characteristics. The program really does nothing for an industry that is experiencing declining demand for its products. It is possible that different types of industries respond to different kinds of incentives.

The results of the McDonald (1993) study of the Illinois enterprise zone program suggested some more general implications for policy. First, the focus of the enterprise zone program on depressed areas of the state has been lost because there are now 88 designated zones in the state. The program will be less successful at stimulating investment and employment growth in depressed areas if other areas of the state also contain enterprise zones. Second, the emphasis on subsidizing capital investment should be reconsidered. The results of the study suggest that the subsidies in the program are successful at stimulating growth in enterprise zones in a growth sector that is capital intensive—the distribution sector. Other types of incentives are needed to attract other sectors to enterprise zones. For example, larger wage subsidies and job training programs might be needed if the objective of the program is to stimulate more employment in enterprise zones. Finally, the state of Illinois did not keep records concerning the cost of the enterprise zone program. It was not possible to retrieve data on the sales tax exemptions and the state income tax deductions and credits earned by the participating firms. The lack of this information means that the benefits of the program could not be compared to the costs. It also means that the responses of the firms could not be estimated as a function of the magnitudes of the incentives in the program.

The studies surveyed by Bartik (1991) also include two studies of incentives to attract foreign investment and one study of export promotion programs. Both policies were found to be effective. The study by Coughlin and Cartwright (1987) of state manufacturing exports found that $1 of added state spending on export promotion increased exports by $432! Bartik (1991) examined the studies of public services and public infrastructure and found that education expenditures and infrastructure had positive effects more often than other forms of public spending. More research on these and other local economic development policies is needed, and it is likely that this area of research will be an active one for some years to come. One clear need is for greater use of the experimental method in the evaluation of economic development policies.

Bartik's (1991) examination of the research on local economic development policies convinced him that those policies probably do have positive effects on employment. The next question he asked was how that employment growth was of benefit to local residents. Bartik's book contains extensive empirical research on the various impacts of employment growth in urban areas during the period 1979–1986. An increase in employment in an urban area will reduce unemployment and increase labor force participation of the current residents, but most of the new jobs will be taken by migrants to the urban area. Bartik's summary (1991, p. 95) is that, in the long run, 6 to 7% of new jobs will be filled by unemployed residents, 16% will go to residents who enter the labor force, and migrants will take 77 to 78% of the new jobs. These results are very important because they say that a one-time increase in employment will reduce unemployment and increase labor force participation permanently. Furthermore, a 1% permanent increase in employment increases average earnings by 0.4%, but real wages per hour for a given occupation do not increase. The one-time increase in employment also permits some residents to move to better-paying occupations. This effect is strongest for black, less-educated, and younger workers. What is more, Bartik's evidence is that the effects of an employment increase are highly progressive; the lowest-income people have the highest percentage gains in earnings. The long-run earnings gains from a 1% increase in employment by quintile found by Bartik (1991, p. 173) are:

Quintile	Percent Gain in Earnings
1	4.64
2	0.66
3	0.42
4	0.32
5	0.21
Average	0.41

Clearly, Bartik's findings come close to saying that about the best thing that can be done for poor people is to increase overall employment in the urban area. He makes no distinction between the different sources of employment growth; he has estimated the effects of the actual employment growth in the urban areas included in the study over the period 1979–1986. Most of that actual employment growth was, of course, in the service sector. Bartik (1991) takes the view that the competition among localities in economic development policies is not necessarily wasted effort. If localities with the economies that are the most depressed are also the most active in economic development policy, economic activity will tend to shift toward those areas. This result is both efficient and equitable because underemployed people are being put to work, and the poorest workers reap the largest benefits.

Bartik (1994) has completed another study that demonstrates the same idea. In this study job growth from 1979 to 1988 in an urban area increased income for the poorest 20% of the households by more than the average household. A 1% increase in employment over this decade increased labor income for the lowest 20% of households by 2.6%, while the gains for the other quintiles were (in order, from low to high) 1.4%, 1.2%, 0.6%, and 0.5%. Bartik (1994) concluded that policies to stimulate job growth in an urban area are progressive as long as the public cost per job created is not too high and provided that those costs are financed by taxes (e.g., income or sales tax) rather than by cuts in welfare spending.

We reach the end of this section with the finding that local economic development policy can be both efficient and equitable, provided that those policies result in employment gains in the more economically depressed areas. This is an important finding, and it is why this book has devoted so much material to the topic of urban economic growth and development. However, at this time we do not know much about how the cost side of these policies compares to benefits.

G. LOCAL ECONOMIC DEVELOPMENT POLICY IN PRACTICE

Most of this chapter has been written as if it is possible to have a coherent economic development strategy for an entire urban area. In Section C it was noted briefly that for the most part, economic development policy is carried out by local governments and by state governments. In this section we take a look at policy at both levels, starting with local government.

Local Governments and Economic Development

In most major urban areas in the United States there is no local government that encompasses all, or even most, of the urban area. There are a few exceptions, such as Indianapolis, Minneapolis–St. Paul, and Houston, but these are indeed the exceptions. The other basic fact is that local governments still depend heavily on the local real estate tax (and on local sales tax revenue and local charges and fees). The result is that local governments within an urban area have an incentive to compete against one another for commercial and industrial development rather than engage in policies to increase the growth of the entire urban area.

Consider a numerical example in a form similar to the "prisoner's dilemma" game. Suppose that an urban area has two counties, Central and Edge, and each county can pursue three kinds of economic development strategies: (1) do nothing, (2) try to draw firms away from the other county (using tax breaks, etc.), and (3) engage in efforts to assist existing firms in the county to grow and to attract new businesses. Table 14.3 shows the outcomes in terms of the number of jobs in each county for the nine possible combinations of strategies. If both counties do nothing, Central has 500 jobs and Edge has 200 jobs. If the counties only try to draw firms away from each other, their efforts cancel out (and are wasted). If only one county tries to draw firms away from the other, 100 jobs will move. If that county, instead, engages in efforts to assist existing firms to grow and to attract new businesses, 50 new jobs will be created. It is more difficult to have success with these creative efforts than it is simply to draw firms away from the adjacent county. The rest of Table 14.3 is filled in using these assumptions.

Now we are ready to play the game of local economic development. For example, if Edge engages in efforts to attract business from Central while Central works to create new jobs, the net result is 300 jobs (200 + 100) jobs in Edge and 450 jobs (500 − 100 + 50) in Central. The message from this example is simple; the urban area has more total jobs (250 + 550) if *both* counties work to create new jobs. But *each* county has a stronger incentive to go after the jobs in its sister county because that strategy leads to more jobs in that county *regardless* of what strategy is followed by the other county. This is the dilemma of the game of local economic development. What can be done about this inherent problem? Leaders are needed who can see the possibilities for the urban area as a whole, and incentives are needed for local policies to be cooperative rather than competitive.

The problem described above is particularly acute when the suburban jurisdictions are playing the game to attract jobs away from the central city. Central cities are the home of most of society's social and economic problems: poverty, crime, fiscal difficulties, and many others. These problems are discussed at some length in Chapter 16, but for now it is worth noting that efforts of the suburbs to attract jobs from the central city will tend to make those problems worse. As it is, suburbs have an incentive to do things that will make central city problems worse.

TABLE 14.3 Local Economic Development Game

| Central County | Edge County | | |
	Do Nothing	Draw Firms from Central	Create New Jobs
Do nothing	200[a]	300	250
	500	400	500
Draw firms from Edge	100	200	150
	600	500	600
Create new jobs	200	300	250
	550	450	550

[a]The top number is jobs in Edge County; the bottom number is jobs in Central County.

What do central cities do in response to the decline in their job base? New York City is a good example of a central city that is an active player of the game. According to the *New York Times* (July 5, 1995), during the period January 1994–July 1995 the city approved 11 deals that give $348 million in sales tax breaks to various companies. New York City has also expanded its programs for low-interest financing, energy subsidies, property tax breaks, and other benefits. The city began its aggressive program in the early 1980s in response to the exodus of firms to New Jersey and Connecticut. Some major firms, including CBS, Morgan Stanley, First Boston, the New York Mercantile Exchange, and the New York Times, have received large benefits not to leave the city. The use of property tax breaks is especially popular because they are easy to administer and require no direct expenditure of city funds. The term *tax expenditures* is used to describe tax breaks for firms. A program known as the Industrial and Commercial Incentive Program was created in 1981 and provides property tax breaks to companies that build, move to, or expand in any of the four boroughs other than Manhattan. (The area of Manhattan above 96th Street is also eligible for the program.) More recently, a program was begun to provide property tax breaks under special circumstances for firms in central and lower Manhattan. Those special circumstances include the building of "smart" buildings that are highly efficient in their use of energy.

Walzer and P'ng (1995) report on the results of a survey that was conducted in 1984 by the International City Management Association to determine the economic development strategies and techniques used by cities in the United States. Usable responses were received from 491 cities, and almost half (44.4%) reported that they did have an economic development plan as of 1984. One strongly suspects that this fraction is higher today. The most popular policy tools used by these cities are:

Tax-exempt bonds	48.3%
Direct loans to private business	25.3%
Tax abatement	25.1%
Loan subsidies	22.4%

Smaller numbers of cities also used direct cash contributions to business, provision of in-kind goods or services, loan guarantees, donations of unused real property, deferred tax payments, and sale to the city and lease back of real estate. The changes in the federal tax laws in 1986 restricted the use of tax-exempt bonds by local government to manufacturing firms, so this tool has declined in importance. It is likely that the use of these other policy tools has increased since 1984.

Economic development incentives have become part of the game of local politics. The executives of major recipients of local tax breaks and other assistance are sometimes major contributors to the political campaigns of local candidates. This fact draws attention to some obvious problems. The potential exists for firms to buy influence and, ultimately, tax breaks in the guise of "economic development" policy.

On the other side of the coin, public officials have learned that firms do not necessarily keep the promises they make to retain and/or create jobs when they accept local tax breaks and other forms of assistance. Newer versions of economic development programs include requirements that firms make commitments about jobs and that benefits can be lost if those commitments are not met. The local government must also monitor the performance of those firms to ensure compliance. The city of New York has run into problems with the performance of some of the firms that have received tax breaks and other benefits, and the city has imposed stronger performance requirements and instituted closer monitoring of performance. But do not lose sight of the fact that all of New York City's efforts are designed to prevent further movement of firms to New Jersey and Connecticut! By the way, the state of New Jersey apparently has no intention of standing by and doing nothing while New York City expands its economic development efforts. Read the *New York Times* for further moves in the game.

As major central cities such as New York City work to keep the jobs that are already there, many local governments in the suburbs and the sunbelt are working to attract new firms. Many of those efforts meet with little success, but some localities have a great deal of success—and success can create its own problems.

Consider the case of Rio Rancho, New Mexico. Rio Rancho is a suburb of Albuquerque that is a big player in the economic development game. In the early 1980s they attracted a large Intel plant that makes semiconductor chips. Note that the Silicon Valley firm, Intel, sought a cheaper site away from the San Francisco area for its manufacturing operations. The deal that attracted the plant includes the provision that Intel does not have to pay any real estate taxes for 30 years. Then, in 1993, Rio Rancho landed the huge Intel plant that makes the Pentium Chip, the main component in some of the best personal computers. The deal to land the Pentium plant includes:

1. Exemption from real estate taxes for 30 years
2. Lower state corporate income tax rate
3. Exemption from the gross receipts tax on equipment purchases
4. Recruitment and training of workers
5. Deep discounts on moving and storage fees and utility deposits for Intel employees who are moving in
6. Guaranteed fast action on such things as building permits

Rio Rancho is also very effective in recruiting smaller firms. They have a recruiting team of experts who will go anywhere to cut a deal. Their team includes a city planner, a banker, and a builder, so Rio Rancho can promise that a firm can plan, gain approval, and build its facility in four months.

Rio Rancho is wildly successful in the economic development game, but its municipal services have not kept up with its job growth. As of 1995 the town has no high school, and its middle school has an enrollment that is double the planned capacity of the building. The high school students are bused to an overcrowded school in Albuquerque. The failure to build schools stems from the fact that the school district relies on real estate taxes, but Intel and other firms are exempt from this tax. The real estate tax in Rio Rancho on residential property is at the limit permitted by state law, but the tax collections fall short of their needs. Intel points out that their employees earn high incomes and pay income and sales taxes to the state, so the problem is with the system for financing schools and is not caused by Intel and the other firms. In any event, success has its pitfalls.

State Governments and Economic Development

Since the 1970s most state governments have become very active in the economic development game. The first states to play the game were the southern states that worked to attract industry from the north starting in the 1950s, but by the 1970s nearly all of the states realized that they had to be in the game. Some states have actually designed very creative economic development strategies that are adapted to their particular circumstances. A book edited by Fosler (1988) entitled *The New Economic Role of American States* contains several useful case studies that describe how states responded to the need for economic development. A few examples from Fosler (1988) will give you a flavor of what has been going on.

In response to the decline in the domestic auto industry, in the 1980s the state of Michigan designed a comprehensive strategy to update its industrial base by promoting research and development, product development, venture capital, and helping workers retrain for the new industrial jobs. The focus is on creating new products and new businesses, not on attracting firms from elsewhere. In the 1990s (after the recession of 1990–1991) Michigan has done very well in participating in the growth of manufacturing in the midwest.

Tennessee has followed a strategy of attracting firms to the state. Tennessee has inherent advantages that derive from its location near the center of the nation and from its low wages and level of unionization. The Tennessee government has been helpful to businesses that are in need of a location for a new plant, and its low-key approach has been quite attractive to Japanese auto firms. Tennessee attracted several Japanese auto plants as well as the General Motors Saturn plant by using relatively modest financial incentives coupled with an atmosphere of patience and trust. Tennessee has been successful in attracting branch plants of major manufacturing firms, but this success has left the state with a relative lack of business services. A large and diverse business services sector helps a local economy create new firms, so Tennessee may wish to rethink and modify its strategy.

As a final example of a state's strategy, the state of Minnesota has long followed a policy of developing its own human resources through high-quality education at all levels. Economic pressures on some of its older industries, such as agriculture and mining, have led the state into some more conventional economic development incentive programs and "smokestack chasing." Some observers of the Minnesota scene are very skeptical of these targeted incentive efforts and argue for a return to the older strategy of keeping the public sector focused on the quality of the basic public services that it provides. In any event, Minnesota succeeded in attracting the Mall of America, the nation's largest shopping mall. It is brilliantly located adjacent to the state's major airport in the suburbs of Minneapolis, so shoppers can fly in from anywhere in the midwest for a day (or more) of shopping. The Mall of America is more than just a shopping mall; it has hotels, live entertainment, and an indoor amusement park. This mall is the wave of the future, it would seem.

The message of Fosler's (1988) book is that states are, and probably will continue to be, the most creative players in the local economic development field. You may find that state government will be an exciting place to work in the future. If you do go to work in state government, try to remember what you know about urban economies and their problems. Be sensitive to equity considerations as you pursue growth for your state.

H. SUMMARY

This chapter is a broad survey of local economic development policy. It began with a discussion of the basic goals of any economic policy—efficient use of resources and equity in the distribution of income. A more efficient use of resources occurs when there is a gain in the welfare of one person with no reduction in the welfare of someone else. It was pointed out that perfectly competitive markets can produce an efficient intertemporal allocation of resources (i.e., an efficient amount of investment in future productive capacity). However, all of the reasons for the failure of markets to be efficient in a static economy also operate over time. The standard problems of monopoly, public goods, externalities, and lack of information still apply. Furthermore, there is the added problem of social risk versus individual risk. Investments in future productive capacity can be highly risky for an individual firm, but the risk for society is less because that social risk is spread out over many firms. This observation suggests that some investments, such as investments in new technologies, should be subsidized because individual firms are applying discount rates to future returns that include a risk premium that is too high from society's point of view. In short, strong arguments can be made on efficiency grounds for economic growth policy.

The goal of equity in the distribution of income requires that the society agree on the nature of that goal. Reasonable people can have widely differing views about this goal, and often a difference in policy recommendations stems from different views about the goal of equity. For example, some would place very heavy weight on increasing the incomes of the poorest members of the society, while others would distribute the weights more evenly. Given these overall goals of economic policy, the specific goals of local job growth and an increased tax base were examined. The view is offered that job growth that employs unemployed or underemployed workers offers benefits on both efficiency and equity grounds. This same point of view has been promoted for the national economy in a recent book by Baily, Burtless, and Litan (1993) entitled *Growth with Equity*. If an urban economist is looking for a slogan, "Growth with Equity" has a good ring to it. Baily et al. recommended a package of programs at the federal level to stimulate commercial research and development activity, increase net investment in plant and equipment, and improve the education and skills of the labor force.

The choice of goals leads to the selection of an overall economic development strategy and the policies to be pursued in support of that strategy. A strategy to increase growth with no special reference to the poorest members of the urban area leads to one set of policies, while a strategy to emphasize economic opportunity for the disadvantaged can lead to another package of policies. A policy can be categorized according to the underlying factor in economic growth that it enhances. From your study of Chapters 10 to 14, you know that these underlying economic growth factors are:

- Export demand
- Import substitution
- Capital (private and public)
- Labor force and population
- Education and training
- Technical change: new products, new production processes, and diffusion of new technology
- Entrepreneurship
- Amenities
- Agglomeration economies: urbanization economies and localization economies.

One topic that is debated by experts in local economic development is whether the local programs should select *target industries* as the focus of much of the strategy and policy. A target industry is one that will respond well to policy initiatives because of the existence of market failure of some sort (e.g., localization economies or individual risk that is high compared to social risk). At this point it is not clear that local officials are very adept at selecting good targets, but it is also true that the use of scarce resources for economic development programs may require that some choices be made. Some economic development policies can be of a general nature (e.g., improvements in basic education, general training in entrepreneurship, support for cultural, social, and recreational amenities, provision of good public services at low tax rates, etc.). Indeed, it is quite possible that general policies of these kinds represent the best use of scarce public and philanthropic resources. However, many local economic development officials cannot resist the urge to select target industries. Some analytical methods are offered to assist in this selection.

The final topic in the chapter is the evaluation of economic development strategies and policies. Evaluation research in this field is, for the most part, in its infancy. A good deal of research has concentrated on the effects of local taxes on economic activity, and recent studies generally have found that variations in local taxes for small jurisdictions within an urban area can have sizable impacts on business location. The figure obtained by Bartik (1991) in his survey of the research is that a 1% decrease in local taxes, compared to the rest of the urban area, can result in about a 1.9% increase in economic activity. This finding is consistent with discussion of the local public sector in Chapter 9. State and local taxes are less powerful influences on the location of economic activity across states and urban areas.

The only other local program that has been studied very much is the state enterprise zone program. As of 1991, 37 states had enterprise zone programs, but very few of those programs had been subjected to an evaluation of decent quality. The study of the Illinois enterprise zone program by McDonald (1993) found that the program did stimulate employment in the distribution sector (wholesale trade and transportation) in the enterprise zones. However, total employment did not increase in the zones compared to other areas. Bartik's (1991) survey of other evaluation research found that other policies, such as export assistance and programs to attract foreign investment, had positive effects.

Clearly, more research on the effects of economic development policies is needed. Assuming that effective policies do exist, Bartik's (1991) examination of the impacts of employment increases on the local labor market produced striking results. Job growth does most of the right things. A one-time increase in employment reduces the unemployment rate, increases the rate of labor force participation, increases earnings, and produces the greatest benefits for the poor. In short, labor resources are used more efficiently and the distribution of income becomes more equitable. The favorable effects of local economic growth in general, and employment growth in particular, are sufficient justification for devoting four chapters of this book to these topics.

The real world of economic development policy at the local level often consists of competition between jurisdictions within the same urban area. This competition can be harmful because it comes at a cost of a lost opportunity—the opportunity to devise strategies that will enhance the growth of the entire urban area. This problem of policy coordination and cooperation has not been solved in most of America's major urban areas, but some state governments have developed creative economic development strategies that are more in keeping with the message of this chapter.

EXERCISES

1. Suppose that you are the economic development czar of your urban area. You have decided to pursue the goal of increasing the per capita income of residents of the urban area (without regard to income distribution), and your strategy is to support growth by selecting target industries.
   (a) Select a package of specific policies from Table 14.1 that is consistent with this strategy.
   (b) Conduct an analysis of the manufacturing sector of that local economy along the lines shown in Table 14.2 to identify possible candidates for target industries in manufacturing. Conduct the study at the two-digit SIC code level.

2. Contact a public economic development agency that operates within an urban area of your choice. This agency might be a department of the central city government, for example. What are the primary goals and strategies of this agency, as nearly as you can determine? Are they smokestack chasers? Do they concentrate on industry retention? Do they have a more comprehensive economic development strategy? Was it difficult to find out about basic goals and strategies? What are the policies used to support that strategy? Are policies being pursued that seem to be in pursuit of no coherent strategy?

REFERENCES

Baily, Martin, G. Burtless, and R. Litan, 1993. *Growth with Equity*. Washington, DC: The Brookings Institution.

Bartik, Timothy, 1991. *Who Benefits from State and Local Economic Development Policies?* Kalamazoo, MI: W.E. Upjohn Institute.

————, 1994. "The Effects of Metropolitan Job Growth on the Size Distribution of Family Income," *Journal of Regional Science*, Vol. 34, pp. 483–501.

Bernstein, Richard, 1990. "The Restructuring of Manufacturing within the Philadelphia Region," in W. Stull and J. Madden, eds., *Post-industrial Philadelphia*. Philadelphia: University of Pennsylvania Press.

Blackstone, Erwin and Kathleen Carr-Possai, 1990. "Growth and Change in Health Care Employment within the Metropolitan Area," in W. Stull and J. Madden, eds., *Post-industrial Philadelphia*. Philadelphia: University of Pennsylvania Press.

Coughlin, Cletus and P. Cartwright, 1987. "An Examination of State Foreign Export Promotion and Manufacturing Exports," *Journal of Regional Science*, Vol. 27, pp. 439–449.

Erickson, Rodney, 1992. "Enterprise Zones: Lessons from the State Government Experience," in E. Mills and J. McDonald, eds., *Sources of Metropolitan Growth*. New Brunswick, NJ: Rutgers University Press.

Fosler, R. Scott, ed., 1988. *The New Economic Role of American States*. New York: Oxford University Press.

Greenwood, Michael, 1981. *Migration and Economic Growth in the United States*. New York: Academic Press.

Henderson, J. Vernon, 1986. "Efficiency of Resource Usage and City Size," *Journal of Urban Economics*, Vol. 19, pp. 47–70.

Hoover, Edgar and R. Vernon, 1959. *Anatomy of a Metropolis*. Cambridge, MA: Harvard University Press.

James, Franklin, 1991. "The Evaluation of Enterprise Zone Programs," in R. Green, ed., *Enterprise Zones: New Directions in Economic Development*. Newbury Park, CA: Sage Publications.

McDonald, John, 1987. "Crime and Punishment: A Social Welfare Analysis," *Journal of Criminal Justice*, Vol. 15, pp. 245–254.

————, 1992. "Assessing the Development Status of Metropolitan Areas," in E. Mills and J. McDonald, eds., *Sources of Metropolitan Growth*. New Brunswick, NJ: Rutgers University Press.

————, 1993. "Tax Expenditures for Local Economic Growth: An Econometric Evaluation of the Illinois Enterprise Zone Program," *Public Budgeting and Financial Management*, Vol. 5, pp. 477–505.

Mier, Robert, 1993. *Social Justice and Local Development Policy*. Newbury Park, CA: Sage Publications.

Muth, Richard, 1971. "Migration: Chicken or Egg?" *Southern Economic Journal*, Vol. 37, pp. 295–306.

Newman, Robert and D. Sullivan, 1988. "Econometric Analysis of Business Tax Impacts on Industrial Location: What Do We Know and How Do We Know It?" *Journal of Urban Economics*, Vol. 23, pp. 215–234.

O'hUallachain, Breandon and M. Satterthwaite, 1992. "Sectoral Growth Patterns at the Metropolitan Level: An Evaluation of Economic Development Incentives," *Journal of Urban Economics*, Vol. 31, pp. 25–58.

Rawls, John, 1971. *A Theory of Justice*. Cambridge, MA: Harvard University Press.

Solow, Robert, 1970. *Growth Theory: An Exposition*. New York: Oxford University Press.

Stull, William and J. Madden, 1990. *Post-industrial Philadelphia*, Philadelphia: University of Pennsylvania Press.

Walzer, Norman and P. P'ng, 1995. "Incentives and Economic Development: An Empirical Analysis," Research Memorandum, Illinois Institute of Rural Affairs, Western Illinois University.

C H A P T E R

15

Urban Growth and Changing Location Patterns

A. INTRODUCTION

This is a capstone chapter. The basic economic functions of urban areas were discussed in Part I of the book, and in Part II we examined the details of urban location patterns. Part III was devoted to the economic growth and development of urban areas. Now is the time to put all three of these topics together to examine the changing nature of urban areas. It is not possible to combine *all* that has been learned about all three topics, but urban economists have done a pretty good job of knitting the three topics together to provide a fairly comprehensive explanation of how urban areas are evolving. Some of the economic and social problems that are associated with the current evolution of urban areas are discussed in Chapter 16.

There are three studies that represent serious empirical attempts to provide the synthesis that is needed. Each book has a title that is a bit long-winded but gives you a good idea of the nature of the study. The first effort is by R. D. Norton and is titled *City Life-Cycles and American Urban Policy* (1979). The second study, by Katherine Bradbury, Anthony Downs, and Kenneth Small, followed Norton by only three years and is titled *Urban Decline and the Future of American Cities* (1982). The most recent work is by Thomas Stanback, Jr. and carries the title *The New Suburbanization: Challenge to the Central City.* (1991). From Norton's title we can see that his emphasis is on the idea that cities (i.e., urban areas) have life cycles in a manner that is similar to the life cycles of firms and industries, a topic that was discussed in Chapter 11. The title used by Bradbury et al. conveys the idea that the decline of the central city is their main concern. It turns out, however, that their work provides a fairly comprehensive approach to urban growth and changing spatial patterns. Finally, Stanback's more recent work emphasizes the role of the "new" suburbanization, the suburbanization of employment into large employment subcenters (i.e., edge cities). Together these three studies provide a good empirical overview of the evolution of urban areas and of the evolution of research on the evolution of urban areas. The easiest way to grapple with this topic is to review the three studies one at a time and then to summarize their findings. That is the plan of this chapter. By the way, I also recommend that Stanback's book be read as part of the course in urban economics.

Recall the discussion in Chapter 1 of stages in economic research. To review, these five stages are:

1. Accumulation of data
2. Examination of data and determination of important facts
3. Formulation of economic model to explain those facts
4. Estimation and testing of the model
5. Use of the model for forecasting, policy analysis, and/or normative analysis

The three studies reviewed in this chapter are all devoted to stages 2 through 4 of this list. The topic under study is the similarities and differences in the spatial evolution of urban areas in the United States since the end of World War II. Each of these three books is an attempt to examine data to reveal patterns and phenomena that call for explanation through an economic model. An economic model is then formulated and estimated. The three studies come up with somewhat different facts to be explained, economic models to explain those facts, and empirical results. The topic is not one for which there exists a "standard" model that everyone is using. Rather, this is another topic that is somewhat in an unsettled scholarly state. As we shall see, the differences in the three studies can be explained, in part, by when each study was completed. We begin with the earliest of the three.

B. R. D. NORTON AND CITY LIFE CYCLES

Norton (1979) began with the observation that older central cities lost population in the period 1950–1975 but that younger central cities gained population during this period. Some old central cities, such as St. Louis, Pittsburgh, Detroit, Buffalo, and Cleveland, experienced huge population losses, while San Diego, Phoenix, and Houston showed large gains in population. At the time some argued that the old cities were obsolete and that large areas within their boundaries had essentially been abandoned by all except the poor. Norton pointed out that the central cities that declined the most are "artifacts" of the age of industrialization, a period of roughly 1880 to 1914. During this time period of rapid urbanization in the United States we did not so much build great urban areas as we built centers of manufacturing based on industrial agglomeration economies. Norton argued that such urban areas (and their central cities) are especially vulnerable to changes in the larger economy compared to the great urban areas of Europe that have a much longer and diverse economic history. The economic logic of industrialization of that time produced centralized urban areas within an industrial region (the northeast).

So the story begins prior to World War II with a dominant group of urban areas in the northeast that are centers of manufacturing (and other things, as well). Up until that time these older urban areas had successfully performed the role of being incubators of new industries and technologies. Some industries would die out or move away, but they would be replaced by new industrial activities that rejuvenated the local economy. However, the decades after World War II saw the migration of a good deal of the incubator function to newer urban areas in other parts of the nation, especially to California and Texas. Norton argued that this shift in the incubator function could not be reversed, and some of the older urban areas collapsed. This story sounds plausible, but the proof is in the empirical work.

Norton conducted his study by assembling data on the 30 largest urban areas as of 1970 and then ranking them according to their population levels in 1910. Table 15.1 shows these 30 urban areas and several variables for each. Norton calls the 12 urban areas at the top of the table members of the industrial age class. Eleven of the 12 are in the northeast; only San Francisco is not in this region. The next six are a mixed group of urban areas that includes Los Angeles, Washington, DC, Milwaukee, Kansas City, New Orleans, and Seattle. The bottom 12 are called young urban areas because they had not yet grown to prominence as of 1910. Ten of the 12 are in the sunbelt. Indianapolis and Columbus are in the northeast but can be considered to be young urban areas. We shall see that these two urban areas stand out among northeastern urban areas.

The first variable listed in Table 15.1 is the percentage of total employment in the urban area in 1950 that was in manufacturing. The average for the 12 industrial age urban areas was 34.6%, while the average for the young urban areas was 18.9%. The two groups of urban areas were performing sharply different economic functions in 1950.

The next three variables listed in Table 15.1 pertain to population growth from 1950 to 1975. The population growth for the urban area is shown first; the average for the 12 industrial age urban areas was 32%, while the 12 young urban areas grew at an average of 111%. The next variable shows the growth of the population of the central city in each urban area. These growth figures include the effects of any expansions in the boundaries of the central cities that took place during the period 1950–1975. The 12 industrial age cities declined by an average of 21% over these 25 years, while the 12 young urban cities grew by an average of 124%. Part of this huge difference can be attributed to the fact that the young central cities were able to annex territory and the industrial age cities were not. The percentage increase in land area of the central city is shown in the next column of Table 15.1. The industrial age cities increased their land areas by an average of only 2%, while the young cities expanded their land areas by 704%! It should be noted that much of this annexation was "preemptive" in the sense that the city annexed territory in advance of population growth.

Norton summarized the information on population growth in a particularly clever way. He used the population growth data for 1950–1970 for the 30 urban areas to estimate a linear equation that relates population growth in the central city to population growth in the urban area and the increase in land area of the central city over the period. This estimated relationship is

$$CPOPGRO = -61.9 + 1.1UPOPGRO + 0.06L,$$

where CPOPGRO is the percentage growth in the population of the central city from 1950 to 1970, UPOPGRO is the corresponding growth figure for the urban area (including the central city), and L is the percentage increase in the land area. The R^2 value for this estimated equation is 0.88; the equation explains 88% of the variation in central city population growth for the 30 urban areas. All three coefficients (in-

TABLE 15.1 Thirty Largest Urban Areas in 1970, Ranked by Population in 1910

	Mfg. Emp., 1950 (%)	Population Growth (%), 1950–1975		Area Annex 1950–1975 (%)	Income City/Suburbs, 1974 (%)	Housing Built before 1939 (%)	Population Density[a]
		Urban	City				
Industrial age							
New York	30.8	5	−5	0	77	53	6.7
Chicago	37.7	35	−14	7	78	49	5.3
Philadelphia	35.6	31	−12	1	83	53	5.3
Boston	28.7	54	−21	0	82	65	4.0
Pittsburgh	38.0	5	−32	2	93	55	3.1
St. Louis	33.0	32	−39	0	81	44	4.1
San Francisco	19.4	46	−14	2	101	38	4.4
Baltimore	30.9	47	−10	0	80	42	5.1
Cleveland	40.5	29	−30	1	68	46	3.0
Buffalo	39.7	22	−30	5	83	58	5.1
Detroit	46.9	40	−28	0	80	38	4.6
Cincinnati	33.4	35	−18	4	96	48	3.3
Indeterminate							
Los Angeles	25.6	67	38	3	100	23	5.3
Washington, DC	7.4	97	−11	0	na	22	5.0
Milwaukee	42.9	41	4	90	83	46	2.7
Kansas City	24.5	49	3	292	91	38	2.2
New Orleans	15.6	54	−2	0	92	36	5.2
Seattle	19.8	67	4	18	111	30	3.0
Young urban areas							
Indianapolis	33.1	59	67	580	100	37	2.2
Atlanta	18.3	104	32	256	85	18	2.7
Denver	16.8	128	17	70	104	27	3.6
Columbus	25.0	69	42	338	89	32	3.4
Memphis	20.5	50	67	169	118	22	3.4
Nashville	22.9	50	143	2208	109	24	1.3
Dallas	18.4	110	87	176	111	15	2.0
San Antonio	11.6	80	89	279	75	24	3.5
Houston	21.4	142	123	206	101	15	3.1
Jacksonville	13.1	93	162	2436	119	21	1.5
San Diego	15.7	185	131	225	108	17	3.1
Phoenix	10.4	267	522	1499	100	9	2.2
Class means							
Industrial age	34.6	32	−21	2	84	49	4.5
Young	18.9	111	124	704	102	22	2.7

[a]*Population density is measured in thousands per square mile.*

Source: Table compiled from data obtained from Norton (1979).

cluding the constant term of −61.9) are highly statistically significant. Look carefully at this equation and see what it says. First, it says that an increase in the growth of the population of the urban area of 1% actually increased the population growth of the central city by 1.1% (although the 1.1 is not significantly different from 1.0). In Table 15.1 it is obvious that the growth of the central cities is related to growth at the metropolitan level, but this equation says that the effect is 1 : 1 in percentage terms. However, the estimated equation also says that if the urban area did not grow at all and if the central city annexed no territory, the population of the central city would have *decreased by 61.9%*. No urban area had zero population growth, so this did not happen. Another way to interpret the equation is to find the increase in the population of the urban area that results in no change in the population of the central city. Assuming annexation is zero, this growth for the urban area is 57%; if UPOPGRO = 57, then CPOPGRO = 0. Finally, the coefficient of the annexation variable says that an increase in the land area of the central city of 1% increased its population growth by 0.06%.

Norton gave his empirical result an interpretation that is related to the population density function from Chapter 5. He argued that during the period 1950–1970, there was a strong tendency of population to move to the suburbs in all urban areas because of declining intraurban transportation costs and rising real incomes. This means that the population density function was getting flatter and the peak population density was falling, as was shown in Chapter 5 for the case of Chicago. On the other hand, population growth will shift the population density function up—density will tend to increase at all locations. The change in population of the central city is the net outcome of the two forces: suburbanization and growth of the urban area. Recall that this was the basic idea behind the discussion of population change in the New York, Los Angeles, and Chicago metropolitan areas in Chapter 1 as well.

Norton also estimated the same equation separately for the white and nonwhite (i.e., mainly black) populations. The results for the white population are very similar to the results for the total population shown above and are that

$$\text{WCPOPGRO} = -67.2 + 1.0\text{WUPOPGRO} + 0.08L,$$

where the R^2 value for the estimated equation is 0.89. The equation for the nonwhite population shows the rather different result that

$$\text{NWCPOPGRO} = 8.9 + 0.9\text{NWUPOPGRO} + 0.02L,$$

where the R^2 value is 0.60. Neither the constant term nor the coefficient of L is statistically significantly different from zero in this equation. The equation simply says that the nonwhite population growth of the urban area translates into an equivalent growth in the central city. The nonwhite population was not moving to the suburbs during this period in any significant numbers.

Norton then looked at the period 1970–1975. During these five years, population in the 12 industrial age urban areas declined by an average of 1%, and their central cities fell by 9% on average. The 12 young urban areas had population growth of 11%, and the central cities gained 2% in population. The estimated equation for this period is

$$\text{CPOPGRO} = -8.6 + 0.6\text{UPOPGRO} + 0.3L,$$

with an R^2 value of 0.66. The coefficient of UPOPGRO of 0.6 says that the effect of population growth at the level of the urban area may have weakened somewhat in the 1970s. Nevertheless, there was still a strong relationship between the growth of the central city and its urban area. One criticism of Norton's method is that he made the growth of population in the central city a function of population growth in the urban area, which includes the central city. In other words, the independent variable (UPOPGRO) partly *is* the dependent variable.

The last three columns in Table 15.1 show some additional characteristics of the 30 urban areas. The next column shows the per capita income in the central city in 1974 relative to the per capita income in the suburbs. A figure of 100 means that these two income figures were equal and a figure of 77 says that the per capita income in the central city was 77% of the suburban income level. The average figure for the 12 industrial age urban areas was 84, while the average for the 12 young urban areas was 102. In other words, per capita income levels were lower in the central cities than in the suburbs for the industrial age urban areas, but such was not the case for the young urban areas. This result stems, at least in part, from the ability of the young central cities to annex territory.

The last two variables in Table 15.1 show the characteristics of the housing stock in the urban area as of 1970. One column shows the percentage of the housing stock that was built before 1939; about half (49%) of the housing in the industrial age urban areas was built before 1939, but only 22% of the housing in the young urban areas dates from before 1939. The population density is one consequence of the timing of construction of the housing stock. The average population density per square mile in the 12 industrial age urban areas was 4500 in 1970, but the average density in the 12 young urban areas was only 2700.

Norton's examination of employment growth in these 30 urban areas was not quite as exhaustive as his study of population growth. He gathered data on manufacturing, wholesale, and retail trade and selected services for 1948 and 1972 for the urban areas and their central cities. This leaves out about 44% of total employment. He estimated his standard equation for employment growth in the central city as a function of employment growth in the urban area and annexation, with the result that

$$CEMPGRO = -46.6 + 1.0 UEMPGRO + 0.03L,$$

with $R^2 = 0.93$. Note that this equation says that if $L = 0$, employment growth in the urban area (in the industries included) needed to be 46.6% to keep employment in the central city constant over the period 1948–1972. This equation demonstrates clearly the potentially devastating effect on the central city of slow employment growth in the urban area. For example, employment growth in the urban area of a seemingly respectable 25% would have meant a decline of employment in the central city of 21.6%. The actual average figures for the 12 industrial age urban areas were 17% employment growth in the urban area and a 24% decline in the central city. The 12 young urban areas had, on average, employment growth of 160% in the urban area and 138% in the central city. The 12 young urban areas have central cities that annexed a great deal of territory, of course.

Norton (1979) succeeded in showing the powerful connections between growth in the urban area and the fortunes of the central city. Growth that was sufficiently robust was able to offset the forces of suburbanization, but the urban areas that date from the industrial age did not have that kind of growth. As stated previously, Norton attributed this slow growth of the industrial age urban areas to the decentralization of the economic incubator function away from the old industrial northeast. The industrial age cities were at a later stage in their life cycles than the young urban areas. The life-cycle hypothesis was discussed critically in Chapter 11, but Norton's empirical results stand as strong indicators of the relationship between urban area growth and the plight of the central city. Norton's results are also profoundly discouraging for those who wish to formulate policies to address the economic problems of the industrial age central cities. Norton basically includes no policy "handles" in his analysis. There was a certain inevitability about the decline of the industrial age central cities that (perhaps) smacks of Marxism. What do you think about that idea?

It is worthwhile to pause to consider Norton's study in terms of the five stages of economic research. The basic facts that were of concern to Norton were the growth (or decline) of the central city and the growth of the entire urban area. He had no particular concern with the suburbs other than as the loci of much of the growth of the urban area. His basic facts included the observation that the older, industrial urban areas (and their central cities) had grown slowly compared to the newer urban areas (and their central cities). However, he did not formulate and test a model that explains why these urban areas differed so sharply in their rates of growth. Rather, he was more concerned with formulating and testing models of the *consequences* of different urban area growth rates on central cities. He took those differences in urban area growth rates somewhat for granted.

C. THE COMPREHENSIVE MODEL OF BRADBURY, DOWNS, AND SMALL

The book by Bradbury et al. (1982) reports on a major research project that was undertaken at the Brookings Institution, a major independent research organization located in Washington, DC. The study, which was supported both by the Ford Foundation and the U.S. federal government, was prompted by increasing problems experienced by the large central cities in the 1970s. The study was done at a time when it was widely assumed that the federal government has major responsibility to "save" the central cities and their low-income populations. But when policymakers turned to the research literature, they found a lack of empirical findings that could be used as a guide for policy. Decisions regarding the allocation of billions of dollars for various federal programs were being made based on unverified notions of how urban areas and central cities grow and decline. The title of the study, and many of the descriptive data in the book, refer to declining central cities. However, the real heart of the book is the formulation and testing of a fairly comprehensive model of growth for urban areas and their central cities. Their important facts included growth rates for both urban areas and their central cities, and their economic models included explanations of growth at both levels. As such, theirs is a more complete effort than that of Norton (1979). In short, the researchers took the policy concern of the day with certain central cities and turned the project into something more general and of a higher order of scientific value. People who value research are always looking for that kind of opportunity, and you readers should bear this point in mind as you pursue careers in urban affairs.

Bradbury et al. (1982) based their empirical tests on data from 120 large urban areas (population greater than 100,000) for the period 1960–1975. Their first test was to replicate Norton's equation for the change in the population of the central city. All of their tests pertaining to central cities held the boundaries constant. They found that for 1960–1975,

$$CPOPGRO = -16.9 + 0.71UPOPGRO + 1.01ANNEX$$

where ANNEX is the percentage increase in the population due to annexations over the period. The R^2 value for this equation is 0.87. The equation shows that if the population of the urban area failed to grow and there was no annexation, the population of the central city would have declined by 16.9% over 15 years, which translates into a decline of 1.2% per year. The coefficient of UPOPGRO of 0.71 is statistically significantly lower than 1.0, so it says that an increase in the growth rate of the urban area's population increases the growth rate of the central city by 0.7%, a result that is similar to Norton's finding for 1970–1975.

Bradbury et al. (1982, pp. 84–119) viewed their first task as providing explanations of growth in population, employment, and income per capita for urban areas. They did not formulate a comprehensive model of economic growth such as that presented in Chapters 11–14 of this book, but their models perform reasonably well in statistical terms. A summary of their results for population growth of an urban area from 1960 to 1970 is as follows:

1. Employment growth is the most powerful factor in population growth.
2. Urban areas in the north with larger black populations grew faster. The migration of blacks from the south to the north was a major factor in the 1960s.
3. People were attracted to urban areas with higher incomes per capita and warmer weather.
4. Greater population density in 1960 was associated with lower population growth.
5. The natural rate of population increase (births minus deaths) had a positive, but not statistically significant, effect on population growth.

The equation that contains these results has an R^2 value of 0.90. The main finding is that employment growth is the main driver of population growth. The coefficient of employment growth is 0.74, which says that a 1% increase in employment growth over 10 years produced a population growth rate that was 0.74% higher.

What determined employment growth? Their results are that:

1. Population growth, through both natural increase and migration, was the most powerful factor in total employment growth. The estimated coefficient is 0.88.
2. Three variables had positive but weak impacts on employment growth; these were per capita income level, percentage change in income per capita, and a favorable industry mix in 1960 (to capture export demand changes).
3. Population density and local taxes per capita had negative effects on employment growth.

The R^2 value for the estimated equation is 0.88. Note that employment and population growth interact. Proper statistical methods were used to estimate the independent effect of population growth on employment growth, and vice versa. An independent increase in population growth of 1% increased employment growth by 0.88%, and an independent increase in employment growth of 1% increased population growth by 0.74%. An increase in population increases both the supply of labor and the demand for labor (through the demand for local goods and services). An increase in employment growth draws more migrants to the urban area, as discussed in Chapter 13.

The results for the growth in real income per capita are striking:

1. Employment growth drives real income per capita, but population growth through migration or natural increase reduced the rate of growth of real income per capita.

2. Urban areas with higher incomes per capita in 1960 or a greater proportion of jobs in trade, construction, transportation, and utilities had lower rates of income growth per capita.

3. Urban areas with larger black populations had larger per capita income growth rates.

The main finding is that real per capita income growth was driven by employment growth and moderated by population growth.

Together, the results for the growth of urban areas in Bradbury et al. (1982) provide ringing endorsement of the basic neoclassical growth model presented in Chapter 11. Employment growth drives the local economy, and employment growth is itself largely driven by the supply of labor and the demand for local goods and services created by that increase in supply. However, Bradbury et al. (1982) did not provide the more comprehensive explanation for urban employment growth that was assembled in Chapters 12 and 13 and summarized in Table 14.1.

Their next task was to study the economic fortunes of the central city. Bradbury et al. (1982) hypothesized that both interurban and intraurban factors are important. The growth of the urban area as a whole should be very important, but disparities between the city and the suburbs should also play their parts. The analysis of population growth is a study of the percentage change in the population of the central city *minus* the percentage change for the urban area over the period 1960–1970 (i.e., the growth of the central city compared to its urban area). The question asked concerns the factors that caused the population growth in the central city to be faster relative to the urban area. In other words, the variable measures the extent to which the urban area did not decentralize. The results are that:

1. More rapid employment growth in the central city, relative to the suburbs, decreased decentralization.

2. Several variables tended to increase decentralization; percentage increase in per capita income in the urban area, high central city income relative to the suburbs, more old housing (built before 1929) in the central city relative to the suburbs, percentage of the population of the central city that was black, and the extent of housing construction in the urban area in excess of population growth.

3. One variable had a negative effect on decentralization—a variable which indicates whether the school district that served the central city also served some of the suburbs.

In other words, the urban area tended to be less decentralized if the city had greater employment growth, low income, fewer black people, newer housing, and a school system that also served some of the suburbs. Slower growth in the urban area in income per capita and housing construction also helped the city catch up. The income variables pertain to the ability of people to move to the suburbs; households with high and rising incomes move to the suburbs. The other results are self-explanatory.

Next they looked at the percentage employment growth in the central city minus the growth in the urban area. Once again, the variable measured reductions in the tendency for decentralization. They found that:

1. Employment growth was less decentralized if population growth was less decentralized.

2. Employment growth was more decentralized if there was a higher unemployment rate in the city (compared to the suburbs), if the total amount of employment in the urban area was larger, if the share of employment in the city was larger, and if employment growth in the urban area was less.

3. More rapid growth in per capita income in the city, relative to the suburbs, reduced decentralization.

The bottom line for employment growth in the central city is that it was a function of urban area growth factors, central city growth factors, and intraurban variables. The individual factors that contributed to employment growth in the central city, along with their signs, were:

Variable	Sign
Urban area factors	
Population growth	+
Growth in real income per capita	−
Per capita income level	+
Population density	−
Industry mix effect	+
Local taxes per capita	−
Total employment in urban area	−
Central city growth factors	
City population growth	+
City growth in real income per capital	+
Intraurban factors	
City minus urban area unemployment rate	−
City share of urban area jobs	−

This list tells us how to have a central city that does poorly on employment growth. First, be located in a large urban area that has slow population growth, high income, rapid income growth, high population density, high taxes, and a bad mix of industries. Furthermore, be a city that starts out with a large share of the jobs in the urban area, is losing population, has slow income growth, and high unemployment. In short, be Detroit, Cleveland, Buffalo, or others that you can name. The population growth rate of the urban area is a big determinant of the employment growth in the central city, but several other variables also had significant effects. The broad policy conclusion is that a central city is not just prisoner to the growth rate of the urban area. Some factors that can be influenced in the long run by policymakers in the central city make a difference (e.g., local taxes, rate of population loss in the central city, and industry mix).

D. STANBACK LOOKS AT THE NEW SUBURBANIZATION

One thing that is particularly striking about the work of Norton (1979) and Bradbury et al. (1982) is their seeming disinterest in the suburbs. For one thing, they have nothing to say about the spatial pattern of suburban growth. One might reinterpret their studies to say that the suburbs are the engines of growth for an urban area (not the central cities) and that promoting the growth of your urban area might involve promoting suburban growth. The remedy for this oversight is provided by Stanback's book (1991), a study of 14 of the largest urban areas for the period 1969–1987. Stanback is familiar with the trends in the composition of employment by industry and the nature of various types of suburban employment subcenters, so his research is considerably more current than the other two. The generality of his results is limited by the small number of urban areas that were studied, but the findings are still quite valuable.

Stanback's proposition—his compilation of important facts—is that the economies of the suburbs have become much broader in recent years and that the relationship between the central city and the suburbs has changed significantly. These changes have taken place within the context of a national economy that has undergone dramatic change as well. The transformation of the U.S. economy, as we have seen, involves a large shift in the composition of employment away from industries that produce goods to those that produce services. Furthermore, the goods-producing industries increasingly have needed producer services such as transportation and communications, wholesaling, finance, advertising, and the professional services of accountants, lawyers and management consultants. A great deal of this transformation is associated with the use of computer technology in all phases of the production of goods and services. The shift of the economy toward the production of services has taken place in urban areas that were experiencing decline in the industrial sector of the central city and beginning to develop suburbs with more diverse industrial and office employment bases. Further, the labor force was expanding rapidly as the baby boom generation and more women sought employment. Stanback notes three important resulting changes in urban areas that have taken place since the 1970s:

1. The downtown areas of major cities have been transformed and rebuilt by the growth of the service sector. The downtown employers still rely on commuters from the suburbs, although some downtown workers have decided to live in certain areas of the central city.

2. The new suburbanization has created large centers of employment and agglomeration economies that place the suburbs in direct competition with downtown and other older employment centers. Suburban employment centers have become the centers of economic growth in urban areas.

3. The demand for workers has shifted in favor of workers with higher levels of education and training.

Except for the last of these three points, all of this has also been discussed extensively in Chapter 7. These changes in the economy of urban areas have created even greater challenges for the central city outside the downtown area because employers find that such locations (e.g., old industrial areas) are not suitable for service sector jobs.

Some of the basic data for the 14 large urban areas in the Stanback study are shown in Table 15.2. The table includes data on the annual rate of employment change for the central county (or counties in the case of New York City) for the periods of 1969–1979 and 1979–1987, data on population change, and amount of the central county that is actually in the central city. This last variable is the proportion of

TABLE 15.2 Fourteen Large Urban Areas, 1969–1987

| | Employment Change (%), Annual | | | | Population Change (%), 1969–1987 | | |
| | 1969–1979 | | 1979–1987 | | | | City/County Population[a] |
	Central County	Suburbs	Central County	Suburbs	Central County	Suburbs	
New York	−1.3	2.2	1.2	2.9	−0.40	0.12	1.00
Chicago	0.4	3.5	0.3	3.5	−0.19	1.99	0.57
Philadelphia	−2.0	2.2	−0.2	2.8	−0.95	0.75	1.00
Los Angeles	2.3	6.9	2.0	4.3	1.10	2.69	0.40
Atlanta	2.1	5.2	2.1	7.3	0.23	3.68	0.72
Boston	−0.3	2.1	1.6	3.0	−0.53	0.24	0.86
Cincinnati	1.1	4.0	1.1	3.1	−0.27	1.16	0.44
Columbus	2.6	2.3	2.7	1.0	0.68	1.36	0.65
Dallas	3.7	5.3	3.7	7.5	2.06	5.68	0.58
Detroit	−0.6	3.7	−1.6	2.5	−1.22	1.00	0.52
Minneapolis	2.6	3.3	2.4	2.3	0.16	1.75	0.39
Pittsburgh	0.5	1.6	−0.2	−0.6	−0.91	0.01	0.29
St. Louis	−0.8	2.6	−2.9	3.3	−2.31	0.87	1.00
Washington, DC	0.4	3.9	0.9	4.8	−1.12	1.73	1.00

[a]*Variable is the ratio of central city to central county population.*
Source: Table compiled from data obtained from Stanback (1991).

the population of the central county that was in the central city in 1980. The table shows that as you would expect, the rates of growth in employment were greater in the suburbs than in the central city.

The data can be used to estimate an equation in which the employment growth in the central county is a function of the employment growth in the suburbs. This equation should include a correction for the amount of the central county that is actually in the central city because the part of the central county that is not in the central city will behave like suburbs. The data on the 14 urban areas for the two time periods were combined to yield 28 data points, and the estimated equation is

$$\text{CEMPGRO} = 1.27 + 0.43\text{SEMPGRO} - 2.82\text{CCPOP\%},$$

where CEMPGRO is the annual rate of employment growth in the central county, SEMPGRO is the corresponding growth rate for the suburban counties, and CCPOP% is the percentage of the population of the central county that resides in the central city. The R^2 value for this estimated equation is 0.67. The coefficient of SEMPGRO is highly statistically significant and says that if the growth rate of employment in the suburbs is 1% higher, employment growth in the central county will be 0.43% higher. This result suggests that employment growth in the suburbs generates employment growth in the central county. The coefficient of CCPOP% is also highly statistically significant and tells us that the growth rate of the central county is lower if it is more closely identical to the central city. For example, a central county that is twice the size of the central city (CCPOP% = 0.5) had an employment growth rate that was 1.41% higher than a central county that is identical to the central city (CCPOP% = 1). To put the point another way, if the central city that is half of the central county had been able to annex the rest of the central county, its employment growth rate would have been 1.41% higher.

A similar result is found for population growth for the 14 urban areas from 1969 to 1987:

$$CPOPGRO = 0.08 + 0.45SPOPGRO - 1.48CCPOP\%.$$

The R^2 value for this estimated equation is 0.65. An increase in the growth rate of the population of the suburban counties of 1% increased the growth rate of the central county by 0.45%, and a central county that is identical to the central city grew by 0.74% less than a central county that is half central city and half suburban.

Stanback's research documents some of the details of employment change in central counties and suburbs. Employment increases in the central counties were largely in finance, insurance, and real estate and in services—the types of employment that prefer the downtown location. Large employment declines occurred in central county manufacturing. Suburban employment growth was robust on a broad front, and manufacturing employment in the suburbs generally was stable. These results mirror the observations that were made in Chapter 7 of this book.

Stanback (1991) went on to describe the employment growth in the suburbs in terms of the emergence of agglomeration economies much in the same manner that was done in Chapters 3 and 7. Stanback found it helpful to distinguish the types of suburban employment centers in the manner that was introduced by the urban geographers Hartshorn and Muller (1992). Suburban employment clusters can occur as:

- Linear patterns along freeway corridors
- Retail corridors
- Centers around regional shopping malls
- Old town centers
- Office centers
- Centers with mixed uses (such as retail, hotel, and office)
- Specialized centers (e.g., airports, hospitals, military centers, or universities)
- Corridors of high-tech firms

Stanback (1991) also cited another study of suburban employment centers by Cervero (1989), which is an examination of 57 centers across the nation as of 1987. Cervero found that white-collar employment dominated in his sample of employment subcenters; clerical employees made up 22% of workers in the centers, technical workers were 20%, followed by administration (15%) and management (14%). Manufacturing workers (13%) and sales workers (12%) and others (4%) were smaller fractions of the workers. The task of producing and processing information tended to be the dominant activity. Some of the establishments located in suburban employment centers were "back office" operations that specialize in maintaining, updating, retrieving, and using the records of clients and customers. These operations send out bills and receive and record payments, for example.

Cervero (1989) classified the 57 employment centers in his sample into six categories:

1. Office parks, with low density and a parklike environment
2. Office concentrations, with high densities
3. Large-scale developments with mixed uses (commercial, office, light industry)
4. Moderate-scale developments with mixed uses
5. Suburban cities, which have much the same full set of activities as central business districts
6. Large-scale corridors of office development

Consider two examples of Cervero's suburban cities. One is called the North Dallas Parkway, a development shaped by two freeways located 12 to 15 miles north of the Dallas CBD. The Parkway area contains 17 million square feet of office space in more than 150 office buildings as well as substantial amounts of commercial and manufacturing space in an area of 5.6 square miles. Eight hotels and three shopping malls are located there. As of 1987 the Parkway area employed about 60,000 workers and has the potential to house 65,000 more. The Parkway area competes directly with downtown Dallas for the best office tenants. Another example is the remarkable Tyson's Corner, located 12 miles west of downtown Washington, DC at an intersection of two major highways near Dulles Airport. Tyson's Corner is the largest agglomeration of offices and commercial activity in Maryland and Virginia, except for downtown Washington, DC and downtown Baltimore. As of 1987, some 60,000 workers were housed in 15 million square feet of office space. Tyson's Corner boasts several hotels with convention facilities, a major shopping mall, several shopping centers, and a high-rise apartment building. Cervero (1989) noted that Tyson's Corner was suffering from traffic congestion and a shortage of low-wage workers. Despite these problems, Cervero noted that it was likely that Tyson's Corner would expand.

Cervero's book includes discussions of many other cases of suburban employment centers, including detailed discussions of the centers in the Seattle, Chicago, and Houston urban areas. One of his main concerns is to find methods for reducing the growing problem of traffic congestion in and around these centers. His hope is that more people can be induced to take some form of public transportation, but it is clear that it will be difficult to achieve a significant increase in the use of public transit because the residential locations of the workers in the suburban employment centers are quite spread out. What remains impressive about these employment centers is their rapid expansion and their potential for further expansion.

The growth of some suburban centers has been nothing short of phenomenal. For example, two suburban office centers in the Atlanta urban area each have more office space than that in downtown Atlanta. Stanback (1991) did not have data to permit an examination of these various kinds of suburban employment centers; instead, he examined several suburban counties that he called *magnet counties*.

Stanback's magnet counties were defined on the basis of a high and rising ratio of employment to population; an employment/population ratio of about 0.6 served to identify such a county in 1987. Magnet counties tended to have high proportions of employment in manufacturing and retail trade, but they also had substantial employment bases in wholesaling, transportation, FIRE (finance, insurance, and real estate), and services, including business services. Downtown is still the dominant source of FIRE and legal services, but the suburbs offer a wide variety of business services that are part of their agglomeration economies.

Because of the development of the diverse suburban economy, the suburbs face some problems. As Cervero (1989) found, the two problems that are cited most often are traffic congestion and the imbalance between jobs and housing opportunities. Another problem with suburban development has emerged more recently. Since a good deal of suburban employment growth has been concentrated in certain employment centers, some suburban municipalities have not gained the business tax base that they feel they need to offer their residents good public services at reasonable tax rates. The complicated decisions that are made by local governments were discussed extensively in Chapter 10, and the uneven pattern of suburban employment growth has made the problems faced by some local governments even more complicated.

The success of suburban developments since the 1970s has raised the question of whether the suburbs really "need" the central city any longer. Are the economies of the suburbs and the central city sufficiently independent that the suburbs would be capable of the same growth rate even if the central city were to disappear? Stated in this way, the question sounds absurd. Nevertheless, just what do the suburbs gain by their association with their central city? Ihlanfeldt (1995) has done a careful review of the evidence on this question and found that there are several connections that are potentially important. He placed these connections into four general categories:

1. The conditions in the central city influence the perceptions that outsiders have of the urban area. These perceptions can influence their willingness to make investments in the urban area as a whole.

2. Central cities provide amenities of various kinds that are valuable for all residents of the urban area. These amenities include cultural, recreational, and educational facilities. For example, the city of Chicago has the Chicago Symphony, the Lyric Opera, the Art Institute, the University of Chicago, the world's greatest outdoor museum of office building architecture, sports, and much more. Many other central cities are not so blessed, of course.

3. The central city may provide a "sense of place" or a sense of community pride for all who live in the urban area. This point is difficult to study empirically, but that does not mean that community pride is not important.

4. Central cities still offer certain types of agglomeration economies that are not available in the suburbs.

The bulk of the existing empirical evidence pertains to agglomeration economies in the central business districts of major central cities. The basic idea is that face-to-face contacts are important for a variety of activities in the business and public sectors and that location in the central business district offers a lower cost for making those contacts. What are the services provided in the central business district for firms located in the suburbs? A recent study by Schwartz (1992) examined the purchase of five business services by firms in the New York, Los Angeles and Chicago urban areas. Those five services are actuarial consulting, auditing, banking, investment banking, and legal services. He found that firms located in the suburbs relied primarily on central city firms for these services. The majority of suburban companies relied on the central city for these services, and very few companies in the central city relied on suburban providers of these services. Suburban firms in the Chicago urban area relied on the central city more than did their counterparts in Los Angeles and New York, and reliance on the central city by suburban firms was generally greatest in the case of legal services. Ihlanfeldt (1995) suspected that this reliance on the central city for such services may be eroding over time. More research needs to be done in other urban areas and for different time periods to gain a more complete picture of this matter. Nevertheless, the reliance of the suburbs in the three largest urban areas on the central city for accounting, banking, and legal services is impressive. These services are included in the category of urbanization economies that was introduced in Chapter 3.

E. SUMMARY

The studies by Norton (1979), Bradbury et al. (1982), and Stanback (1991) represent the changing nature of the research on urban growth and changing spatial patterns. Norton (1979) focused on the plight of the central city as it depended on the growth rate of the urban area. He provided no empirical test of a model of growth for an urban area. Instead, he appealed to the idea of a life cycle for an urban area. This model has been criticized in Chapter 11 on the grounds that the empirical evidence in support of the model is weak and subject to alternative interpretations. In particular, the idea that the incubator function for new businesses has decentralized away from the traditional manufacturing belt of the northeastern United States is obviously correct. The question is why it happened. Several reasons come to mind, such as:

1. The location of specific types of human capital
2. Federal government spending in the sunbelt during and after World War II
3. The emergence of agglomeration economies in urban areas in California, Texas, and other places
4. The invention of air conditioning
5. Low factor costs
6. The decisions of southern states to join the modern economy rather than relying on an economy of low-wage labor and share cropping.

Nevertheless, Norton (1979) provided powerful evidence of the effect of slow growth in the urban area on the central city during the period 1950–1975. Dramatic improvements in urban highways and rising incomes, coupled with slow growth in the urban area, were a recipe for large absolute declines in population and employment in the central city. The population that was lost from the central city was, for the most part, large numbers of the white middle class. Norton (1979) also emphasized the role of the ability of the central city to annex territory; the old cities that date from the industrial era lack this critical ability.

Bradbury et al. (1982) began their study by providing empirical models of population and employment growth for urban areas. Their growth models are not as comprehensive as the modified neoclassical growth model presented in Chapters 12 and 14, but their results made it clear that urban economic growth depends on the growth of the labor force and the demands for locally produced goods and services that result from population growth. They included the effect of the industry mix of the urban area to capture the changes in the demand for exports. Also, high local taxes per capita were consistently associated with lower growth.

They then examined how rapidly the central city grew compared to the urban area as a whole. The population growth rate in the central city (compared to the urban area) was reduced by old housing, a larger black population, greater growth in incomes, greater amounts of housing construction in the suburbs, slower employment growth in the central city, and a school system that serves only the residents of the central city. These results clearly are what one would have expected. Employment growth in the central city (compared to the urban area) was retarded by low population and income growth in the city, high unemployment in the city, and a large share of total employment in the city. Central city employment growth was also slower (compared to the urban area) in larger urban areas and in urban areas that experienced slower employment growth.

The results for the determinants of urban growth and the growth of the central city relative to the urban area as a whole were combined into a master list of factors that influenced growth in the central city. Those factors can be grouped as urban area variables, central city variables, and intraurban variables that compare the central city with the suburbs. A summary of these factors was provided in Section C.

The more recent work of Stanback (1991) gave emphasis to suburban development, which was, by then, serving as the driving force of their urban economies. Both employment and population growth in the central city seem to be associated with the growth rates of the suburbs. Much of the new economic activity is being located in the suburbs, especially in the various types of suburban employment centers that have grown up since the 1970s. That new economic activity is concentrated in the categories of business services, wholesale trade, transportation and communications, corporate offices and research facilities, back office establishments, hotels and convention centers, and FIRE. The employment base of the suburbs no longer consists largely of retail trade and light manufacturing (in industrial parks). The fortunes of the central city appear now to depend on the success of the suburban employment centers and on its own central business district. As Schwartz (1992) found, the central business district still provides accounting, banking, and legal services for firms all over the urban area. However, because the central business district is inherently somewhat limited in its ability to expand and the rest of the central city is not attractive to employers, the suburban employment centers serve as the major points of growth. In some urban areas, such as Atlanta and several others, the center of economic gravity had already shifted to the suburbs when Cervero (1989) looked at them in the late 1980s. The implications of this shift for some economic and social problems are discussed in Chapter 16.

As a final word on the three major studies discussed in this chapter, note how the focus of attention shifted over time. The Norton (1979) study is primarily concerned with the fortunes of central cities, especially the industrial age central cities versus the newer central cities. In the Bradbury et al. (1982) study the focus shifts partly to the urban area as a whole. They were interested in understanding the underlying causes of urban growth first, and then they examined the fortunes of the central city. Their model of urban growth is quite simple—indeed, much simpler than the models presented in Chapters 11 to 14. Nevertheless, they recognized that concern for the central city must begin with a better understanding of the principles of growth for urban areas. The most recent study by Stanback (1991) brings us to a full consideration of the suburbs and the role that they play in urban growth. We are beginning to understand how modern suburbs function as sources of growth for urban areas, but much more research is needed. We still need to (1) collect more data, (2) uncover more important facts, (3) formulate more economic models, (4) estimate and test those models, and (5) use the models for forecasting, policy analysis, and normative analysis. There is much to be done for those of you who care to try to do it.

EXERCISE

1. You have gathered a great deal of information about a particular urban area of your choice. Now is the time to pull together that information on population and employment growth and location patterns to tell a more complete story. Tell the story of your urban area (in brief outline). Be sure to discuss particular industries as well as suburban employment centers (if any). How does this urban area fit with the Norton (1979), Bradbury et al. (1982), and Stanback (1991) results?

REFERENCES

Bradbury, Katherine, Anthony Downs, and Kenneth Small, 1982. *Urban Decline and the Future of American Cities*. Washington, DC: The Brookings Institution.

Cervero, Robert, 1989. *America's Suburban Centers*. Boston: Unwin Hyman.

Hartshorn, Truman and P. Muller, 1992. "The Suburban Downtown and Urban Economic Development Today," in E. Mills and J. McDonald, eds., *Sources of Metropolitan Growth*. New Brunswick, NJ: Rutgers University Press.

Ihlanfeldt, Keith, 1995. "The Importance of the Central City to the Regional and National Economy: A Review of the Arguments and Empirical Evidence," *Cityscape: A Journal of Policy Development and Research*, Vol. 1, No. 2, pp. 125–150.

Norton, R. D., 1979. *City Life-Cycles and American Urban Policy*. New York: Academic Press.

Schwartz, Alex, 1992. "Corporate Service Linkages in Large Metropolitan Areas: A Study of New York, Los Angeles and Chicago," *Urban Affairs Quarterly*, Vol. 28, pp. 276–296.

Stanback, Thomas Jr., 1991. *The New Suburbanization: Challenge to the Central City*. Boulder, CO: Westview Press.

C H A P T E R

16

Urban Dimensions of Economic and Social Problems

A. INTRODUCTION

Our urban areas are the home of many of the nation's economic and social problems. An important purpose of studying urban economics is to have a deeper understanding of those problems. Your study of urban economics will enable you to place urban problems in a larger context because you understand many of the economic forces at work behind the problems that we see. A deeper understanding of the economic sources of urban problems will also permit you to consider policy alternatives with a keener sense of what the goals of policy might be, and what will work to help solve those problems and what will not.

The purpose of this chapter is to review some of the major urban problems of the day. The economic forces that underlie each problem are discussed, and some issues of policy are addressed. The urban problems included are:

1. Poverty and the plight of the urban "underclass"
2. Mismatches between job and housing location patterns
3. Housing for low-income households and homelessness
4. Crime
5. Central city fiscal problems

The first three of these topics all have to do directly with the causes and consequences of poverty in urban areas, especially in the larger central cities. One can think of the other two, crime and central city fiscal problems, partly as consequences of poverty in large central cities as well. Given such a menu of topics, we do not provide an optimistic note upon which to conclude the book. It is not for nothing that economics is called the "dismal science."

In Chapter 15 we discussed the relationships between the urban economic growth of recent years and the spatial patterns in urban areas. The older urban areas

■ 461 ■

of the northeast have experienced slow growth and loss of employment in the manufacturing sector along with the movement of jobs and middle-class households to the suburbs. The centers of growth in these urban areas are now in the suburban employment centers. Urban problems are not confined to the older urban areas of the northeast, but clearly the problems of the central city are exacerbated by this pattern of events that is characteristic of northeastern urban areas.

B. POVERTY AND THE URBAN UNDERCLASS

Poverty in the United States was not a major issue for public policy until the 1930s. It was not a major issue in the 1920s, when at least 50% of Americans could have been classified as poor. Prior to the 1930s relief for the poor was left to private charities and, to a lesser degree, local and state governments. The coming of the Great Depression in 1929 and the election of Franklin Roosevelt as president in 1932 changed all that. An examination of the Great Depression is beyond the scope of this book, but a few numbers will give you an idea of the motivating forces behind what Roosevelt called the "New Deal." From 1929 to 1933 the GNP dropped 31% in real terms, investment dropped to an amount that was less than capital depreciation, employment fell by almost 20%, and the unemployment rate shot up from 5% to 25%. The Great Depression shaped the attitudes and opinions of most of those who lived through it.

The people of the United States turned to the federal government to solve economic and social crises of the 1930s. The federal government took on many new responsibilities that carry on to this day. As you probably know, the English economist John Maynard Keynes provided the economic theory behind the idea that the national government must assume some responsibility for the overall performance of the economy. However, most of Roosevelt's New Dealers were pragmatic people who did not care about economic theory. They were trying to respond to immediate problems. Here is only a partial listing of the programs that were created in the 1930s:

- Federal Emergency Relief Agency provided emergency money for state and local relief agencies.
- Works Progress Administration (WPA) and Civilian Conservation Corps (CCC) employed millions of people on public works projects.
- Agricultural Adjustment Act (AAA) provided programs to support farmers and prices for farm products.
- Tennessee Valley Authority (TVA) and other programs provided electricity to the rural population.
- Social Security System provided pensions for retired or disabled people.
- Fair Labor Standards Act instituted a minimum wage.
- National Labor Relations Act (NLRA) gave workers the right to organize labor unions and to bargain collectively with employers.
- Aid to Families with Dependent Children (AFDC) became the nation's basic welfare program.
- Federal Housing Administration (FHA) helped people with average incomes become homeowners (as discussed in Chapter 9).

These and many other programs were established in the 1930s, and this partial list makes it clear that the New Deal was addressed to the entire nation. A majority of the population was in poverty, and most people were at risk of losing their jobs, farms, or homes.

The nation did not really recover from the Great Depression until World War II called for the federal government to spend amounts of money that were unprecedented. The economy of 1939 and 1940 was operating at a level of GNP that was far below its capacity. In 1944 all governments (federal, state, and local) spent an amount equal to 52% of the GNP, but the total amount of private spending in 1944 was roughly equal to the private spending in 1939!

World War II left the U.S. economy in a dominant position in the world, and as we have seen, the period of the late 1940s to the late 1960s was a period of growth and prosperity for the nation. However, by the late 1950s it became evident that growth and prosperity were not reaching down to a substantial minority of the population. The nature and extent of poverty had changed from the 1930s, so poverty became a different kind of problem for public concern and for public policy. For the first time we began to define the problem of poverty, to measure the extent of poverty (and its changes over time), and to design policies that focus specifically on the minority of the population that is in poverty.

Definitions of Poverty

The first task was to define poverty. There is no ideal definition of poverty, but its definitions are of two basic types. One type of definition attempts to set an absolute standard for poverty that is based on an assessment of the minimum amount of income needed to sustain a healthy and minimally comfortable life. This approach might involve figuring out for households of various sizes a minimal budget for food, housing, health care, and so on. The other approach is to define a poverty standard that is relative to the average standard of living in the nation. We might decide, for example, that poverty is defined as a household income level of less than 40% of the average for households of a given size. The idea is that people feel deprivation in relative terms, based on what they see around them. In addition, the definition of poverty probably should be based on a time period that is longer than one year. Many people in their early 20s (e.g., college students) who live in their own separate households have incomes that are low only temporarily. Other people have incomes that fluctuate from year to year, and they plan their lives and consumption expenditures accordingly. The problem of how to define poverty can never be resolved in a manner that satisfies everyone, but some sort of official definition is probably needed.

One or more official definitions of poverty are needed because we need to measure the extent of poverty and to assess the effectiveness of programs intended to alleviate poverty. Economists in the federal government set about establishing an official poverty standard, and they decided to use an absolute (rather than a relative) criterion. Their method is fairly simple. The U.S. Department of Agriculture computes the minimum annual cost of a nutritious diet for low-income households, and then that number is multiplied by 3 because poor households spend about one-third of their incomes on food. Note that the official poverty line is defined as *annual money income*. The poverty line varies by size of household, and is updated annually to account for changes in food price and for general inflation.

The official poverty definition has been widely criticized for many years. It takes into account only the cost of food; it ignores the cost of other essential consumer goods, such as housing, clothing, and transportation. The definition ignores assets and noncash sources such as food stamps, housing assistance, publicly funded medical care, and noncash gifts, and it also ignores taxes, tax credits, allowances for child care, and premiums paid for medical care. Despite these shortcomings, the official poverty data are used to allocate certain categories of federal funds to the states and local governments.

The poverty line for 1993 was set as a function of household size as follows:

One person	
Under age 65	$ 7518
Age 65 and over	6930
Two persons	
Under age 65	9414
Age 65 and over	8740
Three persons	11,522
Four persons	14,763
Five persons	17,449
Six persons	19,718
Seven persons	22,383
Eight persons	24,838
Nine or more persons	29,529

As you can see, the poverty line is set at a lower level for the elderly. Why is this done? My conjecture is that the elderly need to eat less than others to maintain a healthy diet. What do you think about these poverty standards? Do they appear to be reasonable given what you know about the cost of living? Is an income of $14,763 a sensible standard for a family of four with two adults and two children? By the way, as of 1993, the minimum wage in the United States was $4.25 per hour. One full-time year-round job at this wage generated an income of $8500. To put it another way, a single wage earner needed to make $7.38 per hour (40 hours per week for 50 weeks) to enable a family of four to reach the poverty line. Remember that these figures pertain to 1993, so you need to adjust them for inflation.

The Basic Facts of Poverty in the United States

The official poverty line was established by the federal government in the early 1960s, and the first year for which an official poverty rate was computed is 1959. The history of poverty in the United States from 1959 to 1993 based on the federal standard is shown in Table 16.1. This table reproduces most of a table in a government report, and it contains a lot of numbers. You have encountered many tables with economic data in this book, and by now you should have enhanced your skill at interpreting data presented in tabular form. Take a few minutes to look at this table, and then formulate some important facts that it contains. This sort of exercise illustrates

TABLE 16.1   Poverty in the United States, 1959–1993

Year	All Persons		All Persons in Families		Persons in Female-Headed Families		Unrelated Individuals	
	Number (millions)	Percent	Number (millions)	Percent	Number (millions)	Percent	Number (millions)	Percent
1993	39.3	15.1	29.9	13.6	14.6	38.7	8.4	22.1
1992	38.0	14.8	29.0	13.3	14.2	39.0	8.1	21.9
1991	35.7	14.2	27.1	12.8	13.8	39.7	7.8	21.1
1990	33.6	13.5	25.2	12.0	12.6	37.2	7.4	20.7
1989	31.5	12.8	24.1	11.5	11.7	35.9	6.8	19.2
1988	31.7	13.0	24.0	11.6	12.0	37.2	7.1	20.6
1987	32.2	13.4	24.7	12.0	12.1	38.1	6.9	20.8
1986	32.4	13.6	24.8	12.0	11.9	38.3	6.8	21.6
1985	33.1	14.0	25.7	12.6	11.6	37.6	6.7	21.5
1984	33.7	14.4	26.5	13.1	11.8	38.4	6.6	21.8
1983	35.3	15.2	27.9	13.9	12.1	40.2	6.7	23.1
1982	34.4	15.0	27.3	13.6	11.7	40.6	6.5	23.1
1981	31.8	14.0	24.8	12.5	11.1	38.7	6.5	23.4
1980	29.3	13.0	22.6	11.5	10.1	36.7	6.2	22.9
1979	26.1	11.7	20.0	10.2	9.4	34.9	5.7	21.9
1978	24.5	11.4	19.1	10.0	9.3	35.6	5.4	22.1
1977	24.7	11.6	19.5	10.2	9.2	36.2	5.2	22.6
1976	25.0	11.8	19.6	10.3	9.0	37.3	5.3	24.9
1975	25.9	12.3	20.8	10.9	8.8	37.5	5.1	25.1
1974	23.4	11.2	18.8	9.9	8.5	36.5	4.6	24.1
1973	23.0	11.1	18.3	9.7	8.2	37.5	4.7	25.6
1972	24.5	11.9	19.6	10.3	8.1	38.2	4.9	29.0
1971	25.6	12.5	20.4	10.8	7.8	38.7	5.2	31.6
1970	25.4	12.6	20.3	10.9	7.5	38.1	5.1	32.9
1969	24.1	12.1	19.2	10.4	6.9	38.2	5.0	34.0
1968	25.4	12.8	20.7	11.3	7.0	38.7	4.7	34.0
1967	27.8	14.2	22.8	12.5	6.9	38.8	5.0	38.1
1966	28.5	14.7	23.8	13.1	6.9	39.8	4.7	38.3
1965	33.2	17.3	28.4	15.8	7.5	46.0	4.8	39.8
1964	36.1	19.0	30.9	17.4	7.3	44.4	5.1	42.7
1963	36.4	19.5	31.5	17.9	7.6	47.7	4.9	44.2
1962	38.6	21.0	33.6	19.4	7.8	50.3	5.0	45.4
1961	39.9	21.9	34.5	20.3	7.3	48.1	5.1	45.9
1960	39.9	22.2	34.9	20.7	7.2	48.9	4.9	45.2
1959	39.5	22.4	34.6	20.8	7.0	49.4	4.9	46.1

Source: U.S. Bureau of the Census (1995).

one of the critical skills an economist must develop, the ability to pull information from data. You will (I hope) recall from Chapter 1 that this is the second step in the creation of knowledge in an applied field such as urban economics. I am fond of saying, "The data never speak for themselves." (The word *data* is plural; the singular is *datum*.) You and I must speak for the data.

Now let me give you my summary of important facts in Table 16.1.

1. The poverty rate in 1959 was 22.4% of the population, and the poverty rate among people who lived in female-headed households and among unrelated individuals was much higher (almost 50%). Although this fact is not shown, it is obvious that the poverty rate among people who lived in male-headed households was much lower than the average.

2. The current (1993) poverty rate of 15.1% is lower than the poverty rate in 1959, but I would regard this decline in the poverty rate as surprisingly small. Also, note that the total number of people in poverty was about the same in these two years (39 million).

3. A closer look at the data over time reveals that the poverty rate declined sharply in the decade of the 1960s to 12.1% in 1969. Indeed, the sharp drop in the poverty rate began in 1961–1962. The poverty rate remained in the rather narrow range 11 to 12.6% from 1969 to 1979, and then it increased in the early 1980s to 15.2% in 1983. This increase in the poverty rate was almost certainly caused by the deep recession of that period. The poverty rate drifted down after 1983 to 12.8% in 1989, but afterward it increased steadily to the 15.1% of 1993. Note that the all-time low for the poverty rate was 11.1% in 1973. What reasons would you hypothesize to explain this fact?

4. The poverty rate among persons in female-headed families declined from 50.3% in 1962 to 38.2% in 1969, but since then basically this percentage has been stuck in the high 30s. Recent years have seen some increase in this poverty rate, from 35.9% in 1989 to 38.7% in 1993. These data almost succeed in speaking for themselves, but we could add that people in female-headed families are at very high risk of being in poverty. Also, the 7.0 million persons in poverty in female-headed families constituted 17.8% of the population in poverty in 1959, but that percentage had increased dramatically to 37.3% in 1993. The total number of people in poverty was about the same in 1959 and 1993, but the number in poverty in female-headed families had more than doubled to 14.6 million.

5. The poverty rate among unrelated individuals declined steadily from 1959 46.1% in 1959 to 21.9% in 1979. Many of the unrelated individuals are elderly, and the growth in Social Security benefits that began in the 1960s certainly helped this group. The nation has had far more success at reducing the poverty rate among unrelated individuals than among persons who live in female-headed families. However, the poverty rate among unrelated individuals has remained in the fairly narrow range of 19.2 to 23.4% since 1979. Indeed, the 19.2% recorded for 1989 is 1.4% below the next-lowest figure (20.6% in 1988).

Table 16.1 provides a look at poverty over time, and it does highlight the poverty rates of people in female-headed families and unrelated individuals. However, there are many more ways to "cut" the data by population group. Table 16.2 has been prepared so that we can look at several different groups of people for just one year, 1993. Tables 16.1 and 16.2 thus represent the two traditional methods that economists use to present and study data. The two methods are called the time-series ap-

TABLE 16.2   Poverty Rates for Persons and Families, 1993

	Number in Poverty (millions)	Poverty Rate (%)
Persons		
Total	39.3	15.1
White	26.2	12.2
Not of Hispanic origin	18.9	9.9
Black	10.9	33.1
Other races	2.2	18.8
Hispanic origin[a]	8.1	30.6
Persons by age		
Under 18 years	15.7	22.7
18–24	4.9	19.1
25–44	10.2	12.2
45–54	2.5	8.5
55–59	1.1	9.9
60–64	1.1	11.3
65 years and over	3.8	12.2
Persons by place of residence		
Inside metropolitan areas	29.6	14.6
Inside central cities	16.8	21.5
Outside central cities	12.8	10.3
Outside metropolitan areas	9.6	17.2
Northeast	6.8	13.3
Midwest	8.2	13.4
South	15.4	17.1
West	8.9	15.6
Families		
Total	8.4	12.3
White	5.5	9.4
Not of Hispanic origin	4.0	7.6
Black	2.5	31.3
Other races	0.4	16.8
Hispanic origin[a]	1.6	27.3
Families by type		
Married couple	3.5	6.5
White	2.8	5.8
Black	0.5	12.3
Hispanic origin[a]	0.8	19.1
Female householder, no husband present	4.4	35.6
White	2.4	29.2
Black	1.9	49.9
Hispanic origin[a]	0.8	51.6

[a]*Persons of Hispanic origin may be of any race.*

Source: U.S. Bureau of the Census (1995).

proach and the cross-section approach. What does the cross-section approach shown in Table 16.2 tell us?

Once again, take a few minutes to form your own opinion of what important facts are contained in Table 16.2. Are you finished? Here is my list.

1. The poverty rate of white people is relatively low at 12.2%, and even lower (9.9%) if white persons of Hispanic origin are excluded from the computation. The poverty rates for black people and people of Hispanic origin are both over 30%.

2. The next group of figures shows the poverty rate by age group, and the group with the highest rate of poverty (at 22.7%) is *children* (people under age 18). The sensational way of saying it is that almost one out of four children in the United States lived in poverty in 1993. Surely there are serious consequences for our society in the long run because so many of our children live in poverty at any given time. At 12.2%, the poverty rate for the elderly is actually somewhat below the overall average. The poverty rates in 1993 for children broken down by group are not shown in Table 16.2, but they were:

White	17.8%
Black	46.1%
Hispanic origin	40.9%

3. The next two sets of figures show that the poverty rate is higher in central cities than in suburbs or outside metropolitan areas, and that poverty is more prevalent in the south than in the other regions of the nation. A more detailed examination of poverty in urban areas is provided below.

4. The final sets of data refer to families rather than to individual persons. In 1993, 12.3% of families were in poverty. The poverty rates were 9.4% for white, 31.3% for black, and 27.3% for Hispanic families. As you would expect, the poverty rate was much higher among female-headed families than among married couples. The poverty rate was 35.6% for all female-headed families in 1993, but the rate was 49.9% for black and 51.6% for Hispanic female-headed families.

Table 16.2 includes the fact that the poverty rate is higher in central cities than in suburbs or nonmetropolitan areas. It is also true that poverty in central cities tends to be concentrated in certain areas within central cities and that this tendency toward the concentration of poverty has been increasing in some urban areas. Some recent studies define an *extreme poverty census tract* as one in which at least 40% of the population is in poverty. Several studies have shown that the number of extreme poverty tracts in central cities increased dramatically in the 1970s and the 1980s, as did the concentration of poverty in those tracts. These trends are particularly evident for the black population. Jargowsky (1994) estimated that the number of extreme poverty tracts for the black population increased by 54% from 1980 to 1990. He also reports that the proportion of poor blacks who live in extreme poverty tracts increased from 37% to 45% over this decade. This concentration of black poverty in the 1980s was particularly strong in certain cities, including Detroit, Milwaukee, Cleveland, Pittsburgh, and Buffalo. But cities on the east coast (especially New York, Philadelphia, and Newark) actually saw reductions in the number of black extreme poverty tracts and the concentration of poverty in those tracts. It appears that these differences are related to the rate of economic growth of the urban area, but this is an idea that needs to be tested.

Effects of Taxes and Transfers on the Poverty Rate

As we have seen, the official definition of poverty is based on before-tax money income from all sources except capital gains. This definition omits the effects of taxes and the value of noncash transfers (e.g., food stamps, public housing, Medicare, and Medicaid). The U.S. Bureau of the Census (1995) annually conducts a careful study of the effects of various taxes and transfer programs on the poverty rate. Some of their illuminating results are shown in Table 16.3. The bottom line on these results is

TABLE 16.3 Effects of Taxes and Transfers		
	Persons in Poverty (millions)	*Poverty Rate (%)*
Definition 1	39.3	15.1
Definition 2	60.6	23.4
Def. 1 less government cash transfers		
Definition 3	60.1	23.2
Def. 2 plus capital gains, employee health benefits, and EITC and minus income and payroll taxes		
Definition 4	41.7	16.1
Def. 3 plus nonmeans-tested government cash transfers		
Definition 5	40.5	15.6
Def. 4 plus value of medicare and school lunches		
Definition 6	37.6	14.5
Def. 5 plus means-tested government cash transfers		
Definition 7	31.5	12.1
Def. 6 plus value of medicaid and other means-tested government noncash transfers		
Number removed from poverty by:		
Nonmeans-tested cash transfers	18.4 million	
Capital gains and health insurance benefits	2.0	
Earned income tax credit	1.8	
Federal and state income taxes and payroll tax	−3.3	
Means-tested cash transfers	2.9	
Means-tested noncash transfers	6.1	

Source: U.S. Bureau of the Census (1995).

that the poverty rate for 1993 is reduced by around 20% (from 15.1% to 12.1%) after capital gains, taxes, and noncash transfers are included.

The official poverty rate is listed at the top of Table 16.3, and then several adjustments to this rate are made in succession. The first adjustment (Definition 2) is to subtract out *all* government cash transfer payments and to recompute the poverty rate based on the money income that remains. Government cash transfer programs include:

- Social Security payments (and U.S. Railroad Retirement)
- Unemployment compensation
- Education grants (Pell grants)
- Aid to Families with Dependent Children (AFDC)
- Supplemental Security Income (SSI)
- Veteran's benefits

Social Security is, of course, the pensions paid to the elderly and to the disabled under the Social Security System. Unemployment compensation is the joint federal/state program that pays temporary benefits to workers who have been laid off. AFDC is the main welfare program that primarily pays benefits to female-headed families with dependent children. SSI is a transfer program that is run by the Social Security System for the elderly who are poor and do not qualify for regular Social Security benefits. Education grants and veteran's benefits are received by the relevant special groups.

Table 16.3 shows that if all of these government transfer programs are subtracted, the poverty rate would be 23.4%. The number of people in poverty jumps from 39.3 million to 60.6 million. This figure of 23.4% is based simply on a subtraction of government transfers from the money incomes of households. No account is taken of the possibility that households would respond to the loss of government transfer payments by acting to increase other forms of money income—by working more, for example. Nevertheless, this first result in Table 16.3 gives us a pretty good idea of the extent to which all government transfer programs reduce poverty.

The next line on Table 16.3 is an intermediate step that shows the net effect of five items: income from capital gains, employee health insurance supplements (treated as part of total employee compensation), the earned income tax credit (EITC), federal and state income taxes, and the payroll (Social Security) tax. The only item in this list that needs comment is the earned income tax credit.

The current federal income tax includes a tax credit to workers who make low wages. A tax credit reduces one's tax liability and, in the case of the EITC, can result in the receipt of money from the federal government if one has a low income tax liability. The tax credit for the worker who has no children is very low, but the worker with one child can earn a sizable tax credit. Here is how the EITC works (as of 1994). If the worker has one child, the EITC increases by $163 per $1000 of earnings up to a maximum tax credit of $2038 at earnings of $7750. The tax credit remains at $2038 for earnings between $7750 and $11,000, and then declines by $160 per $1000 of earnings to zero at earnings of $23,750. A person with a taxable income of $7750 owed $1159 in federal income taxes in 1994, so the tax credit of $2038 would mean that such a person would actually receive a check from the Internal Revenue Service for $879. The EITC effectively removed workers with earnings less than about $12,000 from the federal income tax roles, and actually provided a small *negative* tax to most of them. However, note that the EITC is indeed a tax credit for *earnings*. People who have no earnings do not benefit from the program, so EITC is not a welfare (or income maintenance) program.

As Table 16.3 shows, the net effect on the poverty rate of the five adjustments in Definition 3 is very small. As shown at the bottom of the table, the inclusion of capital gains income and employee health insurance benefits puts 2.0 million people above the poverty line, and the EITC moves 1.8 million people above the poverty line. However, the federal and state income taxes and the payroll (Social Security) tax put 3.3 million people below the poverty line, so the net effect is to reduce the number of people in poverty by 0.5 million.

The next step (Definition 4) adds back in the government cash transfers that are *not* means tested. *Means tested* is the term used to describe transfer programs in which eligibility and benefits are based on the income (or wealth) of the potential recipient. The government cash transfer programs that are not means tested are Social Security payments (and Railroad Retirement), unemployment compensation, and most veteran's benefits and education grants. By far the largest program in this category is Social Security, and eligibility for this program is based on working on jobs that were covered by the program. Inclusion of these income sources brings the poverty rate down from 23.2% to 16.1%. In short, the Social Security System is the nation's largest antipoverty program. Most of its payments are made to the elderly, but the program also covers people with disabilities.

The next line in Table 16.3 (Definition 5) adds in the value of Medicare, the federal health care program for the elderly. This addition reduces the poverty rate to 15.6%. The value of Medicare included is not the cash amount paid by the government for health care for the elderly, but is, rather, an estimate of the value of Medicare benefits to the individuals in the program. The idea is to figure out how much income would have been spent on medical care in the absence of the program. This is called the *fungible value* of the benefits, and is assumed to be zero if the household has an income that is less than an estimated amount Y_b needed for basic food and housing needs. If household income exceeds Y_b, the value of Medicare is assumed to equal the difference between actual income and Y_b (up to the actual Medicare benefit). The same method is used below to evaluate Medicaid benefits.

The next step (Definition 6) is very important. It shows the reduction in the poverty rate that results from the inclusion of *means tested* government cash transfer programs (i.e., the public welfare programs). These programs include Aid to Families with Dependent Children (AFDC), Supplemental Security Income (SSI), and public relief programs operated by the states. The largest of these programs is AFDC. The cash public welfare programs reduce the poverty rate from 15.6% to 14.5% and raise 2.9 million people above the poverty line. As we shall see below, most welfare recipients are still below the poverty line.

The final step shown in Table 16.3 (Definition 7) adds in the value of Medicaid and other means-tested government noncash transfers. Medicaid is the health care program for the poor. The other programs included in this category are food stamps, rent subsidies (e.g., public housing, Section 8 housing, etc., as discussed in Chapter 9), and the reduced-price and free school lunch programs. Medicaid is counted at its fungible value, as discussed above in the case of Medicare. The other programs are counted at their cash amounts. These programs result in a substantial reduction in the poverty rate, from 14.5% to 12.1%. Six million people are raised above the poverty line by Medicaid, food stamps, and the other programs. This final line in Table 16.3 perhaps is the best available measure of the poverty rate because it includes the effects of the income and payroll taxes and adds in the noncash government transfer programs as well. Recall that the official poverty rate in 1993 was 15.1%, but this adjusted figure is 12.1%.

The final adjustment to the poverty rate shown in Table 16.3 has also been computed for all the population subgroups. Some of those adjusted figures are as follows:

	Official Poverty Rate (%)	*Adjusted Poverty Rate (%)*
All people	15.1	12.1
Age under 18	22.7	17.5
Age 65 and over	12.2	9.5
White people	12.2	9.8
Age under 18	17.8	13.5
Age 65 and over	10.7	8.4
Black people	33.1	26.3
Age under 18	46.1	36.7
Age 65 and over	28.0	20.5
Hispanic people	30.6	24.2
Age under 18	40.9	31.6
Age 65 and over	21.4	13.6

The series of adjustments shown in Table 16.3 reduces the poverty rate for all people by 20% (from 15.1% to 12.1%), and the poverty rates for each of the large racial/ethnic groups (white, black, Hispanic) are also reduced by 20%. These adjustments also cause the poverty rates for various subgroups to be reduced by about 20%, with the exceptions of black and Hispanic elderly people. Their poverty rates are reduced by 27% and 36%, respectively. This larger reduction in poverty rates of the elderly might have been expected since one of the major adjustments is the addition of the fungible value of Medicare benefits.

Table 16.4 shows the total amount spent, the number of recipients, and the average benefit level for each of the major income transfer programs in 1992. The Social Security program is by far the largest of these programs. In 1992 total outlays were $285.1 billion to 41.5 million recipients. The recipients received an average of $589 per month. Total outlays for Medicare were $129.2 billion: $80.6 billion for hospital bills under Part A of Medicare and $48.6 billion for doctors' bills under Part B. Enrollment in Part A is automatic for senior citizens and others who are eligible for Social Security, but enrollment in Part B is voluntary and required a payment of $37 per month. (This required payment has since been increased.) Nearly all who are eligible elect to enroll in Part B, so total payments for Part B were $14.7 billion.

The programs that are targeted at the poor include Aid to Families with Dependent Children. AFDC had total outlays of $24.9 billion in 1992 (state and federal out-

TABLE 16.4 Major Income Transfer Programs, 1992			
Program	Outlays (billions)	Number of Recipients (millions)	Benefit Level (average)
Social Security	$285.1	41.5	$589/month
Medicare	129.2		
Medicare A (hospital)	80.6	34.7 enrolled	$2341/year
Medicare B (doctor)	48.6	33.1 enrolled	$1448/year
	(−14.7)	(enrollees pay $37 per month)	
Earned Income Tax Credit	8.2		
Aid to Families with Dependent Children	24.9	13.6 persons (4.7 families)	$388/month
Medicaid	118.2	28.3 enrolled	$4100/year
Supplemental Security Income	17.9	5.6	$336/month
Food Stamps	22.8	25.4	$68/month per person
Child Nutrition	6.1		

Source: U.S. House of Representatives, Committee on Ways and Means (1993).

lays) to 4.7 million families with 13.6 million persons. The average benefit was $388 per month per family, or $4656 per year. Most AFDC recipients are also enrolled in the Food Stamp program. The total cost of this program was $22.8 billion in 1992, and the benefits were $68 per month for each person. These two basic programs that transfer income to poor families thus cost $57.7 billion, which was about 1% of the gross domestic product. The finances of a welfare family are discussed in detail below.

The other very large program is Medicaid, the program that pays medical bills for the medically indigent, which includes AFDC recipients, elderly poor people, and disabled people. The total benefit payments of $118.2 billion were split roughly equally among these three groups. However, the portion of Medicaid that has been growing most rapidly is payments for nursing homes for the elderly who have little income and no assets. The elderly person in a nursing home must sell all assets and spend the proceeds before he or she is eligible for Medicaid. The other programs listed in Table 16.4 are the Earned Income Tax Credit, Supplemental Security Income, and Child Nutrition (including school lunches). These programs cost a total of $32.2 billion in 1992.

Causes of Poverty

Table 16.1 shows that poverty rates have changed over time, and Table 16.2 shows that the poverty rate varies enormously by population group. Hypotheses about the causes of poverty must address both sets of facts.

Changes in the poverty rate over time are caused largely by three factors: (1) macroeconomic and labor market conditions, (2) demographic/social changes (e.g., increase in the proportion of households headed by females), and (3) changes in public policy. A substantial amount of research has shown that the poverty rate is sensitive to macroeconomic conditions. For example, Blank and Blinder (1986) found that an increase in the unemployment rate for males of 1% increased the poverty rate by 0.7%. For an economist the first order of business in fighting poverty is keeping the unemployment rate low. Also, you know from Chapter 11 that the rate of growth of the American economy slowed down in the early 1970s. Wages of many workers, especially those without higher education, have stagnated or even declined in real terms. The increase in the inequality of income tends to increase the poverty rate. Macroeconomic policy is beyond the scope of this book, but the discussion of economic development policy for urban areas in Chapter 14 is relevant to fighting poverty.

Changes in the poverty rate are partly driven by social and demographic changes. We have seen that people who live in households headed by females are at very high risk of being in poverty. Thus an increase in the relative size of this group will increase the overall poverty rate. Here the evidence is overwhelming. The population of the United States increased by 35.5% from 1965 to 1993, but the number of people living in households headed by females increased by 131.3%. In 1993, 14.6% of the population was living in households headed by females, and that proportion had increased from 8.6% in 1965. It is evident that far fewer women than men are able to earn enough money to escape poverty, so this trend toward more households headed by women makes it difficult to reduce the poverty rate. The status of women in the labor market is a subject that deserves a lengthy discussion, but that discussion is beyond the scope of this book. The topic of women in the labor market is normally included in courses in labor economics.

A purely demographic factor that tends to increase the overall rate of poverty is the recent rapid growth of the Hispanic population. As we have seen, people of Hispanic origin have a risk of being in poverty that is much higher than average. The proportion of the population that is of Hispanic origin increased from 6.56% in 1980 to 9.02% in 1990. Unless people of Hispanic origin are able to reduce their risk of being in poverty, the continued growth of this group will put upward pressure on the overall poverty rate.

The last factor to consider is changes in public policy. We saw that the poverty rate dropped sharply in the 1960s. That drop can be explained partly by the reduction in the unemployment rate that took place at that time. However, there was a large expansion of the income support system in the United States at that time as well. Moffitt (1992) has provided a careful recounting of the history of means tested transfer programs, and some of the most significant findings are as follows.

1. The AFDC caseload increased from 3.0 million recipients in 1960 to 8.5 million recipients in 1970 and 11.3 million recipients in 1975. Eligibility criteria were reduced, and welfare rights organizations made the effort to inform potential recipients of their rights under the law.

2. The number of recipients of food stamps increased from 0.4 million in 1965 to 4.3 million in 1970 and 17.1 million in 1975. The program was transformed from a minor program for the use of agricultural surpluses into a major means-tested transfer program.

3. The Medicaid program was created in 1965, and the number of recipients was 15.5 million in 1970 and 22 million in 1975.

The number of recipients in all three of these major means-tested programs leveled off after 1975. It is clear that this major commitment on the part of government, largely the federal government, to income support for the poor resulted in a reduction in the poverty rate. Also, the Medicare program was created in 1965 to provide health benefits for the elderly population. At the same time the Social Security System started to increase benefits at a rate that exceeded the rate of inflation. These policy changes greatly reduced the poverty rate for the elderly.

Moffitt (1992) also shows that since 1975, the real value of the total of AFDC, food stamps, Medicaid, and housing assistance has declined. The decline in the real value of AFDC benefits per recipient household actually began in 1970, and by 1985 the real decline in the average AFDC benefit was about 30%. The cause of this decline is the simple fact that states failed to increase benefit levels along with inflation. The consequence of this failure of benefits to grow with inflation is that the welfare package (AFDC, food stamps, Medicaid and housing assistance) is, over time, less capable of moving the household above the poverty level. The response of welfare recipients to this state of affairs is discussed below.

Now let us turn to the cross-section variations in the rate of poverty. Why does poverty vary so dramatically across population groups in the United States? All of the determinants of the incomes of individuals and households matter. Any reasonably complete list of these factors will include:

- Education level
- Job training
- Work experience
- Age and age discrimination
- Natural ability and intelligence
- Motivation
- Union membership
- Racial discrimination in the labor market
- Sex discrimination in the labor market
- Occupational segregation in the labor market
- Family background factors
- Geographic mobility (or immobility)
- Racial segregation in housing, leading to spatial limitations on job opportunities

The importance of education and training was emphasized in Chapter 13, and some of the other factors in this list are discussed in this and the next section of the chapter. The net effect of all of these factors is a distribution of income that leads to the differences in the poverty statistics shown in Table 16.2. As you know, members of the black and Hispanic minority groups and women suffer from relatively high rates of poverty.

The poverty rate in 1993 was 15.1% of the population (or 12.1% if you prefer the adjusted figure). The overall rate of poverty is a major national problem, but perhaps the most distressing aspect of the current poverty problem is the increasing concentration of poverty in certain areas of major central cities in the form of what has been called the *urban underclass.*

The Urban Underclass

The urban underclass consists of the groups of people who believe that they have little or no hope of joining the mainstream of American life in which people work for a living and look forward to their futures. The urban underclass displays behavioral symptoms that include:

- High unemployment
- Poverty
- Crime
- Illegitimacy
- Dependence on welfare
- Drug addiction and alcoholism
- Family instability
- Female-headed families
- Teen age pregnancy
- Dropping out of school and poor education
- Low aspirations and low self-esteem
- Poor health
- Early death

Many people suffer from one or more of these problems at some times in their lives, but for the underclass these behaviors are the way of life. In their controversial book *The Bell Curve* (1994), Richard Herrnstein and Charles Murray add that many of the people in the underclass also have low IQs (intelligence quotients) as measured by standard tests. There is no general agreement about how to define and measure the underclass in precise terms. But however the underclass is defined, a disproportionate number of the urban underclass is black. The existence, and apparent growth of, the urban underclass in the past 30 years is a tragedy of immeasurable magnitude that confounds everyone.

Many social scientists have tried to understand the forces that perpetuate and increase the urban underclass. The leading scholar of underclass life is the sociologist William Julius Wilson. Wilson published two books that have had a major impact on thought about race and class. In the first book, *The Declining Significance of Race* (1978), Wilson argued that a growing number of blacks are being incorporated into the mainstream of modern middle-class American life, but that many are being left behind. The biggest social problem in America is no longer race, but class, especially the urban underclass. The emergence of the black middle class in large numbers is the reason that Wilson thinks that race, by itself, is of declining significance.

In the second book, *The Truly Disadvantaged: The Inner City, the Underclass, and Public Policy* (1987), Wilson elaborated his thoughts on the urban underclass. Wilson documented the sharp increases in some of the symptoms of underclass behavior that have occurred since the 1960s. In 1960, 33% of black children were not living with two parents, and by 1988 that figure had increased to 61%. The number of black children born to an unwed mother increased from 23% to 61% during the same period. [However, Jencks (1992) pointed out that the main reason for this increase is the reduction in births by married women.] As we have seen, because families headed by women have a high risk of being in poverty, 46% of black children and a majority of black children under the age of 6 (52%) now live in poverty. In 1960, 51% of black women in the 15–44 age group were married, and that fraction had dropped to 29% by 1988.

Wilson argued that economic and social factors in the inner city can account for at least some of the growth in underclass behavior. He pointed out that poverty and unemployment have become more concentrated in certain areas of the inner city because those who are able to move out of such areas do so. The older black neighborhoods have lost their middle-class residents, so the remaining residents have lost contact with people who personify middle-class values. The loss of decent jobs, primarily in manufacturing, from inner city areas has reduced the employment prospects for black men. Wilson introduced what he called the male marriageable pool index, which is the number of employed men per 100 women in a particular age group. That index stood at 68 for black men aged 20–44 in the north in 1960, and it dropped to 56 by 1980 [Wilson (1987, p. 97)]. In contrast, the index for white men in the same age group in the north was 89 in 1960 and 86 in 1980.

Hammer (1992) has tested Wilson's hypotheses in a more rigorous statistical framework. Hammer posited the following model of labor force and family-related behavior:

1. Reductions in blue-collar job opportunities reduce the labor force participation of males.

2. Reductions in male labor force participation reduce both the number of females who marry and the number of children who are born. The number of families headed by women increases.

Hammer tested these hypotheses using data on changes in the variables from 1970 to 1980 for 76 large urban areas. The model was estimated separately for blacks and whites in the 16–34 age group. He found that, as hypothesized, the decline in blue-collar employment for blacks was strongly related to the drop in black male labor force participation. The decline in the share of black women who were married with spouse present was strongly related to drop in male labor force participation. The change in the fertility of black women was positively related to the change in the proportion of women who were married as expected, but the drop in male labor force participation actually increased fertility (as was not expected). Hammer's explanation for this last result is that fertility may decline in urban areas where blacks had greater success in moving to middle-class status (i.e., where male labor force participation increased). The results for whites came out generally as expected, but the magnitudes of the effects are considerably smaller for whites than for blacks.

Hammer used his empirical results to trace through the effects of a loss of 1000 blue-collar jobs for both blacks and whites. The loss of 1000 blue-collar jobs by blacks led to a decline in the labor force participation of black men of 253, while the same loss of blue-collar jobs by whites reduced male labor force participation by 114. The number of black females with husbands present dropped by 104 (compared to 78 for whites). Whites responded to these changes by having 119 fewer children, but black children increased by 137. These changes resulted in 84 more female-headed families for blacks versus only 13 for whites. Based on Hammer's analysis, the loss of blue-collar jobs in urban areas appears to have had powerful effects on the black family and, in contrast to expectation, actually increased black fertility relative to what otherwise would have happened.

The linkages between the economy and underclass problems seem to be clear enough, but most researchers in the field think that the economic problems are insufficient to explain the massive changes that have taken place in society. Some blame the growth of the urban underclass on the welfare system, but as Ellwood (1988) and Moffitt (1992) pointed out, welfare programs have become less generous since the 1970s as the underclass problems have continued to grow. There is much that we do not know about the causes behind the underclass phenomenon, and economists (and others) must be modest in their claims of having the explanation at hand. Nevertheless, it is clear that the changes in the urban economy that were described in Chapter 15 are implicated.

Life on Welfare

What sort of life do members of the urban underclass lead? This question cannot be answered because the underclass does not make itself available for detailed study. However, thanks to an ingenious study by Kathryn Edin that is reported in Jencks (1992), we have a pretty good idea about how welfare mothers live. Edin interviewed a nonrandom sample of 50 welfare mothers in Cook County, Illinois during 1988–1990 to find out how they get by on their meager welfare checks. The sample is not random because she had to interview people who would trust her. The sample was determined by the contacts of acquaintances.

The 50 welfare mothers had an average of 2.1 children and received a welfare check that was an average of $324 per month. They also received food stamps worth $200. Twenty-eight of the women resided in unsubsidized housing and paid an average of $364 per month in rent and utilities. The remaining 22 who lived in subsidized housing paid only $123 per month in rent and utilities. The average food expenditure was $250 per month, so the food stamp allotment was not enough. Other expenses included clothing, laundry, cleaning supplies, school supplies, transportation, furniture, and so on. Average expenses for all of these other categories averaged $351 per month. Welfare mothers who did not live in subsidized housing had expenses of $940 per month, and those who lived in subsidized housing reported expenditures of $840 per month, compared to an average welfare check and food stamp allotment of $524.

Where does the rest of the money come from? Almost half (43%) of the additional $316 or $416 in cash came from resident boyfriends, absent fathers, relatives, or friends. An equal amount (44%) came from money earned by the women themselves. Seven women had salaried jobs under another Social Security number, and 22 others had part-time jobs that were off the books (bartending, babysitting, catering). Five women sold drugs, and five worked occasionally as prostitutes. Of the five who sold drugs, one sold crack cocaine and was murdered shortly after the interview. The remaining 13% of the "supplemental" income came from various sources, including student loans. Not one of the 50 women lived just on the welfare check, food stamps, and subsidized housing. Only four reported any of the additional income to the welfare authorities. It is illegal not to report the additional income, but welfare authorities do not go looking for violations.

The only way a welfare mother can even come close to surviving without extra income is to live in subsidized housing. The option that is much preferred is the subsidized housing under the Section 8 program (as discussed in Chapter 9). These apartments are owned by private individuals or organizations and are scattered throughout the city and inner suburbs. However, very few units of this type are available and there is a long waiting list. The other option is public housing in Chicago, but much of this is horrible and dangerous. The waiting list is fairly short for public housing, but the welfare mothers in Edin's sample evidently will do almost anything to avoid having to live in public housing. The welfare officials tacitly permit them to acquire the income necessary to stay out of public housing.

The choices facing the welfare recipient can be depicted in a standard diagram that shows the labor–leisure trade-off. Figure 16.1 measures leisure time on the horizontal axis and income on the vertical axis. The total time budget for a person is assumed to be 480 hours per month (30×16). Utility increases as one moves in the northeastern direction in the diagram from indifference curve IC_1 to IC_2, and so on. Consider the average welfare recipient from Edin's data who lives in unsubsidized housing. The family receives $524 in AFDC and food stamp benefits each month, and this amount is shown on the diagram. The total money income of the family is $940 per month, and about half of the additional money (or $208) is received from others: boyfriends, other family members, and so on. The rules of the AFDC program

FIGURE 16.1 Welfare participation and work

require that these funds be reported to the administrators of the program, and the AFDC benefit is supposed to be reduced by that amount. The welfare recipients in Edin's study do not report this income, so the family now has an income of $732 per month, as shown on Figure 16.1. Next, the welfare recipient considers working to earn additional money. The rules of the AFDC program regarding the taxation of earnings (the benefit reduction rate) for the first year on AFDC are rather complex, but after one full year on AFDC, benefits are supposed to be reduced by the amount of the earnings. In other words, the benefit reduction rate is 100%! No wonder the women in Edin's study failed to report their earnings.

Figure 16.1 depicts the various cases. If all the rules of AFDC are followed, the AFDC family has an income of $524 per month regardless of the amount of time the woman works. The budget constraint is a horizontal line at an income of $524. If the unearned income received from other people is not reported to the authorities but earnings are reported, the AFDC family has an income of $732 regardless of the amount of time spent working. Now consider the option of working.

If the woman chooses not to receive AFDC and food stamps, assume that unearned income is $208 from other people. Suppose that the woman's wage rate is $5.00 per hour. The budget constraint starts with $208 and 480 hours of leisure. Income can be increased by $5.00 for each hour of leisure given up, so Figure 16.1 shows that the slope of the budget constraint is -5. If the woman chooses to be on AFDC and food stamps and to abide by all of the rules of the program, the monthly income will be $524. The woman who chooses *not* to be on AFDC and food stamps can reach this level of income by working 63 hours per month (or about 16 hours per week). Which option is preferable? The answer depends on the woman's preferences, which are drawn to make the option of *not* participating in AFDC and food stamps the preferred choice. The woman who makes this choice attains utility level IC_2, compared to IC_1.

Figure 16.1 depicts some better options. First, consider the option of participating in AFDC and food stamps and *not* reporting the unearned income received from others. Now the family has $732 per month. Including the $208 of unearned income received from others, the woman would have to work 105 hours per month (or about 26 hours per week) to have an income of this amount. Figure 16.1 is drawn so that participating in AFDC and food stamps, and not following all of the rules, is preferable to working and not receiving AFDC and food stamps (IC_3 versus IC_2). This choice is made presuming that it is extremely unlikely for the woman to be penalized for not following the rules of the AFDC program. Finally, consider the best option of all. Suppose that the woman receives AFDC and food stamps and fails to report *any* other forms of income, including her own earnings. As Edin's study indicated, this is done by working under another Social Security number or working in the underground economy (where the few records that are kept are not available to the AFDC officials). The woman who makes this choice begins with a total of $732 in unearned income, and then decides how much time to work at a wage of $5.00 per hour. Edin's study showed that these families had an average income of $940 per month, so the woman earned $208. This level of earnings requires about 42 hours of work per month (about 10.5 hours per week). Figure 16.1 shows that this combination of $940 of income and 42 hours of work maximizes utility on indifference curve IC_4, given the constraint under which the woman must operate and given that the woman really does not face a penalty for failing to follow the rules of the AFDC program.

C. THE SPATIAL MISMATCH HYPOTHESIS

The Urban Transportation Problem (1965), a book by Meyer, Kain, and Wohl, stated that the really serious urban transportation problem is the fact that the residents of the inner city do not have easy access to the jobs in the suburbs. Kain (1968) elaborated this point in a classic article. Kain's hypothesis really has three parts:

1. Housing segregation affects the distribution of black employment.
2. Housing segregation reduces job opportunities for blacks.
3. The process of suburbanization makes the problem worse.

Kain's (1968) statistical tests confirmed the first point; residential location does affect the spatial distribution of employment. Blacks are viewed as being constrained in their choices of residential location by a segregated housing market, and this constraint is bound to have an influence on their job choices. This may or may not be particularly injurious to economic opportunity. What if urban blacks are constrained to live in areas in the city where there are many jobs? This was pretty much true in the 1950s, the time when the data used by Kain were collected. The social problem arises from Kain's other two hypotheses, but his empirical evidence in 1968 on these points was not completely convincing. However, it has now been established pretty definitively that all three of Kain's hypotheses are correct for teenagers. The evidence is not fully convincing at all for adult male workers. It is worthwhile to review briefly the research that has been done on these important issues.

Kain (1968) tested his first hypothesis above by examining the racial composition of workers in a small zone (in Chicago or Detroit) as a linear function of the distance of that zone from the black housing area and the racial composition of the *residents* of that zone. The statistical significance of the distance variable (with a negative sign) confirms what can be called the *direct effect* of housing segregation on employment. Given that blacks have restricted residential location choices, the costs associated with distance will create the negative effect. The statistical significance of the racial composition of the residents of the zone (with a positive sign) is evidence that employers tend to hire workers who reflect the racial composition of the neighborhood in which the firm is located. This effect can be called the *indirect effect* of housing segregation on employment because it says that the movement of jobs from black to white residential areas will reduce black job opportunities apart from the effect of distance. The movement of jobs to distant, white suburbs is therefore doubly harmful to black job opportunities. Kain's (1968) empirical evidence indicated that both effects might be important.

Kain's study initiated a great deal of research, which has centered basically in two areas. First, several labor economists have argued that while residential segregation restricts the opportunity to hold some jobs, the consequences for employment are relatively insignificant compared to other factors that influence job opportunities for blacks, such as the relative lack of education and training and racial discrimination. Second, it has been argued, most notably by Offner and Saks (1971), that the indirect effect of residential segregation on black job opportunities may be either positive or negative. It may be the case that residential integration will reduce disproportionately the jobs available to blacks because of the propensity of employers to hire workers who reflect the racial makeup of the surrounding residential area.

The labor market studies that are critical of Kain used different research strategies, but they all began with the observation that the demand for labor was stronger in central cities than in suburban areas. (This is no longer true in many urban areas.) Blacks were confined to residential locations that happened to be accessible to jobs. Noll (1970, p. 501) examined the spatial distribution of jobs in major urban areas in the 1960s and concluded that "jobs, particularly for the less skilled, are easier to find in the central city." Furthermore, studies by Lewis (1969) and Fremon (1970) demonstrated that the population in urban areas generally decentralized more rapidly than did total employment during the 1953–1967 period. We now know that the reverse was true in the 1970s and 1980s; jobs "moved" to the suburbs more rapidly than did the people in these more recent periods. Friedlander (1972, p. 194) summed up the evidence at the time by noting that "the employment problems of city residents may be more affected by suburbanites commuting to the city for employment than by movement of jobs to the suburbs." However, the real problem that was faced by minority residents of the central city may have been that employment opportunities in blue-collar and semiskilled and low-skilled jobs were moving to the suburbs so rapidly that a surplus of labor in these categories developed in the central city. This is the skills mismatch hypothesis. Several studies demonstrated that there had indeed been substantial shifts in the occupational mix of jobs in central cities. The most comprehensive study was done by Wilson (1979). Using the 1% public use samples from the 1960 and 1970 censuses for the 25 most populous states, he showed that there had been absolute declines in the craftsman, operative, and laborer categories in central cities over the period, while professional, sales, clerical, and service employment increased in central cities. Wilson did not determine whether these changes implied an increasing mismatch of skills between central city labor demand and supply, but it seems reasonably clear that the mismatch increased.

Partly because the direct test of the mismatch hypothesis requires a great deal of information about the supply of and demand for skills, a number of labor economists and other researchers have examined wage rates, earnings data, and unemployment rates for central city and suburban workers. However, as Wilson (1979) pointed out, evidence based on wage rates and other labor market data must be evaluated with care. There are four groups of black workers to be examined: those who live and work in the central city, those who live and work in the suburbs, those who live in the central city and work in the suburbs, and those who live in the suburbs and work in the central city. The best comparison to test Kain's hypothesis is, holding other factors constant, to examine the wages of workers who live and work in the suburbs with those who live and work in the central city. Workers who commute from the central city to the suburbs, for example, may only take jobs that pay more than the worker's expected wage because of the higher commuting costs involved. In other words, the data on wages earned by commuters from city to suburbs may contain a severe selection bias in the positive direction. Wilson (1979) made the appropriate comparisons and found that in both 1959 and 1969 the wages of blacks who lived and worked in the suburbs were not higher than the wages of blacks who lived and worked in the central city, holding constant schooling, experience, and industry. However, a more recent study by Price and Mills (1985) used data from the 1978 Current Population Survey and found that both black and white men who lived in the central city earned 6 to 8% less than their suburban counterparts, holding constant the effects of a large number of personal characteristics, industry, and amenities. Black workers who lived in the city earned 13% less than comparable white men who lived in the city, and black suburban residents earned 16% less than their white suburban counterparts. However, a more recent study by McMillen (1993) found no evidence of the effect of the spatial mismatch on the earnings of black male workers in the Detroit urban area in 1980 because he found that blacks who worked in the central city had higher earnings there than if they had worked in the suburbs. Similarly, blacks who worked in the suburbs had higher earnings there than if they had worked in the central city.

Leonard (1987) conducted a study of black male employment in Chicago and Los Angeles using establishment data for 1974 and 1980 available from the Office of Federal Contract Compliance. The Chicago sample consists of 1191 establishments that were observed in both years at their same locations. Regression analyses showed that the proportion of blue-collar employees in an establishment who were black males was strongly negatively related to the distance of the establishment from the border of the black residential area. Furthermore, this negative gradient in Chicago actually was steeper in 1980 than in 1974. No allowance was made for the movement of the border of the black residential area from 1974 to 1980, so the effect of the distance variable was actually underestimated. Furthermore, no attempt was made to consider the effects of establishments that decentralized over this period. It is telling that employment of black males in blue-collar jobs remained constant in the 547 suburban establishments in the sample of 1191 given that total blue-collar employment in these establishments increased by 2.3% over the period. One might have expected that black workers would have been able to increase their ability to compete for suburban blue-collar jobs.

Ellwood (1986) completed an important study of the employment of male teenagers in metropolitan Chicago in 1970. This study is discussed in some detail because it has received a good deal of publicity. The study was designed to address two related issues: the effect of proximity to jobs on labor market outcomes, and whether the proximity effect can explain some of the differential in employment opportunities between black and white youth. Teenagers were chosen for the study because of concern for this group and because it is reasonable to assume that their residential locations are exogenous to the employment outcome. Many teenagers (even those not in school) live with their parents or guardians. However, Ellwood (1986) made no effort to determine whether the teenagers in his data lived at home. Two empirical research strategies were followed. The first used Census Tract data for 1970 and examined the employment rate for out-of-school male youths aged 16–21 living in the tract as a function of job accessibility, education, and demographic variables. The second approach used the special 1970 Census Employment Survey (CES) of low-income areas in Chicago.

The results using the Census Tract data indicate that employment rates were lower in tracts with more poor families, blacks, Spanish-speaking people, and children in single-parent families. Teenage employment for those not in school was greater if more teenagers were in school. The variable to measure job accessibility is the ratio of jobs (blue-collar and service) located in the community to workers who live in the community. The variable is a measure of local demand relative to supply, and its regression coefficient is positive and statistically significant. But as Ellwood (1986) pointed out, the magnitude of the coefficient is very small. The coefficient says that if a neighborhood were changed from one with two workers per job to one with two jobs per worker, the employment rate of male teenagers would increase by less than 1 percentage point. This finding is consistent with the idea that locational factors are of minor importance compared to racial discrimination, education, and training.

The Census Employment Survey of 1970 was conducted on the west and south sides of Chicago. Blacks and whites in low-income areas were surveyed, and the survey was designed to gather information on the labor market. As Ellwood (1986) pointed out, this survey provides a natural experiment because access to employment was much higher on the west side than on the south side of Chicago. Ellwood (1986) simply calculated mean values for young black men (age 16–21) who resided in these two areas. The sample sizes are only about 100 for each area. The labor market outcomes for out-of-school young black men in the two areas are very similar. The employment (unemployment) rates were 51% (38%) for the south side and 54% (35%) on the west side. The outcomes for high school dropouts were very similar in the two areas. However, Ellwood (1986) did not point out that there may have been some differences in labor market outcomes for those young men who had graduated from high school. The employment (unemployment) rate for this group was 71% (19%) on the south side and 80% (10%) on the west side. The small sample sizes mean that these differences are not statistically significant, but the figures suggest that high school graduates did better on the west side than on the south side and that dropouts did poorly in both locations.

Ellwood (1986) was also able to use the CES data for the west side to compare labor market outcomes for black and white males who resided in the area. This tabulation reveals that the employment rate (unemployment rate) was 79% (11%) for whites and 54% (35%) for blacks who were not in school and in the 16–21 age group. Furthermore, the percentage of whites who had graduated from high school was 29% compared to 34% for blacks. Again it appears to be race, not place.

Another approach to labor market studies was followed by Mooney (1969) and Masters (1974, 1975). Using a cross section of urban areas, these studies related a measure of economic well-being of blacks to the degree of residential segregation and other variables. These studies failed to find an important relationship between these two variables. However, Kain (1974) has criticized both of these studies on the grounds that the measures of segregation used do not adequately measure the access of blacks to jobs. A related study by Moffitt (1977) examined changes in city/suburban relative wages for a cross section of urban areas for 1960–1970. The study found that wage rates in the central cities actually increased slightly relative to suburban wages during the period because of the extensive movement of the white population to the suburbs. Central city residents would thus appear to have had somewhat better wage opportunities in 1970 than in 1960.

The empirical evidence from the labor market appeared to be inconclusive until a series of studies was conducted by Keith Ihlanfeldt and David Sjoquist on urban teenagers. Ihlanfeldt (1992) has reviewed the literature and presented the Ihlanfeldt–Sjoquist findings. His review of the literature reveals that the studies that rejected Kain's hypotheses used flawed methods of some sort. For example, the Ellwood (1986) study is criticized on four grounds:

1. The measures of access to employment may have been measured with error.

2. It may not be true that the residential locations of the teenagers in Ellwood's study are exogenous. If residential location and work location are determined together, the effect of residential location will appear to be zero.

3. The comparison of white and black youths from the CES did not adequately control for other factors.

4. The comparison of black youths who lived on the west and south sides may be flawed because it is not clear that residence on the west side provided better access to jobs that could be held by black youth.

In contrast, the research by Ihlanfeldt and Sjoquist (1990, 1991) show that poor access to employment is a significant factor in the low employment rates of black youth in a large number of urban areas. The measure of access to jobs that was used is the average travel time of low-wage workers who lived in the same residential zone as the youth in question. Only youths who still lived at home with a parent or guardian were included in the studies. The results for Philadelphia are that an increase in travel time of 1 standard deviation reduced the probability that a black youth had a job in 1980 by 4.0 to 6.3%. The effect of this same change on white youth was −3.8 to −5.1%. The difference in access to jobs between whites and blacks accounted for 33 to 50% of the difference in employment rates between the two groups. The studies by Ihlanfeldt and Sjoquist are superior to previous studies because they used a better measure of access to jobs, because they included only youths who live at home, and because their use of data on individuals permitted them to include a large number of control variables for individual and family characteristics. The results reported by Ihlanfeldt (1992) show that black female teenagers and Hispanic youths of both sexes faced roughly the same problem with access to jobs as black males. At this point the work of Ihlanfeldt and Sjoquist is the definitive research on the narrow issue of access to jobs and chances for employment among black and Hispanic teenagers who still lived at home. The question for all black and Hispanic workers remains open. Is it race, or is it place for other groups of black and Hispanic workers?

Jencks (1992) argues rather persuasively that for adult males, it is race and not place. Most teenagers are qualified only for jobs with low wages. It makes sense that they are not willing to search far and wide and to make lengthy commutes to jobs that pay very little. Other groups, such as women with children and adult men with little education, are probably in the same boat. The argument is not convincing for adult men with at least a high school diploma. These men conceivably can qualify for reasonably good jobs, including suburban jobs in manufacturing, construction, transportation, wholesale trade, and so on. As Jencks (1992, p. 123) puts it, "Distance is a problem only when employers let it become one." Distance is not a barrier for white men with at least a high school education. Firms in the central business district have no difficulty recruiting men who live in the suburbs, and people who work in the suburbs rarely live close to work. A good job pays enough to permit the worker to purchase a car; commuting is our way of life. Employers do not advertise their blue-collar jobs in places that are known to blacks in the inner city because they do not wish to hire these workers.

Jencks (1992) also provides a refreshing perspective on the problems that teenagers face in the labor market. He points out that variations in the employment rate of black and other teenagers can be explained by aggregate changes in demand and supply. For example, the boom in the Massachusetts economy in the 1980s reduced the unemployment rate of blacks to 5.6%, and Freeman (1991) found that tight labor markets substantially reduce unemployment among black teenagers. Macroeconomic evidence also shows that a high level of aggregate demand and a low unemployment rate benefit minority and teenage workers. The problem is that we are reluctant to crank up aggregate demand enough to bring the unemployment rate down to levels such as 3.5 or 4% because we fear accelerating inflation. However, it is also true that the demand for unskilled labor has weakened as the supply of such labor has increased. This is the problem that labor economists used to call structural unemployment. The "structure" of demand for labor has changed (i.e., employers now demand more verbal, mathematical, and analytical skills than before). At the same time the suppliers of labor have been slow to adjust. In some areas the supply of unskilled labor has been expanded by the immigration of Hispanic workers and other groups. The entry of the baby boom generation and many women into the labor force also tended to increase the supply of workers at all levels, especially at the unskilled and semiskilled levels. In the 1980s there was something of a shortage of college-educated workers (at least in some fields) and an oversupply of workers with lesser skills. At this point in time the society is trying to grapple with the problem of how to upgrade the skills of our fellow Americans so that they can better match the demand for labor. Businesses, schools, colleges, and government in general are all engaged in a wide variety of serious efforts to understand and deal with this problem.

Since the 1960s a debate has been going on about how to address the spatial mismatch problems discussed in this section. The policy debate also has some relevance to the problems of urban crime and underclass behavior as well. The debate has been framed as *ghetto development* versus *ghetto dispersal*. I find the use of the word *ghetto* somewhat distasteful, but the idea is that policies might focus on building up the economy of the inner city as compared to policies designed to move low-income and minority households to locations where economic opportunities are better. Another shorthand phrase is bringing jobs to people or moving people to jobs. There is no reason why a comprehensive strategy cannot try to do both, but it may be useful to begin with a broader perspective.

Chapter 14 is a lengthy discussion of economic development strategy and policy for an urban area. An economic development strategy can be framed to provide greater or lesser benefits for the low-income residents of the inner city, but as Bartik's (1991) empirical results indicate, an effective strategy for economic development of any sort will generate enhanced economic opportunities for the residents of the urban area. It should be clear that the first thing to do is to put in place an economic development strategy that is designed to put some emphasis on low-income households. The evidence reviewed in Chapters 14 and 15 and in this chapter shows that economic growth at a sufficient rate in an urban area will translate into growth in the central city as well. Many people criticize what they derisively call *trickle-down economics*, but economic growth cannot be bad, and in a growing local economy it is easier to create opportunities for lower-income people. Let us work to expand the pie, and let us also try to make sure that some of the increase goes to the poor. With that said, what about ghetto development versus ghetto dispersal?

If politics is the art of the possible, so is urban economic development. Is it possible to generate economic growth and development in the inner city outside the downtown area? Perhaps it is, but the efforts to do so in urban areas that have experienced little growth overall have not been very successful. Inner-city development efforts surely work better when the urban area is experiencing robust growth. That was the message from the study of enterprise zones in Cook County, Illinois that was discussed in Chapter 14. The one group of industries that was attracted to the inner city is wholesale trade and transportation, an industry group that was experiencing appreciable growth in the urban area as a whole. If the economic development strategy includes targeting of industries for special programs, a program of inner-city development should then target those industries that are experiencing substantial growth and that also would consider such a location. In particular, attempts to induce manufacturing to locate in the inner city of an urban area that is growing slowly are wasted efforts. It probably is true that even when the urban area is growing, some special inducements will be needed to attract firms to the inner city. It would seem that some modest inducements are in order to bring about the result. Economic growth in the inner city might mean better job prospects for teenagers and women, at least. An improvement in job prospects for women might have a direct impact on the poverty rate, as discussed in Section B.

The conclusion is that some selective efforts to generate economic development in the inner city seem to make sense, but these policies are likely to work only after policies to promote the growth of the urban area as a whole have been put in place. In addition, the problem of structural unemployment of minority workers and others with low levels of education and training need to be addressed with labor market policies that will enhance educational and training opportunities. A full discussion of these matters is beyond the scope of this book, but the inherent difficulties must not be understated. Heckman (1994) points out that between 1979 and 1989, the earnings of male high school dropouts per week dropped by 13%, high school graduates earned 4% less, and college graduates increased their weekly earnings by 11%. Heckman (1994) estimated the amount of investment in human capital that would restore the earnings of the high-school dropouts and graduates to their 1979 levels. If the rate of return to investment in human capital is 10%, which is a decent rate of return to any investment, each high school dropout would require an investment of $25,000 (in 1989 dollars) and each high school graduate would require $10,000 in human capital investment. The grand total for all males in these two categories is $426 billion (in 1989 dollars). Needless to say, high school dropouts do not have $25,000 to spend (and earnings to forgo) to make the needed investment. They will need assistance from the public sector to obtain the education and training just to restore their earnings to 1979 levels, but the government is not contemplating a program of anything like the magnitude that Heckman suggests.

But what about ghetto dispersal? It turns out that there is solid evidence of the benefits of a limited program of ghetto dispersal. The best studies of the strategy of ghetto dispersal have been done on an unusual program in Chicago [Rosenbaum (1993)]. In 1976 the Supreme Court of the United States ruled that because the Chicago Housing Authority (the public housing agency in Chicago) had employed racially discriminatory policies in selecting locations for and administration of public housing, it must offer a program of rent certificates that permits the residents of public housing to move out to other locations. This program has succeeded in helping black people move to middle-class white suburbs; since 1976 some 4000 families have participated in the program, and over half have moved to white suburbs. The evaluation studies compare those who moved to the suburbs to those who moved to another location in the city. This technique is a reasonable method for controlling for the level of motivation of the family. The adults in the study are women, and the ones who moved to the suburbs had a higher employment rate than did those who moved to a city location. Among those who claimed that they had never been employed before, 46% of suburban movers got jobs compared to 30% of city movers. (Note that moving out of public housing increased employment for both groups.) More important, the children in the families that moved to the suburbs did extremely well. These children were more likely to be in the college track in high school, to attend college, or to be employed full time if not in college. Those who were employed were far more likely to have decent earnings and job benefits (such as health insurance). After a period of adjustment to the higher standards that are imposed in suburban schools, the black students did much better in suburban schools than did their counterparts in city schools. The families that moved to middle-class suburbs, where the streets are pretty safe, jobs are plentiful, and schools have fairly high standards, learned how to take advantage of this better environment. In short, Rosenbaum and his associates have shown us that there is reason for hope.

The research that is available gives us a pretty clear message. The urban area with serious problems in its inner city should formulate and pursue a strategy of economic growth and development that includes some emphasis on attracting business to the inner city. At the same time, policies that move inner-city residents to the suburbs provide positive results and should also be followed.

D. HOUSING FOR LOW-INCOME HOUSEHOLDS AND HOMELESSNESS

In Chapter 9 it was pointed out that the most serious problem facing low-income households in the housing market is the cost of housing compared to (reported) income. The discussion of the urban underclass in Section A included an examination of how 50 welfare mothers manage to provide for their families. The problem of housing loomed large in that discussion. Welfare mothers in Cook County, Illinois who did not live in subsidized housing paid an average of $364 per month in rent and utilities (electricity and natural gas for heat), an amount that was roughly equal to their welfare checks. Their solution to the problem of a severe shortage of money was to get income from a variety of other sources that were not reported to the welfare authorities (or to other government agencies, most likely).

The related problems of "affordable" housing and homelessness have been very much on the policy agenda in recent years. Let us begin with a discussion of the problem of homelessness and then turn to a broader examination of the urban housing market.

Several different attempts have been made to count the number of homeless people. The number will depend, of course, on the definition of homelessness that is used. The official definition of homelessness that was written into the McKinney Homeless Assistance Act of 1987 defines the homeless as:

1. Persons who lack a fixed, regular, and adequate nighttime residence (e.g., those who use a tent, a highway underpass, a car, a sleeping bag on the street).

2. Those whose nighttime residence is a temporary shelter or other institution that provides temporary housing, or a place not intended for human sleeping accommodations (e.g., a hallway in a public building).

This definition includes people who are living temporarily in welfare hotels or in shelters for battered women as well as those who are in homeless shelters. A narrow definition would include only those who sleep in homeless shelters and exclude those who are in other forms of temporary accommodations. On the other hand, what about people who are doubling up in housing units or others who live in very crowded conditions? The number of people in these two categories also indicates a serious problem of access to housing that is affordable.

Many attempts have been made to estimate the number of homeless people, a group of people who are difficult to count because often they do not wish to be counted. The 1990 Census placed the number of homeless on the streets or in shelters at approximately 250,000 for the nation (as of March 1990). The U.S. Department of Housing and Urban Development (1984) used four independent methods to estimate the number of homeless and came up with a range of 250,000 to 350,000 as of 1984. HUD also produced estimates of the homeless population for 60 cities in 1984. These estimates vary from 535.1 per 100,000 population in the city of San Francisco down to 6.8 per 100,000 in Fall River, Massachusetts. The top 10 cities for homeless rates among the cities in the 1984 HUD study were as follows:

City	Homeless per 100,000
San Francisco	535.1
Los Angeles	412.0
Miami	348.8
New York	346.2
Chicago	323.9
Worcester, MA	259.9
Fort Wayne, IN	208.1
Las Vegas	205.0
Houston	200.7
Seattle	187.2

Note that the three largest cities in the nation (New York, Los Angeles, and Chicago) were in the top five. These and other large cities have sizable absolute numbers of homeless people; for example, a rate of 412 per 100,000 in Los Angeles (population 3.5 million) translates into 14,400 homeless people on any given night. The McKinney Act of 1987 was passed to address the immediate problems of this sizable group of people by providing funds for homeless shelters, some funds for the rehabilitation of single-room occupancy dwellings, and some funds for community efforts to assist the homeless. However, many advocates for the homeless argue that the McKinney Act was a good start but that more is needed.

If the number of homeless people is about 250,000, who are they? The HUD studies did not provide data on the characteristics of the homeless, but a fairly comprehensive national study by Burt and Cohen (1989) did. Their estimates of the homeless population are:

	Proportion
Sex/family status	
Single male adults	0.68
Single female adults	0.09
Male adults in families	0.01
Female adults in families	0.07
Children	0.15
Race	
Black	0.41
White	0.46
Hispanic	0.10
Other	0.03
Medical/criminal history	
Ever in mental hospital	0.19
Chemical dependency	0.33
Ever in prison	0.24

Note that most of the homeless in their study were adult males, but that 15% of the homeless were children. Homeless people suffer from high rates of mental illness and/or chemical dependency (e.g., addiction to alcohol), and they are disproportionately black. Presumably all of the homeless are eligible for food stamps, but only 12% of the homeless adults in the Burt–Cohen study received them. Only 3% of homeless adults received welfare benefits (Aid to Families with Dependent Children). The homeless in their study had very little cash income; the (reported) median for single adults was $64 per month and $300 for homeless families.

Now that you have a picture of the plight of the homeless, let us turn back to economic analysis to gain some insight into the causes of homelessness. It is obvious that many of the homeless have severe personal problems that take the homelessness issue beyond economics, but it turns out that economic factors can explain a good deal of the variations in homelessness. Nearly all homeless people share one characteristic; at the time they are homeless they lack sufficient income to afford housing. More people will become homeless if the incomes of the poor decline and/or if the cost of housing rises. Both of these happened in the 1980s.

It is helpful to use a model of the rental housing market that is similar to the one introduced in Chapter 9. Figure 16.2 shows a market for low-quality rental housing with a vacancy rate. The demand for such housing is curve *DD*, and the supply in

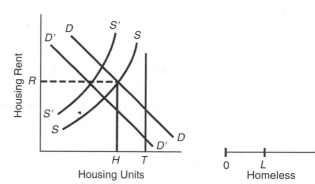

FIGURE 16.2 Market for housing and homelessness

the short run is *SS* (with a total stock of units *T*). Housing rent is set at *R*, the number of units occupied is *H*, and the number of vacant units is *T − H*. It is assumed that with rent at *R*, there are *L* households that are homeless, as shown on the right-hand diagram. The total number of low-income households is *H + L*. We have the seemingly anomalous situation of homeless people and vacant housing units at the same time.

Now let us consider alternative changes in the model that all tend to increase the number of homeless households.

1. Suppose that the cost of providing housing rises because of increases in utility rates or other costs. The short-run supply curve shifts up to *S′S′*, housing rent rises, the number of occupied units drops, and the number of homeless households increases.

2. Alternatively, suppose that the incomes of poor households decline, and this translates into a drop in the effective demand for housing units of low quality to *D′D′*. The housing rent will fall, but so will the number of occupied units. Homelessness increases.

3. A third case is relevant in many older cities. Suppose that the housing for low-income households is old and depreciating. Units are removed from the stock when they become no longer fit for habitation, so both the total number of units (*T*) declines and the short-run supply curve (*SS*) shifts to the left. Housing rents rise and homelessness increases. Housing units can also be removed by redevelopment, but according to the filtering model, the construction of new units (in excess of the growth of the number of households) should free up other units for use by lower-income households.

4. An even more sophisticated argument has been made by Apgar (1990). He argued that households in the lower-middle class are having greater difficulty becoming homeowners. Their incomes are not rising very much, if at all, and the cost of housing is rising. These trends mean that new houses are not being built and that households are failing to vacate rental housing. The filtering mechanism is not working. Low-income households are therefore caught in the squeeze caused by the high demand for rental units.

Some of the implications of this model were tested by Honig and Filer (1993) using the data on cities collected by U.S. Department of Housing and Urban Development (1984). As noted above, the rate of homelessness varied very widely across cities, so Honig and Filer looked for economic variables that can explain that variation. They found that the rate of homelessness was positively related to the housing rent for low-quality housing units and negatively related to the vacancy rate for units of that type. As you might have expected, they found that recent employment growth had a strong negative effect on homelessness. Economic growth helps again! Also, they found that homelessness was lower if AFDC payments per recipient were greater. Homelessness may not be entirely an economic problem, but economic variables clearly influenced the rate of homelessness in the expected ways. It appears that based on the results obtained by Honig and Filer (1993), homelessness can be treated to a considerable degree as if it were just an economic problem. Indeed, the two most powerful variables in their analysis were the housing rent level (for low-quality units) and employment growth.

E. URBAN CRIME

Compared to other economically advanced countries such as England, Japan, and Germany, crime in the United States is at shocking levels. In 1994 the homicide rate in the United States was 9.4 per 100,000 population, but the rates in European countries were 1.1 in England, 1.1 in France, 1.2 in Germany, 1.3 in Sweden, and 2.6 in Italy. The Federal Bureau of Investigation keeps track of serious crimes with victims that are reported to the local authorities in seven categories: murder, rape, aggravated assault, robbery, auto theft, larceny-theft, and burglary. Between 1960 and 1980 the reported amount of crime in the United States in these seven categories per capita *tripled* from 1867 crimes to 5950 crimes per year per 100,000 population. Most crime researchers think that this increase is exaggerated because, in earlier years, some police departments did not have adequate systems for recording crimes and reporting them to the FBI. Nevertheless, no one thinks that crime did not increase sharply between 1960 and 1980. Crime per capita has declined slightly since 1980, but a crime rate at this level means that, on average, everyone in the United States will be a victim of a serious crime every 17 years.

Facts About Crime in the United States

A more detailed picture of crime in the United States since 1960 is shown in Table 16.5. The murder rate doubled from 1960 to 1980 from 5.0 to 10.2 per 100,000, and the murder rates in the 1990s are over 9 per 100,000. The crime rate for rape increased by more than four times, although this increase probably reflects an increase in the reporting of rapes as well. The robbery rate also increased by more than four times, and the rate of aggravated assaults increased by more than five times. The rates of rape, robbery, and aggravated assault have increased nearly continuously since 1960. The rate of burglary more than tripled from 1960 to 1980, and since then it has declined by 35%. Larceny-theft tripled from 1960 to 1980 and has remained fairly constant since then. Auto theft almost tripled from 1960 to 1980, took a brief decline in the mid-1980s, and then increased in the 1990s.

Homicide is, of course, the most serious crime of all and the crime with the best data because nearly all homicides are reported. The homicide rate increased from a low point in 1960 to 5 per 100,000 to 10.2 per 100,000 in 1980. Since then the homi-

TABLE 16.5 Crime in the United States, 1960–1993 (Crimes per 100,000 Population)

Year	Murder	Rape	Robbery	Assault	Burglary	Larceny-Theft	Auto Theft
1960	5.0	9.5	59.9	85.1	502.1	1024	181.7
1965	5.1	12.0	71.2	109.8	653.2	1314	254.6
1970	7.8	18.5	171.4	163.0	1071.2	2079	453.7
1975	9.6	26.3	220.8	231.1	1532.1	2805	473.7
1980	10.2	36.8	251.1	298.5	1684.1	3167	502.2
1985	7.9	37.1	208.5	302.9	1287.3	2901	462.0
1990	9.4	41.2	257.0	424.1	1235.9	3195	657.8
1993	9.5	40.6	255.8	440.1	1099.2	3032	605.3

Source: U.S. Department of Justice, Federal Bureau of Investigation, *Crime in the United States*. Washington, DC: U.S. Government Printing Office, various issues.

cide rate has dropped slightly, but because the total population has increased, the total number of homicides in 1993 was about the same as in 1980: 24,530 in 1993 compared to 23,040 in 1980. About 54% of serious crime is larceny-theft, such as shoplifting, stealing from the auto, picking the pocket, larceny in business or consumer affairs, and so on. Larceny can be a very serious matter for the victim, but the other crimes are worse.

Some basic facts about murder are worth recounting. All of the following facts pertain to murders in 1993. First, murders are committed with firearms. In 1993, 69.6% of all murders (i.e., 16,200 murders) were committed with the use of a gun. Knives were used in 12.7%, blunt instruments in 4.4%, and personal physical force (e.g., hands, feet, pushing the victim) in 5.0%. Other means (including unknown means) accounted for 8.3% of all murders. For example, poison was used in 9 murders (0.04%). The means of choice for suicide victims is also often a firearm, by the way. In my opinion this huge number of murders committed with firearms is a national scandal that we strangely seem unable to address.

The victims of murder are predominantly male (77%) and black (51%). About 49% of all murder victims are males between the ages of 15 and 34; and 34% of all murder victims are black males between the ages of 15 and 34. The single demographic group with the highest murder rate is black males aged 20–24; their murder rate is 206 per 100,000, which is 22 times the overall average rate of 9.4 per 100,000. Murderers are also predominantly male and black. Of the offenders in 1993 for whom the sex is known, 91% are male. Only 1742 murders were known to have been committed by a female in that year. Among the offenders for whom sex and age are known, 62% are males between the ages of 15 and 29. Blacks make up 56% of murderers for whom the race is known, and black males between the ages of 15 and 29 are 41% of all murderers for whom sex, age, and race are known.

It is fair to say that many of the residents of large urban areas in the United States live in fear of crime. It is also true that the news media, especially local television stations, play up crime stories and probably make people more afraid than they otherwise would be. However, it may be that the effect of the news media can be overstated. A major topic of conversation among people who live in urban areas is the crime that they have experienced or seen themselves. As a piece of advice from this author, college students who live on their own in dormitories or student apartments should not assume that they are immune to crime. You should at least be taking the normal precautions of keeping doors and cars locked, not leaving things within easy reach of thieves, and being aware of your surroundings. You have almost certainly been told these things since you were a small child, but they bear repeating. Our society has changed. I grew up in the 1950s in an urban area of about 80,000 people, and crime was never a concern. As far as I can remember, we did not lock our door.

Crime rates are higher in major central cities compared to other places, especially the suburbs of those same central cities. Table 16.6 has been prepared as a comparison of crime rates in eight large central cities and their suburbs for 1993. There is no other way to say it; some of the comparisons are shocking. The first metropolitan area in the table is Atlanta. The murder rate in the central city of 50.4 per 100,000 population is 7.4 times the murder rate in the suburbs. The disparities between the central city and the suburbs of Atlanta are not as great for some of the other crimes; they are as follows:

Rape	3.9 times larger in central city
Robbery	7.2
Aggravated assault	10.1
Burglary	2.6
Larceny-theft	2.0
Auto theft	3.3

Note that the disparities are smaller in the nonviolent property crimes of burglary, larceny, and auto theft. This is a general pattern that exists in all of the other seven urban areas shown in Table 16.6.

Table 16.6 contains a great number of facts, and it is interesting to pick a few out. For some reason several crime rates are lower in Cincinnati, both central city and suburbs, than in the other urban areas. It would appear that Cincinnati should advertise its relative lack of crime. The largest disparity in the table between a central city and its suburbs is the murder rate in the Detroit metropolitan area. The murder rate of 56.8 per 100,000 in the city of Detroit is 17.8 times the murder rate in the suburbs. Indeed, the murder rate in the suburbs of Detroit of 3.2 per 100,000 is actually rather low. In contrast, the murder rate in the city of Los Angeles is only 2.0 times the murder rate in its suburbs. The disparities between central city and suburbs are generally smaller in the Los Angeles and Phoenix metropolitan areas than in the other six urban areas. Research is needed on these variations in central city–suburban crime rate differences. But the bottom line on Table 16.6 is that crime is not just a little higher in major central cities compared to their suburbs; crime is *much* higher.

Causes of the Increase in Crime

Criminologists have investigated the factors behind the jump in crime rates between 1960 and 1980. One big factor is the baby boom. The bulk of crimes is committed by young men, so the high birth rates of the late 1940s and 1950s meant a large increase in the number of crime-prone individuals in the 1960s and early 1970s. However,

TABLE 16.6   Crime Rates in Urban Areas, 1993 (Crimes per 100,000 Population)

City	Murder	Rape	Robbery	Assault	Burglary	Larceny-Theft	Auto Theft
Atlanta	12.2	42.4	369	500	1495	4280	896
Central city	50.4	122.1	1500	2367	3267	7754	2287
Suburbs	6.8	31.0	208	233	1242	3783	697
Baltimore	17.2	49.7	636	653	1387	3733	800
Central city	48.2	• 91.1	1688	1166	2442	5655	1449
Suburbs	4.1	32.1	189	425	938	2917	523
Cincinnati	3.8	53.5	202	314	870	3132	258
Central city	10.6	122.3	634	765	1677	4655	562
Suburbs	1.7	32.5	70	177	624	2669	165
Dallas	14.6	59.0	326	546	1416	4051	877
Central city	30.4	95.9	711	905	2011	5195	1674
Suburbs	5.4	36.5	91	327	1052	3353	391
Detroit	15.8	n.a.	400	564	1056	3310	1042
Central city	56.8	n.a.	1332	1274	2264	4198	2751
Suburbs	3.2	n.a.	113	346	684	3037	515
Los Angeles	21.3	40.3	722	899	1272	2717	1378
Central city	30.5	50.3	1090	1204	1425	3378	1695
Suburbs	15.4	34.1	491	708	1177	2301	1179
Philadelphia	12.0	31.0	327	292	765	2170	758
Central city	28.1	50.3	739	437	969	2517	1525
Suburbs	4.6	22.1	139	226	672	2013	407
Phoenix	9.6	36.8	205	555	1629	4307	1046
Central city	15.2	42.7	331	758	1984	4657	1498
Suburbs	5.2	32.3	109	400	1356	4040	691

Source: U.S. Department of Justice, Federal Bureau of Investigation, *Crime in the United States:* 1993. Washington, DC: U.S. Government Printing Office, 1995.

demographic changes cannot account for the entire increase in crime during this period. By one estimate [Chaiken and Chaiken (1983)], only 46% of the increase in the volume of arrests could be attributed to growth in the total population and changes in its age composition. However, empirical models that make use only of demographic data have been very successful in forecasting (if not explaining) crime rates.

One example of a crime forecasting model was estimated by Fox (1978). He was able to forecast various components of the FBI crime index very accurately using a model that contains only three variables:

1. Percentage of the population that is nonwhite and aged 14–17
2. Percentage of the population that is nonwhite and aged 18–21
3. The consumer price index

Fox's model presents a rather stark depiction of the role of young black males in the perpetration of crimes, at least the ones that are reported to the FBI. The good news in the short run is that the drop in the birth rate (from a peak of 3.8 children per woman in the late 1950s to a low of 1.8 children per woman in 1976) means that crime rates should tend to be lower into the 1990s.

If purely demographic changes can account for only a fraction of the increase in the crime rate that took place during the 1960s and 1970s, what other factors were involved? This is the issue upon which criminologists have focused their attention, and they have some pretty reasonable answers. Young men are most prone to commit crimes between the time they reach puberty and the time they assume adult roles and responsibilities. This period of time has been growing longer because the age of the onset of puberty has been falling, and because of the increase in schooling needed to function in the modern economy, the age of the assumption of adult responsibilities has been rising. However, this factor does not appear to explain the sudden increase in crime during the 1960s and 1970s. Another factor that surely is involved is the decline in proportion of children in two-parent families. This decline in the role of fathers translates into a decline in the control that families have over teenage males. The timing of the sharp increase in the number of one-parent families in the 1960s and 1970s corresponds to the increase in the crime rate. The increase in the degree to which poor blacks are segregated in central cities is implicated as well. The role of the breakdown of social control in urban underclass communities is reasonably clear. Urban street gangs of mainly black and Hispanic young men dominate some neighborhoods and perpetrate a great deal of crime.

The factors behind the increase in crime discussed so far are demographic and sociological in nature, so they fail to pinpoint the direct causes of crime. The fact is that most young men in crime-prone groups do not commit serious crimes, and it is grossly unfair to label an individual on the basis of membership in a demographic group. We know that crimes are committed by a small minority of the population and that a large number of violent crimes are committed by a small fraction of those who commit crimes. This group has been called *violent predators* by Chaiken and Chaiken (1983). They commit a very large number of robberies and assaults. Violent predators are different from other offenders. They began committing crimes at a young age and were likely to have committed both property crimes and crimes of violence frequently before they were age 18. They tend to be more socially unstable than other offenders; few are married and they have trouble holding jobs. But perhaps their most important characteristic is their drug use. In the 1960s and 1970s use of heroin was common among violent predators, and many of them combined heroin use with use of amphetamines, barbiturates, or alcohol. Violent predators also are often involved in drug dealing. In the 1980s and 1990s the use of cocaine became the largest drug problem. Offenders commit property crimes to pay for drugs, but it is also known that drug use can lead to the commission of violent crimes. In short, it appears that the increase in the number of violent predators, many of whom are multiple drug users, can account for the sudden and disproportionate increase in crime in the 1960s and 1970s *and* for the failure of crime rates to decline substantially in the 1980s and 1990s.

Is it possible to identify violent predators? Chaiken and Chaiken (1983) found that it is very difficult to identify them from their official records. Records of juvenile offenders are, by design or by accident, often not very informative. And because we need to identify violent predators at an early age, they usually do not have very extensive adult criminal records. The prospects for identifying and directing actions at the violent predators are not very good. It is true that violent predators cannot commit crimes when they are in jail, but the jailing of many more juvenile offenders may increase the criminality of those who are not violent predators.

Economics and Crime

What does economics have to say about crime? The foregoing list of serious crimes includes four—robbery, auto theft, larceny, and burglary—that are economic crimes. Indeed, these four crimes make up 92% of all serious crimes. Most criminals, even the violent predators, are in the business of committing crimes for monetary gain. It is useful to think of criminals who commit crimes for economic reasons to be governed by economic incentives; the criminal commits a crime if his evaluation of the potential gain exceeds his evaluation of the loss that he may incur. By the way, the use of the male gender in the previous sentence is realistic; most crimes (not just murders) are committed by males. The gain to the criminal is the value of the loot that is acquired, of course. The loss to the criminal is the jail sentence and possible fine that will be imposed if he is caught and convicted of breaking the law. The possible loss really consists of two parts: the probability that the criminal will be caught and have a penalty imposed, and the size of that penalty. Numerous studies by economists have shown that criminals respond to both of these components, and some studies [e.g., Witte (1980)] showed that increasing the probability of punishment (rather than increasing the size of the punishment) has the larger effect on the crime rate. This last finding means that the difficult and expensive work of apprehending and convicting criminals has a larger effect than does an increase in prison sentences. However, both of these policies are costly because prisons are expensive to build and to run.

The probability that an offender will actually suffer punishment depends on the probability of arrest, the probability of conviction given that he is arrested, and the probability of punishment given that he is convicted. The probability of arrest for a *single* nonviolent offense is known to be quite low, although offenders who commit many crimes eventually will be caught. According to the Federal Bureau of Investigation, the fractions of crimes (percents) cleared by arrests in 1993 are as follows:

Murder	66
Rape	53
Aggravated assault	56
Robbery	24
Burglary	13
Larceny-theft	20
Auto theft	14

These figures pertain to offenses that have been "cleared" by the police by the arrest of an offender. The arrest of a single offender may "clear" several crimes that are on the books because the offender can be identified as the perpetrator of all of those crimes. Suppose that the probability of arrest for a single burglary is 0.05, but the offender committed five burglaries. The probability that he is *not* caught is $0.95 \times 0.95 \times 0.95 \times 0.95 \times 0.95 = 0.77$, so the probability that he is caught is $1 - 0.77 = 0.23$. A burglar who commits 20 burglaries has a $1 - 0.36 = 0.64$ probability of being caught, for example.

Forst (1983) conducted a detailed study of the dispositions of arrests for felonies. He found that of 100 felonies, 35 were sent to the juvenile justice system.

Of the remaining 65, 40 were accepted for prosecution. The 25 who were not prosecuted either were innocent or were guilty but could not be prosecuted for lack of evidence. Of the 40 who were prosecuted, 32 were convicted and 20 of these served
time in jail. Therefore, Forst's (1983) estimate is that if you are arrested for a felony
and are considered to be an adult by the criminal justice system, you have a 0.49
probability of being convicted and a 0.31 probability of serving time in jail. Punishment in the United States is neither swift nor sure.

Potential victims of economic crime can also be thought of as responding to
economic incentives. People protect their homes with better locks, security alarm
systems, and other devices. They also buy guns. To protect their cars they buy alarms
and a well-known device that attaches to the steering wheel. People protect themselves when they are away from home largely by reducing their exposure to dangerous situations. These are rational responses to crime. It is also clear that crime has an
effect on real estate markets, especially the residential market. Thaler (1978) found
that crime rates have a negative effect on residential property values, and Mills
(1992) found that crime in the central city increased the rate at which people moved
to the suburbs.

The question of economic efficiency and crime was raised by Becker (1968) in
a classic article. Becker's point is that as long as crime has a marginal benefit for
criminals that declines with the amount of crime committed, it is not worthwhile to
prevent all crime through expenditures on police, courts, and prisons. If the crime
rate is driven down to very low levels, there still are criminals out there who find that
the benefits of crime exceed the cost to them. The cost of preventing crime at the
margin is, at some point, greater than the cost of the crime to the victim. Figure 16.3
shows this last point graphically. The marginal cost of crime prevention is a declining
function of the crime rate; the greater the number of crimes, the lower is the cost of

FIGURE 16.3 Optimum crime rate

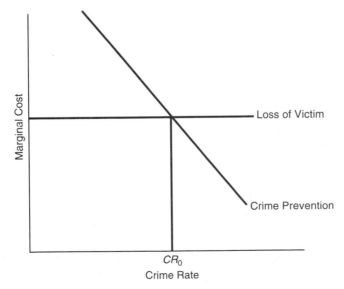

CR_0
Crime Rate

reducing the crime rate. This marginal cost of crime prevention is so labeled on Figure 16.3. The marginal cost of crime to the victim is assumed to be a constant amount in the figure, and the optimum amount of crime is crime rate CR_0. Note that the optimum crime rate rises if the marginal cost to the victim falls or if the marginal cost of prevention rises.

The analysis in Figure 16.3 presents the basic idea of an optimum crime rate, but it fails to depict the interaction between criminals and potential victims. Balkin and McDonald (1981) have devised a model of street crime that captures the idea of criminal–victim interaction. *Street crime* is crime that takes place outside the home (or workplace) and involves a direct confrontation of criminal and victim. Street crime can include murder and rape, but most often it is robbery or assault. Balkin and McDonald suppose that street crime is important enough to make ordinary citizens alter their behavior. They assume that people have two types of activities; one type of activity exposes them to street crime, and the other type of activity does not. The amount of time that one is exposed to street crime might be the amount of time spent outside after dark plus the amount of time that is spent during the daytime in areas where street crime can occur. It is assumed that the demand per day for activities that expose one to street crime is inversely related to the risk of being a victim. Here the correct measure of risk (i.e., the "price" of this activity) is the probability of becoming a victim of street crime *per unit of time exposed* to crime. The demand for the activity that exposes potential victims to street crime is depicted in Figure 16.4 as curve *DD*.

Now consider the perpetrators of street crime. They spend part of their time outside looking for potential victims. We shall take the probability of apprehension and conviction and the prison sentence as given for the moment. If there are very few potential victims who expose themselves to street crime, it will take a long time for a street criminal to find a victim. The criminal will have a low probability of finding a victim in a given amount of search time. On the other hand, if there are many potential victims out there, the criminals will be able to find more victims per unit of time spent searching. It is hypothesized that there is a function that relates the amount of time that street criminals are out there searching for victims and committing crimes to the rate at which victims can be found per hour spent. This is, in effect, the "wage rate" for the criminals. Suppose that this supply curve of criminal effort shows that the crime wage rate and the supply of time to criminal activities are positively related.

It was suggested that the probability of finding a victim is positively related to the amount of time that potential victims spent exposed to street crime. Therefore, the horizontal axis of Figure 16.4 is labeled "exposure time of potential victims" *and* "probability of finding a victim per unit of search time for criminals." An amount of exposure time by potential victims translates directly into a success rate for criminals. These two variables are measured in different units, but those two different units of measurement can both be displayed on the horizontal axis. Now consider the vertical axis of Figure 16.4, which is labeled "probability of victimization per unit of exposure time." This probability of victimization is determined directly by the amount of time that criminals devote to searching for victims and committing crimes. Both of these variables can be displayed on the vertical axis. Once again, the two variables are measured in different units, but a given amount of time supplied by criminals for criminal activity translates into a victimization rate. The two axes can therefore carry labels that correspond to the variables in the function that depicts the

FIGURE 16.4 Market for street crime

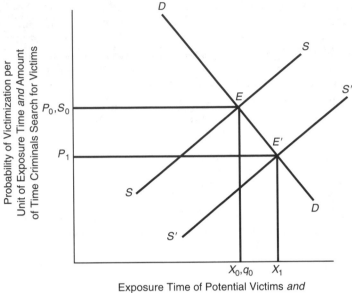

Exposure Time of Potential Victims *and*
Probability of Finding a Victim per
Unit of Search Time

supply of criminal effort: the probability of finding a victim, and the amount of time devoted to searching for victims and committing crimes. The supply of criminal effort is shown in Figure 16.4 as curve *SS*.

The equilibrium in this market for street crime is where the two functions intersect at point *E*. At this point the behavior of potential victims is consistent with the behavior of criminals. The equilibrium amount of time exposed to crime is X_0 and the probability of victimization per unit of time exposed to crime is p_0. Note that the actual crime rate for the time period (e.g., one day) in question is p_0 times X_0. Criminals spend amount of time S_0 in criminal activity, and they have a "success rate" of q_0 per unit of time spent "working" as street criminals.

Crime control policies can enter the model by altering criminal behavior. Suppose that more police officers are put on the streets so that the probability of apprehension and conviction rises. This change means that at any level of success rate for criminals (on the horizontal axis in Figure 16.4), the supply of time to criminal activities will fall. This drop in the supply of criminal "labor" is shown as curve $S'S'$. The decline in the amount of time devoted to criminal activity results in a new equilibrium point at E'; the citizens have increased the amount of time they are exposed to crime because the probability of victimization per unit of exposure time has dropped. However, the actual crime rate can rise or fall. Recall that the actual crime rate (per day) was p_0 times X_0. Now the actual crime rate is p_1 times X_1, which can be greater than, equal to, or less than the old crime rate.

What does this last result mean? It says that making an area safer (in terms of the probability of victimization per unit of time exposed to crime) may bring a lot of people out and exposed to crime so that the actual number of crimes rises. The story is analogous to the case of air travel. In the early days of air travel the accident rate per passenger mile was high, and few people chose to fly. Air travel was made much safer, a lot more people decided to fly, and more people (let us suppose) were involved in accidents. There are certain very dangerous places in urban areas where few crimes take place because hardly anyone is foolish enough to go there. This model has important implications for the allocation of crime prevention resources. If the objective is to reduce crime, the crime prevention resources should be allocated to the places with the highest actual crime rates. On the other hand, this policy would tend to ignore places that have relatively low crime but are extremely dangerous. In such places the residents are trapped inside their homes by the real fear of crime. A policy of allocating police resources to these areas will make the residents better off by permitting them to take back their streets, but there may or may not be actual reductions in crime.

In this section we have presented a brief introduction to the economic analysis of urban crime. Crime is perhaps the most pressing of urban problems, and it should be clear that economic analysis can make a contribution to the understanding of the motivations of criminals and potential victims. Economic analysis also provides some guidance for policy in that the economic motivations of criminals must not be ignored. The research shows clearly that criminals respond to punishment that is swifter and surer. However, it is far less clear that criminals can be induced away from a life of crime by positive economic incentives.

A good deal of research has examined the possible link between unemployment and crime. Freeman (1983) reviewed the studies up to the early 1980s and found that there is a relationship between higher unemployment and/or lower labor force participation and increases in crime. However, the link between the labor market and crime is far from sufficient to explain the rise in crime that took place during the 1960s and 1970s or the variations in crime rates from place to place. There are many reasons for us to pursue a policy of low unemployment rates and to provide improved economic opportunities for potential criminals (and everyone else) in general. One outcome of such a policy may be to reduce crime somewhat, but it is also clear that crime is a more complex social issue about which economists probably have little to say at this time. For example, a social experiment called the Supported Work Experiment [Manpower Demonstration Research Corp. (1981)] provided ex-offenders with subsidized employment and social service support. This effort had no significant effect on subsequent crime (recidivism) or on the ability of the participant to get a job in the long run compared to a control group. The reasons for this failure surely involve a complicated set of economic, social, and psychological factors. At this time we do not know how to prevent the creation of violent predators, and we do not know how to turn violent predators into productive citizens.

F. CENTRAL CITY FISCAL PROBLEMS

In a narrow sense a city's fiscal "problem" is that expenditures exceed revenues by an amount that is large enough to make people think that a city is not a good credit risk. City officials wake up one morning and discover that the lenders are no longer willing to bail them out with short-term loans to cover the deficit. What do they do then?

They can declare bankruptcy and refuse to honor their debt obligations. This strategy is not a good idea because it is likely that the city's ability to borrow will be negatively affected for many years. The better idea is to put in place a plan that includes a package of expenditure reductions, tax increases and other revenue "enhancements," and restructuring of debt. The idea of restructuring debts is to lengthen the repayment period so that current payments are reduced.

The city of New York was pushed to the brink of bankruptcy in 1975. However, we now know that New York was a special case that is not indicative of problems faced by other central cities. New York was (and is) required by the state of New York to pay 23% of the expenditures on welfare and medicaid for city residents. Most cities pay none of these expenditures—the federal government pays half and the state pays half. Also on the expenditure side, New York City offered an extensive set of city services (including its own complete university system with very low tuition) and had powerful public-employee unions that had succeeded in increasing wage rates in the public sector. On the revenue side, the city was by state law not permitted to increase its real estate tax rate. The city was progressively getting into trouble in the early 1970s by borrowing large sums of money to cover current expenses, a policy that technically was illegal. The city also had a substantial amount of unfunded pension liability from the retirement pensions that had been promised to public employees. The house of cards came tumbling down in the recession of 1975, a time when federal aid to the city was also being cut. The banks refused to lend any more money to New York City. To resolve the crisis the state and federal governments stepped in to guarantee New York's bonds, and the federal government granted loans to New York in exchange for a program of austerity. In short, New York was trying to do too much and was guilty of shaky fiscal practices.

Now let us turn to the tragic case of East St. Louis, Illinois. East St. Louis is the old central city on the Illinois side of the Mississippi River across from St. Louis, Missouri. It is a very small city (population 45,000 in 1990) that has a population that is largely black. It is surrounded by suburban municipalities, so it has no ability to annex territory. The city once had a sizable economic base that included a major stockyards and meatpacking industry. That economic base is completely gone. The downtown office buildings are across the river in Missouri. In short, East St. Louis is a city that consists entirely of badly depressed inner-city areas. The tax base of East St. Louis is insufficient to pay for anything remotely like decent urban public services: schools, police and fire, public health, and so on. The city is in fact a ward of the state of Illinois. In effect, the state is operating the government of the city. East St. Louis is the living, barely breathing worst-case scenario. In recent years the city was sued by a citizen who charged that brutality had been committed by the police force. The citizen won his case and was awarded a substantial amount in damages which the city was unable to pay. The citizen was given title to city hall by the court until such time as other financial arrangements could be made. East St. Louis is obviously another special case.

Do central cities in general have fiscal problems? Some researchers, such as Clark (1985), point out that in the narrow sense, they really do not. A central city government can live within its means by carefully balancing the various demands on the budget with its revenue sources. The city can also take steps to try to strengthen the local economy as discussed in Chapter 14, although the payoff to these activities will take years to materialize. It is evident that since the New York fiscal crisis of 1975 (and other fiscal crises experienced in Cleveland and a few other cites at about the same time), central cities have learned how to avoid fiscal crises, narrowly defined.

Central cities are avoiding fiscal crises, but Ladd and Yinger (1989) argued that what they are not doing is providing a standard package of public services at a standard local tax rate. Ladd and Yinger constructed an index of fiscal health for central cities that is based upon the assumption that a city offers a standard array of public services with a tax package that amounts to a tax of 3% on local income. The cost of the standard array of public services was determined by local conditions. The index measures how far the city falls short of this fiscal package as a percentage of the implied budget. The index for 1988 was −83% in New York City, −38% in Los Angeles, −45% in Chicago, −35% in Philadelphia, and −64% in Detroit. The central city must make up for this implied deficit by aid from the state (and to a far lesser extent, the federal government), higher taxes, and/or lower spending on services. The cities in fact do make up for this shortage of funds using some combination of these strategies. The Ladd–Yinger index provides an interesting measure of the stress that city officials are under. They are under heavy pressure to find more revenue from state and federal sources. They constantly hear complaints about local taxes and fees from their constituents, and they are also forever being told that the public services, especially the schools, are inadequate.

What are the sources of the fiscal stress that has been documented by Ladd and Yinger (1989)? By now you should be able to answer this question. Your answer will probably include the following:

1. Loss of commercial and industrial tax base,
2. Retention of low-income population with heavy demands for public services such as education, health care, and housing,
3. High crime rates, which require more police and criminal justice facilities,
4. Aging infrastructure, which requires expensive maintenance and rehabilitation,
5. Population loss, which means that fixed costs must be spread over a smaller population and tax base,
6. Old buildings, which create more fire hazards and demolition expenses,
7. Inability to annex new territory.

By the way, the loss of middle-class taxpayers to the suburbs may not have a strong negative effect on the fiscal situation of the central city. Middle-class households pay taxes, but they also demand public services. Indeed, the rule of thumb is that middle-class households and the houses that they own cost more in public services than they pay in taxes, largely because they send children to school. The trick is to get middle-class households that do not place demands on the public school system to live in the city.

What are the policy alternatives to address the problem of fiscal stress on central cities? One alternative is to permit the central city to annex territory or somehow to have access to the tax base of the urban area. As Norton (1979) showed, some central cities in the sunbelt, such as Houston, Nashville, Jacksonville, and Phoenix, have been able to annex large amounts of territory. For example, under Texas law, Houston has extraterritorial rights over areas within 5 miles of its city limits. In this area new municipalities cannot be created and existing municipalities cannot annex territory without the approval of Houston. Houston has taken advantage of this system to prevent the creation of separate suburban municipalities. In a few other cases, most notably in Minneapolis–St. Paul, the urban area has a metropolitan governmental structure that requires the sharing of some of the tax base. A third option is to have state governments provide more support for the central cities. But what if none of these options can be made to work? Political power in many urban areas has shifted to the suburbs away from the central city. Suburbanites often have little enthusiasm for being taxed to provide better services for the central city. There are many central cities that find themselves in this position, and it means that they must daily fight the budget battles. One typical outcome is that expenditures per pupil in the public schools are generally lower in the central city than in suburban areas (with the exception of some poor suburbs).

G. SUMMARY

In this chapter we have provided a brief tour through some of the most pressing economic and social problems in urban areas. There are other problems that could have been included, such as youth gangs, drugs, guns, low school achievement, pollution, welfare policy, and so on. The choices of poverty and the underclass, housing–jobs mismatch, homelessness, crime, and central city fiscal problems were selected because of their close connection to the type of economic analysis developed in this book. Nevertheless, I am convinced that economic analysis also makes a contribution to the understanding of many other urban problems.

Your task, should you choose to accept it, is to go forward and use economics to improve our understanding of urban areas and their economic and social problems. Urban economic analysis can be used to serve those who seek to make money in urban real estate and in other lines of business. Urban economic analysis also can be used to serve those who attempt to govern urban areas more efficiently and equitably, and those who would hope that the conditions of the urban poor can be improved. Your training in economics tells you that each of these uses of economic analysis will be a part of an agglomeration of knowledge that is more than the sum of its parts.

EXERCISES

1. Look up the urban area of your choice in the study of homelessness by Honig and Filer (1993). Be sure to select an urban area that is in their study. How many homeless people are reported? This study also identified two other serious housing problems for a large number of urban areas. What are these problems, and what are their magnitudes for the urban area of your choice?

2. Look up the city of your choice in the FBI Uniform Crime Reports data in *Crime in the United States*. What has happened to crime rates in recent years? Has crime declined since 1980? Have some categories of crime increased in recent years?

3. Look up the central city of your choice in the study by Ladd and Yinger (1989).

What is value of their index of fiscal health for this central city? Why is it low (or high)? What does this finding imply for taxes and quality of public services in this case?

REFERENCES

Apgar, William, Jr., 1990. "The Nation's Housing: A Review of Past Trends and Future Prospects for Housing in America," in D. DiPasquale and L. Keyes, eds., *Building Foundations: Housing and Federal Policy*. Philadelphia: University of Pennsylvania Press.

Balkin, Steven and J. McDonald, 1981. "The Market for Street Crime: An Economic Analysis of Victim–Offender Interaction," *Journal of Urban Economics*, Vol. 10, pp. 390–405.

Bartik, Timothy, 1991. *Who Benefits from State and Local Economic Development Policies?* Kalamazoo, MI: W.E. Upjohn Institute.

Becker, Gary, 1968. "Crime and Punishment: An Economic Approach," *Journal of Political Economy*, Vol. 76, pp. 169–217.

Blank, Rebecca and A. Blinder, 1986. "Macroeconomics, Income Distribution, and Poverty," in S. Danziger and D. Weinberg, eds., *Fighting Poverty: What Works and What Doesn't*. Cambridge, MA: Harvard University Press.

Burt, Martha and Barbara Cohen, 1989. *American Homeless: Numbers, Characteristics, and the Programs That Serve Them*. Washington, DC: The Urban Institute Press.

Chaiken, Jan and Marcia Chaiken, 1983. "Crime Rates and the Active Criminal," in J. Wilson, ed., *Crime and Public Policy*. San Francisco: ICS Press.

Clark, Terry, 1985. "Fiscal Strain: How Different Are Snow Belt and Sun Belt Cities?" in P. Peterson, ed., *The New Urban Reality*. Washington, DC: The Brookings Institution.

Ellwood, David, 1986. "The Spatial Mismatch Hypothesis: Are There Teenage Jobs Missing in the Ghetto?" in R. Freeman and H. Holzer, eds., *The Black Youth Employment Crisis*. Chicago: The University of Chicago Press.

———, 1988. *Poor Support*. New York: Basic Books.

Forst, Brian, 1983. "Prosecution and Sentencing," in J. Wilson, ed., *Crime and Public Policy*. San Francisco: ICS Press.

Fox, James, 1978. *Forecasting Crime*, Lexington, MA.: Lexington Books.

Freeman, Richard, 1983. "Crime and Unemployment," in J. Wilson, ed., *Crime and Public Policy*. San Francisco: ICS Press.

———, 1991. "Employment and Earnings of Disadvantaged Young Men in a Labor Shortage Economy," in C. Jencks and P. Peterson, eds., *The Urban Underclass*. Washington, DC: The Brookings Institution.

Fremon, Charlotte, 1970. *The Occupational Patterns of Urban Employment Change*. Washington, DC: The Urban Institute.

Friedlander, Stanley, 1972. *Unemployment in the Urban Core*. New York: Praeger.

Hammer, Thomas, 1992. "Economic Determinants of Underclass Behavior," in E. Mills and J. McDonald, eds., *Sources of Metropolitan Growth*. New Brunswick, NJ: Rutgers University Press.

Heckman, James, 1994. "Is Job Training Oversold?" *The Public Interest*, No. 115, pp. 91–115.

Herrnstein, Richard and Charles Murray, 1994. *The Bell Curve: Intelligence and Class Structure in American Life*. New York: Free Press.

Honig, Marjorie and R. Filer, 1993. "Causes of Intercity Variations in Homelessness," *American Economic Review*, Vol. 83, pp. 248–255.

Ihlanfeldt, Keith, 1992. *Job Accessibility and the Employment and School Enrollment of Teenagers*. Kalamazoo, MI: W.E. Upjohn Institute.

Ihlanfeldt, Keith and D. Sjoquist, 1990. "Job Accessibility and Racial Differences in Youth Employment Rates," *American Economic Review*, Vol. 80, pp. 267–276.

———, 1991. "The Effect of Job Access on Black and White Youth Employment," *Urban Studies*, Vol. 28, pp. 255–265.

Jargowsky, Paul, 1994. "Ghetto Poverty among Blacks in the 1990s," *Journal of Policy Analysis and Management*, Vol. 13, pp. 288–310.

Jencks, Christopher, 1992. *Rethinking Social Policy: Race, Poverty and the Underclass*. Cambridge, MA: Harvard University Press.

Kain, John, 1968. "Housing Segregation, Negro Employment, and Metropolitan Decentralization," *Quarterly Journal of Economics*, Vol. 82, pp. 175–197.

———, 1974. "Housing Segregation, Black Employment, and Metropolitan Decentralization: A Retrospective View," in G. von Furstenberg, ed., *Patterns of Racial Discrimination*, Lexington, MA: D.C. Heath.

Ladd, Helen and J. Yinger, 1989. *America's Ailing Cities: Fiscal Health and the Design of Urban Policy*. Baltimore: Johns Hopkins University Press.

Leonard, Jonathon, 1987. "The Interaction of Residential Segregation and Employment Discrimination," *Journal of Urban Economics*, Vol. 21, pp. 323–346.

Lewis, W., 1969. *Urban Growth and Suburbanization of Employment*, Washington, DC: The Brookings Institution.

Manpower Demonstration Research Corp., 1981. *Final Report of the National Supported Work Demonstration*. New York: MDRC.

Masters, Stanley, 1974. "A Note on John Kain's Housing Segregation, Negro Employment, and Metropolitan Decentralization," *Quarterly Journal of Economics*, Vol. 88, pp. 505–519.

———, 1975. *Black–White Income Differentials: Empirical Studies and Policy Implications*. New York: Academic Press.

McMillen, Daniel, 1993. "Can Blacks Earn More in the Suburbs? Racial Differences in Intra-metropolitan Earnings Variation," *Journal of Urban Economics*, Vol. 33, pp. 135–150.

Meyer, John, J. Kain, and M. Wohl, 1965. *The Urban Transportation Problem*, Cambridge, MA: Harvard University Press.

Mills, Edwin, 1992. "The Measurement and Determinants of Suburbanization," *Journal of Urban Economics*, Vol. 32, pp. 377–387.

Moffitt, Robert, 1977. "Metropolitan Decentralization and City–Suburb Wage Differentials," *International Regional Science Review*, Vol. 2, pp. 103–111.

———, 1992. "Incentive Effects of the U.S. Welfare System: A Review," *Journal of Economic Literature*, Vol. 30, pp. 1–61.

Mooney, Joseph, 1969. "Housing Segregation, Negro Employment, and Metropolitan Decentralization: An Alternative Perspective," *Quarterly Journal of Economics*, Vol. 83, pp. 299–311.

Noll, Roger, 1970. "Metropolitan Employment and Population Distribution and the Conditions of the Urban Poor," in J. Crecine, ed., *Financing the Metropolis*. Beverly Hills, CA: Sage Publications.

Norton, R. D., 1979. *City Life-Cycles and American Urban Policy*. New York: Academic Press.

Offner, Paul and D. Saks, 1971. "A Note on John Kain's Housing Segregation, Negro Employment, and Metropolitan Decentralization," *Quarterly Journal of Economics*, Vol. 85, pp. 147–160.

Price, Richard and E. Mills, 1985. "Race and Residence in Earnings Determination," *Journal of Urban Economics*, Vol. 17, pp. 1–18.

Rosenbaum, James, 1993. "Closing the Gap: Does Residential Integration Improve the Employment and Education of Low-Income Blacks?" in L. Joseph, ed., *Affordable Housing and Public Policy*. Champaign, IL: University of Illinois Press.

Thaler, Richard, 1978. "A Note on the Value of Crime Control: Evidence from the Property Market," *Journal of Urban Economics*, Vol. 5, pp. 137–145.

U.S. Bureau of the Census, 1995. *Income, Poverty and the Value of Noncash Benefits: 1993*. Current Population Reports, Series P60-188. Washington, DC: U.S. Government Printing Office.

U.S. Department of Housing and Urban Development, 1984. *A Report to the Secretary on the Homeless and Emergency Shelters*. Washington, DC: Office of Policy Development and Research, HUD.

U.S. House of Representatives, Committee on Ways and Means, 1993. *Overview of Entitlement Programs: 1993 Green Book*. Washington, DC: U.S. Government Printing Office.

Wilson, Franklin, 1979. *Residential Consumption, Economic Opportunity, and Race*. New York: Academic Press.

Wilson, William, 1978. *The Declining Significance of Race*. Chicago: The University of Chicago Press.

———, 1987. *The Truly Disadvantaged: The Inner City, the Underclass, and Public Policy*. Chicago: The University of Chicago Press.

Witte, Ann, 1980. "Estimating the Economics of Crime with Individual Data," *Quarterly Journal of Economics*, Vol. 94, pp. 57–84.

Appendix: Review of Some Mathematics and Microeconomic Theory

Some fundamental results in microeconomic theory and mathematics are used repeatedly in this book, so this appendix provides a discussion of all the results that you will need to read the book. All of the concepts will be familiar to one who has studied intermediate microeconomics and one term of calculus. Some of the material will be new to those of you who have not taken these two courses — you will need to study this appendix carefully. Students who are taking the slightly abbreviated course described in the Preface can omit Section G.

A. SOME BASIC MATHEMATICS OF FUNCTIONS

Basic concepts in mathematics are presented first. Economics always makes use of functions, an example of which is

$$Q = f(K,L).$$

This equation says that the quantity of output (Q) is a function (f) of the quantities of inputs capital (K) and labor (L). A function means that for a given combination of K and L, there is only *one* value of Q. An example of a linear function is

$$Q = 5K + 7L.$$

If $K = 1$ and $L = 5$, $Q = 40$. An example of a quadratic function is

$$Q = K^2 + 5L.$$

Another example of a function is

$$Q = 4KL.$$

Often in economics, one is interested in finding out how much the variable on the left-hand side of a function changes when a variable on the right-hand side of the function changes. Throughout the book the symbol δ denotes "change in." From the linear function above which says that $Q = 5K + 7L$, we know that Q changes by 5 when K changes by 1, or

$$\frac{\delta Q}{\delta K} = 5.$$

Similarly, if $Q = 4KL$, the change in Q when K increases by 1 can be written

$$\frac{\delta Q}{\delta K} = 4L.$$

■ **508** ■

What about the change in Q as K increases in the function $Q = K^2 + 5L$? This question is a bit more complicated, but a simple rule can be found. A helpful way to write this equation is

$$Q = K(K) + 5L.$$

If K increases, both of the K's increase, which means that

$$\delta Q = K\delta K + (\delta K)K,$$

or

$$\delta Q = 2K\,\delta K$$

and

$$\frac{\delta Q}{\delta K} = 2K.$$

Notice that K is multiplied by its original exponent, 2, and the exponent on K is now 1. This is an example of the exponent rule for finding derivatives in calculus. The more general rule is: If $Q = K^b$, then

$$\frac{\delta Q}{\delta K} = bK^{b-1}.$$

This result can be demonstrated if we write

$$Q = K \times K \times K \times \cdot \cdot \cdot \times K \qquad (b \text{ times}),$$

so that

$$\delta Q = \delta K(K^{b-1}) + \delta K(K^{b-1}) \cdot \cdot \cdot + \delta K(K^{b-1}) \qquad (b \text{ times}).$$

Therefore

$$\frac{\delta Q}{\delta K} = bK^{b-1}.$$

Often, we wish to know how Q changes if both K and L change. The linear form $Q = 5K + 7L$ yields the simple result that

$$\delta Q = 5\delta Q + 7\delta L.$$

The change in Q in the multiplicative form $Q = 4KL$ can be found by varying K and L separately and adding the two changes together, or

$$\delta Q = 4L(\delta K) + 4K(\delta L).$$

One final mathematical concept is needed. This idea, known as the *chain rule*, applies when K on the right-hand side of a function for Q is itself a function of some other variable X [i.e.

$$Q = f(K),$$

and

$$K = g(X),$$

where g indicates a different function with K as a function of X]. The basic result of the chain rule is that

$$\frac{\delta Q}{\delta X} = \frac{\delta Q}{\delta K}\left(\frac{\delta K}{\delta X}\right).$$

Suppose that $Q = 6 + 5K$ and $K = 2X$. We have

$$\frac{\delta Q}{\delta K} = 5,$$

$$\frac{\delta K}{\delta X} = 2,$$

and

$$\frac{\delta Q}{\delta X} = 10$$

by the chain rule. This result can also be obtained by substituting for $2X$ for K in $Q = 6 + 5K$, which yields $Q = 6 + 10X$. Obviously, $\delta Q = 10\delta X$.

B. PRODUCTION THEORY

These mathematical concepts can be used to demonstrate some of the basic results in microeconomic theory. Begin with the production function

$$Q = f(K,L).$$

The change in output when one of the inputs is changed (holding the other constant) is called the *marginal product* (MP) of that input, which can be written

$$MP_K = \frac{\delta Q}{\delta K}$$

and

$$MP_L = \frac{\delta Q}{\delta L}.$$

Here it shall be assumed that the marginal product on an input declines as more of the input is used; this is the *law of diminishing (marginal) returns*. Figure A.1 shows a marginal product curve for labor. Note that the curve is drawn so that at some point, the marginal product of the input falls to zero and then becomes negative. The idea is that, holding other inputs constant, adding more of the worker will eventually create a situation in which one more worker hampers the ability of the other workers to produce output.

Given the production function, we can also define the average product of an input, or

$$AP_K = \frac{Q}{K}$$

FIGURE A.1 Average and marginal product

and

$$AP_L = \frac{Q}{L}.$$

An average product curve for labor is also shown in Figure A.1. The average product is rising if the marginal product exceeds the average product, and the average product is falling if the marginal product is less than the average product. If average product equals marginal product, the average product is not changing. This is what I like to call the *old average–marginal relationship*, a concept that you learned in the basic microeconomics course.

The change in output if both inputs change is

$$\delta Q = MP_K(\delta K) + MP_L(\delta L).$$

If K and L change so as to leave output the same,

$$\delta Q = 0 = MP_K(\delta K) + MP_L(\delta L).$$

This equation defines an isoquant, the curve that shows the various combinations of inputs that produce the same output level. Figure A.2 shows a set of isoquants. The *slope* of the isoquant can be found by solving the equation for the trade-off between K and L, which is

$$\frac{\delta K}{\delta L} = \frac{-MP_L}{MP_K}.$$

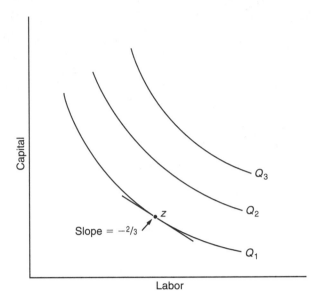

FIGURE A.2 Isoquant map

This is the familiar result that the slope of the isoquant is the ratio marginal products times -1. See the isoquants in Figure A.2. The slope gives the trade-off between capital and labor that holds output constant. For example, suppose that $MP_K = 3$ and $MP_L = 2$ at point z in Figure A.2. If you increase the labor input by 1 unit, how much capital can you subtract and keep output constant? Increasing the labor input by one unit increases output by 2 units, so you can subtract $\frac{2}{3}$ unit of capital and hold output constant. The figure $\frac{2}{3}$ is just

$$\frac{MP_L}{MP_K} = \frac{2}{3}.$$

C. THEORY OF THE FIRM

Suppose that the firm with the production function wishes to maximize profits (π). The firm faces a demand curve and must pay for the two inputs. The quantity demanded (Q) is a function of the price that is charged, or

$$Q = g(P).$$

For example, suppose that

$$Q = 100 - 2P.$$

This demand curve is shown in Figure A.3.

Profits equal total revenue minus total costs. Total revenue (TR) is the price of output times the quantity sold, and total costs (TC) are the sum of the expenditures on each input, or

$$\pi = TR - TC = PQ - TC = PQ - rK - wL,$$

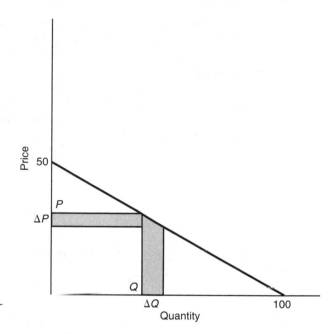

FIGURE A.3 Demand function

where *r* and *w* are the prices that the firm must pay for the use of capital and labor. The firm must decide how much output to produce, so we wish to know how profits change as output is increased. The profit-maximizing level of output occurs where the additional profit generated by producing 1 more unit of output has dropped to zero. One result needed is that

$$\delta\pi = \left(\frac{\delta TR}{\delta Q}\right)\delta Q - \left(\frac{\delta TC}{\delta Q}\right)\delta Q = 0.$$

The change in total revenue when output changes is called *marginal revenue (MR)*, and the change in total cost when output changes is called *marginal cost (MC)*. Therefore,

$$\delta\pi = 0 = MR\,\delta Q - MC\,\delta Q,$$

and the change in profits $(\delta\pi/\delta Q)$ drops to zero where

$$MR = MC.$$

This is the familiar condition for maximizing profits that you learned in the basic microeconomics course. The result is normative; it says that to achieve the goal of maximizing profits, the firm *should* produce where marginal revenue equals marginal cost. In more general terms, the firm sets output where the marginal benefit of output (the marginal revenue) equals the marginal cost.

Take a closer look at marginal revenue. Recall that total revenue is *PQ*, which means that the change in total revenue consists of two parts; that is,

$$\delta TR = Q\,\delta P + P\,\delta Q.$$

These two components are depicted in Figure A.3. As Q is increased we see that $P \, \delta Q$ is a positive number and $Q \, \delta P$ is a negative number (because P must be reduced so that more output can be sold). Marginal revenue is the net outcome of these two offsetting forces.

We also know that Q is a function of P, written $Q = g(P)$. However, we are contemplating changes in Q, not P. We need to invert the demand function and instead make P a function of Q. This can be done if Q always declines as P increases, because P then will always decline as Q increases. Write down the inverted function as

$$P = g^{-1}(Q).$$

For example, if $Q = 100 - 2P$, then

$$P = 50 - \frac{Q}{2}.$$

The change in P can be written simply as

$$\delta P = \left(\frac{\delta P}{\delta Q} \right) \delta Q.$$

The term $\delta P / \delta Q$ is just the slope of the demand curve, and it has a negative sign. Substitution of this expression for δP into the equation for δTR gives the result that

$$\delta TR = Q \left(\frac{\delta P}{\delta Q} \right) \delta Q + P \, \delta Q.$$

Marginal revenue is given by

$$MR = \frac{\delta TR}{\delta Q} = Q \left(\frac{\delta P}{\delta Q} \right) + P.$$

This equation simply says that the marginal revenue is the price of output plus an adjustment for the fact that the price had to be reduced in order to sell more output. The reduction in price ($\delta P / \delta Q$) is multiplied by Q.

If the firm is in a perfectly competitive market for output, the price does not have to be reduced to sell more ($\delta P / \delta Q = 0$), and

$$MR = P.$$

A closer look at marginal cost is also useful. Recall that

$$TC = rK + wL.$$

There are two simple ways to increase output—use more capital or hire more labor. Suppose that more labor is used, so

$$\delta TC = w \left(\frac{\delta L}{\delta Q} \right) \delta Q.$$

The expression $\delta L / \delta Q$ is the amount of labor that is needed to produce one more unit of output, which is just the inverse of the marginal product of labor ($\delta Q / \delta L$). Therefore,

$$MC = \frac{\delta TC}{\delta Q} = \frac{w}{MP_L}.$$

Recall Figure A.1, which depicts MP_L. The declining MP_L as output rises translates into a *rising* marginal cost of output, as shown in Figure A.4.

A sensible firm will use the cheaper method for increasing output. Suppose that more capital is hired instead. The same logic produces the result that

$$MC = \frac{\delta TC}{\delta Q} = \frac{r}{MP_K}.$$

The firm's managers know that something is amiss if these two figures for marginal cost are different. If the marginal cost of increasing output by using more capital exceeds the marginal cost of increasing output by hiring more labor, the firm should cut back on its use of capital and hire more labor. These changes can keep output at the same level and reduce total costs. Therefore, a firm that is maximizing profits must have

$$\frac{r}{MP_K} = \frac{w}{MP_L}.$$

This condition can be rewritten as

$$\frac{MP_L}{MP_K} = \frac{w}{r},$$

which is the familiar condition that for profit maximization, the firm should have the ratio of input prices equal to the ratio of marginal products. This is another normative proposition. Recall that the ratio of marginal products is the slope of the isoquant times -1. Figure A.5 shows this condition graphically.

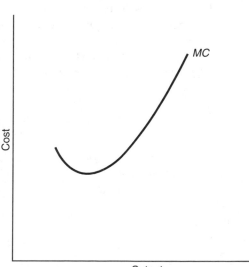

FIGURE A.4 Marginal cost

FIGURE A.5 Cost minimization in the long run

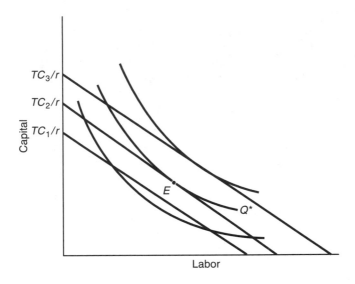

In Figure A.5 the firm has a target of producing an output level of Q^*. The parallel lines on the diagram are *isocost* (equal total cost) lines with slope $-w/r$. Each line is based on the equation $TC = rK + wL$, so that

$$K = \frac{TC}{r} - \left(\frac{w}{r}\right)L.$$

Given a level of TC, the straight line for K as a function of L is defined. Varying TC produces the set of parallel lines shown in Figure A.5. The firm minimizes cost in the long run by selecting point E on the Q^* isoquant. Point E is defined by a tangency between the Q^* isoquant and an isocost line. The lowest possible total cost occurs at point E.

As a final exercise with the theory of the firm, return to the condition that $MR = MC$ for the maximization of profits, and substitute for MR and MC from the foregoing results. The new statement is that

$$MR = Q\left(\frac{\delta P}{\delta Q}\right) + P = \frac{r}{MP_K} = \frac{w}{MP_L} = MC.$$

This group of equations can be manipulated to produce some interesting results, two of which are that

$$MR(MP_K) = r$$

and

$$MR(MP_L) = w.$$

The left-hand sides of these equations are called the marginal revenue product of capital and labor, respectively. They tell us the amount of added revenue that is gener-

FIGURE A.6 Demand for an input

ated when the firm uses 1 more unit of capital or hires 1 more unit of labor. Figure A.6 shows the marginal revenue product for labor. Maximization of profits means that this added revenue is set equal to the price of the input. If the last unit of an input hired is generating more revenue than it costs, the firm is not maximizing profits and more of the input should be hired. (Note the use of the word "should" again.) In Figure A.6 the price of a unit of labor is w, and profit-maximizing employment is L^*.

If the firm sells output in a perfectly competitive market, then $\delta P/\delta Q = 0$, and the conditions reduce to

$$P(MP_K) = r$$

and

$$P(MP_L) = w.$$

The left-hand sides of these equations are called the *value of the marginal product*, the added output produced by the marginal unit of the input times the price of the output.

D. THEORY OF THE CONSUMER

The basic theory of the consumer is used to examine how households allocate their resources and respond to changes in their economic circumstances. The theory contains two separate elements: the preferences of the consumer for various economic goods, and the budget constraint that the consumer faces.

Consumer preferences are summarized in the utility function, the function that describes the consumer's level of well being as a function of the amounts of economic goods consumed. For example, the utility function for a particular consumer might be written

$$U = U(x_1, x_2, x_3, \ldots, x_n),$$

where x_1 through x_n are various economic goods, such as housing, food, clothing, and leisure time. The utility function says that for a given combination of the goods, the consumer achieves some unique level of utility.

Now suppose that the amount of one of the goods (x_1) changes. We can write

$$\delta U = \left(\frac{\delta U}{\delta x_1}\right) \delta x_1.$$

What do we know about the crucial quantity $(\delta U/\delta x_1)$? The usual assumption is that we know only that $(\delta U/\delta x_1)$ is greater than zero; we do not know by *how much* utility increases when x_1 increases. We do not presume that utility is measurable in the same sense that we presume that output in a production function is measurable. What we *do* assume is that the utility function can tell us how much of one good can be substituted for another good to keep utility *constant*.

Suppose that good x_1 is decreased and that good x_2 is increased so as to keep utility constant at some level. We can use the mathematics of functions to write

$$\delta U = \left(\frac{\delta U}{\delta x_1}\right) \delta x_1 + \left(\frac{\delta U}{\delta x_2}\right) \delta x_2 = 0$$

because the net change in utility is zero. This is the basic equation for an indifference curve, the curve that shows the combinations of x_1 and x_2 (given certain amounts of the other goods x_3 to x_n) that yield the same level of utility. The equation can be solved to yield

$$-\frac{\delta x_1}{\delta x_2} = \frac{\delta U/\delta x_2}{\delta U/\delta x_1}.$$

The negative sign on the left-hand side has to be there because we know that δx_1 is a negative number, δx_2 is a positive number, and the right-hand side of the equation is greater than zero.

The quantity $(\delta U/\delta x_1)/(\delta U/\delta x_2)$ is called the *marginal rate of substitution* of x_1 for x_2 because it tells us the amount of x_1 that can be given up when x_2 increases by 1 unit so as to keep utility constant. The marginal rate of substitution is -1 times the slope of the indifference curve shown in Figure A.7 because this figure has the quantity of x_1 on the vertical axis and the quantity of x_2 on the horizontal axis. The standard assumption is that the indifference curve is bowed in toward the origin of the graph as shown. This shape implies that the amount of the good x_1 that is substituted for another unit of x_2, to keep utility constant, *declines* as the amount of x_2 increases and x_1 decreases. This is a sensible assumption because it means that as the consumer has more of x_2 and less of x_1, he is less willing to trade away x_1 for more x_2 as utility is being held constant. The shorthand method for stating this assumption is to say that the marginal rate of substitution declines.

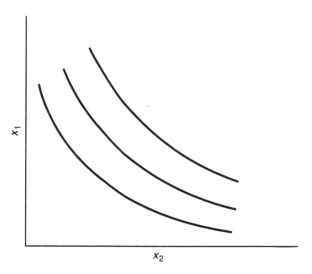

FIGURE A.7   Indifference curves

An indifference curve for goods x_1 and x_2 is assumed to exist for each level of utility, so a family of indifference curves can be drawn on the same diagram, as shown in Figure A.7. A higher level of utility corresponds to higher indifference curves, of course, because both of the goods are assumed to be *goods*.

Now we turn to the other half of the story—the budget constraint. We assume that the consumer has a given amount of resources to allocate to the goods in the utility function. The usual problem involves allocating a given amount of money income to the various consumer goods that can be purchased in the market. For simplicity suppose that there are only two such goods, x_1 and x_2, and that the consumer has an amount M to allocate to purchases of these two goods. To proceed we must know the prices of these two goods. Suppose that they are p_1 and p_2, respectively.

We now have all of the information needed to write down the budget constraint for this problem, and it is

$$M = p_1 x_1 + p_2 x_2.$$

Amount M is spent only on the two goods. The budget constraint can be placed on Figure A.8 by solving the budget constraint for x_1 in terms of x_2. This solution is

$$x_1 = \frac{M}{p_1} - \left(\frac{p_2}{p_1}\right) x_2.$$

As an exercise, confirm that this equation is correct. This new equation says two things very clearly. First, if the consumer buys no units of x_2, the amount of x_1 that can be purchased is M/p_1. This makes perfect sense—the maximum amount of x_1 that the consumer can buy is M divided by the price of x_1. Second, the equation says that if x_2 is increased by 1 unit, x_1 must be reduced by p_2/p_1 units.

Consider a numerical example to reinforce this second point. Suppose that the price of x_1 is \$2 per unit and that the price of x_2 is \$6 per unit. If the consumer decides to buy 1 more unit of x_2, he will spend \$6 more dollars on x_2. Where can he find \$6? He can find \$6 by reducing his purchases of x_1 by 3 units because each unit of x_1 has a price of \$2. Note that $p_2/p_1 = 6/2 = 3$.

FIGURE A.8   Budget constraint

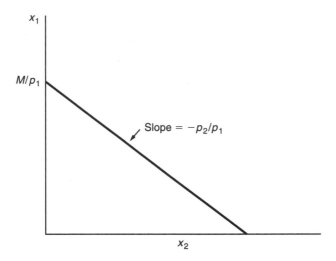

We bring the indifference curves and the budget constraint together in Figure A.9 and present a graphical solution to the consumer's allocation problem. The objective of the consumer is to get the most utility possible from his purchases, so the idea is to get to the highest indifference curve that is possible given a budget of M. The highest feasible indifference curve is labeled IC^* in Figure A.9; it is the indifference curve that comes into contact with the budget constraint only at one point. Note that indifference curves below IC^* come into contact with the budget constraint *twice*, and that indifference curves above IC^* do not touch the budget constraint at all—they cannot be reached.

FIGURE A.9   Consumer equilibrium

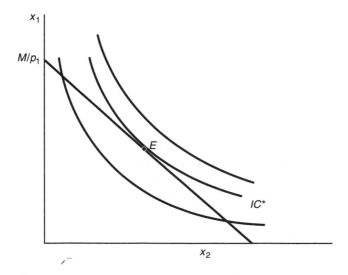

Indifference curve IC^* comes into contact with the budget constraint only once because the two curves are tangent—their slopes are equal at point E. Recall that the slope of an indifference curve is -1 times the marginal rate of substitution, and the slope of the budget constraint is $-p_2/p_1$. Therefore, the mathematical expression for the maximization of the consumer's utility subject to the budget M is

$$\frac{\delta x_1}{\delta x_2} = -\frac{p_2}{p_1} = -MRS_{12},$$

where MRS_{12} is the marginal rate of substitution of x_1 for x_2.

One different application of this model of the consumer is used in the book. In this application x_1 is assumed to be money income (M) and x_2 is leisure time (L, measured in hours). People regard both of these as goods, so the indifference curves are of the usual sort. The only tricky part is the budget constraint. Here the constraint is the number hours the person has to devote to leisure time and to activities that yield money income.

Suppose that the person has total time T per week to devote to leisure (L) and work, and suppose that he can earn wage rate w at work. The equation for his budget can therefore be written as

$$M = w(T - L) = wT - wL.$$

Here M is graphed on the vertical axis and L is shown on the horizontal axis of Figure A.10. The slope of the budget constraint is $-w$, which means that if the person increases leisure time by one hour, $\$w$ of money income must be given up. This case is depicted in Figure A.10. The maximization of utility occurs at point E. In this case point E represents an allocation of time to its competing uses—work and leisure.

FIGURE A.10 Allocation of time to work and leisure

E. EFFICIENCY AND THE MARKET ECONOMY

So far only a single firm or household has been considered in this review of microeconomic concepts. Let us broaden the picture to consider the interests of an entire economy, focusing on the market for a single good. That good has a demand function

$$Q = g(P)$$

and an inverse of the demand function

$$P = g^{-1}(Q).$$

The demand function tells the quantity demanded at each price, while the inverse demand function tells the price offered at each quantity. In other words, the inverse demand function indicates that someone out there in the market for the good is willing to pay a particular price for the next unit of the good. That willingness to pay is lower the greater is the quantity. The inverse demand function can therefore be interpreted as the marginal benefit curve for the good in question. The inverse demand curve has been depicted in Figure A.11 and labeled "marginal benefit."

If the good is produced under conditions of perfect competition, the supply curve of the good is also the marginal cost curve for the industry. This is the fundamental result for supply that is taught in the principles of economics course. The marginal cost curve is also depicted in Figure A.11. The competitive market equilibrium price and quantity is also the point at which the marginal benefit of the good to its last purchaser is just equal to the marginal cost of the good. The perfectly competitive outcome is therefore an efficient outcome, in the economic sense that it is the level of output at which it is not possible to make someone better off unless someone else is made worse off. To see this point, suppose that suppliers are ordered by the

FIGURE A.11   Equilibrium in a competitive market

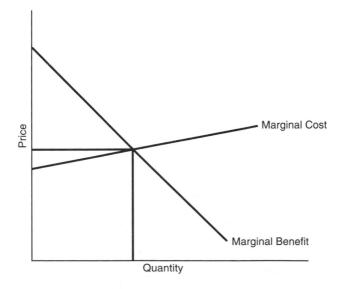

Pope to increase the quantity supplied beyond the competitive equilibrium output shown in Figure A.11. There are benefits attached to this increased output, but the cost to the producers of producing the additional output exceeds that benefit. The Pope notices his mistake and orders the consumers of these additional units to pay the suppliers for their expenses. This transfer keeps the suppliers on the same level of well being, but the consumers are now worse off because they have had to transfer to suppliers an amount of money in excess of the value of the additional benefits of the good.

Alternatively, suppose that the output of the good has been restricted by a monopolist. A monopolist sets output where marginal cost equals marginal revenue and then sets price from the demand curve so that

$$MC = MR < p.$$

Refer to Figure A.12. The monopolist faces demand curve DD and has a marginal revenue function MR. She maximizes profits by equating MR and MC at output level Q^* and sets the price P^* from the demand curve.

At the monopoly output the marginal cost is less than the marginal benefit of the good, represented by the price as read from the inverse demand function. This is clearly an inefficient allocation of resources because there is room for a consumer to bribe the monopolist to produce more of the good. A clever bribe can make both the consumer and the monopolist better off. For example, at output Q^*, a clever consumer could make a private deal to offer a price of $P^* - 1$ for the next unit of output. Suppose that the other consumers do not learn of this private deal. The consumer is better off because she gets to consume 1 more unit of the good at a price below her marginal benefit, and the monopolist is better off because the price paid exceeds the cost of producing that additional unit. Bribery can continue until the marginal benefit of the good is just equal to the marginal cost. At this point the consumer has no further room to make a bribe.

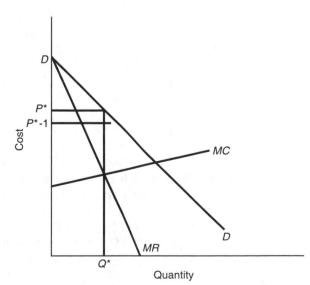

FIGURE A.12 Monopoly price and output

The monopoly example in the preceding paragraph is closely related to the basic idea of cost-benefit analysis. In the cost-benefit analysis of a public good or service the idea is to produce more if the marginal benefits exceed marginal costs, or if

$$\frac{MB}{MC} > 1,$$

the marginal benefit/cost ratio exceeds 1. If the benefits and/or costs of the public good extend beyond one year, we must compare the present value of the stream of benefits to the present value of the stream of costs. The benefits and costs that occur in the future must be discounted by an interest rate that represents the willingness of society to trade the present for the future. For example, if society is willing to wait one year to receive benefits only if 5% interest is paid (in real terms), benefits in amount MB that occur one year in the future have a present value of $MB/(1.05)$. A finding that MB/MC exceeds 1.0 means that enough benefits exist to pay all of the costs of the public good and have something left over. This means that the potential exists for the project in question to make someone better off while leaving no one else worse off. Projects that do not at least have this potential should be rejected.

F. INTEREST AND DISCOUNTING

The concepts of compound interest and discounting are used frequently in urban economics and real estate, and in everyday life as well. As an educated person, you *must* understand these ideas. There is no alternative. The basic ideas are presented here, and they are used often in the body of the text. Some sophisticated compound interest and discounting concepts are developed in the appendix to Chapter 9.

Suppose you know that your local bank is paying a 5% interest rate on one-year certificates of deposit. This means, of course, that if you deposit $100 today, you will receive $105 one year from today. The formula for this computation is

$$A_1 = A_0(1 + r),$$

where A_1 is the amount one year from today, A_0 the initial deposit, and r the interest rate expressed as a decimal (e.g., 0.05).

Now answer the following question. If you can answer this question, you understand the basic idea from which all of the rest of the ideas follow. Given that you, or anyone else, can earn 5% on bank deposits, what is the most you are willing to pay for a promise to pay you $100 one year from today? Are you willing to pay $100 now? Of course not, because you can put your $100 in the bank and have $105 one year from today. What about $99? If you put $99 in the bank today, you will have $103.95 one year later. So what is the answer? The answer is $95.24. If you were to put $95.24 in the bank at 5% interest, you would have $100 in one year. You can always earn interest on your money at the bank, so a promise to pay $100 one year from today is worth $95.24 today.

How did you (or I) get the answer of $95.24? This amount is, in fact, equal to 100/(1.05), or 100/(1 + r). This computation is just a manipulation of $A_1 = A_0(1 + r)$ to read

$$A_0 = \frac{A_1}{1+r}.$$

If we know A_0, we use the top formula to compute A_1. If we know A_1, we use the bottom formula to compute A_0, the initial deposit needed to produce A_1.

Now suppose that you decide to roll over your certificate of deposit for a second year, and suppose that the interest remains at 5% for the second year. (The interest rate probably will have changed in a year, but ignore this complication.) In two years you will have an amount that is computed as

$$A_2 = A_1(1+r) = A_0(1+r)(1+r) = A_0(1+r)^2.$$

If the initial deposit is $100, the amount in two years is $110.25. This is compound interest because you earned interest on your interest earnings. You earned $5 in interest in the first year, and you earned $0.25 on that $5 in the second year in addition to the $5 in interest on your original deposit of $100.

Now answer the question: How much is the promise to pay $100 in *two* years worth *today*? Manipulation of the formula above produces the answer:

$$A_0 = \frac{A_2}{(1+r)^2} = \frac{100}{(1.05)^2} = 90.70.$$

This is the answer because if you were to deposit $90.70 today at 5% interest, you would have $100 in two years. Use your pocket calculator to check this out.

The next step is to compute the current value of a promise to pay $100 one year from today *and* $100 two years from today. You already know the answer to this one. You add $95.24 and $90.70 to get $185.94. The more general formula for this computation is

$$A_0 = \frac{A_1}{1+r} + \frac{A_2}{(1+r)^2},$$

where A_1 and A_2 are the amounts to be received at the end of one and two years. This is, in fact, a general formula for the computation of the *present value* of a series of payments.

Suppose that the series of payments extends for 10 years. The present value of that series of payments is computed as

$$PV = \frac{A_1}{1+r} + \frac{A_2}{(1+r)^2} + \cdots + \frac{A_{10}}{(1+r)^{10}},$$

where the $\cdots$ stands for the third through the ninth terms.

What if the series of payments goes on forever? Does a series of payments ever go on forever? Sure. Land in an urban area never wears out. The payments of land rent for the privilege of using the land go on forever. The present value of an infinite series of payments is

$$PV = \frac{A_1}{1+r} + \frac{A_2}{(1+r)^2} + \cdots + \frac{A_{\infty-1}}{(1+r)^{\infty-1}} + \frac{A_\infty}{(1+r)^\infty}.$$

Note that the payment in time period "infinity" is A_∞, and that this amount is divided by $(1+r)^\infty$, which is a number that is infinitely large (because $1+r$ is greater than 1). Therefore, the present value of A_∞ is actually zero.

The formula for the present value of an infinite series of payments simplifies very neatly if the amount that is paid each year is a constant amount A. Now the formula is

$$PV = \frac{A}{1+r} + \frac{A}{(1+r)^2} + \cdots + \frac{A}{(1+r)^{\infty-1}} + \frac{A}{(1+r)^\infty}.$$

Multiply both sides of this equation by $(1+r)$ to obtain

$$(1+r)PV = A + \frac{A}{(1+r)} + \cdots + \frac{A}{(1+r)^{\infty-2}} + \frac{A}{(1+r)^{\infty-1}}.$$

Subtract the top equation from the bottom equation to obtain

$$(1+r)PV - PV = A - \frac{A}{(1+r)^\infty} = A.$$

Remember that the present value of amount A to be received an infinite number of years from now is zero. Therefore,

$$rPV = A,$$

or

$$PV = \frac{A}{r}.$$

The present value of an infinite series of payments equal to A is just A/r. For example, if $A = 100$ and $r = 0.05$, then $PV = 2000$. An investment of $2000 at 5% interest forever will produce an infinite series of payments of $100.

G. MATHEMATICS OF EXPONENTIAL FUNCTIONS

Exponential functions are used frequently in urban economics (and in economics in general) to create models of economic growth, urban population density, and many other economic phenomena.

We define e as the limit, as m approaches infinity, of

$$\left(1 + \frac{1}{m}\right)^m.$$

It so happens that e equals about 2.718 and is known as the *base of the natural logarithms*. To convince yourself of this numerical result, use your pocket calculator to compute the expression above when $m = 5$, $m = 10$, $m = 15$, and so on.

The natural logarithm of a (positive) number is the power to which e is raised to get the number, or

$$x = e^{\ln x}.$$

Here $\ln x$ means *natural logarithm*, the logarithm with base e.

Consider a compound interest problem where amount A earns interest rate r per year, and interest is compounded m times per year. Then the value (V) of A after t years is

$$V = A\left(1 + \frac{r}{m}\right)^{mt}.$$

For example, if $m = 1$ (annual compounding), $V = A(1 + r)^t$; if $m = 2$ (semiannual compounding), $V = A(1 + r/2)^{2t}$; with quarterly compounding, $V = A(1 + r/4)^{4t}$; and so on. This formula can be written as

$$V = A\left[\left(1 + \frac{1}{x}\right)^x\right]^{rt},$$

where $x = m/r$. This result follows from the standard laws of exponents, and the proof is left as an exercise. This last formula means that

$$V = Ae^{rt}$$

as m approaches infinity (since x approaches infinity as m approaches infinity). This is the standard formula for exponential growth of amount A at interest rate r with continuous compounding. A graphical example is shown in Figure A.13.

For exponential decay, we can write

$$V = A\left(1 - \frac{r}{m}\right)^{mt} = A\left[\left(1 + \frac{1}{x}\right)^x\right]^{-rt},$$

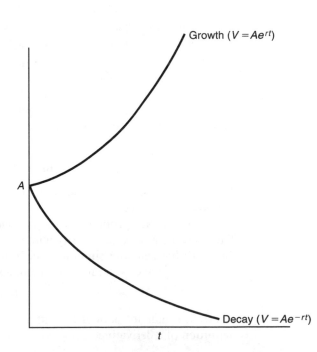

Growth ($V = Ae^{rt}$)

Decay ($V = Ae^{-rt}$)

FIGURE   A.13 Exponential growth and decay

where $x = -m/r$. This means that

$$V = Ae^{-rt}$$

as m approaches infinity. This is the standard formula for exponential decay at rate r with continuous compounding, and Figure A.13 shows an example. Note that the value of the function (V) declines by the same percentage in each time period, which means that the actual numerical value of the *decline* gets smaller and smaller as time passes.

These exponential functions have important properties that make them very convenient functions for empirical work. In particular, if $V = Ae^{rt}$, then

$$\frac{\delta V}{\delta t} = rAe^{rt},$$

or

$$\frac{(\delta V/\delta t)}{V} = r.$$

Similarly, if $(\delta V/\delta t)/V = r$, then $V = Ke^{rt}$ (where K is some constant). In other words, if the percentage rate of change per time period is r, then V with continuous compounding at any time period is $V = Ae^{rt}$, where A is the initial value (at time zero).

The basic exponential growth and decay functions are very useful in urban economics. For example, population density in an urban area is usually described reasonably well by the exponential decay function written

$$D(x) = D_0 e^{-gx},$$

where $D(x)$ is population density at distance x from the central business district, D_0 the hypothetical population density at distance zero, and g is called the density gradient. From the discussion of changes above we know that

$$\frac{\delta D(x)/\delta x}{D(x)} = -g,$$

or that the percentage decline in population density per unit distance is g. Also, the exponential decay function for population density can be written in logarithmic form as

$$\ln D(x) = \ln D_0 - gx.$$

The natural logarithm of population density is a linear function of distance to the central business district.

This change property of the exponential function can be proved quite easily. These proofs require familiarity with basic calculus and can be skipped. Let us begin the proof by using the simplified function $V = e^t$. We define the natural logarithm as the power to which e is raised to obtain a specified (positive) number, or

$$\ln V = t,$$

where ln stands for natural logarithm. It is easy to show that $dt/dV = 1/V$. From the definition of a derivative,

$$\frac{dt}{dV} = \text{limit (as } V \text{ approaches } N) \text{ of } \frac{(\ln V - \ln N)}{V - N}$$

$$= \text{limit } \frac{\ln(V/N)}{V - N}.$$

This result follows because the logarithm of a quotient (such as V/N) is the same as the difference in logarithms. Here N is simply some specific value for V at which we have chosen to find the derivative. Next define $m = N/(V - N)$. Now we have

$$\frac{dt}{dV} = \text{limit}\left(\frac{m}{N}\right) \ln\left(1 + \frac{1}{m}\right),$$

a result that follows because $1/m = (V - N)/N = V/N - 1$. Therefore,

$$\frac{dt}{dV} = \text{limit}\left(\frac{1}{N}\right) \ln\left(1 + \frac{1}{m}\right)^m.$$

As V approaches N it so happens that $m = N/(V - N)$ approaches infinity, so

$$\frac{dt}{dV} = \frac{1}{N} \ln e = \frac{1}{N},$$

since the natural logarithm of e itself is 1. Remember that N is a value of V that V approaches in the definition of the derivative. This simple result can be inverted to yield

$$\frac{dV}{dt} = N,$$

which means that the derivative of $V = e^t$ is always itself!

Now if $V = Ae^{rt}$, we can find dV/dt by using the chain rule for derivatives, which states that

$$\frac{dV}{dt} = \frac{dV}{dz}\left(\frac{dz}{dt}\right),$$

where z is some intermediate function. In this case let $z = rt$, so $V = Ae^z$. This means that $dV/dz = Ae^z$ and $dz/dt = r$, so

$$\frac{dV}{dt} = rAe^{rt}$$

and

$$\frac{dV/dt}{V} = r.$$

Solutions to Selected Exercises

CHAPTER 3

1. a. Cost per ton is $175 if the trees are transported, compared to $160 if firewood is transported. Thus, the trees should be cut into firewood at the forest. You actually only needed the transport cost data to determine the cost-minimizing location.

   b. If the price of firewood is $150, it is not profitable to produce, but at a price of $175 a profit can be made.

2. a. With 23 customers, the median is customer #12 located 25 miles from Lubbock.

   b. With 27 customers (10 in Amarillo), the median customer is #14—still at 25 miles from Lubbock.

   c. Now with 27 customers (4 more in Lubbock), the median customer is *in* Lubbock.

3. a. There are 11 customers. The profit-maximizing equilibrium locations are both at the median customer (#6). Any other location is not an equilibrium because one vendor has an incentive to move. Aggregate travel costs are

$$(1/2)2(5+4+3+2+1) = 15 \text{ cents.}$$

   b. The socially optimal location pattern is to have the vendors locate at the one-quarter and three-quarter points along the beach. These points correspond to customers #3 and #9. Aggregate travel costs are

$$(1/2)2(2+1) + (1/2)2(2+1) + (1/2)3 = 7.5 \text{ cents.}$$

   However, this location pattern is unstable because either firm can increase sales by moving toward the center.

4. a. $AC = 10 - .001 \, Q$ [because $TC = q(ac)n$].
   $TC = n(10q - .001qQ)$. Now $Q = nq$, so
   $TC = Q(10 - .001Q) - Q(AC)$.

   b. $TC = 10Q - .001Q^2$, so
   $MC = 10 - .002Q$.

   c. The industry produces where $AC = P$, so $Q = 1000$, $AC = 9$, and $MC = 8$.

   d. No localization economies means that $AC = 10$ and $Q = 980$.

CHAPTER 5

1. Initial value $= R/r = 10,000/.05 = \$200,000$. With the tax

$$V = (R - tV)/r, \text{ where } t \text{ is the tax rate, and}$$

$$V = R/(r + t) = 10,000/.08 = \$125,000.$$

2. a. Marginal cost of distance is ($4/8)250 = $125 per mile per year.
   b. Marginal benefit of moving one mile farther out is 3,000($.05) = $150 per mile per year. Thus MC of travel is less than the marginal benefit of travel, and the household should move farther out.
   c. Locational equilibrium requires that

$$3,000 \, (\delta R/\delta x) = 125, \text{ so}$$

$$\delta R/\delta x = \$.0417 \text{ per mile.}$$

3.

Distance	Gross Density
0	7,500
1	6,140
2	5,027
4	3,370
10	1,015
3.14	4,000
8	1,514

4. a. The bid-rent function with profits equal to zero is:

$$\text{profit} = 0 = pQ - TC = \$1000 - 100(.25)x - \text{other costs} - \text{rent/acre,}$$

where x is distance to CBD.
Other costs are $5 per unit, or $500, so

$$\text{rent/acre} = R = 500 - 25x.$$

   b. $R = 500 - 25x = 100$, or $x = 16$ miles.
5. a. The second industry has "other costs" of $10 per unit, so:

$$\text{profit} = 0 = 1500 - 75x - 750 - R, \text{ or}$$

$$R = 750 - 75x.$$

   b. The two bid-rent functions cross at $x = 5$.
6. If the Urban Growth Boundary prohibits residental use beyond it, then the market rent falls to the agricultural rent at this distance.

CHAPTER 6

1. a. For the land rent function, let $x =$ distance to the CBD. The slope of the land rent function is $-2t$. The area of the city is PK, so the radius x^* of the city is found as

$$PK = \pi(x^*)^2, \text{ or } x^* = (PK/\pi)^{0.5}.$$

The key to the problem is to realize that land rent at the CBD ($x = 0$) equals travel cost at x^*, which is

$$2tx^* = 2t(PK/\pi)^{0.5}.$$

Thus the land rent function is

$$R(x) = 2t(PK/\pi)^{0.5} - 2tx.$$

b. Aggregate land rent is the volume of the land rent cone with base equal to the area of the city and height equal to land rent at the CBD, or

$$\text{AGG } R = (1/3)PK[2t(PK/\pi)^{0.5}] = (2/3)t(PK)^{1.5}/\pi^{0.5}.$$

Aggregate travel costs equal the volume of the cylinder of base PK and height of the land rent function at the CBD *minus* the aggregage land rent, so aggregate travel costs are 2 times the aggregate land rent.

c. A decline in marginal travel cost t reduces the land rent at the CBD and flattens the rent function because

$$R(x) = 2t(PK/\pi)^{0.5} - 2tx.$$

In other words, land rent *falls* everywhere in the city except at the edge, where it is still zero.

d. The results in answer c happened because the population of the city is fixed, as is the land area of the city (fixed at PK). Land rent at the edge of the city is always 0, and the amount of transportation cost *avoided* by living at any given location in the city has *declined*.

2. a. Equation c says that the marginal cost of moving a marginal distance away (t) equals the marginal benefit of this move $[R'(x)l_D(x)]$, the savings in land rent.

b. $l_D(x) = B/R(x)$, so
$R'(x)/R(x) = -t$
The land rent gradient is a constant percentage change per unit of distance, and this percentage change is just equal to the marginal transportation cost.

c. From equation (6), setting $L_D = L_S$,

$$N(x)/L(x) = 1/l_D(x) = R(x)/B.$$

Thus the population density gradient is $(1/B)$ times the land rent gradient.

d. If t rises, the population density gradient gets steeper.

e. This model is the same as the graphical model, except that the CBD is a dimensionless point and the population density in this model refers to households per unit of land area rather than population per unit of land area.

CHAPTER 7

3. a. $S/L = (\mu/1 - \mu)v/r = (1/3)v/r$.
b. $E/L = [(1 - \alpha - \beta)/\alpha(1 - \mu)]v/w = (4/3)v/w$.
c. For example,

$$\ln(E/L) = \ln(4/3) + \ln v - \ln w$$

The natural log of employment density is just a linear function of the natural logs of the two input prices, with coefficients of 1.

4. a. Potential gross income equals $2,250,000 per year, and effective gross income (with vacancy rate of 10%) is $2,025,000.
   b. Net operating income (NOI) is EGI minus expenses of $1,001,250, or NOI = $1,023,750.
   c. The market value of the building is $10,237,500 with a cap rate of 10%, or $9,306,818 with a cap rate of 11%.

CHAPTER 8

1. a. $\ln T_{ij} = .5(\ln 100) + .2(\ln 200) - 2(\ln 5)$
      $= 2.30 + 1.06 - 3.22 = .14$, so
      $T_{ij} = 1.15$.
      If distance is 10, then $\ln T_{ij} = -2.25$ and $T_{ij} = .1$ (i.e., trips fall from 1 to 0).
   b. If both O and D double in size, then $T = 1.88$; T does not double because the exponents of O and D add up to a number that is less than 1.

2. a. Probability of using the auto of 0.5 means that

   $$\ln(P/1 - P) = \ln(1) = 0 = -8(t_a - t_b) - 2(m_a - m_b).$$

   Thus any combination of $(m_a - m_b)/(t_a - t_b) = -4$ leads to $P = 0.5$.
   c. The value of reductions in commuting time is 4 cents per minute.

3. a. Define m as the departure time in minutes after 8 A.M. Commuting time is therefore

   $$CT = 15 + 0.1m + .04m^2.$$

   The value of the commuting time is $5CT$.
   Time spent at work before 9 A.M. is $60 - m - CT$, and the cost of this time wasted is $3(60 - m - CT)$. The total cost of time is therefore $5CT + 3(60 - m - CT)$. Substitution for CT produces

   $$\text{Total Cost} = 75 + .5m + .2m^2 + 180 - 3m - 45 - .3m - .06m^2$$

   $$= 210 - 2.8m + .08m^2.$$

   Minimization of total cost requires that $\delta TC/\delta m = -2.8 + .16m = 0$, or $m = 17.5$ (minutes past 8)
   b. Commuting time is computed from the CT function, and it equals 29 minutes.
   c. Arrival time is thus 8:46.5.
   d. If the cost of time spent at work increases to 3.1 cents per minute, departure time changes to 19.14 minutes past 8, commuting time increases to 31.6 minutes, and arrival time is now 8:50.74

4. a. $D = 80/2 = 40$ cars per mile.
   b. $V = DS = 40$ cars per mile times 50 miles per hour,
      $= 2,000$ cars per hour.

5. a. Supply is $AC = 10 + 4V$ and demand is $V = 46 - P$, so

$$P = 46 - V \text{ and } AC = P, \text{ or}$$

$$10 + 4V = 46 - V, \text{ which yields } V = 7.2.$$

   b. Marginal cost is $10 + 8V$ and $V = 4$.

6. a. $(1/S) = 1 + 0.03V$ in minutes per mile. Substitution into the demand function yields $V = 2,000$.

   b. If average travel time is $1 + 0.03V$, the total travel time is $V(1 + 0.03V)$ and marginal travel time is thus $1 + 0.06V$.

   c. Optimal traffic volume is found by substituting into the demand function, or $V = 1,172$.

   d. The optimal congestion toll is the difference between average and marginal cost at optimal V. This difference is $0.03V$, which is 35.16 minutes.

CHAPTER 9

5. Substitution of 0.4 for A and m_L in the final formula for t yields $t = 0.12$ (instead of 0.14).

6. a. If $Y = 15,000$ and $p = 100$, then

$$H = 500/10 = 50 \text{ and } HP = \$5,000.$$

   b. If $Y = 20,000$, then $H = 666.7/10 = 66.67$ and $HP = 6667$.

   c. If $p = 70$, then $H = 500/8.367 = 59.76$.
   $HP = 70 \times 59.76 = \$4183.20$. Total expenditures fall because demand is inelastic.

7. a. $V = (6,000 - 4,000)/0.05 = 40,000$.

   b. Market value is still $40,000. Compute present value of rents received at end of years 1, 2, and 3, and house sold for $40,000 at end of year 3.

   c. Selling price of $50,000 adds $8,636 to present value.

CHAPTER 10

2. a. The price for a household is $5,000/125 = 40$.

   b. $G = 100 - 0.5p = 80$ units.

   c. Tax bill $= 80 \times 5000/125 = \$3,200$.

3. a. The median voter is a household with demand equal to $G = 50 - 0.5p$. The price for a household is $5,000/300 = 16.67$, so $G = 41.67$ units.

   b. The tax bill for each household is $pG = 694.6$.

4. a. $V = R/(r + t)$, so the demand function translated into $V - Q$ space is $V = 125,000 - 12.5Q$. Setting supply equal to demand yields

$$50,000 + 2.5Q = 125,000 - 12.5Q, \text{ or}$$

$$Q = 5,000.$$

At $Q = 5,000$, $V = 62,500$, and $R = 5,000$.

b. If t increases to 0.04, then $Q = 4,000$, $V = 60,000$, and $R = 6,000$. Under the old situation (with $t = 0.02$) the tax was $0.02 \times 62,500 = 1,250$. The new tax is $0.04 \times 60,000 = 2,400$. The tax increased by 1,150, of which 1,000 is paid by the tenants in the form of higher rent. The owner pays 150 of the increase in the tax, which makes sense because the present value of 150 per year is $150/.06 = 2,500$, which is the decline in the value of the house.

6. This change in AFDC policy will reduce spending on welfare, as shown in Figure 10.8. This is a prediction that can be tested in a few years.

CHAPTER 11

1. a. $T/B = 2.4$, so local multiplier is 2.4. An increase in basic employment of 3,000 would yield an increase in total employment of 7,200.
   b. This forecast assumes that $L = a + bT$ with $a = 0$, so the multiplier is B/T. The forecast also assumes that B and L workers are paid equally.

2. a. With this function for imports $[M = 0.23(1 - t)Y]$, then

$$Y = C + I + G + (X - M)$$

$$Y = 100 + .9(0.7)Y + 650 - 0.161Y$$

$$0.531Y = 750$$

$$Y = 1,412. \text{ The values for } C, T, \text{ and } M \text{ follow.}$$

   b. The multiplier for Ruston is $1/0.531 = 1.88$.

3. a. $y = 0.25k + 0.75l + t$. Successive substitution for k, l, and t yields $y = 8.625\%$.
   b. The growth rate can be decomposed as follows:

Labor force	3.75%
Natural growth	1.50
Migration	2.25
Capital	1.875
Local saving	0.625
Migration	1.25
Technical change	3.00

4. a. $\delta Y = \alpha A e^{rt} L^{\alpha-1} K^{\beta} \delta L$, so substitution into the definition of elasticity $(\delta Y/\delta L)(L/Y) = \alpha$.
   The same procedure works for K.
   b. $\delta Y/Y = \delta A/A + E_K(\delta K/K) + E_L(\delta L/L)$
      $= r + \beta(\delta K/K) + \alpha(\delta L/L)$
      because $A e^{rt}$ grows at rate r.
   c. The growth rate of Y is 3.25%.

5. a. Larger employment growth tells potential migrants that they have a better chance of finding a job when they arrrive.
   b. $\delta E = \alpha\theta/(1 - \alpha\beta) = 0.625\theta$.

c. Note that the denominator in the equation for δE is $1 - \alpha\beta$. If $\alpha\beta > 1$, then this denominator is negative, which yields a nonsense result. If $\alpha\beta > 1$, an increase of θ makes M increase without limit.

6. a. The technical coefficients are:

	A	B
A	0.1	0.714
B	0.3	0.143

b. Gross output is the total value of output of an industry, which also equals the total value of *all* of the inputs.

c. $A = 0.1A + 0.714B + X_A$
$B = 0.3A + 0.143B + X_B$

d. If final demand for A increases from 40 to 50, then

	A	B	Final Demand	Gross Output
A	11.5	53.8	50	115.3
B	34.6	10.8	30	75.4
VA	69.2	10.8		
Total	115.3	75.4	80	190.7

Gross output of A increased by $15.3/10 = 1.53$, and gross output of B increased by $5.4/10 = 0.54$. Value added increased by $10/10 = 1$, of course.

e. There are no exports because there are no imports; all output is sold locally.

CHAPTER 12

1. Static localization economies exist because the industry has increasing returns to scale $(0.75 + .04 = 1.15)$. Dynamic localization economies exist because industry growth is a function of the employment level. Static urbanization economies exist because industry growth is a function of employment growth in the urban area (holding other factors constant), and dynamic urbanization economies exist because industry growth depends on the level of air service.

2. a. Because the coefficient of $\ln E_0$ is less than 1.0, the dynamic localization economy is of the weaker form; employment in the base year leads to greater employment growth in absolute (but not percentage) terms.

   b. The model includes no variable that captures a static localization economy effect.

   c. The Pop variable tells us that the industry is also subject to a dynamic urbanization economy.

CHAPTER 13

1. a. The trainee invests $1,500 for an annual return of $750, so the private rate of return is 50% per year. For society the cost is $7,000 and the annual return is $1,000, so the annual return is 14.3%.

b. The trainee now has a cost of $6,500, which is to be compared to a benefit stream with a present value of $750/0.06 = $12,500. The person will enroll.

2. The idea is to compute the costs and benefits as of the date of high school entry. The worker has a stream of benefits of $4,000 for seven years that begins at the end of year 5, and then an infinite stream of benefits of $7,000 per year that begins at the end of the twelfth year. Costs consist of four years of $12,500, discounted back to the entry year.

4. Projects V, W, and Y can be chosen and will yield benefits of 50, compared to 48 for projects Z and W.

Index